I0532471

CAPTURED FREEDOM

The Thrilling True Story of
POWs Escaping the Grasp of the Rebels

STEVE PROCKO

Captured Freedom
The Thrilling True Story of POWs Escaping the Grasp of the Rebels

ISBN: 9798988024408

Published by
There's History Around Every Bend
Ocala, FL

CapturedFreedom.com

Cover design by Eric Labacz
LabaczDesign.com

What They Are Saying About *Captured Freedom*

A Civil War–era photograph reveals a sprawling true story of suffering and survival in Procko's nonfiction work…Although the author refers to the book as a work of narrative nonfiction in the introduction, imaginative descriptions are sparingly used, and they effectively enhance a small number of pivotal moments.

Kirkus Reviews
https://www.kirkusreviews.com/book-reviews/steve-procko/captured-freedom/

The Civil War is chock full of remarkable true stories, and *Captured Freedom* tells one that beats them all. Procko's detective work uncovers the lives of an amazing group of escaped prisoners, and tells their adventures with a narrative flair. Everyone will learn something they didn't know about the Civil War in the pages of this book.

Dr. Lorien Foote
Patricia & Bookman Peters Professor in History
Texas A&M University

Narrative nonfiction aficionados will greatly enjoy *Captured Freedom,* which Civil War buffs will find a special treat. Exhaustively researched, richly anecdotal, and well-written.

Joseph Wheelan
Author of Libby Prison Breakout, The Daring Escape from the Notorious Confederate Prison; and 10 other books of historical nonfiction

Procko delivers. While prison and escape stories are a staple of Civil War literature, *Captured Freedom* adds a fresh approach; readers will become immersed in the various stories of these nine men and the Southern Unionist sympathizers who helped them.

David A. Powell
Author of the award-winning trilogy on The Chickamauga Campaign

The details of this adventure come to life. The photograph…becomes personal and poignant. The people are no longer characters in a picture, they are heroes. They are family. They are the new American spirit of a country reborn in the blood of its sons.

Eric Rosenbaum
Member of the Union County Historical Society
Elk Point, South Dakota

A well-researched book, *Captured Freedom* delves into the personal biographies of literally dozens of individuals, but also brings insight to the Confederate prison system. Another interesting addition is a glimpse at two obscure Union regiments, the 2nd and 3rd North Carolina Mounted Rifles. This book is a welcome addition to any Civil war library, particularly those collections on prisons and escapes.

Tom Parson
Park Ranger
Shiloh National Military Park

As the Senior Vice President of the Chicago History Museum, I encountered the image that graces the cover and animates this well-researched book by Steve Procko many, many times. The photograph is in the museum's amazing collection of Civil War materials. But I had no idea that the museum had gotten the story of this image so profoundly wrong and was sharing a wildly inaccurate narrative about these impressive Union soldiers and their guides. In *Captured Freedom*, Procko corrects the record, telling the true story and honoring the men who posed for this photograph over 160 years ago.

John Russick
Interim President & CEO
Levine Museum of the New South

Steve Procko is the kind of historian who knows that all history is local, that all history resides in the story of individuals. A dogged researcher, Procko breathes life into a Civil War-era photograph and, in so doing, illuminates the intensely personal, life-altering decisions made by Americans amid this crucible.

Adam Alfrey
Assistant Director for Historical Services
Public Library - East Tennessee History Center

Written with an impressive degree of depth and detail, the reader gets to know (each man) and follow their experiences as citizens, soldiers, prisoners, and escapees. Each experience is described with crisp prose that allows the reader to understand the extreme challenges that these men faced. The author has taken great care to cite sources of information, but this work does not read as a dry academic account. It is a very readable account of an unknown story of people experiencing great change and challenge.

Janet Elizabeth Croon
Editor of The War outside my Window: The Civil War Diary of LeRoy Wiley Gresham

A great book about an early and long forgotten version of the great escape. It would make a great film.

Joseph Bilby
Author and assistant curator of the New Jersey National Guard and Militia Museum

Historians live for "rabbit holes" and Procko fell into a big one! Procko takes something as seemingly simple as a dusty old photograph and by digging a bit deeper uncovers a fascinating story of survival and perseverance that up until now had remained lost to time…. It is rare to find a page-turning story that is also a historical reference work but Procko pulls it off.

Raymond Johnson
Chicago's History Cop

A picture really is worth a thousand words, and many tell the most fascinating stories! The Civil War-era photograph that inspired Captured Freedom is a perfect example, and Procko's well-researched work of narrative nonfiction is as compelling as it is informative.

Cheri Todd Molter, Research Historian and Content Development Specialist
NC History Center on the Civil War, Emancipation & Reconstruction

About the Cover

About the front cover: The photograph of the twelve ragged men was taken in Knoxville, Tennessee, on the morning of January 2, 1865. The nine Union officers had just checked in at Provost Marshal General Samuel B. Carter's headquarters on Gay Street in Knoxville. The other three men—mountain guides that helped them through the mountains of North Carolina and Tennessee—accompanied them. In the building right next door to Carter's headquarters, on the third floor, was Theodore M. Schleier's studio. Less than twenty-four hours after crossing Union lines, Schleier posed the twelve men and Captured Freedom in his iconic photograph.

The photograph on the cover was digitally captured from the only known original albumen print. Courtesy of the Charles Hoffman family.

About the back cover: A photographic composition by the author from a photograph of Mark M. Bassett created in the first decade of the twentieth century by Bach Studios of Peoria, Illinois, courtesy of the Local History and Genealogy Collection, Peoria Public Library, Peoria, Illinois with special thanks to Christopher Farris. Throughout his life Bassett cherished the photograph of "twelve ragged men with determination strong on their faces," which he kept on the mantle in the parlor of his Peoria home.

For my parents,
Mike and Irene Procko

In war some persons seek adventures;
others have them in spite of themselves.

Major Samuel H. M. Byers
5th Iowa Infantry – 1911

About the Escape Route Map

Hundreds of Union officers escaped from Camp Sorghum while it was in operation from early October to early December 1864. The men in the front cover photograph did not all escape together but eventually came together toward the end of their tramp in the mountains of Western North Carolina.

This map divides the men into two POW groups. In the POW Group 1, Lieutenants Mark Bassett, Thomas Young, and Allie Stewart escaped on November 10 with six other officers. After thirteen days of walking past plantations and through the swamps of the Saluda River basin, the group of nine decided they were too large and visible so broke up into three smaller groups. All the men in the other two groups were recaptured in North Carolina, though two escaped and made it to freedom in the middle of January 1865.

Lieutenant Lem Dobbs was the only officer in "The Photograph" that did not escape from Camp Sorghum. He escaped from the Richland County jail in Columbia, South Carolina, on November 21, along with a Union private. They traveled more quickly than Bassett's group, caught up with them, and met guide Flem Cison at Dunns Rock, North Carolina, around the beginning of December.

POW Group 2, for the most part, followed the path of POW Group 1, then took a slightly different route when they neared the border of North and South Carolina, bypassing Dunns Rock and coming down into Cashiers Valley, North Carolina, where they met the Zachary family.

The 5th Iowa Boys—Major Marshall, Captain John Page, and Lieutenant Michael Hoffman—escaped together on November 24. Henry Fowler escaped on the same date but traveled with a different group of escapees, following along the same route.

The last one to escape on November 26 was John McAdams, who likely traveled with one or two other escapees. McAdams also followed the 5th Iowa Boys' route.

All nine escaped Union officers in the front cover photograph did not come together until they met Kit Ledford near Hayesville, North Carolina, in the last days of 1864. They then all made the final push to freedom, arriving in Sweetwater, Tennessee, to catch the train to Knoxville at 2 p.m. on New Year's Day 1865.[1]

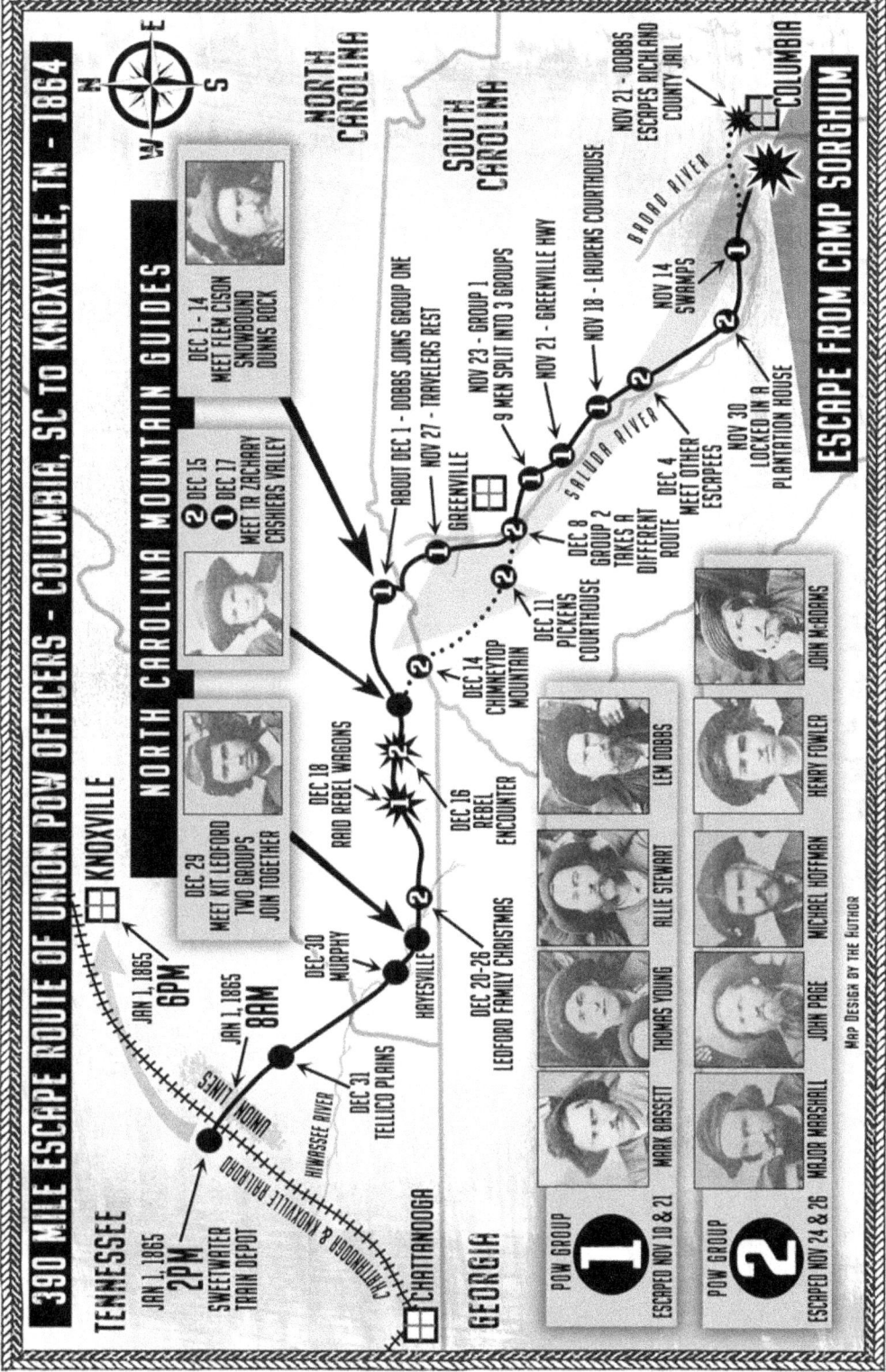

390 MILE ESCAPE ROUTE OF UNION POW OFFICERS - COLUMBIA, SC TO KNOXVILLE, TN - 1864

ESCAPE FROM CAMP SORGHUM

NORTH CAROLINA MOUNTAIN GUIDES

TENNESSEE

KNOXVILLE

JAN 1, 1865 6PM

JAN 1, 1865 8AM

DEC 31 - TELLICO PLAINS

HIWASSEE RIVER

UNION LINES

JAN 1, 1865 2PM - SWEETWATER TRAIN DEPOT

DEC 30 - MURPHY

DEC 29 - MEET KIT LEDFORD - TWO GROUPS JOIN TOGETHER

DEC 20-26 - LEDFORD FAMILY CHRISTMAS

HAYESVILLE

DEC 18 - RAID REBEL WAGONS

DEC 16 - REBEL ENCOUNTER

DEC 15 - MEET TR ZACHARY - CASHIERS VALLEY
DEC 17

DEC 14 - CHIMNEYTOP MOUNTAIN

DEC 11 - PICKENS COURTHOUSE

DEC 1 - 14 - MEET FLEM CISON - SNOWBOUND - DUNNS ROCK

ABOUT DEC 1 - DOBBS JOINS GROUP ONE

NOV 27 - TRAVELERS REST

GREENVILLE

NOV 23 - GROUP 1 - 9 MEN SPLIT INTO 3 GROUPS

DEC 8 - GROUP 2 TAKES A DIFFERENT ROUTE

NOV 21 - GREENVILLE HWY

NOV 18 - LAURENS COURTHOUSE

DEC 4 - MEET OTHER ESCAPEES

NOV 30 - LOCKED IN A PLANTATION HOUSE

SALUDA RIVER

NOV 14 - SWAMPS

BROAD RIVER

NOV 21 - DOBBS ESCAPES RICHLAND COUNTY JAIL

COLUMBIA

NORTH CAROLINA

SOUTH CAROLINA

GEORGIA

CHATTANOOGA

CHATTANOOGA & KNOXVILLE RAILROAD

POW GROUP 1 - ESCAPED NOV 10 & 21

MARK BASSETT

THOMAS YOUNG

ALLIE STEWART

LEM DOBBS

POW GROUP 2 - ESCAPED NOV 24 & 26

MAJOR MARSHALL

JOHN PAGE

MICHAEL HOFFMAN

HENRY FOWLER

JOHN McADAMS

Map Design by the Author

N E W S

Contents

Introduction

THIS IS A BOOK INSPIRED by a single photograph.

When I first saw the front cover photograph, I had just finished the manuscript for my first book, *Rebel Correspondent*. I was continuing some research for a documentary I was making for the "There's History Around Every Bend" video series. This particular video was titled "1864: Chaos in the Mountains," which tells the story of several skirmishes during the Civil War that pitted neighbor against neighbor in the North Georgia and Eastern Tennessee mountains.

While trading messages over the course of a few days regarding some details of that story that were pertinent to my documentary with members of **a** Facebook Civil War group, I received a text message response from Sam Houston, which included an attachment featuring the photograph that now is prominently featured on the front cover of this book. Surprisingly, even though this was on a social media website accessed by people from all over the country, if not the world, Sam Houston turned out to be a neighbor living just a few miles from my cabin on Stanley Creek in the North Georgia mountains.

> **Steve:** *That is an amazing image - who are they?*
>
> **Sam:** *I have a GG uncle, David Ledford, who was killed by rebels while guiding escaped Union prisoners of war through the mountains to Union lines.*
>
> *He was from Cherokee County, NC. He was killed in December 1864 in Tennessee.*
>
> *He is buried in the old Ledford cemetery near Shooting Creek, NC; he was killed at Tellico Mountain, TN. He served in the 2nd NC Mounted Infantry U.S. This is his widow's application for a pension.*
>
> *His brother Jason was in the same regiment.*
>
> *This is a photo taken by the Union Army at Knoxville. David Ledford is identified in this group of Union officers who had escaped from a Confederate Prison in SC. David had guided them through the mountains. David is 2nd row far left. The man with his arms on David's shoulders is the colonel in charge of the group.*
>
> **Steve:** *Is that where you got the history about his death, or did the family pass down an oral account as well?*
>
> **Sam:** *Some from both: There are family stories about the Home Guard hanging Nancy by her thumbs in an attempt to find out David's location.*
>
> **Steve**: *How did you get the photo?*
>
> **Sam:** *My aunt Mae had it when she passed away. The family had moved to Ga from the Hayesville, NC area when she was a girl.*
>
> **Steve:** *Were they from NC or GA?*
>
> **Sam:** *NC they lived not far from the Ga line.*
>
> **Steve:** *Would you mind if I do some research into this?*

So from that text message, with its remarkable photograph, came this book.

As I began researching and identifying the men in "The Photograph," I soon came across a couple of other versions of it as well. They were different in the sense that they were clearly printed on other kinds of photographic paper, which meant they had likely been made at different times. I wondered, *which is the earliest version, and who was the photographer who took the picture*?

I also found out the exact version of the photograph that Sam Houston's family had in their possession was also in the Library of Congress, having been donated to the institution by Mrs. Louise S. Ernst on August 17, 1944. In fact, when I later asked Sam if there were any markings on the back of his family's photograph, he said there was an "LOC" stamp, which meant Sam's family copy had been made by the Library of Congress after 1944. Then I discovered the Chicago Historical Society also had the same photograph in their collection, but it was a different print, and they had incorrectly identified the men as Rebel soldiers—all from Morgan's Raiders.

I soon realized that not only was there a story to be found in the history of the men within "The Photograph," but there was also a story to be found in "The Photograph" itself.

This is a work of narrative nonfiction.

The genre provides a lot of latitude to the author's telling of a story. The approach I have taken for this book is to always follow the facts. It is deeply researched and based on a mountain of evidence sleuthed on a fact-finding journey that took more than eighteen months. Everything within quotations was written or said by the people indicated. There are no fictional characters in this book. Without having the benefit of interviewing the participants, as all my subjects were no longer alive, I wanted to tell this epic story, covering broad swathes of the Civil War without limitations.

Nevertheless, I believe *Captured Freedom* follows the tradition of "new journalism" in how a story is told. James E. Murphy, the late journalism professor at Southern Illinois University, described "new journalism" in 1974 as "an artistic, creative, literary reporting form with three basic traits: dramatic literary techniques; intensive reporting; and reporting of generally acknowledged subjectivity."[2]

Several of the men in "The Photograph" wrote accounts of their experiences after the war. One kept a diary and carried it with him when he escaped. Other soldiers captured with the men also kept diaries and mentioned their comrades or wrote their accounts of their shared experiences as POWs after the war. By pulling together and comparing all these first-person accounts, I was able to triangulate the story, and these facts are backed up by hundreds of sources.

Newspaper archives had tidbits of the story, like breadcrumbs placed along the way. Even small details such as weather and phases of the moon were researched. Detailed family trees were compiled for each man, helping to understand their family histories, what became of them after the Civil War, and how they lived their lives. The descendants of each man were searched, and many of them were found and contacted. So much time had passed so most were unaware of their ancestor's story. Others knew of and had copies of the front cover photograph stored away in musty places, able to point out which man was their ancestor.

One had the only original print of the photograph I was able to locate, and allowed an art conservator to inspect it and create high resolution digital images. And one still had the original letters written over a hundred years ago between two of the men in "The Photograph." "We're a family of pack rats," she said. Thank God for that.

This is a true story about a group of Union POWs who escaped and survived the Civil War.

"Every picture tells a story..." and this picture tells way more than just one.

Steve Procko
Blue Ridge, Georgia

Every Picture Tells a Story

THEY HAD MADE IT.

Lieutenant Michael Hoffman's thoughts spun around and overflowed in his head. Like fireworks, the synapses were all lighting up in his brain at the same time. He felt euphoric, with a tremendous sense of relief. Now the possibilities were endless. Though he hadn't touched a drop of alcohol, he felt drunk or, as he called it, "boozy." But this was pure adrenaline.

New Year's Day 1865 had been one of the most eventful and exciting days of his life, and now it was behind him. The burden of the invisible, hair-trigger pistol he had carried for the last thirty-five days, loaded with bullets named "stress" and "anxiety" had magically disappeared. It had taken that long for Hoffman and two other comrades, Major William Stanhope Marshall and Captain John Elijah Page, to make their way the give-or-take 360 or so miles on foot in the dead of winter. They had made a successful escape from Camp Sorghum, the wretched Confederate Prisoner-of-War (POW)[3] camp located in Columbia, South Carolina. Now they were in Knoxville, Tennessee.

All three were members of the 5th Iowa Infantry Regiment, and had stuck together since November 25, 1863, when almost half of the officers and enlisted men of their regiment were captured by Rebel General Braxton Bragg's forces at the Battle of Missionary Ridge[4] during the Chattanooga Campaign.

Hoffman and Page were both in Company D, which was made up of men from Marshall County, Iowa. They had spent more than thirteen months as POWs together, and it was now finally over. Hoffman's only problem was that all the activity in his brain was occurring in the middle of the night. Tossing and turning, he couldn't sleep.

"We were so elated and lighthearted over our successful escape and the prospects of soon being at home that we could not sleep much. The joys of a year had come to us," said Hoffman.[5]

★ ★ ★

FOR THE FIRST TIME IN WEEKS, he found he was actually content. Being clean, warm, and well-fed was something he had dreamed about for more than a year. Countless meals lovingly made by his mother, Lydia, had been cooked up in his imagination, conjured in a cruel attempt to stave off the ever-present hunger as a POW in the multiple Rebel prison camps where he had been housed.

Outside, on this second day of the new year, it was brutally cold; temperatures hovered in single digits. But Hoffman was cocooned under a warm blanket, lying on a rickety army cot in Knoxville's Asylum U. S. Army General Hospital. Also in the room were at least fifteen others, as was evident by the snoring and other nocturnal body sounds.

Their group was made up of twelve POW Union officers, a Union private, and the three local scouts they had met while walking across North Carolina. The scouts were all supporters of the Union; two of them had deserted the Confederate army they were forced to join. These brave North Carolinians had risked their own lives, as well as their families' well-being, to help him and his friends.

The danger came from helping the POWs on the last stretch of their escape to Union lines through the rugged mountains of Western North Carolina and Eastern Tennessee. The mountainous region was in a state of chaos, though no major battles between the Union and Confederate armies were fought there. Bands of home guards supporting both sides of the fight terrorized the citizenry and engaged in combat against each other. With Union POWs flooding the area in escaping from Columbia, South Carolina, the home guards were on the hunt.

The Asylum U. S. Army General Hospital or "soldier's hospital" was housed in the building known as the Deaf and Dumb Asylum; its cornerstone had been laid in 1848 and had been used first by Confederate and then by Union armies during the Civil War. It didn't matter which side occupied Knoxville; the war was brutal, and both sides desperately needed hospitals. At the time, the hospital was located on the appropriately named Asylum Avenue, which today is known as West Summit Hill Drive, near the intersection of Western Avenue and Broadway. The building still stands today and houses the Lincoln Memorial University's School of Law. In 1865 it was just a few blocks west from the Provost Marshal General Samuel P. Carter's Headquarters, where the former POWs had checked in upon their arrival on New Year's Day by train into Knoxville.

Normally, army cots made from cotton canvas nailed to a flimsy-looking, folding wooden frame with accompanying itchy-rough army blanket in an army hospital would not have been the most desirable accommodations. But to former POWs, it must have felt like being in a luxury suite lying on a thick cotton-filled mattress snuggling with one of their mother's soft, hand-made quilts in one of the finest hotels in Chicago. Hoffman had seen the city of Chicago in 1855 when his parents and six other siblings made their way from western Pennsylvania, where they were all born, to settle in Marshalltown, Iowa.

As the dawn lightened the morning skies on Monday, January 2, 1865, the group of thirteen now-former-POWs and their guides all lay back in their cots for a moment, staring at the ceiling of the soldier's hospital, taking it all in. They were indoors, no longer exposed to the harsh elements, and no longer subject to capture or worse by the pursuing Rebel companies and bushwhackers they had dodged for weeks. They were finally safe, and because they'd been deprived of decent food for months, they were ravenously hungry. Soon they all climbed out of their cots and wrangled some breakfast, which they no doubt savored.

MORE THAN 2,800 UNION POWS had managed to escape from South Carolina in the winter of 1864-65,[6] striking out in all directions of the compass. Some traveled north toward the North Carolina mountains in the general direction of Union lines and Knoxville, Tennessee. This route proved to be the most successful. Others headed west toward Atlanta, which after September 2, 1864, was in Union hands. Some had heard that Sherman was heading toward Columbia, South Carolina, and set off south in an attempt to rendezvous with the celebrity general and his army as they headed northeast from Savannah. Or they went south toward Port Royal at Hilton Head Island. Heading southeast toward the South Carolina coast, still more POW escapees made it to the coastline near Georgetown, South Carolina, where they would try to signal Union gunboats out in the Atlantic Ocean.

"They seem to be everywhere," reported South Carolina's Edgefield Advertiser on November 30, 1864, "They actually cover the land like the locusts of Egypt."[7]

So by the beginning of 1865, the post commander at the Asylum U. S. Army General Hospital had no doubt greeted them and was happy to provide his flimsy cots to many other former POWs who had escaped from South Carolina in the last months of 1864.

"The next morning he gave us an entire new suit of blue soldier clothes," said

Downtown Knoxville 1865 from the south looking north
This photograph is one of a panorama of four photographs
taken by Theodore M. Schleier.

Hoffman.[8] Soon there was a discussion among the former POWs about their new blue uniforms and what to do with the clothes they had arrived in across Union lines the day before, which were best described as odorous rags.

General Samuel P. Carter
Photograph by T. M. Schleier

Then someone threw out an idea, and a plan was hatched.

"Before discarding our old ones we put them on and went up town in search of a photographer," recounted Hoffman.[9]

The staff of the Asylum U. S. Army General Hospital stopped and paused for a brief moment staring at the sight of this band of twelve, all still dressed in the rags they had arrived in, exiting the building. They walked down the steps of the soldier's hospital with a cold wind blowing constantly from the north. Turning to the east onto Asylum Avenue, they headed a few blocks toward Gay Street, Knoxville's main thoroughfare.

"No caravan in passing through the streets would have excited any more curiosity than we did," said Hoffman.[10] Knoxville citizens walking through downtown that morning stopped and stared at the sight. The first thing they needed to do was check in with Provost Marshal General's headquarters, where each of their names were recorded in a ledger. Now they were recognized as soldiers again, POWs no more. As they were emerging from the building where two Union Privates stood at attention with rifles at their sides, someone in the group noticed that right next door was a photographer's studio. *How convenient*, he thought. *This is just what they were looking for.*

PHOTOGRAPHER THEODORE M. SCHLEIER is the most likely suspect that morning to take the photograph of the dozen oddly dressed men. The thirty-two-year-old's photography studio was indeed located right next door to Provost Marshal General Samuel P. Carter's headquarters on South Gay Street. Catering to Union soldiers in Knoxville, Schleier had even photographed Carter himself.

He had opened his Knoxville studio in January 1864. "Headquarters for Pictures," announced the *Knoxville Whig and Rebel Ventilator*, "Mr. T. M. Schleier, Artist from Nashville, has established a branch gallery...next to General Carter's headquarters where he is ready to furnish every style of picture such as photographs, cartes de visites, stereotypes, etc."

Theodore M. Schleier
Date unknown

Born in Prussia and immigrating to the United States around 1852, Schleier fled Europe and his inevitable conscription into the Prussian Army at the start of the German Revolution. As soon as it was allowed, he became a naturalized citizen of the United States. The stout, solidly built Prussian-American stood five foot, five inches tall with intense hazel eyes.

Schleier began his career in New Orleans, opening a daguerreotype salon in the late 1850s. Another New Orleans photographer, James Andrews, clearly did not appreciate the competition. After several heated verbal confrontations, the rivalry turned into a full-blown brawl. Andrews kicked in the door of Schleier's studio and proceeded to beat Schleier with an iron poker, injuring him seriously, and smashed all his photographic equipment. Schleier filed suit and lost, recovered from his injuries, and rebuilt his studio. For a while he remained in New Orleans, continuing to market his artistic daguerreotypes.

By the late 1850s, Schleier had relocated to Nashville, Tennessee, taking on an opportunity to affiliate himself with the Southern Photographic Temple of Fine Arts, the established studio of Charles C. Giers, a fellow Prussian-American photographer. By 1862 or 1863 he had established his own independent gallery in Nashville and, with advancing photographic technologies, sold his wares to Union soldiers who passed through the Nashville area for much of the Civil War. He was responsible for a large output of individual soldier cartes de visites (CDVs) with his Nashville studio imprint. "Photographs of all sizes in india ink, oil or water colors. Daguerreotypes and other pictures copied to any size. Landscapes, views, camps, etc. taken at short notice," according to an advertisement on the imprint found on the back of the CDVs he created. He would eventually have studio galleries in Nashville, Knoxville, and Chattanooga.

The sign on the exterior of the building read "T.M. Schleier's Picture Gallery." The twelve men entered the building and climbed two flights of stairs, their sore legs complaining with each step, before arriving on the third floor where they knocked on the door. Moments later, the studio door opened, and photographer Theodore M. Schleier paused for a moment staring with interest at the motley crew. "There were twelve of us who had our picture taken in the group, four of our party for some reason or other not being with us," said Hoffman.[11]

The Union officers hailed from regiments from all around the United States; 1st Lieutenant Michael Hoffman was with his fellow 5th Iowa Infantry comrades, Major William Stanhope

Advertising on the back of a
T.M. Schleier cartes de visite (CDV)
Circa 1870s

Marshall and Captain John Elijah Page. The other officers included 2nd Lieutenants Alfred Shelby Stewart and Thomas Payne Young of the 4th Kentucky Mounted Infantry; 1st Lieutenant Mark M. Bassett of the 53rd Illinois Infantry; 1st Lieutenant Lemuel Davis Dobbs of the 19th United States Colored Infantry (USCI); 1st Lieutenant Henry M. Fowler of the 15th New Jersey Infantry; and 1st Lieutenant John McAdams of the 10th West Virginia Infantry. Along for the ride and rounding out the group were the three North Carolina guides, Julius Ketron "Kit" Ledford from near Hayesville, NC; Joseph Fleming "Flem" Cison from Dunns Rock, NC; and Thompson Roberts "T.R." Zachary from Cashiers Valley, NC.

The group piled into Schleier's studio, interesting odors emanating from their ragged clothing mixed with the chemical fumes common to the photography trade that permeated the place. They were literally and figuratively the dirty dozen.

Schleier's studio was located on the top floor of a three-story building that featured a pool hall on the first floor and a community gathering space known as Ramsey's Hall on the second floor. Like most photographer's studios in the 1860s, it featured natural lighting sources, a large skylight and window array that could be opened and closed to allow light into the studio space.[12] The group soon were hustled together into three rows backed up against a plain, light-toned studio background. But first, Schleier had to go into his darkroom to prepare the glass-plate negative.

The technique Schleier was using at the time was known as wet-plate collodion. Creating a collodion negative was potentially more valuable to photographers like Schleier because a negative allowed for multiple copies of an image to be easily made, which resulted in additional sales. For Schleier, the man who owned the "Headquarters for Photography," twelve people in one photograph might make for a lucrative day. This was one of the largest group of subjects that he had photographed inside his studio. It would take all the space the studio had, requiring him to back up his camera in order to fit them all into the frame.

He removed the camera's lens cap and then threw the dark focusing cloth over both his head and the back of the camera. The focusing cloth created a darkened pocket at the back of the camera where a piece of ground glass was attached, which allowed him to see his subjects through the camera's lens and to focus and frame the image. He viewed the twelve men upside down on the ground glass, then, satisfied with the composition, removed the focusing cloth from the camera's back, replaced the lens cap, and attached the sensitized wet-plate collodion holder to the camera. Schleier was now ready to make the photograph.

A large skylight array above and behind the photographer and his camera front-lit the twelve men. The scene was so wide that a cast-iron drainpipe was visible in the right of frame, while other studio props pushed to the side edge into the left of frame. He told his subjects that they would need to hold perfectly still, then mentally calculated the exposure time—a couple of seconds in length. Any longer would make it hard for his subjects to hold still. Any movement would make them blurry in the photograph.

The ragged bunch brace to steady themselves. Each wears a hat—a cornucopia of different styles. Their clothes are full of holes; the knees of their pants are torn and reveal a patchwork of mismatched layers beneath. The shoes that can be seen on the men in the front row are falling apart, yet somehow remain miraculously attached to their feet. Having not yet had the time to trim them, many sport long beards. Others have little or no facial hair at all because they are so young. One had little facial hair because of genetics; he had indigenous Cherokee blood in his veins.

Major Marshall coyly turns his cap sideways, then with a smirk drapes his arms over Kit Ledford's shoulders. Lieutenant McAdams rests his elbow on his right knee and places his right hand to the side of his face. Lieutenant Bassett folds his arms and takes on a serious expression of concern; his mind is elsewhere, thinking about personal matters. Lieutenant Young leans his left arm on Captain Stewart's shoulder while gripping the walking stick in a still-gloved right hand. He had become quite frail from his time in Rebel prisons and his exposure to the frigid winter elements during his escape, Young had needed the walking stick to lean on and navigate the treacherous mountain terrain just two days earlier; now he feels at peace. Captain Stewart crosses his arms, resting his elbows on his thighs, and sits up straight. In the last row at the far right, Tom Zachary puts his hand on Flem Cison's shoulder and holds steady, preparing for what is possibly the first photograph he has ever had taken—Zachary is just fourteen years old. The men collectively hold their breath and freeze, as if a Rebel picket is but six feet away instead of the Prussian-born photographer behind a camera.

Schleier opens the light-protective slide of the wet-plate collodion holder attached to the back of the camera. His German-accented voice tells them all to hold still. He expertly removes the lens cap and mentally counts off the seconds exposing the sensitized glass plate to the light of the twelve men focused on its surface. One, two, three, four. In 1865 there is no sound of a shutter clicking, just silence. Then he quickly replaces the lens cap, ending the exposure, and closes the light-protective slide of the plate holder.

The photograph now taken, the men all relax and collectively release their breath. It feels good to feel relaxed. Cigar smoke continues to waft through the studio as Major Marshall cracks a joke and they all laugh, relaxing a bit more.

But there is one more step. To confirm that the photograph was a success, and the negative is good, Schleier needs to process the negative. Until he confirms this, the men wait in case another negative needs to be exposed.

Quickly, he removes the plate-holder from the back of the camera and heads back into his darkroom to process the image. Slowly, in about three to four minutes, it emerges. With trained eyes, he sees a negative image of twelve men staring back at him. He knows it's a good photograph.

A serendipitous moment, a couple of seconds forever frozen in time. This group of twelve had only known each other for a few days, having come together on December

28, 1864, near Murphy, North Carolina, though over the preceding months they had all crossed paths at some point in the various Rebel POW prisons they were all being held in. Within a few hours they would scatter out in all directions—except to the south. Within a day they would have leave papers in hand and would be finally heading home. The oldest was thirty-one years old, the youngest just fourteen. Some would never see each other again.

Theodore M. Schleier hadn't just successfully captured a photograph of twelve ragged men.

He had indeed Captured Freedom.

**Photograph made on Monday, January 2, 1865,
in Knoxville, Tennessee, by Theodore M. Schleier**
*Digital capture from original albumen print originally owned by Michael Hoffman.
Courtesy of the Charles Hoffman family.*

Back Row: Major William Stanhope Marshall, 5th Iowa Infantry;
1st Lieutenant Henry M. Fowler, 15th New Jersey Infantry;
1st Lieutenant Michael Hoffman, 5th Iowa Infantry;
Thompson Roberts "T.R." Zachary, North Carolina guide.

Middle Row: Julius Ketron "Kit" Ledford, North Carolina guide;
1st Lieutenant Lemuel Davis Dobbs,
19th United States Colored Infantry (USCI);
2nd Lieutenant Thomas Payne Young, 4th Kentucky Mounted Infantry;
Joseph Fleming "Flem" Cison, North Carolina guide.

Front Row: 1st Lieutenant Mark M. Bassett, 53rd Illinois Infantry;
1st Lieutenant John McAdams, 10th West Virginia Infantry;
2nd Lieutenant Alfred Shelby Stewart, 4th Kentucky Mounted Infantry;
Captain John Elijah Page, 5th Iowa Infantry.

Chapter One

Mark M. Bassett – 53rd Illinois
January 1862 to July 1863

THE DAY BEGAN JUST LIKE the one before it. The morning of July 1, 1863, Mark Mitchell Bassett's company manned the sharpshooter's line, their Springfield rifles ready, hundreds of fingers aquiver on each of their weapon's respective triggers. Another day of holding the line, pushing up against the Rebels, who were pushing right back with all the men they had, desperately trying to get out of the city of Vicksburg, Mississippi.

He had never gotten used to sleeping under the conditions of war. The night was always peppered with the occasional sounds of gunshots and other disconcerting noises of the night, keeping him constantly on edge. The twenty-six-year-old was a First Lieutenant in command of Company E of the 53rd Illinois Volunteer Infantry Regiment.

Another day of holding the line.

Poised. Ready.

Lieutenant Bassett and the 53rd Illinois Infantry had been given the task of blocking a potential Confederate escape route at Hall's Ferry Road, which was located on the southeast side of Vicksburg. They had held for thirty-eight days, with duty on the sharpshooter's line since June 9. The weather was humid and steaming hot, Mississippi hot. It had taken a while for the soldiers from Illinois to acclimate to it. Some never had to. Some never did. Both sides were so close they could see and hear each other's conversations, killing time instead of killing each other. One could imagine back-and-forth dialogue discussing such banal topics as the weather:

"Hey Johnnie Reb, you getting hot in there?" yelled the Yankee private to his *counterpart lying balled-up in a hand-dug "cave" at a place known as the Salient works, which was a bulge in the Rebel fortifications.*

"Not me, I love the hot, 'cause I'm from the south. How 'bout you, Billy Yank, the sweat gettin' to you yet?" the Rebel private in a thick drawl verbally fired his *conversational bullet back across the line.*

THE SIEGE OF VICKSBURG officially began on May 19, 1863; the 53rd Illinois arrived six days later, on May 25, to join the fight on the southeast side of the city.

**Private
Herbert E. Ranstead**
Company D
53 Illinois
Photographer unknown

Ulysses S. Grant had decided to dig in and squeeze the fortress city by surrounding it from the north, east, and south, with the Mississippi River providing a wall to the west. Grant's counterpart within the city walls was Confederate Lieutenant General John C. Pemberton. Pemberton and Grant knew each other well, having fought together during the Mexican War. Like so many other confrontations in this war, former comrades were now adversaries.

The 53rd Illinois was just one small part of a giant, half-crescent, 77,000-plus–man line formed to the east of the city. The siege's strategy was to keep the 22,000-plus men of the Confederate army trapped inside Vicksburg, crushing it into submission.[13] The Rebels' fortress-like setting gave a sense of security and comfort—unless the city was completely surrounded and supplies dwindled with no chance of reinforcements. The citizens of Vicksburg were packed in along with the soldiers, suffering the same fate.

By July 1, conditions for the Rebel soldiers and Vicksburg civilians had deteriorated badly. "The Union works and the Confederate works were pretty close together at the last of the siege. In some places they were as close as three or four rods.[14] Looking out over the works we could see the lines of both sides for two miles each way, running over the hills," noted Private Herbert E. Ranstead of Company D, 53rd Illinois. "It was a nice sight at night to look out over the armies and over the city and see the flashes of the small arms and the flash of the gun and mortar boats throwing shell and mortar shot into the city. We could see the flash of the mortar and then see the ball rise up in the air and make a circle through the heavens and then, when near the ground, another flash and boom and all would be still, and so they would be at it all night. The Rebs had to dig caves in the sides of the hills to be in safety from the shell and shot."[15]

By the evening of Thursday, July 2, the Confederate army was getting desperate. Pemberton's division commanders, when polled individually by the General himself, had each come to the realization that their situation was futile. They were looking for a way out of the mess they found themselves in. Talks commenced between the two sides, and General Grant, having the upper hand, issued terms he had become famous for: unconditional surrender.

"The negotiations were going on slowly. During the 2d and 3d of July we would get up on the works three or four times a day when the white flags were up and visit. Pretty soon, way up the line, the flags would begin to go down. Then you would hear everybody shout, 'Look out, we are going to shoot,' and it would not be a minute till all along the line they were shooting as hard as ever," scribbled Private Ranstead in his diary.[16] It was always a good thing to be warned before they started shooting.

By the morning of Saturday, July 4, in a major loss by the Rebels, Vicksburg was ceded to Union forces. By July 8, they controlled the Mississippi River. By the time it was finished, more than 30,000 Confederates soldiers had surrendered. In the terms of the surrender, with the exception of a few officers, all the Confederate soldiers were paroled, not imprisoned. Pemberton himself was taken as a prisoner and exchanged a couple of months later in October 1863.

THIS WAS THE CIVIL WAR merry-go-round. Soldiers became POWs for a while until they were exchanged with a soldier from the other side, then they rejoined the fight. Repeat. "And so it went till the 4th of July, 1863, when the city and the Confederate army were surrendered to the Union forces, and on that day, after the Johnnies had stacked their arms, they were allowed to mingle freely with the men and you would not suppose we were a lot of men that had been trying to kill one another for the last two months. We gave the Johnnies as good a dinner as we could, and had a general good time to celebrate the glorious Fourth," said Private Ranstead.

After forty-five days of siege, the two sides got together for what must have been the strangest 4th of July celebration anyone has ever attended. They celebrated the birth of the nation, in what was at the time a foreign country known as the Confederate States of America, along with those "foreign" soldiers. Even so, a sense of relief passed through the ranks of the 53rd Illinois including Company E and its First Lieutenant, Mark Bassett. It wouldn't last long.

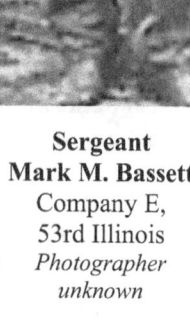

**Sergeant
Mark M. Bassett**
Company E,
53rd Illinois
*Photographer
unknown*

MARK MITCHELL BASSETT was born in Schuyler County, Illinois, on March 27, 1837. His father, Thomas Bassett, was born in Davies County, Kentucky, around 1801 but died young, the same year Mark was born. His mother, Abigail Carlock, who was born in Overton, Tennessee, in 1809, was suddenly a widow, struggling to raise her four children: three boys, including infant Mark, and one girl.

"He passed his boyhood days in Schuyler and Fulton Counties," later claimed the *Peoria Biographical Dictionary*, "enjoying but limited educational means, yet, nevertheless, attaining such proficiency in his studies as to lay a solid foundation...He was brought up on hard labor on a farm."

Schuyler and Fulton Counties were located to the southwest of Peoria, Illinois, on the northern banks of the Illinois River, which was rich midwestern farmland. In the late 1830s the midwestern frontier was drawing settlers from the east. The land, enriched by the Illinois River flood plain, produced soil ideally suited for farming. Bassett worked hard tilling the soil and rafting logs down the Illinois River to the St. Louis market.

His early life of hard labor was also filled with personal struggles and tragedy. In

October 1854 his brother Nathaniel died at age twenty-one. Three years later in August 1856, his mother died at just forty-seven years old. Mark was suddenly on his own with his two older surviving siblings, both married. Brother William moved to Indiana. His older sister, Mary Jane, married Abram Jefferson Markley, had two children, and lived down the road from Bassett.

The year after his mother's death was a busy time for Bassett, giving a glimpse into his character and entrepreneurial drive. Besides farming a plot of land, in August 1857 he went into business with another farmer selling grain and stock in a country store.[17] A short time later he bought out his partner's interest to go it alone, operating the business himself.

He also began courting the daughter of a family friend. This led to a quick marriage when on December 22, 1857, the twenty-year-old Bassett married seventeen-year-old Ohio-born Charlotte Severns. He called his wife by her nickname, Lottie. A son, Nathaniel, was born just seven months after the wedding in June 1858. Bassett was an honorable man. The marriage would produce two additional children, Sarah Jane in 1860 and Charles in 1861.

The 1860 census shows the family was living in Kerton Township with his occupation recorded as a warehouseman, reflecting his country store business, owning $1,400 in real estate. He had no family legacy but was full of ambition and was slowly growing a semblance of financial stability for his young family. At the start of the Civil War his farmstead was just down the road from where Charlotte's father lived.[18]

Her father, Daniel Severns III, was originally from Monongalia County, Virginia. He had settled for a time in the 1820s about 150 miles to the east of Monongalia County to Coshocton, Ohio, where he married Barbara Bucklew in 1830. But Severns had a wandering eye and at the end of the 1830s had started an affair with a neighbor. The tryst resulted in Charlotte being born in 1840. Soon after, looking to clear the air and wanting a fresh start, Severns moved his family west, settling in Kerton Township, Illinois. He acquired several choice parcels of rich farmland. Charlotte was left behind in Ohio with her mother, where her early years were difficult and confusing.

From 1840 to 1850 the Illinois River basin where Severns moved had doubled its population from 190,000 to more than 500,000.[19] In the rich Illinois farmland he prospered, farming corn and serving as a town clerk.

Back in Ohio, in 1852 Charlotte's mother died. Twelve-year-old Charlotte was shipped west to live with her father in Illinois. She would join his family of eight half-siblings, with one additional half-sister born shortly after she arrived. Severns became wealthy by the standards of the time, owning real estate with a value of $11,500 as recorded in the 1860 census.

BASSETT'S INVOLVEMENT in his nation's divisive Civil War began in December 1861 in Ottawa, Illinois. Experiencing what tens of thousands of men were facing when the nation went to war against itself, he traveled northeast, leaving his wife and three young children—a difficult decision that separated a husband from his wife, a father from his children, and the main financial provider from his family. While her husband was at war with no guarantee they would see each other again and as their time apart grew, Lottie Bassett suffered from a stress known by thousands of other soldier's wives. She would rely on her father and stepmother for support, as well as a few others she befriended.

Bassett boarded a steamboat for a 125-mile trip up the Illinois River past Peoria to LaSalle, Illinois.[20] From LaSalle he took a mule-pulled flatboat on the Illinois and Michigan Canal. The canal would take him the final fifteen miles to Ottawa, passing through four locks and a viaduct, which included raising the canal boat's elevation along the way.

In Ottawa, Bassett enlisted into the 53rd Illinois Volunteers. The regiment was organized by Colonel William Hercules Washburn Cushman, a personal friend of President Abraham Lincoln. Colonel Cushman's friendship with the President was notable and publicized for all to see, making him rarefied "Illinois royalty." When Bassett enlisted, he did so with a connection his family believed might also be notable but definitely didn't want it publicized. In fact, it was a family secret he hoped would never be discovered.

In the family's nineteenth-century oral history passed down through the generations, Bassett's maternal great-grandfather was William Hezekiah Lee (1758-1819).[21] His brother was Henry Lee III (1768-1818). Henry's son turned out to be quite famous— none other than General Robert E. Lee (1807-1870).

That made Bassett's maternal grandmother, Mary Ann Lee Carlock (1780-1850), a first cousin to none other than General Robert E. Lee, making the newly minted Sergeant Bassett a first cousin twice removed. When Bassett's grandmother died in 1850, her cousin was a colonel, a famous, well-respected American who had just completed service during the Mexican War. The Carlock clan was proud of their lineage, but just over a decade later that would dramatically change.

"I was named for my maternal grandfather, William Lee, who was a brother of the father of Gen. Robert E. Lee. My middle name was for Gen. Jackson, the hero of the Battle of New Orleans, under whom my father fought," said Bassett's patriotically proud uncle, William Jackson Carlock, at the start of the twentieth century.[22]

At the beginning of the Civil War, Robert E. Lee was offered command of the Union Army. But his loyalties were with his native Virginia, which seceded so he resigned and became commander of the Confederate Army of Virginia in May, 1862. This made Lee an instant traitor to the United States, to which Bassett had enthusiastically sworn his allegiance. Such were the times with families divided and brothers fighting brothers or, in this case, cousins secretly fighting very famous cousins.

There is only one problem with such a passed-down family legend: Oftentimes it is wrong. This was indeed the case with the Bassett-Carlock-Lee family tree narrative: It was incorrect. They were, in fact, not related to Robert E. Lee.[23] Nevertheless, from back in the early nineteenth century through the first part of the twentieth century, the Carlock family thought that Robert E. Lee was a member of their family. Even though today it is proven incorrect, they believed it was true. As a result, it would present a difficulty for Bassett. As a soldier in the Union army, potentially his loyalties could be questioned.

COMPANY E'S 21-YEAR-OLD Armand Pallissard was someone well known to the 23-year-old Bassett. Born in L'Isle en Dodon, France, on January 22, 1840, the five-foot, four-inch tall Pallissard had studied at the premier French military academy, the Ecole Speciale Militaire, located southwest of Paris some 460 miles from his home. The military academy had been created in 1802 by the order of Napoleon Bonaparte.

Pallissard came to the United States with his father, Paulin, arriving on August 4, 1855. Father and son were originally headed to St. Louis, but a cholera epidemic thwarted those plans so they settled near the French-speaking community of Bourbonais, Illinois, just north of Kankakee. They would both would become naturalized American citizens.[24]

Lieutenant Armand
Pallissard
Company E
53 Illinois
Photographer unknown

Armand enlisted in the 53rd Illinois on the same day as Bassett, January 1, 1862, mustering in a notch above Bassett's rank as First Sergeant. The two would become close friends.[25] "Our relations were very close and always the most friendly. He was rather small...young, rosy-cheeked and bright-eyed, vivacious and enthusiastic. I can hear his voice still, which in times of excitement gave a broken French accent to English words, as for instance when there was disorderly talking in the ranks which offended his true military idea of discipline, I can hear him order "silence" in the ranks instead of "si-lence," said Bassett.[26]

On February 27, 1862, the regiment moved to the south side of Chicago where Sergeants Pallissard and Bassett, along with their men, served as guards at Camp Douglas. The Union training facility, named after Senator Stephen A. Douglas, had become a POW camp in early 1862 after the capture of Fort Donelson and Fort Henry in Tennessee, which resulted in a sudden intake of 12,392 Rebel POWs. Success in battle produced prisoners; what to do with them once you captured them proved to be a dilemma for both sides during the Civil War.

By the end of March 1862, the 53rd Illinois moved south toward the fight. From April 29 through May 30, 1862, Sergeant Bassett and the rest of the 53rd Illinois moved south into Mississippi, supporting the Siege of Corinth, mostly performing picket duty with one company participating in the fighting at Russell House. Most of the time the 53rd Illinois faced the hard, cold reality of war with a shovel in their hands, tasked with burial duty in the damp rain.

"We thought it was awful at that time, but I tell you we got used to that, and found a man's life was held pretty cheap in those days at the front," said Private Ranstead.

Sergeant Armand Pallissard, full of ambition, was eyeing the Army as a full-time career; he would write to his father expressing his hopes of soon being promoted to Lieutenant. But he also wanted the war to end, offering his own solution to the expanding conflict that would be personally satisfying to both him and his fellow soldiers. "It would be necessary, in order to end the war promptly, for all the bantering senators and abolitionist representatives who sit in Washington to be obligated to engage themselves in a company like simple soldiers and to exist for eight months on hard bread and coffee," said Pallissard.[27]

For the next four months of 1862, the 53rd Illinois found itself slowly moving west on a serpentine path in and out of Tennessee and Mississippi, passing near Corinth before finally finding itself back in Tennessee near Memphis, fighting in small skirmishes along the way.

By September 21 they were in camp near Bolivar, Tennessee, for almost two weeks, back to taking their meals seated on the ground, soldier-style. Pallissard would write his brother Edward, noting the impact of thousands of soldiers tramping over the lush farmland. "The harvests are beautiful but in a strip of 15 miles from all military posts, federal or confederate, all is eaten, destroyed; all appears desolate when armies pass...my love to all the family; I must end this letter because it is 10:00 P.M. and my light must be extinguished."[28] His last words to Edward proved prophetic.

On October 5, 1862, they had reached the Hatchie River near Metamora, Tennessee, at Davis Bridge. The 53rd were fighting the Confederates on the east bank of the bridge. "The 53rd engaged four times their number of the enemy, who were retreating from Corinth," said Private Ranstead.[29] The 53rd Illinois assisted in running a section of artillery, a Missouri Battery, up the bluff by hand, placing it within fifty yards of the enemy's line. They were so close they could stare into each other's eyes.

The Davis Bridge engagement became the source of the bad blood between Major General Edward O.C. Ord and Brigadier General Jacob G. Lauman. Ord ordered Lauman to send two regiments, including the 53rd Illinois, across the Davis Bridge. Once across, there was not enough room to safely deploy on the opposite side, resulting in soldiers being jammed against each other in the confusion, during which General Ord was seriously wounded. When orders to pull back were given, General Lauman misunderstood and instead sent two more regiments over the bridge, adding to the chaos and causing additional casualties. The Rebels rained lead on the position of the disorganized Yankees.

After marching double quick to Davis Bridge, Company E's Captain Charles M. Vaughn was mortally wounded. Second Lieutenant Mark C. Wheeler was sick and had been lucky enough to be granted a leave of absence, avoiding the battle, which made Pallissard next in the company's line of command.

Wheeler had given Pallissard his sword, and the young Frenchman took his place as acting Lieutenant. While attempting to rally his men who seemed to be faltering in a tenuous position, he waved the sword shouting, "Men stand firm; we must not lose our ground." At that exact moment a canister round tore through his chest, killing him instantly[30] and leaving the men of Company E without a leader at this critical moment.

Major Earl rode up and seeing the men in confusion with no officer shouted, "Who is in command of this Company?"

During the battle Bassett was still a 5th Sergeant and acting as Pallissard's orderly. Private Moses Wilkins, the tallest man in Company E and therefore easiest to spot, yelled out a response to the Major over the continuing fire.

"All the officers are killed or wounded."[31]

Pallissard's body lay nearby, face down in a pool of blood. With Pallissard killed in action, Bassett was the next in the line of command for the company.

Major Earl quickly assessed the deteriorating situation; his gaze fell back to Bassett, yelling to him over the noise of battle. "Throw down that musket, take the sword off that dead officer, and take command of the Company, Sergeant!"[32]

"That officer was Lieutenant Pallissard who was lying on his face in front of us, just as he had fallen dead. Wilkins then took him by his left shoulder and turned him on his back so as to get at the belt fastening, unbuckled the belt and removed it, then turned the breathless body back again on its face just as it fell a few minutes before, then removed sword and fastenings and assisted in putting it on me and then I assumed command," said Bassett.[33]

The 53rd Illinois's loss in this battle was sixteen killed and forty-nine wounded.[34] Among the wounded from Bassett's own company were two neighbors from back home that he knew well, Privates John H. Moore and William Kirk. Their war was over; with disability discharges they returned home to Kerton Township. Moore, who lived close to

Bassett's farmstead, would personally give a firsthand account of the battle to Lottie.

"Never did officers do better; never were men placed under more trying circumstances," said Brigadier General J. G. Lauman in his official report, calling out Major Earl as one of those officers.[35] There were more than 550 total Union casualties, some of which was caused by Lauman's confusion over the orders.[36]

On October 15 Major Seth Clark Earl stepped forward and took command of the 53rd Illinois. The tall, stout, fifty-three-year-old Major Earl had been a merchant in Ottawa, Illinois, as the war began. S.C. Earl and Son was a shop that sold paint, fancy wallpapers, and lamps to the booming population in the region.

Major Seth Clark Earl
53 Illinois
Photographer unknown
Abraham Lincoln
Presidential Library &
Museum

Following Pallissard's death, Bassett's leadership in the regiment was recognized; he officially received a promotion to First Lieutenant of Company E on November 10. Seth C. Earl was promoted to Lieutenant Colonel on November 11. Through the remainder of 1862, the 53rd Illinois continued moving through parts of western Tennessee and Mississippi.

"We spent Christmas at the Tallahatchie River. Most of us had plenty of roasted corn for Christmas dinner," wrote the 53rd Illinois's Private Wilson in a letter published in his hometown newspaper around the holidays. "And, while you were sitting in your houses, looking out at the rain and mud, wishing that there was six inches of snow so you could spend Christmas as it should be spent, we were lounging upon the grass out in the open air, and wondering if they 'missed us at home.'"[37]

ON JANUARY 1, 1863, THE Emancipation Proclamation became the law of the land, and the 53rd Illinois regiment was reshuffled within the chain of command of the Army of the Tennessee, becoming part of a brigade under the command of Colonel Isaac C. Pugh and setting the stage for the battles of 1863.

By January 11, 1863, they were in Moscow, Tennessee, in winter quarters, tasked with guarding the Memphis and Charleston Railroad. As spring came on March 11, 1863, they were moved to Memphis, Tennessee, the staging ground for the Union army's move on Vicksburg.

Two months later, on May 16, 1863, they headed for Vicksburg, Mississippi, passing west of the city to a point where Union forces could safely cross the Mississippi River to the city's south. Then they swung into position on the 25th at Hall's Ferry Road for the siege on the southeast side of the city and hunkered down. Forty-one days later the siege had played out,[38] and they found themselves uncomfortably rubbing elbows with their Rebel enemies.

✯ ✯ ✯

JULY 1 THROUGH 3, 1863, SAW THE Union army's victory at the Battle of Gettysburg in the north. The next day, July 4th, Vicksburg was also won. To the North, it seemed like a turning point.

"After the capture of Vicksburg, Mississippi, on July 4th, 1863, that branch of the Union army to which my regiment belonged was ordered to pursue General Joseph E. Johnston who had been attacking it in the rear, and five days' rations were issued to us," said Bassett, now a First Lieutenant, "but while we were getting ready to break camp thirty-one thousand Confederates, who had surrendered under General John C. Pemberton, thronged over their breastworks and ours, and, as they had suffered from hunger during the siege, we gave them all of our five days' rations."

The relief felt from the victory at Vicksburg was short-lived, and on July 5 the 53rd Illinois, along with several other regiments, were sent east toward Jackson, Mississippi.

"We were ordered to countermarch, and in the awful heat and dust of that sultry soul-depressing semi-tropical sun, with malarial fever burning in my body, I heard the order; rumor said we were going after Joe Johnston," said Edwin L. Hobard who hailed from Colchester, Illinois, and was a private in Company D, 28th Illinois Infantry. "We now have orders to march on Jackson."[39]

Having given up the first batch of rations issued to them, "We received an additional five days' rations and started on the march to Jackson, Mississippi, fifty miles east of Vicksburg, which place we reached on the evening of the 11th," said Bassett.[40]

They marched toward Jackson fast. Too fast. They arrived well in advance of other supporting regiments, camping on the night of the 11th on the west side of the railroad tracks that ran southwest out of Jackson. They were located just one mile from the Rebel earthworks. Johnston's army had fortified the city with a strong line of earthen works extending from the Pearl River to the south of the city and then around the west side of the city to meet the river again on the northeast side of the city.

At around 9 a.m. on the morning of Sunday, July 12, the incessant heat radiated down from the Mississippi sun onto the men of the 53rd Illinois. It blazed directly into their faces as they tried to shield their eyes and get a look east toward the earthworks. It was then that things all went south for Bassett and Company E. A short distance from where they were lined up, there was suddenly heard the sounds of a piano eerily playing a popular nineteenth-century song called "You Shan't Have Any of My Peanuts." No one was singing, but the tune was known to all, and it was likely that some of the men had the lyrics rattling around in their heads as the tune repeated itself, like the 1863 version of "Ninety-Nine Bottles of Beer."

The man who has plenty of good peanuts.
The man who has plenty of good peanuts.
And giveth his neighbor none.
He shan't have any of my peanuts.
When his peanuts are gone.
When his peanuts are gone.
When his peanuts are gone.
He shan't have any of my peanuts.
When his peanuts are gone.

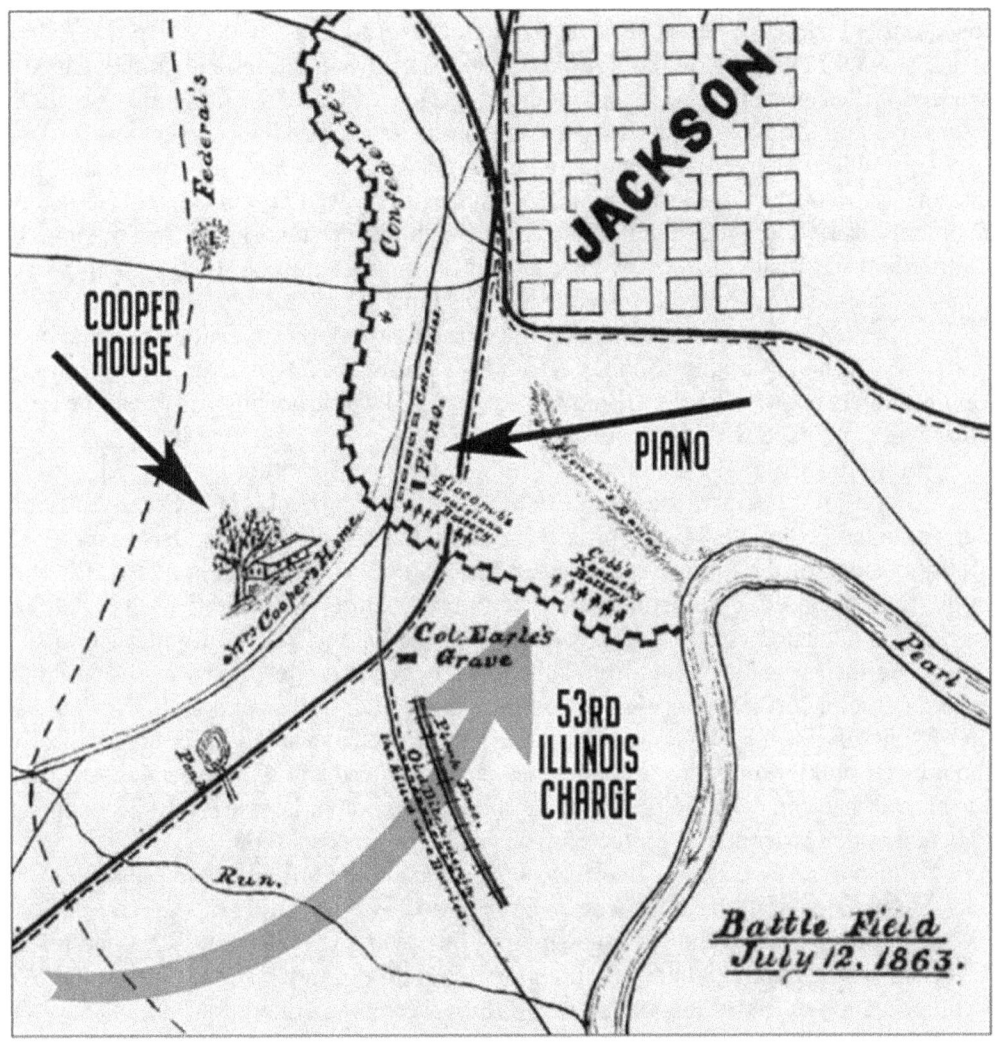

**July 12, 1863 – The disastrous charge on the earthworks
at Jackson, Mississippi, by the 53rd Illinois**
Adapted from map; Library of Congress, Prints and Photographs Division

Nearby stood the recently burned-out shell of a mansion, wisps of smoke still coming from the ruins. The mansion had been in the way, destroyed by the Confederates to improve their field of fire from atop the earthworks. The Cooper family, who were loyal Confederate citizens, agreed to the burning of their home for the cause but had asked the soldiers to help remove whatever belongings they could salvage before their home was torched. One of the items saved was a Chickering "square" parlor piano, manufactured by Yankees in Boston in 1840. The piano was hoisted over the earthworks of the Washington Artillery Battery where it took position near the 5th Company known as Slocomb's Louisiana Battery.[41] Private Andy G. Swain, the 5th's bugler, was the soldier tinkling the ivories.[42]

Then at around 10 a.m., the Rebels began firing down on the exposed Yankees.

"From this point, Colonel Pugh advanced to the skirmish line, which soon engaged the enemy," said Private Samuel M. Howard of Company H, 28th Illinois Infantry. "We moved through dense underbrush across a small creek, and thence onward until we came to a cornfield. Here we halted and dressed up the line, although under sharp fire."

"Colonel Pugh says he did not like the looks of the situation here, and declined to proceed further without specific orders therefor. Hence he sent for General Lauman, the division commander, who thereupon came upon the ground in person and ordered Colonel Pugh to charge upon the main earthworks of the enemy, less than a half mile distant. With a deep yell, learned at Shiloh, which still rings in my ears, these four veteran regiments started on the double-quick for the main earthworks of the enemy, for destruction and death; for we were charging at a terrible angle of the main works, completely enfiladed from our right flank, and supported by nobody," said Howard.[43]

From the Confederate earthworks, the Washington Artillery Battery, consisting of thirty-two-year-old Captain Cuthbert Slocumb's Louisiana Battery, fired down onto the Union soldiers below. The 53rd Illinois's Colonel Earl was killed instantly near the Rebel breastworks, pierced with four canister shot.[44]

Soon after Colonel Earl fell, the 53rd's colors were captured, saturated with the blood of the color bearer, a native of Farm Ridge Township in LaSalle County, Illinois, Sergeant George Poundstone.[45] Initially he was shot through the thigh. His first thought after the shock of the injury was to try and protect the flag from capture. While lying in the field of battle, Poundstone removed the red, white, and blue from its "pike" or flagstaff and stuffed the thirty-five–star flag of the United States of America into his jacket. He then was hit by additional shots to his eye and chest and went down in the futile charge of the earthworks, like so many other men in the regiment. He would lie on the battlefield, his blood saturating the flag, for what was to be hours. Still alive though mortally wounded, Poundstone was captured by Confederates. He was transferred back to Vicksburg where he died eleven days later on July 23. The flag clutched under his coat and protected with his body survives today.

"This was an awful place to charge across," said the 53rd's Private Ranstead. "We had charged almost to the Rebs works, getting so close we could not stand the fire and hail of bullets, so we laid down in a shallow furrow made by a plow. This had been a cornfield. I don't know what they thought we would do here, as there were no orders to retreat, and the first thing we knew the Rebs were swarming all around us and said we were their prisoners."[46]

Captain James E. Hudson of Private Ranstead's Company D had also been mortally wounded in the fight and would succumb to his injuries less than a month later.

"On Sunday, the 12th, our brigade...attacked the confederate breastworks at Jackson and after hard fighting was repulsed with great loss," said Bassett. "Many were killed, among them our Colonel S.C. Earl, from Earsville, Illinois, and many line officers were wounded and captured. I was one of these, having been wounded by a fragment of a bursting shell, though not seriously."[47]

"I never saw such a slaughter as our guns made, they were nearly all killed, captured or wounded. I never saw so many dead men in my life," said twenty-one-year-old Confederate Private Thomas Benton Ellis of Company C, 3rd Florida Infantry.[48] In two years of war, Private Ellis himself had been a prisoner of war, captured and wounded at Perryville, Kentucky, on October 8, 1862. He was exchanged a little over two months later at Vicksburg, MS, earning another ticket on the Civil War merry-go-round.

For the 53rd Illinois it was a disastrous charge, going in the fight with 200 men and officers and coming out with just sixty-six. The number killed and wounded was eighty-eight with forty-six reported as "missing in action." Those "missing" were all prisoners of the Rebels. The officers from the 53rd Illinois included in the group of prisoners were Captain George R. Lodge of Company H, Lieutenant John D. Hatfield of Company K, and Lieutenant Mark M. Bassett. The men were brought up onto the earthworks, all with their hands held up in the air over their heads.

"I had orders to 'charge' and had none to fall back," Captain George R. Lodge would later write his wife from Rebel prison. "I never fall back without orders. I pushed on untill (*sic*), when within about 25 paces of the enemy's work and canon (*sic*), which were handled splendidly, I found not more than a dozen of the Regt. in sight, and the enemy on every side of me as they sallied out in pursuit of our flying men. I surrendered to Major Lash of the 4th Florida Inft."[49]

Again, the sound of the piano was heard, mixing eerily with the rifle fire and cannonading. The music was closer to the captured soldiers now; they could see the instrument perched behind some cotton bails just north of them on the earthworks. A soldier dressed in grey was seated at the piano looking back, glancing toward the new arrivals in blue uniforms with a smug nod, playing the tune "O, Let Us Rejoice."[50] There were no singers, just the piano accompaniment. Perhaps those who knew the lyrics sang them silently in their head.[51]

O let us rejoice in the Lord evermore,
Though all things around us be trying,
Though floods of affliction like sea billows roar,
It's better to sing than be sighing.

Then rejoice evermore, rejoice evermore,
It is better to sing than be sighing:
It is better to live than be dying;
So let us rejoice evermore.

It was certainly better to be alive than dead, but to the new prisoners of war there was not much rejoicing evermore. They were quickly hustled by the Rebel soldiers up and within the earthworks. They could peer down on the battlefield below, and it was not a pretty sight. "We had charged in a half circle" said the 53rd's Private Ranstead, "as this was the shape of the Rebel works, and they told us when we got in they had six thousand infantry massed here and fourteen pieces of artillery. This outfit was firing on this little handful of men for over an hour."

Acting Second Lieutenant Armand Pallissard's sword, passed to him by Company E's Lieutenant Mark C. Wheeler, which was then in October 1862 passed on to Mark Bassett upon Pallissard's death and Bassett's promotion to command of the 53rd's Company E, was captured in the battle. It became a war souvenir to a Confederate officer and subsequently lost to history. "I prized greatly and fully expected to bring it back north, but the fates of war would not have it that way, for it was taken from me when I was made a prisoner in the disastrous charge," said Bassett.

Little did Bassett know this would be the last battle of the Civil War he would take part in. He had served for 557 days since he left Ottawa, Illinois. His fighting days were over.

★ ★ ★

ALMOST IMMEDIATELY, THE GRAVITY of the debacle of July 12, 1863, at Jackson, Mississippi, reverberated through the Union command. All eyes immediately went to General Lauman.

Major General Ord went to Lauman's headquarters right after the disaster, and in his official report to General Sherman dated July 27, 1863, he stated, "I knew nothing of this attack and disaster until it was reported to me about one hour afterward by a member of your staff, Captain James C. McCoy, who had been sent to examine the position taken up by the division...I visited his division immediately. He then reported his total loss about 100. I found the men scattered, except that part which had not been with him, and when I called upon General Lanman to take immediate steps to put the remnant of his command under temporary cover, to call the rolls and gather the stragglers, I found he did not know how to do it."[52]

Captain McCoy stated that from General Lauman's headquarters on the battlefield, he was told to tell General Ord, "I am cut all to pieces."

In a special order by Major General Ord, Lauman was immediately removed from command and replaced.[53] It was the last battle of the Civil War that General Lauman would take part in as well.

For Colonel Isaac C. Pugh, the reckless charge of the earthworks on the orders of General Lauman must have been infuriating.

"I lost in about 80 minutes more than half of my command," wrote Colonel Pugh to his wife on July 29, 1863. "I am in no way responsible for the slaughter of the men under my command. I do not pretend to say who is responsible but somebody is. I think that the conduct of General Lauman and others ought to be investigated. The men feel very bitter towards Lauman and Ord they know that I ordered a halt and did not move until General Lauman ordered the line forward himself."[54]

"It is the strangest thing to me that I am here alive, unhurt," wrote twenty-year-old Isaac Rinaldo Pugh, who was also in the battle, to his mother, Elvina, on July 13, 1862. He was Colonel Pugh's son and a member of the Colonel's staff. Isaac went by his middle name Rinaldo, so as not to be confused with his father. "It is a miracle any of us got off that blood field alive," he said in a second letter to his mother written weeks later.

Rinaldo Pugh would also comment about the grizzly situation that began to become apparent in the hours after the battle. "The very air was filled with shell, canister, grape, spherical case and every other kind of shot...Our dead are unburied and those wounded on the field uncared for. Their cries could be heard all night, praying for help and for water."[55]

The aftermath of the disaster was itself a disaster. The men that were killed and wounded in the battle remained where they fell for more than two days until the afternoon of July 14 when a flag of truce was finally agreed upon. The dead had begun decomposing in the summer heat. The wounded were suffering as well, with many dying during the two days they remained lying in the field of battle. The Confederates who had killed and wounded those left in the no-man's-land below their earthworks had the gruesome task of burying their enemies with a couple of Union officers following along to identify the dead and record their names.[56] The Union dead were buried where they fell.

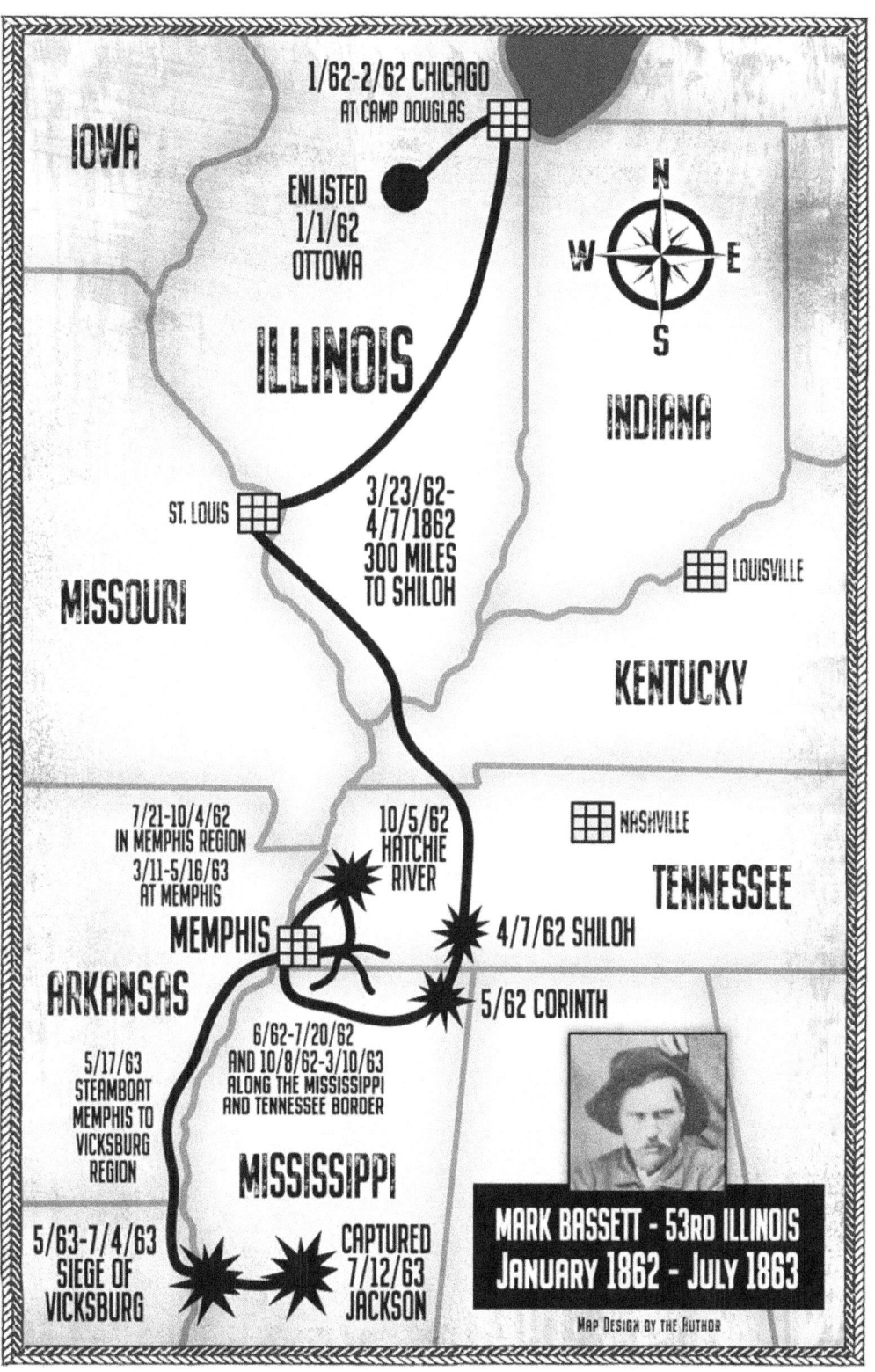

1/62-2/62 CHICAGO
AT CAMP DOUGLAS

ENLISTED
1/1/62
OTTOWA

IOWA

ILLINOIS

INDIANA

3/23/62-
4/7/1862
300 MILES
TO SHILOH

ST. LOUIS

LOUISVILLE

MISSOURI

KENTUCKY

7/21-10/4/62
IN MEMPHIS REGION
3/11-5/16/63
AT MEMPHIS

10/5/62
HATCHIE
RIVER

NASHVILLE

TENNESSEE

MEMPHIS

4/7/62 SHILOH

ARKANSAS

5/62 CORINTH

5/17/63
STEAMBOAT
MEMPHIS TO
VICKSBURG
REGION

6/62-7/20/62
AND 10/8/62-3/10/63
ALONG THE MISSISSIPPI
AND TENNESSEE BORDER

MISSISSIPPI

5/63-7/4/63
SIEGE OF
VICKSBURG

CAPTURED
7/12/63
JACKSON

MARK BASSETT - 53RD ILLINOIS
JANUARY 1862 - JULY 1863

MAP DESIGN BY THE AUTHOR

Chapter Two

MARK BASSETT STOOD ON TOP of the Confederate earthworks that defended the southwest side of the town of Jackson, Mississippi, along with the large group of sweaty, dejected fellow soldiers, most in shock at the turn of events that had occurred over the last hour and a half. Some of the group were wounded seriously and would not make it through the ordeal that would come next. There were no doctors; they were on their own. Bassett himself was only slightly wounded; he would survive. Their entire group were prisoners of the Rebels, who stood with their rifles and pistols ready, staring in amazement at their enemies, now so close they could touch them. Looking down from on top of the earthworks to cornfield turned battlefield below, Bassett could see the devastation left in the wake of the absolutely ridiculous attempt they had just made, trying to charge a force that greatly outnumbered them. Soldiers whom they had breakfasted with just a couple of hours earlier lay dead. The pathetic cries of the wounded still lying on the battlefield asking for help, water, anything, was a cruel accompaniment to the music eerily emanating from the piano just a couple of hundred yards from where they stood. How could this possibly have happened?

★ ★ ★

Captain John D. Hatfield
53rd Illinois, Company H
(Hatfield was promoted to
Captain on 12/18/1864)
Photographer unknown
Abraham Lincoln
Presidential Library & Museum

"THOSE WHO GOT CLOSE to the works were all taken prisoners," said Ranstead, "as before they knew they were in danger of being taken prisoners the Rebels were in the rear of us and ordered us to surrender. One of our boys thought at first that we did not have to surrender for he jumped up and drew his gun to bear on a Rebel and told him to surrender, but one of the men told him to be careful, as he was the fellow who had to surrender."[57]

Ranstead noted in his diary that 104 prisoners were taken; forty-six were from the 53rd Illinois. The 53rd's captured officers—Company E's Lieutenant Bassett, First Lieutenant George R. Lodge of Company G, and Lieutenant John D. Hatfield of Company H—gravitated toward their men, trying to stay together. The same would have happened for the other captured men from the 28th and 41st Illinois and 3rd Iowa regiments.

On Sunday afternoon, after that disastrous morning attack, all the prisoners of war were marched into town near the railway station. A Confederate officer came in and told the POWs that they needed to turn over any money and valuables, which he would place in a haversack for safekeeping. Speaking in hushed tones among themselves, some of the prisoners came up with ways to hide some of their money in their clothes and shoes, thinking that giving up their valuables was not the prudent thing to do. Others went ahead and followed the orders of the Confederate officer. "The others turned their things over to the officer for safe keeping and it proved to be safe, for they never saw their money again," Ranstead wrote sardonically. Then both enlisted men and officers, including Bassett, were marched out and loaded into boxcars. Thus began their tour across the Confederacy. "There was a good deal of guessing as to where we would be taken," said Ranstead.

Not all would survive the ordeal in the stifling summer heat packed into box cars with little water or food. The train loaded with more than a hundred POWs left the station in Jackson headed 150 miles toward the east and the Tombigbee River on the Mississippi-Alabama state line. There they were loaded on a steamboat, which provided a reprieve from the stifling heat of an enclosed boxcar. The steamer traveled southeast on the Tombigbee, almost all the way to Mobile, Alabama, until they reached the point where the Tombigbee met the Alabama River. Then the steamboat made a sharp left-hand turn and headed northeast up the Alabama River, eventually arriving at Selma, Alabama. The trip by riverboat was over 325 miles. At Selma the POWs were unloaded from the riverboat and marched out to a grove of trees.

Soon the Confederate officer from Jackson with the haversack of valuables returned and poured the contents out on a table for the owners to get them. "The first man who got his pocketbook opened it to find his money, but it had taken wings and flown, alas, no one knew where," said Ranstead.

A more pressing problem for the POWs was food. There wasn't any. The Confederate army had not considered the need for rations for anyone other than themselves, so their prisoners went hungry.

Next came another train ride as they were loaded onto another group of boxcars. The train left Selma, averaging between twenty to twenty-five miles per hour. It was torturously slow, and the air heated by the July sun baked down on the enclosed, locked boxcar. Temperatures inside became unbearable, and the POWs were unsure of where they were being taken. It was physical and mental torture. 200 miles and eight to ten hours later, their train pulled into Atlanta.

Delirious from the heat and lack of any sustenance, the prisoners stumbled from the train and were marched to a stockade. Finally, hardtack and a barrel full of hams were brought to the starving group. "Water would not make the hard tack soft, and the hams were packed in ashes and maggots were crawling all through the meat," said Ranstead. "It was eat that or nothing, so we took the meat away from the maggots and did the best we could, for a man is not very particular when he has eaten nothing for three or four days and no prospects of getting anything better soon."

Once again, the POWs were herded back onto boxcars, and when the train left Atlanta, they were still clueless as to where they were headed.

FROM ATLANTA THE SOUTHERN railroad system of 1863 would have had the men heading due east through Augusta, Georgia, then onward through South Carolina. At Wilmington, North Carolina, the train would have turned north.

The next few days saw travel on some very poor railroad tracks. Once again, the train moved painfully slow—so slow that men could jump off the train, walk alongside the moving car and pick berries, then jump back on again under the watchful eyes of armed Confederate soldiers.

Somewhere in the Carolinas a group of Confederate soldiers walked up alongside the railcars and asked if any of the POWs had ever guarded prisoners at Camp Douglas at the beginning of the war. "We told them some of us were at Camp Douglas and guarded prisoners at that time," said Ranstead. "They said they hoped that we would receive as good treatment as they received at our hands at that time. We hoped they would, for we had not seen much good treatment so far."

Finally, on July 20, eight days after their capture, the prisoners arrived in the Confederate capital of Richmond, Virginia. From their capture at Jackson, Mississippi, to their arrival in Richmond, Virginia, the POWs had traveled over 1,300 miles by rail and steamboat through Rebeldom. From the railroad depot they were marched a couple of blocks on 8th Street and then turned right onto Cary Street, heading thirteen blocks southeast to 21st Street to arrive at Libby Prison. "We reached this headquarters of treason on the 20th of this month and after being marched up to this prison were all taken back to a prison just one square from this and opposite Castle Thunder which is the military criminal prison here," said Captain George Lodge of Company G, 53rd Illinois. Castle Thunder was the Confederate prison a block from Libby Prison that was used for civilian, spies, and political prisoners.

"There we were subjected to a search and all our personal effects, such as blankets, oil cloths, haversacks, canteens, belts, and money, which had not been taken at Jackson were taken from us that they could find," said Captain Lodge, "Many of the men had strips round them instead of suspenders, and even these were seized and taken off...And this robbery was committed by the agents, and in the name of the 'Confederate States of America.'"[58]

Once all the prisoners were searched at this staging area, the enlisted men were separated from the officers. For the enlisted men, including the forty-three from the 53rd Illinois, their destination would be Belle Island, located in the James River about three miles west of Libby Prison. Private Ranstead was among them.

They faced sweltering heat. It was reported that the portion of the island on which the prisoners were confined was low, sandy, and barren, baked by the burning rays of a Southern sun. Because the terrain was a part of the James River watershed, the island was a breeding ground for mosquitoes, which carried malaria. The prisoners were herded into a space of around six acres surrounded by an earthworks of about three feet in height. Guards were stationed about forty feet apart and kept watch day and night. There were a few ragged tents, but most of the POWs had no shelter of any kind. More than 10,000 POWs were confined to this desolate space, without a tree to be found. With a spectacular view of the Confederate capitol to its north, as hot as it was in summer, the Belle Island prisoners froze in the winter. Left exposed to the elements, as many as fourteen POWs froze to death in one night.[59] In addition to the horrible living conditions, food was scarce, so the men were starving.

COMPARED TO THE ENLISTED men's situation at Belle Island, Libby Prison seemed like a luxury hotel, but it was still a hellish nightmare. Libby Prison was located along a canal with locks that fed directly into and out of the James River to the southeast of the heart of Richmond. It was one of a group of warehouses known as Tobacco Row before the war; the building was built sometime between 1846 and 1852 and leased by Libby and Sons—Luther Libby and his son George W. Libby, who operated a ship's chandlery out of the large warehouse.

The fact that the infamous prison would take on the Libby name was a bit of bad luck for Luther Libby, who was born in Maine, though he had lived in Virginia since the 1830s and was the owner of two enslaved females.[60] "My father was engaged in the business of ships chandler, grocer, and commission merchant, and had a lease on the building for three years," said Sergeant George W. Libby, who enlisted in the 12th Virginia Infantry CSA. "When the war broke out his business was suspended, as his whole trade was with the North, but he still retained possession of the building, and General Winder, who was in command of Richmond at that time, notified him that he desired the building for a prison and if his goods were not removed within a certain time, he would throw them into the street. Winder took forcible possession of the building and converted it into a prison. The name was derived from the simple fact of the sign of Libby & Son remaining over the door."

With the Libby family shingle hanging from the building, the namesake prison was a large, thick-walled, brick building three stories high on Cary Street with a basement that gave the building a four-story profile on the docks, which faced southwest along the canal and James River.

The three southern men who made the lives of the Libby Prison occupants miserable were its commandant, warden, and chief clerk. They were all in their early 20s; only one of the three was an actual officer in the Confederate army.

The commandant for both Libby Prison and Belle Island when Bassett arrived in July 1863 was twenty-three-year-old Major Thomas Pratt Turner. A man of short stature, Major Turner hailed from Clarke County, Virginia. He had been a student at Virginia Military Institute and then a cadet at West Point in 1860. In his plebe year, he refused to take an oath of allegiance and left the Academy, citing reasons for his refusal to "swear allegiance to a Government I despise and abhor."[61] He immediately joined the

Confederate army where he was assigned to the staff of General Thomas "Stonewall" Jackson as a lieutenant. His first significant assignment came when he was appointed commandant at Libby in 1862. He brashly lobbied for his own promotion, stating, "I was in charge of the two Mil. Prisons at Richmond which position has always before and since been held by officers holding either the rank of Maj. or Capt. holding such a low commission where I regularly have to command those who are so much my superior."[62] This successfully led to his promotion to captain in July 1862, and then to major in November 1862.

Major Thomas P. Turner was young and inexperienced; he really had no clue as to how to run a prison. He countered this incompetence by projecting the illusion of a strict commander and disciplinarian, the result of which was that he was hated by all of Libby's prisoners. "He not only deprives us of little comforts which would greatly mitigate our woes, and cost him nothing," said POW Lieutenant Willard Glazier of the 2nd New York Cavalry, "but he heaps barbarities upon us with Herculean and fiendish strength."[63]

★ ★ ★

Second-in-command and "warden" of Libby prison, twenty-five-year-old "Captain" Richard Randolph "Dick" Turner was known for his cruel temper and severe treatment of the prisoners. He, too, was despised by all of Libby's prisoners. Warden Turner used the military rank of "Captain" and then "Major," but there is no military record of his service; he was most likely a civilian who just happened to have a penchant for torture. Coincidentally, Dick Turner was not related to commandant Thomas Turner, though they were often confused. He towered over his superior by almost a foot. He loved all forms of physical punishment, brutality, and verbal abuse, seemingly taking a sadistic pleasure at devising them. Dick Turner was also described by Lieutenant Glazier as "possessed of a vindictive, depraved, and fiendish nature...there is nothing more terrible than a human soul grown powerful in sin and left to the horrible machinations of the evil one and its own evil promptings."[64]

"Richard, or as usually called, Dick Turner was the inspector of the prison, and acted under the orders of the commander," said prisoner Lieutenant Colonel Charles Farnsworth of the 1st Connecticut Cavalry. "There was nothing too mean for him to do. He searched you when you entered, knocked you down if you grumbled, took your blanket from you if found lying upon it after morning roll call, never spoke of you except as damned Yankees—told you 'you were better treated than you deserved.'"[65]

The third man to make life difficult for Libby prisoners was the chief clerk, twenty-three-year-old Erastus Willey Ross. One of the chores of the short and portly Ross was roll call, counting all the prisoners twice daily. The Libby POWs took great pride in making this process torturous and confusing for Ross by regularly mixing up his roll call numbers. He was soon appropriately nicknamed "Little Ross."

"Ross was insultingly, malignantly bitter toward prisoners at all times and under all circumstances, gnat-brained, pompous, and the ready tool of his brutal superiors. It will be within the limits of the truth to assert that three-fourths of all the officers who came into contact with Ross, while prisoners, utterly despised him,"[66] commented the English-born Captain Adam Dixon of the 104th New York, who was captured at Gettysburg on July 1, 1863, and arrived at Libby around the same time as Bassett and the other 53rd Illinois POW officers.

To protect himself during the roll calls, Ross carried a Bowie knife and revolver and

**Major Thomas
Pratt Turner**
Commandant of
Libby Prison

**Richard Randolph
Turner**
Warden of
Libby Prison

**Erastus Willey
Ross**
Chief Clerk of
Libby Prison

was escorted by two armed guards.[67] The chief clerk would prove to be an enigma to most of the Libby population. His explosive fits of anger led to additional taunting of him by the captors, but to some who interacted with him on a one-on-one basis, he sometimes appeared to be actually on their side. Some POWs would later find that his demeanor was part of a well-planned act. Others would never see that side of Little Ross and would for the rest of their lives hold him in contempt.

Along with the three administrative buffoons of Turner, Turner, and Ross, the prison guards were a motley crew of local militia and rejected Rebel soldiers. To be a reject of the Confederate army that was always in need of manpower meant that you had to really be an incompetent soldier, and these guys were exactly that. One adjutant, three sergeants, one overseer of enslaved labor, one officer of the guard, and sixteen enlisted men, along with the two Turners and Ross, made up a total of only twenty-five men.[68] This band of incompetents ran Libby Prison, guarding a prison population that exceeded 1,000. Most of the POWs would laugh at how inept it all was—if it weren't so deadly serious to be held prisoner there.

Libby had been used by the Confederates as first a hospital and prison at the start of the war, and then exclusively as a prison for Union officers by 1862 with a population of around 700 to 800 prisoners. By the time that Bassett and his fellow officers were inmates there in the summer of 1863, the numbers had grown substantially.

AS THE OFFICERS WERE marched back to Libby Prison after being searched and separated from the enlisted men, they would have heard the shouts of "fresh fish" coming from their fellow prisoners. This was the not-so-subtle code announcing that a fresh batch of prisoners had arrived. Following along on the nautical theme, those who had been at Libby the longest were known as "dry cods," and an exchanged prisoner was known as a "pickled sardine."[69]

One can imagine the despair Bassett and his fellow officers from the 53rd Illinois—Captain George R. Lodge and Lieutenant John D. Hatfield—felt as they entered Libby Prison through the ground floor entrance, passing through the commandant's office, then climbed the banister-less stairs upward toward their new quarters. The stairs were hinged and could be drawn upward like a trap door, keeping the prisoners locked into the floors above.

Another prisoner[70] recalled the words from Dante's *Divine Comedy* as he first ascended the same set of stairs. "All hope abandon ye who enter here." It was the inscription on the sign that Dante described at the entrance to hell, a fitting description of what awaited the prisoners above.

The sheer number of prisoners at Libby made sanitary conditions impossible. Many of the officers imprisoned there looked forward to a potentially short stay as regular exchanges of prisoners cut the time men were held to, at most, a few months. "I took up my abode in that notorious southern hostelry," said Bassett, "and as at that time President Lincoln was calling for more men, and in some way we had knowledge of it and were anxious to be exchanged or, if this could not be effected, were eager to escape and go again to the front."

So as the new POW officers from the 53rd Illinois "checked in" to their new digs, they had the hope that things wouldn't be too bad for them and that they would soon be exchanged. But by the summer of 1863 prisoner exchanges had slowed to a trickle due to the Confederate government's lack of recognition of Union soldiers and officers serving in Black companies. It was a painful realization when they discovered that they were not getting out of Libby Prison anytime soon. "On our arrival there were already about twelve hundred prisoners, all officers," explained Bassett. That meant not only were they at the bottom of a long list, but as more and more men were brought to the prison, conditions were going to get worse.

POWs packed into the top two floors of the former warehouse. "On each floor of this warehouse were three rooms, each of which I should say was 120 feet long by 40 feet wide,[71]" Bassett later explained. "The doors and windows were all heavily iron barred. Our beds were our blankets with our boots for pillows, on the hard floor."

The heavily barred windows presented a serious hazard to the prisoners. The windows offered the only air and light into the crowded upper floors of Libby prison. In an arbitrary rule created by the prison warden, Turner, there was an invisible "dead line" around each window.

"The prison was closely guarded and the rules were very strict and cruelties repeatedly practiced," said Bassett. "When a 'Yank' was seen nearer a window than the dead-line, he was liable to be shot at without warning."[72]

"We were not allowed to go within three feet of the windows to look out; but men could not help this, and were repeatedly fired upon," said another Libby.[73] Many were killed including a prison nurse who, while inadvertently walking too close to a window, was shot in what was later called "target practice" by the guards.

"I was a witness to one such instance," said Bassett. "Lieutenant Forsythe, of the One Hundredth Ohio (from Toledo I think) sat near a window reading a paper when the guard outside below shot him through the head spattering his blood and brains around—no provocation whatever."[74] Lieutenant George Duncan Forsyth had been a POW since September 8, 1863, when he was captured with more than 250 other soldiers at Limestone Station, Tennessee.

To the Libby guards, the sport became known as "to shoot a Yankee." Major Turner commented, "The boys are in want of practice." One of the guards said he had made a bet that before he came off duty he would kill a damned Yankee.

The *Daily Richmond Enquirer* provided this description of the conditions experienced by the occupants: "Libby takes in the captured Federals by scores, but lets none out; they are huddled up and jammed into every nook and corner; at the bathing troughs, around the cooking stoves, everywhere there is a wrangling, jostling crowd; at night the floor of every room they occupy in the building is covered, every square inch of it, by uneasy slumberers, lying side by side, and heel to head, as tightly packed as if the prison were a huge, improbable box of nocturnal sardines."[75]

Depending on the prevailing winds and time of year, the smells produced by Libby Prison and Belle Island would waft through the city of Richmond in a sort of ironic payback for all the suffering of the prisoners held in those institutions. If the winds were from the east, Libby would make itself known to the citizens of Richmond. If the winds came in from the south, Belle Island would remind them of its presence.

The day-to-day life at what one prisoner had named the "Bastille of the Confederacy" began with them awakening at first light, having been sardined or spooned together into the ever-tightening space on the top two floors as the Libby Prison population continued to increase. As the hundreds of ragged men awoke, they began the daily skirmish against the "greybacks"—the coined nickname for lice, fleas, and other vermin that seemed to permeate every nook and seam of their clothing as well as their bodies. "They were the most prolific bugs I ever saw. They were all over us," said Captain George H. Starr of the 104th New York.[76]

After the skirmishing came to an end, it was time for roll call, conducted by "Little Ross," the Chief Clerk who was from Georgia and spoke with the thick southern accent. "Turn out for roll call! Turn out!" he would yell from the bottom of the steps leading to the prisoners contained in the two floors above. As he slowly made his way through the upper two floors with all the prisoners, the POWs would sometimes switch to the next room to be counted again, intentionally throwing off Little Ross's count. He would then have to start over, dragging out the entire process, making him lash out and seek revenge on the captives during the next roll call.

"We have to fall into line for roll call every morning and evening," said Captain Lodge, commenting on the confusion intentionally caused by the prisoners. "This need not occupy more than three minutes, nor would it were it not that some of the men will not start at the word…The clerk had remonstrated a dozen times, but finding his request availed nothing, he brought up this morning an armed squad with fixed bayonets to force us into line at the word and then he kept us waiting about 15 minutes; just to show us, I suppose, how pleasant it is to wait."[77]

After Little Ross was finally satisfied, the men were released to prepare their breakfast, an organized chaos in the first-floor prisoners' kitchen with hundreds of men cooking for their individual mess, each vying for some stove space. There was a large brick fireplace in this room surrounded by a sea of men. They usually cooked everything they had in one pot. "Our food was coarse cornbread, rice and sometimes bacon and beans in whatever degree or staleness the meat happened to be and of the poorest quality," Bassett recalled.

IN APRIL 1863 COLONEL ABEL D. Streight had gained notoriety by leading a force of 1,700 men on a raid into the deep south only to be captured by a smaller force of 500 Confederates under General Nathan Bedford Forrest at Cedar Bluff, Alabama.

He had been a prisoner at Libby since May 1863 and had become a thorn in the side of Libby's two Turners. Known for being very outspoken, Streight officially complained about the condition of the food supplied to his fellow POWs. "The rations furnished by your Government may be as good and as much as it can afford under the circumstances, but in that case it does seem that we should be allowed to purchase the necessary amount to sustain us. It cannot possibly be that it is intended to reduce to a famishing condition 600 prisoners of war. Humanity cannot contemplate such a thing without feelings of the deepest horror, saying nothing of our rights as prisoners of war. Even criminals guilty of the blackest crimes are not, among civilized people, confined for any length of time on insufficient food." Streight's letters complaining about Libby were postmarked to James A. Seddon, the Confederate Secretary of War, as well as Brigadier General Sullivan A. Meredith, the US Army's Commissioner for the Exchange of Prisoners.[78] Meredith made sure President Lincoln saw it as well.

Another situation many POWs found themselves caught in was the tit-for-tat retributions between the two enemy governments. Whenever the Federals would imprison Confederate POWs beyond the traditional confines of the prison as a punishment, the Confederates would randomly select the same number of Federal POWs and subject them to the same punishment. If it was learned that a Confederate prisoner in the north was in solitary confinement, the South would place one of their Union POWs into solitary confinement as well.

Beyond the horrible conditions, the prisoners at Libby faced boredom. To occupy their minds, the POWs engaged in all sorts of games and formed groups to continue their education, which included courses in Latin, Greek, French, German, Spanish, and English as well as Philosophy, Algebra Geometry, Religion, and many other subjects of interest. A debate club was formed, and there was also an informal prison newspaper known as *The Libby Chronicles*. No actual printing of the newspaper occurred but the local news correspondents submitted their "stories" on scraps of paper to the editor, Prison Chaplain Louis N. Beaudry of the 5th NY Volunteer Cavalry, who would read the imaginary newspaper out loud to prisoners who eagerly gathered around him each Friday morning at 10 a.m.

Singing was also a popular group form of entertainment, though song choices could result in punishment. "The Star-Spangled Banner" and "The Battle Hymn of the Republic" would draw the wrath of Warden Turner.

Toward the end of the day, the sparse rations were distributed again, and the chaos in the first-floor kitchen ensued, which was followed by a roll call at 5 p.m. As the sun set the prisoners would turn in. After dark meager lighting was provided by tallow-dips, which were nothing more than a strip of cloth set into a crude container of animal fat, fastened to the heavy posts. Lights out was at 9 p.m., and the tallow-dips were extinguished as the men again slept sardined or spooned together amid hundreds of tortured, foul-smelling bodies. Every half hour through the night the guards outside would shout out their status, providing the prisoners inside with a sense of time. "Eleven-thirty, Post number one, and all's well!" For those POWs having trouble sleeping in the miserable conditions, all was not well. Then the daily cycle would begin again, with little change from the day before.

As time passed a change occurred for most every prisoner at Libby. They were getting thinner, becoming emaciated due to the inadequate food rations. Prison conditions led to disease and perhaps a trip to the first-floor hospital. Over a three-month period in the fall of 1863 the hospital saw 650 patients, of which forty-two died.

"The prevailing diseases [at Libby] are diarrhoea (*sic*), dysentery and typhoid pneumonia," reported a recently exchanged group of Union surgeons in November 1863. "Of late the percentage of deaths has greatly increased, the result of causes that have been long at work—such as insufficient food, clothing and shelter, combined with that depression of spirits brought on so often by long confinement."[79]

One thing that did improve the psyche of a prisoner was writing a letter home and getting a reply, which could include a package of requested food supplies.

JUST FIVE DAYS AFTER climbing the stairs and swallowing hard at the enormity of his situation, Mark Bassett was settling into the accommodations afforded him at Libby Prison and trying to learn how to survive. Back home in Illinois, on Saturday, July 25, 1863, *The Ottawa Free Trader* newspaper published an article describing the battle on the earthworks in Jackson, Mississippi, by the doomed 53rd Illinois Infantry thirteen days earlier. "Heavy News From Jackson: Death of Col Seth C. Earl" claimed the headline. An account of the disastrous events was accompanied by a list of each company highlighting all the killed and missing from the 53rd Illinois. Under Company E, listed as "Killed," was Lieutenant M. M. Bassett's name.[80]

The printing of the incorrect information of those killed and wounded-in-action by *The Ottawa Free Trader* would cause pain and suffering to families all throughout Illinois. Bassett wasn't the only soldier listed as killed-in-action, yet he was very much alive, sitting like a blue-coated sardine, packed in with other POW officers in Libby Prison. The Union army itself didn't know who was actually captured and now held as prisoners by the Rebels after Jackson.

It would take a few days for the news to reach 125 miles south of Ottawa, and then to the cornfields in Kerton Township. The shock from the news was like a bullet to the heart of Mark's wife, Lottie. She had not seen her husband since December 1861, more than a year and a half earlier. The tragic news came to her flowing like tears down the Illinois River along with the painful realization that she was now a war widow with three small children. Nathaniel had turned five on July 15, three days after his father was captured at Jackson. Sarah Jane was two-and-a-half years old, and Charles, who had never even met his father, was one-and-a-half years old.

On August 8, 1863, *The Chicago Tribune* reported a corrected list of casualties from the 53rd Illinois in the Jackson, Mississippi, debacle: "Missing: 1st Lieut MM Bassett, and 2nd Lieut MA Goodfellow, taken prisoner unhurt."[81] It is unclear whether this news ever reached Lottie. It would take months before the first letter written home from Libby Prison by a very much alive Lieutenant Bassett would reach his wife.

Lottie by then had gone through all the stages of grief and was trying to move on with her life and provide for her children. Private John Moore, a member of Bassett's own Company E of the 53rd Illinois, had gotten a disability discharge the year earlier after being wounded at the engagement at Davis Bridge. The six-foot tall, blond-haired, blue-eyed, twenty-three-year-old Moore had even come around to console her when he heard Mark had been killed-in-action. They became close.

Now she was deeply and profoundly shocked a second time. Absorbing the news that her husband was not dead and buried in an unmarked grave somewhere in Mississippi was suddenly an enormous problem for her.

Fortunately for Mark Bassett, he was blissfully unaware of the situation swirling 850 miles away at his homestead in Illinois. Being a prisoner of war was a miserable existence. Relief came only when he was able to conjure pleasant thoughts of home, Lottie, and his three children. It seemed so long ago that Bassett could hardly remember what they looked like.

Chapter Three

**William Stanhope Marshall, John E. Page,
and Michael M. Hoffman
5th Iowa – July 1861 to November 1863**

CAPTAIN JOHN PAGE SILENTLY APPROACHED, crouching as he walked, then took a seat on the ground next to Lieutenant Michael Hoffman, who glanced over and nodded. It was just before midnight on Monday, November 23, 1863. Both officers were focused on getting their company safely across the Tennessee River. Thousands of Union soldiers were bivouacked along the western shore, hidden north of the city of Chattanooga, awaiting a signal to cross the treacherous waters that had delayed their advance. The river was high on its banks, and from the eastern side the voices of Confederate pickets, part of General Braxton Bragg's army, could be heard, sounds muffled by the mist. Low fog and a drizzling rain successfully blocked the scene from being illuminated by a waxing gibbous moon that might have helped the situation. On the other hand, to the thousands of Union soldiers anxiously waiting at that moment, darkness was their friend. Each soldier was told to be as quiet as possible so they would not reveal themselves to the Confederates picketing several hundred yards on the other side of the river.

The Union army had been under siege in Chattanooga since their defeat by the Rebels at the Battle of Chickamauga in late September. The arrival first of General Grant and then Sherman's forces brought hope, as well as thousands of soldiers to defend Chattanooga. The next few days would be their chance to gain revenge, a dish best served in the cold of November to the Confederates.

The Tennessee River was a swollen, angry river made more dangerous by the pitch-black darkness; 116 pontoon boats would act as troop transports across its churning waters. First, an advance party stealthily made the crossing, landing at the mouth of South Chickamauga Creek. Just one shot was fired as they made quick work of capturing and silencing fourteen Rebel picket stations.[82] The errant shot caused no reaction from along the Confederate main line, which was some distance from the pickets. Sherman's gathering forces continued to remain hidden.

"There was an ominous silence in the air, and officers moved about mysteriously, saying but little of the unusual danger about to be encountered," remarked a 5th Iowa soldier named Marsh Byers. "To cross a river in the face of an enemy at any time is hazardous, but to attempt rowing an army over a broad, rapid stream in rude boats, in the darkness of midnight, and with a strong and victorious army on the opposite shore, is a hazard even veterans contemplate with great misgivings."[83]

In the early morning hours around 2 a.m. on Tuesday, November 24, 1863, the signal finally came. Major General William Tecumseh Sherman emerged from the misty darkness wearing a long, waterproof coat, looking on at the large assemblage of his men. Standing close by on the shore, he observed as the boats were loaded with soldiers of the 5th Iowa. "Be prompt as you can boys," he said, "there's room for thirty in a boat."[84]

Company D and the rest of the 5th Iowa Infantry stepped gingerly into the pontoon boats and were quickly caught up in the swirling eddies that carried them across the swollen river south of Chickamauga Creek. They were all part of Sherman's Army of the Tennessee, a regiment in a brigade under the command of Colonel Charles L. Matthies. Sherman's objective was to attack the Confederate's right flank at the northernmost point of Missionary Ridge, a location known as Tunnel Hill.

Samuel Hawkins Marshall "Marsh" Byers
Mahashka Historical Society Archives

"The rude square boats were loaded to water's edge," said Byers, "each contained from twenty to thirty soldiers who sat in the darkness holding their trusted rifles on their knees, in the momentary expectation of a blast of musketry or cannon ball that might sink them to the bottom of the river." In the early morning hours, Colonel Matthies and the regimental staff of the 5th Iowa, which included Major William Stanhope Marshall, would each board pontoon boats crossing with a group of their regiment. Marshall chomped on his ever-present cigar, its smoke melding with the mist.

The thirty-one-year-old Page, who had a brusque, no-nonsense way about him, now sat quietly, looking downstream, staring into the darkness as if in a trance. He was in command of Company D. Hoffman, his second-in-command, noticed that Page often did this after being seriously wounded at Iuka. It seemed a lifetime ago, although it had only been fourteen months. They had been neighbors in Marshalltown, Iowa, at the start of the war.

Hoffman's older brother, Corporal Samuel W. Hoffman, was also in Company D; in short order they had all made the difficult river crossing together. Each crossing took about a half of an hour; while that may seem like a short time, it was just long enough in the rocking, shaking boats for seasickness to set in, and many of the soldiers lost their dinner over the side of the boat—they had few enough rations as it was; they hadn't needed this, too.

In addition to their rifles, most of the soldiers also carried entrenching spades. As morning light slowly faded up, the misty rain and fog continued to provide a veil of cover. More than 8,000 men had successfully crossed and set to work on the east side of the Tennessee River.

At dawn on November 24 the rain continued, and the fog persisted. A small riverboat named The Dunbar came up from Chattanooga to help ferry thousands of additional Federal soldiers across the Tennessee River. The former Confederate riverboat that had been sunk two months earlier, then refloated and repaired, was now employed by the Union army.[85]

The pontoon boats that had initially shuttled the thousands of soldiers across the Tennessee River were now repurposed. By noon they were all aligned side by side, and a wooden roadbed had been built on top to span the river. What had been transport boats twelve hours earlier was now a 1200-foot-long pontoon bridge, erected in amazing speed by the army engineers, which allowed for more of Sherman's army, including its artillery, supply, and ambulance wagons, to cross. But they were running late. That morning Sherman was supposed to attack the northernmost part of Missionary Ridge at the same time other parts of the Federal forces attacked positions to the south. But there was a problem.

The terrain they found themselves in didn't match the maps they had. It was a reconnaissance mix-up, and it delayed things. So for the rest of the day the 5th Iowa would dig in, while General Bragg's Confederate army looked down from the top of Tunnel Hill into the foggy valley below. The Union attack would have to wait until the next day.

AT THE BEGINNING OF JULY 1861, patriotism abounded as Iowa felt a great threat boiling up from the border state of Missouri to its south. The men on the prairie answered the call, and the 5th Iowa mustered in and began drilling at Camp Warren in Burlington, Iowa.[86]

A newly sharpened pencil made the first entry in a newly purchased diary:

> *July 15th, 1861 – Taken into the United States service for three years or during the war by Lieut Chambers of the U.S.A. Lay at Burlington until August 1st, 1861 when I commenced keeping diary.*

The words were written by the hand of newly minted twenty-two-year-old Sergeant Michael Hoffman of Company D. The diary would be carried in his pocket for the next four years. Page joined him in Company D; being a little older, he mustered in with the more senior rank of first sergeant.

Three Iowa lawyers also mustered into the 5th Iowa in Burlington in July 1861. Twenty-nine-year-old William Stanhope Marshall joined Company E as a 2nd lieutenant, along with his best friend Alexander Brown Lewis as the company's fourth sergeant, and twenty-two-year-old Marsh Byers joined Company B as a corporal.[87]

At its formation in the summer of 1861, the 5th Iowa Volunteer Infantry was under the command of another lawyer, thirty-two-year-old Colonel William H. Worthington, who was born in the then-frontier town of Harrodsburg, Kentucky, in 1828 with a family tree that included President James Monroe.[88] In 1857 he moved to Keokuk, Iowa, with his family and opened a law practice. But he was seen as a southern outlier by his new Iowa neighbors. "His sympathies were with his native South. Why he was leading a Northern regiment was a constant mystery to his men," questioned Marsh Byers.[89] That question would dog the Colonel for his entire time as the 5th Iowa's commander.

MARSHALL WAS BORN IN RICHLAND COUNTY, Ohio, on March 17, 1832. He came from a family with roots that ran deep into the United States' earlier forays into war. The family's Ohio farm was a result of land grants issued to William's grandfather John Marshall Sr., who had been a Major in the Continental army under George Washington. His grandson William became the proud owner of the sword presented to his grandfather by Washington himself.[90]

Marshall's parents were John Marshall Jr. and Sarah Stewart. John Marshall Jr., was a veteran of the War of 1812 and claimed to be related to the famous U.S. Supreme Court Chief Justice John Marshall. The claim was actually not true but was a yarn spun by William's father to intrigue his friends and neighbors.

Marshall graduated at age twenty-four from Jefferson College in Canonsburg, Pennsylvania, in April 1856. While in college he was a member of the fraternity of Phi Gamma Delta, which had been founded at the college eight years earlier, with chapters that would later spread nationwide. For a year after college, he and fellow graduate, fraternity brother, and best friend, Alexander Brown Lewis, moved to Louisiana to teach school. The two then relocated to Independence, Iowa, in 1858, where they both received their law degrees. In 1859 Marshall opened a law practice in Independence and hired his friend Lewis to work in his firm. They both left the practice when they enlisted together in the 5th Iowa.[91]

ON OCTOBER 24, 1832, PAGE WAS BORN IN WHITBY, ONTARIO, Canada, a shipping town with a natural harbor on the shore of Lake Ontario, just a few miles northeast of Toronto. Page was the oldest child of Charles Washington Page, who was also born in Ontario, and Eleanor Hugill, who was born in Yorkshire, England. The family grew with the addition of four girls over the next decade, then in 1842, when John was twelve years old, his mother, Eleanor, died. His father remarried to Juliet Nash in 1846, and John soon had five half-siblings. The Page family regularly moved between Canada and the United States, eventually settling in Norwalk, Ohio. They were Americans at heart, with John's grandfather and great-grandfather having served in the War of 1812 and the American Revolution.[92]

At the beginning of the war, Page had been married to his wife, Nancy, for over six years; the couple had two boys, five-year-old Charles and William who was born in July 1861, the same month his father had enlisted.

HOFFMAN WAS BORN IN NEW COLUMBIA, Pennsylvania, on July 9, 1839. Michael was one of thirteen children, four boys and nine girls, born between 1824 and 1853 to Michael C. Hoffman Sr. and his wife, Lydia Wagner. Michael's education was limited to the "four months in a year when it was too cold to work out(side)."[93] In 1855 the senior Hoffman, a milliner by trade, moved his burgeoning family by team and carriage to the frontier town of Marshalltown, Iowa, where hats must have been in short supply. Michael Jr. helped in his father's business and ran a little "up and down" sawmill. The experience as a retail shopkeeper would provide a valuable hands-on education that helped shape the direction of Hoffman's life after the war.

THE FOURTH SIGNIFICANT PLAYER IN THE story of the 5th Iowa was Samuel Hawkins Marshall Byers. He went by the name of S.H.M. Byers, or just "Marsh" Byers, a much easier to remember nickname that most likely came from his fellow soldiers. Byers was born on July 23, 1838 in Pulaski, Pennsylvania, a small town on the Ohio-

Pennsylvania border just east of Youngstown, Ohio. His family had been part of the great American migration westward, hoping for better luck and new opportunities. His father, James Byers, was a brick mason, a valuable occupation in the prairie farming community of Oskaloosa, Iowa, where they settled.

Byers was educated on the Iowa prairie in a one-room public school house and studied to be a lawyer. He was admitted into the Iowa Bar of June 16, 1861, but never had a chance to actually practice law because a few weeks later the military called, and he became a member of the 5th Iowa. Byers was a prolific writer, keeping a diary, like Hoffman, during the war. He is noted for coining the popular phrase and song "Sherman's March to the Sea," which he wrote as part of a poem while he was a POW; it was set to music by a fellow prisoner. In later life he would write extensively about his Civil War experiences but during the war he was the 5th Iowa's poet.

IN EARLY AUGUST 1861, AFTER A few weeks of training at Camp Warren, the 5th Iowa was finally on the move, having received their orders to march. They were headed toward the escalating animosities in Missouri.

Camp Warren was located on the Mississippi River so the easiest way to move a 1,000-man regiment was by steamboat. Each soldier walked across the gangplank and boarded the steamship *Pomroy* carrying his muzzle-loading U.S. Model 1841, Mississippi Rifle with bayonet and an array of supplies strapped to, hanging from, or lashed to their bodies, like human pack animals.[94] One soldier quipped that the weight of all his equipment and rations would have been a respectable load for a mule. They left Burlington just before midnight, traveling on the Mississippi River twenty miles south to Fort Madison. From there they boarded a train that took them another twenty miles to Keokuk, Iowa.

ON AUGUST 9, 1861, HOFFMAN found space on the crowded deck alongside his friend Page and recorded, "We went aboard the *Sucker State* at sunrise for St. Louis." The two tried to enjoy the twenty-four-hour-long, 180-mile trip south on the Mississippi River as passengers of a steamship packed to the railings with "pack animal" soldiers. The next day the hot summer sun baked down on the city of St. Louis as the *Sucker State* made its way for a wharf and docked.

"We landed at 8 a.m., marched for the arsenal through the city which was dry and dusty...we arrived at 9 a.m., and camped under the trees," said Hoffman as he and his men welcomed the shade as a reprieve from the broiling sun.

The arsenal was located on thirty-seven acres, three miles from the center of town within the city limits, on a bluff overlooking the Mississippi River. The entire complex, with its important strategic location, was surrounded by a massive stone wall ten feet high and three feet thick.[95]

THAT MORNING, ABOUT 200 MILES southwest of where the men of the 5th Iowa were resting in the shade, things had finally boiled over. In Springfield, Missouri, the Battle of Wilson's Creek was the first major battle of the Civil War that was fought west of the Mississippi River. Though it was a Confederate victory, the state of Missouri would be in Union hands by the end of October 1861. Except for one problem—Missouri fought with itself through much of the war with renegades, bushwhackers, and guerrilla warfare taking its toll throughout the state.

"Missouri was neither North nor South; she was simply hell," observed Byers, "for her people were cutting one another's throats, and neighboring farmers killed each other and burned each other's homes."[96]

For what was left of 1861 through early 1862 the 5th Iowa spent its time moving through broad swatches of Missouri west of St. Louis. Page and Hoffman worked together drilling the men of Company D; their time was spent marching, picketing, and generally expecting to be attacked by the guerrillas at any moment.

Having experienced no real battles since the regiment formed, along with having plenty of time to drill, had one noticeable benefit. Through months of military training, the 5th became a well-disciplined regiment, gaining the attention of their commanding officers. To the average soldier, though, the constant discipline without being able to apply what was learned in an actual battle was frustrating.

Most Union soldiers thought their enemy was the Rebels or Johnnies, or guerrillas and bushwhackers. But, in truth, their most dangerous enemy was microscopic. Trying to not get sick was a constant battle fought in the periphery of the events of the day by every single soldier on both sides of the argument. More soldiers in the Civil War died from the effects of illness than from the effects of battle.[97] A regiment with ten companies could contain upwards to one thousand soldiers along with their support wagons and animals. The regimental camps became breeding grounds for disease.

✯ ✯ ✯

HOFFMAN REPEATEDLY SUFFERED from the various illnesses brought on by the unsanitary conditions, poor water supply, and questionable food. On November 25, 1861, he recorded that he was "pretty sick, lay in bed most of the day and took some of Dr. Jaynes carminative Balsam, got a cramp in the breast about 1 p.m., very severe pain, went and saw Doc."[98] Hoffman battled the microscopic enemy on and off throughout most of the war. These kinds of ailments were common among a large percentage of soldiers, making their lives miserable.

In mid-December the 5th Iowa had arrived at Booneville, Missouri, where they camped on the old fairgrounds, which would be their winter quarters through the beginning of February 1862. Once again, time was spent sharpening their soldiering skills, but they also found time to write letters home while trying to stay warm in the wintry mix that Missouri threw at them. Eight months in and they still had not seen major battle, but that was about to change.

On February 8, 1862, the 5th Iowa was given orders to move out six days later on February 23; they docked at Cairo, Illinois. Hundreds of soldiers disembarked down the town's busy streets, stretching their legs and enjoying freedom from the confines of a six-day riverboat trip. Hoffman sought out a photographer and had his picture taken.

Sergeant Michael Hoffman
Image made
February 23, 1862,
in Cairo, Illinois
Photographer unknown

After leave in Cairo, they took the steamboat *Fairchild* to Commerce, Missouri, and then the regiment marched forty miles south through swampland to New Madrid, Missouri, arriving on March 3, 1862, to take part in what would be their first significant battle.

New Madrid was located at was known as the Kentucky bend of the Mississippi River and was defended by Confederate forces along the banks of the Mississippi. "Under considerable hardships from bad weather, deficient roads, and floods of water, the passage of the Mingo swamp was made and the siege of New Madrid began," said Byers.

Nearby in the middle of the river was "Island Number Ten," which contained a Confederate garrison heavily fortified with 150 pieces of artillery and defended by 12,000 Confederate soldiers. The name Island Number Ten was logically derived from the fact that it was the tenth island south of the Mississippi's junction with the Ohio River at Cairo, Missouri.

At midnight on March 13, 1862, during a terrific storm, Union troops including the 5th Iowa lay waiting for an assault of New Madrid planned at sunrise. However, Hoffman was not with them; he had been sick for almost a week. "I went to Doc and got medicines, took feavor (*sic*)...I was very sick...laying in my tent all day, Regiment went to fight, I did not go being unwell." Perhaps it was for the best because a severe thunderstorm that night was making life miserable for the troops waiting to assault New Madrid.

"The water in the trenches was knee deep, but the men bore the discomfort without a murmur," said Byers, "at last, daylight came, but instead of battle, a flag of truce."

Knowing an assault was coming, Confederate forces snuck out of New Madrid overnight during the storm and fled both to Island Number Ten and south toward Tiptonville, Tennessee. Union forces marched into New Madrid unscathed, and quickly moved toward Island Number Ten. They attacked from its north side of the island with ironclads in a siege lasting until April 8, when the Confederates gave up the fight and surrendered.

This major Union victory was overshadowed by the Battle of Shiloh, which occurred at the same time 200 miles to the southeast. Following their first major battle at New Madrid and Island Number Ten, the 5th Iowa boarded another steamboat and finally left Missouri for good, as part of a fleet of twenty-two steamers reaching Paducah, Kentucky, then taking the Tennessee River, landing on April 22, just twenty miles northeast of the strategic town of Corinth, Mississippi.

The Siege of Corinth would take place from April 29 through the end of May 1862. The 5th Iowa would be at times just four miles from the center of Corinth, yet they didn't see any notable action. Instead, they found themselves mainly on picket duty throughout the siege and only experienced minor skirmishing with the enemy. Being so close to the action for almost a month resulted in a nervousness among the men, who were probed and prodded by the Rebels but never really got into the fight with them. This resulted in a hair-trigger tension, which culminated in a deadly accident.

AT 2 A.M. ON MAY 22, THE MOON had not yet risen, so it was pitch-black in the woods along the picket lines. A sentry perceived motion in front of his position and, suddenly through the darkness, saw two shadowy figures on horseback. The soldier took them for the enemy and, without calling out a warning, raised his rifle and fired. The officer of the day and commander of the 5th Iowa, Colonel William H. Worthington, fell from his horse. His adjutant who was riding alongside of him sprang to the ground, but Colonel Worthington was dead, the ball hitting him in the forehead and killing him

instantly.[99]

"There were many among us who believed that the colonel had been intentionally murdered," observed Byers. "He was one of the most competent colonels in the army, but among his soldiers he was fearfully unpopular. He was, however, a splendid disciplinarian, but this was something the volunteers did not want."

The unfortunate sentinel who fired the deadly round was arrested, then tried and acquitted. Worthington had died as a result of accidental friendly fire. Taking over command of the 5th Iowa was the Prussian-born Colonel Charles Leopold Matthies.

A week later the Confederate army retreated from Corinth for the remainder of the summer of 1862 as they began their second year of fighting. The 5th Iowa pursued the enemy before returning to Corinth in early June.

At first light on the morning of September 19, 1862, camped six miles from Jacinto, Mississippi, they would finally face their most challenging fight. Information came down the line that the Confederate army was just west of them in Iuka, Mississippi. The 482 men of the 5th Iowa, as part of Rosecrans' two divisions of the Army of the Mississippi, began marching, arriving on the outskirts of town around 2 p.m. and finding a wide enemy line blocking the roads that led into town. Vastly outnumbered, the 5th Iowa, two or three other regiments, and a light artillery battery engaged the Rebels in a fierce battle.

With deadly projectiles flying, Page was suddenly hit. The Rebel bullet struck his left temple, and he crumpled, his body falling in a heap. A couple of his men pulled him to the rear while the fighting continued. Page remained unconscious, blood flowing across his face in what his men thought had to be a lethal injury.[100]

"It was a duel to the death," said Byers. "For hours the blue and the gray stood within forty yards of each other and poured in sheets of musketry...only the setting sun put an end to what was part of the time hand to hand combat."

In the fight Marshall showed his bravery under fire; he didn't flinch as he issued commands throughout the regiment. The battlefield was blanketed in smoke as a cacophony of blasts exploded all around him, with his men's rifles delivering their response. Through incredible luck the incoming enemy fire missed Marshall, and he emerged from the battle unscathed.

This would mark the third time the same Confederate regiment, the 3rd Louisiana, stood eyeball to eyeball with the 5th Iowa in a "duel to the death." It didn't go well for the Cajuns.

"In less than three hours, out of two hundred and thirty-eight men who went into the fight, one hundred and fifteen were killed and wounded," said one Rebel soldier from the 3rd Louisiana.[101]

"It was a bloody battle from 4 p.m. till dark," said Hoffman, who took roll call the next morning without Page, who had been taken to the regimental hospital. The ugly wound to Page's temple had left a deep gash, but he was alive. Roll call showed that Company D had two killed and sixteen wounded at Iuka. Hoffman returned to the battlefield to take another look at the horrible sight, walking among the dead and hoping to find somebody alive.

"The casualties in my regiment were seven commissioned officers killed, and eight wounded and thirty-four enlisted men killed, and one hundred and sixty-eight wounded, out of four hundred and eighty-two who went into battle. In commanding my regiment before the enemy, I was nobly assisted by Lieutenant Colonel Sampson, on the right, Adjutant Patterson, acting Major, on the left, and Lieutenant W. S. Marshall, acting Adjutant, all of whom behaved most gallantly, repeating my commands and steadying and cheering on my brave boys through the engagement," reported Colonel Charles Matthies to the Union command.[102]

Marshall's best friend and fraternity brother from his college days, Alexander Brown Lewis, was another of the severely wounded. He would be evacuated to Keokuk, Iowa, succumbing to his wounds five months later on February 25, 1863. "Lieutenant Lewis while fighting as each fought, like a hero, received a dangerous wound in the hip...After the intimacy that existed between us for the last ten years, my regard for him resembles more that of a brother than a stranger. For three years we sat together in the same class, met together in the same societies, roomed and ate together, shared the toils and enjoyed with each other the pleasures of youth, and all the bright anticipations of the great unknown future that lay before us," said Marshall of his friend, whose "unknown future" had become sadly snuffed out.

Page spent four days in the regimental hospital at Iuka, then rejoined his company, sporting a bandage wrapped around his forehead covering the gash on his left temple. The gunshot wound to his head had been a close call, the difference between life or death measured by less than an inch. Page would never be the same, suffering headaches and bouts of vertigo. The injury affected his personality; he became more brusque and sometimes would just stare off into the distance, appearing deep in thought.[103]

They returned to Jacinto to recover and by the beginning of October 1862 had orders to march to Corinth to guard Pittsburg Landing Road well to the southeast of the action during the Battle of Corinth on October 3, 1862. "Company D was up all night...noise and bustle all last night with heavy cannonading early in the morning," said Hoffman, "the battle was desperate from 10 a.m. till 12...Rebels got badly whipped—loud cheering all along the lines."

After the Confederates retreated, the 5th Iowa would be part of Grant's first attempt to take Vicksburg in what was known as the Mississippi Central Campaign. In December when Union supply lines were cut, they were all forced to retreat to winter quarters at Memphis. They all took time to write letters home. The days were cold but were also peaceful since the enemy was in their winter quarters as well.

On New Year's Day 1863 the men in the 5th Iowa speculated on what would come next. "I enjoyed the last year pretty well, though I have been sick considerable," said Hoffman. "I expect to see this war close in about one year but would not be surprised of it would close sooner!"[104] It would be wishful thinking for the twenty-four-year-old soldier, who in the preceding year had witnessed the horrors of war firsthand.

In the eighteen months since they had enlisted, card-shuffling of the ranks due to injury and death had brought changes to the ranks of the 5th Iowa. Marshall enlisted as a 2nd lieutenant and soon became regimental quartermaster, then adjutant lieutenant before leapfrogging to major. Byers went from quartermaster sergeant to lieutenant and then was promoted to Marshall's old job as adjutant, when Marshall became a major. Byers would find himself working side by side with Marshall in the regimental staff and develop a great respect for the stoic officer. Page and Hoffman both enlisted as sergeants in Company D; in eighteen months Page had been promoted to captain and Hoffman to 2nd lieutenant and were leading Company D.

For the 5th Iowa, the war was on hold for the winter, and the only enemy was bad luck. One cold morning a big tree crashed down with a loud cannon-like report directly onto two tents, badly wounding the unlucky occupants resting inside. A few days later another unlucky soldier accidentally shot himself when he tossed his pistol under his bunk. Time seemed to come to a standstill, as if it were holding its breath; the men grew anxious as they suffered from cabin fever.

IN SPRING 1863 THE SOLDIERS of the 5th Iowa were happy to finally be out of winter quarters and were ordered toward Vicksburg, the best fortified city in the two Americas. But Captain Page wasn't with them. While the injury he had sustained at Iuka had healed, leaving an inch-long scar on his left temple, the damage to his brain caused by the concussion continued: vertigo, bouts of dizziness and weakness, reaction to sounds, even a nervousness he couldn't shake. Today, it would he would most probably have been diagnosed with post-traumatic stress syndrome combined with what was likely an undiagnosed fractured skull caused by the bullet. Page was sent for rehabilitation to a hospital in Memphis on March 25 as the rest of the regiment went to Vicksburg; he wouldn't return to the regiment until mid-July.[105]

HOW TO MOVE THE LARGE NUMBER of Union forces south to engage the Rebels at the fortress-like city of Vicksburg had become a challenge. The solution was a hair-brained scheme dreamed up by Army engineers to open a gap in a levee along the Mississippi River at Yazoo Pass. Then the entire army would float along the flood waters produced by the breech and travel hundreds of miles south through the swamps by way of the Coldwater, Tallahatchie, and Yazoo Rivers all the way down to Vicksburg where they hoped to flank the Confederate positions, ending up on dry land. The scheme became appropriately known as the Yazoo Pass expedition.

When the engineers first opened the levee, the mighty Mississippi River was almost eight feet higher than the surrounding land at Yazoo Pass. The ensuing conflagration of water blasted open a gap in the levee almost eighty yards wide. As the Mississippi poured through the new opening along its shoreline, the force of the water surging through was so powerful that it proved to be unnavigable for days. Finally, once the waters settled down, the army began sending a flotilla of Union boats, shooting through the opening. It was a hell of a ride.

The 5th Iowa took their turn, boarding the schooner *Armada,* one of ten similar small boats loaded with other regiments near Helena, Arkansas. The cut in the river levee boiled and raged, its white waters shooting logs and debris into the hellish rapids created by the narrow passageway.

Marshall, Hoffman, and Byers held on for dear life as the *Armada* shot through the cut. "Our engines are working backward, and we enter the crevasse slowly, but in five minutes the fearful, eddying current seized us, and our boat was whirled round and round like a toy skiff in a washtub," said Byers. "Not a soul of the five hundred on board the boat in this crazy ride was lost. Once in the lake we stopped, and with amazement watched other boats, crowded with soldiers, also drift into the whirl and be swept down the pass. It was luck, not management, that half the little army was not drowned."

For the next two weeks the small boats loaded with soldiers slowly plodded along, attempting to make their way to Vicksburg. The soldiers stuck on board spent their time lying around the boat and playing lots of poker for "drinks & Segars (*sic*)." Marshall nervously strolled the deck assessing his men, who, besides card playing and smoking, had nothing to do but sleep and eat. They were making only four to five miles a day of progress as they floated past stately southern plantation mansions, each standing alone like southern sentinels on their own individual islands protected from the floodwaters. Hoffman had time to read a book titled *Pauline of the Potomac*, a barn burner of a read centering on the cross-dressing female Union scout and spy, with ready access to Gen. McClellan.[106]

The Union command who approved the plan soon realized that as the time passed, the flood waters were slowly receding. All their men were about to become stuck in the muddy marshland, inside landlocked boats miles from Vicksburg. Orders were given to turn around and get out of the receding flood waters as quickly as possible. The boats all returned to Helena seventeen days after they had left. With the potential of a disaster during the Yazoo Pass debacle averted, they would have to come up with another plan.

By the middle of April, a simpler plan to get to Vicksburg was ready. They would travel down the Mississippi River, get well past Vicksburg, then circle around the east side of the city. They tested the plan under the cover of darkness. After the moon set on April 16, a small fleet of Union steamers, barges, and gunboats successfully ran the Confederate blockade at Vicksburg. Its batteries fired relentlessly down upon them as they passed and, in the process, turned night into day. Upriver on a tug sat General Grant listening to the cacophony. A little further downstream General William Tecumseh Sherman floated in the darkness, also listening to the thunderous roar and watching the explosions caused by the Rebel cannons. Like a few weeks earlier at Yazoo Pass, eddies in the current spun some of the small boats around multiple times right in front of the batteries, but all made it past Vicksburg unscathed.

Six days later the 5th Iowa took the same wild ride and were soon below Vicksburg. They got off their boats and marched a good sixty miles along the west side of the Mississippi River, crossing back over the river near the town of Bruinsburg, Mississippi.

From then on everything must have seemed like a blur. The army moved quickly, skirmishing as they went, with the goal of surrounding the east side of Vicksburg. But on May 12 a battle at Raymond, Mississippi, changed General Grant's plans for going after Vicksburg right away. He decided to first take care of Confederate forces located to the east of him at Jackson, Mississippi, worried that if he didn't do so his army might be sandwiched between Vicksburg and Jackson by Confederate forces.

On May 14 at Jackson, Mississippi, the thundering sounds of cannon mixed with actual thunder and lightning of a severe thunderstorm raging at the same time.

"Shortly, we formed line of battle, and in rushing to the left through a great cane-brake, while we were advancing in battle line under a fire of musketry, the order was given to lie down. We obeyed quickly. How closely, too, we hugged the ground and the depression made by a little brook," said Byers. While everyone was pressed against the ground, Marshall was close behind all of them, sitting tall in the saddle on his horse, taking in the scene, "He had no orders to dismount. I could glance back and see his face as the bullets zipped over our heads or past him. He sat on his horse as quiet as a statue, save that with his right hand he constantly twisted his mustache. He looked straight into the cane-brake. He was a brave man." Marshall twisted his mustache as a subconscious nervous action.

Union forces took Jackson splitting the Confederates led by General Joseph E. Johnston and Lieutenant General John C. Pemberton. Johnston retreated northeast toward Canton, Mississippi, while Pemberton dashed off westward on the double toward Vicksburg, with Union forces giving him chase.

Two days later, on the morning of May 16, they caught Pemberton at Champion's Hill, a plantation twenty miles east of Vicksburg.[107] The 5th Iowa found itself in the line of fire at the edge of an open field that rose to a ridge full of Rebel soldiers, firing down from above.

"Zip! zip! zip! came the Rebel bullets, and now and then a boy in blue would groan, strike his hand to a wounded limb or arm, drop his gun and fall to the rear; or perhaps he fell in his tracks dead, without uttering a word," said Byers.[108]

General Grant and his entourage rode up right behind the 5th Iowa's position and surveyed the situation. His intuition about the possible dangers of his army being sandwiched between Vicksburg and Jackson had been correct. Byers took a moment to look over his shoulder and observe the General.

"He leaned against his little bay horse, had the inevitable cigar in his mouth, and was calm as a statue. Possibly smoking so much tranquillized his nerves a little and aided in producing calmness. Still, Grant was calm everywhere; but he also smoked everywhere."[109]

The order was given to fix bayonets, then forward, double-quick! The 5th Iowa charged up the hill to a point where they were just 100 yards away from the Rebel line.

"There was no charging further by our line. We halted, the two lines stood still, and for over an hour we loaded our guns and killed each other as fast as we could," said Byers.[110]

Many on both sides fell dead or wounded. Hoffman was one of the casualties, slightly wounded by shrapnel to his side.

The action raged on until finally Pemberton's Confederate forces turned west in a rapid retreat toward Vicksburg while another Confederate division headed in the opposite direction, back toward Jackson.

The Battle of Champion's Hill and at Big Black River on the next day were Union victories, fights on the razor's edge that, had they gone the other way, would have completely changed what was to come because they forced the Confederates into the fortifications of Vicksburg where they would hunker down and become trapped.

Lieutenant Hoffman was left to his own devices with his injury; because the wound was relatively minor, he was capable of handling it himself. At Champion's Hill the two-story white-frame plantation house located 800 yards northeast of the bald-crested hill was pressed into service for a short time as a Union Hospital. Hoffman stopped there to have his wound examined and bandaged.

On the evening of the Battle of Champion's Hill Hoffman slept in an old log house near the field of battle. The next morning he began limping gingerly westward over the ridge in the direction of another Union field hospital, taking in the horrible sights of the previous day's carnage.

He had few rations and in the next few days cooked what he could find, mostly sweet potatoes and beans, camping overnight with another Iowa regiment. "I marched 10 miles to our division hospital, my wound is sore, there is cannonading along the line," he recorded on May 20.[111] For the next four days the sounds of the heavy bombardment were thrown back and forth by both sides as the Siege of Vicksburg had begun. The display of artillery occupied Hoffman's attention as he lived off beef broth and recuperated.

He eventually found his way back to Company D. Still sore and bandaged, he had recovered enough to rejoin the fight. The 5th Iowa found itself in the center of the Union forces, pushing against Vicksburg from the east. They were just seven miles north of First Lieutenant Mark Bassett's Company E and the 53rd Illinois, fighting together in the siege of Vicksburg.

For the next four weeks the regiment lived in rifle pits and trenches. Hoffman maneuvered Company D's sharpshooters to fire on the Rebel breastworks; cannons from each side threw thousands of projectiles in each direction. Each day Hoffman would move his men slightly from the prior day's position, sometimes just a few yards, to try and gain an advantage.

Amid all the insanity there a little humanity survived. At night Rebel and Union soldiers on picket duty sometimes paused and exchanged tobacco or coffee. It was a common occurrence in the war that a soldier might find himself fighting against family members on the other side. Such was the case with a drummer in the 5th Iowa who was bold enough one evening to meet a Rebel relative at the picket line and accompany him on a private nighttime tour inside the fortifications of the besieged city. They strolled up and down its darkened streets before returning back to the Union lines. This was dangerous stuff, and the story of the drummer's tour was kept from the officers, as blood was thicker than army discipline.[112]

During the day they were hunkered in 400 yards from Rebel lines with the incessant roar of cannons and rifle fire. One night, under torrential rains, Marshall, with a force of 200 men, dug new ditches and built breastworks in the mud. At daybreak the cannons and rifle fire began anew. And so it would continue day after day, night after night.

By late June there was increasing concern once again that Joseph Johnston's Confederate army might attack from the east and sandwich the Union army against the Rebel breastworks at Vicksburg. As a precaution, the 5th Iowa once again marched back toward Jackson on a clear moonlit night, settling in eleven miles to the east at Black River. The perceived danger was warranted; a few weeks later Mark Bassett and many of the 53rd Illinois became POWs under reinforced Confederate forces at Jackson.

Finally on July 4, 1863, Vicksburg was surrendered. The 5th Iowa was moved into the city, given guard duty, and set up a camp at Randolph and Locust Streets, just a few blocks from the fortress-like bluffs on the Mississippi River. Page returned from his hospital stay in Memphis, much recovered from his injuries. They would stay in Vicksburg through the brutal heat of August and into early September before finally receiving orders to head back toward Memphis.

In the fall the 5th Iowa was part of Sherman's Army of the Tennessee in the 2nd Brigade led by Colonel Charles L. Matthies, the regiment's former commander. They spent most of the month of October in and around Memphis, recovering from Vicksburg and biding their time.

Meanwhile, 300 miles to the east in Chattanooga, the Union army was cut off, trapped, and in need of supplies. They desperately needed help.

Starting on October 29, 1863, marching twenty miles a day from Memphis, it took almost a month for Sherman's forces to make it to the outskirts of Chattanooga. Because of the meanderings of the river and mountains near Chattanooga, they crossed the Tennessee River twice to reach their objective. They arrived at the extreme north point of Missionary Ridge and were in position in the early morning hours of November 24.

Sherman's orders called for him to mount an attack on the Confederates the morning of the 24th. But that morning, when he and his officers reached the summit of Billy Goat Hill, which they assumed was the farthest northern point on Missionary Ridge, they found themselves staring across a ravine through a steady rain. The Confederate army was on the other side. Through a bit of bad reconnaissance, they had not realized that Billy Goat Hill was detached and separate from Missionary Ridge.[113] They weren't ready to attack the enemy. So they stood there soaking wet, listening to the sound of thunder coming from about twelve miles to the south. It was Union cannons being fired at Confederate forces as they went on to take Lookout Mountain.

Page and Hoffman were 300 feet below the north side of Billy Goat Hill, where they could hear the thundering sounds in the distance as well. The 5th Iowa spent the rest of the day digging in, throwing up fortifications, and taking turns standing picket in the wet woods, without the warmth of a fire while starting to run short on rations.

As Tuesday afternoon faded into twilight, it was decided that Sherman's attack would be delayed until the next morning. After sunset, the rain let up, the skies began to clear, and the temperatures began to drop.

In the cold, wet darkness, in fits and starts, Marshall, Page, Hoffman, and Byers managed to get a little shut-eye. A chill wind would occasionally blow, helping stir up the fog layer that surrounded them in the valley just enough to suddenly reveal clear skies and a full moon. For a minute or two the moon illuminated things all the way up to the top of Billy Goat Hill, and then the fog would return along with the darkness.

At around 11 p.m. Marshall stirred and lay back, watching the fog part to reveal a moon that had turned a deep blood-red color. He was witnessing a near total lunar eclipse—an ominous sign at the start of a long and eventful twenty-seven hours that he would remember for the rest of his life.

Chapter Four

5th Iowa – Prisoners of War
November 1863

IT WAS A BITTER COLD ON THE MORNING of Wednesday, November 25, 1863. The first light of the sun, diffused through the scrim of a grey sky, provided no warmth to the Major, Page, and Hoffman, as well as the thousands of soldiers in blue. Heavy fog had returned in the valley, greeting the dawn with a damp, piercing consistency like a chilled sauna. A frigid breeze blew; the cold front that had produced the misty rain that provided cover for Sherman's army's amphibious crossing of the Tennessee River in the early morning hours of November 24 had moved southward.

The rest of Sherman's forces were positioned at the very northwest side of Missionary Ridge, the long defensive mountain that ran for miles all the way into Georgia. The Federal line ran down through Chattanooga, sandwiched between the Tennessee River and the Ridge's slopes. The day before had seen a major battle at Lookout Mountain, with a win by Union forces. Sherman was supposed to have attacked Tunnel Hill on the 24th as well but, due to a geography snafu, he was delayed. The Union command was crouched atop Billy Goat Hill, staring across a ravine toward Tunnel Hill, which rose up to the south, aptly named for the Chattanooga and Cleveland Railroad tunnel that passed under the mountain at that location. The 5th Iowa was bivouacked at the northwest base of Billy Goat Hill, which shielded them from the enemy, their backs against the tracks of the Western & Atlantic Railroad.

Sometime after 8 a.m. the 5th Iowa and ten other regiments received orders to move and position themselves on the west side of Tunnel Hill. This line was to support the flank of other regiments to the north who were about to attack. The 5th had taken any cover they could find, lying down looking to the east across an open, level field about one third of a mile wide. The field offered no protection from the Confederate sharpshooter fire coming above, and at some point they all knew they would have to charge across it. At the end of the field, through the fog, was a white structure that formed a barely visible outline in the white-on-white landscape. It was the John G. Glass family home located at the western base of Tunnel Hill; the farmstead's other outbuildings stood nearby. The line immediately registered their locations and potential to provide cover when the order came to charge. The actual railroad tunnel that the hill was named after was tucked into a depression in the side of the hill, just to the south of the farm, with the tracks hidden from view, providing another potential place to find cover. It was also a place where the Confederates could hide if they decided to charge down from the top of the hill to counterattack.

At around 10:30 a.m. the valley fog finally cleared, and the sun broke through, warming the men's faces as they looked up the 320-foot slope to the top of Tunnel Hill. It was the cue for the battle to begin.

A force of 1,100 Union soldiers charged down the ravine and climbed the steep slope to the top of Tunnel Hill's north side, only to find that the Confederate forces had repositioned themselves slightly to the south along the ridge overnight. For the next few hours they fought the Confederate soldiers of General James A. Smith's Texas Brigade. General Smith would be wounded in both thighs.

Shortly afterward the order was given for Colonel John M. Loomis's Union forces to attack from the west. Made up of the 90th Illinois, also known as the Chicago Irish Legion, they raced across the open field under heavy artillery and rifle fire. Gunfire hailed down, and cannons boomed from the top of the Ridge as they were fired down on by the Confederate soldiers of the Texas and Tennessee Brigades. Soldiers of the Irish Legion were mowed down in the carnage. They reached a point between the Glass farmstead and rail line approach to the tunnel and took cover, hunkering down, the path through the open field marked with their dead and wounded.

By 11 a.m. the Confederates sent down a counterattack by the 29th and 56th Georgia Infantry that pushed Loomis's forces back past the Glass farmstead, which they also set on fire. Members of the Glass family, as well as several enslaved individuals they owned, had all taken refuge in the cellar of the home when the battle started. Terrified and caught in the crossfire, the group, which included several young children, was all flushed out as the home was set on fire. They ran across their farmland westward to the Union lines as the rain of cannon and gunfire continued around them. Replacing the fog of an hour earlier, smoke hung over the battlefield from cannons, guns, and burning farm buildings.

At noon a second attack by Union forces of the 27th and 73rd Pennsylvania took their turn rushing across the open fields to help Loomis's forces and push the Confederates back up Tunnel Hill. Once again, cannon and gunfire rained down from above. At the height of this round of battle, an order was mistakenly given, and the 27th Pennsylvania stormed up the ridge, almost reaching the top. They were raked with fire from above and then pinned down, forced into positions all along the slope, their bodies pressed against the ground, taking what little shelter they could find in the roughness of the terrain. Confederate soldiers at the top of the ridge were so close they were able to throw stones down onto the Union troops just yards below them.

At 1 p.m. the Confederates counterattacked again, this time with the 29th and 34th Georgia Infantry charging down from the above, all the way back to the burned ruins of the Glass farm. At times soldiers found themselves engaged in hand-to-hand combat, blue and gray uniforms blurring together until one fell or both fled. This back-and-forth attack, then counterattack fighting, continued into the afternoon with the heaviest casualties on the Union side.

At 2 p.m. the 5th Iowa joined the fray. They were given the orders to fix bayonets and "take that white house," which by then was nothing but charred, blackened remains of the Glass's log home. They moved through a narrow skirt of protective trees and arrived at the open field leading to the base of Tunnel Hill toward the Glass farmstead. The Major raised his saber, "glittering in the sun (it) made an excellent mark for the enemy's artillery."[114] The 5th Iowa charged across the open field, all the time under enemy fire with cannon balls storming down from above. "Behind us our own batteries (forty cannon) were firing at the enemy over our heads, till the storm and roar became horrible," said Marsh Byers.[115] The Major, Marsh Byers, Page, Hoffman, and the rest of the 5th Iowa raced toward Tunnel Hill under extreme Rebel fire. Soon they all reached the bottom of Tunnel Hill, rising more than 300 feet above them, the northernmost part of Missionary Ridge. The enemy fire suddenly became even more intense.

Within a short time they, too, were charging up the steep ridge until they reached a point where they had to lie down to continue firing up toward the top. Then the worst happened.

"That moment someone cried, 'Look to the tunnel! They're coming through the tunnel,'" said Marsh. "Sure enough, through a railway tunnel in the mountain the gray coats were coming by hundreds. They were flanking us completely."[116]

From Marsh's perspective halfway up the ridge, it appeared that the Confederates were streaming out of the railroad tunnel below them to the south. But, in fact, this new counterattack by Rebel soldiers of the 39th and 34th Georgia and 7th Texas Infantry came charging down from the top of Tunnel Hill at a position south of the tunnel, hidden from the Union soldiers' view by the terrain. Then they paused in the ground depression the railroad tracks followed, using it as cover, before sweeping across the battlefield past the remnants of the Glass farmstead, and charged back up the hill.

The 5th Iowa, outnumbered and pinned down, unable to move, was overtaken from their right and rear. They didn't stand a chance.

AS THE REBELS QUICKLY OVERWHELMED the 5th Iowa, many soldiers were killed where they lay, pinned against the mountain. Soon those left alive had no choice but to surrender. The regimental colors fell to the ground. Private John Whitten of Company H rushed to raise them, but he was surrounded, and the colors captured along with Whitten and his brother Josiah. The brigade commander, Colonel Matthies, was wounded in the head and left sitting against a tree in the field of battle. Though he would survive his wounds, his head injury proved to be too much; he resigned his commission in 1864. Those captured were marched up the top of Tunnel Hill at the point of a bayonet.

"I took a blanket from a dead comrade near me, and at the point of the bayonet I was hurried up the mountain," said Marsh. "We passed lines of infantry in rifle pits and batteries that were pouring a hail of shells into our exposed columns. Once I glanced back, and— glorious sight!—I saw lines of bluecoats at our right and center, storming up the ridge."

Colonel Jabez Banbury
Circa 1862
Photographer unknown

It was too late. Over the incessant barrage of heavy fire came the yell "Retreat, Retreat!" from English-born Colonel Jabez Banbury who had taken command of the 3rd Brigade after Colonel Matthies was wounded. Those who escaped did so through a shower of balls and yells from the enemy to halt, rushing back past the remains of the Glass farm, and then across the open field to the west again.[117]

Eighty-two officers and enlisted men of the 5th Iowa were among almost 300 Union soldiers captured at Tunnel Hill. Eight 5th Iowa officers were captured including Major William Stanhope Marshall, Captain John E. Page, Lieutenant Michael Hoffman, and Adjutant Marsh Byers, along with Captain William F. Pickerill, Captain Elias B. Bascom, Lieutenant John W. Huffman, and Lieutenant John W. Austin. They joined several other officers from other regiments. For the 5th Iowa, the entire battle was over in less than an hour.

Company E's 40-year-old 2nd Lieutenant William Staughton Peck, who remarkably wore a size 20 boot, somehow survived Missionary Ridge unscathed and avoided capture. "I had my usual luck not a scratch but I done some of the prettiest running you ever saw. A foot 14 inches long at times was an advantage for every time I took up my foot it left the Rebs so much further behind...I have wished sometimes that I was wounded, then I could have the satisfaction of showing how I had suffered, blead (*sic*) & died for my Country...I have been in every battle that the Fifth has been in but I have not received a scratch or lost a drop of blood," remarked a very lucky, large-footed Peck[118] who ran to safety across the open field in the opposite direction from which he had charged an hour earlier.

THE POWS WERE QUICKLY gathered together in a hollow on the opposite side of Missionary Ridge, their captors conveniently robbing their prisoners of anything of value. Confederate General John C. Breckinridge, who had served as the fourteenth Vice President of the United States under James Buchanan, came in among the prisoners of the 5th Iowa. He purchased a pair of Yankee gauntlets from Marsh for fifteen dollars in Confederate money.[119]

Though the 5th Iowa had large numbers captured, the Union forces won the battle, and the Confederate forces fell into retreat. As night came, Page shot a glance behind him as he walked alongside Hoffman. He could see Union fires on top of Tunnel Hill, and all the captives could hear the cries of victory. A Confederate captain issued a command to the prisoners under his charge that they must walk as rapidly as possible eighty miles south to Kingston, Georgia. The prisoners began walking along the railroad ties with the steel rails pointing southward and armed Rebel guards on either side. Many hadn't had much sleep in days and somehow grabbed sleep as they marched. They had to move in a hurry because the Federal army was right behind them. But Union soldiers were not fast enough to catch up to the new POWs of the 5th Iowa.

Lieutenant William Staughton Peck
Photographer unknown

In the darkness the skies had finally cleared, and a full moon illuminated the retreating Rebels as they headed south with their prisoners of war. "I was taken prisoner on the 25th day of Nov. 1863 about 4 o'clock in the evening and we was marched until 3 o'clock in the morning and made 17 miles and camped near Ringgold, Ga.,"[120] observed Private John Whitten.

The prisoners would march south into North Georgia, passing through Confederate General Bragg's headquarters at Dalton on November 27. It rained heavily for the next few days as they followed the train line and marched through Tilton, Resaca, Calhoun, and Adairsville. Finally on November 30, after marching seventy miles with limited rations and bayonetted rifles prodding them down the railroad tracks, they arrived at Kingston, Georgia, where they were loaded onto cattle cars. The train passed through the towns of Cartersville and Marietta, reaching Atlanta at 9 p.m. that night.

The rumor mill on board the train worked overtime, trying to figure out which prison they were headed for. Anywhere they ended up would be miserable, and the best to hope for was for a prisoner exchange as soon as possible. When they reached Atlanta, the Confederate authorities held them on Tuesday, December 1, trying to determine their fate. They were given rations of corn meal, beef, and salt but were not provided with a means to cook their first significant meal since they were captured. The morning of December 2 saw additional cruelties; they were issued five days' worth of hard tack rations, then their canteens were taken from them. Hard tack with no water to help soften it was a difficult chew. Once again, they were packed into cattle cars, headed east, and arrived in Augusta, Georgia, at 2 a.m. the next morning. They were headed toward Richmond. After a day of camping under guard on the banks of the Savannah River, they boarded their boxcars again. On December 4 they passed through Columbia, South Carolina. Early morning on December 5 they were in Charlotte, North Carolina. They changed cars at sunrise on December 6 near Salisbury, North Carolina, and were soon passing through Raleigh traveling toward Virginia.

By midnight on December 8 they were at Petersburg, and at sunrise they reached Richmond. As they crossed the large railroad bridge over the James River, they could look down onto the sandbar in the middle of the river below.

"We passed Petersburg last night, and this morning as the train crossed the James River bridge we saw thousands of our poor Northern soldiers freezing and starving on a wet sand-bar down in the river, known as Belle Isle," said Marsh Byers.[121]

By this time in December 1863, Belle Island contained almost five thousand ragged, emaciated Union soldiers with little shelter, exposed to the harsh winter elements. Brothers John and Josiah Whitten would soon join the mass of suffering humanity.

"After riding through Rebeldom in box and cattle cars for thirteen days we were landed in Richmond, Va. Here we were divided, the men put on Belle Island, and the officers, thirteen in number, were put into Libby prison," said Hoffman. "There were already in the prison nearly one thousand officers from all parts of the Union army, who had been captured during the summer, the most of them at the battles of Gettysburg and Chickamauga."[122]

In fact, the 5th Iowa had been moving nonstop for some forty days since they left Memphis on October 29. They had marched 300 miles to find themselves captured at Chattanooga on November 25, and then traveled on foot and by train as POWs for more than 750 miles to arrive in the capital of the Confederacy.

AT LIBBY PRISON THEY were soon introduced to Major Thomas P. Turner, the prison commandant. "Gentlemen, it becomes my duty to relieve you of all money and valuables in your possession, before you enter the prison," Turner said. "Fork it out or be chained in the dungeon."[123]

"We were taken into one of the large rooms of Libby, used as an office and prison reception room, we were searched very closely by two rebel sergeants and all of our sidearms, sword belts, pocket knives and greenbacks that had not already been taken were then taken from us," said Hoffman. "We asked why our money was taken and the reply was that it would be returned to us on our release or exchange... Our little party, however, did not furnish them much; only about four or five dollars. We were expecting to be searched before we arrived there and those who had money had it secreted. Capt.

Page had forty dollars in greenbacks which he secreted between the souls of his shoes. The shoes were old and worn on the bottom so that the soles would separate and between these he slipped the greenbacks, except one dollar. This he left in his inner vest pocket as a ruse. They found that one but not the forty."[124]

Libby Prison – Richmond, Virginia
Circa 1865 after the end of the war – *Library of Congress*

Once their names were recorded by chief clerk Erastus W. Ross, they were marched up the stairs and greeted by emaciated, hungry fellow POW officers to the Libby welcoming initiation call, "Fresh Fish, Fresh Fish!"

Though the POWs of Libby Prison were malnourished, the hunger they exhibited upon the arrival of new prisoners was for information. The "Fresh Fish" calls were peppered with questions. "Where were you captured?" "Any word on prisoner exchanges?" "How is the war going?"

Among the voices sounding out the welcome was Lieutenant Mark Bassett of the 53rd Illinois, who had experienced the same initiation when he entered Libby just five months earlier.

TO BASSETT, FIVE MONTHS seemed like five years. He had become accustomed to the daily routine, and the arrival of new prisoners always broke the monotony. Bassett was troubled. It had taken months to get a letter from his wife after he had written her shortly after arriving at Libby Prison. The reply from Lottie left him hollow and confused. Something wasn't right; he felt it in his gut. It compounded the hunger pains that he constantly felt in his stomach. As most POWs at Libby, he had written to ask for his family to send supplies.

For Lottie Bassett back home in Illinois, the letter had come from a ghost. She thought her husband had been killed; his first letter to her from Libby proved he was very much alive. It complicated her life. Believing she was a widow with three small children, she had begun a new relationship with John H. Moore, who had served in the 53rd Illinois[125] under her husband until he was disabled and came home. She lived in a small farming community where everyone knew everyone's business. Soon everyone would know the shocking news of her betrayal, including her POW husband.[126]

BYERS ALSO HAD A LOCAL newspaper report him as killed-in-action shortly after Missionary Ridge. "An occasional paper from the North finds its way into the prison, and from one of these I learn that I was killed (?) at one of the recent battles," said Byers. "Gratifying intelligence, truly! But I am convinced of the untruthfulness of the statement, having just pinched myself, and find that it is I, and that I still live! Libby, bad as they say it is, is still an improvement on being killed."[127]

When the Major, Page, and Hoffman, along with the other new POW officers from Missionary Ridge, first arrived at Libby, the first thing they were advised to do was to write home and ask for supplies.

Most all the prisoners received packages with supplies from home. They were delivered to Richmond on a truce boat that traveled from Fortress Monroe, located to the east where the Chesapeake Bay, Potomac, and James Rivers all met, and City Point, a few miles down the James River at the head of the tidewater. The truce boat conveyed mail between prisoners of either side. Letters were left unsealed so they could be inspected. Any letter with news of the war was not allowed to pass. A lot of these packages and the items within had things hidden in them, like greenbacks.

Since most of the packages were looted by Commandant Turner, Warden Turner, and the Rebel guards, it wasn't long before they discovered that money was also hidden among the supplies.

"They were dragged and unloaded in front of Libby," said Hoffman. "The boxes and barrels opened, examined, and if agreeable were sent into the prison and the man's name called and the box given him. It was found by close calculation that about one third of the goods turned over to the rebels for their delivery were stolen and appropriated for their own use. These goods consisted largely of canned goods, sweetmeats, and trinkets. These were generally taken as they were scarce and hard to get in Rebeldom and if found for sale it would take almost a basketful of rebel money to buy them. Enough however, reached us so that our cravings for rebel rations were considerably diminished. Those who were successful in getting supplies from home would donate rebel rations to the more unfortunate ones who did not get anything from home."

Once word got out to his family as to where he was, the Major would regularly receive a box of his trademark cigars. One cigar in the box displayed a particular mark that clued the Major that perhaps he shouldn't smoke it. When he examined the cigar more closely, a twenty-dollar bill was found wrapped in the center of the tobacco. The Major would pocket his find and reroll the cigar so he would not waste its precious tobacco.[128]

The rations furnished by the Rebels were sparse. They consisted of a steamed loaf of corn bread about the size of a brick, perhaps a little thicker and certainly a great deal heavier, made of very coarse cracked meal with many whole kernels in it. About twice a week there was some fresh or corned beef and about half a cup of red sand beans, sometimes a little salt.[129]

Five members of the 5th Iowa— Captains John Page and Elias Bascom, along with Lieutenants Marsh Byers, Michael Hoffman, and John Austin—would "bunk" together on the floor of the overcrowded east room on the third floor.[130]

About a week after their arrival on December 14, 1863, Commandant Turner issued an edict, just in time for Christmas, that no more packages received by the truce boat for the prisoners would be allowed, effectively shutting down an important asset for the POWs. It was seen as a sadistic blow. The packages began to pile up in a warehouse building located east of the prison across from a narrow vacant lot in full view of the prisoners. So close but so far. From time to time guards could be seen going into the warehouse and emerging with pilfered item from the ever-growing cache. These items sent from loved ones at home or fellow soldiers from their own regiments provided additional nutrition sorely needed by the POWs.

The one wish any prisoner wanted more than any package from home was to be exchanged. They soon found that as the Richmond winter chilled the massive Libby Prison complex, that wish was not going to be granted anytime soon.

Chapter Five

John McAdams – 10th West Virginia
December 1863

THE NIGHT OF SATURDAY, DECEMBER 19, 1863, was as black as the coal they mined in the newly created state of West Virginia, and the temperatures were bone-numbing. Lieutenant John McAdams, age twenty-eight, didn't like the predicament he found himself in. A column of more than 2,500 cavalry soldiers was stretched out for miles in the ice and snow approaching Covington, Virginia. The cavalry at the front of the column had just made it onto James River Turnpike, which under the current conditions was a barely usable road slick with ice. To the south, Ritch Patch Road was an even more miserable track that the rear of the column with the supply wagons, ambulances, and Lieutenant McAdams found itself on. They were slogging along miles away from the column's front, about to make a left-hand turn onto a country path. Known only to the locals, it was a shortcut that branched off of Ritch Patch Road to meet the Turnpike.

The ice made it difficult for both ambulance and supply wagons to move forward with the rest of the column. Men had to march along each side of the wagons, supporting them by pushing hard with their shoulders into the wagon's side to prevent them from tipping.[131] Their luck was quickly running out.

McAdams was a member of the 10th West Virginia Volunteer Infantry, and in October he had been detached from his regiment and detailed to thirty-one-year-old General William Woods Averell's[132] Brigade. Averell, a West Point graduate, was also a connoisseur of the game of chess,[133] a skill that would serve him well as a General.

McAdams, having proved himself a competent multitasker since he became an officer, was given charge of the Averell regiment's ambulance corps, which was how he found himself in the current miserable predicament at the end of a long train of cavalry soldiers, in a pack of

Brigadier General
William Woods Averell
Library of Congress
Mathew Brady's National
Photographic Portrait
Galleries

ambulance and supply wagons, scrambling away after a highly successful raid on the Confederate infrastructure. However, unfortunately, McAdams and his ambulances were bringing up the rear, the last men at the back of a very long train. The front didn't know exactly how far back the rear was, and vice versa.

Four days before, on the afternoon of Wednesday, December 16, Averell had successfully conducted a raid of the town of Salem, Virginia, designed to muck up the Confederate supply lines down to Knoxville. This was McAdam's second raid under Averell since taking command of the ambulance corp. The Salem raid had started on December 8, and the regiment had thus far traversed over more than 250 miles of rugged mountains under terrible winter weather conditions. After the 2,500-men-strong raiding party struck the hornet's nest in Salem, an angry enemy, thousands of men strong, chased after them with a vengeance. Averell found himself surrounded and desperate to avoid capture, looking for the fastest way out of Rebeldom and back to the safety of West Virginia. Initially, the Confederates were hot on his trail, but Averell's skill at chess had enabled him to pre-visualize the enemy's moves, confusing them by creating multiple diversions. It had slowed the enemy down. Confederates still buzzed all around him; they just weren't quite sure where he was.

Colonel William L. "Mudwall" Jackson
Photographer unknown

The odds were against Averell; he had been effectively surrounded by upwards of 12,000 Confederate troops. To his east were the brigades of Generals Fitzhugh Lee and John D. Imboden. To his west was General John Echols. To his north, in the general direction of the Turnpike where he was heading, were troops under the command of Colonel William Lowther "Mudwall" Jackson, a cousin of General Thomas "Stonewall" Jackson. Lee had been a classmate from Averell's West Point days; the two knew each other well. They and the other commands had battled Averell in earlier conflicts conducted along the tenuous, new Virginia-West Virginia border in the rugged Appalachian Mountains.

Mudwall hoped to surprise Averell. He had received intelligence on the afternoon of the 19th that Averell's Raiders were very close to his position at Clifton Forge. Mudwall thought he would finally have Averell trapped if only he could cut off his lone escape route over Island Forge Bridge, just a few miles west of his headquarters.

When heading north, just before Ritch Patch Road reached the James River Turnpike and the Jackson River, there was a fork in the road. Go to the right, and you headed to Clifton Forge where Mudwall's troops were waiting just a mile away at a fence barricade they had recently placed in the road. Go to the left, and there was a narrow path the locals used as a shortcut to connect to the Turnpike and Island Ford Bridge if you were heading toward Covington. Averell's raiding party desperately wanted to get over that bridge, which was his only means of escape, and Mudwall Jackson knew it.

As the sun went down, the temperatures plummeted, and the shortcut to the left had been reduced to a ditch full of ice. Part of Averell's main body of cavalry soldiers had already taken that road single-file, slip sliding as they went. In the darkness they passed through a culvert under the railroad tracks that ran parallel to the Turnpike and emerged onto the Turnpike itself. Looking to the east they saw the Confederate fence barricade about a half mile away. The Rebels were warming their hands over a fire, looking westward in the darkness with their faces clearly seen aglow in the fire's light. They were waiting for the enemy, yet completely unaware of its presence.

Averell's advance scouts had found this nifty little shortcut; it was the perfect, stealthy way to avoid Mudwall. It meant Averell could turn the tables and surprise the Rebel general. His knights were a move or two ahead because for some reason Mudwall was not aware of this shortcut. "A considerable force of the enemy, by some route that had never been explained to me...threw themselves between me and the bridge," which was how Mudwall Jackson explained why he was unaware of the shortcut in his report after the incident.[134]

Looking to the west, about a mile away, was the Island Ford Bridge, guarded by a small Confederate welcoming party of about ten Rebel soldiers from the local Alleghany Home Guards.[135] These guards held torches to illuminate the bridge's structure, the lone escape route that crossed over the Jackson River five miles east of Covington.[136]

The Rebel soldiers on the bridge had been ordered to rig three large piles of kindling at key points so they could quickly set it ablaze. They were just awaiting the word to apply their torches and cut off Averell's escape route.

Suddenly riding out of the shadows on the Turnpike, coming from the direction of the bridge, a Confederate courier appeared. Averell's advance party couldn't believe their luck. The courier, who was on his way to Mudwall Jackson, was quickly captured, and the messages he carried gave Averell some important strategic information as to the positions of the enemy in either direction, as well as intelligence as to where they thought he was.[137]

Averell placed one of his companies at the Turnpike's junction with the Ritch Patch Road shortcut—the culvert under the railroad tracks provided cover—to challenge the enemy from approaching his rear from the east. Then the bulk of his cavalry charged westward on the Turnpike toward Covington, hoping to quickly overwhelm the small welcoming party of Confederate soldiers at the Island Ford Bridge.

Averell's men had been pushing their horses to the limit ever since they rode out of Salem. Many of the soldiers' uniforms were frozen solid against their bodies when they finally arrived at the bridge at 9 p.m. that Friday night. The sheer number of men in Averell's charging cavalry easily overwhelmed the Confederate bridge guards who scattered from the scene before they were able to light their fires to destroy the bridge. Averell's men then captured the bridge, leaving a company behind to guard it. It would take several hours to move the entire column over the bridge.

Because the rear of Averell's brigade stretched out into a several miles long mass of freezing horses and soldiers, by 1 a.m. on Sunday, December 20, McAdams was still miles from the bridge. The slow-moving ambulances hadn't even made it to the shortcut turnoff. Luckily, these rear wagons had some protection. The 14th Pennsylvania Cavalry were acting as their guards. Only three of McAdam's ambulances were occupied; the rest were empty. Their progress had been painfully slow in the pitch-black darkness.

Finally, McAdams could make out up ahead the fork in the road. And he suddenly became aware of an approaching soldier on horseback waving to them to take the road to the right—not the left. The ambulances obediently followed the soldier's lead.

John McAdams was born in Wheeling, Virginia, on August 22, 1835, the first-born son of Robert McAdams and his wife, Susan McCune Adams. Robert and Susan would produce thirteen children, six of whom would survive into adulthood.[138] Robert McAdams was in the "trucking service" running an express wagon around the region.

His branch of the McAdams family had lived in the United States since before it was the United States, having come over from Scotland and Ireland in the early 1700s. Several McAdams had served in the Revolutionary War, with one branch of the family tree settling around Wheeling and the other in Indiana in the early part of the nineteenth century.

In 1853 the Baltimore and Ohio Railroad connected Wheeling, Virginia,[139] with the east. The industrial mill town located on the Ohio River, in what was known as the northern panhandle of Virginia, was wedged between the borders of Ohio and Pennsylvania. Due to the jutting of Virginia's boundaries northward, in order to provide access to the Ohio River the town was actually located north of the Mason/Dixon line. It also was home to a piece of engineering that, as an expressman driving a wagon, John's father, Robert, would have been familiar with. The Wheeling suspension bridge when it was completed in 1849 was the largest suspension bridge in the world. Its design would be a precursor to the Brooklyn Bridge in New York.

BY THE 1850S WHEELING HAD become a melting pot of different cultures, with large Irish and German populations drawn to the work that the mills provided. Some additional McAdams cousins arrived from Ireland during this time, like hundreds of thousands of fellow Irish during the Great Famine, or as it was known in the United States, the Irish Potato Famine. They lived a block away from their cousins in Wheeling's working-class 4th Ward.

As John McAdams came of age, he began working for the railroad, eventually becoming a locomotive engineer. In the late 1850s he married Mary C. Ryland in a ceremony held twenty miles east of Wheeling in Claysville, Pennsylvania. Their first-born son, Charles, came along in February 1861; the McAdams family lived next door to Mary's parents in a block full of coopers, wagon makers, and coppersmiths.

As the tensions that led to the Civil War grew, the state of Virginia's sentiments over secession became clear. Wheeling found itself the focal point of the area of Western Virginia that was strongly anti-slavery and against secession. In mid-May 1861, a month after Fort Sumter and the beginning of the Civil War, the Wheeling Convention was held with twenty-seven northwestern Virginia counties represented. It was agreed that if Virginia officially seceded from the Union, which it did under a statewide referendum confirmed on May 23, then a second convention would be held in June 1861 to determine the fate of the western counties. The result when the second meeting occurred was a condemnation of secession as treason, and the formation of a new government called the "Restored Government of Virginia" with Francis Harrison Pierpoint, a supporter of Abraham Lincoln and an opponent of the secession, elected governor.

Aside from lobbying the Union for statehood for the loyal western part of Virginia to remain in the Union, one of the primary jobs embraced by Governor Pierpont in the summer of 1861 was the recruiting of West Virginia men to form Union regiments. Since the State of West Virginia did not exist yet, these regiments became known as "Loyal" Virginia Regiments, as in loyal to the Union. Confederate Virginia would refer to them as "Bogus" Virginia Regiments.[140]

On August 28, 1861, John McAdams, along with William McAdams who was one of his recently arrived Irish cousins, went into town and enlisted as privates in Company K, 1st West Virginia Cavalry.[141]

Their regiment was composed of hard-working men, mainly from the towns of Wheeling, Morganton, and Clarksburg. Some spoke with German accents, and others, like his cousin William, in a thick Irish brogue. To John, it was all comforting and felt just like home. Immigrants made America, and now a native-born son and immigrant cousin would try to prevent the nation from tearing itself apart.

The area composed of the northwestern counties of Virginia during this time was full of infighting between the majority of citizens favoring allegiance to the Union and their minority neighbors who wanted to go along with the newly formed Confederate States of America. For the remainder of 1861 and the first few months of 1862, the 1st West Virginia Cavalry (Union) was tasked primarily with fighting Confederate bushwhackers and guarding the strategically important Baltimore and Ohio Railroad in the mountains of West Virginia.

In spring 1862 John McAdams was appointed lieutenant by order of Governor Pierpont to fill an empty position in a new regiment. He had been in the army for just over six months. The expanding Union army in Western Virginia needed leadership, and they clearly saw that quality in McAdams. He was separated from his cousin William and reassigned to the 10th West Virginia Infantry, which was also tasked with guarding the railroad in the mountains of West Virginia. In November 1862 McAdams was appointed regimental quartermaster; he oversaw all the supplies required by the regiment, including clothing, food, and horses.

On the last day of 1862 President Lincoln signed a bill admitting West Virginia into the Union, officially recognizing it as the thirty-fifth state on June 20, 1863.

McAdams was detached from the 10th West Virginia in the spring of 1863 to serve as aide-de-camp to Colonel George Hay, commander of the 87th Pennsylvania Infantry Regiment. It was another regiment responsible for guarding the railroad but in an area further to the east. This assignment as the personal assistant to the Colonel was a position of increased responsibility and relocated McAdams from the West Virginia mountains to Winchester, Virginia. He was soon appointed as acting adjutant of Hay's regiment. It was another step up. This new position would have placed him in an interesting physical location in the lead up to the Battle of Gettysburg and its aftermath had Colonel Hay not become sick and been granted a surgeon's medical disability discharge in the same month of McAdams' appointment. Lacking a colonel for whom to act as adjutant, McAdams was sent back to Beverly, West Virginia, to supervise in the construction of fortifications through the summer of 1863.

About the time that Lieutenant McAdams' service under Colonel Hay was coming to an end, Brigadier General William Woods Averell was moved to the Army of West Virginia to command the Fourth Separate Brigade, which included McAdams' regiment. Owing to the rugged mountains of West Virginia where the brigade would operate, fast movement through the terrain was particularly important. Through the summer Averell converted some infantry companies to mounted infantry and cavalry companies.[142] Being on horseback was preferable to being on foot.

"The intention was to organize a force that would be able to meet the confederate partisan rangers on their own ground, and as our regiments were so intimately acquainted with all the ins and outs of the warfare in the mountains, they were selected for this exceedingly difficult and arduous task," said a cavalry soldier in the brigade.

In August 1863 Averell conducted the first of three major raids launched over the Appalachian Mountains from the newly minted state of West Virginia into Virginia. The first raid in mid-August destroyed the Confederate infrastructure, then engaged in a battle against a larger Confederate force under the command of Colonel George S. Patton, grandfather of WWII General George S. Patton. Averell had to retreat to avoid capture, returning to his headquarters in Beverly, West Virginia.

McAdams' supervision in the construction of fortifications was completed at Beverly at the same time Averell arrived there looking for an officer to command the brigade's ambulance corps. McAdams was chosen to fill the position, giving him a front row seat, albeit on a seat in the front of an ambulance wagon located in the rear of the column, for General Averell's two important raids aimed at the Confederate infrastructure in the coming months. It was an interesting juxtaposition for a locomotive engineer used to riding up front.

In the first year of the Civil War, the creation of the ambulance corps was a medical innovation that had saved thousands of soldiers' lives. A particular ambulance design that would have been familiar to Lieutenant McAdams was done in his adopted hometown of Wheeling.

Through the collaboration of Union General William S. Rosecrans, who was living in Wheeling at the time; Major Jonathan Letterman, a surgeon and medical director of the Army of the Potomac; and a Wheeling wagon and carriage building company, a new kind of ambulance was created. It became known as the Wheeling or Rosecrans

FIG. 461.—The "WHEELING" or "ROSECRANS" ambulance wagon.

The "Wheeling" or "Rosecrans" Ambulance

ambulance.[143] The 750-pound ambulance was pulled by just two horses and could carry upwards of a dozen men in seated position, or two to four men lying down. Its lighter weight and suspension system made it well-suited for the mountains. [144]

Averell's second raid began on November 6, 1863, at Droop Mountain, some twenty miles north of Lewisburg. Leading almost 4,000 Cavalry, Infantry and Artillery soldiers against smaller Confederate forces, he commanded the battle that began around

11 a.m. and was over with the Confederates fleeing south toward Lewisburg by 4 p.m. Lieutenant McAdams's ambulance corps was busy with ninety-three wounded in the battle.

Averell's third raid on Salem, Virginia, came in December 1863. The primary objective was to cut off the Confederate supply and communication lines along the Virginia and Tennessee Railroad that went down to Knoxville, Tennessee, where Union General Burnside was under siege by Confederate General Longstreet. When the raid was planned, the target of Salem, with its railroad and Confederate supply warehouses, was so important that Averell was ordered to accomplish this task even it meant the total destruction of his army.[145] Five days after Averell's raid was underway, the Knoxville campaign had come to an end; then, Longstreet withdrew and went into winter quarters.

McAdams and his ambulance corps at the rear of an army of nearly 3,300 soldiers started out from New Creek (Keyser, WV) on December 8, and the entire raiding party followed a difficult path high up, along the ridges that formed the backbone of the Appalachians.

Another strategy that Averell employed was stealth; traveling under the cover of darkness when navigating the tops of the mountains was particularly difficult. "It was evident the enemy was thoroughly confused as to our purpose, and no one was in our front to oppose us or carry the news ahead," said one of his raiders.[146]

ON THE NIGHT OF MONDAY, DECEMBER 14, in a little log cabin deep in the woods between Sweet Springs and New Castle, about thirty miles north of Salem, a group of Rebel soldiers gathered together for the wedding of their friends, George and Polly.

George was a Rebel private, and the intimate affair was attended by the groom's fellow soldiers, primarily members of the 22nd Virginia Infantry with a few 30th Virginia Sharpshooters thrown in for good measure. The bride had a complement of friends there as well, young women eager to be a dance partner with a soldier in one of the few fun social events in the middle of a war.

The Rebel soldiers were part of Echols Brigade. For the last few days several of their regiments had searched unsuccessfully for Averell's Raiders. They had a special grudge against these particular Yankees. Many of their numbers had been defeated by Averell at Droop Mountain a month earlier. The casualty count for the 22nd Virginia was more than 100, and the Rebel army of Southwestern Virginia was almost destroyed.

Monday had been a tough day for the men, riding around in the ugly, miserable cold rain through Monroe County, West Virginia, and Alleghany County, Virginia—a place many of the men knew well as it was where a lot of them were from. They were home. George and Polly's wedding was a welcome break from the miserable, lousy, stinking war.

It was almost pitch-black outside the cabin; its windows cast a warm light. A small sliver of moon was setting just as the ceremony got underway. Polly, a young teenage bride, stood radiant in the glow provided by the fireplace. George looked at his soon-to-be bride and smiled. He knew they wouldn't have much time together, just one night, but that was enough. Then he had to go back to being a soldier. He hoped the war would soon be over and things could return to the way they were. He would farm, and they could have a family together.

"I now pronounce you man and wife," proclaimed the fifty-three-year-old Reverend

Andrew Jackson Elmore as George kissed Polly, and everyone cheered. A fiddle player began a crisp reel, filling the cabin with music, and the bride and groom began to dance. No one in the group was aware in the slightest that a few more wedding guests were also present, watching from outside while sitting on horseback.

"One of our scouts, who was dressed in a confederate uniform, came galloping back and said, 'Boys, there's some fun ahead. The rebs are having a big dance in that cabin,'" said twenty-one-year-old regimental Quartermaster Sergeant Elias F. Seaman. General Averell employed this ruse of dressing his scouts in the enemy's uniform often. It was highly effective, though incredibly dangerous, and could even be deadly if the soldier was captured because he would be looked upon as a spy and executed. Averell's Raiders had succeeded in finding some of the men who had been on their trail before the Rebels succeeded in tracking them down.

The party to celebrate the wedding was just getting started, with the food having just been placed out for all the guests, when the cabin was suddenly surrounded by wedding crashers.

"I was in command of the squad, and soon as we were sure of everything I went forward to the door and ordered the crowd to surrender. You never saw a company more completely thunderstruck," said Sergeant Seaman. "About twenty Johnnies, as soon as they could collect their wits, were compelled to release their fair partners and yield themselves up to less agreeable company."

Both Reverend Elmore and the groom were taken as prisoners.[147] The uninvited guests then helped themselves to the food laid out for the wedding celebration, since many of the actual guests were now indisposed. The Rebel prisoners watched as "less agreeable company" thoroughly enjoyed a dance or two with the female guests. Then it was time to leave.

"Fall in line," barked Sergeant Seaman. The Rebel prisoners reluctantly left the warmth of the cabin and stepped into the cold night air. The bride and groom were left to themselves for a moment, as only a small group of guests remained, all watching as the wedding came to a tragic conclusion.

Polly clung desperately to George, tears welling in her eyes.

"We have just been married, sir; and you're not going to take George away from me now, are you?" said Polly to the Yankee sergeant.

Seaman assured Polly that her husband would be treated well and doubtless, within a few months, would be exchanged so they would be reunited.

George squeezed tightly, holding his bride closely, not wanting to let go. He kissed her, then released her from his embrace and slowly moved to the door, glancing back one last time.

"Good-bye, George, good-bye," said Polly. "God bless you."[148]

She never saw her husband again.

AVERELL'S RAIDING PARTY REACHED the outskirts of Salem in the morning of Wednesday, December 16. It had taken eight days and more than 200 grueling miles to get there.

At 10 a.m. a strike force of 350 men on horseback and two three-inch guns were sent forward as fast as they could gallop into town. The targets of the main raiding party were the telegraph lines, the railroad, and the provisions stored by the Confederates in town. Most of Salem's citizens emerged from their homes to see what the ruckus was all about, only to swiftly go back inside to hide from the "damned Yankees."

The telegraph lines were cut and poles burned. Through a Confederate patrol, captured just prior to reaching Salem, word had come that a troop train would arrive soon. Averell's men dismounted and prepared for the arrival of the train with one of their guns aimed straight down the tracks. When the train came into sight, the first shot missed, then a second shot was blasted diagonally through one of the train cars. The panicked locomotive engineer reversed the train, which began traveling backwards as fast as possible. A third shot was fired and whizzed past the locomotive and its startled engineer, missing as the train disappeared around a bend.

Now attention was placed on the train tracks and infrastructure. Railroad tracks, four miles eastward and twelve miles westward, were torn up, set into piles with wooden railroad ties, and burned to melt the iron, then bent to make them unusable. The depots with cars standing on the tracks, the water tower, the turntable, and various supplies were all torched. Five railroad bridges were destroyed.

Finally, the massive Confederate supply warehouses located adjacent to the train depot were broken into; some of the supplies were drawn by Averell's men for use on the trip home. Then the rest was burned in a massive fire.

The raid at Salem was lightning-fast, taking just six hours. Averell's Raiders departed as quickly as they arrived, heading north out of town on the same road they had come in. They were all sleep-deprived and exhausted. The last eighty miles into Salem had been traversed in just thirty hours. So, seven miles north of Salem, the column stopped for the night for a much-needed rest.[149]

Then a cold rain began.

It would continue for more than two days, swelling all the rivers and creeks and soaking the constantly moving mass of men, horses, and their ammunition. Averell was faced with a critical decision on how exactly to get back home. "Two ways were left, both difficult and obscure; one to the southwest...through Monroe and Greenbrier Counties; the other northeast to Covington and Fincastle Pike, which I took, as it was the most direct and dangerous, consequently the safest," said Averell.[150]

At sunset, appearing to stop for the night, Averell's men started campfires and, as soon as they were raging, continued moving north again "in the darkest and coldest night we had yet experienced," said Averell. The temperatures eventually dropped below zero. The tactic fooled the enemy's scouts. While the Rebels thought that Averell's men were camped and sleeping, they were able to travel an additional thirty miles further north, where they arrived just fifteen miles south of the Island Ford Bridge at noon on Saturday, December 19, capturing the bridge around 9 p.m.

McAdams and the men in the pack of wagons and ambulances stuck in the rear of the column could not have known that Averell had seized the Island Ford Bridge; their hope was that the rear of the column would soon catch up and get across the bridge to safety. But it was not to be. In the darkness of the early morning hours, Confederate troops attacked the bridge, exchanging fire with the Yankee company left to defend it and capturing a few of Averell's men. But the Rebels were driven back, and the raiders managed to continue to hold the bridge.

Sleep-deprived and bone-weary, McAdams urged his ambulance's two horses forward. Two more ambulances carrying additional wounded soldiers followed close behind, and all three passed to the right at the fork in the road. The raid on Salem to this point had not seen many wounded soldiers, though there were many injuries due to exposure to the extreme cold.

LYING PROSTRATE, OVERCOME WITH extreme exhaustion in the back of one ambulance, was Vienna, Austria-born Lieutenant Leopold Markbreit, the regiment's acting assistant adjutant general. Also with the ambulances was its chaplain, Captain Andrew W. Gregg.

Close by the ambulance and supply wagon pileup, fumbling around in the darkness on horseback, rode Lieutenant Colonel John J. Polsley, the son of the first Lieutenant-Governor of the "Restored Government of Virginia," Daniel H. Polsley.[151] A shadow on horseback approached Polsley, who mistook him for one of his own men. Polsley froze when a gun was placed up to his head with the man whispering, "Unless you surrender immediately, I will blow out your brains."[152]

The ambulances plodded along the icy road, then through a different culvert under the railroad tracks, emerging onto the James River Turnpike heading to the east. It was so dark and miserably cold that the uniform colors of men on horseback leading them through the shadows were not identifiable. In the dim light everything was shades of gray, and McAdams thought the men on horseback were wearing blue. He had no idea that the rest of their regiment was heading in the opposite direction while they were heading into a trap. About a mile straight ahead was the fence blockade across the turnpike manned by Mudwall Jackson's men. Mudwall had finally managed to capture part of Averell's raiding party.

"Three ambulances were captured in this way, and some of the men in them did not know they were prisoners until the next morning," said Sergeant Seaman, who was with the wagons and ambulances in the rear of the column.[153]

After the sun rose on December 20, Averell's guards on the Island Ford Bridge were again being fired at by the Rebels. They had no choice but to torch the bridge to prevent them from retaking it. An order was given to burn the supply wagons and ambulances that remained on the east side. Sergeant Seaman quickly circled the wagons and set them aflame.[154]

This action left a small group of Confederate soldiers between the 14th Pennsylvania Cavalry and the now smoldering Island Ford Bridge, with more Confederates coming toward their rear, racing down the Turnpike. The 14th Pennsylvania was now separated from the regiment, trapped on the east side of the Jackson River with Rebels at their front and back. The Rebels issued an ultimatum to surrender at 8:30 a.m. but the commander of the 14th refused. His men began yelling, "The 14th Pennsylvania Cavalry never surrenders![155]" In the time it took to exchange communications refusing to surrender, a scouting party for the 14th located a narrow, icy pathway that led a few hundred yards south to Holloway's Ford. The ford was normally easily crossed, but after days of steady rain and cold, it was about forty yards across with a swift dangerous current,

The men of the 14th Pennsylvania quickly fled along this newfound escape route where almost 500 soldiers successfully crossed the Jackson River. In the raging waters several men drowned during the crossing. Swept downstream with his hands bound was one of the Rebel prisoners, the groom captured at his own wedding prior to the raid on Salem,[156] his gray Rebel coat blending with the churning gray waters until he disappeared beneath its surface, his body never to be found. The 14th Pennsylvania

Cavalry eventually caught up with the rest of Averell's raiding party a few days later.

McAdams, still seated in his ambulance, saw the dark, smoky column that rose to the west. Confused, he looked down at men dressed in blue. They were pointing their weapons at him and the others in the three ambulance wagons. They were Rebels wearing Union blue, posing as Federal soldiers.[157] McAdams soon found himself at Confederate General Mudwall Jackson's headquarters next to Clifton Forge's railway depot. He was now a prisoner of war. Over the course of the day, the other Union soldiers captured by Mudwall's men were assembled at the railroad station; they would all spend a cold night without a fire, on bare, frozen ground, wondering what kind of hell was coming next.

"There were 114 of us cooped up near the station house at Jackson River station...before we started via Stanton for Richmond and starvation,"[158] said a litter bearer from McAdams' ambulance corps. The actual number of enlisted men captured was sketchy with different numbers reflected in different accounts. In total, five officers—Lieutenant Colonel John J. Polsley; Captain Andrew W. Gregg, the regiment's Chaplain; Lieutenant AAG Leopold Markbreit; Lieutenant John McAdams; and Lieutenant Caleb H. Casdorph—were part of the total number of POWs captured.[159] [160]

Lieutenant Casdorph, who was part of the 8th West Virginia Mounted Infantry during the Salem Raid,[161] had been captured at some point near Island Ford Bridge.

The Four Other Officers Captured Along With
Lieutenant John McAdams at Jackson River

Lieutenant Colonel John J. Polsley	Chaplain / Captain Andrew W. Gregg	Lieutenant AAG Leopold Markbreit	Lieutenant Caleb Casdorph
Photographer Unknown	*Courtesy of Steve Cunningham Charleston, WV*	*Courtesy of Steve Cunningham Charleston, WV*	*Courtesy of James Casdorph*

Upon his capture, Lieutenant Markbreit was singled out by Mudwall Jackson to be initially sent to his headquarters in Warm Springs, Virginia, to await negotiations for a prisoner exchange.[162]

"The Confederates took us about half a mile further down the river to an old shed, where we were kept until the morning of the 20th...on the 22nd we started in the direction of Staunton," said one twenty-three-year-old private.

Two days after they were captured, the POWs left Jackson River station on foot. For two days they were marched eastward thirty miles through the rugged mountains.

"We arrived at a little station on the railroad known as Goshen, where they ordered us into rickety, old box cars, and with a creaky, old engine started for Staunton, and arrived there about sunset that evening," said the private. "Early Christmas morning, we marched down to the depot and again ordered aboard a train of cars—good coaches for once— and started for Richmond, a place we had long wanted to get to but not under the escort of a military guard, but as triumphant victors in capture of the Capitol *(sic)* of the Confederacy."[163]

They arrived in Richmond around 8 p.m.;[164] then, the entire group of new POWs was moved to Scott Prison, which was located between Main and Cary Streets about a block from Libby Prison, for processing by the Confederate prison authorities. At least this was a brick building, offering some cover from the torturous winter weather. The arctic-like winter cold they had experienced through much of the Salem raid continued, and the winds blowing off the James River in Richmond cut through the men like an icy knife.

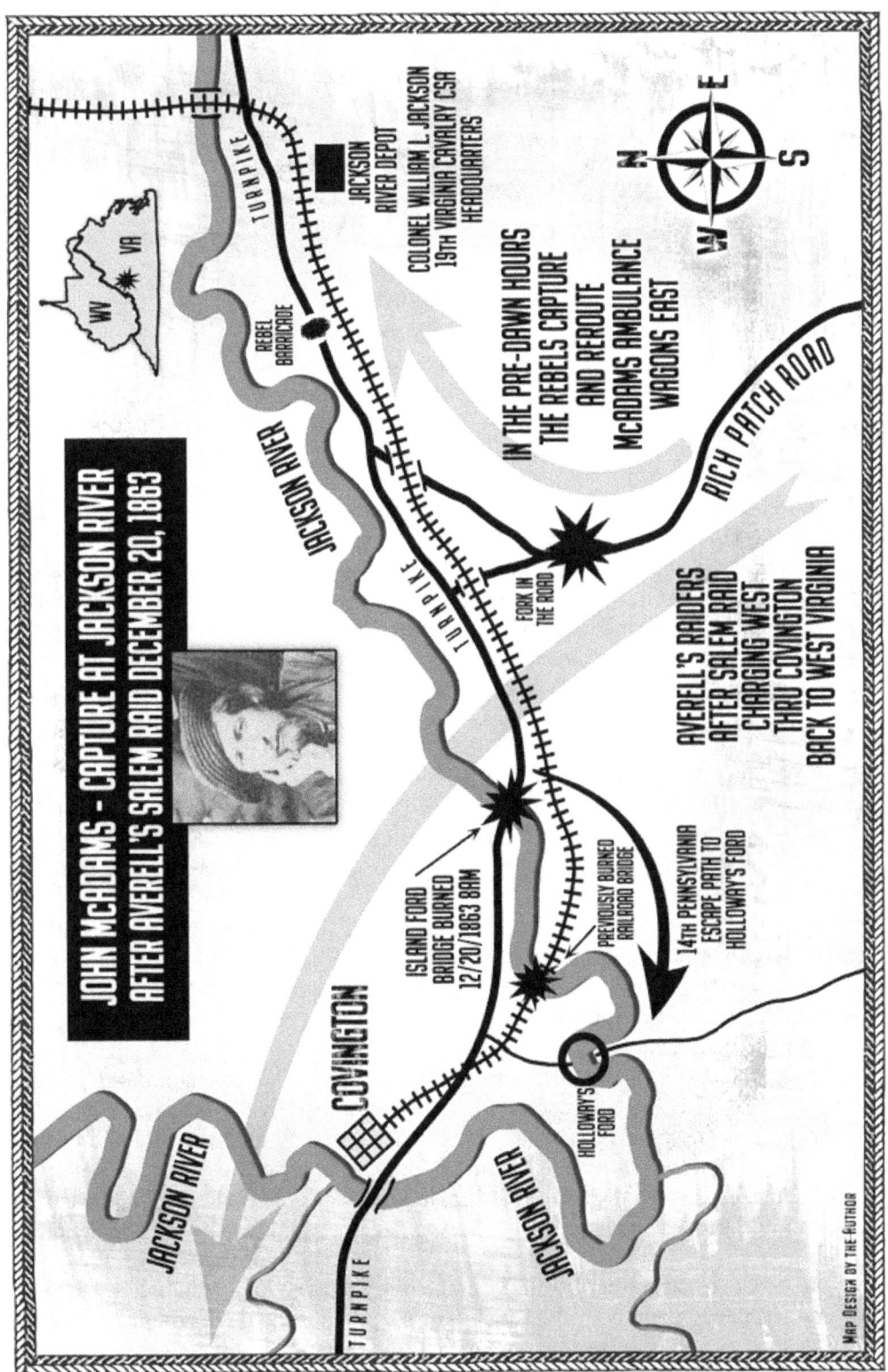

JOHN McADAMS – CAPTURE AT JACKSON RIVER
AFTER AVERELL'S SALEM RAID DECEMBER 20, 1863

JACKSON RIVER DEPOT

COLONEL WILLIAM L. JACKSON
19th VIRGINIA CAVALRY CSA
HEADQUARTERS

IN THE PRE-DAWN HOURS
THE REBELS CAPTURE
AND REROUTE
McADAMS AMBULANCE
WAGONS EAST

REBEL BARRICADE

TURNPIKE

JACKSON RIVER

TURNPIKE

FORK IN THE ROAD

RICH PATCH ROAD

AVERELL'S RAIDERS
AFTER SALEM RAID
CHARGING WEST
THRU COVINGTON
BACK TO WEST VIRGINIA

ISLAND FORD
BRIDGE BURNED
12/20/1863 8AM

PREVIOUSLY BURNED
RAILROAD BRIDGE

14th PENNSYLVANIA
ESCAPE PATH TO
HOLLOWAY'S FORD

COVINGTON

JACKSON RIVER

HOLLOWAY'S FORD

JACKSON RIVER

TURNPIKE

WV VA

N E S W

MAP DESIGN BY THE AUTHOR

Chapter Six

Libby Prison
December 1863 to February 1864
Illustration by Lieutenant Colonel
Federico Fernández Cavada

"Christmas! at that name, what pleasant visions come thronging to the prisoner's mind, visions of home and hearth, – of mince pies, plum-puddings and bon-bons, of Christmas trees and child-laughter, and pretty little rosy mouths, sweeter for the sugar plums, puckering into Christmas kisses! What prison-thoughts, that laugh at the rebel bars and bayonets, go traveling by swift air lines, afar off into cozy cottages among the northern snows, and over wide prairies into western homes, north, south, east and west– over the whole land...The north wind comes in reeling in fitful gushes through the iron bars, and jingles a sleigh-bell in the prisoner's ear, and puffs in his pale face with a breath suggestively of odorous egg-nog.

Christmas Day! a day that was made for smiles, and not for sighs–for laughter, and not for tears,–for the hearth, and not for prison."[165]

Lieutenant Colonel Federico Fernández Cavada
114th Pennsylvania Infantry

BY CHRISTMAS EVE, THURSDAY, DECEMBER 24, 1863, Libby Prison was bulging at the seams with more than 1,200 Union officers. The battles fought over the last six months at Gettysburg, Chickamauga, and Missionary Ridge had produced a large crop of prisoners for both sides; for the citizens Richmond, the capital of the Confederacy, it was becoming a nuisance.

Within Libby itself, the first floor fronted Cary Street. The main entrance and front door to the prison was at the corner of 20th and Cary Streets, which led into the commandant's office and guardrooms. The prisoner's kitchen was in the middle section of the first floor, and the east side of the first floor was the prison hospital. A set of stairs with no banister led to the upper floors and could be retracted, like a trap door, preventing access to the kitchen except when it was allowed and containing the prison population to the floors above.

"The middle room on the first floor is our cook and mess hall," reported Lieutenant George Duncan Forsyth of the 110th Ohio. "The mess hall is fitted with rough pine tables with seats such as you have seen at picnics, all stationary. In my mess which is No. 6, we have old rye coffee served at 9:30 a.m. and dinner at 4 p.m."[166]

Confederate coffee was another concoction that served as a replacement for the real thing. "It was made out of roasted, or rather burned, cornbread; vile stuff it was, but then it had the merit of being hot; the heel of a molasses jug helped to allay its bitterness. After a time I grew to like it," said one Union Captain.[167]

The Four Floors of Libby Prison – View looking to the east,
the road where the horse is would be 20th Street.
The road in the foreground was along the canal and the James River,
sometimes called Canal or Dock Street.
C – Cellar; 1 – Ground Floor with entrance on Cary Street;
2 and 3 – Prisoner's Areas
Library of Congress – Post War 1865

The second and third floors were approximately 105 feet by forty-five feet and had been divided up into three rooms per floor. The second-floor ceiling was just seven feet tall with the third-floor ceiling being vaulted, following the lines of the roof above. The cathedral ceiling made the overcrowded space feel a little roomier, though the room's occupants considered the third floor a cathedral straight out of hell. The first room on the west side of the third floor was Colonel Streight's room. Immediately below him on the west side of the second floor was General Milroy's room. The two rooms were occupied by the earliest inmates at Libby. A total of 1,466 of Streight's raiders were captured at the end of his infamous raid in May 1863, though most all had been exchanged except for four senior officers and Streight himself.[168] A large contingent of Milroy's men were captured at the Second Battle of Winchester in June 1863, so the room was named in his honor even though General Robert H. Milroy was never captured, and thus had never set foot into Libby.

The middle room on both the second and third floor was known as the upper and lower Cumberland Army or "Chickamauga" rooms. The east room on the second and third floors was known as the upper and lower Potomac Army or "Gettysburg" rooms. The POWs tended to congregate together based on the battles in which they were captured in, as well as the regiments of which they were members. What little attempts to make the space clean were daily mopping by Black workers enslaved by the

THE
LIBBY PRISON
MINSTRELS!

MANAGER,	LT. G. W. CHANDLER.
TREASURER,	CAPT. H. W. SAWYER.
COSTUMER,	LT. J. P. JONES.
SCENIC ARTIST,	LT. FENTRESS.
CAPTAIN OF THE SUPERS,	LT. BRISTOW,

THURSDAY EVENING, DEC. 24th, 1863.
PROGRAMME.
PART FIRST.

OVERTURE—"Norma".........................TROUPE.
OPENING CHORUS—"Erneni"...............TROUPE.
SONG—Who will care for Mother now Capt. SCHELL.
SONG—Grafted in the Army.............Lieut. KENDALL.
SONG—When the Bloom is on the Rye Adjt LOMBARD
SONG—Barn-yard Imitations...............Capt. MASS.
SONG—Do they think of me at Home...... Adjt. JONES.
CHORUS—Phantom..............................TROUPE.

PART SECOND.

Duet—Violin and Flute—Serenade from "Lucia,"
Lieuts. Chandler and Rockwell
Song and Dance—"Root Hog or Die,".........Capt. Mass
Banjo Solo..............................Lieut. Thomas
Duet—Dying Girl's Last Request, Adjt. Lombard & Jones
Magic Violin...............Capts. Mass, Chandler and Kendall
Song—My Father's Custom.................Lieut. McCaulley
Clog Dance................................Lieut. Ryan

RIVAL LOVERS.

JOE SKIMMERHORN..........................Capt. MASS
GEORGE IVERSON..........................Lt. RANDOLPH

PART THIRD.
COUNTRYMAN
IN A
PHOTOGRAPH GALLERY.

PROPRIETOR............................Capt. MASS
BOY...................................Lt. RANDOLPH
COUNTRYMAN............................Maj. NEIPER

MASQUERADE BALL.

MANAGER...............................Adjt. JONES
DOOR-KEEPER...........................Capt. MASS
MUSICIAN..............................Lt. CHANDLER
MEMBER OF THE PRESS...................Lt. RYAN
MOSE..................................Lt. WELSH
BLACK SWAN............................Lt. MORAN
BROADWAY SWELL........................Lt. BENNETT
RICHARD III...........................Capt. McWILLIAMS

THE WHOLE TO CONCLUDE WITH A
GRAND WALK AROUND.

Performance to commence at 6 o'clock.

ADMISSION FREE--Children in arms not admitted

Adjt. R. C. KNAGGS,
Business Agent.

Confederate prison staff. Often the water would freeze to the floor as fast as it was splashed onto it. On a rainy day the floors would stay wet all day, and the men ended up sleeping on the wet surface.[169]

At the southern end of each of the rooms was the common latrine. This was nothing more than a water spigot and a long sink or trough. If the winds blew in from the south, the stench wafted throughout the prison living space.

The 53rd Illinois's Lieutenants Mark Bassett and John D. Hatfield were mess mates and bunked in the second-floor middle "Chickamauga Room." Lieutenant George R. Lodge, also from the 53rd Illinois and captured with Bassett and Hatfield, had taken up quarters upstairs in the third floor's east "Gettysburg Room." Why Lodge chose to occupy the upper floor was a mystery. The 5th Iowa's Major William Stanhope Marshall, Captain Elijah Page, and Lieutenants Michael Hoffman and Marsh Byers were also mess mates together in the third-floor's east "Gettysburg Room."

The cellar, which fronted the canal and the James River, was divided into three sections. It was actually at ground level because of the slope down to the James River and canal, so when looking at Libby from the water, the building appeared as four stories tall. The west cellar was initially used for cooking, then the Rebels moved the cooking area up to the first floor, and the space was used as a morgue. The middle cellar was used for storage, a carpenter's shop, and contained the Libby windowless dungeon, directly against the cellar's northern wall. "The rear and darker part of the middle cellar was cut up into cells, to which were consigned those of our numbers who were guilty of infractions of rules of the prison," said one Libby prisoner, "dungeons dark and horrible beyond description." Some of those tortured in the basement cells were put there in a "tit-for-tat" reaction to what was happening to Confederate prisoners in the north. If word got out of punishment inflicted on several

Rebel officers at Camp Douglas, the Union POW camp in Chicago, then warden Turner would randomly select the same number of Union POWs and throw them into the Libby Prison dungeon. What this form of sadism actually accomplished was hard to say. A prisoner was still a prisoner, though in the dungeon he was a tortured prisoner. The east cellar was full of damp, rotting straw and used for commissary storage. There were so many rats in that part of the cellar that it became known as "Rat Hell."

Things were getting so bad with the overcrowding that at 9 p.m. when the call of "Lights Out, Yanks" came and the tallow-dips that provided a dim, meager light were extinguished, every square inch of floor space was occupied by a malnourished POW. Some shared blankets, and all lay side by side on the hard floor surface, each man "spooned" against the man next to him in order to maximize the available space. Each group of spooning men had a man in charge or "spoon-captain." When the hard floor was too much for the men's right side, an order was given by the spoon-captain, "Attention, Squad Number Four! Prepare to spoon! One, two, spoon!" at which the entire squad would flop over to their left side.[170] The sound of hundreds of tired bodies resonating through the hard floor like a wooden drum.

The benefits of this "spooning" arrangement in the dead of winter was also that it provided much-needed warmth to all the soldiers attempting to get some rest. After "Lights Out" it was dark and bitterly cold. At Libby, though all the windows had metal bars in their openings to prevent escape, they had no glass in them so the winter winds that blew down the James River howled through the prison, providing an unwanted, frigid cross-ventilation through the second and third floors and keeping the inside temperature roughly equal to the outside one. At some point during the winter, they placed fabric over the opening, which didn't help at all.

There were no Christmas gifts shipped from home for the POWs at Libby to be unwrapped. That was because the regular pipeline of packages shipped to the prisoners had been shut down by Commandant Turner as a cruel punishment with no explanation just a few weeks earlier. So the provision packages sent to the prisoners piled up in a warehouse building directly east of Libby, regularly looted by Confederate guards and soldiers, just across an empty lot for all the prisoners to see. The existing supplies had dwindled, and the prospects for anything resembling a Christmas dinner were bleak. Yet the prisoners found ways to lift their spirits. They staged a Christmas concert by the Libby Prison Minstrels on Christmas Eve. The event was held in the first-floor prison kitchen. "Last night the Libby Minstrels gave an entertainment which was very creditable to them. They had their Programme *(sic)* printed in regular style," said Lodge.[171]

"Among the musical instruments was a bass viol, violins, guitars, banjoes, clarinets, and down even to bones," said Hoffman, "They had organized a concert troupe, and on Christmas they rendered a concert. They gave the rebel sergeant a few complementaries for the loan of a plank from which to erect staging. He and his friends came in and enjoyed it hugely. The singing and music was a great source of comfort through Libby. One thousand or more men from all parts of the Union were randomly thrown together in prison were as U.S. officers, but at home they were doctors, merchants, mechanics, farmers, lawyers, ministers, etc. representing all professions and trades, so when in Libby there was a ready hand for almost anything."[172]

"Christmas in prison!" exclaimed Marsh Beyer, "The day is cold and gloomy; we have little but fuel for fire, so comfort is out of the question. I am thinking of the bright and happy firesides, today, in the far-off North."[173]

Fantastical Christmas meals were created in the minds of the prisoners to ward off their hunger. These visualizations provided a distraction but not a relief from the gnawing in their stomachs.

"Christmas!!!" exclaimed Lodge. "Little did I think when I came here that I was to spend my Christmas here. I should have had but a sorry dinner had it not been this morning Lt. King came and invited me to dine with his mess, which invitation I promptly accepted. We had roast turkey with applesauce, mashed potatoes, pumpkin pies, cheese, crackers, and coffee. The turkey was excellent, very well cooked, and we had a good dinner."[174]

Lodge's actual dinner was more than likely a soupy gruel made of the daily corn bread ration with perhaps a salty piece of rancid bacon. Bassett would comment, "Our food was coarse cornbread, rice and sometimes bacon and beans in whatever degree of staleness the meat happened to be and of the poorest quality."[175]

"I am invited out today to a Christmas dinner. Good!" said Cuban-born Lieutenant Colonel Cavada of the 114th Pennsylvania Infantry. "When I say I am invited out, I mean over there in the north-east corner of the room: I shaved my face, and combed my hair this morning for the occasion. I am promised a white china plate to eat from!"[176]

Cavada was an artist who sketched his surroundings at Libby. Living in Philadelphia at the start of the war, his artistic skills made him a natural recruit for the Union Army Balloon Corps. From up to 1,000 feet in the air, he would sketch the enemy's movements while aloft, while at the same time providing the Rebels with a large target in the air at which to fire their guns. Somehow, by sheer luck, he had avoided being hit by the numerous mini-balls shot skyward in his general direction. He was captured with his regiment during the Battle of Gettysburg, though by then he had given up his wartime hot air balloon adventures.

ON CHRISTMAS, AS THE DAY FADED into evening twilight, the Union officers and enlisted men of Averell's Raiders who had been captured at Jackson River near Covington, Virginia, five days earlier arrived in frigid Richmond. Since it was dark, the Rebels temporarily moved the arriving prisoners to Scott Prison, just a block away from Libby.

Early Saturday morning, December 26, 1863, following the standard processing procedures by the Confederate army, Lieutenant John McAdams, Lieutenant Colonel John J. Polsley, Chaplain Andrew W. Gregg, and Lieutenant Caleb H. Casdorph were separated from the enlisted men and sent to Libby Prison. The enlisted men were sent to Belle Island, where there was virtually no shelter, with temperatures that were below freezing on most nights during December 1863. Many of the men were later shipped south to the Confederate prison at Andersonville, Georgia after it opened in February 1864. It is believed that of the total number of Union enlisted men captured during Averell's Raid on Salem, only about twenty-six survived the war.[177]

At Libby Prison McAdams and the other officers entered the door on the ground floor and were marched into the long, main entrance room. McAdams glanced to the door to his right that had a small card pinned to it with an inscription scrawled, "Office of the Commandant." At that moment the door opened, and Major Thomas Turner emerged to begin the interrogation process. In the room waiting for him were Warden Turner and Little Ross, ready to administer the indignities delivered onto all Yankee officers entering Libby for the first time.

When it was over, from the back part of the room, the trapdoor stairway mysteriously appeared from above, pivoting down from the ceiling.

"That's all, gentleman," shouted Little Ross. "Now, please march up the stairs and make yourselves at home." McAdams and his comrades slowly climbed the stairs, their senses taking it all in, stunned by the sheer number of prisoners packed into the upper two floors.

The day after Christmas McAdams and his comrades excitedly told their captive audience of fellow captives their firsthand account of General Averell's Salem Raid, which by then had become front page news in the North. The POWs at Libby were well aware of General Averell's exploits. Though copies of the *Richmond Enquirer* were not allowed in Libby, they were nevertheless readily available and eagerly read by all. To their delight, General Averell seemed to be making the Rebels jittery.

Chaplain Gregg was soon singled out. Because he was a member of the clergy, and by the sheer good fortune that upon his arrival there was a need to relieve the overcrowded conditions of the prison, he was paroled and sent down the James River in the flag-of-truce boat on December 27. His total time as a prisoner of the Confederacy: one week. "The truce boat at this time made weekly trips between the north and south or between Fortress Monroe and City Point; the latter a few miles down the James River from Richmond at the head of tide water," said Lieutenant Hoffman. Chaplain Gregg would soon rejoin his regiment and report back on the conditions that the POWs were faced with at Libby Prison, as well as his treatment in general by his captors.

Lieutenant Leopold Markbreit, AAG soon joined the rest of the men at Libby who had been captured after General Averell's Salem Raid and after his exchange through General "Mudwall" Jackson headquarters in Warm Springs, Virginia, fell through.

For the remainder of the week, the new prisoners acclimated to Libby Prison. On New Year's Eve, back home in Wheeling, West Virginia, the *Wheeling Daily Intelligencer* would report:

Capture of Lieut. McAdams By The Rebels–*Lieut. John McAdams of this city, who accompanied the late expedition of Gen. Averill (sic) to Salem, Virginia was captured by the rebels and is now doubtless in Richmond. The following letter to Mrs. McAdams conveys the intelligence with other matters of less local interest.*

Beverly, West Virginia
December 25, 1863

Lieut. McAdams was captured at Jackson's River, along with General Averill's (sic) Adjutant General (Capt. Markbreit[178]) Lt. Col Polsley of the 8th Va. and the Chaplain of the 8th, They captured three ambulances. The balance of the ambulances and the rest of the train we burned. I am sure that the Lieutenant was safely captured. I mean by this he was not wounded. The Brigade is just coming into town. The above I learned from William McCane, who says that he was close to the Lieutenant at the time he was captured.

Hoping the above is satisfactory, I am with much sympathy. Very respectfully,
your ob't sev't
M.S. Hall
Lt. Col 10th Va. Infantry

Lieut. McAdams belongs to company G, 10th West Virginia Infantry, and was in charge of the ambulances at the time of his capture. Lieut. Col. Polsley is a son of Judge Polsley, ex-Lieutenant Governor.

Back home in Wheeling, McAdam's wife, Mary, tightly hugged her two-year-old son, Charles, clenching the Colonel's letter tight in her hands, tears streaming down her face, thankful that her husband was alive.

Polsley would write to Major Hedgeman Slack of his regiment, "You now doubtless heard of this, from the Chaplain, an account of my capture. I have been doing quite well as to be expected, but am very anxious to get out of this...If the Chaplain has not sent me a box of provisions, I hope you will be kind enough to attend to it...Markbreit, McAdams and Casdorph are all well and doing well."[179]

"December 31st, 11 o'clock at night! The old year is almost gone. We have been allowed to keep lights burning in the prison later tonight, than usual. I have spent the day, and thus far the night—in reading the "Unionist's Daughter"—a history of many of the thrilling events occurring in Tennessee" recorded Byers in his diary. The book was written by Mrs. Metta Victoria Victor who created what was known as the "dime novel," publishing more than 100 of them in her lifetime.

New Year's Day 1864 saw Libby Prison more crowded than ever before, with a crush of POWs arriving daily. "Yesterday three hundred and sixty-two Yankee,

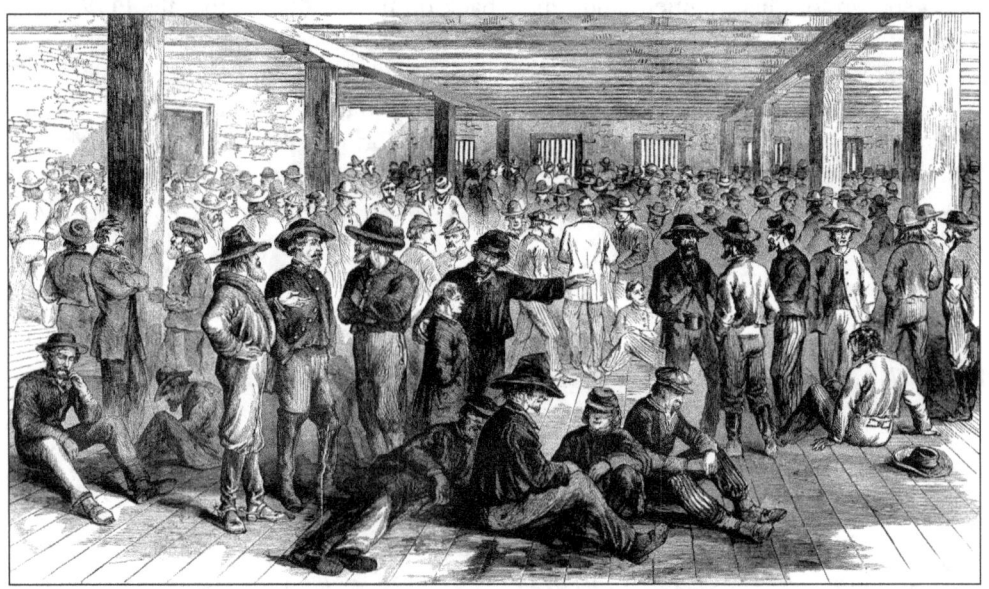

The crowded conditions of Union POWs inside Libby Prison
Frank Leslie Illustration – 1896

belonging to Burnside's force, captured by General Longstreet in East Tennessee were received at the Libby prison via Danville railroad," reported the *Richmond Enquirer*.[180]

"Did I think I should ever write this date in this vile place. Well! The prospects are present that I will write it many times and maybe 1865 before I get out of here. Last night the Rebs allowed us to have our lights until 11 o'clock, and then we put them out and sang patriotic songs from that until after twelve. The day is cold and bright and beautiful," said Captain George Lodge.[181] Lodge, along with Bassett and Hatfield, had been prisoners together at Libby for almost six months.

With the holiday season as a prisoner at Libby Prison now at an end, the monotony of day-to-day life resumed. Most officers' minds were filled with thoughts of escape. But Libby was pretty much escape-proof, which was why it was chosen by the Confederates in the first place as a prison for their valuable Union officer POWs.

In October 1863, the ever-outspoken Colonel Abel D. Streight of the 51st Indiana Volunteers, and one of the highest-ranking Union officers held at Libby Prison, had hatched a brute force escape scheme. With Richmond housing more than 15,000 enlisted and 1,200 officer POWs all around the Confederate capital, the idea was to create a revolt that would overwhelm the guards and take over the city. Streight knew the numbers and his plan was no bluff.

Though it would obviously have resulted in a high number of losses, the simple fact was that there were a lot more Union prisoners in Richmond than there were Confederates guarding them, and with the increasing numbers of POWs arriving daily, the percentage of prisoners to guards made the odds of success look pretty good to Streight.

Lieutenant Alva C. Roach was one of Colonel Streight's remaining officers from the 51st Indiana captured with him who had not been exchanged. Roach's explanation of how the plan was to work was to "proceed to the arsenal, take possession, and arm and equip ourselves with the guns and accoutrements found there; then release all the prisoners confined in and around Richmond, form them into companies, regiments and brigades, and, if possible, take prisoners Jefferson Davis and his Cabinet, and other leading rebels then in the city, and then march en masse down the Peninsula until we should arrive within our own lines."[182]

Simple.

Streight's "brute force" escape plan also employed the help of Elizabeth Van Lew, a Unionist spy. Van Lew's home was located on the south side of East Grace Street between 23rd and 24th and had a view down to the James River and the prison just six blocks away. Van Lew would on occasion visit Libby and provide food for prisoners in the hospital, a practice that was stopped by an increasingly suspicious Commandant Turner in early 1863.[183] Van Lew's spy ring consisted of Richmond citizens, enslaved and formerly enslaved individuals, and paid informants. She was also astute at keeping watch on the Confederate forces throughout Richmond and had the means to get that intelligence back to Streight in his third-floor Libby Prison lair.

But the sheer number of people who were "in the know" and involved in the planning of the escape caused the Confederates to become aware of it. The plan was abandoned. "We had traitors in our midst who put the rebel authorities on alert only a few days before the attempt was to have been made," suggested prisoner Captain Isaac Newton Johnston of the Sixth Kentucky Volunteers.[184]

Just before Christmas 1863, Streight attempted another escape along with Captain Benjamin Read of the 3rd Ohio. Streight had been passed a note, appearing to come from a Libby guard, that said guard would be amenable to allowing him to escape for the low price of 100 dollars in greenbacks and two silver watches. The affair was likely a ruse planned by Libby's commandant Major Turner in order to catch Colonel Streight in the act, and perhaps take advantage of the situation as a means to get rid of the thorn in his side once and for all. In the early-morning hours, Streight and Read slipped to the ground from an upper floor window of the prison using a rope made of blankets. Despite having provided a guard with the requested bribes, the man yelled out an alert, and the escapees were surrounded and immediately captured. They were shackled in irons and placed into

Libby's notorious cellar dungeon. It was from this location that Colonel Streight and Captain Reed would have been serenaded by the Libby Prison Minstrels, from the floor directly over the dungeon cells, singing as loud as they could on Christmas Eve 1863. They would be housed in Libby's dungeon for a total of twenty-two days before being released in mid-January 1864.

THE NEW YEAR BEGAN WITH THE Libby inmates very much aware of Streight and Reed's unsuccessful escape. What the majority of the POWs did not know was that another escape plan had been hatched two months earlier and was now making significant progress. The difference between this plan and Streight's "brute force" plan was there would be very few "in the know."

The plan: They would dig their way out, escaping by a tunnel.

The original plan was conceived sometime in late October 1863 by thirty-three-year-old Pittsburgh resident Colonel Thomas Ellwood Rose of the 77th Pennsylvania, along with twenty-seven-year-old Kentucky-born Captain Andrew G. Hamilton of the 12th Kentucky Cavalry.

Rose, who had been captured at the Battle of Chickamauga on September 20, 1863, was hobbled by a broken foot he had suffered at Murfreesboro, Tennessee, months before his capture. Even with this disability, he had successfully escaped the POW train that was taking him to Richmond from Georgia in Weldon, North Carolina, only to be recaptured a day later. The Colonel was a man just itching to escape and get away from the damned Rebels.

Rose arrived at Libby Prison on October 1 by private railroad car surrounded by his own contingent of guards, due to his escape attempt. He was part of a wave of nearly 250 Chickamauga Union officer POWs.[185] His group of prisoners added twenty-five percent more to the population of an already overcrowded Libby.

Hamilton was captured at Jonesborough in Eastern Tennessee. He arrived at Libby two days before Rose. Both ended up in the second-floor "Chickamauga Room," with Bassett and Hatfield.

Shortly after each man arrived, they independently set about exploring to see if they could find a means of escape. They became aware of each other when, at the same time one evening, both were closely investigating the windows of the third floor as a possible way out. A few evenings after the first encounter, they independently snuck down into the Libby cellar during a storm and bumped into each other again. In the pitch-black darkness, lightning illuminated the surroundings every few minutes. One particular flash froze them both in time, staring at each other. It became clear they were thinking the same way so decided to work together.[186]

Soon after the discovery of Streight's "brute-force" plan prison, officials began changing the access points and tightening security. They increased the guards, tore up and sealed stairways, and walled off doorways. The prisoner's kitchen in the cellar was permanently consolidated to the first-floor's middle room. This completely cut off prisoner access to the cellar. Rose and Hamilton immediately began to view this as a new opportunity. One flaw in the Rebels' new security plan was quickly noticed: They didn't post a guard inside the cook room at night. "Hamilton and myself cut our way down into the carpenter shop, out of which we prepared to make our dash for liberty," Rose said. "A party of us went down into the shop for this purpose on more than one occasion, but the unexpected shifting of prisoners prevented this attempt."[187]

The "dash to liberty" would have been to stroll out the cellar door onto Canal Street when the timing of the guard's positions was just right. But the opportunity never presented itself, so another means had to be thought up. Before long both men had similar plan in mind. "We both arrived at the conclusion that there was only one way for us to get out of the prison, and that was to dig out," said Hamilton.[188]Colonel Rose was a civil engineer by trade, and Hamilton was a carpenter and mason. Together, both men had the skills to construct a tunnel.

WITH THE CONFEDERATES' TIGHTENED prison security, the east third of the cellar at Libby, known as "Rat Hell," became completely sealed off from the center cellar room. It was only accessible from a door directly on Canal Street, which ran along the canal parallel to the James River. The room was large and so dark you couldn't see into its deep recesses. It was also disgusting. Every time the outside door was opened, the enormous population of rats hidden from view under the putrefying hay would go into a panic, squealing loudly and causing the floor of the cellar to undulate like a hay pile from...hell. The advantage was that no Confederate guard wanted to spend much time down there. "Rat Hell" was the perfect venue for a team of tunnel diggers since it was minimally accessed by the Confederates, leaving the tunnelers with privacy to work. In addition, dirt from the tunnel could be easily hidden under the rotting straw. Wisely, Rose settled on a team of about fifteen men, sworn to secrecy, to excavate the tunnel. Working in three groups of five, the number of men with knowledge of what was happening was kept small. With the less people in the know, there was less chance of discovery.

First, they had to gain access to the east cellar. Rose and Hamilton removed bricks from the first-floor prisoners' kitchen fireplace in such a way that it created an S-curve through the fireplace's back wall, and then arched downward to access to the east cellar. "The material was so cut that after the hole was completed it could be replaced and removed at will, and not a vestige of the work be seen when the material was replaced and soot was thrown down,"[189]said Rose, crediting the ingenuity to Hamilton's masonry skills. This allowed men to work at digging a tunnel in "Rat Hell" without fear of discovery. A rope was converted into a rope ladder by Hamilton to make the access through the fireplace easier.

They had minimal tools. A 100-foot piece of rope, a pen knife, an old chisel, a wood box, and a few other items. Rose and Hamilton had kicked around several ideas on tunneling out of Libby from the moment the two first arrived. The digging soon was underway. Through a trial-and-error process, the tunnelers dug their way through several failed attempts. The first tunnel was dug down below the cellar floor under the building's foundation southward toward a large sewer that ran parallel to the canal. Digging below the water table, the tunnel quickly flooded due to its proximity to the canal and James River. Water and raw sewage rushed into the tunnel, almost killing Rose who was pulled out by his feet just in time.[190]

Coincidentally, Confederate General John Hunt Morgan—who with his men had successfully escaped Ohio State Penitentiary in the middle of downtown Columbus by digging a tunnel into an air shaft beneath their cells using pilfered cutlery—inspected Libby Prison on January 8. "He is a rakish-looking chap," remarked Byers, "but is gentlemanly for all that. He spoke kindly to us, and appeared to sympathize with us in our misfortune, remarking that 'the South was being disgraced by its cruel treatment of prisoners.'[191] He made those comments while just two stories below his feet in "Rat Hell" Colonel Rose's team was strategizing which direction to dig next.

Two other attempts were made, each one failed. It is remarkable none of the tunnelers were killed in any of the failures, though several of the tunneling team were

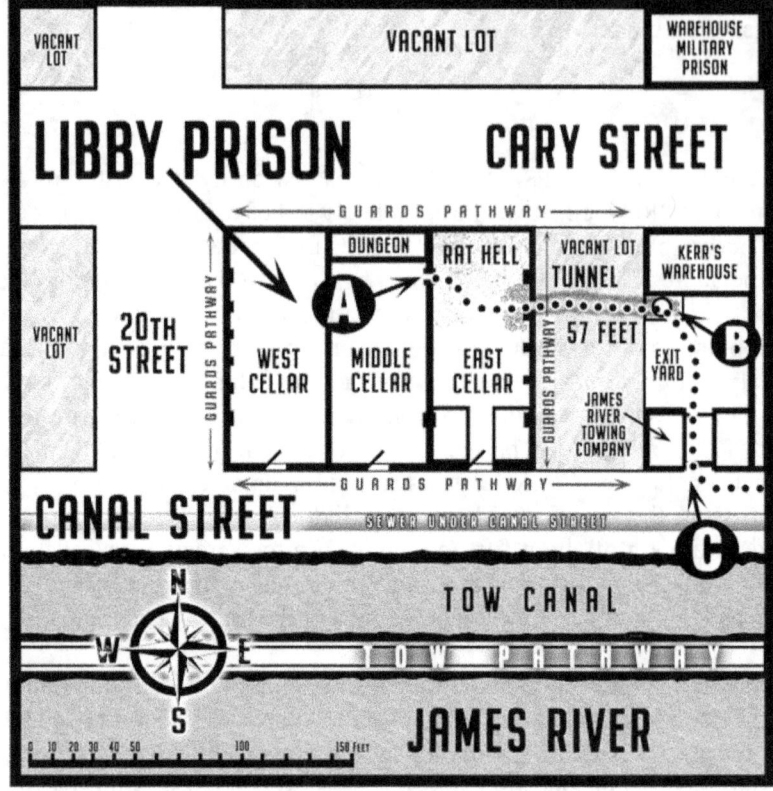

1864 Floor Plan of the Cellar of Libby Prison and Tunnel Path
A – Break through into cellar from the
prisoner's kitchen fireplace on floor above
B – End of tunnel where escapees emerged
C – Direction escapees took east on Canal Street
Adapted by the author from March 1883, Century Magazine

discouraged and gave up. Rose soon replaced them with others.

"The profound darkness of the place caused some of them to become bewildered when they attempted to move about, and as absolute silence had to be observed, they could not find their way to places where they were needed, or even find their way out of the cellar, and, what was worse, as the cellar was very large and no one must speak above a whisper, it was a matter of great difficulty to find them. I sometimes had to feel all over the cellar to gather up the men who were lost," said Rose.[192]

Finally, after more than two months of failed attempts, in mid-January, shortly after Confederate General Morgan's visit, a new scheme was devised. They would dig from the northeast corner of the cellar, as far away from the river as they could get. Here, the outside of the bottom wall was about six feet underground by the natural grade of the land sloping down to the river from Cary Street.

This plan had the men tunneling under a vacant lot almost sixty feet to the east, ending between a couple of buildings—Kerr's warehouse on Cary Street and the James River Towing Company on Canal Street. The target for where the escapees would emerge from the tunnel was just inside a tobacco shed, behind a fence that would conveniently shield them from view.

Digging for this new route began on January 23, 1864. Once again, there were only fifteen men, made up mostly from the original tunnel crew and a few replacements. Three work groups of five amazingly took just seventeen nights to successfully dig the tunnel.[193] "The earth we dug through was composed of compact sand, nearly as hard as rock. There was therefore, no danger of caving in...In order to draw the dirt out of the tunnel as it was dug, we used a wooden spittoon with a clothes-line tied to it so the digger could pull it in with him while at work, and the man at the mouth of the tunnel could pull it out when filled," said Rose.[194]

"The only difficulties experienced in making this excavation resulted from a lack of tools and the unpleasant feature of having to hear hundreds of rats squeal all the time, while they ran over the diggers almost without a sign of fear," said Hamilton.[195]

While digging continued in the cellar below, prison life in the odd and random world of Libby continued. The daily routine always started and ended with a roll call conducted in the prisoner's quarters in the upper floors by Libby's Chief Clerk Erastus "Little" Ross and his crew of intimidating guards. During the tunneling work, sometimes the tunnelers were not in their quarters during roll call, and the POWs upstairs would

Digging the Tunnel
February 1894, Worthington's Magazine

intentionally mess with Little Ross's count by circling back through the lines and having themselves counted twice. It became a game the prisoners loved to use to antagonize the man. Most didn't know the value of this ruse to the tunnelers below but getting Little

Ross to turn red in the face while screaming and cussing "damn Yankees!" in his harsh southern drawl was something to look forward to.

After one roll call, Little Ross singled out Captain Benjamin F. Lownsbery of the 10th New York Cavalry, striking him sharply in the stomach with his index finger. "You blue-bellied Yankee, come down to my office. I have a matter to settle with you," he barked. A totally confused Lownsbery followed Ross down to his office on the first-floor corner of the prison. When they arrived, there was no one in the office, but a guard stood outside the prison's front door on the sidewalk that ran along Cary Street. Ross looked up at Lownsbery and pointed behind the counter, then left the room.

"I stepped behind the counter and found a Confederate uniform, and I lost no time in getting into it, although it was too small for me. Then I walked out the door. It was just after dark, and Ross and the sentry were walking down the sidewalk, I ran across the street to a vacant lot which had brush growing upon it. As I did so, a colored man stepped out and said, 'Come with me, sah, I know who you is,' and he took me to Miss Van Lew's house on Church Hill. Miss Van Lew told me the roads and where to take to the woods to escape the pickets and to go down the James River, and I could, perhaps, before morning reach a place of safety where I could escape to our troops," said the surprised Captain.[196]

Little Ross was hated by just about every POW in Libby. But what the prisoners did not know was that he was the nephew of Franklin Stearns, a wealthy Richmond distiller and Unionist who was part of Elizabeth Van Lew's spy ring. The distillery was located at 15th Street between Main and Cary Streets just five blocks from Libby. Little Ross was working under "deep cover" and was, by far, the best kept secret in Libby. He was also a hell of an actor.

At the beginning of February by an arbitrary order from Major Turner,[197] the prisoners were restricted in writing their letters to six lines, but the "rule of six" was successfully evaded for a considerable time by the use of invisible ink, usually in the form of lemon or onion juice.[198] The technique was discovered when another POW wrote a letter limited to the regulation six lines and added a PS that said, "Now my dear, read this over, and then bake it in the oven and read it again." After that, all letters send out of Libby by prisoners were carefully inspected and subject to heat sources to find any hidden messages.

As the tunnel quickly progressed, a new problem arose. As it got longer, there was less breathable air at the point where the digging was taking place. One tunneler posted at the entrance to the tunnel in the cellar would "fan" air into the tunnel. But as the tunnel got longer, fanning from thirty or forty feet away didn't really help. The lack of oxygen caused the digger's candles to snuff out, plunging them into darkness and forcing them to scramble backwards out of the tunnel and into the cellar.

"As the work approached completion the difficulty of breathing in the tunnel was greatly increased, and four persons were necessary to keep the work moving. One man would go in and dig awhile, when he came out nearly exhausted another would enter and fill the spittoon, a third would draw it to the mouth of the tunnel, a fourth would then empty the contents," said Captain Isaac Newton Johnston, one of the tunnelers.[199]

As the tunnel construction moved along, Bassett and Hatfield, who were housed in the second-floor Chickamauga Room along with the main tunneling crew, became curious. "We begun to be suspicious there was something going on in the kitchen at night. We watched and would see a man standing in front of the stoves; back of these was a fireplace. One night we discovered a hole in the fireplace," said Hatfield.

Bassett was a Freemason. He stepped up to the man, found he belonged to the same order, and said, "How are you getting along with your work?"

"We are getting along slow," the man answered. "It is hard digging. We are troubled a great deal by the foul air."

Bassett and Hatfield later discovered the man was Captain Hamilton. The next morning Hamilton asked the two men if they could "help out" upstairs. "We have to account for two men in the roll call, you two men can do that tomorrow," he said.

Hamilton then explained to Bassett and Hatfield how to get to the rear at roll call. The POWs formed in a long line of rows, four men deep. As Little Ross would count each man in front, he would multiply by four. Bassett and Hatfield would each playfully push the last man at the back of a row over one row as the lines were forming and then hold a hat, balanced on their hand, in his place in the back row. Amid the chaos hundreds of soldiers jostling and forming lines, the "hat trick" made up for the two missing soldiers, who remained hidden in the cellar digging.[200]

The newly created exit hole was exposed in the open lot, not under the tobacco shed, and on the wrong side of the protective fence. The loud noise caused by the falling stone also attracted the attention of one of the guards. McDonald quickly ducked back down into the tunnel just as a guard came to a stop in front of the open lot and stared into the darkness. McDonald held his breath, sure that he had been discovered. Then the guard turned and continued his march back to the west, convinced the sound was created by one of those damned rats. McDonald quickly made his way through the tunnel back to the cellar.

The tunnelers quickly devised a solution to plug the hole using some old working garments.[201] When viewed through one of Libby's third-floor windows looking down into the lot, the surface breach looked like just another rathole with a piece of refuse sticking out of it, and no one was the wiser. Two days later, on Tuesday, February 9, McDonald and Rose succeeded in tunneling to the planned exit point under the tobacco shed. The final tunnel was fifty-seven feet long and just two feet wide by two and a half feet tall.

Emerging inside the tobacco shed, escapees would cross to a gate next to the Towing Company's office, and then time their exit onto Canal Street. There were two gas lamps nearby that dimly illuminated the area around the gate. Over many nights, carefully watching in the shadows of a second-floor window with a view down onto Canal Street, Rose had studied the sentry's marching pattern in order to understand the routine. The ever-present guards marched exactly forty-five paces eastward, stopping about twelve feet from the Towing Company's gate, then did an "about face," turning back in the opposite direction, marching the same forty-five paces to the west. Forty-five paces east, then forty-five paces west, a monotonous routine repeated over and over. Knowing this, an escapee would need to wait until the "about face" to the west occurred, which placed the guard's back to the gate, then quietly emerge onto Canal Street and walk away from the guard to the east.[202]

It was shortly after dark between 7:30 and 8 p.m. on February 9 when Rose and Hamilton were the first to escape.[203] They were followed by fourteen additional groups made up of the original tunnel diggers and others. Two men every ten minutes made their way successfully through the tunnel and away from Libby.

"In fact so well had Rose and his party secreted their nearly two months of terrible labor from the general population of Libby, that I had lain down for the night without the remotest suspicion that such a work had been done; nor did I learn of the existence of the

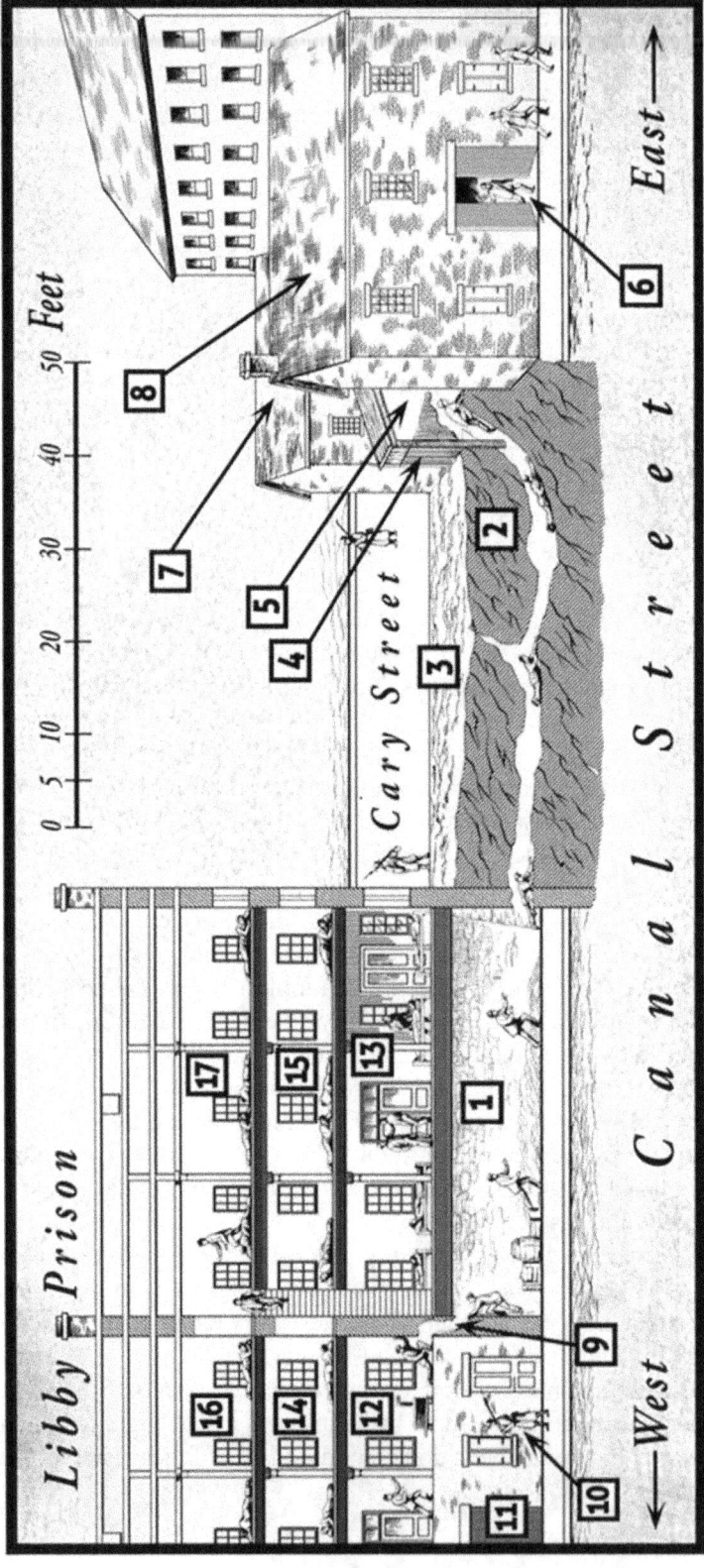

Libby Prison and the Tunnel Path From Canal Street Looking North

1: East Cellar "Rat Hell"; 2: Path of Tunnel; 3: Open Lot; 4: Fence; 5: Tobacco Shed; 6: Exit Gate onto Canal Street; 7: Kerr's Warehouse; 8: James River Towing Company Office; 9: S-shaped Opening into East Cellar from first floor Kitchen Stove; 10: Regular Guard walking west on Canal Street; 11: Center Cellar; 12: First Floor Kitchen and Dining Room; 13: First Floor East, Hospital; 14: Second Floor, Lower Chickamauga Room; 15: Second Floor, Lower Gettysburg Room; 16: Upper Chickamauga Room; 17: Third Floor, Upper Gettysburg Room

Adapted from March 1883, Century Magazine Illustration

tunnel until more than an hour after Col. Rose and his diggers had passed out on Feb. 9, 1864," said Lieutenant Frank E. Moran.[204]

Upstairs in the second-floor Chickamauga Room, the 9 p.m. "Lights Out, Yanks" order had been called out by the guards down below. Bassett and two messmates, Hatfield and Lieutenant Henry Crawford of the 2nd Illinois Cavalry, were part of a small group of POWs who were "in the know." They had been patiently waiting to make their way down to the tunnel. Now was the time.

BASSETT DESPERATELY WANTED TO ESCAPE. He had recently received word from back home in Kerton Township, Illinois, that soon after his capture, in August 1863, his wife Charlotte had begun a relationship with another man, six-foot-tall, blond-haired, blue-eyed, twenty-three-year-old John H. Moore.[205]

Bassett knew Moore well. Eighteen months earlier, the man had been a private in then-Sergeant Bassett's very own Company E of the 53rd Illinois. Moore had been discharged with a disability on October 19, 1862, following the Battle of Davis Bridge. Ironically, this was the same battle that resulted in Bassett's promotion to lieutenant. After his discharge, Moore went back to Kerton Township, recovered from his wounds, and resumed his life as a farmer. By fall 1863 Moore began playing house with Lottie Bassett, knowing his higher-ranked, former comrade had either been killed or was a Rebel POW.

Flash back to the summer of 1863 and you could almost sympathize with Charlotte's mindset. She was in shock, thinking she was a newly minted widow. After all, Mark had been killed-in-action, the gut-wrenching facts had even been reported in the local paper.[206] With three young children to raise, Charlotte was grieving while at the same time needing to provide for the children Then a couple of months after she was told her husband was dead, she was gut-punched with an even greater shock. She received a letter from Mark postmarked from Libby Prison in Richmond. The final blow by the end of 1863 was that Charlotte was pregnant by Moore. She confided the news to twenty-two-year-old Mary A. Schreffler; Charlotte had gotten herself into quite a predicament. Schreffler was a friend of both Mark and Charlotte and, while Bassett was away at war, had lived as a boarder at various times in the Bassett home, helping Charlotte with the children.

In January 1864, as Bassett was involving himself with the Libby Prison tunnel planners, Charlotte was hoping to solve one problem by having an abortion in the Bassett home in Kerton Township. The procedure was performed by thirty-nine-year-old Dr. William Kirk, [207]another man Bassett would have known well. Amazingly, he, too, had been a private under Bassett. Kirk was discharged on October 16, 1862, a few days before Moore, also following the Battle of Davis Bridge. Dr. Kirk returned to Kerton Township, recovered from his wounds, then resumed his medical practice.

The letter sent to Mark from home detailed the whole mess. His anger raged, but he kept it contained within. How could she have done this to him? What about his children? In a prison packed with 1,200 fellow officers, he told no one, internalizing and walling off the pain in its own dungeon cell. His escape from the thoughts of this personal crisis were replaced with thoughts of escaping through the tunnel.

The first thirty men to escape did so in an orderly, methodical manner. Because they timed their exit onto Canal Street following the directions from Colonel Rose's observations, the guards never saw any of them. Streight, who was not aware of the tunnel's construction until it was almost finished, found himself by pure chance in the first wave of thirty escapees. The fifteen men responsible for digging the tunnel either went with a fellow digger or chose another POW as their escape partner. Major McDonald chose Streight, but as this first group stealthily moved through the tunnel, timing their movements with great precision, Streight almost plugged up the entire escape operation. Literally.

Tipping the scales at 225 pounds, the six-foot, 2-inch-tall Colonel Abel Streight was a large-framed man who had received a continuous supply of provision boxes while in prison. He might have been the only man to gain weight as a Libby prisoner. After a couple of unsuccessful attempts, Streight had to remove most of his clothes and tie them to his foot, dragging them behind as he crawled through the narrow tunnel. At several bottlenecks McDonald had to push him from behind. Streight eventually emerged from the tunnel's exit, red-faced and sweaty from the exertion. He stood shivering for a few moments, catching his breath. Exposed to the cold night air, he quickly redressed as McDonald emerged. The two disappeared into the night, meeting a couple of additional escapees a short distance away, before heading for a preplanned rendezvous point. There they met New Hampshire-born Abby Green, another Richmond Unionist, who led them to a safe house on the northern outskirts of Richmond.

The exciting buzz quickly filtered out to the rest of the Libby population. There was a tunnel and men were escaping! Bassett, Hatfield, and Crawford quickly made their way to the first-floor kitchen, entering a mob scene of excited prisoners. Desperate men were jammed around the opening in the fireplace that led down to the cellar below. It had turned into chaos, with fellow POWs fighting each other to get through the tight entrance and down to the tunnel. As quickly as they could, men jammed themselves down the S-shaped access hole through the fireplace's brick. The noise emanating from all the excitement threatened to reveal them to the guards. The regular rodent population in "Rat Hell" was stirred into a frenzy, causing the rotting straw to pulsate with their screeching and scurrying.

Bassett, Hatfield, and Crawford made it down the rope ladder into the east cellar, seeing the tunnel for the first time, as other POWs piled up in front of the tunnel's entrance. For Bassett, it was the first real hope he had felt in all the months he had suffered in the damned prison. Here was their ticket to freedom. Hatfield went first; then, Bassett followed. The space was so claustrophobic they tried to not have too many in the tunnel at the same time. But everyone was too excited. Too afraid they would miss out on the opportunity. Too worried they would have to return upstairs to their life at Libby Prison. It became a mad scramble.

Initially, the three men had agreed to travel together, but as Hatfield emerged from the tunnel ahead of Bassett, he was startled upon seeing a guard just forty feet away. He thought he had been spotted and panicked. "I said, come boys, let's go! and I started through the warehouse and on the other side of the street. I looked around and could not see either of them. I supposed at the time they were captured," said Hatfield.[208] The guard continued his walk, unaware of the events occurring so close by, and made his regular turn and headed back westward. But Hatfield was unaware of the guard's routine and immediately made his break, heading into the darkness of Canal Street without Bassett and Crawford.

"From the upper floor you could see the fugitives pop out of the tunnel, cross the yard, clear the gateway to the street, and disappear into the dark," said one prisoner.[209]

In the third-floor upper east Gettysburg Room, the POWs from the 5th Iowa—Marshall, Page, and Bascom, along with Hoffman and Byers—were all bedded down, eyes heavy, sleep approaching, packed in the usual "spooning" formation. But this time, when the "Prepare to spoon. One, two, spoon!" order was given, the men became aware of the noise of excited whispers in the darkness. Something was up!

The Cellar Tunnel Entrance in "Rat Hell"
February 1894, Worthington's Magazine

Four stories below them, passing through the cold, narrow tunnel felt like a crawl through a mile-long grave. The stale air within the space was full of the exhaled breaths of the men who had just crawled through shortly before. Finally, emerging into the crisp, pure air felt like a slap to the face.[210]

The temperatures were near freezing, and most of the escapees were clothed in rags, "When I could see stars above me I heard someone breathing heavily behind me down the tunnel, and waiting a moment found it was my old friend, Lieutenant Henry Crawford of Havana, Illinois, my own neighborhood, so we started together," said Bassett.[211]

The forty-three-year-old Lieutenant Crawford had been a practicing physician before the war. He had been at Libby longer than Bassett, having been captured while on a scouting expedition on June 11, 1863, at Hernando, Mississippi. He was also not in the best condition to begin a journey into the frigid swamps east of Richmond, having suffered reoccurring bouts of dysentery in his months of captivity in Libby.

With the surge of adrenaline, brought on from their sudden freedom, both men were euphoric. Less than an hour earlier, Bassett had been lying on the hard floor of Libby Prison's Chickamauga Room spooning to keep warm. Now he was freezing. But he was free.

Chapter Seven

MARK BASSETT SLOWLY STOOD FROM the crouched, guarded position he had been in after emerging from the tunnel and extended a hand to Crawford as he climbed up from the hole. The two carefully peered over the top of the fence that shielded them from the guards who were making their regular east-to-west rounds up and down Canal and Cary Streets. One guard was walking away from them, heading west. They quickly moved to the arched entranceway of the James River Towing Company and pressed themselves against the wall, peeking again to the west. The guard was coming back toward them, and they froze. They heard his footsteps on the cobbled street surface getting nearer. Sixty feet, fifty feet, forty feet, then the footsteps stopped, and the guard shouted out, starling the two escapees, "Eleven o'clock and all is well." He turned and began heading west, away from the men.[212]

Now was the time as the two carefully emerged from the entranceway and began walking casually to the east. In the late evening hours of Tuesday, February 9, the temperatures were close to freezing, but the skies were clear. The moon was just two days old, a waxing crescent that had set just after sunset. So aside from two gas streetlamps close to where they had just slipped through the building's main entrance, darkness would help hide them as they moved down Canal Street.

"I stood in the dark at an upper window and watched the prisoners as they came out at the farther end of the tunnel and slipped away. I did not try to enter the tunnel when I heard of it; there was already five times as many men in the cellar as could possibly get away by daylight," said Byers.[213]

Like all the escapees, Bassett and Crawford were wearing the clothing in which they had been captured, which had become quite ragged over time and offered little warmth. More than a hundred ragged escapees moving through Richmond at night might have drawn suspicion.

But their attire didn't; many Confederate soldiers were ragged themselves, and confusing things even more, some of them sported parts of Union uniforms they had acquired by various means. So the new additions to the city streets appeared quite normal.

Bassett and Crawford's biggest challenge was to get out of Richmond as fast as they could. The route most prisoners took was almost due east out of Richmond, about fifty miles toward Williamsburg where the Federal lines were. The first part of the route required maneuvering around the heavy fortifications that protected the city. Then there were multiple layers of pickets along a difficult route featuring very swampy terrain and two icy rivers, the Chickahominy and Pamunkey Rivers.

Rose and Hamilton, the tunnel's designers, were the first two out. They had gone east one block down Canal Street, then turned north a couple of blocks before turning back to the east again. It was here where they became separated when a guard at a Confederate hospital asked where Rose was from. Hamilton continued walking, ignoring the guard and giving the appearance that the two men were not traveling together. He managed to travel eight miles before sunrise, finally stopping well east of Richmond near a half-frozen swamp.[214] Rose was detained for a half hour and somehow talked his way out of his predicament. But by then Hamilton was gone. The broken foot Rose had experienced a year earlier began to ache. He hobbled on alone toward the Richmond and

View From Canal Street With Libby Prison (left)
James River Towing Company (right).
It is from the arched entrance to the James River Towing Company
that the 109 escaped from Libby Prison, heading east (to the right) away from Libby.
Library of Congress – circa 1865

York River Railroad tracks, which became the main artery used by escapees to navigate their way out of Richmond.

In the first hours of escape, all the men needed to pass unnoticed through the Rebel lines surrounding the city of Richmond. "The feat was accomplished before daylight by our assuming to be in search of fuel to make a fire to warm by; so picking up bits of wood here and there were supposed to be freezing 'Johnnies' and were not challenged," said Bassett.[215]

Colonel Abel Streight and Major Beden McDonald, who also got away before Bassett and Crawford, planned a different approach. They would travel within the Unionist spy network located in the Confederate capital. Shortly after crawling out of the Libby escape tunnel, they rendezvoused with Captain William W. Scearce, a member of Streight's 51st Indiana, and Lieutenant John Sterling of the 30th Indiana, another one of the tunnelers. Just blocks from the prison the four met up with Abby Green, a transplanted northerner living in Richmond, who then led the Colonel's escape party to John Quarles' farm, located in the northern outskirts of Richmond. Once there, they were helped by Lucy Rice, another Unionist, and hidden away for the next week. During this time Rice would return to Richmond and bring Elizabeth Van Lew to the safe house to meet the four Union officers.[216] The three Unionists were working independent of Van Lew's spy network, but in performing the risky task of moving Colonel Streight's escape party through Richmond, they soon became part of her spy ring.

The odds that 109 escapees could move through the enemy's capital under the cover of darkness and not have a few of their numbers captured were impossible. The one advantage they all had was that for quite a while the escape itself remained undiscovered, which gave them all a head start. Even with this advantage, two escapees reportedly

Major Beden McDonald
as he appeared on reaching
Union lines with a chisel in
hand, which he had used in
tunneling out of Libby
Prison. The Major's hands,
made sore from digging
the tunnel, were tied up
with old cloths.
*Worthington's Magazine
February 1894*

drowned though the drowned men's exact names were never reported, so it draws into question whether the two dead men were actually escapees.[217] Seven more were captured during the first day. The first unfortunate escapee to be captured and returned to Libby was Captain Junius Gates of the 33rd Ohio, who was discovered near Bottoms Bridge, which crossed over the Chickahominy River twelve miles east of town.[218] Two of the escapees found themselves in the swamps east of Richmond; as they emerged from the water willows, they encountered a field of ice. The swamps had frozen over in the bitter cold. As they slipped and slid their way onto the ice, they heard a cracking sound, then found themselves breaking through the thin, frozen surface, suddenly finding themselves in freezing swampy water up to their armpits. They would make their way to a hammock rising out of the ice and slush and collapse exhausted and soaked, their teeth chattering, as the first light of dawn began to glow to the east.[219]

BACK AT LIBBY ON THE MORNING after the escape, a perplexed Little Ross repeated the daily roll call over and over again. His numbers kept coming up more than 100 men short, and he gave a great performance feigning anger at the Yankee scoundrels and delivering a tongue-lashing of swear words in his thick Southern drawl. With Little Ross spending the morning hours trying to reconcile the rollcall numbers without alerting his superiors to the missing men, the delay provided additional time for the escapees to get further away from Richmond. Perhaps this was Little Ross's strategy. The remaining prison population still totaled more than 1,000 men, all packed into the upper two floors of Libby. With each new attempt at a rollcall, some would intentionally move back around the crowded packs of men, only to be counted again. Little Ross, who increasingly became more and more frustrated, expressed deep outrage with more cussing and shouting at the prisoners. It was a command performance. It wouldn't be until late morning on Wednesday, February 10, that the prison's commandant, Thomas P. Turner, was finally told of the missing prisoners and would come to understand the enormity of his predicament. Little Ross kept counting and counting into the afternoon. "The alphabetical roll call occupied all day," recorded Hoffman.[220]

"This morning, according to the rollcall, one hundred and nine men are missing (some make the number more). There is great consternation among the officials, who are unable to determine how it was done. The Inspector, with mounted guard, dashed past the prison today in search of the fugitives," wrote Libby prisoner Captain Junius Gates of the 33rd Ohio in his diary.

Finally, the alarm was sounded throughout Richmond, and its citizens became aware that they had a big problem. There were 109 Yankees loose in their midst. Search parties were put together on Thursday, February 11, more than twenty-four hours after the first escapees emerged from the tunnel. The three Richmond newspapers, the

Examiner, Enquirer, and *Whig*, all had a field day. This was slow-motion "breaking news" in a time when the term meant something. Soon the newspapers began reporting the names of the men who had been successfully captured and returned to Libby each day. They gave a great amount of newsprint in speculating about the whereabouts of the hated Colonel Streight, even incorrectly crediting him as the mastermind of the tunnel escape.

"As might have been expected, the papers of this morning give a full account of the escapade the night before last. The number escaping were six colonels, six lieutenant colonels, seven majors, thirty-two captains, fifty-nine lieutenants. They call it the greatest escape during the war," wrote Libby prisoner Colonel Fredrick A. Bartelson of the 100th Illinois.

> *Couriers were early dispatched in every direction, and the pickets double posted on all the roads and bridges. It is quite evident that the escaping prisoners have scattered and are travelling (sic) singly or in pairs, or are laying up in the houses, or hiding-places, provided for by the disloyal element to be found in and about Richmond. Doubtless many will be re-captured, but we fear too many will escape for the credit of the Confederacy. We believe the largest number of them are yet in Richmond, and will seek to steal off one by one in various guises other than that of the Yankee. It is fortunate that the leak was discovered when it was, or the exodus would have been continued last night, and night after night, until there would have been no Yankees to guard.*
>
> **The Richmond Examiner**
> **February 11, 1864**

On the second and third nights of their escape, while the citizens of Richmond were going crazy, Bassett and Crawford had managed to make it twenty-five miles east. They were looking to run into the Pamunkey River and then follow the waterway southeast all the way to the Union lines. Polaris, the North Star easily found in Ursa Major, served as a guide in the pitch-black night, giving the escapees some sort of reassurance that they were headed in their planned direction. They made their way across open fields, away from the roads, and tramped through briars that tore at their already ragged clothing. There were bloodhounds and anxious Rebels crisscrossing the countryside everywhere. In addition, Confederate pickets were already guarding the approaches to Richmond from the east, even before the escape. Hoping to avoid all this, they kept to the woods and swamps, traveling at night away from public roads. At sunrise on one day, Bassett and Crawford climbed a tree and remained hidden in it all day.[221]

"We headed for the White House, eastward on the Pamunkey river, where we believed the Union troops to be," said Bassett. White House was the Richmond and York River railway bridge over the Pamunkey. It was named after the nearby White House plantation, which had been owned by Martha Dandridge Custis, who became the owner upon the death of her husband, Daniel Parke Custis in 1757. Twenty-seven-year-old Martha would marry a twenty-six-year-old French and Indian War veteran named George Washington in the house on January 6, 1759, and the couple would live in the home for the first two years of their marriage. At some point before the Civil War, the original White House building was torn down and replaced by a new one. In 1857 it was inherited by Robert E. Lee's son William H. F. "Rooney" Lee. On June 27, 1862, the plantation was burned by Union forces. Its blackened remains were a landmark known by both sides.

The bridge over the Pamunkey River at White House was heavily fortified and, with the news of a wave of escaped Union officers headed eastward, Bassett and Crawford's luck ran out. "On the fourth night out, when we supposed we had passed beyond the probable danger of re-capture, we neared a cabin where there must have been Confederates who discovered us, for soon they had blood hounds out after us," said Bassett.[222]

"We carried sticks of ironwood, which we used as staves, and these were also our only weapons of defense, and with these we beat the hounds so they would not follow our scent, for they were trained to hunt in packs and when the leader is hurt the pack scatters. The scars where one of them grabbed the calf of my leg are still visible. In the fright and confusion consequent upon such a 'surprise,' we ran into an extended line of Confederate pickets, and two South Carolinians who seemed to our astonished eyes like

giants with mammoth double-barreled shotguns, persuaded us to stay our flight."

By Saturday, February 13, they had tasted freedom for four days and had gotten within twelve miles of Union lines. They were sent back to Libby and, like all the returning escapees, thrown into the cellar dungeon, which was now packed beyond its capacity. The Saturday *Richmond Enquirer* would publish Bassett's and Crawford's names in the daily list of Yankee fugitives; they noted that at that point 34 of the 109 escapees had been recaptured.

Lieutenant John D. Hatfield, who was right in front of Bassett and Crawford as they made their way through the tunnel, was one of the first escapees to successfully reach the Federal lines. He arrived at Williamsburg on Sunday, February 14, at around 9 p.m., the fifth night of the escape, having traveled a total of fifty miles.

On Monday, February 15, as snow fell in Richmond and the temperatures throughout the region plummeted, *The Richmond Enquirer* would report to the citizens of the Confederate capital, who were starved for any news on the escape:

Lieutenant
John D. Hatfield
53rd Illinois

"It was extensively rumored yesterday, that the notorious Colonel Straight (sic) had been wounded and captured, on the canal, above and west of the city, and was on his way down. The manner of his capture was embellished according to the fancy of those giving currency to the report. The leavanting (sic) Colonel may have been taken, but he certainly had not reached the city at sundown yesterday."

The Richmond Enquirer
February 15, 1864

But the newspaper was completely wrong. While the entire town was in a panic and travel by the escapees was at its most dangerous, Streight's group was still hiding out at John Quarles' "safe house" farmstead on the outskirts of Richmond. The Union army was made aware of Streight's location by Elizabeth Van Lew's spy network and had strategically planted a fake story that was published in northern newspapers, claiming that the Colonel had successfully made it to Fortress Monroe and was safe.[223] Two days later, on Wednesday, February 17, Streight, McDonald, Scearce, and Sterling finally left the Richmond area equipped with supplies and revolvers. Under the cover of darkness, in brutally cold weather in which the daytime temperature had climbed to just 12 degrees Fahrenheit, the four escapees traveled along with a guide and two Confederate deserters.[224] Slowly, they made their way north along the route of the Brook Turnpike, then along the pathway of the Richmond, Fredericksburg, and Potomac Railroad.[225]

On Saturday, February 13, the weekend after the escape, Colonel Rose's foot continued to slow his progress. He was in intense pain limping his way alone, yet on the same day as Bassett and Crawford's capture, he had managed to get forty miles to the east of Richmond to a crossroad known to the locals as Burnt Ordinary. Named after a Revolutionary War tavern known as John Lewis's Ordinary, in 1780 it received its name when it was burned to the ground. Eighty-four years later the remains of the burnt brick Ordinary were still there, marking the crossroads. One of those roads led south to freedom, just ten miles away. On this Saturday Rose's problem was that there were Confederate picket lines covering the area.

"Suddenly came upon a spot where a picket had been posted the night before. As I was now so close to Williamsburg, it became a question with me whether it was a Union or a rebel picket. I soon discovered by the tracks that the men had been fronting toward Williamsburg, and therefore concluded that it had been rebel. I now became exceedingly cautious and withdrew to the woods. I kept on through the woods in a southeast direction until I came to an open space. Here, to my great joy, I saw a body of United States troops moving on the road to my left. I sat down very much exhausted and awaited their approach," said Rose.

But just as freedom was within his grasp, the main body of Federal troops he had seen had suddenly paused, then he heard a noise behind him and upon turning saw three men in Union uniforms, standing like pickets on the same road the Federal troops had been approaching on. Assuming they were an advance party for the US troops he had seen further down the road, he began walking toward the larger body.

"When I had walked about fifty or seventy-five yards, I came again in sight of the three men in the road, who now saw and challenged me...As soon as I came close to them, I saw that I was entrapped, even before they spoke. Their manner indicated that they were in great fear of the troops that had halted below."[226]

The three men were Confederate soldiers disguised in Union blue. One of the men forced Rose in the opposite direction, across the open field and back into the woods.

"I sprang suddenly upon him, disarmed and prostrated him, fired off his piece, and started to run toward the troops, and would easily have escaped had it not been for my lameness. The man I had disarmed did not attempt to follow me, nor did the two we had left in the road. On the contrary, these two ran across the field diagonally to the rear; but several other men whom I had not seen before sprang up from behind the fence on the side of the field opposite to the road. They ran so as to intercept my approach to the troops. Two or three of them outran me and struck me with their muskets. This prostrated me, and they all rushed around me. I heard one of them say, 'Be quick; the Yanks are right here.'" [227]

Colonel Rose, the chief planner, designer, and leader of the tunneling crew, had been captured by Confederate pickets just a few hundred yards away from the Union lines. It was a crushing defeat for the Colonel, who was beaten by rifle butts during the capture. Bloodied and shackled, he was soon back in the Libby Prison, confined to the cellar, a place he was intimately familiar with, and just yards away from his now infamous tunnel. But now he was in the dungeon located in the cellar's center room. Libby's Commandant, Turner, had him placed in solitary confinement for several days, though by this time the rest of the dungeon cells were full of other recaptured POWs. Knowing that the chief architect of the tunnel himself had been recaptured, beaten up, and now was suffering in the prison dungeon brought on a depressing funk throughout the prison population.

★ ★ ★

THROUGH AN ODD SET OF CIRCUMSTANCES shortly after his return, a series of prisoner exchanges began occurring again between the Confederate and Union armies, paroling officers of the higher ranks. Ironically, had Rose not escaped, he probably would have been one of those exchanged. Now, he was the last colonel remaining at Libby prison although, with all the new prisoners constantly arriving at Libby, that wouldn't last for long.

Colonel Thomas E. Rose
Author's collection

Captain Andrew G. Hamilton
Artist unknown

Two days later on Tuesday, February 16, at a place close to where Colonel Rose had been captured and a week after the Libby tunnel escape, Hamilton, Rose's closest partner in the tunnel escape scheme, successfully made it to the Union lines near Williamsburg.[228] He was immediately sent to Washington.

By then Hatfield had already been sent up the Potomac to Washington, D.C., where he had been debriefed and taken time to relish his newfound freedom. A few days later it was time to head home, and Hatfield walked into the Baltimore and Ohio train station just north of the U.S. Capitol where he would board a train heading west toward Chicago. Boarding the train at the same time was none other than Hamilton. The two officers traveled together, comparing their escape stories along the way. Then Hamilton changed to a train headed for Kentucky at Crestline, Ohio, and Hatfield continued to Chicago.[229] At the same time when he escaped Libby in February 1864, Hatfield had completed his three years of service with the 53rd Illinois. After a short furlough, he reenlisted, mustering in as a veteran of the 53rd in Ottawa, Illinois. He would return to the war and participate in the Atlanta Campaign and Sherman's March to the Sea. Hatfield was promoted to captain in late 1864.

FROM 8 P.M. ON TUESDAY EVENING, February 9, until the early morning hours of February 10, 109 men escaped through Colonel Rose's tunnel. By the time it was all over, fifty-nine successfully made it back to the Union lines and freedom. Two men supposedly drowned,[230] and forty-eight were recaptured.

As a comparison, the three tunnels created by POWs and Stalag Luft III, the German POW camp of World War II and the subject of the 1963 film "The Great Escape," were much more elaborate pieces of engineering. Four times deeper at more than thirty feet and five times longer at approximately 300 feet, seventy-six POWs escaped with three successfully making it to freedom. Of those recaptured, fifty were shot on orders from Adolf Hitler.

MARK BASSETT FOUND HIMSELF SHACKLED and stuffed into the darkened Libby prison dungeon. The dungeon, located in the center room in the cellar of Libby, contained four small cells with padlocked doors and was against the north wall of the space, which was the Cary Street side of the prison. The rooms were approximately ten feet by two feet each and had either no windows or a window that had been covered with a plank of wood from the outside and nailed shut.[231] During the daylight hours perhaps a small ray of sunlight might stream through the crevices between wooden planks blocking the window, but otherwise the cells were in complete darkness. A single communal open bucket, which was emptied every few days, served as the latrine. The smell in the space was indescribable. The numbers of recaptured escapees grew until the dungeon cells were packed with all forty-eight of them. The conditions were appalling. "The recaptured officers refused to answer questions, and at last the brutal Turner had thirty of us packed in a twelve-foot square dungeon," said Lieutenant Moran, one of the recaptured POWs who barely survived the harsh treatment himself.[232]

"We were returned to our former boarding place, and we were crowded into the underground dungeons reeking with filth and vermin of all sizes up to river rats. I say crowded...there was not room for each body to rest on the dirt floor of the dungeons, Heads rested on others' bodies and knees were drawn up to give room for others' limbs to pass under them—and there was no release from this cramped position," said Bassett. "Here our fare was less sumptuous than before and consisted of cornbread and water only."[233] Some prisoners in the first-floor kitchen directly above the dungeons loosened a floorboard to be able to pour down water or drop a morsel of food to the mass of fellow prisoners below.[234]

The great escape through the tunnel at Libby prison brought a heightened awareness to the plight of all the Union POWs held throughout the south. With this awareness came a lot of anger and a desire for retribution. Both sides had issues with the treatment of their prisoners, having never had to deal with the sheer numbers of POWs they were now facing. But in the south by 1864, the treatment of prisoners had tragically deteriorated.

The ramifications of the Libby tunnel escape would resonate throughout both Richmond and Washington. In addition, the attention it brought to the Libby Prison administrators, who were already a group of incompetents, created a new atmosphere bordering on paranoia.

"The great escapade through the tunnel seems to have completely destroyed the mental equilibrium of our young Commandant of the Prison, Major Turner. He seems determined that not another prisoner shall escape from his clutches and spares no precaution to ensure our safe-keeping. The iron bars in the windows have been strengthened...Major Turner seems to have been suddenly seized with the frantic idea that we might tunnel ourselves out of a third-story window, or that we might be constructing a huge balloon wherewith to elevate ourselves from the roof of the prison," quipped Cavada, himself formerly of the Union Balloon Corps.[235]

From the moment the first few Libby escapees made it to the Union lines, they began to give accounts about what they had experienced and how they had come to escape. They would all repeat the need to do something to free the POWs held in Richmond, who were struggling to survive under harsh and oftentimes sadistic treatment. What the returning POWs didn't know was that as they were crawling through the tunnel at Libby to escape, there were already several plans being discussed in Washington to raid the Confederate capital of Richmond and liberate all the Union prisoners held there.

The Union army was well aware that, as bad as Libby Prison was, Belle Island was even worse. Something of an attempt at raiding Richmond to free the prisoners had been tried just a few weeks earlier. Just before the Libby tunnel escape, General Butler brought his men up the Virginia Peninsula toward Richmond, but the raid failed before it could even get started.

In the middle of February 1864, another plan was rapidly moving forward. With all the returning officers' testimonies of the horrible prison conditions and the Union command having a lot of time on their hands to plan and scheme on a strategy while they sat in winter quarters, a new raid plan quickly developed.

Chapter Eight

The Grand Raid
February 1864 to March 1864

Two long weeks had passed since Lieutenant Mark Bassett and fellow tunnel escapee Lieutenant Henry Crawford had been recaptured and thrown into the tiny dungeon cells at Libby. The dungeon was filled with fellow tunnel escapees. The men were flopped across each other, barely able to stretch their legs. It was almost pitch-black in there so when light did enter the space it could be blinding, which caused the men to cry out with complaints. They had all exhausted the telling of their stories to each other of what they had done and where they had gone following their daring escape and subsequent recapture. Many had made it so close to the Union lines that they could see the boys-in-blue in the distance, only to be jerked back into Libby dungeon hell.

In Washington, D.C., the officers who had successfully escaped through the tunnel and made it over the Union lines each repeated the same litany of complaints. Shocking testimony told of their treatment at the hands of the Rebels. The names of Commandant Turner, Warden Turner, and Little Ross were infamously written into the record as the evil purveyors of physical and psychological torture. The trio were the damned Rebels responsible for the suffering and deaths of some of their friends and fellow officers. Something needed to be done by somebody, and it needed to be done soon. That somebody became Union General Hugh Judson Kilpatrick, who through his own self-promotion and lobbying found himself in the right place at the right time.

**General
Hugh Judson
Kilpatrick**
Library of Congress
Photographer unknown

General Kilpatrick presented quite a character. He dressed flamboyantly and had the reputation as being a lady's man with a morally questionable reputation. Just twenty-eight years old and vertically challenged at five-feet, seven-inches tall, the 1861 West Point class valedictorian was described as "a little man, with loud, swaggering voice, full of fun and profanity, florid face, square, prognathous jaw, firm, large mouth, prominent Roman nose, quick, deepset *(sic)*, piercing, fearless gray eyes, full, square forehead, large round head, large ears, dark, thin, and short hair."[236]

Kilpatrick also presents an interesting family tree, which in future generations would include great-granddaughter, fashion designer Gloria Vanderbilt and great-great grandson, journalist Anderson Cooper.

As the commander of the Army of the Potomac's Third Division, Cavalry Corps, he was also known to be sometimes reckless and aggressive. Kilpatrick had earned the interesting nickname of "KilCavalry" for his penchant for throwing his troops into dangerous, precarious situations.

The audacious plan hatched by Kilpatrick proposed for an exciting, "lightning-strike" cavalry raid. About 3,500 to 4,000 of his men would charge Richmond from the north while, at the same time, a second force of around 500 men would sweep around the west side of the Confederate capital and counterpunch, approaching from the south.

In addition, forces under General Benjamin Butler, already located on the south part of the Virginia peninsula at Fort Monroe, would swoop up the peninsula and attack from the east. The precise synchronization of three forces arriving at the same time was crucial to the plan's success. The three-pronged charging, sweeping, punching, and swooping attack was all targeted to begin in the late morning of Tuesday, March 1.

In Washington, after Kilpatrick made the rounds selling his plan, it was finally approved by President Lincoln himself. It should be noted that at the same time he dreamed up the scheme and while pitching the plan to the President in early 1864, Kilpatrick was also probably not of sound mind. He was numb, still stricken with grief from the personal tragedy of the loss of his entire family in a little less than two months. His young wife, Alice Shailer Kilpatrick, was just age twenty-two when she died on November 22, 1863. Less than two months later, his seventeen-month-old son and namesake, Judson B. Kilpatrick, died.[237] Deep in grief, Kilpatrick buried himself in carrying out his plan.

Colonel Ulric Dahlgren
Photographer unknown
c1863

At six-feet tall with a head full of light auburn hair, the thin, twenty-one-year-old Union Colonel Ulric Dahlgren cut a handsome and striking figure. A Kilpatrick opposite, "Ully" was the son of Admiral John Dahlgren, who held a patent for the "Dahlgren gun," an advanced bottle-shaped, muzzle-loading naval ordnance, and a close acquaintance of President Lincoln. With his admiral father's notoriety and successes, Ulric Dahlgren was raised with privileged status, rubbing elbows with men of power. In May 1862, with little experience other than being part of a home-guard unit, he was given his initial commission as a captain in the army through a note signed by the President and expedited by Secretary of War Edwin Stanton. Prior to the war, his family knew most everyone in Washington, D.C. They were even personal friends with Senator Jefferson Davis and his wife, Varina. As a newly commissioned captain, the younger Dahlgren was inexperienced, arrogant, and full of himself. He also seemed to have a poor sense of direction, which would prove to have tragic consequences.

Kilpatrick and Dahlgren were already acquainted with each other. Just after the Battle of Gettysburg, Captain Dahlgren served as an aide to Kilpatrick. At the lead of a company charging under Confederate fire into the main square of Hagerstown, Maryland, on July 6, 1863, Dahlgren was wounded when a ball struck his right ankle and passed through the top of his foot. Two weeks later, after an infection set in, his right leg was amputated at the knee. After eight months of recovery, which included a visit to his bedside by President Lincoln and a quick, leapfrog promotion to colonel, Dahlgren was still a weak man, moving gingerly on crutches and unable to mount his horse without the aid of others. Though he was clearly not ready for combat, seething beneath his calm demeanor was the need to seek revenge for the loss of his leg. He was fitted with a state-of-the-art wood-and-cork prosthetic leg[238] and began making the rounds in Washington, D.C., expressing his availability to rejoin the fight, when he got wind of an upcoming operation headed for the Confederate capital and led by none other than Kilpatrick, his old commander.

On February 18, 1864, Dahlgren traveled sixty miles southwest out of Washington by train to Brandy Station, Virginia. After being helped onto his horse, he gingerly rode the five miles to Kilpatrick's headquarters near Stevensburg, Virginia, to lobby the general for the opportunity to take part in the raid. Kilpatrick welcomed Dahlgren's return and likely viewed the young colonel as a more controllable choice to join in on his raid than another officer under his command, twenty-five-year-old Brigadier General George Armstrong Custer. Kilpatrick and Custer were rivals who each enjoyed the spotlight and had come to not much like each other. Kilpatrick would now use Custer in a way that wouldn't steal attention from himself. If Kilpatrick were successful in this raid, he wanted the glory to be heaped down on his reputation, not that of his rival.

Kilpatrick knew that more than 13,000 Union POWs in Richmond greatly outnumbered the Rebels who were guarding them. He also thought that Richmond, with Confederate forces still in winter quarters, was poorly defended. His primary objectives were to free the Union prisoners in Richmond and to seize the Confederate capital, along with capturing President Jefferson Davis and his cabinet. What could possibly go awry?

Kilpatrick would also use General Custer and some of his forces in a diversionary expedition. The tactic would keep Custer at a distance from the grand raid. Custer would aim his cavalry column to the southwest toward Charlottesville, Virginia, hoping the action would draw the Confederates to him and allow Kilpatrick's cavalry column to rush into Richmond relatively unmolested. Along the way, Kilpatrick's Raiders were tasked to destroy railroad depots, tracks, barns, mills, and anything they deemed of value to the Confederacy. They would also toss thousands of handbills printed with President Lincoln's amnesty proclamation, blanketing the landscape as they embarked on a nineteenth-century social media campaign. The target audience for the handbills, advertising Lincoln's plan to reunite the Union, were Confederate troops and the Southern civilian population,.

The problem with Kilpatrick's multipronged plan was in the details, including the rush to get things underway, the lack of actual planning, and making sure all the officers in charge knew what was expected of them. Aside from the noble goal of freeing the POWs, not much thought was given to how they would provide for the men once they were freed. Most of the POW population were malnourished, emaciated, and sick, with little clothing in the middle of what had become a brutal winter. Additionally, the Union upper command was apathetic; they seemed to not be on board with the whole idea of Kilpatrick's raid. Finally, Kilpatrick had problems keeping the plans for the raid secret since he was too busy talking it up to everyone who would listen. Even with all its problems, by the end of February the raid had momentum that could not be stopped.

Ulric Dahlgren would write a letter to his father the admiral before the raid began, in the event he did not return:

There is a grand raid to be made and I am going to have a very important command. If successful, it would be the grandest thing on record and if it fails many of us will 'go up'. I may be captured or I may be 'tumbled over,' but it is an undertaking that if I was not in I would feel ashamed to show my face again, with such an important command...if we do not return there is no better place than to 'give up the Ghost.'[239]

Ulric Dahlgren

On Saturday, February 25, 1864, four days after Dahlgren's arrival at Kilpatrick's headquarters, one of the Libby POW tunnel escapees serendipitously came wandering into Brandy Station, Virginia. It had taken sixteen days for English-born, thirty-nine-year-old Lieutenant Godwin Scudamore of the 80th Illinois to reach the Union lines.

Where most escapees had headed east upon escaping through the tunnel at Libby, Scudamore headed into Goochland County, Virginia. The county, just west of Richmond, was the home to some of the area's largest and richest plantations. By the time Scudamore arrived, the area was crawling with Confederates desperately looking for any escapees.[240]

Four days out of Richmond, Scudamore found himself hiding from search parties, repeatedly diving into ditches and ravines in just the nick of time, when he heard men on horseback approaching. It was so cold that the clothes froze to his back. Finally, starving and suffering from exposure in the harsh winter elements, his legs gave out, so he lay huddled in a fetal position trying to keep warm, fading in and out of consciousness.

"Chop, chop, chop."

The sound of several axes meeting wood woke him from his delirium.

"Chop, chop, chop."

Captain Godwin Scudamore
A lieutenant at the time of his escape, he was promoted to Captain on 7/10/1864.

Scudamore snapped awake and managed to crawl out of a ditch on his hands and knees to find a group of enslaved Black men chopping lumber. They soon noticed him lying prone on the ground and immediately knew, from the heightened presence of soldiers in the area, that he had to be one of the Yankee escapees. Martin Roberson,[241] one of the lumbermen in the work party, was actually a freedman, being paid in some way for his labor.[242] Well known to both Black and White folks living in the area by just his first name, "Martin" lived close to the Dover plantation, where his wife, Baker, was reportedly enslaved.

Martin walked over to Scudamore, who lay exhausted on the cold ground. He bent down to the Union officer, whispering in his ear.

"Go away out of sight, and I'll come back for you after dark."

"That night, the same man came and took me to his cabin. He kept me there seven days before I could walk again," said Scudamore.

Scudamore spent three days recuperating, right under the nose of Confederate Secretary of State James A. Seddon, being taken care of by people enslaved at Seddon's plantation known as Sabot Hill, located right next to the Dover plantation. When the lieutenant was finally able to travel, Martin had agreed to guide him all the way north to the Union lines, arriving at Brandy Station, Virginia.

"I know three-quarters of the way to the Union Lines. I will go with you," he said.[243]

With the Kilpatrick raid scheduled to begin just days after their arrival, the officer and his guide were quickly sent to General Meade's headquarters for a debriefing to learn about the conditions along the route they had just traversed.

Regarding his guide Martin Roberson, while being debriefed by Meade, Scudamore told the General, "He helped me make my way back to the Union Lines."

"I cannot allow him to go any farther. I need him to guide Kilpatrick's cavalry. We are going to make a dash on Richmond," Meade replied.[244]

With his knowledge of the area west of Richmond, it was determined by Meade's staff of advisors that Roberson would be valuable in helping Dahlgren's forces get across the James River, allowing him to attack Richmond from the south.

John C. Babcock, who was the Bureau of Military Information (BMI) interrogator who had interviewed Roberson to extract valuable intelligence, sent a letter to Dahlgren the day before the raid was to begin.

> *Dear Colonel: At the last moment I have found a man you want; well acquainted with the James River and up...Question him five minutes, and you will find he is the very man you want.*[245]

John C. Babcock

On the margin of the letter was written:

> *He crossed the Rapidan last night, and has late information.*

Martin signed on and agreed to show Dahlgren's column a safe way down into Goochland County, hoping to receive a substantial cash payment that they offered him. All he had to do to cash in was to successfully find them a way over the James River.

Sunday, February 28, 1864, was chosen as the day the "Grand Raid" would be launched. At 2 a.m., eighty-five miles to the east of Kilpatrick's headquarters at Stevensburg, Virginia, the group under the command of Colonel Abel Streight, the last of the Libby tunnel escapees, finally reached the banks of the Potomac River. Their journey had taken almost two weeks,[246] but they successfully arrived at a rendezvous point near Blackistone Island, which was the location of a lighthouse in the Potomac River. They were rescued by the steamer *USS Ella*,[247] a picket, patrol, and dispatch vessel that was part of the Potomac Flotilla and were taken up the Potomac to Washington, D.C.

After arriving in the Capital, Colonel Streight, the former captive guest of the Hotel de Libby, wasted no time. Within a couple of days he would give a detailed report on Rebel prison conditions to the House Committee on Military Affairs in Washington, D.C., detailing how the Confederates treated their prisoners of war. Parts of Streight's report would be published in *the New York Times* and then find its way into newspapers throughout the north.

> *My officers, together with something near 1,000 other United States officers, are confined in a large warehouse building, with the average space of about twenty-five square feet to each man. This includes all room for washing, cooking, eating, sleeping and exercising. They have no bunks, chairs or seats of any kind furnished them, consequently they both sit and sleep on the floor...*
>
> *The rations furnished both officers and men by the rebels consists of about one pound of cornbread made from unbolted meal, and one fourth pound of poor fresh meat per day. The meat has been issued to the prisoners but about half the time since the 1st of December last...*
>
> *When I arrived at Richmond, to about the 1st of December, all the enlisted men were taken to Belle Island, and turned into an enclosure like so many cattle into a slaughter pen. Very few of them had any tents or shelter of any kind, and the few tents furnished were so poor and leaky as to render them little better than none. All prisoners are taken to the Libby when they first arrive in Richmond, for the purposes of counting them and enrolling their names. Consequently I had a fair chance to see their condition when they arrived. Fully one-half of the prisoners taken since May last were robbed by their captors of their shoes, and nearly all were robbed of their overcoats, blankets and haversacks...*
>
> *Under the building known as Libby prison is a large cellar, in which they have*

several cells partitioned off. Several of them are without any light, but some of them have windows below the pavement. These cells are used for the purpose of confining securely such of the prisoners as the authorities may fear will attempt to escape, as well as such as may chance to offend some of the many petty officials and prison attaches. Some of our unfortunate men are confined in these filthy holes, on one pretext or another. It is the uniform practice to feed any and all persons sent to these cells on bread and water only...

At the time I was taken to the cell there were six of our men confined in one of these cells for attempting to escape. They had been there for six days without blankets, and two were very sick. They were released at the end of seven days of confinement...

It is impossible for me to enumerate in this communication gut a few of the many acts of barbarity which have come under my notice, though I have endeavored to give you a sample of such as will enable you to form a correct conclusion relative to the treatment our unfortunate men are receiving at the hands of the inhumane people with whom we are at war. They seem lost to every principle of humanity, and it is my candid conviction that their brutality to our prisoners is only measured by their fears.

A.D. Streight
Colonel Fifty-first Indiana Volunteers[248]

Also that Sunday Captain John Page of the 5th Iowa would write a letter to his wife, Nancy, whom he called Nan, acknowledging the box of food he had received the day before. Page's messmate Michael Hoffman recorded the receipt of Page's box in his diary the same day. The men shared what little food was sent from home, and so the arrival of a box was big news. Nan had gotten a couple of letters with the Libby Prison address from her husband since his capture in Chattanooga, confirming he was still alive. She was trying to provide for their two small sons at their home in Marshalltown, Iowa, with its barn out back full of her husband's harness making tools, reflecting his occupation before the war. She craved to have him back home and hear the sounds of him working in that barn. They had two boys together, seven-year-old Charles, who had some memories of his father, and three-year-old William, who had been born right as his father had enlisted. John Page got to see his newborn son for a brief instance; then, he was off to war. Page would send his pay back home but had been in the fight from the beginning, which included surviving a serious gunshot wound to his left temple at Iuka that left him a different man.

Libby Prison Richmond, Va Feb 28th 1864.
Dear Nan
I am as well as usual, I received my box yesterday. It was in very good condition I have not room to give you an inventory, I am obliged to all persons concerned in making up the box. You may think it surprising when I tell you that my mess eat the loaves of bread today, we have a way of resuscitating it no matter how moldy. I cannot write you much for the Confederate eyes to read, be sure, and, attend to Charley's schooling at present, but good bye,
From your affectionate husband

John E. Page
Capt 5th Iowa[249]

AT AROUND NOON, WITH THE WEATHER unseasonably warm but windy, Kilpatrick and Dahlgren's "Grand Raid" got underway with more than 4,000 cavalry soldiers heading south toward Richmond. They were all hell-bent on freeing the officers at Libby Prison as well as the enlisted men at Belle Island. Custer headed west to provide a diversion. It would take them more than twelve hours to move all their forces. The cavalrymen, four riders wide, began at a trot at about five miles per hour but soon were running at a full gallop of sixteen miles per hour.[250] For Kilpatrick's raid, timing and speed were everything. Each horse and man carried a combined weight of around 1,200 pounds. By design, the sound and fury of a cavalry column racing south presented itself to those it charged past as a powerful, unstoppable force.

As a comparison, passenger trains in Virginia during the Civil War averaged a speed of around twenty miles per hour.[251] Where the iron horse snorted out clouds of steam through the process of creating mechanical motion, thousands of living and breathing cavalry horses and their riders produced clouds of exhaled breath, which condensed in the cold air like an organic fog.

The next day Dahlgren's men would split from Kilpatrick's and head on a slightly different path south, aiming to cross over the James River west of Richmond and then circle back around to attack from the south.

After riding all night with minimal stopping, by late afternoon on Monday, February 29, General Kilpatrick and his charging column arrived at Beaver Dam Station, a strategic depot on the Virginia Central Railroad. They proceeded to destroy almost five miles of track and all the buildings, creating an inferno and smoke column visible for miles around and unwittingly drawing attention to their presence. Passengers on a Confederate train approaching from the south saw the smoke, and its engineer quickly put the train into reverse, getting away from a few cavalrymen who tried to chase after them. This action ended any semblance of stealth for Kilpatrick. The train, traveling backwards toward Richmond, rushed south to the next station south on the tracks and telegraphed the alarm that Yankee raiders were on their way. It also began to turn cold, spitting a variety of different types of precipitation on all the raiders. It would make their lives miserable and changed the course of events by causing the timing of the raid to go awry.

When the warning of an approaching Yankee cavalry raid reached Richmond, the Confederate capital went into a panic. Libby Prison was a little over three weeks removed from the tunnel escape, and commandant Major Thomas P. Turner and his second in command, Warden Dick Turner, were ordered by the provost marshal of Richmond, Confederate Brigadier General John H. Winder, to immediately execute a plan to mine the entire prison from underneath.[252] Using their enslaved work force, several kegs of powder were placed under the prison in a hole dug in the center of the cellar. The order was to blow up all the prisoners should Kilpatrick successfully breach the Confederate line and make it to the heart of the capital.[253]

"Libby and every damned Yankee in it would have been blown to hell before they should have been released," said Warden Turner to one of the POWs.[254] The news they were all sitting on a bomb rapidly spread through the prison population.

Captain George R. Lodge would record in his diary the same: "Today they have done the most villainous thing of the war. Richard Turner, the Prison inspector (Warden), told one of the prisoners, Adjutant R. C. Knaggs,[255] that they had placed a mine of 300 pounds of powder under the centre of the building so that if our cavalry where to come in, they could spring this mine and blow us into Eternity before we could be released."[256]

"It was the desperate determination of Major Turner to blow us up sooner than allow us to be liberated by Kilpatrick's raiders," added Lieutenant Cavada.[257]

All the Rebels were on edge. The prisoners knew something big was happening so they began to taunt and threaten the prison commandant, Major Turner, sending him anonymous, threatening notes informing him that unless he became more lenient in his treatment of prisoners, they would "cut his throat."[258] Realizing the number of POWs versus the number of guards was greatly in the favor of the Yankees, Turner's increased nervousness began to take its toll.

"Turner issued the following order: Hereafter all clothing hanging on the windows will be confiscated; and men seting *(sic)* on the windows or laying their hands on the bars of the window will be liable to be shot. I see two sentinels cock their guns at us today very strict. Richmond all in excitement the Federals making a raid," recorded Lieutenant Michael Hoffman in his diary.[259]

Shortly after the order was announced, a Confederate officer on duty in the lower part of the prison stuck his head out of a window to speak with one of the guards. The guard mistook him for a Yankee prisoner and shot him dead.[260]

AT SUNRISE ON TUESDAY, MARCH 1, Dahlgren's column had made it to Goochland County, west of Richmond, to an area filled with wealthy plantations along the James River where Libby tunnel escapee Scudamore had met Martin, the Black guide they had acquired just before the beginning of this adventure. Martin had tried all morning to find Dahlgren's men a good crossing point over the James River. There was a ford over the river right at Dover, but the river was swollen from the rains, making the crossing impassable. The young Colonel had lost his patience and didn't buy that the lousy weather conditions and a flooded river were acceptable reasons for being unable to get his men over the James. Looking to place blame on someone, he began questioning whether Martin was really a knowledgeable guide; perhaps Roberson was actually a

**Lieutenant
Reuben Bartley**
Dahlgren's Signal
Officer
Photographer unknown

planted spy, intentionally misleading them toward inevitable failure.

"Up to this, our success had been remarkable—two nights and one day in the Confederate lines and not a shot had been fired at us. We were beginning to think we would go right through with the whole programme *(sic),* but now things took a turn that looked rather bad for us," remembered Lieutenant Reuben Bartley, Dahlgren's signal officer.[261]

The men were all cold and muddy, and the James River was angry and swollen from the rain. So they took the opportunity to visit the Dover, Sabot Hill, and several other of the area's wealthy plantations, warming up a little while acquiring fresh horses and taking advantage of the free breakfasts the plantations' owners offered, after a little encouragement, to the hungry Yankees. Many soldiers pocketed the silverware as parting gifts.[262]

By noon, and fifteen miles from the center of Richmond, their guide Martin was beginning to panic, having still not found a place for Dahlgren's men to ford the river and knowing that he had run out of viable options.

It was foggy, with the James River creating its own localized atmosphere. Rain continued to antagonize the soldiers. Colonel Dahlgren's plans were going awry so, needing a fall guy, the young Colonel's unreliable guide became the target of his frustration and anger. He announced to his men that their guide Martin was a traitorous spy, who had been intentionally misleading them all along and purposely slowing them down. Passing quick sentence, Daglgren ordered the ultimate penalty, that Martin be immediately hung. He looked to one of his scouts, twenty-one-year-old Anson B. Carney of the 5th US Cavalry, to carry the order out.[263]

Near Powell's Tavern, an establishment that had been visited by Lafayette in 1824, Martin Roberson was executed. Along the river road, Martin was bound on his horse. Using either a rope or leather strap thrown over an oak tree, Carney slapped the horse's rear. Minutes later, Martin's lifeless body slowly swung back and forth in the misting rain as the last of Dahlgren's men gazed upon it as they rode by.

"It seems that Colonel Dahlgren intended to cross the James River by ford, to which his guide promised to guide him," said one of Dahlgren's officers, "There was neither ford nor bridge; the guide had known it, and in his indignation the Colonel hung him." [264]

One of the last riders in the column cut Martin's body down, and the guide was left lying by the side of the road. Ironically, there was a ford over the James a few hundred yards south of Powell's Tavern, though the waters were too high as a result of the rains. Stuck on the north side of the James River, Dahlgren's column continued along Plank Road, heading east toward Richmond.

Shortly after Roberson's death, Dahlgren's raiders began to hear the sound of cannons coming from the east. Kilpatrick was right on time, arriving as planned at the outer edge of Richmond at 10 a.m. Spreading out and testing the Rebel pickets, by 1 p.m. Kilpatrick was but a few miles from the center of the capital. He set up a couple of cannons on the Brook Turnpike and began firing them at the Confederate lines. He had his band play "Yankee Doodle," which no doubt incensed the enemy, and the Rebels quickly responded.

At Libby Prison, just five miles south of Kilpatrick's position, the POWs all heard the cannonading in the early afternoon as well. Cheers rang out as the bells of all Richmond's churches began ringing wildly, adding their high notes to the booming bass notes being made by the cannons. There was an excitement as speculation of a raid on the Confederate capital telegraphed through the crowded prison population. The officer POWs quickly organized themselves into attack parties and planned an all-out assault that would have them rushing the guards, attacking some of the other prison buildings including Belle Island, releasing their captives, and seizing the arsenal. All this action was occurring even with the knowledge of the explosive filled basement a few floors under their feet.

"Desperate work this is for unarmed men," said one POW, "but, then, they were willing to take desperate chances in order to reach the arms up at the arsenal, and it would be understood that after the guards had poured in their first fire they would not have time to reload before they were overpowered by the weight of numbers...For the first time since my coming to Libby all the prisoners were in high spirits."[265]

"General Kilpatrick is now racing around the city, and fighting rebels wherever he can find them," recorded Marsh Byers from his perspective sitting on the bare rough floor in Libby's penthouse (third floor) level along with other POWs from the 5th Iowa, Major Marshall, Captain Page, and Lieutenant Hoffman, "The citizens' home guards and soldiers are all armed and fighting the bold raiders, who they fear will release the prisoners and burn the city."[266]

UNABLE TO GET OVER THE JAMES RIVER and attack from the south side of Richmond as was the original plan, Dahlgren attempted to head east toward the sounds of the cannons in order to join Kilpatrick. Kilpatrick spent the afternoon fighting from a position so close to Richmond that they could see the city's church spires, with the motion of the bells visibly moving within some of them.

Kilpatrick was waiting for some indication that Dahlgren was attacking the city from the south, but the attack never came; he had no idea where Dahlgren was. Dahlgren, at that moment, was lost, but, in fact, the two men were only about eight miles from each other, with a maze of country roads separating them.

General Benjamin F. Butler's men never showed up on the southeast side of Richmond as the third prong of Kilpatrick's plan of attack. In fact, his troops hadn't even left the Williamsburg area and wouldn't do so until midnight. Butler had sent a message the day before at 6 p.m., stating that he was sending his men. The message closed with "Is this approved?" It seemed like General Butler might not even have been aware that the raid was already underway.[267]

Having been roughed up by the Rebels all afternoon without the planned support of Dahlgren, or Butler, Kilpatrick quickly decided he was fighting a losing proposition. The raid he had hoped would shower him with accolades had fallen apart. At around 6 p.m. he called it quits, packed up his cannons, and retreated toward the east, crossing Meadow Bridge over the Chickahominy River as fast as he could. In Kilpatrick's report after the battle he would write, "The enemy charged...and considerable confusion ensued."[268] It was a surprising outcome after all of Kilpatrick's bluster, and his men were dejected. For an officer tagged with the reputation of being reckless and aggressive, rushing in from the north and facing the enemy at its doorstep for less than eight hours and then calling it a day was a remarkable outcome.

The sounds of battle that had felt so close now completely disappeared. It became deathly silent at Libby; a light snow accumulated on the landscape through the evening, dulling all the sounds around them.

"There was no sleep in Libby that night, nor did the guards passing through with their lanterns wonder why the men were not lying down. It seemed as if day would never come. As the dreary black hours crept on our spirits sank lower and lower," said a Libby POW. "So ended in disaster a raid that promised much."[269]

At 1 a.m. on Wednesday, March 2, the weather was miserable as Kilpatrick's forces had made their way to the east side of Richmond and continued pushing toward the safety of the peninsula.

Dahlgren's men were pushing east also, though half of his men had become separated from him. They were all lost in a maze of backcountry roads full of Confederates, at times skirmishing with them in the darkness.

At Libby prison the muffled sounds of fighting returned, but now it was coming from the east, further away than the day before. "This would have been exciting enough under any circumstances," recorded Lieutenant Cavada, "but our anxiety was not a little heightened by the well-authenticated information that the cellars of the prison had been mined. Some one, as I sat up in my blankets listening to the cannonading, whispered tremblingly in my ear, that he had it from the very best authority, that a soldier was sent down to where the kegs of powder were buried, regularly every half hour during the night, with a lighted candle, to see if the fuse was all right."[270]

For the Kilpatrick-Dahlgren raiding parties, it would prove to be a very long day.

"Our little command kept well together, and when we came to a small band of rebels we charged right through them. This was quite often, for I think we made as many as 10 such charges that day," said scout Anson B. Carney who had been seriously wounded the night before.[271]

At sunset the separated rear of Dahlgren's column finally caught up with Kilpatrick and camped at Tunstall's Station on the Richmond and York River Railroad. It had been seventy-two hours and 113 miles of tough riding on horseback in miserable weather conditions with minimal sleep since they had left together on the raid. Now they were all finally reunited except for Colonel Dahlgren and about ninety of his men, who had gone further east and were about to be surrounded by Rebels while running low on ammunition. Though they didn't know it at that moment, Kilpatrick and Dahlgren were only five miles apart, separated by two rivers.

As night progressed, a mixed band of about 150 Confederates,[272] made up of local home guards, cavalry, and infantry soldiers, continued to follow Dahlgren's men, then managed to divide Dahlgren's small force and get in front of them.

Just after 11 p.m. it would all come to an end just north of King and Queen County Courthouse.[273]

Unbeknown to Dahlgren's men, Confederates lay hidden in the pine trees on either side of the road, and just ahead of them in the darkness a couple of their cavalry soldiers on horseback blocked the road, waiting to ambush Dahlgren as he walked into their trap.

As Dahlgren's men slowly moved toward the roadblock, they became surrounded on three sides. Unaware of the danger, Dahlgren called out to the men on horseback waiting in the middle of the road ahead, "Surrender or I will shoot you." They were to be his last words. He aimed his pistol and pulled the trigger. The gun misfired.

"Almost instantly a volley was fired into our left flank along our line by the enemy who lay in ambush not over twenty feet from the road. This stampeded us for about one hundred yards, every horse in our column turning to the rear. When we pulled up we found that Dahlgren was killed,"[274] said Lieutenant Bartley who was right next to Dahlgren when he fell. Falling from his horse, the Colonel landed in the ditch next to the road with his feet up against a fence and tree.[275]

A sheet of gunfire poured out from the pine trees on either side of the road. Just a few feet away from the others, Colonel Dahlgren had been killed instantly, his body riddled with up to five bullets.[276] More fire poured down from the flank and rear of the column. Finding cover in the pine trees, what remained of Dahlgren's forces were surrounded.

While the Yankees scattered backwards from the scene where their commander fell, the Confederates who ambushed the columns emerged from the trees to examine Colonel Dahlgren's body, which lay on the road where he had fallen. A group of Rebels rifled through the dead officer's pockets, taking the money they found. A pinky ring caught the attention of a cavalry private. When he couldn't remove the ring normally, he took it by slicing off the Colonel's finger.

An area doctor removed Dahlgren's artificial leg when he examined his body, impressed with its quality. The famous prosthesis would begin its own journey through Rebeldom. The doctor's noble objective was to show the leg to a prosthesis manufacturer in order to improve on Confederate artificial legs. But before he had a chance to do so, Lieutenant James Pollard, who was in the group of men who fired upon and killed Dahlgren, took the artifact from him.

A twenty-seven-year-old schoolteacher, "Captain" Edward W. Halbach, along with fourteen of his students, were part of the local home guards that witnessed the ambush.[277] One of the students, thirteen—year-old William Littlepage, was bold enough to rifle through Dahlgren's pockets and found a cigar case and cache of interesting papers, which he quietly pocketed.

Shortly after the teacher and his students sought cover in a safe area and set up camp for the night. As they lay in their blankets on the frozen ground, Littlepage pulled out Dahlgren's pilfered cigar case.

"Mr Halbach, will you have a cigar?" said William, offering the case to his teacher.

"No, but where did you get cigars in these hard times?" asked Halbach.

William then told them all he had got them out of the pocket of the Yankee that had been killed, along with some papers.

"Well William, you must give me the papers, and you may keep the cigar case," said Halbach.

In the darkness William continued telling them that the dead Yankee had a wooden leg, which brought the attention of a Rebel Lieutenant camping with the group, who, upon overhearing the conversation, suddenly became excited and said, "How did you know he has a wooden leg?"

"I know he has," replied William, "because I caught hold of it and tried to pull it off."

"We were a strange medley of regulars, raw troops, old farmers, preachers, schoolboys, etc.," said Halbach.[278]

In the morning of Thursday, March 3, Littlepage was finally able to look at the papers he had recovered off the dead Yankee's body the night before. They sure seemed important, but there was a small problem; William did not know how to read. The teenager handed the papers to his teacher. As Halbach scanned them, his eyes widened. In the upcoming days the papers and their explosive contents would reverberate through the leadership of both sides of the conflict. [279]

Halbach quickly found Lieutenant Pollard and let him read Dahlgren's papers. They described the entire plan for the Kilpatrick raid, with the details of Dahlgren's column coming in from the south side of Richmond, the main objective of freeing the prisoners at Belle Island first, then crossing over the James River, setting the officers held at Libby Prison free, and destroying the bridges and then to "burn the hateful city, and do not allow the Rebel leader, Davis, and his traitorous crew to escape." A separate page labeled "special orders" contained the additional explosive statement: "once in the city, it must be destroyed, and Jeff Davis and Cabinet killed." Pollard's commander, upon seeing the papers, ordered the Lieutenant to take them to Richmond and deliver them immediately to General Fitzhugh Lee.

Pollard raced to the Rebel capital with the Dahlgren papers and prosthetic leg, delivering them to General Lee. Then a few months later on June 24, 1864, in a bit of Civil War karma, Pollard lost his own right leg after being wounded.[280] He somehow reacquired Dahlgren's prosthesis, but when it did not fit him, he bartered a deal with another Rebel officer, who had also lost a leg, for the price of a new prosthetic. That other officer would proudly advertise that he was wearing the damn Yankee Dahlgren's artificial leg to all who cared to hear, and likely those who didn't. The trade would come back to haunt the man shortly after the war when he was pursued by detectives in search of the device. The Rebel officer willingly gave up the leg, and it was returned to Dahlgren's father, the Admiral.[281]

Back at Libby, the excitement and anticipation of the last few days suddenly came to a crashing halt. "When daylight came, bringing with it a prisoner, who told of the failing of Kilpatrick's expedition, the reaction that became despair to so many set in. So terrible was the disappointment that the men did not care to speak about it, but paced the floors in silence and with clouded brows," said a Libby POW.[282]

THE DAILY MONOTONY OF PRISON life soon returned. Finally, a few of the prisoner's provision boxes sent from home began to find their way to the starving men. Commandant Turner had sequestered the parcels for weeks, mentally torturing the prisoners because they could actually see them in a building just to the east of the prison. For starving prisoners, the supply boxes from home were critical in helping increase their caloric intake.

Lt. Colonel John Polsley, Captain Leopold Markbreit, and Lieutenants John McAdams and Caleb Casdorph—making up the group of West Virginia POWs from December's Averell Raid on Salem, Virginia—were all messmates and had remained together in the crowded prison. After three months all the West Virginians were physically suffering from the horrible conditions.

"I have not been very well," said Polsley in a letter to his wife, Ellen, whom he called Nellie. "Dear Nellie, for some little time–having a disease peculiar to the Prison similar to the Scurvy in some aspects–but am recovering from it gradually."[283] Polsley did indeed suffer from scurvy. Its simple cure, vitamin C, was not something any prisoner could easily add to his diet.

The prison rumor mill had started to circulate that prisoner exchanges might resume soon. "We are looking for a boat up today with prisoners for exchange and I hope that it may be my fortune to get off either on it or the next one," said Polsley. This was the nature of life for the POWs. Anything positive to raise their spirits and bring hope was welcomed. The country was at war with itself, raiders were lurking in the distance, and danger was right under their feet. They were all caught in a whirlpool of events that swirled and spun in a different direction every day.

By Friday morning, March 4, in King and Queen County, all the remaining members of Dahlgren's raiders had been captured, gathered together and marched to Richmond. As the identity of Dahlgren himself became known, some additional thought was given to what had been done with the Colonel's body. It was decided to exhume his body from its shallow grave and place it in a pine coffin made by a local carriage maker.[284]

As the days progressed, authorities in Richmond decided the gravity of the papers that were found on Dahlgren's body required for them to order the Colonel's remains to be sent to Richmond to be formally identified. The series of documents, which included the damning one titled "Special Orders and Instructions," ordering the execution of Jefferson Davis and his cabinet, which were written in the Colonel's own handwriting and found on Ulric Dahlgren's body, became forever known as the "Dahlgren Papers." The controversy they caused would resonate for years.

In Washington, Kilpatrick and Dahlgren's raid was considered a failure.

Over the ensuing weeks the raid's details were dissected by the Union command, and Kilpatrick himself would put a spin on it, trying to bring attention to the raid's minimal successes. His commander, Major General George G. Meade, summed up Kilpatrick's efforts: "On reaching the city General Kilpatrick found himself opposed by infantry and artillery, which, in his judgment, rendered any attempt at forcing an entrance extremely hazardous. He accordingly made no serious attempt to enter, but, after some slight and insignificant skirmishing, withdrew his command and hurriedly made his way to Williamsburg."[285]

By Saturday, March 5, all the Richmond newspapers published the Dahlgren Papers, and the Confederate capital was abuzz. The Confederate government would provide copies of the Dahlgren Papers to foreign governments, seeking favor for their cause.

Confederate Secretary of War James A. Seddon, whose Sabot Hill plantation home had been visited by Dahlgren and his raiders a few days earlier, was incensed after studying the incriminating documents. "My own inclinations are toward the execution of at least a portion of those captured at the time Colonel Dahlgren was killed, and the publications of these papers as it is justified...General Bragg's views coincide with my own on this subject," said Seddon in a letter to General Robert E. Lee.[286]

For Lee, the discovery of the Dahlgren Papers couldn't have come at a worse time. His twenty-six-year-old son, William Henry Fitzhugh Lee, who was known as Rooney Lee, had been shot in the thigh on June 9, 1863, at Brandy Station and captured while recuperating two weeks later at Hickory Hill, Virginia. He was sent to a Union POW prison at Fort Monroe in Hampton, Virginia, and then to New York. Right as the Kilpatrick-Dahlgren raid was occurring, there was an agreement to exchange Rooney for General Neal Dow, who was being held at Libby Prison.

AT LIBBY, SATURDAY WAS LIEUTENANT Hoffman's turn at cooking duty for his messmates, which included Major Marshall and Captain Page. For the prisoners, the exciting possibilities brought forth by the raid had faded away and were then followed by disappointment and depression. The prisoners had not yet heard of Colonel Dahlgren's fate. Some who were aware that they all would have been blown up had the raid succeeded breathed a sigh of relief. But the prison commandant let sleeping dogs lie, leaving the kegs of gunpowder buried in the cellar.

In the scramble for men to defend Richmond, most of the Libby guards had been sent to help fight off the Kilpatrick raiders. "The old guards...were replaced with the city guards, a lot of little boys with little red caps on who the very day commenced by carrying guns cocked and were frequently heard to remark that they meant business," said Hoffman. "Major Turner seemed to be aware that these young guards might shoot some of us...the oldest man at Libby had one of his ears shot off for accidentally laying his hands on the window bars."[287]

By nightfall the officers who were captured when Dahlgren was killed finally arrived at Libby as newly minted POWs, including scout Reuben Bartley.

The new prisoners were introduced to the check-in protocol repeated on every new

Libby "guest." "We were taken into the hall and searched and everything we had taken from us. All my precious papers, money, knives & my diary, signal book and all that I had. I was told that in all probability we would be hung pretty soon as murderers and that we should not receive the treatment of prisoners of war for we were nothing but felons...(We) lay all on the floor all night in the hall," recorded Bartley in his diary.[288]

For the Libby management of Turner, Turner & Ross, the new rush of prisoners created an overcrowded dungeon dilemma. The four small cells were still bursting at the seams with more than forty men, most who had been recaptured after the tunnel escape. Now they had a new wave of POWs from the failed Kilpatrick and Dahlgren raid to contend with.

As Sunday morning dawned Robert E. Lee recognized the danger of Secretary Seddon's inclination to execute the new Union prisoners that resulted from the Kilpatrick raid and its potential to block the exchange that was already in motion to spring his son. He quickly responded back to Seddon on Sunday afternoon. "I cannot recommend the execution of the prisoners that have fallen into our hands. Assuming that the address and special orders of Colonel Dahlgren correctly state his designs and intentions, they were not executed, and I believe, even in a legal point of view, acts in addition to intentions are necessary to constitute a crime."[289]

Around noon ten POWs from the raid were ordered down into the dungeon and packed into one of the ten by twelve dungeon cells. The entire dungeon was so full that some of the men who had been there after being recaptured from the tunnel escape were allowed to return to the main prison population to make room for the newcomers. Unfortunately, this group did not include Lieutenant Mark Bassett.

On Sunday evening Colonel Ulric Dahlgren's body arrived in Richmond by a freight train in the pine box coffin that was constructed for him two days earlier. Stenciled on the rough wooden boards of the coffin's flat lid was his name "Ulric Dahlgren."[290]

At Libby Prison on Monday morning, March 7, after roll call, the official word went out that there was to be an exchange of POWs. It was the only way to ease overcrowding with more Union POW officers arriving daily. Considering the events of the last week, it was a remarkable emotional lift for all the prisoners. Lieutenant Michael Hoffman recorded that forty-eight officers left the prison. Included in the group was Lieutenant Federico Fernández Cavada.

"The happy voyage down the James River to City Point—the first glimpse for so many months, of our dear old flag flying from the truce boat—loud cheers for it...I am not dreaming, but I am once more substantially and positively–F R E E!" said Cavada.

Down in the dungeon four Black Union enlisted soldiers, recently captured on the Virginia peninsula while on their way to help find Kilpatrick,[291] were added to the cell holding the Kilpatrick POWs.[292] Warden Turner, always looking for ways to make his prisoners more miserable, thought that being crammed into the dungeon with Black POW soldiers would be taken as an insult to the White POW officers. It was not. One of the POW's, a major, commented that he "infinitely preferred the company of loyal negroes than that of white traitors."[293]

Just a few blocks southeast of Libby, Dahlgren's body was put on ghoulish display in Richmond for the public to see at the York River train depot. "A number of citizens visited the depot...as gratification of a morbid curiosity," reported the Richmond Sentinel. All the Richmond newspapers would report further on the event the following day on the big story.

The body of Col. Ulric Dahlgren, killed in the swamps of King and Queen, by the 9th Va. Cavalry, was brought to the city Sunday night and laid at the York River depot during the greater part of the day yesterday, where large numbers of persons went to see it. It was in a pine box, clothed in Confederate shirt and pants, and shrouded in a Confederate blanket. The wooden leg had been removed by one of the soldiers. It was also noticeable that the little finger of the left hand had been cut off. Dahlgren was a small man, thin, pale, and with red hair and a goatee of the same color. His face wore an expression of agony.

About two o'clock, P. M., the corpse was removed from the depot and buried—no one knows, or is to know, where.

Richmond Whig
3/8/1864

Word spread within Libby of the treatment and mutilation of Dahlgren's corpse, and the POWs fumed, but there was nothing they could do but curse the damned Rebels—which they did, over and over again under their breaths.[294]

Then, under the cover of darkness, Dahlgren's body was removed from the depot in a wagon driven by four mules and taken to Oakwood Cemetery, where it was secretly buried in an unmarked grave. Confederate officials in charge took care that the cemetery was empty so that no one would witness the exact place of burial. Another newspaper would print an inaccurate, propagandized account the next day:

"Where that spot is no one but those concerned in its burial know or care to tell. It was a dog's burial, without coffin, winding sheet or service. Friends and relatives at the North need inquire no further; this is all they will know-he is buried, a burial that befitted the mission upon which he came."

The Richmond Examiner
3/9/1864

The exact spot of Dahlgren's grave was a concern to more than just the few Confederate officials who witnessed his burial. Though the plan was to bury the Colonel's body so no one could ever find it, as the burial took place at close to midnight, a Black cemetery worker secreted himself behind a tree, hidden from view, and was spying on the group of Confederates as the burial took place. Soon after the burial party had left, he would secretly mark the grave in such a way that it could be later found.

Chapter Nine

Libby Life
March 1864 to May 1864

MARCH 1864 SLOWLY TICKED BY as winter held Richmond in its grasp; six inches of snow blanketed the Rebel capital, and the prisoners at Libby continued to starve.

Lieutenant Mark Bassett, still serving time in the overpacked dungeon for his escape attempt, was wasting away, along with his fellow cellmates. The days seemed to blur together; how long his sentence would be was unknown. He could do nothing about his wife, Lottie, and her infidelity. He was no longer allowed to write or receive letters. He felt utterly and totally helpless.

The food situation remained as inconsistent as ever, less than 600 calories per day. That was approximately the amount of nourishment, if you could call it that, in the rations each Libby prisoner received: a half loaf of coarsely made cornbread with the cob ground with the grain. It was ten ounces, roughly five inches square. The batter was prepared in open troughs where it attracted flies, which ended up being mixed and baked in like winged raisins. Sometimes they received a few ounces of rice or peas.[295] It was a starvation diet, one that led to multiple diseases as the body was deprived of the nutrition it required.

Prisoners would go for weeks without a scrap of meat, which when they did receive it was usually rancid. Captain Frederick Memmert of the 5th Maryland Infantry approached Warden Dick Turner to complain about the lack of food. Turner harshly brushed aside his complaints, saying, "That's good enough for you. Our prisoners are just as badly treated by your fellows as you are here. I wish to kill you off. If I had the command, I would hang every God-damned one of you."[296]

Other officers who received packages from home would sometimes share some of their valuable food supplies with other officers who received nothing. Without the support of his comrades, Bassett could not survive on the meager rations Libby Prison provided.

"Rations are cornbread, a little turnip and cabbage averaging about one turnip to two men, I go hungry continually," wrote Hoffman.[297]

The controversy caused by the Dahlgren Papers continued through the spring of 1864. The US government scrambled to explain their contents, ultimately claiming the documents were forged. Two weeks after his return, Kilpatrick himself would write, obviously knowing Dahlgren would forever be unavailable to respond on his own behalf, "that paper was endorsed in red ink, 'Approved,' over my official signature. The alleged address of Colonel Dahlgren published in the papers is the same as the one approved by me, save so far as it speaks of 'exhorting the prisoners to destroy and burn the hateful city and kill the traitor Davis and his cabinet.' All this is false and published only as an excuse for the barbarous treatment of the remains of a brave soldier."[298] Kilpatrick was relieved of his command and sent to the west to join General Sherman, who a few months later would set his sights on Atlanta and environs further southeast toward Savannah.

One of the officers traveling with Dahlgren who managed to evade capture was Captain John McEntee, a Bureau of Military Information (BMI) officer. At the BMI McEntee was second in command under General Marsena Rudolph Patrick and worked as an undercover Union spy, regularly traveling behind the Confederate lines by any means necessary. Most of the scouts on the Kilpatrick-Dahlgren raid came from the BMI and were under his command, including Anson B. Carney, the man tasked with the execution of Dahlgren's guide Martin. When McEntee was interviewed a week after the raid back over the Union lines, he stated that, in his opinion, the Dahlgren Papers were true and that these were things that Dahlgren had personally told him while on the raid.[299]

Several of the Kilpatrick raiders now huddled together as POWs in Libby's dungeon. They were all silent about the Dahlgren Papers except for the whisperings among themselves. On Friday, March 11, as a result of the overcrowded dungeon, an additional special cell was partitioned off in one corner of the main prison's first-floor kitchen to hold these new prisoners,[300] and the Kilpatrick raid group was moved into this new space. Four more officers captured near Fort Hudson were added to the already crowded cell. They were all USCI officers: Captain Thomas Thornton of Philadelphia, Lieutenant Edwin Y. Brown of Boston, Lieutenant George B. Coleman of New York, and Lieutenant Lewis R. Titus of Vermont.[301]

Both chambers of the Confederate Congress had passed a resolution in May 1863, signed by President Jefferson Davis, as a response to the Emancipation Proclamation. "Every white person being a commissioned officer, who were in command of Black men in military service were guilty of inciting servile insurrection, and shall, if captured, be put to death or otherwise punished." The Libby prison officials assumed the Kilpatrick crew would all soon be executed; Warden Dick Turner couldn't have been happier.

After a few weeks the Black enlisted prisoners were sent to other Confederate prisons. Forty-three-year-old Corporal Armstead, a barber before the war, died as a POW under the horrible conditions at Salisbury Prison on February 15, 1865, of starvation and exposure, leaving behind a wife and three children. Twenty-one-year-old Private Lewis died at home of typhoid, nineteen days after being released from prison on March 3, 1865.[302] Thirty-five-year-old Private Corne was sent to Andersonville, Georgia,[303] and Private John H. Thomas disappeared into some other part of Rebeldom. Neither Corne nor Thomas were ever heard from again.

General Robert E. Lee would write a letter to Union General George Meade asking whether the designs and instructions in the Dahlgren Papers were authorized by the United States government or by Dahlgren's superior officers, and whether they had the approval of those authorities.[304]Lee delayed sending the correspondence for a couple of weeks, until April 1, after his son Rooney had finally been exchanged for Union Brigadier General Neal S. Dow.

Admiral Dahlgren in the years after the war would take up the cause of his son Ulric, claiming that the Dahlgren Papers were forged. The principal evidence offered was the misspelling of the name Dahlgren as "Dalhgren" with the "h" and "l" flipped in his son's own signature. The odd-looking signature is likely caused by ink that bled through the paper from the other side or through the rudimentary process of making photographic copies of documents in 1864.

Shortly after the event, commenting on whether the Dahlgren Papers were fake, General Meade would offer the most damning opinion, "This is a pretty ugly piece of business...I regret to say Kilpatrick's reputation, and collateral evidence in my possession rather go against this theory."[305]

There was an irony in the controversy created by the papers found on the dead colonel's body. The Dahlgren Papers called for the execution of the Confederate president and his cabinet and the destruction of Richmond, for which the Confederates now feigned outrage. Union forces scrambled to understand what the true Kilpatrick-Dahlgren plans for the raid on Richmond actually included, then let the matter stay unresolved. They knew the answer was that the Dahlgren Papers were the real deal. At the same time had Kilpatrick succeeded, the Confederates had planned to kill more than 1,200 Union officers held at Libby Prison by igniting the kegs of gunpowder in the prison's basement. The United States Sanitary Commission visualized what the explosion of Libby might have looked like, had it occurred. "Lifted bodily in the air, and let down in one stupendous crash and ruin upon the living forms of twelve hundred helpless men."[306] There was outrage on both sides: the outrage of war.

When the enslaved cemetery worker hid and watched where Colonel Ulric Dahlgren was buried on the evening of March 8, it set into motion within the Richmond spy network under Elizabeth Van Lew a plan to recover the remains and move them elsewhere for safekeeping. On April 2, 1864, in what was appropriately described as a dark, stormy night, four men went into Oakwood cemetery and exhumed Dahlgren's body. The remains were moved to a farmhouse outside of Richmond where they were examined and then transferred to a metallic coffin. Elizabeth Van Lew herself viewed the corpse. The next day it was concealed in a wagon full of peach trees and carried to the farm of Robert Orrock, further northwest of town near Hungary Station on the Richmond, Fredericksburg, and Potomac Railroad, where it was reburied. A peach tree was planted at the burial site to mark the spot.

At the same time the spy network accomplished the recovery of Dahlgren's body, Union officials were negotiating with the Confederates for the return of the Colonel's body to his father, Admiral Dahlgren, through an exchange boat to Fortress Monroe. On April 6 Confederate officials went to Oakwood cemetery equipped with shovels and proceeded to open the grave. After digging to the prescribed depth, they stood back, looking down into the hole with astonishment. The grave was empty.[307]

Colonel Dahlgren's remains were retrieved from the Orrock farm after the war and interred in the family plot in Laurel Hill Cemetery in Philadelphia, Pennsylvania. Ulric is buried next to his father, the Admiral, who died in 1870.

The episode of the raid and the Dahlgren Papers made it even more clear that the burden of housing thousands of prisoners of war within the capital of the Confederacy was an enormous problem. Richmond was already a large, important military target; add in all the Union prisoners, and it just made the target that much larger and desirable. The local newspapers began to offer their opinions that a change needed to be made.

It is to be wished that Government will never again collect a multitude of prisoners in and about this city, as it provokes raids on the capital, and it is much more expensive to feed them here than in Georgia or Western North Carolina.

Richmond Whig
3/24/1864

MARK BASSETT WAS FINALLY RELEASED from the Libby dungeon in early April, having spent eight weeks in confinement. He was quite shaky as he climbed the stairs, returning him to the upper floors with the rest of the prison population. His time in the dungeon had left him emaciated, and he had been physically beaten. It was pure joy to finally be able to stretch, stand vertically, and move about, albeit within a prison population that still exceeded 1,200 Union officers.

The Confederate government had gotten the message and were getting ready to make a change. The citizens of Richmond were thinking "good riddance." One Libby prisoner began to hear the buzz that the entire prison population was going to be moved and came up with an intriguing thought, "If a man is too sick to move, will they carry him South, keep him in Richmond, or specially exchange him?" He decided to pull "the old soldier dodge" and feign being sick in hopes of being exchanged.

At rollcall the next morning, he told the guard that he couldn't get up.

"Rheumatiz?" the guard asked.

"Rheumatism of the worst kind," replied the prisoner.

"Well that's regular old hell," replied the guard sympathetically, "I had it myself down Fredericksburg way, more'n a year ago, an the touch of a blanket at night druv me wild...I'll report you."

"Yes," said a doctor in response to the prisoner who tried to look sick and excited at the same time, "You will be sent North tomorrow."[308]

It had worked! That night he couldn't sleep and dreamt of all the great meals he would soon be eating. At 7 a.m. on May 4 a guard entered Libby hospital and read the names of those who would go down the James River on the flag-of-truce boat. The prisoner, a captain from a western state, felt his body buzz with electricity as his name was called. They were ordered out onto Cary Street where he looked up at the barred windows of Libby.

★ ★ ★

FROM ABOVE MEN WERE shouting "Goodbye" and "See the President and hurry up the exchange" to the sick prisoners below. Soon they were marched on board the flag-of-truce boat. As they made their way down the James, they passed the city's fortifications and continued their way around the obstructions that had been placed in the river to prevent Union gunboats from moving on Richmond.

"Boom, boom, boom!"

An advance boat escorting the flag-of-truce steamer rounded a bend a few hundred yards out front. It suddenly began engaging with a Confederate battery along the shore. Both sides fired heavily back and forth at each other, while the flag-of-truce boat came to a complete stop and tried to stay out of the fray. The battle lasted less than ten minutes when suddenly a terrific explosion lifted the advance boat clear out of the water. It was a Confederate torpedo that struck the Union escort boat. Its wreckage soon covered the James, along with floating dead bodies.

This was a disaster! The flag-of-truce boat quickly turned around on the James River and headed back toward Richmond.

"I reckon," said another invalid watching on the deck next to his startled companion, "you'd rather be back in prison than blowed up like them other Yanks was that we just saw."

"No," said the captain, "I would a thousand times rather be blown up or shot to pieces than to return to that hell of Libby again."

As the flag-of-truce boat returned to the docks near Libby, everyone on board could see that there was a great commotion coming from the prison. Prisoners lined up on Cary Street with armed guards barking commands at their side. Libby was being emptied of all its prisoners. The Cary Street group began marching toward railroad cars that would take them South.[309]

"We could always tell by the stir, excitement and fast walking on the streets of Richmond when things were pressing a little too hard on the front," said Hoffman. "The rebs thought best to take us out of Richmond. When we were taken out of Libby prison, being five months to the day since our little party was captured at Missionary Ridge and put into Libby, it seemed like so many years to us, and yet there were others there that morning who had been in there more than twice that length of time without ever setting foot outside. It was well for us we got out when we did for Libby, like the confederacy itself kept going down from the first day we went into it."[310]

The danger had always been there. Housing a huge POW population in the Confederate capital made it an obvious target for raids. Richmond's Provost Marshal General John H. Winder was the cranky, short-tempered sixty-four-year-old career military officer in charge of the Confederate prisons. When asked about the caliber of his prison system, he once proudly claimed that his prisons were killing more Yankees than Robert E. Lee.[311] Shortly after the Kilpatrick raid, Winder ordered all prisoners moved south. Libby would continue to be used as the clearinghouse and place of temporary confinement for recently captured soldiers, but they would soon be rerouted to more secure locations in the bowels of the Confederacy.

It took several days for all the POWs to be sorted and packed into rail cars and sent to Danville, Virginia, and then ultimately further south to Georgia. The enlisted men at Belle Isle would be sent to Andersonville. The officers would be transferred to a new prison in Macon. They numbered in the thousands.

Brigadier General John H. Winder, Provost Marshall, Richmond, Va.
Photographer unknown

For the POW captain who, by pretending to be sick, thought he was going home on the flag-of-truce boat, the plan rapidly changed. The day after he arrived back at Libby, all the sick POWs were reexamined by Confederate doctors, who realized they were being hoodwinked by several of them. The disappointed captain was soon sent with the healthy prisoners southward, away from Union raiders hell-bent on freeing them all, ultimately ending up in Macon, Georgia.

On May 5 it was the POWs from the Averell raid on Salem, Virginia's, turn to move. They were rounded up and marched onto Cary Street, ready to head south. Polsley, Markbreit, McAdams, and Casdorph were lined up together.

Suddenly, Markbreit was singled out and sent down into Libby's subterranean dungeon. He had been chosen at random with three others to serve as hostages to prevent the execution of four Confederates captured in Kentucky. It was another tit-for-tat retribution by the Libby management.

Polsley immediately wrote to Union authorities as he was leaving Libby Prison regarding Markbreit's situation. Markbreit remained at Libby while his messmates marched away. It would be a long, hot summer during which time he wrote, "My situation could not be worse. I have become so weak and broken down from close confinement and want of food that I can hardly walk. Our daily ration consists of one-half pound of corn bread, one-half pound of boiled beans, and about two or three ounces of bacon...I cannot say how long we shall be able to live on such rations...."[312]

Markbreit would remain in the Libby dungeon until January 1865 before he was finally exchanged, his health broken. He would eventually recover from the ordeal and be appointed as the United States Minister to Bolivia by President Grant. He was the mayor of Cincinnati at the time of his death in 1909.

Bassett and McAdams marched away from Libby in another pack of POWs headed for the train, glancing back and looking at their infamous lodgings one last time before it passed out of sight. A crowd of Richmond citizens gathered and watched as hundreds of Yankees walked toward the railway depot. They were loaded onto boxcars, packed in like cattle. Bassett still had trouble walking and was torn with emotions about his escalating problems at home, about which he was helpless to do anything.

Two days later on May 7, Marshall, Page, Byers, and Hoffman were ordered up just after midnight and told to pack up and be ready to leave at a moment's notice.

"Richmond is not a safe place for prisoners," said Byers, "for the first time in nearly six months, I breathe the pure air of heaven. Oh how glorious, how delightful! Libby farewell; we will not forget you soon; we will remember you even in our dreams, and hope we may yet see you ornamented with the Stars and Stripes."[313]

THE SEVERAL HUNDRED POUNDS of black powder housed in barrel kegs mining the cellar bowels of Libby Prison, threatening everyone in the general vicinity, was secretly removed in May by order of General Winder after all the prison population had left.[314]

Hoffman would record in his diary, "All bustle and excitement, left Libby at daylight, good fresh air, feel better than in Libby. (They) put 44 of us in one box car and I got on top."

In the hot, stifling heat, it was poor Virginia pine-barren country that Hoffman observed slowly passing by from his perch on the top of the prison train box car as he traveled from Richmond to Danville.[315] The breeze cooled his face as he filled his lungs with a deep breath of fresh air, nervously facing an uncertain future.

Chapter Ten

Henry M. Fowler – 15th New Jersey
August 1862 to May 1864

COCOONED IN HIS BLANKET TO WARD off the cold, sixteen-year-old Corporal Henry M. Fowler awoke at dawn on Saturday, December 13, 1862. He and the rest of Company K, 15th New Jersey Volunteer Infantry, were encased in a dense fog just like the day before and camped in the remains of an orchard that had been heavily cratered by artillery fire.[316] Some of the men had bedded down curled up in the craters, hoping they would provide protection from injury should something explosive be thrown their way. The voices of Fowler's fellow soldiers could be heard speaking in hushed tones all around him. But so dense was the mist that he could barely see his outstretched palm.

The 15th was a Fowler family affair, with five Fowlers in the regiment, including Henry's brother, Private Albert G. Fowler and their forty-nine-year-old father Sergeant-Major John P. Fowler. Soldiers within the regiment whispered of nepotism behind the Fowlers' backs.

The 15th New Jersey was part of General Ambrose Burnside's Army of the Potomac, numbering 120,000 soldiers. The regiment was green with little battle experience. Their brigade was made up of six New Jersey regiments and quickly became known as the Jersey Brigade. The 15th had crossed the Rappahannock River over a pontoon bridge the day before and camped in the orchard remains on the west side of the river. Through the night the Fowlers had tried to sleep through the sounds of axe blows cutting away the nearby trees and brush, clearing the way for what would come. Being close to the river made it damp; when mixed with the December chill, fog was produced most mornings.

Out in front of them, at the top of the hill that rose up from the river to the west, was Robert E. Lee's Confederate army of Northern Virginia, along with a force of more than 75,000 men. Lieutenant General's Stonewall Jackson and James Longstreet's forces were closest to the Jersey Brigade's position. The tracks of the Richmond, Fredericksburg, and Potomac railroad marked the approximate location of the Confederate picket line. Down the hill, a short distance toward the river, was the Richmond Road, which ran parallel and close to the railroad tracks.

Fowler's regiment was ordered forward to a point just past Richmond Road to relieve the Union pickets that were located close to their Confederate counterparts along the railroad tracks. This was the first time they had seen any action, and they obeyed the order as inexperienced soldiers would, quickly standing up and marching upright in a tight military unit as if on parade toward the picket line. This was quickly answered by some very happy Confederate sharpshooters, who took advantage of the situation and fired on the foolish Yankees. Fowler and the rest of his comrades dove quickly to the ground and crawled on their bellies. The learning curve is quick when the lesson is unforgiving and deadly. They were lucky that no one was hit.[317]

In the dense fog the sounds of a massive army of men could be heard moving west, fellow Union soldiers coming up from behind them on either side. Soon the fog's fate was decided, and it quickly cleared. The sun shone brightly, revealing three Grand Divisions of the Union army—left, center, and right—more than 100,000 men strong. The army stretched for more than five miles, from the north of Fredericksburg to an area well below the town to the south. The 15th New Jersey was just a small part of the Left Division on the south end, located near a small creek called Deep Run that flowed back to the Rappahannock.

Once the fog cleared and they were able to see their enemy, Confederate artillery fire began raining down on the Union forces. The fighting went on all day, with Union forces attempting to climb the hill toward the crest. Looking down from a higher vantage point at the scrambling Yankees coming toward them from below gave the Rebels the upper hand. Yet, in the first few hours, the position of the Jersey Brigade was insulated by the fighting to either side of them. They used little of their ammunition, only occasionally firing at the enemy.

At around 3 p.m. things changed, and the 15th was ordered forward with the objective to capture a position at the railroad tracks, which was cut through the bank of the hill.

Under heavy fire members of the 4th and 15th New Jersey charged up the hill, pushing back the Confederate 6th North Carolina and taking their position, along with twenty-five Rebel prisoners.

All the soldiers took cover in the cut in the hill made by the railroad tracks. As the position was taken, Sergeant-Major John P. Fowler stood up on the tracks to survey the scene. Fowler was a tall man at six feet; a Rebel sharpshooter quickly had the easy target in his sights and fired. The bullet struck the elder Fowler in the thigh, severing his femoral artery. Both Henry and Albert rushed to their father's side as gunfire continued around them. Because they were pinned down in the cut on the hill made by the railroad tracks in the confusion of the moment and were unable to stem the massive flow of blood, their father was dead in less than five minutes.[318]

The railroad tracks they had just taken minutes before suddenly saw a Rebel counterattack by members the 54th and 57th North Carolina. The 15th New Jersey was forced to retreat to their original position along Richmond Road, leaving Sergeant-Major Fowler's body behind on the tracks.

"The Rebel pickets made a charge on ours and were met at 25 or 30 yards by a murderous fire from our boys...we lost 3 men killed and 10 wounded," seventeen-year-old Lieutenant Ellis S. Hamilton of Company E, and grandson of a former New Jersey Attorney General would write. "Sergeant Fowler's body was first captured by the Rebels and robbed of his watch and purse but not his saber."[319] The Rebels relinquished the body, and members of the 15th New Jersey quickly buried the deceased Sergeant-Major close to their new lines.

Sunday and Monday saw the Union attempt at Fredericksburg fail. The demoralized 15th New Jersey fell back to the ravine near the remains of an orchard where they had first camped and counted their losses. Some of the wounded went to a nearby house being used as a field hospital.

As the 15th prepared to retreat from south of Fredericksburg on the morning of

Tuesday, December 16, Sergeant-Major John P. Fowler's body was exhumed from its makeshift grave. When they moved out, his two sons accompanied the wagon carrying their father's body as it crossed the Union pontoon bridge over the Rappahannock. They would walk with the wagon for a few miles until they all reached White Oak Church, Virginia, where the regiment would camp. Henry and Albert watched the wagon disappear as the road crested a hill.[320] Then they both turned and slowly walked back to camp, feeling lost.

HENRY MEAD FOWLER WAS born on July 30, 1846, in New York City, the second son of John P. Fowler and Sarah Glover Fowler. By June 1861, the John P. Fowler family had grown to nine with the birth of twins, John and Julia. The entire brood lived in Hardyston, New Jersey, where John was a farmer as well as a lumberman, sporting a physique sculpted from constantly swinging an axe.

The extended Fowler family was quite large throughout New Jersey at the beginning of the Civil War. Their roots extended back before the Revolutionary War when ancestors served in the New York Militia. Henry's grandfather was the brother of Dr. Samuel Fowler, a well-known scientist/physician, US Congressman, and entrepreneur who developed one of the largest ore-producing facilities, located in Franklin, New Jersey.

In August 1861 Henry's father enthusiastically joined one of his cousins, also named John Fowler, in the 1st New Jersey Cavalry. John P. Fowler mustered in as Captain of Company M, which was made up of many fellow lumbermen from the area. Cousin John, who was also a Hardyston resident, joined the 1st New Jersey Cavalry as a second lieutenant in Company K, then became the regimental Quartermaster. John P. Fowler also brought along his oldest son Albert, who was just sixteen and only five-feet, five-inches tall but, with his father's genetics, was a rapidly growing young man.

The 1st New Jersey Cavalry's biggest problem when they finally came together as ten companies encamped near Washington, D.C., in September 1861 was that they were undisciplined and completely unprepared for military service. The regiment's commander, Colonel William Hasltead, was almost seventy years old and had no clue how to command a cavalry regiment. Confusing things further, the other officers did not understand how to shape their recruits into soldiers, and the recruits, preferring the comforts of life at home, didn't understand the concept of following orders. Though extremely patriotic in support of the Union, they were basically slobs, camping outdoors for the first time with no idea of what they were doing. Their camp was an unclean health hazard. Many enlisted men became sick from the lack of knowledge of the most basic sanitary requirements needed to keep hundreds of soldiers healthy.

One day for no particular reason Colonel William Halstead, the regiment's commander, simply left camp and never returned.[321] It was suggested that Quartermaster Fowler's brother, forty-three-year-old Colonel Samuel Fowler, assume the command of the wayward regiment. Though he helped in recruiting the men for the 1st New Jersey Cavalry, Colonel Fowler wasn't part of the regiment, and the idea of him as their new commander didn't go over well with the other officers.[322] Soon the name Fowler was persona non grata.

After several months of insubordination and court martial for disciplinary reasons, things had not improved, and the entire regiment was still unfit for duty. No division commander was interested in the roughly 1,000 incompetent soldiers, so they remained encamped where they first started, in military limbo. And soon it was 1862.

Quartermaster Fowler had had enough of the craziness of the 1st New Jersey Cavalry: "Things impossible and possible are expected of me; an order given one moment is contradicted the next, and everything that goes wrong is laid to Quartermaster Fowler."[323]He resigned on February 10.

Colonel Samuel Fowler
15th New Jersey
Volunteers
*Photographer and
date unknown*
*Department of Defense,
Adjutant General's Office
(Civil War),
Cartes-de-Visite, 1861-
1890s. New Jersey
State Archives,
Department of State*

His cousin, Captain John P. Fowler, was ordered before the Board of Examiners in Washington, D.C. Having no appetite for military discipline, he failed an examination for fitness to serve as an officer. [324] He quickly and quietly resigned as well, though his son Albert was stuck in the 1st New Jersey Cavalry until his father could figure a way out for him.

Both John Fowlers returned home to their respective families in Hardyston, New Jersey.

But this was not the end of the family's participation in the war. In July 1862 the Fowler clan decided again to give it a go. This time forty-three-year-old Colonel Samuel Fowler, the same man rejected by the 1st New Jersey Cavalry, was given the task by Governor Charles Smith Olden to recruit a regiment of ten companies of volunteers. It would become the 15th New Jersey Volunteer Infantry. Brother John, the former Quartermaster of the 1st New Jersey Cavalry, became a Second Lieutenant in Company K and by October had transferred to take command of the Jersey Brigade's ambulance corps.

Cousin John P. joined as Sergeant-Major of Company K and brought along his son Henry, who was just fifteen years old. Henry wouldn't turn sixteen until July 30, so they waited until August 25 to muster him in as a Corporal. John P.'s oldest son, seventeen-year-old Private Albert G. Fowler, would join his father and brother when he finally finagled a transfer out of the whacky 1st New Jersey Cavalry in October.

By the end of August 1862, the 15th New Jersey came together at Flemington, New Jersey, and was composed of thirty-eight officers and 909 enlisted men.[325]After training for most of September they were attached to the 1st Brigade, 1st Division, 6th Army Corps, Army of the Potomac which was beginning its Maryland campaign pursuing Robert E. Lee's Confederate army of Northern Virginia. The 15th New Jersey spent its time mainly in the rear of the massive army, seeing little to no action. Right as things got underway, typhoid fever struck several of the officers of the 15th, including its regimental commander Colonel Samuel Fowler. By November 1 he was so ill he had to be left behind at a home in Bakersville, Maryland, with a regimental doctor to watch over his health.[326]

On November 5 the Army of the Potomac saw the sacking of its commander, General George B. McClellan, and the naming of his successor, General Ambrose Burnside. Burnside immediately began planning a massive movement on Richmond that would begin with a fight with Robert E. Lee at Fredericksburg.

In December the 15th New Jersey found itself moving into place on the east side of

Fredericksburg, Virginia, along with more than 100,000 other Union soldiers, awaiting the arrival of pontoon bridges to allow them to pass over the Rappahannock. Tension was building, and while they waited, they could see Lee's army to the west, its numbers also building along the high ridge that ran parallel to the river, looking back across at them.

Finally, several pontoon bridges were in place, and thousands of soldiers began the orderly crossing of the river. It wouldn't be until December 12 that the 15th New Jersey crossed. John P. and his two sons marched over the pontoon bridge with the rest of their company. It was the last full day they would all be together; the next afternoon Henry and Albert would experience the shock of their father's death on the railroad tracks south of Fredericksburg.

Building a Pontoon Bridge at Fredericksburg
December 11, 1862
Alfred Rudolph Ward
Morgan collection of Civil War drawings
Library of Congress

While the Fowler boys mourned the loss of their father, Robert E. Lee's Army of Northern Virginia came away with a victory. In an area called Marye's Heights directly west of Fredericksburg, General Burnside ordered a bayonet charge toward the Confederate line, a stone wall at the foot of the heights. Protected behind the wall lay Confederate forces, all armed with rifles. The slaughter went on for hours with not one Union soldier making it to the wall. The blundering, indecisive strategic mistakes of General Burnside led to a crushing defeat for the Union forces.

IN THE AFTERMATH OF THE DEATH of their father, the Fowler brothers returned to camp. The entire regiment was stunned by the Army of the Potomac's disastrous loss in what was the 15th New Jersey's first real battle as the two Fowler brothers dealt with the disastrous loss of their father. The Union army was also trying to understand the epic failure; Burnside's forces at Fredericksburg had vastly outnumbered Lee's. Yet, Lee had won, and a depression set in all through the ranks of the Union side as winter approached. The 15th went into their winter quarters at White Oak Church, Virginia.

After the death of their Sergeant-Major, the 15th passed the hat and collected $150, which was sent to Sarah Glover Fowler, John P.'s widow. In addition to her two sons fighting in the regiment, there were seven younger children back home who were now her responsibility alone.

Just before the Battle of Fredericksburg, Sergeant-Major John P. Fowler had been in line for promotion to second lieutenant. Now the Governor of New Jersey gave the commission to his sixteen-year-old-son Henry, who became one of the youngest officers in the 15th New Jersey.[327] It was not taken well by some members of the regiment. In the *Hunterdon Republican*, Private William M. Thompson of Company G wrote that Fowler's promotion "shows the benefit of having influential relatives."[328]

In late January 1863 General Burnside decided to attempt some revenge on Robert E. Lee for the loss at Fredericksburg. Burnside thought that Lee wouldn't be expecting his attack since both armies were in winter quarters. He ordered the 15th New Jersey, along with 150,000 other Union soldiers who by then were warm and comfortable in their winter quarters, to head back west across the Rappahannock.

During the Civil War both armies basically placed the war on pause once winter came. There was a reason for this, besides being warm and comfortable. It was impossible in the horribly muddy road conditions of winter to efficiently move thousands of soldiers, wagons, horses, cannons, and everything else needed to wage war. So most large engagements were stopped during the winter.

General Burnside apparently didn't consider this and sent his army out anyway. Sure enough, the weather had turned the roads into rivers of mud, and the army bogged down for five days as Lee watched from his winter quarters to the west, no doubt chuckling to himself. Bogged down and stuck on muddy roads, after several days Burnside threw in a muddy towel. The debacle became forever known to his soldiers as the "Mud March."

The 15th New Jersey marched back in ankle-deep mud that covered most everything they owned and headed back to their winter quarters. Upon arrival, they discovered their camp had been ransacked and reduced to a mud pit for no particular reason by a Union cavalry regiment who had also participated in the Mud March. The depression within the regiment was even worse than after Fredericksburg. Several soldiers went so far as to inflict injury on themselves in order to get out of service and go home.[329]

At the end of January, General Joseph Hooker became the new commander of the Army of the Potomac, ending Burnside's disastrous command. Hooker was very popular with his soldiers, and spirits soon improved throughout the army.

Colonel Samuel Fowler, who was still suffering the effects of typhoid fever, rejoined the regiment for the Battle of Fredericksburg. Terribly weak, he was unfit for duty and was only a spectator to the battle. He accompanied his men on the Mud March but was not recovered fully from typhoid so was exposed to the cold, wet, and mud during the march, which likely did his condition no good. Unable to command, Samuel Fowler was mustered out of service in March 1863 and returned home. During this time the 15th decided to move the winter camp a short distance from its original location to a spot a little higher and less mud-prone. As an honor to their former commander, the new digs became known as Camp Fowler.[330]

At the end of April 1863, it was decided to make another go at Fredericksburg. The 15th New Jersey left their winter quarters with 447 enlisted men, thirteen officers, and five field and staff.[331] Their ranks had certainly diminished in the last eight months.

General Hooker took most of his army around Fredericksburg to the northwest, crossing the Rappahannock and eventually coming in behind Robert E. Lee's position near Chancellorsville, Virginia. The 15th New Jersey was left behind just south of Fredericksburg along with the First Corps.

They all once again crossed the Rappahannock over the now-familiar pontoon bridge at Franklin's crossing south of Fredericksburg, setting up pickets within 400 feet of the Confederate line. Both sides dug in with rifle pits. After a couple of days up front on picket duty, the Jersey Boys were relieved and pulled back to the river. Soon an order by General Hooker was read to all the regiments; it charged up the troops in advance of the battle to come.

On May 2 the 15th re-manned the rifle trenches, and soon cannonading could be heard coming from Chancellorsville just eight miles away. It didn't go well, and Major General Joseph Hooker was wounded, suffering a concussion that knocked him senseless for the next few days. By day's end Union forces were on the defensive.

For the 15th and the rest of the division, their battle began on Sunday, May 3, with an assault on the Confederate positions west of Fredericksburg; by 11 a.m. the army had taken Salem Heights. By late afternoon, having marched several miles west, they arrived near Salem Church, crossing into some cleared fields toward a peaceful-looking wooded area. At about 100 feet from the edge of the forest, the Rebels hiding inside opened fire. The 15th charged in and pushed into the woods about 100 yards, coming to within thirty yards of the enemy positions. The battle would go on until dark with the 15th being relieved several times, only to charge into the fray again.

In the middle of the fight, Company K's Lieutenant John Fowler, brother of the 15th's former commander Samuel, was severely injured in his shoulder. Advised to go to the rear to seek medical attention, he said, "No, I will stick with my men."[332] As the fighting intensified, he was hit a second time. "He was cheering on his men; he was seen to pick up a rifle and shoot five or six times. He was struck in the left side, near the heart, and fell to the ground dead."[333] As the fighting continued, his body was left in the field of battle and eventually buried where it fell. The rest of the regiment fell back, carrying the wounded, and camped for the night in the open battlefield.

Reforming a picket line on Monday morning, May 4, they provided support to various batteries as the day progressed. The Battle of Chancellorsville was another loss for Union forces, and they began withdrawing to the east side of Fredericksburg. The 15th crossed back over the Rappahannock once again in the early morning hours of May 5, returning to where it had winter quartered near White Oak Church.[334]

Over six months the Fowler family's ranks in the 15th New Jersey had been reduced to two: Henry, now a lieutenant, and brother Albert, a private. At Salem Heights the total number of soldiers in the ranks of the 15th had been reduced by one third in just five days with forty-four killed, 126 wounded, and four missing.[335]

The Chancellorsville Campaign was over, and another Union general commanding the Army of the Potomac had been defeated due to a series of bad decisions. Once again, Robert E. Lee had chalked up another Confederate victory with an army half the size of his enemy. Soon Lee would plan an offensive move toward Pennsylvania. In the meantime thousands of Union soldiers slogged back across the Rappahannock to the same positions they had been in just a week earlier, their number diminished as they were looking back across the river at the same Rebels.

At the start of June 1863, Lee's Army of Northern Virginia began to march toward Pennsylvania. The 15th New Jersey was left along the Rappahannock, where they again crossed at Franklin's Crossing on the pontoon bridge and set up pickets, did some reconnaissance, dug in, and traded occasional shots with the Confederates. So familiar were the two enemies with each other by this point that the regimental bands often serenaded each other at night.[336]

BY MID-JUNE EVERYTHING changed. The entire Jersey brigade was ordered to close up shop and get back across the river. This time they removed the pontoon bridges and loaded them into wagons as they left. But in the confusion of moving eastward, not everyone got the message. Albert and another of Company K's privates, Lewis L. Kent, had slept through the night in a shelter tent on the west riverbank, oblivious that with the pontoon bridges removed their only means of crossing the Rappahannock had disappeared. The next morning they were roused from their sleep by a Confederate officer who peeked into their tent and greeted them with a good morning. The dazed men became prisoners of war and were sent south to Richmond.[337]

This left Henry as the last Fowler in the 15th.

A few days later the 15th New Jersey was on the march. On June 18 they were outside of Washington, D.C., at Fairfax Court House, then went onward to Hyattstown, Maryland, arriving June 28. Upon arrival they received the news that the Army of the Potomac's commander, Joseph Hooker, had resigned and was being replaced by Major General George G. Meade. Lee's army had made its way to the Shenandoah Valley, then moved northeast reaching Chambersburg, Pennsylvania, on June 28. The Rebels continued moving in Pennsylvania, setting up for the showdown at Gettysburg.

On Wednesday, July 1, the 15th New Jersey was encamped at Manchester, Maryland. In ten days they had marched more than 120 miles while twenty-five miles to their northwest the Battle of Gettysburg had begun. On Thursday morning, July 2, they marched to Littlestown, Pennsylvania, nine miles from the heat of the battle. They could hear the sounds of artillery and gunfire in the distance. At the end of the day they were marched to a hill just north of Little Round Top where they occupied a position on the southern end of the Union line.[338]

From that position as Friday, July 3 dawned, every indication was that they would soon see action. At around 2 p.m. Pickett's Charge[339] began to their north, announcing itself with the horrific sounds of battle resonating down the line. Smoke and dust rose in the distance. After about an hour came the culmination of the Battle of Gettysburg; then, everything got quiet.

On Saturday, July 4, some of the 15th New Jersey went out on picket duty and moved through the battlefields, stunned by the carnage all around. By evening the entire regiment was on burial detail, seeing firsthand the sights and smells of the Battle of Gettysburg. That afternoon and into the evening a heavy rainstorm hit Gettysburg—a punctuation to the storm of battle witnessed there over the last few days. It cleansed the landscape, soaking Henry and the rest of the men of the 15th New Jersey.[340]

On Sunday, July 5, the Jersey Brigade moved out, leading Meade's forces southwest in cautious pursuit of Lee's army. The next day another brigade took the front, and the

Jersey Boys moved to the rear. Both armies had suffered greatly at Gettysburg, their numbers diminished by the dead and wounded. Through the rest of July the Jersey Brigade followed as part of the Army of the Potomac on a route south through Maryland and into Northern Virginia, paralleling the movement of Lee in the Shenandoah Valley and finally settling in around Warrenton, Virginia, on July 25. They would remain there through much of August as Union forces recovered from Gettysburg.

In mid-September they moved twenty miles southwest to Culpeper, Virginia, and on October 5 another twelve miles down to Rapidan, Virginia. On October 13 Albert, who had been captured in May, was exchanged and returned to Company K. He was greeted by his brother Henry at Mitchell's Station, Virginia.[341] Private Fowler told his comrades tales of his miserable existence through the heat of the summer as a POW at Belle Island on the James River in Richmond. Being a POW for almost four months at the hands of the Rebels was the worst experience of his life. He was happy to be back, even if it wasn't actually home. Henry listened to his brother's story with keen interest and noticed how much thinner he was.

For the remainder of 1863, the Army of the Potomac and the Army of Northern Virginia would test each other in minor clashes. The last was an attempt at Mine Run, Virginia, in late November.

The 15th New Jersey went into winter quarters near Brandy Station, along with the rest of the Army of the Potomac, about twenty miles northwest of Fredericksburg in early December. They would remain there until April 1864.

Time was spent trying to stay battle-ready, drilling and recovering from over a year spent tramping over Northern Virginia, Maryland, and Pennsylvania. The 15th also was indirectly involved in the Kilpatrick "Grand Raid" at the end of February, tasked with marching southwestward to Culpeper Court House as part of a diversionary tactic, hoping to draw the Rebels' attention. They witnessed Custer's cavalry, 1,500 strong, as they galloped on past through their lines on their way to Charlottesville, then saw them return mud-covered and miserable a few days later. The 15th reached their destination, mud-covered themselves, and turned back and tramped through the snow the six miles back to Brandy Station and back into their winter quarters.

March 1864 marked the arrival of newly-promoted Lieutenant-General Ulysses S. Grant, who now commanded all the armies of the United States. General Meade still retained the command of the Army of the Potomac, but Grant arrived and shared his headquarters, which meant that Grant scrutinized everything Meade did. The Army of the Potomac's division were all juggled about. The Jersey Brigade, made up of the 1st, 2nd, 3rd and 15th New Jersey Infantry regiments, now added two additional regiments, the 4th and 10th New Jersey Infantry.

As spring came, drilling to stay sharp continued, but the men did find time for a little relaxation. The 15th New Jersey was able to put up a group of athletes from among the regiment to form a base ball[342] team. They played this new game against other regiments also in winter quarters.

On May 3, 1864, the 15th New Jersey were headed for an area known as the Wilderness, a dark, dense forest located south of the Rapidan River and north of Spotsylvania Court House where the Kilpatrick raid had passed just two months earlier.

For two days—from 5 a.m. on Thursday, May 5, through the morning of Saturday, May 7—the two armies with more than 180,000 men under Ulysses S. Grant and Robert E. Lee pounded each other. At times the fighting was so intense that the thick forest caught fire, and wounded men lying among the dense growth and unable to move were burned alive.

In the early morning fog of May 6, Captain Ellis S. Hamilton awoke. As he stood up, he was immediately hit by a Minié ball that passed through both thighs.[343] The 15th New Jersey took some additional casualties and was surrounded by intense fighting. But a direct attack never came. By nightfall they pulled back and took up a defensive position.

The next morning, Saturday, May 7, dawned hot with clear skies. While some skirmishing still continued, the Battle of the Wilderness was over, resulting in a draw, even though once again the Union army outnumbered the Confederate army by almost two to one. But instead of retreating away from Lee, Grant ordered his army forward toward the Army of Northern Virginia. The Army of the Potomac was playing offense and moved about fifteen miles south toward the crossroads known as Spotsylvania Court House. Robert E. Lee anticipated the move and made it down to the crossroads first, erecting formidable earthworks north of the crossroads.

On Sunday the 15th marched through Chancellorsville, then turned south. In the distance they could hear the sounds of fighting.

At the beginning of the Battle of Spotsylvania Court House on May 9, Major General John Sedgwick, the commander of the VI Corps, of which the 15th was part, was killed-in-action by sharpshooters. Sedgwick was directing the placement of artillery positions, and the sharpshooters were approximately 1000 yards away from the General and his staff. His reported last words were: "They couldn't hit an elephant at this distance."[344] He was hit below his left eye and never regained consciousness.

The focus of their attention in the early evening of May 10 was the Confederate entrenchment with a salient point that wrapped around the terrain known as Laurel Hill. From this entrenched, raised position, the Rebels looked out from three sides onto the surrounding open field some 600 yards wide. From above, the bulging, curved defensive position had the appearance of a Muleshoe. The entrenchment also featured an abatis, a mass of felled trees with branches sharpened and placed in front of the fortifications that acted like organic barbed wire.[345]

Fighting for the strategic position began at around 6 p.m. when twelve Union regiments totaling 5000 men charged the Muleshoe. The men at the front of the charge were killed instantly by Rebel gunfire. Union forces succeeded on breaching the salient but were then pushed back into the open field when the Confederates mounted a counterattack, and soon Union forces were ordered to retreat.

On Thursday, May 12, another attempt to take the Muleshoe was made, this time by 20,000 Union soldiers. The first wave of the attack that began at 4:30 a.m., in the driving rain, was aimed at the center of the Muleshoe. The Yankees successfully made it over the salient, and for a time, split the Confederate army. The Rebels responded with another counterattack, and it was the 15th New Jersey's turn to join the battle, charging the Muleshoe as part of a second wave of attack.

THE 15TH WAS POSITIONED behind the first wave of soldiers in the woods watching the battle at the Muleshoe. When the first attack occurred, they moved forward into position ready to charge. It set the stage for what was forever known as the worst battle in the regiment's history. "Terrific day of awful, murderous conflict! Combine the horrors of many battlefields, bring them into a single day and night of twenty-four hours, and the one of May 12th includes them all," wrote the regimental chaplain, Alanson A.

Haines.

"As soon as we appeared, charging over the open plain, they poured upon us their deadly, concentrated fire," said Chaplain Haines. "In the short space of time required to cross the flat, two hundred men were stretched lifeless, or helpless with wounds, upon the ground."

The 15th raced across the open field, soaked by the rain. When they reached the abatis, they got tangled up, all the while taking on fire. Finally, they cleared through the abatis's debris and charged up and over the Muleshoe's embankments. All the way men fell, either slipping in the mud or hit by gunfire and killed instantly or wounded. The Rebels' second line further on the earthworks continued to fire on the Yankees coming over the salient. Henry Fowler was hit in the knee and fell to the ground on the inside of the Muleshoe.

Spotsylvania Court House 1864
Photographer unknown

The 15th was in a terrible position at a bend in the Muleshoe known as the "Bloody Angle," fighting face to face with Rebel and Yankee shooting and bayoneting each other. "One man was wounded in the charge," said Chaplain Haines, "but reached the work and laid down upon it, with his head at such an elevation that the bullets of the enemy could strike him, and the whole cavity of his skull was filled with leaden missiles."[346]

It was an impossible position to maintain, with too many casualties; dead bodies were piled layers deep on top of each other. The 15th New Jersey was ordered to fall back. The fight at the Muleshoe salient seemed like an eternity but had only taken a half hour.

"No experience during the whole time the 15th was in service was more destructive than the half hour, from ten o'clock to half-past ten, of the morning of May 12th," said Chaplain Haines. "Forty bodies, or nearly one-fifth of the whole regiment, lay on the breastwork, in the ditch, or in the open space in front."[347]

The 15th New Jersey's casualties from the Battle of Spotsylvania Court House were seventy-one killed, 157 wounded, and thirty-six captured.[348]

When it was over the next morning at 3 a.m., the battle had raged for almost twenty hours.[349]Henry Fowler had somehow survived the unsurvivable. Lying on the ground inside the salient, at some point during the day he managed to crawl deeper into the Muleshoe to get away from the carnage, only to be captured by the Rebels as they withdrew and formed a new line.

In the morning light Henry, who was now a POW, was taken to Spotsylvania Court House with the other captured Yankees, many of whom were also wounded. He found himself reclining against a pillar of the building in a daze, looking at his wounded knee and trying to wrap his head around what had just happened. A Confederate surgeon was making his rounds, doing triage among the wounded. He slowly made his way up to Henry, giving his knee a quick glance.

The doctor told Fowler he was gonna have to take the leg off.

Fowler pleaded with the man to not take his leg.[350]

In one of the doctor's hands was a bottle of chloroform, in the other a rag. He doused the rag with the liquid and held it over Henry's mouth and nose. Soon everything went black.

Miles away Henry's brother Albert ran back to the woods where the 15th had been staged prior to the bloody battle on the Muleshoe. What he had seen would be forever burned into his memory. He frantically searched for his younger brother Henry but couldn't find him.

The next morning after exhaustion finally let him sleep, Albert tried to process the enormity of what he had experienced. He had witnessed the death of his father the year before, and now, as far as a he could tell after looking through all the hospital tents, he came to the conclusion that his brother Henry was likely one of those bodies lying dead atop the salient. With Henry missing, now Albert was the last Fowler remaining in the 15th.

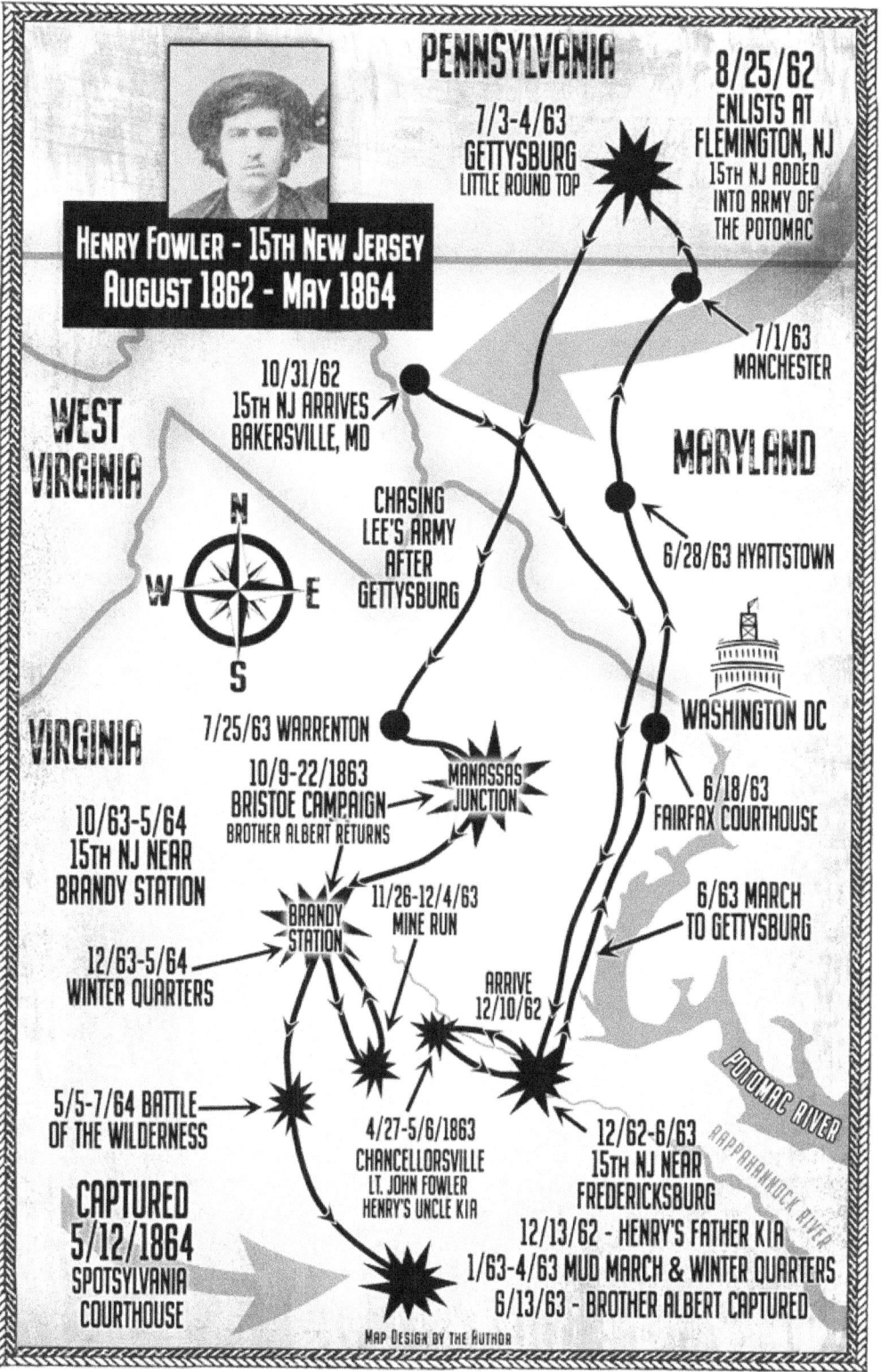

Henry Fowler – 15th New Jersey
August 1862 – May 1864

PENNSYLVANIA

8/25/62 ENLISTS AT FLEMINGTON, NJ
15TH NJ ADDED INTO ARMY OF THE POTOMAC

7/3-4/63 GETTYSBURG
LITTLE ROUND TOP

7/1/63 MANCHESTER

10/31/62 15TH NJ ARRIVES BAKERSVILLE, MD

WEST VIRGINIA

MARYLAND

6/28/63 HYATTSTOWN

CHASING LEE'S ARMY AFTER GETTYSBURG

N W E S

VIRGINIA

7/25/63 WARRENTON

10/9-22/1863 BRISTOE CAMPAIGN
BROTHER ALBERT RETURNS

MANASSAS JUNCTION

WASHINGTON DC

6/18/63 FAIRFAX COURTHOUSE

10/63-5/64 15TH NJ NEAR BRANDY STATION

BRANDY STATION

11/26-12/4/63 MINE RUN

6/63 MARCH TO GETTYSBURG

12/63-5/64 WINTER QUARTERS

ARRIVE 12/10/62

5/5-7/64 BATTLE OF THE WILDERNESS

4/27-5/6/1863 CHANCELLORSVILLE
LT. JOHN FOWLER HENRY'S UNCLE KIA

12/62-6/63 15TH NJ NEAR FREDERICKSBURG

POTOMAC RIVER

RAPPAHANNOCK RIVER

CAPTURED 5/12/1864 SPOTSYLVANIA COURTHOUSE

12/13/62 - HENRY'S FATHER KIA
1/63-4/63 MUD MARCH & WINTER QUARTERS
6/13/63 - BROTHER ALBERT CAPTURED

MAP DESIGN BY THE AUTHOR

Chapter Eleven

POWs in the Heart of the South
May 1864 to July 1864

AS THE TRAIN ARRIVED IN THE DANVILLE, Virginia depot, Hoffman jumped down from the top of one of the boxcars, joining the stream of hundreds of other former Libby POWs marching into Danville's prisoner-of-war camp located in the center of town. It was Sunday, May 8. The trip from Richmond had taken almost twenty-four hours on terrible rails, with the locomotive huffing and puffing, hauling the loaded boxcars behind them at barely twelve miles per hour.[351]

The Danville prison camp was made up of six brick buildings, former tobacco and cotton warehouses appropriately numbered "1" through "6" overlooking the Dan River. As Bassett hobbled along in a crowd of fellow POWs, along with his messmate from Libby, Lieutenant Henry Crawford, and several other Illinois officers, he thought the buildings looked similar in some ways to Libby. Suddenly, Bassett collapsed to the ground. His stay in the notorious Libby dungeon had broken him, and in his weakened state his body just gave out and fell in a heap. His fellow POWs stopped and helped him to his feet, one standing on either side supporting him as they continued their march.[352] He wasn't the only officer from more than 1,000 ragged men who would collapse on that day. Each time fellow POWs would help the men back up. Months of inadequate food and shelter had a cumulative effect on the body and soul.

McAdams and the rest of the West Virginia POW contingency happily stretched their legs after the ride in the jammed, stifling boxcar, though soon they would all groan at the overcrowded conditions they were subjected to at Danville.

Marshall, Page, and Byers all joined Hoffman as he walked, looking skeptically at their new digs from the outside. "Put five hundred in one building, very crowded, poor accommodations...got meat for the first time since April 1st," said Hoffman. "We have not enough room to spread our blankets."[353]

Meat for the first time in more than a month was a reason to celebrate. As they filed into the building, they didn't know if this new home was to be permanent. It turned out it was just a temporary stopping point. On Thursday, May 12, all the POWs were awakened at 2:30 a.m., marched in the rain back to the train depot, and loaded like wet rats onto cattle cars. As the sun rose, the prison train left Danville and was soon in North Carolina.

Once again, it was painfully slow travel because of the poor railbeds. This new section of the Confederate railroad, designed as a shortcut to the south, was not finished. At sunset the men got off the train and were marched by armed guards five miles to where the tracks began again. Then at midnight they got back on another set of railcars, arriving in Greensboro, North Carolina, at sunrise on Friday, May 13. They changed trains again and pulled into Charlotte, North Carolina, around 5 p.m.

EARLIER ON FRIDAY THE 13TH, at Spotsylvania Court House, Virginia, 300 miles northeast of the POW train making its way to Charlotte, North Carolina, Lieutenant

Henry Fowler groggily awoke. It was his lucky day. His body quickly jumped with a panicked start as he looked down at his injured leg. It was still there. The pant leg was cut open and revealed a dirty, bloody bandage on his wounded knee; he was in some pain but would manage. The Rebel doctor hadn't amputated his leg after all.[354] Even though he was now a POW, this was the best news of his life.

The battle his regiment had fought at the Muleshoe salient north of Spotsylvania Court House the day before had pushed the Confederate army backwards a little—a soft counterpunch by General Grant saying that this time the Union army wasn't retreating.

"Let's go, Yanks," yelled the Rebels at their prisoners. Fowler forced himself up onto his feet, grimacing while picking up a stick to act as a crutch. He hobbled along with other prisoners while the more injured men were loaded into wagons. They began a march southwest headed for Gordonsville, Virginia, some forty miles away, to a train that would take them into the deep south. It would take the prisoners until late Saturday, May 14, to walk to Gordonsville and be loaded onto boxcars. They would arrive late the next day Sunday, May 15, in Lynchburg, Virginia.

THE LIBBY POWs WERE MAKING progress along the Confederate railway system headed south. They left Charlotte, North Carolina, soaking wet once again in the pouring rain, at 1:30 a.m. on Saturday, May 14, traveling all day and arriving in Columbia, South Carolina, after dark. Changing to yet another train, they loaded into some very tightly packed boxcars and traveled overnight Saturday and all the next day, Sunday, May 15, arriving in Augusta, Georgia, at 6 p.m. In Augusta they were mercifully unpacked out of what had become their boxcar prison and allowed to camp overnight in the cars of another train with the doors open. At least the train wasn't moving, and they had dry blankets.

The POW train was abuzz with the news that Sherman's army was also in Georgia; they wouldn't have known that he was fighting the Battle of Resaca that day, about 200 miles from the POW train. But knowing the Union army was relatively near raised the men's spirits; some may have thought that perhaps the time remaining spent as prisoners would be short-lived.

Finally, at 4 p.m. on Monday, May 16, the train left Augusta and made an overnight run to its final destination at Macon, Georgia. Since they had left Richmond, the trip had offered many opportunities for the men to escape. It was a risky proposition. A few men were successful in jumping off the train at just the right moment. Some were seen jumping from the cars and shot at by the Rebel guards; firing their weapons from the moving train was challenging and didn't meet with much success. Some were immediately recaptured; only a lucky few got away. Those that did found themselves in the heart of Rebel territory, unsure of exactly where they were and hundreds of miles from Union forces. Still, planning to escape, as well as actually executing the plan, was another way to raise one's spirits. Sometime during the night of the last leg into Macon, Page of the 5th Iowa and Lieutenant John W. Wright of the 10th Iowa jumped off the train and escaped together.

"Page escaped!" recorded Hoffman in his diary.[355] His other friends from the 5th Iowa didn't learn of the escape until they all arrived in Macon at 8 a.m. on Tuesday, May 17. It caused great excitement. Somewhere on the roughly 120-mile train line that ran from Augusta to Macon, Page and Wright were free men, trying to figure out how to get north without being caught. Between them and the Union lines stood Milledgeville, at the time the capital of Georgia, as well as Atlanta. It wasn't going to be easy.

In Macon the men were marched a few blocks to Camp Oglethorpe. The locals were not exactly thrilled at the prospect of more than 1,000 dirty Yankees being relocated into their town. "COMING—We learn from railroad authorities that twenty-four carloads of Federal officers will arrive in Macon this (Tuesday) morning...These are the same started some time ago from Richmond for Danville, and at present writing have reached Augusta, on the way here. As the last Richmond papers announced the exchange of prisoners resumed, we hope it will not be long before they are sent home,"[356] reported the *Macon Daily Telegraph*.

The exchange of prisoners had come to an end, with just a few exceptions, when General Grant, who was firmly against the concept of exchange, took control of the Union army. "Every man we hold, when released on parole or otherwise, becomes an active soldier against us at once either directly or indirectly. If we commence a system of exchange which liberates all prisoners taken, we will have to fight on until the whole South is exterminated. If we hold those caught they amount to no more than dead men," said Grant.[357]

The next day the Macon newspaper would add four more train cars of POWs to the story: "Twenty-seven carloads of Federal officers arrived here yesterday morning and are now at Camp Oglethorpe. Thirty-two of the gentlemen escaped on the way, as was supposed about Millen."[358]

Located in the first third of the route of the Central of Georgia Railway from Augusta to Macon, Georgia, and Millen, Georgia, was where the spur line to Augusta met the main line from Macon to Savannah. When the train slowed to take on water or wood for the boiler, it offered an opportunity for some men to escape. Based on the trip time of sixteen hours, it meant that Page and Wright would have jumped from the train around 9 to 10 p.m. on Monday night, May 16. Thirty-two Union escapees tramping their way through Central Georgia made for large, very visible targets. Even though the men had a good ten-hour head start, the Rebels began successfully tracking them all with bloodhounds.

On May 23, six days after jumping the train in the middle of the night west of

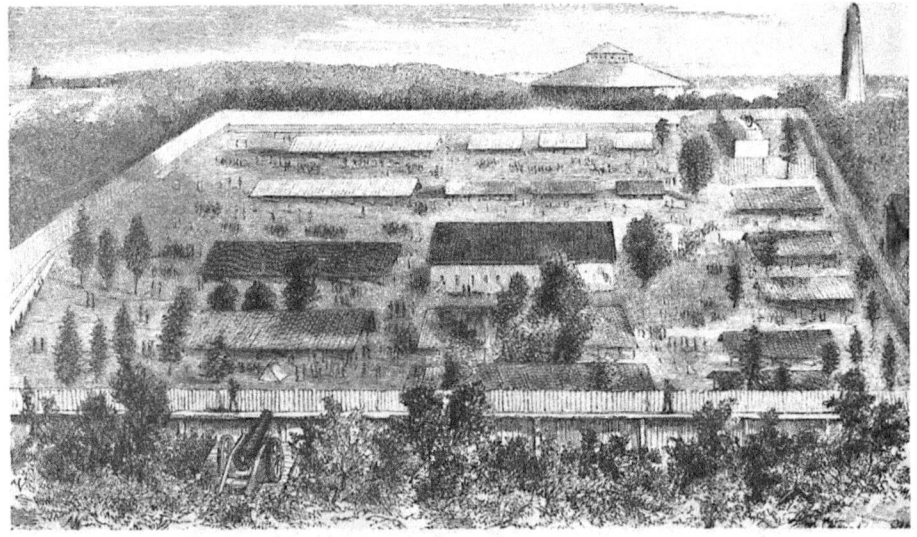

Camp Oglethorpe; Macon, Georgia[413]

Augusta, Page and Wright were recaptured. They had given it a go, but the Rebels were thick in the middle of Georgia, close to the state capital of Milledgeville.

CAMP OGLETHORPE REPLACED LIBBY PRISON as the POW camp used by the Confederacy to hold Union officers. The idea was that it would be less of a target for the Union forces, being so deep into the south. The enormity of what was about to happen in Georgia over the next three months had not been considered by the Rebels. Atlanta fall to the Yankees? Impossible!

The camp was an open stockade and occupied a square spit of land of almost three acres. It was located on the southwest end of Macon on the site used as the town's fairgrounds and militia training since the 1840s. "We were placed in a sand pit," said Byers. "We have no barracks of any kind, and at present our shelter from the sun or rain, is our blankets—stretched over pine sticks...the weather is beginning to get very warm."[360] The camp's perimeter featured an outer twelve-foot-tall fence. Mounted on the outer fence, three feet below its top, was a platform that allowed the guards to patrol around the perimeter looking down into the prison camp. Fifteen feet inside of this was a six-foot-high inner fence known as the dead line. Prisoners were not allowed to approach within six feet of this fence. In one corner of the camp was a spring, fed by a creek, which was used for drinkable water. Downstream from the spring was the open sewer with boards strategically placed over the creek to form an "outdoor privy." There was one seventy-by-forty-foot one-story frame building in the center of the camp and several long sheds sixty to one hundred feet long by sixteen feet wide that provided shelter but were not enclosed.[361]

More than 1,000 Union POW officers were marched out of the Macon railroad depot in two long lines all the way to the prison camp. The mass of humanity was "ragged, unwashed and unshaven, with rags of dirty parts of undergarments barely covering them, with repulsive unhealed wounds, sores and such large wolfish eyes," commented Luther G. Billings, the recently captured paymaster of the paddlewheel steamer *USS Water Witch,*[362] on his first impression of his fellow prisoners.[363]

Organizing the prisoners into squads of 100 with individual messes of twenty men helped control the distribution of the meager food rations.[364] The officers tried to stay close to the men from their respective regiments or divisions or, like in Libby, relative to where they were captured. Bassett and Crawford of the 53rd Illinois formed their mess with other Illinois regiments captured around Jackson, Mississippi. Marshall, Page, Hoffman, and Byers of the 5th Iowa grouped with others from the Battle of Chattanooga. Finally, Posley, McAdams, and Casdorph of the 8th and 10th West Virginia regiments paired with Army of the Potomac POWs.

WHEN THEY REACHED ITS ENTRANCE and passed under the sign reading "Camp Oglethorpe," they were startled and stared in disbelief. Standing next to the front gate, looking over the throng of arriving prisoners, was their much-hated former Libby commandant, Major Thomas P. Turner. Grumbling could be heard throughout the packed-in POWs.

"This human monster stood at the gate to count us as we passed in," said one prisoner.[365]

Bassett felt his blood pressure rise as he passed by, glancing at Turner with disbelief. Was that bastard still going to be in charge of their lives? Luckily, Bassett and the rest of the POWs would soon find out that their much-despised former commandant was only visiting Macon temporarily.

Turner was at Camp Oglethorpe on a grand inspection tour of all the Georgia prisons. He had just toured Andersonville and, of course, had found its conditions to his liking, meeting with Captain Henry Wirz who had taken over the position of commandant in late March.[366] He ended his tour at Camp Oglethorpe just as his former Libby prisoners arrived in Macon. It was merely a cruel coincidence. The next day Turner boarded a train and returned to Richmond to give a report to his commander, Brigadier General Winder, that all was well. Left in charge as commandant at Camp Oglethorpe was Captain W. Kemper Tabb, who had been with the train that had hauled the men from Libby.[367] Tabb would manage to raise the ire of all his prisoners, employing sadistic protocols similar to Turner.

The next day, Tuesday, May 24, Hoffman would record in his diary: "Fried mush for breakfast, one hundred fresh fish arrive, one man died in hospital, funeral preached this P.M. Baked Austin a cake, Page and Lieut. Wright returned from their escape, looks for rain." So numbing had Hoffman's existence as a POW become that he noted Page and Wright's return as if they had taken a short vacation and were just being welcomed back home.

Around the same time that Page and Wright were brought into Camp Ogelthorpe, Henry Fowler and the other officers taken prisoner at the Battle of Spotsylvania Court House finally arrived in Macon. They had traveled by train from a Confederate prison in Lynchburg, Virginia, and headed to Danville, following the same route down to Georgia that the Libby prisoners had taken. Lucky for Fowler, his leg injury was on the mend and had not become infected. He walked through the main entrance of Camp Oglethorpe with just a slight limp to the sounds of "Fresh Fish."

With no shelter, the month of June was spent by the wave of newly arrived prisoners securing building materials and constructing sheds to serve as barracks. They also immediately began digging tunnels and planning to check out of Camp Oglethorpe at their earliest opportunity. Bassett kept himself busy with the rest of the men, building a raised open structure with a roof to protect them from rain. His prior tunnel experience also helped to keep his mind occupied. The move from Richmond to Macon had disrupted the regular mail and package supply lines. In the confusion of war, some letters and packages would never find their way to their captives' addressees. Bassett's link to the outside world and news from home came from his sister. Letters from his wife, Lottie, had become few and far between. The volume of mail that got through in July was tiny; most prisoners received nothing.[368]

"We had been hard at work digging a tunnel by which to make our escape," said Byers. "It was four feet under the ground, an extended under the dead line and by the sentry-boxes, a distance of seventy-five feet It was ready for use, when some spy revealed it, and we were discovered-weeks of labor thus being lost."[369]

When the tunnels were discovered by the Rebels, Commandant Tabb had two twelve-pound cannons mounted into two corners of the perimeter fence pointing inward toward the POWs.[370]

Shortly after, in a fortuitous change, Tabb was replaced as commandant by Captain George C. Gibbs, tasked with the repair and discipline of Camp Oglethorpe.[371] In quick order, Gibbs became another hated Rebel authority figure to the POWs as well. They soon made him a colonel.

On a mid-June evening Byers went down to the part of the spring that served as the camp's privy to explore his escape options. As he walked in the darkness, a sentry on the platform behind the perimeter fence watched his movements, taking aim. Another man, twenty-eight-year-old Lieutenant Otto Gerson of the 45th New York,[372] approached Byers. "I had not stood there long when Capt. Grierson (*sic*) came down and stopped near the spring by me," said Byers. "He had only been there a minute when the flash of a gun blazed out of the darkness...he only gasped 'water, water.'" The Captain was dead.

Deep down Byers knew the bullet had been meant for him. "I am determined to escape from this prison hole, or lose my life in the attempt," said Byers.[373]

He would soon get his chance to escape.

HOFFMAN SPENT MUCH of his summer suffering from intestinal indignities, namely, dysentery. A large portion of the camp was dealing with the same malady, along with typhoid fever and scurvy. An increased numbers of prisoners were dying, Hoffman, who was volunteering as a nurse in the prison hospital, recorded the simple progress of the disease, leading to the death of Lieutenant Lewis C. Priest of the 72nd Indiana in his diary. On June 24 he was very sick; by June 28, at 2:30 PM, Priest died. The next day, June 29, he was buried on a ridge southwest of the camp that was used for burials.[374]

When he wasn't fighting illness, Hoffman was carving chess pieces from bone and scraps of wood, anything to pass the time. It was the steamy doldrums of summer, Macon in July. Life as a POW was monotonous, and the heat just added to the suffering. Most of the prisoners in Camp Oglethorpe were bored out of their skulls. Every day was the same; it started with roll call at 9 a.m. The same tricks played at Libby to screw up the count were played at Oglethorpe. There was constant chatter about when exchanges might begin again. For Bassett, July 12 began his second year as a POW. It was depressing, almost breaking his spirits. But he always held the prospect of being exchanged in his mind, and with that came hope.

In mid-June Byers had conceived an audacious, risky plan of escape and began to implement it. Through an amazing stroke of luck, he had somehow traded for a rebel uniform, which fit him like a glove. On July 16 right after roll call, carrying a paper and pencil like an important Rebel soldier involved in tabulating the count, Byers convincingly walked to the prison stockade gate and knocked on its door. In the distance his fellow 5th Iowans—Marshall, Page, and Hoffman—watched. hoping they wouldn't soon hear the report of a gun.

"What do you want?" asked the Corporal.

"We are bothered about the rolls, Sir, and I am going out to see the officer of the guard."

The Corporal stepped aside and, just like that, Byers walked out of Camp Oglethorpe heading into Macon. The prison was located on the south end of town, and Byers strolled like a soldier on furlough northwest, straight down the middle of Pine Street through the heart of Macon, taking in all the sights. Byers knew he had to get out of town and head north. He spent the next two days in cornfields and swamps, making his way along the route of the northbound Macon and Western Railroad. When a train made a stop to refuel close to where he was hiding, he jumped on board and was soon comfortably seated, heading toward Atlanta.

"Who are you...Let me have your fare, sir!" the train conductor asked.

"A Confederate soldier, sir, of the Ninth Alabama Infantry, on my way to Atlanta, to join my regiment," answered Byers, "I am a Southern soldier, out of money, and cannot pay you; but I must ride to Atlanta. Besides, you do not dare put a soldier off the train." Byers' heart was pounding in his chest. The conductor rolled his eyes and continued to the next passenger.

In the early-morning hours before daylight of Monday, July 17, the train pulled into the center of Atlanta. As the sun rose Byers was startled to find that the train yard was full of Rebel cavalry. He quickly jumped into an empty barrel. He would remain there for hours until the cavalry rode away, emerging dehydrated and starving. He would later view the timing of his arrival as either fortuitous or unlucky. He was smack dab in the middle of the lead up to the Battle of Atlanta. The Confederate army was digging in to defend the city against Sherman's onslaught. Byers, dressed as a Rebel soldier, was dug in as well, hiding from the Rebels in an abandoned house.

Byers had memorized everything he could about the 9th Alabama Infantry. "Samuel Hawkins, Company B, Ninth Alabama, part of General Benjamin F. Cheatham's Division," said Byers. "When questioned in other parts of the army in regard to my regiment, I pass muster amazingly."

His only problem was that the actual 9th Alabama Infantry was in Virginia fighting Grant's army, and at that particular moment, while he was in Atlanta, they were just outside of Petersburg, Virginia. Also, Cheatham's Division in the Battle of Atlanta was made up entirely of Tennessee regiments. Aside from those two glaring mistakes, Byers somehow blended in and bluffed his way around his predicament.

He soon became aware that something big was about to take place the next day, which was Friday, July 22. He was determined to use the chaos of the battle to make it through the lines—if he could avoid getting shot. "I followed the rear of one of the Divisions, as an Ordinance Sergeant, thinking the rebel lines would be repulsed, when I could lie down and remain on the ground until the Federal lines came up," said Byers.

Unfortunately for Byers, the Rebels won that particular part of the battle where he had hidden himself. In that fight the highest-ranking member of the Union army, General James B. McPherson, was killed when he was shot in the back while fleeing Rebel skirmishers.

The next morning on Saturday, July 23, Byers made his way through town, then northwest toward the Chattahoochee River, stumbling through the woods trying to locate the Federal line. It was so close; he could almost taste freedom.

"Surrender and hold up your arms!" barked a Rebel soldier, his rifle raised and pointed directly at Byers. "Who are you?" A small group of soldiers on picket duty came up behind the first soldier.

"Samuel Hawkins, Company B, Ninth Alabama...my horse, which was a borrowed one, broke loose and ran into the woods, and I am hunting him," Byers replied as he raised his hands into the air.

"Do you know, sir, that you are almost into the jaws of the yankees, who are not five hundred yards from here?" said the Rebel soldier.

"Indeed!" replied a surprised Byers, thinking to himself, "so damn close." He had made it to within 500 yards from the Federal lines; he could see the Chattahoochee's waters. On the opposite shore he could also see the movement of soldiers and the distinctive blue shade of their uniforms.

So. Damn. Close.

He didn't know it at the time but the men he saw across the river were part of General McCook's Division who were getting ready for a raid south of Atlanta. Located in this army of thousands of men was the 4th Kentucky Mounted Infantry, along with Second Lieutenants Thomas Payne Young and Alfred Shelby Stewart. The three soldiers were unaware that on this warm Saturday afternoon their paths would soon cross.

Provost Marshal, Colonel Benjamin Jefferson Hill
Photographer unknown
Before 1861

Almost immediately Byers aroused suspicion. Things didn't seem right about where he was and what he appeared to be doing. His story seemed fishy, and the Rebels decided to search him while the first soldier kept his rifle pointed at Byer's head. With no papers to vouch for his identity, the jig was up.

"Boys, take the prisoner to General Ross immediately, and tell him I send him a man believed to be a yankee spy," said the soldier with the rifle.

Being in the uniform of the enemy tagged him as a spy, and in the middle of the Battle of Atlanta, being within enemy lines dressed that way could carry potentially deadly consequences. He had made it to within 500 yards of Union lines. He also had a great deal of valuable intelligence gathered by living with the enemy for more than a week in the heart of Atlanta. He could be hung!

Action around Atlanta continued. As they tried to figure out who Byers actually was, for the next two days he was bounced around the Confederate army of Tennessee to Brigadier General Lawrence Sullivan Ross, then Division Commander William Y. C. Hume to General John Bell Hood himself, and finally to the Confederate Provost Marshal, Colonel Benjamin Jefferson Hill.

"Your name, prisoner, if you please," said Colonel Hill.

"I am a federal prisoner, sir, who escaped from Macon, but was recaptured in the woods yesterday," replied Byers.

"Well," said the Colonel, "I am most sorry you did not get through. You deserve a better fate than to be returned to prison; but I hope you get exchanged. War is very bad, but prison is worst; but it is my duty, and I will send you back to prison in Macon," said the Colonel.

An hour later he was on a train headed to Macon. The next morning on Wednesday, July 27, Byers, stripped of his Rebel gray uniform, walked back into Camp Oglethorpe in his underwear.[375] It made for quite a sight.

AFTER THE BATTLE OF ATLANTA on July 22, Sherman began repositioning his army to cut off supplies to the besieged city. While all this was going on just ninety miles to the north of Macon, the Union was also beginning to test the waters south of Atlanta. Camp Oglethorpe and its Union officers were a valued target. Not wanting a repeat of the debacle by Kilpatrick's raiders in the spring, Provost Marshal General Winder, who was in charge of all Rebel prisons, decided that Macon was not secure.[376] He quickly came up with another southern city that would keep their captives safe from liberation and serve the Confederacy in two ways. The city was Charleston, South Carolina. First, it was more secure than their current lodgings. Second, it would act as a deterrent to the enemy, who at the time had been shelling the city for more than ten months. They had moved a small group of POWs in June for this purpose. Now they would move more than 1,000 Union POW officers from Macon to Charleston. Perhaps placing such large numbers of Yankees directly in the line of fire would be just the thing to stop the shelling.

Chapter Twelve

Alfred S. "Allie" Stewart and Thomas P. Young Jr.
July 1864

THE 4TH KENTUCKY MOUNTED INFANTRY saddled up in the early morning hours of Wednesday, July 27, 1864, as the regiment's buglers finished the last notes of "Boots and Saddles."[377] Nineteen-year-old Lieutenant Thomas P. Young of Company A and twenty-nine-year-old Lieutenant Alfred S. "Allie" Stewart of Company K each moved their respective companies out from where they had camped near Mayson's Church, just west of Atlanta. The damn war had depleted their regiment's numbers; now there were a little more than 300 of them. They all closed in on a pontoon bridge that had been set across the Chattahoochee River.

It was turning out to be a slow start to what should have been a fast-moving cavalry raid. The bridge created a bottleneck, slowing the progress for almost 2,000 men on horseback—all members of Brigadier General Edward M. McCook's Division. Young and Stewarts's companies each waited their turn, dismounting and leading their horses across the bridge before remounting and heading northwest. All the while Confederate pickets watched the Yankees from strategic points along the south shore of the river. Finally, all the men and horses were on the other side. Then they took up the pontoon bridge and hauled it with them at the rear of the column on mule-drawn wagons, slowing the process that much further. The route they were taking required them to cross the river twice to avoid the Rebels. They had to haul their own bridge along with them. Now they were waiting on the mules.

In the prior weeks the Union army had successfully shut off the railroad supply lines into Atlanta from the west, north, and east, leaving the single Macon and Western Railroad as the only way the Confederate army could get supplies into the city. Cut off this last supply line, they would have to surrender Atlanta or starve to death.

GENERAL SHERMAN HAD DEVISED a dual-pronged raid.[378] From the west side of Atlanta, he would send General McCook's Raiders, roughly 3,500 soldiers and horses. From the east near Decatur, Georgia, General George Stoneman and 2,100 horsemen, along with another 3,000 under General Kenner Garrard, would join in under Stoneman's command.

Two days later, a little over twenty miles south of Atlanta, McCook and Stoneman would meet at Lovejoy Station of the Macon and Western Railroad and destroy everything they could get their hands on, boxing in Atlanta and Confederate General

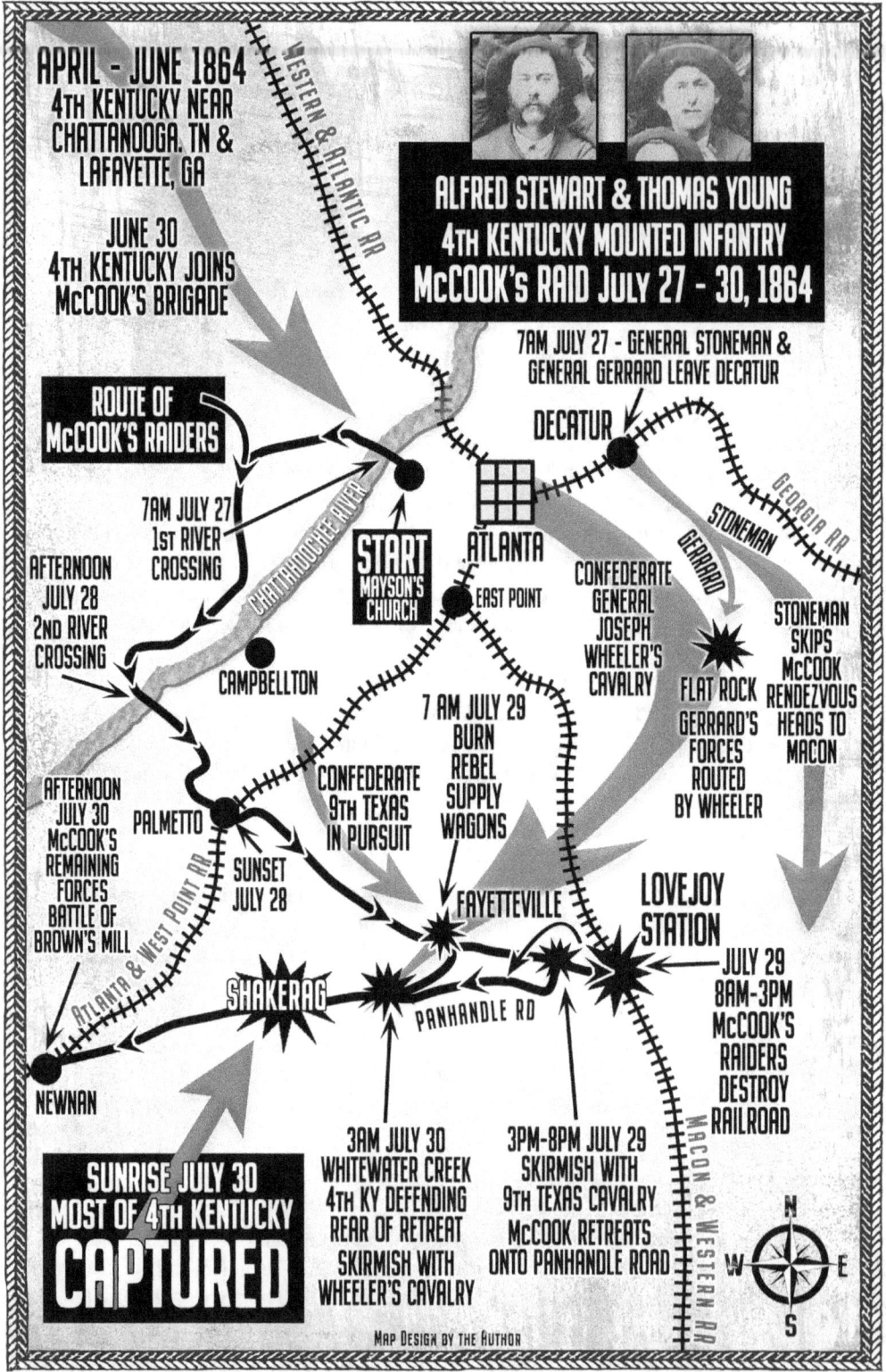

Hood's soldiers. Sherman wagered that if the raid worked, it would be the final straw that would quickly cause the fall of Atlanta.

The day before the raiding parties left their respective camps, a twist added to the plan. General Stoneman requested permission from General Sherman that after rendezvousing with McCook and destroying the southern Rebel supply lines into Atlanta, his forces be allowed to continue sixty miles south to Macon and free all the Union POW officers held at the Camp Oglethorpe prison. Then, if that was successful, he would continue southwest to the notorious Andersonville Prison and liberate the prisoners there as well. Sherman agreed to Stoneman's mission to free the POWs, as long as the McCook and Stoneman part of the plan had successfully been accomplished.[379]

Standing between both McCook and Stoneman's raid was the Confederate cavalry under General Joseph Wheeler, some 10,000 horsemen strong.

By the evening of July 27, McCook's men were still stuck on the north side of the Chattahoochee River, waiting for the mules. McCook was going to be a day behind his scheduled rendezvous with Stoneman.

Stewart sensed the slowness of everything as they moved along the river's north bank to Smith's Ferry, six miles south of Campbellton, Georgia. The 4th Kentucky had once been an infantry regiment. They had upgraded to mounted infantry at the beginning. of 1864. No doubt about it, riding a horse to the fight beat marching to the fight any day. Stewart, Young, and the rest of McCook's 3,500-man army camped the night, awaiting the pontoon bridges to be reassembled the next morning.

It would take until the afternoon of Thursday, July 28, before McCook's pontoon bridge was reassembled across the Chattahoochee so his men and horses were finally able to cross the river for the second time at Smith's Ferry. This time leaving the pontoon bridge and mules behind, McCook's Raiders were quickly on the move, arriving at Palmetto, Georgia, by sunset.

Knowing they were still behind schedule the McCook's Raiders rode all night. West of Fayetteville, Georgia, Young's Company A was among the first to see a massive pack of Confederate supply wagons lined up end to end on either side of the road for almost five miles leading into town. The Rebels had placed their wagons on the west side of town, thinking that the Yankees would be coming from the east.

More than 1,000 supply wagons were quickly overrun by McCook's Raiders, then looted and burned. A large cache of Confederate officer's personal trunks had been packed in some of the wagons, which the raiders had quickly rifled through, helping themselves to desirable spoils before tossing them back on top of the burning wagons.[380] Hundreds of mules were slaughtered. Surprised Rebel quartermasters, clerks, and teamsters were captured.[381] It all occurred with little or no fight; for the rest of the day a massive five-mile-long smoke column climbed high into the sky and could be seen for miles.

A decision made two days before, on Wednesday, July 27, by General Stoneman, who would become the Governor of California after the war,[382] ultimately determined the raid's outcome. Unfortunately, it was the wrong decision. Stoneman took it upon himself to alter the plan approved by Sherman. After riding fourteen miles south, he bolted toward Macon with around 2,200 of his men, aiming straight for Camp Oglethorpe and skipping Lovejoy Station. He left behind Garrard's division, which was about twenty miles northeast of Lovejoy Station, hoping that Garrard would cover his rear as he headed to Macon and then to meet McCook.

Not bothering to relay word of this to General McCook, Stoneman's decision left

McCook on his own and in the dark. The General was clearly excited by the prospects of glory and prestige that would be heaped upon him if he were successful in freeing the POWs in Macon and Andersonville. The name "Stoneman" would be boldly plastered in the headlines of the northern newspapers.

There was just one problem. When General Garrard watched the dust kicked up by Stoneman's raiders disappear down the road heading south, he began to head toward the rendezvous with McCook. That evening at around 10 p.m. Confederate General Joseph Wheeler and his cavalry personally greeted Gerrard's cavalry. In short order Gerrard's forces were routed and driven back toward the east side of Atlanta, leaving Stoneman exposed and McCook out of luck. At midnight Wheeler sent the bulk of his forces chasing after Stoneman and kept one regiment under his command to take on McCook.

By 7 a.m. on Friday July 29, McCook's Raiders finally reached Lovejoy Station, the main target of the raid. They were a day late, expecting to find that Stoneman and his men had beaten them there. Instead, they found no sign of Stoneman at all. McCook immediately sent out scouts to the east looking for Stoneman. After all, 5,000 men on horseback should be easy to find. Meanwhile, McCook's Raiders wasted no time, quickly destroying five miles of telegraph lines, tearing up miles of railroad track, and torching Confederate supplies, working into the early afternoon.[383]

Not long after they left, McCook's scouts returned at a gallop. They hadn't found Stoneman's Cavalry; they had found the enemy. It was Wheeler who was headed their way. It was time to move. McCook's Raiders mounted up and began heading back west. Once again, it was slow going, with the men of the 4th Kentucky Mounted Infantry bringing up the rear, anxiously looking back over their shoulders as they got underway.

ALFRED SHELBY "ALLIE" STEWART was born in Kentucky on May 7, 1835, to William Stewart and Dorcas Wilmot. William Stewart had immigrated from Ireland in 1811 and married Virginia-born Dorcas Wilmot in Mercer, Kentucky, in 1816. Allie was the youngest of the Stewart children and had two brothers: Robert, born 1820, and William Jr., born in 1829. His sister, Elisabeth, was born about 1830. Their father, William, was a farmer in Danville, Kentucky, southwest of Lexington. Allie's two older brothers, Robert and William Jr., also became farmers, married, and established families in Danville.

Allie's ambitions were focused on something other than farming; he attended nearby Centre College in 1857. By 1860 he was working as a merchant, boarding in a room at the home of his boss, William C. Lucas. The prosperous, Irish-born Lucas owned a retail establishment in Danville and was just eleven years Allie's senior. In 1860 the Lucas household was a busy one, with five children ranging in age from six to thirteen years as well as three boarders including Allie and a servant. William Lucas's eldest daughter, thirteen-year-old Anna Jane Lucas, would often talk with the twenty-five-year-old Allie. It was a schoolgirl crush for the girl who went by the nickname of "Nannie."

Thomas Payne Young Jr. was born in Danville, Kentucky, on November 18, 1844, the namesake son of Kentucky-born parents Thomas Payne Young Sr. and his wife, Mary E. Moran. He was sandwiched in age between two other siblings: an older sister, Ann, and a younger sister, Julia. Tom's father was an attorney and judge in Danville and was well connected in Kentucky politics. Judge Young also owned two enslaved individuals in 1860, a sixty-year-old male and a forty-year-old female.

As the Civil War broke out in 1861, Tom Young and Allie Stewart were neighbors, living just a few blocks away from each other in Danville. By the summer of 1861 the order was given by the Governor to raise three volunteer infantry units in Kentucky. Sporting the best military name in Kentucky, Captain Speed S. Fry, a judge in nearby Mercer County and a Mexican-American War veteran, was promoted to colonel of the Kentucky militia and tasked with the job of raising a regiment. His 4th Kentucky Volunteer Infantry recruited men from all around the area. He chose John T. Croxton, another attorney living in Paris, Kentucky, which was located northeast of Lexington, as his second in command, Both Croxton and Fry were close acquaintances with Judge Young, Tom's father.

The leaders of Kentucky had a decision to make before any regiments could come together. They had to decide which side Kentucky was on, or perhaps they would remain neutral. The 4th Kentucky Volunteer Infantry weren't allowed to set up camp until elections took place to decide the question. The results of the election showed support of the Union by seventy-five percent of the voting population.[384]

Judge Young agreed to allow his son Tom, who was just sixteen years old, to sign his name and enlist in his good friend Colonel Fry's new Union regiment. When Tom signed up, he was six-feet tall and gave his age as eighteen years old. The judge went along with the small indiscretion; after all, these were patriotic times. Both Young and Stewart officially enlisted in Company A on Sunday, August 7: Stewart as a sergeant and Young as a corporal. To Stewart, who was always the youngest in his family with two older brothers, Tom became the younger kid brother he never had—except Tom was taller.

The regiment came together to train, drill, and learn to be soldiers at Camp Dick Robinson, named after the owner of the parcel of land the camp was set up on a few miles northeast of Danville. Almost immediately a camp-wide measles outbreak stopped the new recruits in their tracks, requiring the citizens of Danville to come to their rescue. Orders were given to separate infected soldiers from healthy ones and to evacuate unaffected regiments. A few of the cases were fatal.

Thinking Camp Dick Robinson jinxed or worse, in October 1861 the regiment moved twenty miles southwest of Danville to Crab Orchard, Kentucky. Shortly after arriving, typhoid broke out, once again causing deaths among the soldiers before they had seen any action and requiring the citizens of nearby Lebanon, Kentucky, to come to their rescue as well.

During the time at Crab Orchard, Stewart's experience as a clerk back in Danville got him transferred and appointed to the regimental command staff, then promoted to regimental commissary sergeant, requiring him to leave Company A and his friend Tom. Stewart's new job had him acting as the "foreman" of the commissary storehouse, which could be an actual building in winter camp or a group of six-mule wagons as part of the packtrain when the regiment was on the move. He supervised the slaughtering and butchering of cattle used to feed the men and the drawing of rations, along with their preparation and distribution to the entire regiment.[385]

Corporal Young became sick in December, likely from typhoid, and went back home to Danville to recover. His mother, Mary, nursed him back to health. It took two long months before he could rejoin the regiment in February 1862. The bout with the illness weakened Young's general health for the remainder of the war. While he was recovering at home, the 4th Kentucky finally entered the fray.

On January 19, 1862, their brigade moved thirty miles south in a cold, foggy rain to a miserably muddy place called Logan's Crossroads. At dawn the 4th Kentucky was attacked and pushed back by part of Confederate Brigadier General Felix Zollifcoffer's command.

On that particular day Zollifcoffer had chosen to wear a white raincoat, which covered his Confederate uniform, hoping for protection from the incessant drizzle and perhaps allowing him to blend in with the fog. He also was wearing a blue hat, which was a little odd for a Rebel General.[386] Riding on a gray horse through the fog, he became confused, wandering over the lines and thinking that the 4th Kentucky was actually another Rebel regiment firing on his men.

The soldiers of the 4th, all under cover and engaged in the fight, watched as this odd man dressed in white and wearing a blue hat, which gave him the appearance of being on their side, approached their position on horseback from the direction of the Rebel fire. Zollifcoffer, who was nearsighted, rode right up to Colonel Fry, thinking he was castigating a subordinate officer for firing on his own army and ordering him to cease fire.[387]

Suddenly, one of Zollifcoffer's aides came galloping out of the fog from the Rebel lines, firing his pistol at the Kentuckians.

"It's the enemy, General," the aide cried out.[388]

Colonel Fry stared in amazement at Zollifcoffer, and then he and a group of Union soldiers fired at the confused Rebel general, killing him instantly in a barrage of gunshots with two bullets to the head, one to the chest and one to the thigh.[389] Fry himself was slightly wounded in the exchange.

The general's death caused tremendous confusion within the Rebel regiments and soon their line collapsed. They were in a panicked retreat, leaving all kinds of supplies as they ran. Later feigning outrage, the Confederates claimed that Fry had committed murder, forgetting that they were fighting a war. Zollifcoffer's death would forever mark Colonel Fry and the 4th Kentucky as a regiment actually willing to kill the enemy in battle.

In spring 1862 the 4th Kentucky moved down into Tennessee toward Nashville, eventually reaching Pittsburg Landing, just to the northeast of Shiloh. The entire 1st Division, Army of the Ohio arrived at the end of the second day of the battle when the fighting was over. Not taking part in the action, they witnessed its horrors as they helped dig the graves of the fallen.

In late April they then moved toward the vital railroad lines at Corinth, Mississippi. Once again, they didn't see any significant action, just light skirmishing while on picket duty.

During the summer, Stewart, Young, and the rest of the 4th Kentucky, as part of the 44-year-old Major General Don Carlos Buell's Army of the Ohio were tasked with repairing railroad lines to the east of Corinth.

Then from September to early October 1862, they pursued General Braxton Bragg's Confederate army through Middle Tennessee and back up into their home state.

The Rebels had their sights set on the Union supply lines provided by the Louisville and Nashville Railroad and ended up sixty miles to the east of Louisville. For 300 long miles all the way back into Kentucky, Buell's army ran parallel to Braggs, cautiously prodding him along the way but never seeming to really want to stop his advance northward by actually engaging in battle. The General's lack of ambition to attack the fast-moving Rebels, whose speed and ominous path seemed to project further north than just Kentucky, was not lost to his superiors in the Union command.

Even the Governor of Kentucky became worried that Louisville might fall to the Rebels. The politicians in Ohio were getting nervous about Cincinnati, calling out their "Minute-men or Squirrel Hunters."[390] They came to defend Cincinnati by the thousands and no doubt had a large impact on Southwestern Ohio's indigenous squirrel population. Everyone was frustrated with Buell's lack of action against the Rebels. "March where you please, provided you will find the enemy and fight him," said an exasperated General Henry W. Halleck, hoping Buell would be more aggressive.[391]

When the Union army finally arrived in Louisville, they were exhausted, dehydrated, and footsore, suffering under warm weather conditions and limited drinking water supplies. Most disconcerting to Stewart and Young was that in their move northward, the Rebels were getting close to their hometown of Danville. They worried for the safety of their families, knowing that the two armies were destined to clash. "That odd poke-easy general of ours has allowed the thieving rebels to overrun the best portion of the State and they are in full possession of our homes," an unhappy Kentucky soldier wrote about General Buell in his diary.[392]

In an odd prelude to the approaching battle, the senior Union command had given up on Buell's leadership, or lack thereof, and relieved him on September 29. He was to be replaced by his second-in-command, General George H. Thomas, but an embarrassed Thomas postponed taking over until the battle was over. Buell moved some of his army southeast to end up ten miles west of Danville, near the town of Perryville, Kentucky.

It would all be decided at The Battle of Perryville on Wednesday, October 8, which would be one of the bloodiest battles of the Civil War, ultimately deciding who would control the State of Kentucky for the rest of the conflict.

On the Confederate side, Bragg's army had a force of just under 17,000. On the Union side, Buell's had a force outnumbering the Rebels by almost three to one. But in a clearly flawed strategy, he would end up utilizing only 22,000 of them.

It took a couple of days for both sides to get themselves into position, elbowing each other as they went and testing each other's strengths and weaknesses. Bragg was convinced he was facing a much smaller number of Yankees. He was wrong. At the same time Buell was convinced he was facing a larger number of Rebels. He, too, was wrong. Buell positioned his men into three columns along three roads northwest of Perryville.

The Union first column was to the north along Benton Road. The second column in the middle was on Springfield Pike, and the third column to the south was along Lebanon Pike. The 4th Kentucky was part of the second column, located as usual in the rear, just a mile west of Buell's headquarters, which was located in a comfortable log home owned by the Dorsey family.

In an ominous prelude to the fight, the afternoon before the battle Buell injured his leg when he was thrown from his horse. The action began in the morning of October 8, with the Rebels aimed at the Union first column. Bragg himself arrived late-morning to direct his generals. His plan was to try to get around both flanks to surround the first column. An impressive wave of Confederate artillery fire started at 12:30 p.m. It was followed at 2 p.m. by a charge of the Confederate troops, accompanied by the "Rebel Yell," directed at the center of the first column. The Rebels were met with a storm of extremely loud gun and artillery fire, and the battle raged.

Through it all Buell was at his Dorsey House headquarters, unaware that there was even a battle underway, resting his injured leg. Through what was later identified as a bizarre phenomenon called "acoustic shadow,"[393] the wind, terrain, and temperature acted in such a way as to muffle the sound of the fighting. So even though he was just a couple of miles away from all kinds of very loud, heated action, including fierce cannonading that went on for a couple of hours, the General didn't hear a thing. Buell spent the afternoon quietly reading a book at Dorsey House and leisurely having lunch with a close friend, completely oblivious to everything happening around him.

During that time the Union first column got pushed back over a mile and was mauled by Hardee's forces, suffering great casualties. Finally, at 4:30 p.m. when advised that the Rebels had been attacking for hours on the battlefield, Buell was incredulous and couldn't believe it. Reinforcements were finally ordered for the battered first column. But by the time they got there, the battle was over.[394] Through it all Stewart, Young, and the rest of the 4th Kentucky performed picket duty near Buell's headquarters, seeing no action.

In the darkness In the darkness, Confederate General Leonidas Polk became turned around somehow and crossed behind the Federal lines on horseback. Thinking the Yankees were his men, he began yelling at them to cease fire as he assumed he was encountering friendly fire. It could have ended badly for the officer, much like what had happened to the Rebel General Zollifcoffer nine months earlier, if the general hadn't suddenly realized his mistake and bluffed his way back to the Confederate lines, yelling at the Yankees through the darkness, "Cease fire, cease fire."[395] Even though he had won the battle the day before, early the next morning at 2:30 a.m. General Bragg was given the intelligence of how badly outnumbered his forces were and wisely chose to quietly retreat.

At sunrise Buell's army found the town of Perryville deserted; the Rebels had picked up and left, leaving their dead and wounded behind. They retreated through Stewart and Young's hometown of Danville, causing significant panic, but they were not there long. General Bragg was convinced that surely the Yankees would soon be chasing after them, considering how vastly outnumbered his side was. General Buell made sure Bragg's instincts were wrong.

Edward Stanton, the Secretary of War, ordered a military commission to investigate the incompetence at Perryville, along with the lack of will or ambition by Buell to chase Bragg's army, letting the Rebels escape. The results delivered late in the year were inconclusive and, aside from losing his command, no action was taken against Buell, though he never commanded troops again. He resigned his commission in June 1864.

After Perryville, Stewart and Young got to visit their families in Danville, relieved that they had survived their short run-in with the Rebels. With all the wounded on both sides, Union forces were using the Danville courthouse as a hospital.

"The people generally, being loyal, made many demonstrations of joy at being once more delivered from rebel rule, by waving numerous flags," recorded a Union soldier.[396]

Their visits with their families were short. The 4th Kentucky was moved 200 miles back into Tennessee settling in around Nashville, where they spent the remainder of 1862 and first half of 1863. Their primary job was guarding the railroad supply lines. Young was given a desk job working as a clerk for the 4th Kentucky's Adjutant. Stewart continued his job as a regimental commissary sergeant.

In May 1863 eighteen-year-old Corporal Thomas P. Young was now a veteran with almost two years of war experience under his belt. That experience was mainly bringing up the rear, never actually fighting face to face with the enemy and working at his new desk job, albeit in a tent. One afternoon while sitting in the Adjutant's tent near Nashville, Young penned a letter home to his father, asking for some suggestions on what he might do to get himself promoted to Lieutenant.

Judge Young reached out to his political network on behalf of his son, and on May

29 Corporal Young received a telegram from his father's friend and former regimental commander, Brigadier General Speed Fry. The General had been ordered back to Lexington, Kentucky, where he would remain for the rest of the war with the 4th Kentucky, left under the command of Colonel John T. Croxton.

I have a commission for you as Lieutenant on Recruiting Service. Show this to Col Croxton and get an order from Gen'l Rosecrans to let you come home - have your discharge papers made out.

Speed S. Fry, Brig General[397]

Corporal Young, as instructed, promptly filled out the discharge papers and took it along with the telegram to Croxton, no doubt a busy man who responded up the chain-of-command the next day, a little befuddled.

I do not understand from Gen'l Frys dispatch the nature of the position tendered Corp Young— if it is a commission from the Governor in any organization I would recommend his discharge.

John T. Croxton, Colonel[398]

Nevertheless, Young got his discharge papers. During the summer of 1863 as Stewart and the rest of the 4th Kentucky remained in Middle Tennessee guarding the trains. Young was home in Danville, recruiting men for the Union army, his sights set on becoming an officer.

It didn't take long before the young corporal wrote back to his unit. But in the couple of months he was away, he was unsure who was in command so he addressed the letter to the "Officer Commanding 4 Ky."

Danville, Ky
July 24th 63
Officer Commanding 4 Ky.

Dear Sir
    I have written you twice since I left the old Fourth, but have never received any reply to either letter. I have got a sufficient number of men recruited to entitle me to a Lieutenancy - and will assure you that I get my commission in a few days. As soon as my commission was returned to me at D. [Danville] I referred the matter to the Adj't Gen'l of the Army through General Porter. As soon as my papers are returned from W. Pity, I will return to my company if they are not properly arranged. I received permission for the Gen'l to remain here until I heard from my papers.
    I will get Gen'l Finnell or Colonel Bird to write to you advising you as to my conduct here and my authority for remaining,
    Hoping you will get me sufficient time to get my men into camp and get my papers arranged. I remain.

Very Resp't
Your most Obedient Serv't
Thomas P. Young Jr.[399]

It turned out the officer in command of the 4th Kentucky was still Colonel Croxton, who, perhaps taken aback by demands coming from a corporal, never responded to Young's third letter either. By August, Young was absent without leave, and his time in Danville was up. In September 1863 he returned to Middle Tennessee where the 4th Kentucky was still located, guarding the important supply chain for the Union army. He resumed the same desk job he had left in the spring, a clerk for the adjutant. He remained a corporal. The job was safe and rarely placed him in the line of fire, which was perfect for a young man who still suffered the long-term side effects from his battle with typhoid eighteen months earlier.

Through almost two years of war, the 4th Kentucky had managed to skirt the edges of significant conflict. They had seen the horrible results of major battles and even taken part in the gruesome burial details in those battle's aftermath. By sheer luck, however, they had managed to be in the periphery. That would all change in September 1863 at the Battle of Chickamauga.

The lead-up to Chickamauga had the 4th Kentucky move south into Georgia from Middle Tennessee. This battle would see a more evenly matched fight with General William Rosecrans and the Union Army of the Cumberland's 60,000 men against General Braxton Bragg's Army of Tennessee's 65,000 men.

The Brigade the 4th Kentucky was under the command of their original regimental commander, Colonel John T. Croxton. They found themselves camped in the valley near Ringgold, Georgia, on the night of Friday, September 18.

After providing all the men in his regiment with several days of rations, Stewart moved with his six-mule supply wagons—along with all the other regimental quartermasters and sergeants and their supply wagons—from the Army of the Cumberland to the west side of Missionary Ridge, where Young was also located in regimental headquarters. The area was known as the Chattanooga Valley; it was there where they were all staged, in a safe place, one mountain west of where the danger was and where all the action would take place.

At daylight Saturday morning the 4th Kentucky marched five miles toward the West Chickamauga Creek, in search of Confederate troops who had reportedly crossed over the creek. The brigade ran into some of Confederate Cavalry General Nathan Bedford Forrest's men, who had dismounted and were serving as infantry.

It was the beginning of the Battle of Chickamauga with the 4th Kentucky seeing the first action.

In the first few hours, Croxton's brigade pushed Forrest's men backwards, only to be pushed backwards themselves. The fighting was intense with Croxton's brigade taking on tremendous casualties. The fighting continued to escalate with intense action between both armies that would continue all day. By nightfall the lines were drawn with the Union forces on the west side of LaFayette Road and the Confederate forces on the east. Both sides were exhausted.

On Sunday, September 20, the fighting began again with the Union forces playing defense to repeated attacks by the Rebels. Croxton's brigade was positioned on the Union's left, along the southern edge of the property owned by Private Larken H. Poe, who was fighting in the Confederate 4th Georgia Cavalry.

Around noon the Confederates charged Croxton's position from 200 yards out. Initially, the Rebels were repelled, but then a full-blown firefight broke out, and Colonel Croxton suffered a serious leg wound and had to be removed from the field of battle. The fighting was so intense that the Poe farmstead was burned to the ground. Poe wasn't there to witness the burning of his home; his regiment, which included his friend Private

Arba F. Shaw,[400] was located far south of the action in LaFayette, Georgia.

Just as the 4th Kentucky began fighting, Union commander General William S. Rosecrans came to the conclusion that Chickamauga was lost. The Rebels had successfully charged deeply into the Union positions, and it was all over.

Through the late afternoon of Sunday, September 20, the Union retreated en masse northwest through McFarland's Gap. The Confederate army would pore their fight onto the Union's left wing under the command of Major General George H. Thomas. His forces held their position, holding open the road through the gap and allowing the rest of the army to safely retreat back to Chattanooga. For this heroism, Thomas earned the nickname "The Rock of Chickamauga."

Stewart and Young, who were at the regimental headquarters with the supply wagons in the valley west of Missionary Ridge during the battle, experienced the sounds of the battle echoing over the mountain. Muffled cannonading and gunfire marked the deaths of many men on both sides. The lengthy supply train joined the rest of the Union army retreating toward Chattanooga as they crossed through McFarland's Gap.

Though the Rebels may have chalked up a victory against the Yankees, Stewart and Young emerged unscathed because they were sheltered a mountain away from all the action.

For the next eight weeks, the Union army was boxed in at Chattanooga. The Rebels took positions on top of Missionary Ridge and Lookout Mountain, looking down on their enemy below, cut off from their supply lines into the city. By placing Chattanooga under siege, they hoped to starve out the Yankees. Rosecrans commanded the Union position in the Chattanooga until Grant replaced him with the "Rock of Chickamauga." General Thomas was ordered to hold the city at all costs.

"I will hold the town till we starve," Thomas replied.[401] Grant himself arrived in Chattanooga in late October, and slowly supplies began to flow into the city from the west over the Tennessee River.

The stage was being set for the Battle of Chattanooga in late November 1864. The 4th Kentucky had spent the weeks between Chickamauga and the Battle of Chattanooga recovering from the beating it took. They went into Chickamauga with 360 men and 19 officers fit for duty. They had suffered with more than 160 enlisted men as either killed or wounded along with 13 of its officers wounded. The regiment's size had been reduced by more than forty-five percent to just a few hundred men.

The Battle of Chattanooga's pivotal final action came on Wednesday, November 25. The 4th Kentucky was a small part of the combined Union Army of the Cumberland and Army of the Tennessee numbering almost 70,000 located at Chattanooga, commanded by General Grant. The soldiers were ready to pay back General Braxton Bragg's Confederates for the beating they had taken at Chickamauga. Grant deployed his forces: General Sherman with more than 20,000 men to the left at Tunnel Hill, General Thomas in the center with more than 23,000 men at Missionary Ridge, and General Hooker with more than 10,000 men who had chased the Rebels off the mountain the day before to the right at Lookout Mountain.

Grant sat perched on Orchard's Knob, just behind Thomas's Center. He was in the middle of it all, watching it all come together to his east through a pair of binoculars. "There he stood in his plain citizen's clothes looking through his double field-glasses apparently totally unmoved...I could hardly believe that here was this famous commander, the model, it seemed to me, of a modest and homely but efficient Yankee general," commented a British journalist on the scene.[402]

The 4th Kentucky was on the northern end of Missionary Ridge, as part of a row of soldiers almost four miles long. Stewart and Young were in the rear with the regimental supply wagons and headquarters near where Grant was positioned, looking at the backs of thousands of soldiers all pointed east toward the ridge.

Grant had given the order for General Thomas to advance on Missionary Ridge at 3:30 p.m. and take the long line of Confederate rifle pits along its western base. At the appointed time the soldiers all began to advance. They soon overwhelmed the Confederate rifle pits at the base, but the position left them vulnerable to Bragg's men at the top of the ridge.

Two miles to their north, Sherman's forces, which included the 5th Iowa, had taken a beating on Tunnel Hill, which resulted in the capture of Major William Stanhope Marshall, Captain John Elijah Page, and Lieutenants Michael Hoffman and Marsh Byers. At about the time of the move on the center of Missionary Ridge, they began to rally as well.

Though it wasn't part of the original orders, for the next hour the 4th Kentucky and the rest of the Union center took it upon themselves to charge 300 to 400 feet to the top of Missionary Ridge, attacking the Confederates. In a little over an hour, they had broken the center of the Rebel line.

When a shocked Grant asked who had ordered the charge up the side of Missionary Ridge, Brigadier General Gordon Granger replied, "When those fellows got started, all hell can't stop them."[403]

Colonel Croxton, who had been seriously wounded at Chickamauga, had recovered enough to join his men at Missionary Ridge, but at the foot of ridge he was wounded again and had to be carried from the field of battle.

When the Yankees made it to the top of the mountain, the Rebels fell into panic and disarray, retreating down the east side of Missionary Ridge. Throughout the night thousands of Confederates marched south into Georgia, carrying what they could and dragging along prisoners. They would go into winter quarters near Dalton, and their prisoners would be shipped to Libby Prison in Richmond. The Union army chased after them briefly but were soon called back by Grant and would stay in Chattanooga for the winter.

In January 1864 many of the roughly 200 surviving soldiers in the 4th Kentucky reenlisted as veterans. Both Stewart and Young did so with their same ranks, sergeant and corporal. With the reenlistment came a much-welcomed reward of a two-month furlough as well as a $400 bounty. From Chattanooga, the veterans of the 4th Kentucky went the 300 miles to Louisville by train, and then Stewart and Young and many other fellow soldiers rode home in wagons.

The people of Danville and surrounding Boyle County celebrated the return of their native sons. There was also grieving by the families who had lost sons in battle or by disease ever since the regiment came together just a little over two years earlier in August 1861. Soldiers from the 4th who had been discharged with disabilities welcomed home their comrades, eagerly listening to the stories of the battles at Chickamauga and Chattanooga so that was all too fresh on the minds of the veterans.

Allie spent his time visiting his siblings and grieving; his father, William, had died in December 1862 while Allie had been off to war. The last time he had seen him was right after Perryville, two months before he died. He also took time to visit his former employer, Danville merchant William Lucas, telling him stories of how a Union army regiment ran its commissary. The visit to the Lucas household also made him take notice of his former boss's sixteen-year-old daughter Nannie, who had gone from being a flirtatious young girl to an attractive young woman in the years he had been gone.

Tom was doted on by his mother, who was worried about his health. His older sister Ann also shared with her brother the news of her engagement to George Sharp, a talented watchmaker living in Danville. Sharp was a neighbor known by Allie as well. The couple planned on getting married in June. *Maybe Tom could get leave to be in Danville for the wedding*, his sister wondered. *Maybe the war would be over by then*, Tom thought.

At the beginning of March 1864 when furlough was up, goodbyes were said, and Stewart and Young met the rest of the 4th at Camp Nelson, Kentucky. Much to the cheers of the returning veterans, the 4th Kentucky had been reorganized while they were on furlough as the 4th Kentucky Mounted Infantry. They would be footsore no more from the countless miles of marching; now they would travel in style on horseback.

They soon moved back south and were positioned around LaFayette, Georgia, guarding the railroad supply lines and nearby Snake Creek Gap, an important route through the mountains east of LaFayette. The spring of 1864 saw the important battles with the Union army, pushing the Confederates south with each successive fight, starting around Dalton, and then all the way down to Atlanta. But the 4th Kentucky spent its time on the sidelines. Stewart and Young returned with the ranks from their old jobs they had before their reenlistment: Young as a corporal and clerk to the adjutant, and Stewart as the regiment's commissary sergeant.

While Corporal Young was in Danville on furlough, he expressed his frustration that more than six months had passed since he was last home, assigned to recruit troops. Yet, the promised promotion to lieutenant had not come through. His father, Judge Young, knew just the right strings to pull.

On May 5, 1864, Colonel John T. Croxton was in his headquarters in LaFayette, Georgia, when he received a letter from the Governor of Kentucky, Thomas E. Bramlette.

Headquarters Kentucky Volunteers
Adjutant General's Office
Frankfort - May 4, 1864

Col. John T. Croxton
Dear Sir:
Personal considerations make me anxious to promote the son of my old friend Col. Young in Danville, but I do not wish to depart from what I regard the correct rule of doing so with the approbation of the commanding officer of the regiment. I enclose a commission to you for Thomas P. Young as 1st Lt. Co. A. 4 Ky Inf. Note Lt. Linney resigned[404], which I leave to you to either return it or deliver it. No entry of promotion will be made until I hear from you. Nor is the commission to be considered issued unless you sanction it. If you do not want to approve it, it will be cancelled. If you approve, you can deliver it to Young. I hope it will meet you approval as I have a personal desire for that it be done…

Respectfully
Tho E. Bramlette[405]

**Brigadier General
Edward M. McCook**
*Mathew Brady
Library of Congress*

One week later, on Thursday May 12, 1864, Thomas P. Young Jr. received his promotion to second lieutenant of Company A. The next day Alfred S. Stewart received a promotion to second lieutenant of Company K.

There would be no more hanging out with the pack mules for Allie and no more pencil-pushing for Tom. They both mustered in at Chattanooga. Due to the attrition rate of officers, Lieutenant Stewart commanded Company K, while Lieutenant Young found himself third in the pecking order of Company A. They would both now be in the middle of the action instead of in the rear.

By the end of June 1864, the Yankees controlled northwest Georgia all the way down to the north end of Atlanta. The 4th Kentucky was ordered to join General Edward M. McCook's Division there. They arrived near Atlanta, just north of the Western and Atlantic Railroad trestle over the Chattahoochee River. From this strategic position, they would watch and skirmish with the Rebels on the south side of the Chattahoochee through most of July. Then came the raid on Lovejoy Station.

In the early afternoon on July 29, smoke from the burning of more than 1,000 Rebel supply wagons earlier in the day still hung in the air nine miles to the west. When McCook's Raiders arrived at Lovejoy Station, McCook had sent out scouts, feeling for Stoneman's pulse and surprised that Stoneman was missing from the scene. Where the hell was he? His scouts returned with the disturbing news that they had run into Wheeler's Confederate Cavalry, and they were headed their way. That news shook up the General. His senior officers saw it in his eyes when they all met to discuss the next move. Was it fear or perhaps just nervous energy? Continue east and meet up with Stoneman, or head back in the direction they came?

By 2 p.m. McCook's Raiders began retreating from Lovejoy Station, their commander deciding to retreat to the west. They had successfully completed their objective of destroying five miles of rails, cutting down telegraph poles and taking the telegraph wire. They also destroyed the depot and its support buildings, two trains loaded with Confederate supplies, and a huge cache of cotton—all impacting the southern supply line into Atlanta as was planned.[406]

McCook had decided to take a slightly different route back, anticipating that the smoldering wagons left at Fayetteville would likely draw attention. A mile and a half west of Lovejoy Station, instead of heading back through Fayetteville they made a left turn onto Panhandle Road, which would roughly parallel the route they had taken inbound, though the quality of the road was poor.

They headed west, hoping to make a rapid retreat back to cross the Chattahoochee River and the safety of the Union lines. But McCook carried a large footprint of approximately 3,500 cavalrymen, along with some captured Rebels acquired along the way and various spoils as well as their own mule-driven pack wagons. They had lost the lightning speed that was important for a raid to be successful. They never really had it from the beginning; his senior officers were aware of this, knowing it made them all vulnerable. They had become targets.

At 3 p.m. McCook took one last look at his men's work at Lovejoy Station and quickly skedaddled. Three last regiments had yet to clear the left turn onto Panhandle Road, making up the rear guard. One of those regiments was the 4th Kentucky, which included Lieutenants Allie Stewart's and Tom Young's companies. They knew that Wheeler's Rebel Cavalry was coming for them from the east, but as they approached the sharp left turn onto Panhandle Road, they were surprised by another Confederate Cavalry regiment rapidly approaching them from the west looking to cut off them off on Fayetteville Road, the road they had come in on that morning. It became a battle to control the intersection of two roads.

They were charged by Confederate Brigadier General William H. "Red" Jackson's 9th Texas Cavalry. The smoking remains of the Confederate supply wagons had definitely caught his attention. The resulting three-hour-long slugfest saw Stewart's Company K along with Company I ordered to dismount and fight to hold the intersection open. The 8th Iowa deployed in a field at the mouth of the intersection as well to block the Rebels from heading down the road the rest of McCook's Raiders were retreating on.

"So far the whole thing had been a sort of picnic," said one member of Company K, "but now a storm was brewing."[407]

The other eight companies of the 4th Kentucky also dismounted and drove the Rebels back down Fayetteville Road providing interference until all of McCook's Raiders had made it onto Panhandle Road.[408] The battle finally ended with the companies of the 4th Kentucky remounting their horses along with the 8th Iowa and rapidly riding off into the sunset down Panhandle Road.

Red Jackson's Cavalry, pushed back and checkmated at the battle of the intersection, turned and headed back toward Fayetteville. They sent word to Wheeler's men that they would race to circle around the slow-moving Yankees and attack them from the west while Wheeler attacked them from the east.

Adding to the confusion, General McCook was trying to move his entire army down an unfamiliar country road in the dark. "The road was a narrow, devious path, crossing innumerable ditches and bogs, and I was led to believe that these obstacles were the cause of delay to the rear of the column," said McCook.[409] They came to a fork in Panhandle Road: go right and you go back to Fayetteville, go left and the road became the sketchier. Knowing the Rebels were in Fayetteville, McCook's men took a left.

It was a warm night with no wind, and soon the summer humidity turned into a foggy haze.[410] In the dark McCook's column had stretched out for eight or nine miles to the west. In the confusion everything had slowed down so that Stewart and Young and the rest of the 4th Kentucky that made up the rear guard of the column had almost come to a complete standstill.

They were stuck in another bottleneck whose cause was quickly discovered: mules. The pack train animals had all fallen asleep, blocking the road behind them. This behavior was a known characteristic of the breed; when they became exhausted, they shut down and became stubborn. Allie knew from his two and a half years of experience as the regimental commissary sergeant that mules answer to no one; the army had to just maneuver around them.[411] An "everlasting train of pack-mules" doesn't belong on cavalry raids, said a frustrated Colonel Croxton.[412]

At 3 a.m. on July 30, the 4th Kentucky, still acting as the rear guard to the column and creeping at a snail's pace, had reached a bridge over Whitewater Creek.[413] Company C was ordered to remain behind for a half hour, then burn the bridge. They set about piling kindling on the center of the bridge and started a nice blaze, lighting up the night.

It was then when Wheeler's Cavalry finally caught up with them. Gunfire came in flashes from the darkness to the east. Company C quickly retreated down the road; they took cover in a ditch, buying a little more time.

A large group of Wheeler's men quickly ran to the bridge and began throwing burning kindling into the creek, trying to save the bridge. The fire illuminated them like sitting ducks. The 4th Kentucky sent a shower of Minié balls down on the Rebels standing on the bridge. Then they quickly mounted their horses and continued west.[414] It took the Rebels an hour to put out the flames and replace the burnt bridge decking before continuing the pursuit.

At 4:30 a.m. the rear of the column had pushed a few miles further west to the Mitchell farm at Shakerag, Georgia. In twelve hours they had traveled just sixteen miles. The 4th Kentucky halted again and dismounted at the top of a hill. They were ordered to barricade the road and hold their position, with Young's Company A and Company I in front and the five other 4th Kentucky companies guarding their backs a few hundred yards behind the barricade.[415]

They all found cover and aimed their Ballard rifles into the darkness toward the east with the rest of their men. The moon had just risen and was in waning crescent, just nine percent illuminated, so it was worthless in providing any light. Soon they again began to exchange gunfire with Wheeler's men. Hundreds of flashes of gunfire coming from the east and the west, freezing the moment like a photograph and showing where the enemy was as well as revealing their own positions. Many of the Ballard rifles, a single-shot breech loading firearm used by the Fourth, became useless, with mechanisms bursting and springs jamming from repeated firing.[416]

As the battle went on, the flashes that first came from the east began to move around the sides of the 4th Kentucky's barricaded position. The blackness of night repeatedly turned into day with constant rifle flashes. It went on for what seemed an eternity.

"Halt! Halt! you Yankee bastards," screamed some of the Rebels charging along their flanks.

"Get out of here, everybody," screamed an anxious Yankee officer.[417]

A few miles up ahead Colonel John T. Croxton, commanding the First Division, stopped and turned back, listening to the distant gunfire. "A number of men of the 4th Kentucky who had escaped, galloped up, reported the regiment completely surrounded," said Croxton.[418] He had been the 4th Kentucky Mounted Infantry's commanding officer at one time and personally knew the men well.

"It was now evident from the swift and rapid movements and formations of the enemy that we were fighting a very superior force. Their right now charged and took the road some 200 yards in rear of the advance position we held upon the road, cutting off nearly the whole regiment," said Lieutenant Granville West of Company C. "But there was no cowardly nor organized surrender; each man fought until he was entirely overpowered by the enemy...of the 24 officers who went out with us, 17 are missing."[419]

The 4th Kentucky regiment fought until they were out of bullets. They repulsed five separate charges by the enemy. They were overpowered, flanked, and then surrounded until it was all over. The majority of the regiment was captured, including Lieutenant Adjutant Charles V. Ray and Lieutenant Granville West's older brother Captain James H. West, who commanded the regiment at the barricade at Shakerag.[420] Granville was lucky and managed to escape.

YOUNG ROSE UP SLOWLY from the ground, along with the other men of Company A near the barricade. There was no place to escape. Stewart with his men of Company K were back a ways; he couldn't believe that the Rebels had come up on them from behind. All the regiment's horses stood nearby, separated from their soldiers, and captured as well. Slowly, Stewart raised his hands, looking into the eyes of a member of the 8th Texas Cavalry who pointed his rifle directly at his chest. Stewart looked up for a moment and saw the stars directly overhead, with pinpoints of light twinkling through the mist. To the east they could all just barely make out an orange glow on the horizon.

It was just before dawn on Saturday, July 30.

Chapter Thirteen

Lemuel D. Dobbs – 19th USCI
July 30, 1864

IT WAS JUST BEFORE DAWN on Saturday, July 30.

The explosion was so powerful that it felt like an earthquake to the roughly 15,000 Union soldiers secretly arranged in four divisions in the early morning hours, positioned just to the east of the underground bomb. Most froze in shock and stared up in amazement.

At 4:44 a.m., the precise moment of ignition, 8,000 pounds of powder caused the Confederate fort known as Elliott's Salient that sat on a hill as part of the Rebel works outside of Petersburg, Virginia, to cease to exist. Along with the fort, hundreds of Rebel soldiers were killed, either buried alive or flung high in the air. One Confederate regiment, the 18th South Carolina, was almost completely obliterated. People felt the ground shake twenty miles away.

The mine had been secretly tunneled underneath the Rebel line to try and bring an end to the Siege of Petersburg, take the city, and end the war. Every big, audacious idea was designed to end the war. They never did.

As the long, flaming, sizzling fuses reached their end and the mine exploded, "A monstrous tongue of flame shot fully two hundred feet in the air, followed by a vast column of white smoke...then a great sprout or fountain of red earth rose to a height, mingled with men and guns, timbers and planks, and every other kind of debris, all ascending, spreading, whirling, scattering," said a Yankee colonel who witnessed the event from 200 yards away from the explosion.[421]

Some of the Union soldiers positioned to make the first charge at the Rebels after the blast were so close to the explosion it caused them to back away. "It seemed as if a portion of this mass must fall on us. Instinctively the troops rose and tried to fall back to avoid this danger," said another Union officer located nearby.[422]

Even though it was early and still fairly dark, behind the Union entrenchments, a full 400 yards from the conflagration, Lieutenant Lemuel "Lem" Dobbs had perhaps the best view of the event. Being farther back, he had a better perspective on the damage the explosion had caused. Even to a seasoned veteran of the war, this was a big deal. It startled him. He stared wide-eyed at the fiery, dusty mushroom cloud filled with ragdoll enemy soldiers as it rose to its destined apogee in the sky, then came crashing back down. Cannons tumbled end over end like little boys' toys. Lem had never seen an explosion so massive. No one who witnessed it had.

Dobbs was a lieutenant in Company C of the 19th US Colored Infantry Regiment

(USCI), which were also known as a US Colored Troops Regiment (USCT). His company of almost 100 Black soldiers sat in the rear[423] behind a covered walkway that was part of the Union entrenchments, along with the rest of their regiment, waiting their turn to charge into the action. They were part of the Fourth Division of the Army of the Potomac, which was composed of two brigades of nine regiments made up of solely Black troops, totaling more than 4,000 men.[424]

When the explosion shook the ground where Lem was positioned, his men, too, were in awe. Then hushed whispers began resonating from his men until it became a battle cry. "No quarter, no quarter!" and "Remember Fort Pillow!"[425] The Fort Pillow Massacre had occurred just over three months earlier. After Confederate forces led by General Nathan Bedford Forrest assaulted and overtook the fort. His troops then slaughtered almost 200 Black Union troops as they attempted to surrender.

The Crater Explosion
Drawing by Alfred R. Waud
Harper's Weekly, August 20, 1864
Library of Congress

Lem glanced back, knowing his men were well-drilled and ready to fight. Then he turned and watched as the first wave of Union soldiers slowly made their way toward the newly-created crater.

LEMUEL DAVIS "LEM" DOBBS was born on April 14, 1842, near Kittanning, Pennsylvania, a small town along the Allegheny River located about forty miles northeast of Pittsburgh. His parents, Bennett Dobbs and Nancy Smith, were also Pennsylvanians, though the family's roots traced to Ireland and Scotland, immigrating to North America in the 1700s. Lemuel's father, Bennett, was an engineer and surveyor. By 1850 the family had settled in Jenks Township, Pennsylvania, a small farming community about 100 miles northeast of Pittsburgh. The family had six children that survived into adulthood: five boys and one girl, with Lem the fifth born. Of his four brothers, three became ministers. Before the start of the Civil War, Lem was a local schoolteacher living in his father's home.

In June 1861 nineteen-year-old Dobbs made the twenty-five-mile trip south from his home to Brookville, Pennsylvania, and enlisted as a corporal into a local militia company known as The Brady Guards. The militia was made up of men from Jefferson County under the command of Captain Evans R. Brady, who had been the editor of the town's newspaper, the *Brookville Jeffersonian*.[426] They numbered around 100 men, representing a cross-section of trades and occupations from the region: farmers, millers, stone masons, machinists, blacksmiths, carpenters, shoemakers, lumbermen, printers, bookkeepers, and teachers. Lem likely mustered with the rank of corporal because he was a teacher, which would be valuable in training the new recruits.

Brady's Guards soon became Company K, the tenth of ten companies of the 11th Pennsylvania Reserve Volunteers. In early June they proudly marched out of Brookville wearing uniforms furnished by the Brookville citizens, bright red blouses and black belts.[427] They were a sight to be seen…for miles and miles.

The "Reserve Volunteer" regiments were intended to stay in the state to repel any invasion by the Rebels over the Mason-Dixon line.[428] Early on the Union needed reinforcements, so they called in the reserves. Lem and the rest of the 11th Pennsylvania Reserves were moved down to a training camp on the outskirts of Washington, D.C., where they quickly traded in their red blouses for government-issued blue. They would stay in camp, training through March 1862.

In the Pennsylvania military bureaucracy when the "Reserve Volunteer" infantry regiments were called up, they were no longer "reserves" so they needed to be designated as regular "Volunteer" infantry regiments. This meant their regimental numbers changed to whatever number was the next available. The 1st Pennsylvania Reserve Volunteers received the 30th Volunteer numeric designation. This meant Lem's 11th Pennsylvania Reserve Volunteers became known as the 40th Pennsylvania Volunteer Infantry.

To confuse matters for all eternity, Lem, his fellow soldiers, and even the Union army itself continued to call his regiment the 11th Pennsylvania Reserve Volunteers, which no doubt caused great consternation with the 11th Pennsylvania Volunteers who were not reserves.

In the spring the 11th Pennsylvania Reserves provided support to the rear in several engagements, primarily doing picket duty. In May they were moved up the Virginia peninsula in support at the Peninsula Campaign at the Battle of Fort Magruder near Williamsburg, Virginia. On June 26 they arrived for the Battle of Mechanicsville, part of the Seven Days Battles, though they primarily did picket duty along the rear of the

Union forces along the Chickahominy River. That evening they fell back to an area near a mill owned by Dr. William F. Gaines.

Friday, June 27, saw the battle that had ended inconclusively the day before moving to the area south of Gaines' Mill, with Brigadier General Fitz John Porter's corps trapped on the far side of the Chickahominy River and outnumbered by almost 20,000 Confederates under General Robert E. Lee. Lee threw all the Rebels he had at the Yankee line in the afternoon, pushing them backwards.

Late in the day the 11th Pennsylvania Reserves, relieving the 4th New Jersey Infantry, were called up to the shifting line. Their orders were to hold it at all hazards. The fighting was intense, in dense woods adjacent to Boatswain's Swamp.

LEM FLINCHED AS HE FELT a Minié ball hit his thigh. He was lucky; it was just a glancing impact in that the ball just broke the skin. He was bleeding, and it stung like hell; but he could still walk. A direct hit to the leg often meant amputation. As the fighting intensified, smoke filled the woods, and it began to get dark. Unnoticed by the officers of the 11th, the Union regiments that formed the line on either side of them were being pushed back, leaving their regiment flanked by Rebels to their left and right. The 11th was ordered to retreat, but it was too late; they and the 5th New Jersey were surrounded and forced to surrender.

Out of Lem's Company K, four were killed. In the first real fighting they had seen in the war, the 11th Pennsylvania Reserves saw fifty-four killed, 118 wounded, and 644 captured or missing, which was most of the regiment. Their commanding officer, Colonel Thomas F. Gallagher, was also captured.[429]

"Our boys were surrounded but fought desperately. Every fourth man in our regiment was either killed or wounded," said Captain Brady.[430]

Gaines Mill ended in a victory for the Rebels, and it likely saved Richmond from capture, which would have changed everything.

With Rebel guns pointed at them, the POWs marched ten miles west from where they were captured through the night. Lem limped along with blood soaking through his pant leg. At 4 a.m. on Saturday, June 28, they arrived in Richmond. The heart of the Rebel capital had heard the rumblings of the battle. At first light they were ordered to march again, this time on a parade through Richmond's streets to the jeers of the local citizens.

The POWs were taken to an open lot near a former tobacco warehouse known as Castle Thunder prison where they were separated by rank. The officers were then sent to Libby Prison, while Lem and the other enlisted men went to Belle Island on the James River.

Belle Island in the heat of summer was hell. Lem and his fellow soldiers suffered tremendously from lack of shelter and little food or water. They all sweltered in the humid heat on the island located in the middle of the James River, with a commanding view of Richmond to the north.

In his first few weeks of captivity, Lem contracted dysentery, becoming weaker and weaker.[431] The sun felt like it was baking his brains, and he was often delirious. Finally, on August 5 the suffering POWs were granted a reprieve and exchanged for an equal number of Rebel prisoners held by the Union. The officers of the 11th Pennsylvania Reserves were exchanged a week later.

The POWs were all marched the nine miles east from Belle Island to Aiken's Landing, the point of exchange between the two sides. Along the way Lem collapsed from sunstroke and exhaustion; the dysentery had taken its toll. He was left with two fellow POWs on the side of the road as the rest of the prisoners continued marching in the hot sun. His comrades used rags dipped into the waters of the James to bring Lem around. They slowly walked on either side of him, supporting his weight, and helped him make it back to the main group of prisoners in time for their exchange.[432] His forty days exposed to the sweltering heat and his bout with dysentery forever changed Lem, leaving him in a weakened state with maladies he would carry with him for the rest of his life.

The men rejoined the 11th Pennsylvania Reserves and were back in the heat of battle at Groveton and Second Bull Run on August 28 to 29, 1862. At Bull Run they were pinned down overnight, under constant fire from Confederate batteries. It was during this battle that Lem suffered another attack of heat exhaustion.

"Being his tent-mate, I was with him in the tent first night after the attack," said Private Orvil T. Minor. "He was out of his head and suffered terrible convulsions." [433]

Lem was sent to Harewood General Hospital in Washington, D.C., where he would remain for eight months until April 1863, convalescing and eventually being given light hospital duty.[434] Harewood was in the northeast part of the capital, which was a place where the poet Walt Whitman volunteered as a nurse during the time that Lem was a patient. President Lincoln was also a regular visitor to Harewood, which was on the four-and-a-half-mile route from the White House to the Soldier's Home where he and his family often stayed.

> *These are not like other hospitals. By far the greatest proportion (I should say five-sixths) of the patients are American young men, intelligent, of independent spirit, tender feelings, used to a hardy and healthy life; largely the farmers are represented by their sons—largely the mechanics and workingmen of the cities. Then they are soldiers.*
>
> **Walt Whitman**
> **New York Times**
> **February 23, 1863**

After Lem returned to his regiment in spring 1863, he again suffered from bouts of heat exhaustion, with convulsions and delirium. This time he was sent to the regimental hospital for a few days. Upon his return he was given the job keeping the regimental books, which kept him out of the sun.

"I put him on light duty and detailed him as my Clerk," said Lem's Captain James P. George. "I at the time having command of the three left companies of my regiment. He was with the company at the Battle of Gettysburg, but unable to do much duty, he was in the fight the evening of the 2nd of July, but after that, I ordered him on as light duty as possible."[435]

At Gettysburg on July 2, 1863, the second day of the battle, the 11th Pennsylvania Reserves found themselves in a column to the right and in front of Little Round Top where they charged forward down the hill and across the valley, driving the Rebels as they went.[436] Throughout the fall 1863 the regiment was involved in the pursuit of Lee's army in and around Northern Virginia with Lem settling into a job that helped finally stabilize his medical condition. Even though he suffered from a lingering disability, he recognized his duty and responsibility. It was noted by officers in the regiment that "Corporal Dobbs doesn't give up."

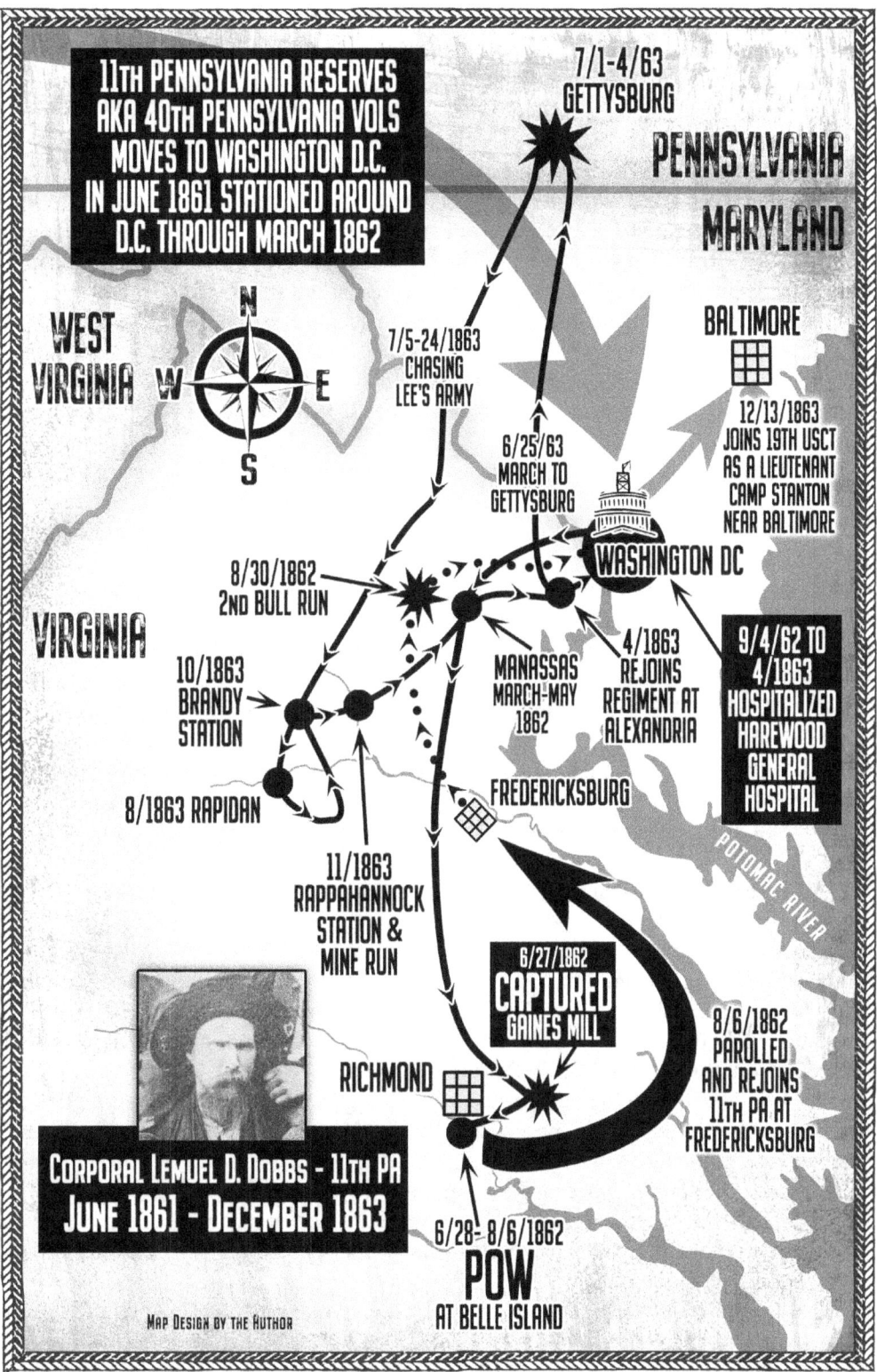

11TH PENNSYLVANIA RESERVES AKA 40TH PENNSYLVANIA VOLS MOVES TO WASHINGTON D.C. IN JUNE 1861 STATIONED AROUND D.C. THROUGH MARCH 1862

7/1-4/63 GETTYSBURG

PENNSYLVANIA

MARYLAND

WEST VIRGINIA

BALTIMORE

7/5-24/1863 CHASING LEE'S ARMY

12/13/1863 JOINS 19TH USCT AS A LIEUTENANT CAMP STANTON NEAR BALTIMORE

6/25/63 MARCH TO GETTYSBURG

WASHINGTON DC

8/30/1862 2ND BULL RUN

VIRGINIA

4/1863 REJOINS REGIMENT AT ALEXANDRIA

9/4/62 TO 4/1863 HOSPITALIZED HAREWOOD GENERAL HOSPITAL

10/1863 BRANDY STATION

MANASSAS MARCH-MAY 1862

8/1863 RAPIDAN

FREDERICKSBURG

POTOMAC RIVER

11/1863 RAPPAHANNOCK STATION & MINE RUN

6/27/1862 CAPTURED GAINES MILL

8/6/1862 PAROLLED AND REJOINS 11TH PA AT FREDERICKSBURG

RICHMOND

CORPORAL LEMUEL D. DOBBS - 11TH PA
JUNE 1861 - DECEMBER 1863

6/28- 8/6/1862
POW
AT BELLE ISLAND

MAP DESIGN BY THE AUTHOR

Back in Washington, D.C., decisions were being made that would alter the path that Lem had found himself on as a corporal/clerk. There had been discussions about using former enslaved men to fight as soldiers in the Union army. The debate had started in 1862 and, on May 22, 1863, resulted in the issuance of General Order Number 143,[437] establishing the Bureau of Colored Troops from which the United States Colored Troops (USCT) was formed.

The regiments of Black Union soldiers would be under the command of White officers. Soon a recruiting effort went out to White soldiers and civilians to fill the need.[438] Several officer selection boards were established throughout the country. It required the applicant to appear before a Board of Examiners and offered a fast track for the right candidates to step from enlisted man to officer.

Applicants were drilled on their knowledge of infantry tactics, army regulations, arithmetic, geography, history, and the sanitary care of the troops, as well as given a medical physical. Applicants had just one chance: If you failed, you could not apply again.

Lem saw this as an opportunity. Once again, it didn't hurt that he had been a teacher before the war and had also in his job as a clerk become proficient at handling the military bureaucracy. In October 1863 he sent in his application and was quickly called before the Board of Examiners in Washington, D.C., for testing.

Lemuel D. Dobbs was commissioned as a Second Lieutenant in Company C, 19th USCI, on November 15, 1863. Through the end of October 1863, 918 people were examined by the board, with only 517, including Lem, deemed qualified to be an officer in the USCI. He was ordered to report to Benedict, Maryland, the location of Camp Stanton, which was the training facility for the new Black soldiers of the 19th USCI.

His first task was to recruit Black men to become Union soldiers. Almost all were former slaves, many recruited from the Chesapeake region of Eastern Maryland including Talbot County where Frederick Douglass was enslaved before he escaped.[439] The 19th USCI filled up its rolls and completed its regimental organization in January 1864.[440]

As a new officer traveling around the area, Lem also had an opportunity to visit Baltimore where he met twenty-one-year-old Catherine Elizabeth Meyers. Her father was a blacksmith, and Catherine worked as a weaver. Her family lived in Towsontown (present-day Towson) located on the north side of Baltimore. Lem called her Kate, and they were married on Wednesday, February 10, 1864, in Baltimore. They likely didn't enjoy much of a honeymoon as Lem was quickly back at Camp Stanton. Kate wouldn't see much of her new husband while the war continued.

The 19th USCI continued to train into the spring, drilling constantly and instilling discipline in the soldiers until they became a tight unit. In late March they took the regiment, which numbered around 750 men, to Harper's Ferry for continued training and for additional recruiting. On a road along the way near Winchester, Virginia, the advanced guard was fired upon, and they returned fire, the first action the regiment had seen. It turned out it was a training exercise secretly thrown at the men by Colonel Joseph G. Perkins, who commanded the 19th USCI.

"It was found that a company of our scouts, dressed in grey, had opened fire on our men to see how they would stand," said a 19th USCI officer. "Our men returned fire and did not flinch."[441]

On April 18, 1864, three regiments of Black troops, including the 19th, made their way to Annapolis, Maryland, by boat to parade through the city and on to Baltimore.

From there they marched west to Washington, D.C., and passed in a column reviewed by President Lincoln and General Burnside from the steps of the Willard's Hotel. They continued marching right out of town, crossing the Potomac River and becoming part of the Ninth Corps of the Army of the Potomac.

Lieutenant Colonel Henry Pleasants
48th Pennsylvania
Property of Ronn Palm Museum of Civil War Images Gettysburg

"The men marched proudly and soldierly, and nothing could be more perfect than their movement, evidencing a great deal of care of their management and drill," said one officer. "Magnificent working and fighting material was in that column. Sturdy, stalwart, able-bodied and healthy men, well disciplined by careful training, proud of their new and novel position, they looked every inch the soldier."

They would spend the next three months guarding supply trains at the Battles of the Wilderness, Spotsylvania Court House, and Cold Harbor. By mid-June they had arrived on the outskirts of Petersburg where the siege operation of the city had started. For the next eight weeks they helped dig the trenches of the Union earthworks and took their turn on picket duty with a large portion of the line under constant fire.

The idea for a tunnel mine dug from the Union works to the Confederate works came from a serendipitous moment when a Colonel overheard the conversation between one of his enlisted men and fellow messmates.

"We could blow that damned fort out of existence if we could run a mine shaft under it," said the private to his buddies.

It turns out that the man who overheard the conversation was Argentinean-born Lieutenant Colonel Henry Pleasants, who was also a mining engineer. The unnamed private was a member of the 48th Pennsylvania, which was made up primarily of anthracite coal miners. For these guys, digging mines was a common topic of conversation at dinner while chewing on hardtack. After a short period of reflection, the Colonel quickly ran the idea up the chain of command.

Three main actors directly impacted the success or failure of the mining of Elliott's salient and the attack: Major General Ambrose Burnside, the architect of the plan and commander of the Ninth Corps, whose men would mount the attack; Burnside's boss, Major General George Meade, who commanded the Army of the Potomac and didn't much like Burnside; and Lieutenant General Ulysses S. Grant, who commanded everyone.

Pleasants told his division commander General Robert Potter, who told Burnside, who then told Meade. With Meade, things briefly stopped as he consulted with his engineers, who told him it was a nutty idea. A tunnel as long as they were proposing wouldn't work, they said, as it couldn't be ventilated properly so the miners would suffocate. But Meade went ahead anyway and tossed the idea up one more notch to Grant, who thought the idea interesting and gave his go-ahead.

THE DIGGING FOR THE MINE BEGAN on June 25, supervised by Colonel Pleasants with the work done by his regiment of Pennsylvania miners. When they got to the point where they were under the enemy's earthworks, the Rebels heard sounds coming from down below, but they could never locate the source. Pleasants' team even solved the ventilation issue, proving the idea wasn't nutty after all. These were experienced miners who were used to being deep in the earth; they weren't going to let the lack of breathable air stop them.

When the tunnel was complete, it stretched 510 feet in what was called the main gallery that was roughly four and a half feet tall and four and a half feet wide. At the end of the main gallery, directly under Elliott's salient, it formed a "T," splitting left and right about thirty-five feet in each direction. Powder was placed in these two galleries with a long, spliced fuse stretched from each of the powder kegs down the main gallery. The entire endeavor was completed on July 26, and the powder and fuses were set in position on July 28.[442]

The original plan of attack, designed by General Burnside, called for the Fourth Division commanded by General Edward Ferrero, composed of his two brigades of all the Black regiments, to take the lead and charge at the Rebels immediately after the explosion. The First Brigade, commanded by Lieutenant Colonel Joshua K. Sigfried, would charge to the right of what was anticipated to be a massive crater. The Second Brigade, commanded by Colonel Henry G. Thomas, would go to the crater's left. The 19th USCI was in the Second Brigade. They were to charge forward as rapidly as possible, widening the breach of the enemy's line as they went, and take the crest 1,300 yards to the northeast known as Cemetery Hill adjacent to Blandford Church. In Burnside's plan, they were not to charge down into the actual crater.

The Black troops would be followed and supported by the remaining three White Divisions. The order would be the First Division commanded by Brigadier General James H. Ledlie, followed by the Second Division commanded by Brigadier General Robert B. Potter, and finally, the Third Division commanded by Brigadier General Orlando B. Wilcox. After taking Cemetery Hill, they would continue onward and perhaps seize Petersburg.

One of the reasons that Burnside chose the Fourth Division to lead was that they were fresh and had seen little action other than guarding wagon trains and digging earthworks. The other three divisions in the Ninth Corps had been subjected to the front lines of the siege on Petersburg and were burnt out. In fact, they were shell-shocked. In Burnside's words, "they had been exposed for forty days to a ceaseless fire and had acquired the habit of sheltering themselves from enemy's missiles." On the other hand, Burnside remarked, the Black troops "were fresh and strong, their ranks full, their morale unexceptionable, and their spirits elated by the thought of the approaching conflict."[443] The Black soldiers were charged up and ready to get into real battle and prove themselves.

In early July all nine regiments of Black troops began intensive training for the precision maneuver they were to execute around the crater and up the hill. In the weeks leading up to the planned explosion, they drilled daily on the techniques they would use to skirt around the crater and move toward the cemetery. By Thursday, July 28, they were ready.

That morning General Meade met with General Burnside to go over the strategy. He told a shocked Burnside that he couldn't "approve of your placing the negro troops in the advance, as proposed."[444] Meade argued that the Black troops would not be as reliable as the White troops. Burnside argued that his White troops were spent, and his Black troops were ready. Meade agreed to pose the question to General Grant. But when he met with Grant a few hours later, he never even presented Burnside's plan. Instead, Meade presented a political hypothesis. If the Black soldiers led the assault and failed, suffering great casualties, there might be a backlash and the appearance of them being careless with the lives of the Black soldiers.[445] Grant chomped on a cigar and considered the observation for a few moments, then went along with Meade's decision.

On Friday, July 29, Meade strolled casually into Burnside's headquarters for a chat, blindsiding Burnside with the information that Grant had agreed with Meade's point of view. Meade ordered the Black troops not to lead the advance. Burnside was to use the White troops.[446] It was a crushing blow for Burnside and the Black troops of the Fourth Division. It was also a very poor decision by Meade, making such a major change to a plan that had been rehearsed for weeks in the final critical hours. It required Burnside to scramble and revise his plan, quickly assigning a different division and bringing them up to speed on their critical role once the mine exploded.

"Both our officers and men were much disappointed, as it was an opportunity to show what they could do," said a 19th USCI officer.[447]

Of the three Divisions of white soldiers, no commander wanted the job, so General Burnside had them draw lots. General Ledlie of the First Division pulled the short straw and won the job though he surely viewed it as a loss. His men would lead the first wave toward the Confederate earthworks after the mine was detonated. He was clueless as to the strategy he needed for the first assault on the Rebels and was left with no time to figure it out and drill his men. They would just have to wing it.

IN THE EARLY MORNING HOURS of Saturday, July 30, all four Divisions were in place as planned. But not a lot of thought was given to the logistics of moving such large numbers of Union soldiers through their own maze of earthworks, some eight-foot deep, over the top of their parapets and down into the land below. They then had to continue through myriad obstacles including all the debris from the explosion that had been tossed around the area and through the Rebel earthworks themselves, which were another maze of unknown passageways. The regiments up front were packed in tight. The regiments behind them were unable to move forward until the ones up front cleared through. It was a massive, claustrophobic traffic jam of sweaty, nervous men.

For Lem and his men in the 19th USCI, being pulled from the lead of the attack was a tremendous disappointment. They went from the front to bringing up the rear of the four divisions, set back from where the mine was set to go off. *It was so typical*, Lem thought, *they always ended up guarding the rear of something.*

At just after 3 a.m., deep inside their tunnel, Colonel Pleasants and his men struck a match and lit three separate fuses. A blue flame burst upward from each, hissing westward down the tunnel. They all quickly ran out of the tunnel. Pleasants had calculated that it would take about twenty minutes from the time they lit the fuses until the mine exploded. Once outside, he took a position on a Union parapet, with a clear view of his target and waited in the darkness.

3:30 a.m. Nothing.

4:00 a.m. came and went.

At 4:15 a.m. Still nothing.

Sergeant Snapper Reese, who had acted as the mine boss for the project, was the brave man who volunteered to reenter the tunnel to see what the hell had gone wrong. He did so carrying a lit lantern.[448]

Reese soon discovered the fuses had died out at a point where they had been spliced together, which was at a point a long way from their appointed destiny. He cut out the splice and lit the fuses again, each sizzling away like a mad rattlesnake. Running as fast as he could while crouched down in the tight four-and-a-half-foot-tall space, at 4:33 a.m. Snapper Reese safely emerged from the tunnel.

Everyone held their breath.

AFTER THE EXPLOSION THAT CREATED The Crater, it was widely understood by the officers in the first wave of Union forces that the first minutes were the most critical for the operation's success. As soon as the explosion occurred, Federal artillery began firing at the Confederate earthworks. A massive amount of firepower lit up the sky and added to the chaos caused by the initial explosion. The sound was deafening. and the smoke created a haze that mingled with the dust from the mine explosion.

The entire event had created such turmoil among the Confederates that they turned and ran away from the area toward Petersburg, expecting some other Yankee-created calamity to follow. It presented a wonderful opportunity to charge quickly through the massive breach in the Rebel earthworks and up the crest toward the cemetery. This was when the chance for success was at its greatest, but the Yankees froze. Nothing happened quickly except for the speed in which the opportunity was lost.

General Ledlie's First Division was completely unprepared for something so powerful going off right in front of their faces. They were beat-up, as General Burnside had noted, and cowered back to protect themselves. When they finally did advance forward, they instantly became a bunch of sightseers. For a few minutes, since no one was shooting at them, they stood in awe. The Crater was massive, creating an irregular rectangular-shaped depression measuring 170 feet long by sixty feet wide and thirty feet deep with steep banks that were difficult to climb out of. The ground around it was a labyrinth of debris, mangled Rebel defense structures, and dead or dying soldiers.

General Meade telegraphed to General Burnside at 6:50 a.m., "What is the delay in your column moving? Every minute is most precious, as the enemy undoubtedly are concentrating to meet you on the crest, and if you give them time enough you cannot expect to succeed."[449]

Finally, the men from the First Division began slowly advancing, but their leader stayed behind. General Ledlie suffered from an affliction of cowardice, and immediately after finally seeing off his men as they finally began advancing, he retired to a bombproof a few yards behind the lines. Bombproofs were protective bunkers with a heavy log roofs and sides, covered with earth, that provided protection from artillery fire.

Ledlie spent almost the entire battle in the bombproof, along with a bottle of medicinal rum given to him by a surgeon after he told the doctor he had been struck by a spent ball when the mine had gone off. It was a lie. He was joined in the bunker by General Ferrero, who commanded Lem's Fourth Division of Black troops, who apparently suffered the same affliction.[450]

As time passed the Rebels began to come back toward The Crater and engage the Yankees who were slowly breaching their line. The Union soldiers in the First Division, now under fire, ran down into The Crater, attempting to use it as cover from the onslaught of fire aimed at them. This proved to be a very bad idea.

Then the Second Division moved in, heading to the right. The Third Division headed to the left of The Crater, fighting Rebel regiments, who had returned to their lines. But in planning to move thousands of men, the Union forces had not provided their men with ladders to get out of their own earthworks. Union soldiers found themselves jammed in and had to climb over their own parapets one or two at a time. Then they had to cross over a dangerous landscape under increasing heavy fire directed by the Rebels from a position to the left of the of the expanding body of Union soldiers in and around The Crater. They got knocked back, many also taking what they believed to be shelter in The Crater, which was rapidly filling with Yankee soldiers.

Finally, it was Lem's turn with his men in the Fourth Division. They tried to move quickly, as they had been trained, but troops from the other divisions were packed against each other in front of them in a bottleneck. The Fourth also moved to the right, making it past The Crater to the Rebel works with the idea of making a rush to the crest of Cemetery Hill.

"No quarter, no quarter" and "Remember Fort Pillow" were the rallying calls of the Black troops joining the battle.

"It was now too late," said one of Lem's fellow officers in the Nineteenth. "Our men were not only exposed to the terrible musketry fire in front, but to an enfilading fire of shell, grape and canister that no troops could withstand.[451]"

It turned into a slaughter. For many of the Rebels, this was the first time they had met Black soldiers in battle. The hate ran to their core, with additional burning-hot anger directed at the White officers for leading companies of former slaves against them in battle. The entire concept was almost too much to fathom for the Rebels.

As the morning progressed, the summer heat tortured both sides. But for the men piled on top of each other in The Crater, it became unbearable. Their canteens were empty, and their ammunition was running low. The Rebels, led by Petersburg-native General William Mahone, rebounded with more vengeance by mid-morning, at one point surrounding the west side of the crater and shooting down into it at will, in what Mahone later called a "turkey shoot."

At around 1 p.m. Mahone ordered a final charge by his men down into The Crater.

The men who found themselves in The Crater couldn't move forward because of the steep, thirty-foot-tall sides. Lem found himself in this pit of hell and was hit, a Minié ball lodging in his chest. As he quickly checked himself, he realized it was another glancing wound. He could survive it if he could just get out of the pit, but he was stuck tight, unable to move. He had reached the point at which he was just trying to survive. That couldn't be said for many of the men from his company stuck there with him. Lem watched in horror as several were bashed in the head with the butt of a Rebel rifle swung with deadly force. Hundreds of White and Black soldiers were desperately fighting, Rebels and Yankees in hand-to-hand combat to the death. The bodies began to pile up on top of each other, Black and White each bleeding the same color: red.

Two soldiers were found dead together, one a White Confederate soldier, the other a Black Union soldier. They were both on their knees with their guns clenched in their hands, rigor mortis having frozen their fingers in a death grip around their weapons. They had thrust their bayonets at the same time, completely running through each other's bodies in synchronized death.[452]

"Our men, who were always made wild by having negroes sent against them," said one Rebel Colonel in the Crater as the battle came to an end, "were utterly frenzied with rage. Nothing in the war could have exceeded the horrors that followed."[453]

Screaming through the carnage a Rebel finally yelled to a Yankee, "Why in hell don't you fellows surrender?" to which came the reply, "Why in the hell don't you let us?"[454]

Even after surrender was accepted, the Rebels murdered many Black soldiers in an uncontrollable rage, completely throwing away their discipline and self-control. It wasn't just killing the enemy during a battle: it was pure, animalistic hate by a group of human beings against their fellow human beings. The Crater became a massive pit of slaughter, fueled by extreme prejudice. Lem, suffering from a wound to his chest, was in a fury over the way his men were murdered by the enemy after clearly surrendering.

By the early afternoon it was over. Lem dragged himself out of the morass; other men, still alive though injured, pulled out with him.

"When we surrendered, I, in common with others, began clambering out of the excavation, up over the boulders of clay to firm ground," said one USCI officer captured with Lem. "As I reached the surface, a Confederate soldier confronted me, saying, "Give me that sword, you damn Yankee!" I of course immediately surrendered my sword, giving him sword and belt and pistol."[455]

They were gathered nearby in the rear of the enemy's line in a low field just outside of Petersburg. The officers separated from the enlisted men. For the entire Fourth Division in the Battle of the Crater, out of more than 4,000 men there were more than 1,800 casualties with 259 killed and more than 1,000 wounded.

In the 19th USCI, the regiment's Lieutenant Colonel Joseph G. Perkins was seriously wounded, and Major Theodore Rockwood was killed in action. In total the regiment saw twenty-two men killed and eighty-seven wounded. Six were missing or captured; some of those missing would never be found as the number of dead within The Crater was staggering, with bodies piled on top of each other. Two other officers in the 19th captured along with Lem were Lieutenant Andrew J. Raymore of Company H and Lieutenant William H. Mix of Company K.

Soon it became apparent to many of the White USCI officers that there was a new danger. The Confederate government, acting on the recommendation of President Jefferson Davis in response to the Emancipation Proclamation, had passed a resolution on May 1, 1863. It declared that every White person being a commissioned officer who commanded, armed, trained, organized, or prepared Black men for military service was guilty of inciting servile insurrection, and should, if captured, be put to death or otherwise punished. It also authorized the enslavement or execution of Black Union troops.

These were the very first White officers who commanded Black regiments to be captured in battle. It was unclear what awaited them. Many tore off the green badge on their hats that identified them as Ninth Corps, 4th Division officers.[456] As they were lined up and their identification taken and written down by their Rebel captors, quite a few claimed they were officers in White regiments. After all, the battle was fought by both Black and White regiments, so who would know? When they came to him, Lem looked down at his own blood oozing through his shirt. He was not willing to hide who he was after seeing his men give up their lives in The Crater.

"My name is Lemuel D. Dobbs, Nineteenth N****rs, by God. You can put it U.S.C.T. as that is the way it is on the muster roll," snarled Lem at the startled Rebel officer. None of the other USCI officers dodged the question of which regiment they belonged to after that. [457]

Most of the prisoners were hurt in some way; they were all dehydrated as well, the result of hours of fighting in the blazing summer sun. Several of them noticed a Rebel officer on a handsome gray horse ride up and pause at the top of the hill. Looking down, he quietly observed the new POWs. Then he turned and rode away. It was General Robert E. Lee.[458]

Lem sat with the other captured USCI officers and looked closer at the wound in his chest. He was lucky that the bullet had been a grazing hit; perhaps it ricocheted off something before lodging on the outside muscles of his left breast. It stung as he examined the raised round bump with his index finger. His blood had dried around the entry point. He fished his knife from his pocket and opened it, holding it tight in his right hand. He braced himself, then grimaced as the blade sliced open his skin and the ball dropped away.[459] Lieutenant Mix stared at Lem, then at his chest where the blood began oozing again. Lem fished the ball off the ground, then folded the knife, placing both back in his pocket. He pushed his already bloodied shirt against the wound, applying pressure to stem the flow of blood.

They remained in the field overnight in the pitch-black darkness under Confederate guard with no food or water. On Sunday morning, July 31, the prisoners—both Black and White— were lined up in a column four men wide, alternating four White officers, then four Black enlisted men until all the prisoners were standing. "Then they marched us all over the town of Petersburg, through the streets, to show us up to the inhabitants," said one POW. "The idea they had in view, I suppose, was to humiliate the officers."[460] Lem had been through this kind of parade before the first time he was captured. This time many of the citizens spit on him.

"That is the way to treat the Yankees; mix them up with the n*****s, they are so fond of them, mix them up," said one Petersburg woman from in front of her home, with two enslaved women standing on either side of her as the parade passed.[461]

That night the POWs were taken to an island in the Appomattox River, which flowed along the north side of Petersburg. The officers were separated from the enlisted men. Many of the Black soldiers were enslaved once again, some having to rebuild the Rebel fortifications they had just destroyed before being returned to their former owners.

Lem and his fellow POWs were given their first food rations since their capture: hard crackers and a piece of rancid bacon alive with maggots. They all spent the night trying to sleep on the bare ground of the island with no shelter.

On Monday morning all the USCI POW officers were packed onto cattle cars and taken to Danville, where they entered the same prison the former Libby prisoners had been held at three months earlier. They would spend a few days there while the Confederate authorities figured out what to do with them.

IN EARLY AUGUST 1864 things were not going well for the Rebels in Georgia. They had begun relocating prisoners from Camp Oglethorpe in Macon while new batches of POWs continued to arrive, and the Yankees were close to taking Atlanta. Now these officers from the Yankee Black regiments presented a dilemma. After several days of discussion, it was determined that Macon was not a good option. They decided to move them to Richland Jail in Columbia, South Carolina.

They arrived in Columbia several days later. It was the middle of the night when the boxcar door screeched open on its rusty track, reaching its end with a loud metallic clank. The fresh air was a relief for the sweaty occupants as Lem stepped down out of the cattle car with fellow 19th USCI officers Lieutenants Raymore, Mix, and the rest of the POWs.

They were marched under guard to Richland County Jail, a three-story building located on Washington Street next to city hall in the heart of Columbia. It was warm and very humid as they walked into a cell on the ground floor, devoid of any furniture with a bare, rough-hewn wooden floor. The jail's masonry walls acted as a heat sink, radiating what it had absorbed from the sun during the day. For a man with a low tolerance for heat stroke, there was no reprieve.

Lem sat down on the rough wood floor and removed his boots, then used them as a pillow, lying down and curling up in a fetal position, exhausted. With his eyes closed, his index finger subconsciously found a nail embedded in a wooden floor plank. His fingernail easily worked its way under the nail's head, and in a few seconds the entire nail slid out. He opened one eye and stared at the rusty thing now sitting in the palm of his hand, then he closed his hand, making a tight fist. Lem then fell into a dreamless sleep as a bead of sweat dripped down his forehead.

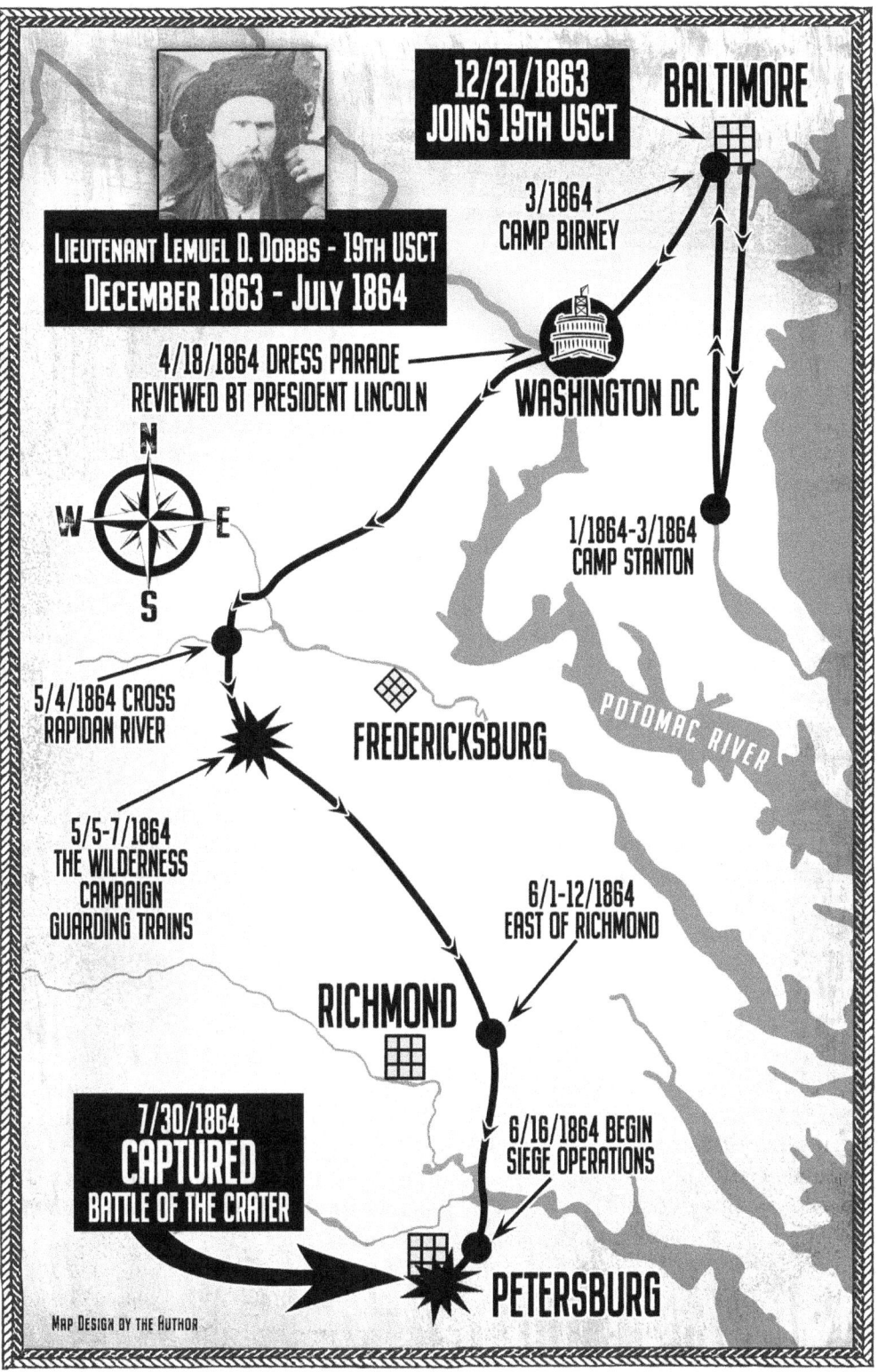

Lieutenant Lemuel D. Dobbs - 19th USCT
December 1863 - July 1864

12/21/1863 JOINS 19TH USCT

BALTIMORE

3/1864 CAMP BIRNEY

4/18/1864 DRESS PARADE REVIEWED BT PRESIDENT LINCOLN

WASHINGTON DC

1/1864-3/1864 CAMP STANTON

POTOMAC RIVER

5/4/1864 CROSS RAPIDAN RIVER

FREDERICKSBURG

5/5-7/1864 THE WILDERNESS CAMPAIGN GUARDING TRAINS

6/1-12/1864 EAST OF RICHMOND

RICHMOND

7/30/1864 CAPTURED BATTLE OF THE CRATER

6/16/1864 BEGIN SIEGE OPERATIONS

PETERSBURG

MAP DESIGN BY THE AUTHOR

Chapter Fourteen

THE FLAMING SHELL ARCHED HIGH through the sky over Charleston Harbor and exploded in a fireball over buildings in the heart of town. The structures, many of them constructed of wood, burst into flames. It was the Civil War form of chemical warfare as the incendiary shells known as "Greek Fire" were made of a mixture of chemicals designed to burn hotly and be difficult to extinguish.

Charleston had been under bombardment by Union forces since August 1863, and by the summer of 1864 the city looked like an apocalyptic battlefield. They fired on the city initially from gunboats offshore, but once Union forces captured Morris Island at the entrance to Charleston Harbor, artillery batteries were quickly positioned there with deadly effect.

Early on a massive 16,300-pound, eight-inch cannon nicknamed "Swamp Angel" began hurling shells four-and-a-half miles across Charleston Harbor. It got its name from its placement in a swamp just 7,900 yards from the city. Even though the cannon was short-lived, firing a total thirty-six shots over a couple of nights, the beast was primarily utilized to terrorize the civilians of Charleston. It worked, and many people packed up quickly and left town. After the cannon failed it was replaced by mortars that continued firing on Charleston for more than a year.

By the summer of 1864, almost every building in the city showed damage from some kind of shelling; the city streets were pockmarked with craters. The "burnt district" was the name of the central business district, which had been gutted by fire. Fort Sumter, where the spark of war was first ignited in 1861, had also been under continuous shelling and was eventually reduced to large piles of rubble. The flagstaff sporting the Rebel flag at Fort Sumter made tempting target practice, and cheers went out from a little over a mile away at the Union batteries on Morris Island as it was repeatedly blown up. It had to be replaced often.

The Rebel solution to the siege of Charleston was to place Union POWs within the line of fire as human shields. They started relocating the prisoners from Macon in June. Fifty high-ranking Union officers were moved from Camp Oglethorpe in Macon to Charleston and placed in the line of fire, surrounded by guards in a citizen's home that had been converted to a makeshift prison.

"For some time it has been known that a batch of Yankee prisoners, comprising the highest in rank now in our hands, were soon to be brought hither to share in the pleasures of the bombardment. These prisoners we understand will be furnished with comfortable quarters in that portion of the city most exposed to enemy fire," reported the *Charleston Mercury* on the arrival of the first batch of Yankees.[462]

One of the officers sent in the first group was Lieutenant Colonel John J. Polsley, a member of Averell's Raiders who had been captured along with Lieutenant John McAdams. After seven months in captivity, Polsley was seriously ill, suffering from the effects of scurvy. After moving to Charleston, the son of the former governor of West Virginia was swapped in a prisoner exchange on August 3.

There had begun to be some exceptions on the exchange log jam. Even during the time that exchanges were placed on hold, there were still a few exchanges that occurred for small numbers of prisoners, specifically the sick and disabled.[463] Being a former governor from a northern state or the general in charge of the entire Confederate army had a great deal of pull in determining who was the fortunate son.

As the summer progressed, the battles pushing toward Atlanta had overwhelmingly favored the north and the Rebels began to think about moving all the Union POW officers to Charleston and placing them in the line of fire by housing them at the Charleston City Jail. When the number of Union officers held at Charleston reached 600, the North ordered 600 Confederate POWs moved to Morris Island and constructed a rustic stockade to house them there in a tit-for-tat escalation. The Rebels used this as a public relations opportunity, naming their soldiers imprisoned at Morris Island as the "Immortal 600."

On Friday, July 29, Union POWs at Fort Oglethorpe in Macon were ordered to pack their meager belongings, cook three days' worth of rations, and be ready to move.[464] To their north, the McCook-Stoneman Raid was underway, but the lack of teamwork between the two Yankee generals led to failure by both. On Saturday, July 30, General Edward McCook had destroyed the railroad infrastructure at Lovejoy Station where he was supposed to meet up with General George H. Stoneman. But Stoneman had other plans and left McCook high and dry, never showing up.

McCook and his raiders ended up waiting around Lovejoy Station all day, wasting precious time, which allowed Rebel forces to catch up with them. Instead of meeting McCook, Stoneman dashed south reaching Dunlap Hill, just four miles northeast of Macon around the same time McCook's forces were at Lovejoy Station. His goal was to free the Union POW officers contained at Camp Oglethorpe. The Ocmulgee River separated Stoneman from Macon and his goal. The Rebels wanted to protect their POW assets by having them ready to move in the event that Stoneman succeeded in getting into Macon.

"We were marched to railroad at 3 a.m. and loaded into the cattle cars," said Lieutenant Hoffman. "We could hear cannonading close by." The shelling they heard came from General Stoneman's forces. The POWs were held in the cattle cars and stayed there until late morning when Stoneman had been driven back. Then they were marched back into Camp Oglethorpe.

BY THE END OF SUNDAY, JULY 31, 1864, Tom Young, Allie Stewart, and the other newly captured officers from McCook's Raiders were separated from the enlisted men and taken on a long march south in the heat of the Georgia summer toward Macon. After several days they reached Griffin, Georgia, just south of the railroad station they had destroyed at Lovejoy. There they were loaded on cattle cars and taken the last sixty miles to Camp Oglethorpe.

Shortly after they arrived as POWs on Thursday, August 4, they finally met up with General Stoneman's men, now fellow POWs, Stoneman himself was the highest-ranking Union officer captured by the Confederacy during the war. The Rebels had trapped and forced him and about 440 of his men to surrender on Sunday, July 31, the day after Stoneman had fired artillery at Macon.

Stoneman's close call at Macon was the final straw, proving to Confederate officials that it was time to move the Union POWs to another location. Within a week the remainder of Camp Oglethorpe was emptied out and all the prisoners sent to Charleston, South Carolina.

IN BALTIMORE, MARYLAND, IN THE FIRST WEEK of August, Kate Dobbs, Lieutenant Lemuel Dobbs' wife, was receiving the news that her new husband had been killed in action at the Battle of the Crater. They had only been married for six months but, in fact, had only seen each other sporadically, a day here or a day there when Lem was in Baltimore recruiting for the 19th USCI. When they got married, they had a day or two to themselves; then Lem had to return to his company. When she considered it, the number of days they had been physically together as a couple, either courting or married, were not much more than could be counted by the fingers on both of her hands. Now Lem was dead, and Kate was devastated. Only Lem wasn't dead; he was a POW sitting in the Richland County Jail in Columbia, South Carolina.

Like Mark Bassett, it would take a while before the facts proving he hadn't been killed in action were sorted. So brutal was the fighting at The Crater, the dead ended up terribly mutilated, piled as many as four or five men high on top of each other. It was impossible to identify many of them. The 19th USCI didn't officially report Lem as having survived The Crater and being held as a POW by the Rebels until September 13, 1864.[465] Kate suffered just like Lottie Bassett, a young woman given the biggest shock of her life by suddenly being made a war widow, then shocked again months later when she received a letter from her husband with a Rebel prison return address.

At the same moment that Kate Dobbs was grieving in Baltimore, Mark Bassett lay in the shade in the middle of the day under an open shed constructed in Macon's Camp Oglethorpe, staring at the rough-hewn texture of the boards that made up the roof. The Georgia summer heat had left him feeling about as low as he had ever felt during his long ordeal as a POW. His situation seemed hopeless. It had taken a while after moving from Libby, but the mail had started flowing again in Macon. Letters from his wife had stopped coming. As Mark lay deep in thought, he was beginning to face the cold and hard fact that his wife had taken up with another man. A tear formed and slipped out of the corner of his eye, mixing with the beads of sweat that were already covering his face as he rolled onto his side and closed his eyes. He knew the Rebels were about to move them all again to another prison. He would be deeper in the south than ever before; he felt like he was in a chasm with no way out.

★ ★ ★

AS IT BECAME APPARENT to the POWs that they were going to be moved again, many began to plan. A trip by train offered an opportunity to escape. Marshall, Page, and Byers joined a group called the "Secret Band," led by a cool-headed captain in the Fourteenth Wisconsin Infantry, whose goal was to attack their guards and seize control of the train, then help their fellow POWs to escape. Along the route about sixty miles from Charleston was the small town of Pocotaligo, South Carolina. About twenty-five miles south of the town the Union army had a foothold along the coast at Port Royal, South Carolina.

All the men had experienced best-laid plans ruined by someone slipping information to the Rebels, either by a stupid accident or a traitorous scheme. Those who joined the Secret Band were required to swear an oath, which Marshall administered to Byers.

"With my hand over my heart I swore to instantly obey every order given to me," said Byers. "I was to ask no questions, but to strike, whenever told; to kill, no matter whom, even were my own brother to be the victim. I was ready to do anything." Each man was to arm himself with a deadly weapon: a club taken from wood in a bunk and hidden under their clothes before leaving Macon, a small pocketknife, or even a fist-sized rock would do.

When the train left Macon, it was loaded with about sixty to seventy prisoners per boxcar. Most cars had four guards stationed inside, and about five on top of each car—all armed with loaded rifles. Every car had a designated "Council of Ten," who were POWs in on the plan.

When the train reached the outskirts of Pocotaligo, the men in the first car behind the locomotive and tender would seize the guards inside and cut a hole in the front of the car large enough to pass through the opening. Then they would uncouple the cars from the front of the train and give a signal.[466]

"At the proper moment...our leader, with three comrades, was to spring through the end of the front car where he was, onto the tender, seize the engineer and fireman and wave a lantern violently as a signal to us to suddenly lay hold of every Rebel soldier on the train," said Byers.[467]

When the train stopped all the prisoners were to rush the guards using their hidden weapons, take them out, and then escape. They figured that a certain percentage of the group would be killed or wounded, but the prisoners outnumbered the guards by such large numbers their odds were quite good. Once the Rebels were killed or captured, they would ditch the train, cut the telegraph lines, tear up the railroad tracks, and make their way through the coastal swamps for about twenty-five miles to the Union position at Port Royal.

The plan progressed exactly as planned with the train leaving Macon after dark on Thursday, August 11. The timing had the attack occurring around 3 a.m. As the hours of travel slowly passed, initial boredom changed to an anticipatory excitement, sharpened by a charge of adrenaline.

"Ten miles out from Pocotaligo our hearts beat in terrible excitement. No one spoke; we only waited," said Byers, "our guards seemed in perfect ignorance of the approaching danger."[468]

For a group of men inside one car, the anticipation became too great; five minutes before reaching Pocotaligo, they literally jumped the gun, easily seizing the weapons from their guards.

"And what are you 'uns going to do with we 'uns?" asked the startled guard staring wide-eyed at the Yankee now pointing his rifle back in his face as the train rushed toward the town.[469]

Everyone was ready, holding their breath, waiting for the signal, and watching for the swinging lantern from the front of the train. Suddenly, the train's whistle sounded its loud familiar screech, causing several POWs to jump. The train shot past the Pocotaligo station, screeching its whistle multiple times and picking up speed instead of slowing.

The signal never came.

"Just before we reached the designated point, the guards on top of the cars were all moved to the roof of the front car, where the plan's leaders were located, with instructions at any unusual noise, to fire through the roof," said a member of the Secret Band.

The lead captain became convinced the plan would fail so he did not set the plan in motion. Someone had snitched and tipped off the Rebels, or someone said something that was overheard. After the big escape plan failed, the men who had seized the guard's guns dropped them onto the floor and disappeared into the sea of bodies packed into the boxcar. The unarmed guards were left unharmed, unable to identify who was who in the darkness. A couple of others couldn't give up and managed to jump from the train outside of Charleston, but all were recaptured.[470]

MORE THAN 1,000 UNION POW officers from Macon arrived in Charleston in the middle of August. Most were initially housed at the Charleston City Jail, a massive three-

The Charleston City Jail
Photographer unknown from an S. T. Souder Stereograph
Library of Congress

story-high stone structure with an impressive four-story turret entranceway and a forty-foot octagonal guard tower. The prison was located in the center of the city on Magazine Street within easy range of Union artillery at Morris Island. The jail compound also had a workhouse and hospital, all of which were filled with prisoners. Inside the main jail building there was a cistern for drinking water and an open latrine/sink. The place stank.

High walls prevented any air from circulating through the building, leaving the latrine's odors to linger throughout the entire jail. In the rear was a jail yard with a sixteen-foot-high fence topped with sharp iron spikes. Initially, prisoners were crowded into this open space with no shelter. Eventually, tents were erected, but ultimately there wasn't enough room at the city jail.

The Rebel solution to the overcrowding was to use nearby Roper's Hospital, an impressive three-story building of Italianate architecture with a view of the Ashley River to its south, to house the POWs as well. On August 13 a few hundred POWs were moved to Roper's. Several prisoners soon became aware that the hospital was where Dr. George Rogers Clark Todd practiced surgery. Todd was First Lady Mary Todd Lincoln's younger brother and very much a Rebel.

"It was a curious situation, that the brother-in-law of the great President should be so attached to the country's opponents," said Byers.[471]

The conditions at Roper's were a great improvement over the City Jail, as the building was relatively new. Marshall, Byers, and Page were moved to Roper's. Hoffman was separated from his fellow 5th Iowa comrades and stayed at the City Jail with Bassett, McAdams, Young, and Stewart.

"It was close to the jail," said Byers, "and the danger of being killed by shells from our own fleet was still very great, though, in fact, few of us were hurt. The yellow fever was a greater scourge than the Yankee cannon. It was a grand spectacle at night—the soaring through the heavens of so many blazing bombshells and their bursting in the city."[472]

Shortly after the Union officers arrived, 7,000 enlisted Union POWs were brought to Charleston by the Rebels. They were housed in the Charleston's Washington Racecourse, which offered no shelter of any kind. The result was that hundreds of the prisoners died and were buried in a mass grave. The Rebel military officials in Charleston were faced with the same dilemma that their counterparts in Richmond and Macon faced. As the POW numbers grew, they had a disproportionate supply of men to guard them. With additional prisoners arriving in large numbers daily, only about 800 men, mainly local troops, were available as guards. Requests from the Rebels in command at besieged Charleston were sent to the Confederate Secretary of War, James A. Seddon, pleading to allow them to ship POWs elsewhere as soon as possible, or perhaps exchange them.[473]

Exchanges of prisoners of war between the two sides had pretty much come to an end in 1863. Prior to it stopping, there was a system that established an assigned value for each soldier so that the exchanges felt balanced when different ranks of soldiers were traded between the two sides. Soldiers of equal ranks were exchanged one-to-one, a captain was worth six privates, while a major general was worth forty privates, etc.

The exchange system had stopped when the Confederates refused to recognize the new Black Union soldiers they captured as prisoners of war for exchange.[474] They viewed the Black soldiers as escaped slaves and wanted to exclude them from the exchange conversation, which was unacceptable to the Union.

With no exchanges to rid themselves of the POWs and get back their own soldiers to replenish their ranks in return, the number of Yankees held by the Rebels continued to grow. The Rebels had problems supplying their own army, let alone providing for thousands of Yankee prisoners. The results were the atrocities at Andersonville and overall deterioration of all their prisons' ability to provide shelter and food. In the north with the Union successes, they accumulated more prisoners with each battle and began to hold more POWs than the South.

The conditions of the POWs held by the Rebels had become appalling, not only for the officers in Charleston, but even more desperately for the enlisted men at Andersonville. This attracted the attention of General Stoneman, one of the newest POWs, and two other Union officers, causing them to write a letter to President Lincoln to try getting the prisoner exchange program moving again. The letter was secretly delivered by a private who hid it in his clothes upon being exchanged. The lone private was a single man exchanged to make up for a deficiency in numbers in a previous exchange.

Stoneman and the two other officers' argument to the President was remarkable.

"Two classes are treated differently by the enemy, the white is confined in such prisons as Libby and Andersonville, starved and treated with a barbarism unknown to civilized nations, the black, on the contrary, is seldom imprisoned; they are distributed among the citizens or employed in Government works. Under these circumstances they receive enough to eat and are worked no harder than accustomed to; they are neither starved nor killed off by the pestilence in the dungeons of Richmond and Charleston." [475]

THEY WENT ON TO ARGUE THAT THE BLACK POW soldier's slavery under the Rebels was "freedom and happiness" and their chances to escape tenfold greater than the imprisoned White Union POW soldier. Finally, they felt that since, in their opinion, there were indeed two classes of soldiers and their circumstances so widely different, then the government should consent to starting the exchanges again for the class of soldiers (White) who were suffering, starving, and dying.

General Grant argued that when exchanges did occur, most Yankee soldiers returned with some degree of health issues brought on first by inadequate food and were in a weakened state. The Rebel soldiers returning to the ranks also had health issues. But, overall, they were in much better shape and ready to return sooner to the fight. One argument on the Union side was why give back soldiers to the enemy ready to fight again when the soldiers they returned were in poor shape, unable to fight? This backward point of view resulted in the deaths of untold numbers of Union soldiers who could have come home alive. In addition, thinking that enslaved men were "free and happy" was just nuts.

The exchange program never resumed fully, but small, random groups managed to act behind the scenes for the remainder of the war. When all the officers got to Charleston, the biggest topic of prison gossip was that they were all going to be exchanged soon and finally go home to their loved ones. It caught the attention of Hoffman when General Sherman personally arranged an exchange of 130 officers with the Rebels. Then a group of naval officers were exchanged, including General Stoneman himself with a few of his staff.[476] It prompted Hoffman to write a letter requesting an exchange himself.[477] He received no reply. The prospect of exchange caused excitement among the prisoners; just talking about it gave the men hope.

In late September Senator John Sherman of Ohio, the brother of General Sherman, sent a letter to Secretary of War Edwin Stanton requesting a special exchange be arranged for Marshall. The Major's father, John S. Marshall, who lived in Mansfield, Ohio, was in feeble health and would likely not live for two more months. In his condition he was unable to look after the extensive business interests of the family, which were in deep distress. Surprisingly, nothing came of the request, and the Major's father survived until April 1866.[478]

At the beginning of October Robert E. Lee wrote Ulysses S. Grant, proposing to resume the exchange program regardless of the color of the POW except if the Black POW was an escaped enslaved person belonging to a Confederate citizen. Grant declined the offer.[479]

AT JUST ABOUT THE TIME thousands of POWs arrived in Charleston, the city was stricken with a yellow fever epidemic. Charleston had become a miserable, dangerous place for the South's citizens and its prisoners.

A shell struck the prison, passed through several rooms, and slightly injured one prisoner. "Last night the city was more severely bombarded than at any time during the siege. The shells averaged one in every two minutes," said Byers. "The yellow fever is still raging in the city. Many rebels who guarded us, have fallen victim to the epidemic. Last night the captain in command of the prison, and his adjutant, died, and were hauled out this morning."[480]

"I have sent an officer to Columbia to endeavor to procure a place of confinement for Federal officers, prisoners, and will send all prisoners from here as soon as possible," telegraphed Confederate General Samuel Jones on September 29 from Charleston to General Samuel Cooper in Richmond.[481] Two days later the Confederate Secretary of War, James A. Seddon, instructed General Winder to send no more POWs to both Savannah and Charleston due to the yellow fever epidemic.[482]

On October 4 the prisoners were all ordered to prepare to leave the next morning. Everyone set about to secure rations. Once again, a trip by train offered opportunities. Many men began discussing how they might jump from the train cars if given the chance. At Roper's Hospital where they were imprisoned, Marshall became the leader in a group of six POWs planning their escape. Besides the Major, there were three others from his 5th Iowa: Page, Captain Elias Bascom, and Lieutenant John Huffman. Joining them were Captain Alvin Alexander and Lieutenant William Kiester of the 103rd Pennsylvania.

At 5 a.m. on Wednesday, October 5, the POWs were once again packed into cattle cars at the train station in Charleston. Marshall's group all made sure they stayed together and boarded the same car. Like the earlier trip from Macon, there were a couple of armed guards inside and several on top of each car. The whistle blew, and they were soon headed for Columbia, South Carolina, a 140-mile trip on a slow-moving train that would take almost twenty-four hours. A half hour after leaving, the train derailed. No one was hurt but it delayed things for several hours.[483]

At 6 p.m. they reached the halfway point at Branchville, South Carolina. It began getting dark, and a heavy rain began to fall. To the POWs packed into the cattle cars, the trip was torturous; the train was moving at less than ten miles per hour. There was little room inside each car, and the men were unable to lie down; they had to stand or squat for the entire trip. A bucket served as a latrine. Once it got dark a single tallow candle provided a flickering dim point of light, aside from the occasional flashes of lightning.

Marshall looked out; his eyes narrowed into slits so he would appear to be sleeping. He studied the two guards standing at the open train car door as they gazed back at the prisoners with bored expressions. They appeared to Marshall to be almost half asleep.

Just after midnight on Thursday, October 6, the train crossed a narrow sixty- to seventy-foot-tall trestle over the Conagree River just south of Columbia. Suddenly, two figures appeared to leap from Marshall's car into the river below. It was pitch-black, and he could barely hear the sound of the splash in the water. The two men who leapt from inside the slowly-moving train car were his guards, and they hadn't jumped of their own accord. They had been pushed.

After the train crossed the river, Marshall, Page, Huffman, and Kiester all silently slipped off the slow-moving train, one after the other every twenty to thirty feet.

"You do not fall, but the earth comes up and hits you," said one escapee on the experience of jumping from a moving train. "I struck first upon my feet, then upon the back of my neck, and then, as it seemed to me, I rolled over several times. Fortunately, the ground was smooth, though very hard. Although terribly jarred and shaken up, none of us were seriously injured, and in a few moments we were standing together on the track."[484]

Then Alexander jumped off the train, and one of the guards on the caboose's rear platform caught a glimpse of his white haversack. He aimed his rifle at Alexander, who was lying as flat to the wet ground next to the tracks as possible. The bullet hit the ground inches from his face, blasting dirt into his eyes.

"Killed that damn Yankee," said the guard as the train passed out of sight into the darkness.[485]

That left Captain Elias Bascom, the last of the Major's group, standing near his car's doorway, holding his breath.

"I jumped about a mile further on, though the guards were all on the lookout," said Bascom. "I rolled up as near the track as possible and lay there until the train was out of sight. About one hundred shots were fired as the train left me. They had a big light on the rear car and could see me plainly as I lay there. Some of the balls passed through my clothing. It was a close call and I think the guard believed me dead or they would have stopped the train and come back for me. After the train was gone I got up and looked around me to see what kind of country I was in. It looked dismal enough. I was in a low flat country five hundred miles from friends with nothing to eat and almost nothing to wear."[486]

Chapter Fifteen

Camp Sorghum – Columbia, South Carolina
October 1864 to November 1864

MARSHALL AND PAGE, AS WELL AS Alexander and Huffman, hid on the side of the tracks in the dark as a steady rain fell and soon soaked them to the bone. A large volley of gunshots sounded just north of where they were hidden. They all knew that Bascom was the last out of their train car and assumed the worst.

They weren't quite sure exactly where they were, though it had to be close to Columbia. There was a large river a few hundred yards down the tracks behind them. Marshall considered the significant rivers from the maps of enemy territory he had committed to memory. The river close to Columbia, South Carolina, was the Conagree. If that was the river their guards had swan-dived into, then they were about twenty miles south of Columbia on the east side of that river. They would have to try to head north and get onto the west side of the river, then figure out where to go from there.

Captain Alexander, temporarily blinded by the dirt from the close-call gunshot fired by one of the guards, lay where he had landed, brushing the particles out of his eyes and letting the rain wash over his face to clear his vision. Soon they were on the move, leaving the railroad tracks at the first crossroad they found and moving down an unknown country road as fast as they could, hoping they were heading north.

Bascom was shaken by the barrage of gunshots fired at him. The Rebel guard thought he had killed another Yankee. As long as the train didn't stop, Bascom was finally free. He searched around in the dark but couldn't locate the others who had jumped before him. So he walked alone in the steady rain all night. Just before sunrise everything slowly faded from pitch-black to a dull gray as the incessant rain continued. But the increased light allowed him to see a ways down the muddy country road, and he spotted men in the distance. They were his fellow escapees.

The men decided that all six of them traveling together was too big a target; they were too easy to spot. It would be best to travel in two smaller groups of three. Marshall, Huffman, and Page would go as one group, and Alexander, Kiester, and Bascom would be the other. Now that it was daylight they would find a place in the woods to hide out and hopefully get some shut-eye. As they walked deeper into the pine forest looking for a good hiding place, they agreed to separate after dark and travel by night.

THE TRAIN ROLLED INTO SOUTH CAROLINA'S state capital of Columbia in a drenching rain around 2 a.m. During the day-long trip from Charleston nearly 100 POWs had managed to escape.[487] Lieutenant Henry M. Fowler of the 15th New Jersey, who had suffered a serious leg wound at Spotsylvania Court House five months earlier, had also made the jump from the train to escape. His leg had healed enough that he wanted to give it a try. After a hard landing, he found himself limping a little as he wandered through unfamiliar pine forests in the dark, getting soaked by the rain in the middle of Rebel South Carolina like the other escapees. Just about all were tracked down and eventually recaptured. A Vermont lieutenant who jumped from the train was hunted and caught by bloodhounds and viciously mauled; he died from the injuries later that day.[488]

The men were kept packed on board the cattle cars until sunrise; then, they were unloaded from the train and herded into an open field near the depot on Gervais Street[489] with no shelter while the rainstorm continued to antagonize them. The total count of prisoners was more than 1,200.

They huddled together for a day as the citizens of Columbia became aware of Yankees in their midst. Some came to see their enemies for themselves and to ascertain whether they indeed had horns as so many suspected.[490] The local authorities had been given no warning that they were even coming. They were guarded by the Columbia Cadets, a group of young men from a local military school.[491]

The next morning they were ordered to be up and ready to march. The ragged mass of miserable, wet prisoners was marched through part of Columbia and out of town, crossing the Conagree River to their new prison home.

"On the way we passed the Confederate money factory. As the girls employed there came to the windows we called to them to throw us a bushel or two, as they could make plenty more," said one POW. "They laughed, threw kisses at us, and for a moment we forgot we were the prisoners, and felt we were going out on a picnic."[492]

"Our blankets and everything we owned was wet as they marched us from town and put us into camp," said Michael Hoffman. "The prison was located two miles up the river, northwest of the city. It was a prison without any previous preparation of any kind—only a patch of ground about three acres, covered by small pine trees. Between this and the river the pine timber was quite thick. No shelter of any kind. The ground for a floor. The sky for a roof."[493]

That night it was so cold that many men could not sleep, and a cold frost formed on the prisoners as they lay on the open ground. Where they were to be imprisoned was really nothing more than a recently cleared, open field, without shelter of any description, surrounded by a pine forest. It was an "imaginary stockade." The prisoners had been moved to the bare ground before the Rebels had a chance to build a real stockade to house them.

One reason for this was that they were moved to Columbia quickly, under the orders of one man—General Samuel Jones, Commander of the Department of South Carolina, Georgia & Florida—who was in charge of things down in Charleston. Jones wanted them out of the city as soon as possible when the yellow fever epidemic hit, so he took it upon himself to move them all north. At the time they thought yellow fever was contagious, not understanding the disease was mosquito-borne. Jones had no authority to ship more than 1,000 POWs north, but it didn't stop him. "They were sent to Columbia without my knowledge or consent," reported a flummoxed Chief of Confederate Prisons, General William M. Gardner to General Braxton Bragg.[494]

The second reason was the Rebels lacked the manpower to get a stockade built quickly. They also lacked adequate guards to make sure the POWs didn't escape. The poorly-supervised prison guards at this new place were made up of the state militia, under-trained fourteen- to seventeen-year-olds and men over age forty-four, some of whom were members of the invalid corps. Columbia, South Carolina, hadn't really been under much pressure from the Yankees—yet.

The prisoners had not been given any rations since they left Charleston. When they came into the imaginary stockade, they were finally provided with rations, giving them an idea of what food would be provided by the Rebels in their new setting. The meager offering consisted of a daily pint of coarse cornmeal with pieces of cob ground into it and a pint of sorghum molasses every five days. The POWs would sift the pieces of corncob from the cornmeal and brown it; then they would brew a prison coffee from it.

Sorghum, a cane plant native to Africa, was introduced into the United States in the 1700s. The liquid of the cane is extracted by pressing it, and the sorghum juice is then slowly boiled to produce a molasses-like sweet syrup. Apparently, they had an abundant supply in Columbia, South Carolina, so they gave it to the Yankees.

As a result of this new addition to their diet, the POWs named their new digs "Camp Sorghum," and the name stuck. Even the Rebels would use the name in their records, though officially it was known as "C. S. Prison, Columbia, S.C." In yet another example of poor planning on the part of their captors, no means was provided to draw individual rations of sorghum. Unless the prisoner owned a cup or bottle of some sort to hold the sorghum syrup, they were out of luck. Perhaps they were expected to take their ration

Camp Sorghum, Columbia, South Carolina
From "Prisoners of War and Military Prisons," 1890[495]

of the viscous, sticky liquid and carry it around the camp cupped in their bare hands. The rations provided were terribly inadequate, a starvation diet far worse than the prior Rebel prisons they had occupied. Many would rely on local sutlers, who sensed they had a new market of more than 1,000 captive men with money to spend. Their wagons soon appeared at Camp Sorghum, selling eggs, butter, flour, and other items that provided critical additions to the POWs' diet and likely was responsible for keeping them alive. Even private citizens, including some of the women in Columbia, arrived at camp selling homemade bread and pies.[496]

The commandant of Camp Sorghum was Lieutenant Colonel Robert S. Means. The son of the former governor of South Carolina had been a member of the 17th South Carolina and was seriously wounded shortly after Gettysburg. He became a member of the Rebel Invalid Corps, which was made up of wounded soldiers who had convalesced but were not likely to ever be well enough to return to the lines. Means was given the job of running Camp Sorghum, a camp that, aside from having more than 1300 prisoners, didn't really exist.

Adding to how unprepared the Rebels were for housing more than 1,000 prisoners at Columbia, there was no water supply within the camp, requiring the prisoners to go outside the guard line to retrieve water.

There were also no latrines, or "sinks," as they were called at the time, within the camp. Men were allowed to go into the woods just outside the guard line in groups to relieve themselves. Most all the POWs were suffering from diarrhea, a cruel side effect of the addition of sorghum to their diets, so it was a common sight to see a hundred men standing in line at the camp entrance, anxiously waiting to go in.[497]

Nothing was convenient about the early days of Camp Sorghum, a work-in-progress prison camp. The work to build their own shelters fell to the prisoners themselves and relied on a bizarre set of rules where the prisoners were "temporarily paroled," allowing them to walk outside the camp in small groups and to go into the pine forest to chop wood to build these shelters. The wood was also used to provide fuel for fires. What could possibly go wrong?

A guard line was established with about seventy-five Rebel guards placed every twenty-five feet, forming a circle around all the prisoners in the middle, with a dead-line twenty feet inside the line of guards. Eight axes and twelve shovels were supplied to the prisoners as construction tools, for the crazy parole system under which the men worked.

"The only shelter we had was of our own making. Some had excavations in the ground over which they built a covering of brush and dirt. Others had blankets and canvas stretched over fly pole. These were promiscuously located all over the camp without any system whatsoever," said Hoffman.[498] Another prisoner with a similar shelter noted that at night four would lie down in their cave-like shelter, then a fifth would squeeze in. When they needed to turn over from one side to the other someone would say "About!" and the odd man would get up and everyone would turn over, then jam back in like sardines in a box.

Within the boundaries of the stockade a few trees remained from the initial clearing of the land. Early on some prisoners gathered under these trees, claiming the spot as "home." "Our little mess located under a tree, and our rule was that one should always be home; but for some cause one day all were absent for a few moments, and when we returned, we could not find where we lived, as our tree had been cut down," remembered one prisoner.[499]

On October 11, four days after the POWs arrived at Camp Sorghum, Page and Huffman came strolling in, checking out their new home, or lack of it, for the first time. They had been captured thirty to forty miles northwest of Columbia the day before. Marshall walked into the camp the next day, having evaded the bloodhounds for several more hours after his traveling companions had been captured. The returning POWs were clearly dejected. But, like the others who had escaped from the train days before and then recaptured, they offered up information on the places they had been and the conditions to expect for future escapees. Their exploits during their brief taste of freedom made for good conversation. It raised all their spirits as they came to know Camp Sorghum. There would definitely be other opportunities for escape.

Of the six in Marshall's group who had jumped the train outside Columbia, three remained free: Captains Alexander and Bascom and Lieutenant Kiester. Along their route north, Bascom had inadvertently become separated from the other two. On Sunday, October 16, Kiester and Alexander were captured in Rutherfordton, North Carolina, 130 miles north from where they escaped. It was too far north for the Rebels to send them down to Camp Sorghum, so they were taken to Danville, Virginia, and then to Libby Prison in Richmond, where they stayed through the winter and then were finally paroled in February 1865.

Bascom was captured on the same day at Asheville, North Carolina, and placed in the city jail. Three nights later he managed to escape again, tramping through the Appalachian Mountains, making it to the Union lines at Morristown, TN, on Saturday, October 29. From there he took a train to Knoxville, Tennessee, where he checked in with the Union Provost Marshal. He had walked more than 250 miles in twenty-two days. Bascom arrived home in Lansing, Iowa, on November 6 and mustered out of the 5th Iowa the next day.

AT CAMP SORGHUM Monday, October 17, was Election Day for the POWs. The true general election pitting the Republican, President Abraham Lincoln, against the Democrat, General George McClellan, wouldn't officially be held until Tuesday, November 8, back home. But the prisoners had all decided they couldn't wait any longer, so held their own unofficial election. The polls opened at 9 a.m. and closed promptly at noon.

It was the most exciting event the men had experienced since arriving in their godforsaken corner of Rebeldom. On Camp Sorghum Election Day, the prisoners took an internal census showing that there were 1,367 men in Camp Sorghum. Lincoln received 1023 votes; McClellan 143, and 204, just fifteen percent, did not take enough interest to cast a vote.[500]

Life within Camp Sorghum began to resemble the life they had experienced in the other Rebel prisons where they had been held. "Our mess would get a turn at the camp kettle about 4 o'clock in the afternoon, when we would have hot mush and sorghum for suppers, cold mush and sorghum for breakfast, while for dinner we ate lots of it and did not kick much either," said Hoffman. "The only problem with it was that the sorghum had too much of the laxative qualities which, when mixed with the mush, made pretty lively food."[501]

It helped that the prisoners had dug latrines within the camp and extended the small creek that ran outside the camp perimeter to within the dead-line so that they had potable water for drinking and bathing. The mail also began to catch up with them, and from the United States Sanitary Commission, a private relief agency in the north, supplies of new clothing arrived in enough quantity that every prisoner got something—even if it was just a handkerchief.

Life at Camp Sorghum could turn deadly on a whim with no consequence to the provocateur.

On the evening of October 20,[502] a young, fifteen-year-old Rebel guard standing watch walked over to the next guard along the line and asked him if he thought he could hit a Yankee from where he was standing. He was pointing to a POW several hundred feet away near a group of prisoners warming themselves at a small fire.

The other guard looked on with a curious interest as his young counterpart lifted his rifle, paused for a second, took aim, and fired. The gunshot loudly echoed through the camp, causing most of the prisoners milling about outside to flinch. Lieutenant Alvin G. Youngs of the 4th Pennsylvania flinched as well, then threw up his hands and fell to the ground, dead.[503] The young Rebel walked back to his post as if nothing had happened with no actions taken against him. The thirty-five-year-old lieutenant was buried in the cemetery outside of the camp, which was beginning to grow.

About three weeks after the Yankee POWs were transferred to Columbia, a member of the staff of the Confederate Inspector General wrote: "I have inspected the camp of the Federal officers here. Lieutenant-Colonel Means, a disabled officer, is in command. He is an efficient officer, attentive to his duties. He should have an assistant. . . . The guard is composed of very raw recruits both as to officers and men, and require constant watching and instruction. . . The present guard is inadequate, 350 men, all very raw. The prisoners have no shelter, and if they are to remain at this place it would be easy to build winter quarters. If the prisoners remain they should be placed in an enclosure."[504]

By late October the Rebels began constructing the walls that would enclose the stockade. "The stockade was made of heavy timbers, somewhat like railroad ties, driven into the ground close together, making a solid wall from 10 to 14 feet high. This well-guarded, made a secure prison," said Bassett. It would be similar to Camp Oglethorpe in Macon when complete. But with inadequate workmen, construction was going to take a while, and the longer it took, the better chance of escape the POWs had. They began to take advantage of the situation.[505]

Aside from those selling goods to the POWs, the rest of the loyal Confederate citizens in the area were not too happy with the Yankee prisoners in their backyard. Plus, there was the yellow fever epidemic, which they all thought was contagious. Why are you shipping contagious, dirty, yellow fever-infested, damned Yankees to our fair city? they asked.

The mayor of Columbia, Dr. Thomas Jefferson Goodwin, stood up for his constituents and wrote a letter to Confederate President Jefferson Davis complaining that the thousands of Yankee prisoners confined at Columbia in both the Richland County Jail and Camp Sorghum were depriving the citizens of the area from purchasing food and had driven up prices. "The said prisoners enjoy privileges through their sutler of purchasing eggs, butter, sweet potatoes and other luxuries apart from the rations furnished them by the Government prisoners...depriving our citizens of the opportunity," said the mayor.[506]

THE GOVERNOR OF SOUTH CAROLINA, Milledge L. Bonham, would weigh in several times, first protesting the location of Camp Sorghum at Columbia and then later opining that there should be no prison camps within twenty to thirty miles of his state capitol.[507]

In late October the Chief of Confederate Prisons, General William M. Gardner, with his blood pressure rising, repeated once again to all concerned that it really wasn't his fault that the prisoners were now in Camp Sorghum. Because, after all, the blame really belonged to General Sam Jones down in Charleston who sent the Yankees to Columbia without his consent.[508]

It didn't matter. The Yankee POWs were in Columbia, like it or not, and they were there to stay—until they began regularly escaping. Then they would be everywhere like locusts.[509]

By late October for most of the prisoners upon waking, their first thought was how they might escape from the cursed, lousy, miserable Rebel prison.

In the month since they had arrived, most had scrambled and constructed some form of meager shelter. But the POWs still needed to regularly cut their own firewood, so the crazy parole system remained in place as the method used to accomplish this task.

Every day multiple firewood crews, always no more than a dozen prisoners at a time for each crew, would march with axes over their shoulders into the thick woods outside of camp. Over the limited time they were allowed outside of the confines of the prison, a crew member would have to march back into camp hauling firewood they had cut stacked in their arms and then return back to the woods to chop more. These repeated back-and-forth trips never had the same number of men from the crew of twelve. If the guards weren't paying attention, it was possible for two crew members to come in with their firewood and for four men to march back out. When the crew's time was up, as long as twelve men returned, no one was the wiser. The next morning during the rollcall, the prisoners would employ the same tactics they had done at Libby Prison by moving around while the roll was called to cover for the men who escaped.

On Friday, November 4, Marsh Byers decided it was time to go home to Iowa. He was accompanied by Lieutenant Amos E. Fritchey of the 26th Missouri. The two had become close friends as they had been captured in the same battle on the same day almost a year before on Missionary Ridge.

As members of a twelve-man firewood crew, Marsh and Amos marched back into camp with their arms full of freshly chopped wood. After dropping off the firewood, they marched back out of camp along with two additional men. Then Marsh and Amos hid themselves away in some brush, and everything appeared normal to the Rebels when they counted twelve men in the crew that marched back into camp with axes over their shoulders.

"The night was cold, dark and windy," said Marsh. "By midnight we heard the hounds after us, but managed to elude them, and secreted ourselves in a corn crib, and slept soundly until 7 o'clock in the morning, when we again took to the woods and traveled most of the day."

It would only be a weekend pass for Marsh and Amos. By this time POWs were escaping every day, and the Rebels had dedicated patrols out every day with bloodhounds. On Sunday, November 6, they were captured ten miles west of Camp Sorghum and marched to the jail in Lexington, where they were placed in cells with a couple of other officers who had also escaped at the same time.

"On the following morning, a company of Rebel home-guards, armed with bowie-knives and shot-guns, came to the jail and marched us back to Columbia," said Byers. They arrived around 3 p.m. "All that we accomplished by our adventure was a break from the monotony of prison life."

Byers' escape put a stop to his firewood crew privileges for a while, which cut off his escape options. The next morning on Tuesday, November 8, he and Lieutenant William M. Morris of the 93rd Illinois decided to build themselves a shelter. Like Amos, William had been captured in the same battle on the same day as Marsh almost a year before at Missionary Ridge. The new shelter was really a hovel scratched out of the bare earth—three feet wide by eight feet and three feet deep—covered with pine boughs and then covered by dirt. In one corner they built a little fireplace to burn pine knots that gave them warmth and light at night and a place to cook.

"It was more like a grave than a house, having just room sufficient to lie side by side to sleep," said Marsh.[510]

That night Marsh and Morris sat up for the greater part of the evening in their new quarters for the first time. Hundreds of miles away in the north, Abraham Lincoln was elected to his second term as President of the United States. The two bunkmates wouldn't know the results of the election for a couple of days, so, instead, they talked over their past and wondered about their future.[511]

Chapter Sixteen

Escape
November 1864

AT THE BEGINNING OF NOVEMBER, daily life at Camp Sorghum offered a taste of how miserable winter might become for POWs living in their meager shelters and wearing tattered and torn clothing. The first couple of days the rain was constant; when it finally stopped, it became very cold and windy.[512] The prisoners were exposed to whatever weather was thrown at them, and it wasn't pleasant. In addition, aside from shivering in the cold, there was also a gnawing empty feeling in their stomachs.

"This was, by all odds, the worst of the prisons we were in, as far as the rebels were concerned, although this condition of things was relieved a little by those of us who were fortunate enough to have a little bit of rebel money," said Michael Hoffman. "A soup bone...would cost us $3; a head of cabbage $1, $2, and $3; a large sweet potato, 25c; peanuts, 50c per cup. These prices, of course, were in Confederate money. This money the prisoner would get in various ways—new prisoners would bring some in; a pair of officer's boots with red tops could readily be traded for a pair of home-tanned red rebel shoes, which would probably wear just as long, and get in addition $50 to $75; the buttons off an officer's coat would get $5 apiece."[513]

Hoffman would buy himself six dollars' worth of meat this way because the Rebels provided no protein to their prisoners at all. The prisoners all knew their health depended on it.

"No meat of any kind was issued to us at Columbia, but we did get some one day unexpectedly. A wild boar rushed out of the woods, it passed the guard and came into camp," said one prisoner.

The entire camp went crazy chasing after the animal when twenty-six-year-old Lieutenant George Brown, a five-foot, eleven-inch-tall Pennsylvanian, timed a leap perfectly as the hog shot past him, diving onto its back and seizing the animal's thick midsection with one arm, then successfully tackling it to the ground. The lieutenant's other hand deftly wielded his knife and, in one quick motion, slit the animal's throat. Before the war Brown had worked at "Isaac Brown's," a dry goods store in Milton, Pennsylvania, named after his father. Without waiting to dress the animal, he began expertly cutting off pieces and throwing them to the crowd. He clearly learned the knife skills he exhibited from the butcher at "Isaac Brown's."

"The smell of fried pork soon pervaded the camp, and fifteen minutes after the boar passed the guard, every particle was devoured," said one happy eyewitness to the event.[514]

After performing his thrilling feat of strength in the capture of the wild boar, the next day Brown escaped from Camp Sorghum. He was on the run for thirteen days, making it all the way to Tennessee before he was recaptured. He was returned to Columbia and placed in the Richland County Jail[515] where another prisoner, Captain Lemuel Dobbs, who was planning an escape of his own with a little help from a friend. Dobbs was going to tunnel his way out.[516]

The boys were always studying up some manner and away of escape," said Hoffman. "The trouble was that when anyone got outside the prison the bloodhounds would soon be on his track and he would be brought back in a few hours. However, if one got out without the rebels knowing it, or creating a disturbance, the chances were one to two on getting into Union lines."[517]

It was said that one way to mess up the sensitive nose of a bloodhound was to smear turpentine on your shoes. In Macon a POW willing to pay Confederate cash asked a Rebel officer if he could get him some, claiming it was to fight off the lice that plagued all the prisoners. The Rebel bought the lie and purchased a half pint of turpentine for him. The POW then carried it with him all the way to Columbia. He doused his shoes with the stuff and was one of the first escapees from Camp Sorghum, successfully making it to Knoxville.[518] But getting turpentine from one of the sutlers that sold food

Chasing a Wild Boar at Camp Sorghum
Artist unknown[519]

from across the "dead line" to the prisoners was impossible.

Mark Bassett was studying the progress that was being made on building the ten- to fourteen-foot-high walls of the stockade that the Rebels desperately needed to get finished to secure their prisoners. They were beginning to make progress, so Bassett began to plan with a group of fellow prisoners how to make their escape attempt.

"On a number of occasions, along about midnight, some fellow would make a run right through the line, expecting that before the guard could recover his gun and shoot with any certainty, he would be too far away to be hit," said Hoffman. "They generally succeeded, but the next day the bloodhounds would be on their track, and they would be brought back the worst for wear."[520]

On Wednesday, November 9, Bassett decided it was time to go for it; they were going to make a mad dash across the dead-line. They would make their escape the next day in the early morning hours. He quickly got word to the others. The group was composed of a total of nine men: Bassett and eight other officers, Lieutenant Thomas P. Young and Lieutenant Alfred S. Stewart, both of the 4th Kentucky; Captain James A. Wilson and Captain Alvah S. Skilton, both of the 58th Ohio; Captain Augustus Dusenberry of the 35th New Jersey; Lieutenant William Henry Harrison Welsh of the 87th Pennsylvania; Lt. Malcolm M. Moore of the 6th Michigan Cavalry; and Lt. John G. Oates of the 3rd Ohio.

THURSDAY, NOVEMBER 10, 1864

"Myself and eight other prisoners arranged to bribe a guard by agreeing to give him $1,800 in Confederate money," said Welsh. But the group were a little light of the $1,800 they needed. "We rolled $400 around a thick wad of brown paper, and handed it to the guard at 2 a.m., then we passed through the guard line skipping away in the dark as rapidly as possible."[521]

The nine escapees rapidly entered the dense tree line as the guard examined and unwrapped the wad of money, discovering he had been short-changed.

He would teach those G-d damned Yankees. He pointed his rifle at the place in the tree line where they had disappeared and began firing into the darkness.

Pow!

The single gunshot in the quiet of the night was loud and woke several of the guards nearby—all had dozed off. Inside the camp few prisoners peeked out from their shelters into the darkness.

Pow! Pow! Pow!

More rifles were fired into the darkened woods by the guards who were closest to where Bassett's group had disappeared. Most of the Rebels were in a daze after being shocked awake by the first guard's initial shot. They had no clue about where they should be aiming, so they all just fired in the same general direction they saw other guards firing. A blue smoke from the gunpowder hung in the air around the guard posts, illuminated by a moon approaching full. Then the guards all quickly reloaded. More guards became aware and fired their rifles into the woods.

Pow! Pow! Pow!

The nine desperate men ran as fast as they could, then dove for the ground at the sound of the first volley. Close, so close. Then there were multiple high-velocity, screaming, shrill sounds as several Minié balls passed directly over their heads, followed by a powerful explosive thud as the ball found a tree, bark splintering in the air at the point of impact. A couple of the men felt the shards of bark rain down on top of them.

"We soon heard shots fired after us by the guards who had spied us," said Bassett. Everyone in the group dropped to the ground as if shot, then they recovered their wits and disappeared into the darkness. "This only served to quicken our steps," he added.[522]

Lungs were screaming for air, muscles were burning, and bodies were broken down by prison life, unaccustomed to this kind of exertion. But this was life or death. So they ran. They ran for what seemed like forever. Then they slowed to a rapid walk, chests heaving. A few vomited from the extreme stress. They continued this way for almost four hours until the sky started to lighten, indicating sunrise was near. They stopped to hide out during the first day, not knowing if an armed group of Rebels might be pursuing them or, worse, their bloodhounds.

FRIDAY, NOVEMBER 11, 1864

"We covered each other with leaves in the woods. The last man had to cover himself as best as he could. We remained in the woods, thus concealed, until evening came again; then traveled all night," said Welsh.[523]

They had somehow made it through their first day of freedom; at sunset they headed into the swamps.

The Congaree River is formed by the confluence of the Broad River and the Saluda River just north of the city of Columbia. The Saluda's pathway is northwest into the foothills of the Appalachian Mountains near Greenville, continuing to a confluence of two branches that takes it to its source near the North Carolina border.

The group of nine men were traveling west, away from the city and Camp Sorghum. The area they were traveling through was part of the Saluda River Valley watershed, which was subject to frequent flooding. Some of the terrain west and northwest of Columbia had a swampy characteristic because of all the river flooding.

"Of course blood-hounds were put on their trail at once, but this danger was escaped by taking to the swamps where at night we plunged forward in water up to our knees and rested in trees during the day," said Bassett. [524]

The soil was rich along the Saluda watershed, and many established plantations dotted the landscape on the higher grounds. The crops raised on these plantations were primarily cotton and tobacco farmed by enslaved men and women. "For the first two or three nights we went toward Atlanta, which was nearly due west, but reasoning that the enemy would probably cover more territory between us and our army at that place, we changed our course to the northwest, hoping to reach Knoxville, Tennessee by crossing the Blue Ridge mountains," said Bassett.[525]

The Saluda became their highway leading them to the mountains, and the enslaved men and women along the way became their guides and provided them with food and shelter in their own cabins located in the slave row of the plantations.

"We traveled only by night and never on a public highway subsisting on yams found in the fields or on cornbread and sorghum obtained from the colored people, who were always our friends and upon whom we could rely," said Bassett.[526]

Throughout November 1864 the POWs were escaping every day from Camp Sorghum; the successful escapees numbered in the hundreds.[527] The prison's security system leaked like a sieve, offering the POWs all kinds of opportunities to sneak out. They were miserable and desperately wanted to get out, with the chance of exchange seeming to evaporate into thin air.

Things in Camp Sorghum were so bad that the day after Bassett's group of nine escaped Colonel John Fraser, one of the senior ranking Union officers, decided to draft a petition addressed to Confederate General William J. Hardee, the commanding General of the Department of South Carolina, Florida, and Georgia, complaining of the conditions the Union POW officers were forced to live in. Before the war Fraser had been Major Marshall's professor of Mathematics at Jefferson College in Canonsburg, Pennsylvania, and the two men knew each other well.

CSM Prison, Columbia, SC
Nov. 1864
Lt. General Hardee
We the undersigned acting in behalf of the federal officers confined in this prison, hereby respectfully submit to you our protest against the treatment which we have received at this place.
As union prisoners of war we have had heretofore almost uniformly good reasons to complain of rations short in quantity & very inferior in quality, of an

extremely inadequate supply of cooking utensils, & of very long detention of letters, monies & boxes from home, but never before we were placed in this prison have we had reason to complain that the confederate authorities had aggravated these standing grievances ten fold by exposing us as they have done here to the inclemency of the weather in a camp in structure kind which not a structure of the humblest kind has been erected for our accommodation.

It is but just to admit that 20 tents & one tent flies were issued about four weeks ago to officers who are charged with the transaction of business connected with the prisoners. But with this exception we have been left for more than five weeks to shift for ourselves the best way we could. During the first fortnight of our imprisonment here, there were only eight very unserviceable axes among 1400 officers, six of which were private property. Subsequently twelve new axes were issued to us by the commandant with of the prison. With these twenty axes, & with 14 spades which were also issued for our use, we have erected such shelters as were practicable under the inevitable embarrassments caused by the restrictions of prison discipline. At present most of us have only very rudimentary shelters of pine branches, but few of us having as yet found it possible to erect substantial log huts which are covered with pine branches & clay. Our great want of adequate shelter makes us all feel the more keenly the other hardships of our prison life. Many officers weak & sickly from long confinement & insufficiently supplied with clothing, blankets & shoes have suffered severely from cold & rain. The want of shelter makes us especially feel the want of proper rations. No meat or lard has been issued to us for the past forty days. The daily allowance to each officer in this camp consists of one (1) pt. of unbolted corn meal, one half pint of molasses, one tenth pint of rice, one fourth of a table spoonful of salt, with occasionally one fifth of a pint of very bad flour. This allowance our experience has convinced us does not furnish adequate food for men in our exposed condition who suffer so much as we do from exposure. In brief, the pressure of our condition here justifies us in saying that annoyance frequently amounting to torment is inflicted upon us in almost every relation of our prison life. This statement will not be considered extravagant coming from officers who are required to 'find' their own shelter with very inadequate tools & under very embarrassing circumstances, who are obliged to cut very hurriedly timber for their fuel & shelters & to carry the material on their backs a distance of several hundred yards from the neighboring woods, who are inadequately fed, who are so scantily supplied with cooking utensils that many of them cannot cook breakfast till late in the afternoon, who are tantalized by the provoking detention of letters monies & boxes from home (only one mail has been received in forty days) & who are moreover denied the benefit of the monies sent them by their friends. Our government has already found it necessary to retaliate in behalf of union prisoners of war by reducing the rations allowed to your compatriots in Northern prisons.

We deprecate the necessity of inflicting additional retaliation by turning fourteen hundred southern officers out of their prison shelters & subjecting them to treatment as nearly as possible identical with that which we receive. In justice to you we will state that we do not believe that you fully realize our condition in this camp. For your un undoubted bravery & great experience & ability as an officer assure us that the generosity of the tried soldier would long ere now have moved you to grant us the redress which we have a right to expect at the hands of the authorities of a civilized people.

In conclusion the foregoing statement we can affirm with truth that we have not exaggerated any thing or set down aught in malice. The gravity of our case has made us very careful that an action in the premises should not be impaired by exaggeration or abuse.

The petition was signed by more than 160 of the Camp Sorghum POWs, including Professor Fraser's former student, Major Marshall, and Captain John Page.

SUNDAY, NOVEMBER 13, 1864

The full moon rose and lit the Richland County Jail's impressive tower as Lem Dobbs walked back to the barracks. Dobbs had concluded, after studying the place for months, that he could escape the Richland County Jail by digging a short tunnel. The jail had also housed Union Navy prisoners before he had arrived, and they had dug several tunnels. Most were detected by the Rebels, but a few were successful. Many of the Navy POWs had been paroled, but he had talked with the few that remained and had gotten an understanding of what they faced.[528] Now that the temperatures were cooler in Columbia, the exertion required shouldn't overstress his body's faulty thermostat. He had become susceptible to heat stroke incidents, a lasting side effect of the conditions he experienced during his last stay in the Rebel prison system.

The main jail to which he had been brought in August was an imposing three-story masonry building.[529] But the place Dobbs was confined in was out in the prison yard in an old wooden barracks. The structure had a wooden floor, and the very first night he had easily removed a nail from the floorboard with just the tip of his finger. Over the next couple of months, always under the cover of darkness while the others were sleeping, he experimented with different locations in the barracks that would be the easiest path out. He recruited another prisoner to help with his plan, Private Albert Hall, who had been also captured at Petersburg that summer, a few weeks before Dobbs was captured at The Crater.

If they removed two rickety old floorboards, they could access the ground under the barracks, which was hidden from the prying eyes of the guards. The tunnel would only need to go a short distance under the wall surrounding the jail complex before emerging into an adjoining garden. They would emerge in the heart of Columbia and then head west out of town as fast as they could. With one man keeping watch while the other dug, they could dig a little each night. It would take about a week. The dirt they excavated could be spread around the area under the barracks. Dobbs and Hall began executing their plan to escape the Rebels, both feeling a renewed energy and believing for the first time in months that they controlled their fate.

FRIDAY, NOVEMBER 18, 1864

Bassett's group of nine escapees was making slow progress north, heading for the mountains in North Carolina. Just over a week after their escape they had traversed about seventy miles. They found themselves in an area just south of Laurens Court House, South Carolina, living on fruit, raw pumpkins, and corn,[530] any kind of crop they could find along the river and in the bottom-land fields of the plantations along the way.

They had also learned that the enslaved men and women in the plantations would help them. The economy based on the planter aristocracy found in this area of South Carolina relied on the commodities of land and enslaved people to work the land. The larger plantations were predictable places for help in that they all had a row of one-room shacks for their slave population. This was where they would seek food and perhaps a place to sleep during the day.

One group of escapees was advised at one plantation to deal only with the field slaves, not the house slaves, because the house slaves were spoiled and would likely turn them into their masters.[531]

The Black plantation population was key to helping guide the Yankee officers through the northwestern part of South Carolina. These suffering people were valuable allies who desperately hoped that the North would prevail and win the war. A POW was likely a prisoner for just a short time and then returned to freedom. The enslaved population of the south had lived most, if not all, their lives never knowing what freedom was. They were hungry to taste freedom and excited by the news the Yankee officers brought to them, especially word on the Emancipation Proclamation.

Most of the plantations were large, with hundreds of acres of tillable land. In this portion of South Carolina, wedged between the large plantations were a few small farmsteads with just a few acres, run by a family of subsistence farmers and perhaps a few enslaved individuals. Throughout the area by this point in the war, most all the White men between age seventeen and fifty were gone, having been conscripted into the Confederate army or serving in local militia units.[532]

"We drew near a plantation one night and after reconnoitering concluded to approach the house and ask for something to eat," said Bassett. His group took a chance and knocked on the door. "A young girl answered our knock and referred our request for 'something to eat' to her grandmother, they two seeming to be the only persons at home. The old lady answered in a snappish manner, that she 'did not have anything to eat in the house. An astonished look on the girl's face and some remark probably contradictory of the elderly woman's that she began to make, decided us to walk in and help ourselves."

At this the old woman began to scream, and Lieutenant Young, a looming figure at six foot tall, walked up to her, putting one arm around her shoulders and his hand over her mouth. He then dragged her over to the fireplace, grabbed a large shovel that was sitting next to it, and began dragging coals out onto the floor. Smoke began to slowly rise from the glowing coals as they singed the wooden floorboards. The woman stopped screaming, eyes wide, becoming fully submissive with her body eventually slumping in Young's arms. Tears welled in the eyes of the young girl and rolled down her cheeks.

"This silenced her, but Young held her until we helped ourselves plentifully to the stores of good things to eat laid up in the adjoining room in great quantities, no doubt awaiting to satisfy the hunger of 'expected guests' from the enemy's ranks," said Bassett.[533]

Once he silenced the woman's screams, he shoveled the coals back into the hearth, and the group made a quick exit into the protective darkness of the woods. Though Young's height provided him with an intimidating presence, he was not well, having never fully recovered from typhoid fever from the early days of the war when he had first enlisted. The effects of the illness would dog him through the entire war, sapping his strength.

MONDAY, NOVEMBER 21, 1864

Over the weekend in Columbia, with all the Yankee escapes occurring at Camp Sorghum, the Confederate General Gardner had been ordered to Columbia to survey another location, away from the city and suitable for a prisoner of war camp.[534] He was hoping that shutting down Camp Sorghum would placate the pressure coming from officials in the South Carolina capital. In a letter to South Carolina Governor M. L. Bonham, the Confederate Secretary of War, James A. Seddon, wrote, "Instructions have been given, in deference to your views, to discontinue construction of prison at Columbia."[535]

At the Richland County Jail on Sunday night into the early hours of Monday, Lieutenant Dobbs and Private Hall had finished their tunnel and were ready to move. They spent the day preparing some rations they could carry with them from their cornbread allotment; it wasn't much but would get them through the next day.

Richland County Jail had between 200 and 250 Yankee prisoners, a mixture of officers and enlisted men. Many of the USCI officers had been segregated there, with discussion and hopes raised by the Rebels that they would be executed. But the repercussions on their own officers being held as POWs by the Yankees if they followed through with a deadly sentence was too great. So they left these special POWs at Richland County Jail instead of moving them in with the rest of the Yankee officers being held at Camp Sorghum. In fact, the Rebels actually weren't quite sure how many Yankees they had at Richland County Jail; there were more actual prisoners in the jail than were listed in the prison books.[536]

"Most of the privates are confined in the yard of the jail, which is formed by a rotten wood fence. Hence the sentinels are the only security against escape," reported one Rebel captain on inspecting the place. "There are also sentinels stationed on the outside of this wood fence. Sentinels, upon examination, exhibit considerable ignorance as to their instructions...Prisoners are not secure under the present arrangement. Stringent and proper instructions are not given to the guard. Prisoners are allowed to purchase eatables and read our papers...Prisoners under the present prison organization I deem insecure."[537]

Dobbs has surveyed the jail in great detail and couldn't agree more with the Rebel Captain's assessment. The place was insecure, and he was the perfect guy to take advantage of that. Late in the evening it would be pitch-black as the moon wouldn't rise until after midnight. That was the moment when he and Hall would quickly crawl through their tunnel and escape into the streets of Columbia. Then they would head west and somehow find their way over the Congaree River before sunrise.

WEDNESDAY, NOVEMBER 23, 1864

Two days northwest of Columbia in the middle of a moonless night, Dobbs and Hall were making their way in the swamps that bordered both banks of the Saluda River. By now there was a steady stream of escapees coming out of Camp Sorghum, but these two men were among the few who had made it out of Richland County Jail. They would hear the barks in the far distance coming from what was likely bloodhounds on the trail of other escapees. But so far they had been lucky, sneaking out of Columbia, then traveling at night and hiding by day.

West of Greenville, South Carolina, Mark Bassett and his eight fellow escapees had run out of luck. They had been following the Saluda River watershed upriver, staying near the swamplands and, on occasion, moving to higher ground to hunt for food and perhaps a place they might lie up in during the daylight hours.

Suddenly, a gunshot rang out in the night, then the barking of bloodhounds. Like the night of their escape, all nine men turned and began running as fast as they could. One tripped over something in the pasture and went sprawling onto the ground. He quickly picked himself up and caught up with the others. They passed through a tree line and entered another field, running as fast as they could. Bassett remembered a similar outcome involving bloodhounds and being recaptured during the Libby tunnel escape. Not this time.

"While crossing a field, we were discovered by Confederate soldiers who were, presumably, at a farm near," said Bassett. "They set out after us on horses with bloodhounds, and though we made as fast time as possible, they were gaining upon us, so we halted and held a whispered council of war and agreed to separate into squads of four, three and two respectively, in the hope that by so doing some of us might get through."[538]

They had to move quickly as they had little time and the sound of the bloodhounds' aggressive barking was clearly gaining on them and getting closer. Perhaps one group would be captured, and the Rebels would be unaware that there were more escapees still out there.

"Lieutenant Oats and Moore made up the squad of two; Captains Wilson, Skelton, Welsh and Dusenberry the four; and Captain Stewart, Lieutenant Young and myself the three; each squad taking different directions," said Bassett. "We three had not gone far when we realized that the hounds were not following us and so continued on our way."

The tactic worked, but it separated the three groups of escapees for good. Each group got away, with some thinking that one of the other groups hadn't. Lieutenant Welsh would firmly believe for the rest of his life that only his group of four got away and all the others had been recaptured. But all three groups somehow evaded the bloodhounds and continued moving northward, all within a few miles of each other, making progress. *Not this time indeed*, thought Bassett. As his panic subsided, his group of three resumed their hike at a more normal pace, managing to get ahead of the other two groups and taking the lead in the race to get to the mountains.

SATURDAY, NOVEMBER 26, 1864

The cadence of men escaping the prison camp through November increased daily. On this Saturday, two days after Thanksgiving, the largest group since the beginning of the month successfully escaped. By month's end more than fifty would check out of the godforsaken accommodations known as Camp Sorghum.[539] One of the reasons for success was the darkness. As the month came to an end, it was closer to the new moon, which occurred on November 29. With the lack of moon and dim nocturnal light came many more opportunities to get away.

Lieutenant John McAdams and two other men, Lieutenant Edward P. Strickland and Lieutenant Joseph D. Zeigler, both of the 114th Illinois, were able to make the run through the guard line in the late hours of the evening and immediately began following the route to the north that so many other escapees had taken. After more than seven weeks in Camp Sorghum, those who were recaptured and returned provided a wealth of information. Their failed escapes became valuable scouting expeditions, giving other prisoners valuable information on the conditions they might face and the directions the failed escapees had taken. The recaptured POWs also gave tips on who could be trusted and how to evade the damned bloodhounds.

McAdams didn't stay with the other two officers and set out on his own, sticking to the swamps, which was the best method recommended by others to evade the bloodhounds.

SUNDAY, NOVEMBER 27, 1864

Bassett, Stewart, and Young continued to plod along, finding themselves west of Traveler's Rest, South Carolina, where the Saluda River forked. The South Saluda went northwest; the North Saluda went northeast. They followed the South Saluda because that would take them to a place where they would enter the North Carolina mountains further to the west.

The weather was steadily growing colder, and their clothing continued to grow more and more ragged as it was exposed to the elements. The escapees were constantly cold since they continued to travel at night and sleep during the day. When they did stop during daylight hours, they couldn't burn a fire as it would draw attention.

Their shoes, which had been repeatedly soaked in the South Carolina swamps, had deteriorated to the point that it felt like they were walking barefoot, offering little protection from the rugged conditions.

They continued to rely on the help of enslaved Black men and women who offered them food, shelter, and advice on directions to take and names of people ahead that would help them along the way.

"The negroes were as true as steel, and had it not been for their assistance, we would have perished in the swamps," said Bassett.[540]

At several different plantations where they had gotten a meal or a place to sleep during the day, they were told that Table Rock was an important landmark, indicating they would soon reach North Carolina.

The terrain had begun to change, becoming hillier, and they could make out ridges in the distance. Table Rock, a distinct flat-topped mountain that was the subject of folklore by the indigenous Cherokee peoples and the landmark they had been looking for each morning when they stopped, was now clearly visible to their northwest.

After traveling close to 150 miles since their escape, they were almost into North Carolina.

MONDAY, NOVEMBER 28, 1864

The Major had decided he had enough and that Monday was going to be the day they would escape. The preceding Friday, November 25, marked exactly one year since he, along with Page, Hoffman, and a large group of other 5th Iowa soldiers, had been captured on Tunnel Hill at Missionary Ridge during the Battle of Chattanooga.

It had been one long year living in four different miserable, lousy Rebel prisons.

There were already a large group of prisoners who had gone out of the camp on the daily parole to collect firewood. Marshall, Page, and Hoffman were not part of this parole group; they were inside the camp. The process of collecting firewood had become an important part of the daily routine and had evolved for efficiency's sake. The men outside on parole chopping wood would bring it to the "dead-line" and then men inside the camp would haul it in and distribute it. This would go on for several hours until enough fuel was gathered. Then it was repeated again the next day. With more than 1,000 prisoners, the need for firewood was endless.

"In our shirt sleeves, with an ax and maul, and a couple of wooden wedges, we walked up to guard No. 1, where all the passing out and in was done, he being a new guard just placed there a few minutes before, and asked permission to pass out again," said Hoffman.

The Rebel guard, an arrogant, young private, was immediately dismissive and refused permission. This prompted Marshall, who after all was a Major, to sternly order the man to call the officer of the day, who kept the records of the parolees. The Rebel private stood glaring at the Major for a long moment, then turned and stomped over to the tent of the officer of the day, which was less than twenty-five yards away. Soon an old man in a butternut Rebel uniform and broad-brimmed hat walked up with the Private trailing behind him, demanding to know what the hell all the trouble was.

"We were on parole that day to cut wood; and we had got hungry, and came in to get something to eat," said Hoffman.

"What are your names?" asked the old officer.

Marshall, Page, and Hoffman gave the names of three other men, who conveniently happened to be three of their messmates and who also just happened to be legally out on parole cutting firewood.

"He pulled his parole book out of his pocket, which contained the names of those paroled for that day, and sure enough there were the names we had given," said Hoffman.

"Guard, let 'em out," said the old Rebel officer to the private who looked

Camp Sorghum Guards Along the "Dead Line"
Illustration by Captain Robert J. Fisher, 17th Missouri[594]

suspiciously at the prisoners with disdain, still doubting their story.

Their plan had worked. Now they would have to execute the second part. Through this entire exchange, several other messmates of the three men watched the goings-on from inside the camp.

"It was understood with our messmates inside...that if our plan succeeded we would each bring in an armful of wood and lay it inside the line and have some excuse to call for our blankets, which were prepared for the occasion," said Hoffman, "We had our coats and a piece of hard-cooked mush enclosed inside our blankets."

Soon Page brought in his armful of wood and called to his mate to bring him his blanket as he wanted to fill it full of nice big chips. Shortly after Marshall and Hoffman approached the "dead-line" asking for their blankets so they could bring in some dry leaves to sleep on. Hoffman's ears were ringing, something that had been happening with frequency ever since they had gotten to Camp Sorghum. Sometimes he had a hard time hearing and would miss what was being said unless he was looking right at the person.[542]

"We then went out about a mile, threw up a big brush pile, crawled into this, and lay there until quite dark. While lying here, a rebel with a dog and a gun passed close by," said Hoffman.

It was a tense moment, the men all buried in the mound of fall leaves, each hoping that the musty, moldy smell of the decaying vegetation wouldn't suddenly cause one of them to sneeze. Somehow their noses remained silent, while the bloodhound with its superior olfactory organ had somehow missed their scent.

"That was a Union dog," said Page.[543]

That night, taking advantage of the darkness, many more POWs ran the "dead line," including Lieutenant Henry M. Fowler. Traveling alone, he, too, had made his way northwest following a familiar path on the route to the Appalachian mountains and freedom.

Fowler made it to the marshland along the Saluda River under the cover of darkness. The swamp waters were extremely cold as he took a step on his bad leg, sinking into the sludge layer up to his calf. Though it was definitely a shock, it actually felt good on the leg, which had now healed from the wound that had almost caused the leg's amputation at Spotsylvania Court House six months before. He was excited and ready for the rigors of a long march to get back to the Union lines to the north.

GENERAL JOHN H. WINDER, the much-despised Rebel in charge of all the South's prison camps, visited Camp Sorghum and exclaimed the place was completely unfit for the purpose. By the time of his visit more than 373 had escaped,[544] most of whom went north toward North Carolina. The Rebels would shut down the place and move the remaining prisoners into Columbia to an old insane asylum in December. The new camp was appropriately called Camp Asylum.

"We were marched into the city and placed in the enclosure belonging to the lunatic asylum," said Marsh Byers. Byers had chosen to not attempt the escape with the Major, Page, and Hoffman. "It is a small lot, one acre in extent, surrounded by a brick wall, twelve feet tall. We have no shelter whatever and the weather is disagreeable." A short time after his arrival in Camp Asylum, having found information from Rebel newspapers gotten from either the guards or suttlers, Byers composed a poem titled "Sherman's March to the Sea." It was put to music by a fellow prisoner, Lieutenant Justus O. Rockwell of Trenton, New York, and then, during a prisoner exchange, the composition was snuck out hidden in the wooden leg of Lieutenant Daniel W. Tower of Farmington, Iowa. Northern newspapers published the poem and song, along with the author's names, and it quickly became a sensation. Back in Asylum Prison, Byers was clueless about his newfound fame.

TUESDAY, NOVEMBER 29, 1864

There were so many escapees strung out on the path from Columbia to the North Carolina mountains that you would have thought they would have constantly been running into each other. But the Saluda River route meandered with twists and bends, offering many places to hide. All the escapees had learned that it was best to avoid all roads and highways following the bottom lands. It was extremely tough going in miserable conditions.

"We soon found it necessary to march single file, one after the other. The night being unusually dark, we could not see anything," said Hoffman as they took turns leading. At that particular moment the Major was out front.

In the extreme darkness up ahead Hoffman and Page heard a splash.

"While tramping along in this way the Major, being in the lead, fell into one of those big open drain ditches, six or seven feet deep. We heard him fall, but it was some few minutes before we could understand what was up...it punched the wind out of him. We pulled him out, but it was some fifteen minutes before he was able to march again."[545]

The Major was just five-feet, nine-inches tall and was soaked to the bone and gasping for air. His shock from the accident turned into uncontrollable shivering as they continued the walk, single file. After a short distance they realized the Major needed to stop. In fact, they all did. It had been a long day, and the adrenaline rush had faded away. At 2 a.m. they hid themselves, spooning together with the Major in the middle to provide warmth. They all quickly fell asleep.

It was the sound of church bells that woke Hoffman shortly after sunrise. Once again, his hearing wasn't quite right, but he definitely heard the bells, even if the sharpness of their sound was diminished.[546] He was so tired that he felt like he could have slept all day, but the closeness of the bells to where they all lay was concerning. After all their efforts the day before into the early morning hours, something wasn't right.

"We discovered we were only five miles from Camp Sorghum," said Hoffman. "We had tramped over twelve miles that night, but were in the bend of the river, which bore us back toward our starting point."

They had eaten their meager rations and were now starving; as POWs they were always starving. At the edge of the woods where they spent the night they spotted a house with smoke coming out of the chimney. Then they spotted a persimmon tree between them and the house and began crawling, their bellies close to the ground.

"We crawled out to the tree on all fours and found it full of nice ripe fruit. We lay on our backs, for if we stood up, we might have been seen from the house, and knocked the persimmons down with stones...We ate all we wanted, and took some back to eat through the day," said Hoffman.

They crawled back into the woods the same way they had gotten to the tree but this time with full bellies, and hid the rest of the day. They all knew that when it got dark, based on their location still being so close to Camp Sorghum, their next goal was to get across the Saluda River and away from Columbia as quickly as possible.

At sunset they set out again and found a boat that got them across the river. Once across, they found a road and began following it, the North Star guiding their way. The night was very dark, making it almost impossible to see anything, and after a short time they ran into a Black man traveling in the opposite direction. The man was appropriately named Moses, and after the initial shock of almost running headlong into each other, they each told their stories. Page said that they had escaped from prison, were trying to get home, and were in need of food. The Major thought perhaps Moses would help them get to the promised land.

"Yes," said Moses, "we heard that the Yankees were all the time getting away." He then helped the men find a hiding spot and said he would come back with food. Then he proceeded back down the road, disappearing in the darkness almost immediately.

"Moses was about 22 years of age quite smart, and a good talker. Said he knew all about the country and roads from there clear up to the Blue Ridge Mountains," said Hoffman. "We found out afterward that he did know something about the roads and country, for in describing the roads to us he said that when we got up near the mountains, in a narrow valley we would come to two jack-oak trees standing in the road just wide enough apart for a wagon to pass through, and right there the road forked: that we should take the left-hand road. This place we found some twelve days afterward, just as Moses had described it."[547]

After midnight Moses suddenly reappeared, his arms loaded with a large load of cornbread, some boiled pork, and a lot of roasted peanuts. After consuming the food, they all shook hands, and the three headed north again along the country road, marching miles until dawn and then going into hiding again.[548]

WEDNESDAY, NOVEMBER 30, 1864

They had been free for just a couple of days, but the Major, Page, and Hoffman were making progress, following the advice of Moses. At around 9 p.m. they came across a large plantation that Moses had mentioned. They approached the row of shack-like slave cabins near the main plantation house; in one of them was some celebrating going on with music and dancing. After a few minutes a man came out, and the three officers approached him asking for Bob, which was the name that Moses had given them. In short order, Bob came out and invited the three inside.

"It was full of colored men, women and children," said Hoffman. "They gave us our supper, after which we remained for quite awhile, they dancing for us, and listening to our stories about the war, etc. They were quite anxious to hear about Abe Lincoln and paid the strictest attention to all we had to say."

Even though they were escaped Yankees, the welcoming nature of their hosts provided a warmth and sense of peace to the three men.

Captain Page sat in silence, taking it all in. After his head injury at Iuka over two years earlier, his personality had changed; he became known as the quiet one, speaking few words. But when he wanted to, he could project a commanding appearance. In the spirit of the moment, Page suddenly stood up and began enthusiastically singing to the stunned audience.

The Major and Hoffman knew he could carry a tune, but the Black faces surrounding the White officers lit up in amazement and then laughter as Page launched into a well-known Northern Civil War tune called "Kingdom Coming."[549]

Say, darkies, hab you seen de massa,
wid de muffstash on his face,
Go long de road some time dis mornin',
like he gwine to leab de place?
He seen a smoke way up de ribber,
Whar de Linkum gunboats lay;
He took his hat, and lef' berry sudden,
and I spec' he's run

De massa run, ha, ha! De darkey stay, ho, ho!
It mus' be now de kingdom coming,
an' de year ob Jubilo![550]

Page brought down the house.

Chapter Seventeen

Flem Cison
December 1864

WHEN THE POWS FIRST ESCAPED from Camp Sorghum, the big plantations they crossed along the way were owned by the planter aristocracy, occupying large parcels of land and relying on their enslaved population for the labor required to raise their crops. When the escapees made it into the mountains of North Carolina there was a marked change in not only the terrain, but in the farms themselves. Western North Carolina was made up mostly of subsistence farmers. Everything grown was consumed by the family that owned the land. Most farmsteads were small and fully self-sufficient, 100 acres or less, with just a few tillable acres devoted to farming due to the ruggedness of the terrain. The structures found on these farms were few, a cabin as the main living quarters, a barn, an outhouse. Only about thirty percent the inhabitants owned slaves.[551]

There was also a large contingent of Union sympathizers in the mountains of Western North Carolina. Having a population of Confederate citizens who stayed loyal to the Union was all the kindling needed for a major conflagration. There were no real major battles fought by the two armies in this region, but the personal, local conflicts were like wildfires, their flames fanned by the larger war that surrounded them on all sides, ultimately engulfing everyone.

"We found them to be rugged, stalwart, mountaineers," said one Union officer who had escaped Camp Sorghum and made it to the area. "Most of them seemed to be determined to die rather than serve in the Rebel army. All the men who were liable to military duty and consequently to conscription spent most of their time in the woods, only coming home for supplies. All of them were heavily armed. Posses of rebels had frequently been sent in there to hunt up these people, but had almost invariably met with defeat, as these mountaineers would band together and ambush them. We were told that they also tried to capture them with bloodhounds, but that also proved a failure; as not one bloodhound brought in ever got out alive."[552]

Then, as the flames seemed to settle, a criminal element entered the vacuum. These criminal bushwhackers managed to terrorize everyone with looting, robbing, and killing. Some families were divided, at times fighting among each other with deadly effect. Neighbors fought fellow neighbors, with the Confederate point of view enthusiastically enforced by local home guard units who hunted for those who were disloyal, who deserted, or for the men of age who failed to answer the mandatory conscription call.

Sheriff
Robert Hamilton
Photographer unknown

SINCE ESCAPING CAMP SORGHUM, it had taken Mark Bassett, Alfred Stewart, and Thomas Young twenty days to tramp almost 150 miles to finally cross into the mountains of North Carolina, entering this new, strange battlefield. The enslaved people helped them and offered guidance as to which paths to take and for whom to ask each step along the way. As they neared the South Carolina state line, one name was mentioned. Sherriff Robert Hamilton of Transylvania County could offer safe passage through the North Carolina mountains.

Transylvania County had been carved out of two other counties in North Carolina in May 1861. Its southern border was the state line. At the same time the county was founded, Hamilton was elected the county's first High Sheriff. His deputy was George C. Neill, first cousin of Hamilton's wife, Rhoda Neill Hamilton. In August 1864 the two men swapped jobs with Neill becoming the sheriff and Hamilton becoming the deputy. The switch didn't matter to the residents of Transylvania County; both men held everyone's respect, and they would both continue to be addressed as Sheriff.

When the very first escapees from Camp Sorghum made it to the mountains in October 1864, they were directed to the forty-seven-year-old Sheriff Hamilton. This first group numbered ten men, including five officers who escaped by jumping from the same train that Major Marshall and Captain Page had on the way from Charleston to Columbia. The other five were some of the first escapees who had run the "dead-line" a few days after all the Union POW officers arrived.

In addition to being hidden by Hamilton, the group also enjoyed dinner in the home of Sheriff Neill. The law in Confederate Transylvania County, North Carolina, was fully committed and dedicated to the Union cause, keeping their views and actions hidden from the citizens of the county who didn't share their point of view.

"We found the sheriff to be a very earnest Union man, who was willing to assist the Union cause in every way he could," said one officer in that group of five Camp Sorghum early escapees.[553]

Hamilton was past the age for service in the Confederate army but, as Sheriff, was required to help the local home guard whenever called upon. This demand placed the Sheriff in a unique position to effectively watch over what the home guard was up to and act accordingly.

"Whenever they called him to turn out he always responded," said the officer. "As their principal duty was to hunt deserters, he said he always tried to manage to send word ahead that they were coming."[554]

So Hamilton was, in effect, a very clever Unionist spy. He and his wife, Rhoda, helped escaped prisoners move through the mountains, using hiding places near their home as a way station that became known as "The Pennsylvania House."[555] They would hide the men for a few days until the sheriff could arrange for like-minded Union men from his network to guide them north or west over the mountains to the Union lines in Tennessee.

Joseph Fleming "Flem" Cison, age twenty-nine, was born and raised in Buncombe County, North Carolina, where his father had received a 100-acre land grant in 1844. Transylvania County was later carved from the part of Buncombe County where they lived, which was known as Dunns Rock.

The Cison family was made up of five children, four boys and a girl, with Flem being the youngest boy. Their next-door neighbors in 1850, when Flem was fifteen years old, were none other than the future sheriff and his wife, Robert and Rhoda Hamilton, fellow subsistence farmers also raising a family of five children. Ten years later, by the start of the war, both of Flem's parents were dead, and the land his father had first acquired as well as other parcels had passed on to the Cison brothers.

One of Flem's brothers, John Ashley Cison, had been conscripted in the Confederate army in July 1863 in the 7th Battalion, North Carolina Cavalry. The battalion was given the awful job of assisting local authorities in the enforcement of Confederate conscription laws and to quell insurrection by attempting to control the bushwhackers. After a couple of months of this, John had given up. He was court martialed and discharged, returning home to Dunns Rock.

This action would have drawn the ire of the local home guard, making John one of those "rugged, stalwart, mountaineers" who, until the end of the war, was forced to spend most of his nights avoiding them in a secret mountain hideout, while during the daylight hours trying to provide for his family. One technique used to allow the men of a family to farm their land during the day was to station the wife on the mountain ridge, overlooking their farmstead and watching for home guard patrols. If she saw something approaching, she would blow a horn to give notice, allowing her husband to go back into hiding.[556]

In November 1863 in Knoxville, Tennessee, while the city was under siege, Flem and a fellow neighbor, William W. Hamblin, were recruited into Company F of the 2nd North Carolina Mounted Infantry (U.S.). Oddly, soon after enlisting at about the same time in early 1864, both men returned to Transylvania County. Hamblin was on detached service duty recruiting for the regiment on the orders of General Kenner Garrard, 2nd Cavalry Division, Army of the Cumberland[557] while also secretly working in Hamilton's network as a mountain guide.[558] Cison returned to his home where he, too, secretly worked as a mountain guide.

In the regiment's records during this time, both men were also listed as deserters, though in November 1864 Hamlin is shown as returning to service. Flem never returned to the 2nd North Carolina, staying home unless he was acting as a guide. Perhaps this had been to disguise them as being Union soldiers while living behind Rebel lines, doing the dangerous job of guiding Union officers through the mountains. After the war both men filed for their veteran's pensions. Maybe working undercover was all part of the plan.

THURSDAY, DECEMBER 1, 1864

When Bassett, Stewart, and Young finally crossed a rugged mountain pass into North Carolina near an area called Dunns Rock, they ran into Flem as they were carefully inquiring for the whereabouts of Sheriff Hamilton.

"In Transylvania County, North Carolina, we came upon a Union man...Joe

Fleming Cison by name," said Bassett, "who befriended us as he did all others in like straits and whose knowledge of all that wild mountain country made him a desirable guide for us, as others had been."[559]

Winter weather had arrived in the mountains, covering the landscape with several inches of snow. Flem found a hideout for Bassett's group as the snow made it impossible to cross the high mountain ridges. As time passed and they waited, other escapees from Camp Sorghum arrived and were added to the group, including Lemuel Dobbs and Albert Hall, who had escaped Richland County Jail in Columbia, South Carolina.

"As we met with the mountaineers they furnished us with guns and revolvers," said Bassett. "Our party was often joined by others, prisoners escaping like ourselves, or by deserters from the Confederate ranks, we numbered at different times from six to twenty or more."

They would spend what seemed like an eternity waiting for weather conditions to improve and hiding from the home guard that was actively patrolling nearby, on the lookout for anyone new who had arrived in the area. Word had gotten to the home guard of the large number of escapees from Camp Sorghum in the last week of November that were likely headed their way.

The escapees were mostly able to make it from Camp Sorghum to the mountains primarily on their own; the river and its swamps were their guides, along with the help they were able to find at the plantations along the way. But making their way through the rugged mountains was difficult because the trails along the tops of the mountain ridges were unfamiliar and dangerous, requiring a guide with knowledge of the terrain such as Flem Cison.

SATURDAY, DECEMBER 3, 1864

While Bassett's group was laid up in the mountains, Marshall, Page, and Hoffman had spent the weekend making progress northward in South Carolina. On Saturday night they had come across a Black man walking down the road in the opposite direction carrying a bucket loaded with eggs. He took them back to the plantation he was enslaved on but was afraid to tell them his name. If the soldiers were captured and knew the names of the people who helped them, those people could easily be killed. At the plantation the man's sister was frying a freshly killed chicken in a cast-iron pan in the fireplace. The aroma wafting through the single room of the slave quarters was almost too much for three cold, starving men, but they would have to wait. She promised them a good meal and a warm place to rest while she finished preparing it; then, they would have to move on. The man said he had to take the eggs to the slave quarters on the next plantation and told them he would be right back.

"She put us in the master's house, a nice two-story frame building. They, "the white folks," were gone, think she said to the war. As she left the room in which she left us she pulled the door closed and locked it," said Hoffman, "This we did not like, but they had proved so true that we concluded not to offer any objections. After groping around the room in the dark we came across a lot of books among them being an old school atlas. We lighted a match and tore out the map of North and South Carolina and put it in our pockets. This proved a fortune to us, and was just what we wanted."[560] The men had a sense of the direction they were headed, and at night, if the skies were clear, they had Polaris, the North Star, as a beacon above. Now they had a map.

Then they heard two gunshots.

Panic raced through the three men's minds. They were locked in a pitch-black room in the "big house" of a southern plantation. Had they missed all the warning signs and walked into a trap? What was their best way to get out of this mess?

Several minutes passed; then they heard footsteps. They all jumped as the key ratcheted in the lock with a metal-on-metal sound, and the door creaked open. The man and woman smiled warmly as they entered the room holding a candle and plates loaded with the freshly fried, mouth-watering chicken. The Major asked where the hell the gunshots had come from.

"He said there were two guards at the fork in the road; that they had stopped him and had taken his eggs and some other things away from him," said Hoffman. The man also said the guards were firing just for fun.[561]

They devoured the fried chicken, sitting in their host's master's parlor, their new friends offering the men advice on whom to seek out next as they continued northward. But the gunshots had unnerved them, and they had a powerful suspicion that they were in danger. The Major considered that shooting three Union officers could be thought of as "firing just for fun" by certain folks. They needed to get out of there immediately.

They thanked the man and his sister and with full stomachs quickly left the plantation. The map showed a railroad line nearby, and they crossed a nearby field toward a line of trees where they found the tracks. The three walked all night between the rails, all agreeing how odd the experience at the last plantation was, alert for the sound of any trains or additional gunshots, which never came. As the sun began to rise, they found shelter in a depression-like gutter next to the tracks that hid them from view, where they would stay and sleep all day.

SUNDAY, DECEMBER 4, 1864

The gutter next to the railroad tracks turned out to not be the best hiding place; it was damp and covered with a sticky red clay. As it began to get dark, the Major, Page, and Hoffman emerged from the ditch, their clothing spotted with reddish mud. With the help of the map they had "borrowed" the day before, they soon approached a large plantation looking for a Black man named "Hamp." The brother and sister from the day before had told them he could help them.

This had become the daily routine, a scavenger hunt looking for one individual along their route who would provide them with food and the name of the next person up the line. The term "underground railroad" was first used in the 1830s to identify the way stations, stationmasters, and conductors that helped enslaved people running toward freedom in the north. The term could be applied to escaped POWs as well, ironically helped by enslaved stationmasters and conductors, in pursuit of their own freedom from their Rebel captors. The charity of the enslaved people forever changed each escapee so desperate to get home. "A bigger-souled people never lived," said Hoffman of the Black men and women who befriended him and his comrades along the way.[562]

In the days since they escaped, the trio had visited "Boles House" where they got supper; another day they were sent to "Bob's House" for a fine breakfast, then on to "Uncle Peter," then to "Domnicks" before experiencing the unnerving fine dinner locked away in "Massa's Parlor." Now they were walking in the dark along the railroad tracks looking for "Hamp."[563]

"We found that the white folks were at home and had not retired yet. This was the first white family we found at home since our escape," said Hoffman. "However, there were very few white families living in the country. The men had all gone to war, and the women and children had all moved to the villages and cities to be better protected from the ravages of war—a much different situation of affairs than was in the north. We flanked the "white folks" house and got around to the shanty where we thought Hamp might live. We were bold enough to rap at the door and inquire for Hamp. He was there all right, and said he was glad to see us; took us in, and after talking a while told us that a squad of rebel cavalry had passed that day and advised us to be careful."

Hamp also told the men that there were Union officers like them nearby in a field also waiting for a meal. So while enough food was prepared for all the escapees, Hamp took the Major, Page, and Hoffman to where the other escapees were hiding so they could meet them.

"Sure enough there were five officers who had got out of Columbia since we had," said Hoffman. The men compared notes as to conditions and things experienced since their escapes. "After a pleasant talk...they brought us our suppers. We thought best not to travel together, so after supper we went our ways as before."[564]

UP IN THE MOUNTAINS CAPTAINS WILSON, Skelton, Welsh, and Dusenberry, who had escaped with Bassett, Stewart, and Young, had safely arrived in Transylvania County. Their group was one of the two breakaway groups from Bassett's original group of nine that had been chased by Rebels on horseback and bloodhounds. As the four officers came down a narrow mountain trail, they ran into John Aiken, another Unionist who was part of Sheriff Hamilton's network.

"I am sorry to tell you, boys, but you are in danger of being captured," said Aiken, "There is a squad of men after you. Go with me and I will conceal you till the chase is over."[565]

He brought the four men to his own log cabin and hid them there for seven days, then moved them into a secluded hollow to the west. It was deep in the mountains, away from the regularly traveled road along a small mountain creek called Little Bear Wallow. They built a small log cabin in a well-hidden spot and spent the next three weeks there. If it weren't for the fact that they were all being hunted, the place offered an idyllic tranquility. The home guard was patrolling all around them, but this spot was so remote that they were never found. Mountain laurel blanketed the steep slopes in an impassable maze unless you were knowledgeable of just the right path.

The four officers didn't know it, but Bassett's group was just ten miles east from their hiding spot. Flem Cison had become acutely aware the danger to the men he was helping seemed to be growing daily. He needed to get them away from the area and guide them to the west, but the winter weather conditions didn't allow it.

THURSDAY, DECEMBER 8, 1864

It was cold and damp, and it seemed nearly impossible to get warm, regardless of how many layers of ragged clothing and borrowed blankets they were bundled in. Bassett, Stewart, and Young, along with Lem Dobbs, Private Hall, and a couple of other escapees who had arrived after Bassett's group, were being hidden in another mountain hollow a few miles from Flem Cison's farmstead at Dunns Rock. They couldn't burn a fire because it would draw attention to them, so they huddled shivering in a quivering mass of smelly humanity. Flem had told them they would be moving soon, but they were stuck because the weather was holding them in, and the home guard was becoming a real threat. They seemed to know there were escaped Union officers close by, but for some reason, perhaps thanks to the sheriff, they just hadn't managed to find them yet.

"A young woman, the promised wife of our guide, Flem Cison, walked four miles alone across the mountain wilds, over the encrusted snow, to warn us not to relax our vigilance, as armed men were looking for us and to bring, us food, returning before daylight lest she should be seen and our hiding place discovered," said Bassett.[566]

Sarah Ann Bagwell was just thirteen years old when she was secreting her way through the mountain laurel to warn Bassett's group of impending danger and to provide them with much-needed food. The war had forced many children on both sides to grow up fast. What wasn't known by the escapees was the emotional pain and turmoil that both Sarah and Flem were experiencing as the war swirled around them. Both appeared calm and stoic, but a constant anxiety remained hidden beneath the surface.

Sarah's father, thirty-nine-year-old James Adolphos Bagwell, had been conscripted into Company K of the North Carolina 62nd Infantry State Troops, CSA, in March 1863. In September 1863 Bagwell was captured at the Battle of Cumberland Gap, becoming a POW of the Union army and imprisoned 650 miles from home at Camp Douglas, Illinois. His wife, Patsy, and their six children had to make do, running their farm without him. John, the eldest son who was just age thirteen when his father was captured, had to take on the duties of the farm or else the family would starve. Knowing the patriarch of the family was a POW, the local home guard kept an eye on them, trying to offer them some protection from the constantly preying riffraff. The family had only received a couple of letters over Bagwell's sixteen months of captivity, assuring them that he was still alive and well.

In an intuitive act in the days after he was first conscripted, Bagwell drafted a letter to his family, just in case he didn't make it home. Patsy would often read her husband's words while alone, with tears running down her face and anger raging in her heart:

James Adolphos Bagwell
Photographer unknown

18 February 1863
> *There are dangers abroad and dangers at home and life is uncertain and death is sure. It seems as if the time has come for me to leave home. It is necessary that I should leave on record some remarks for instructions to my family. They will need my labor but will need my instructions worse.*

> *I want you to live uprightly if you die by it. I want you to live with your heads up, be ashamed of nothing but sin and consider yourselves as good as anybody if you behave yourselves as well. Never pass and insult without just provocation, never make sport of anybody. Don't tell a lie, don't swear, don't steal, pay all your just contracts. Live justly if you die by it.*

> *Remember that my will is for you all to enjoy the good of my labor in my lifetime and after my death also. Don't go in debt so that there will be any claims on my property after*

death.

Remember that I don't want you to be quarreling about it after I am dead and gone. Remember that my will is not like some I have seen. If there is only one dollar, I want it divided between all the children. I want the girls to have as much as the boys. John, don't ever suffer anybody to impose on your little brothers and sisters, wrongfully. Always mind your own business, don't be talking and tale bearing and meddling in other peoples business. Speak evil of no man. I have tried all these things and they will not do to live by nor will they do to die by. Remember this is an abomination in the sight o God.

Remember, a clear and acquitted conscience is better than gold and silver. Don't be ill to one another, be kind and obliging to one another always. Remember, be that little boy and girl that obeys his father and mother. Be faithful and industrious and let me live or die. Get all the education you can. Get all the religious instruction you can. Remember that these things are my desire and will and prayer to All Mighty God.

Father[567]

In early December Bagwell was fighting a different battle, having contracted typhoid fever at the Camp Douglas POW prison. His family never knew. He would not survive, dying on December 20, 1864. He was buried at Chicago City Cemetery and, after the war, reinterred in a Confederate Mound mass grave at Oak Woods Cemetery in Chicago. It would take weeks, well into early 1865, before the family would learn his fate.

At the beginning of November, Flem's oldest brother, forty-three-year-old Joseph Charles Cison, died from yellow fever at his home at Dunns Rock. His surviving siblings, widow Mary, and six children buried him in the church graveyard, grieving in private.

Even with the burden of their own personal struggles planted firmly on their shoulders, both Flem and Sarah dutifully helped the Union officers, even though it put themselves and their families at risk.

SUNDAY, DECEMBER 11, 1864

On Friday the temperatures dropped, and the rain turned to snow and sleet along the length of the route from Pickens Court House in South Carolina to the North Carolina mountains. Stretched out along this route there were almost 100 escaped POWs, all who had gotten away from Camp Sorghum in the second half of November.[568] The winter weather lasted all day.

To the south the Major, Page, and Hoffman, along with McAdams and Fowler, found themselves tramping through two inches of snow. Their feet were freezing, and their shoes were so ragged they provided little protection. McAdams was in agony; the pain to the areas of his feet that had suffered frostbite a year before constantly tormenting him.

In the mountains Bassett's, Stewart's, Young's, and Dobbs' meager shelter was buried in the white stuff and without a warming fire that would improve their situation. They hoped it would be only a few more days until the weather improved and Flem was ready to guide them west from Dunns Rock.

Cison watched as the big flakes of snow fell on the winter landscape from a small window of his cabin. The snow created a peaceful silence, dampening the sounds around them. But he found no solace in the tranquility; he knew he had to get the Union officers out of there.

After the snow had stopped, the Major, Page, and Hoffman had sought shelter and were lucky to be hidden away in a plantation barn with the help of another enslaved man named George, whom they met along the way. They buried themselves deep into the hay to keep warm.

"George marched with us, as he was going our way to his home. He was the most intelligent and best educated of any of the colored men we met. Arriving at his destination he secreted us in the barn in the hay mow, where we had a good sleep until long after day light," said Hoffman.

The Major's group of three would spend the rest of the day in the warmth of the barn, daydreaming of life at home and hoping for normalcy to return to no longer being hunted men. The snow had melted, the temperature was crisp and cool, and the sun returned to a clear blue sky. The men were comfortably buried in the hay in the barn's loft, enjoying a much-needed break and exhausted from the events of the two weeks fighting the elements since their escape.

It brought a sense of longing to twenty-five-year-old Michael Hoffman, a red-blooded young Union officer. He had put things on hold for the war. It seemed like another lifetime, lived long ago by an entirely different person back in Marshaltown, Iowa, where he worked as a retail clerk in the tight-knit Iowa farming community. Working in town, as opposed to being an isolated farmhand, gave him an advantage when it came to the nineteenth-century art of courting. He regularly interacted with women his own age who came into the store and, as a result, had become quite the lady's man. He lay in the barn as a wave of nostalgia passed through him; he missed that worry-free life.

"In looking out through the cracks in the barn, we saw a very large two story house with fine surroundings," said Hoffman. "This being Sunday, and a very nice day, we sat there for quite awhile...Presently two young ladies came out and scampered around. We watched them for some time. White girls looked good to us, as we had not seen any for a long time nor spoken to any for over a year. How we would like to have been in this condition to spend the Sunday with them. But this could not be. We were fleeing Yankees in an enemy's country, uncouth, footsore and ragged."[569]

Eighteen-year-old Lieutenant Henry Fowler, who escaped a few hours after the Major's group, was hiding nearby. Fowler wasn't feeling the wave of nostalgia that Hoffman was; he was just feeling the biting cold.

Lieutenant John McAdams was a few miles ahead of the Major's group, hidden in a thick forest. McAdams lay back, looking up into the clear blue sky. A bird could be seen way up high gliding on the thermal currents, then he closed his eyes and tried to will himself to sleep.

All nine escapees were contemplating their next move. For those not in the mountains yet, they loomed just ahead and could be seen in the distance topped with white, offering proof that they were closer to home.

The Major's group studied their map and found a promising route that would take them northwest over the North Carolina state line, placing them on top of a mountain looking down into the Cashiers Valley. They discussed the route with George when he brought them breakfast to their comfortable lodging in the plantation barn's hay loft. He had hidden their meal in a couple of milk buckets so as not to draw attention. George told them he knew the route was a good one, mentioning a couple of names along the way of people who could help. The last name on George's list was a farmer in the Cashiers Valley between Chimneytop and Rock Mountains.

His name was Zachary.

Chapter Eighteen

T. R. Zachary
December 1864

WEDNESDAY, DECEMBER 14, 1864

Flem Cison had Bassett, Young, Stewart, Dobbs, and several other Union soldiers on alert that they would leave their hiding place just after dark. They'd been snowed in for almost two weeks. Now the weather had cleared, and the skies were a deep blue. The temperatures at night dropped below freezing, which was not the best way to travel when you didn't have warm clothing. Flem had arranged for some rations for each of his charges and hoped to get them over the mountains and down into Cashiers Valley in a couple of days. It was almost thirty miles of tough hiking in the snow-covered mountains and could be treacherous in places where things had iced over.

"We traveled at night, through snow and ice, over Blue Ridge Mountains," said Bassett, "almost frozen being deterred from kindling fires for fear of discovery by rebel scouts that swarmed the valleys."[570]

Thursday, December 15, 1864

The wind was blowing hard, and it was bitterly cold as the 5th Iowa Boys, the Major, Page, and Hoffman climbed the mountain in the darkness. They knew that they had crossed over the state line and were now in North Carolina. They had traveled most of Wednesday night and into the early hours of Thursday morning, covering fourteen miles along this rugged road—if you could call it a road. It was really just a couple of wagon ruts in an icy and muddy path with snow covering the rest of the landscape. The road switched back and forth so many times it was dizzying, and if not for the light of the moon, they surely would have gotten lost and perhaps even fallen off one of the cliffs they had seen along the way. Once during the night they stopped along a cliff's edge, staring down at the snow-covered landscape way down below, which offered little detail in the darkness except the tiny glow of a small campfire that seemed miles away.

They had taken a slightly different route than Bassett, Young, Stewart, and Dobbs, bypassing Transylvania County and ending up a little further to the west. It was an hour before sunrise, and they needed to rest. They were somewhere along the spine of Chimneytop Mountain, which stood at just over 4,600 feet in elevation, huddled together against a hemlock tree, each wrapped in the single ragged blanket they had escaped with, trying to keep warm.

"We went into hiding on top of a high mountain peak from which we could look down and from whence we came as far as the eye could reach," said Hoffman.[571]

The sun soon rose, casting the mountain's dark shadow down into the valley below. The shadows contrasted with the white snow that clung to the mountains, illuminating them so brightly that looking at the east side of the terrain was almost blinding, which caused the exhausted men to squint so as to not hurt their eyes. It was easy to just keep their eyes closed, and they managed to doze off, all the while shivering in the cold.

"Through the day the sun shown brightly, but the wind was so cold and chilly we could sleep but a little, although we so badly needed it," said Hoffman. "We could see a house way down in the valley in the direction we proposed go, so we started on our march quite early."[572]

That high up in the mountain they had little risk of being seen so they set out in the early afternoon, carefully making their way down into the valley. Soon they found the road through the valley heading west and, even though it still was brutally cold, the afternoon sun warmed their bodies, providing some relief as they walked. When they first escaped, the three men would take turns leading as they all hiked. When Hoffman let his comrades know that he was increasingly becoming hard of hearing, the Major and Page thought it was prudent to not let Hoffman lead them anymore, just in case he missed hearing something that would result in danger to all of them.[573]

"After going some distance we came to a log house on the left side of the road and a barn on the other side," said Hoffman. "Just as we got between the house and the barn, a lady who had been milking some cows straightened up surprised."[574]

Sarah Isabelle "Ibby" Zachary remained seated on the small wooden crate she used as a milking stool and stared for a moment at the three men standing in the road. They were dressed in rags, and under other circumstances she might have felt a little panicked, but she had seen other men like them over the last few months: Yankees in need of help. She stood up and walked out of the barn carrying the milk pail and strolled the few steps to the road where the strangers stood, using one hand to pull her coat tight against her body.

The Major greeted the woman and asked if she could tell them the best way to get to Franklin.

Ibby obliged, setting down her milk pail, then picking up a small stick and drawing a map in the dirt road.

Just then the men all jumped, reeling around as the sound of the door to the log cabin creaked opened and an older man stepped out. He pulled on his winter coat at the same time he pulled the door shut behind him, standing on the narrow porch for a moment looking at the strangers and his wife.

Alexander Washington "Andy" Zachary was a husky, stout man just four days shy of his fifty-eighth birthday. Like his wife, he, too, had experienced ragged strangers passing through and slowly walked over to the road.

The Major, Page, and Hoffman stood frozen, considering if they should run. The Major immediately sized up Zachary from the moment he stepped off his porch. The man was older and appeared to have a pleasant demeanor. He wasn't armed. After exchanging pleasantries, the man quickly calmed their fears.

"Gentlemen, I guess I know who you are, and if mistaken I offer an apology. I hear that the Yankees are getting out of Columbia prison pretty fast and I think from your talk that you are some of them. If you are, you need not be afraid for you are in a Union settlement," said Andy.[575]

Ibby carried the pail of fresh milk back into the cabin as the men continued to talk. A few minutes later she emerged again with a dish of apples and passed them around. The men inhaled them, having had little to eat other than what meager rations they had carried since the day before when they climbed Chimneytop Mountain.

Andy Zachary came from a family deeply rooted in the Quaker religion. His parents were Colonel John A. Zachary and his wife, Sarah, who were members of the Deep Creek Friends in Surry County, North Carolina, near the Yadkin River where Andy and his fourteen siblings were born.

The Quakers were devoted abolitionists; they were the first religious movement to condemn the practice of slavery, not allowing their members to own enslaved individuals. They were also pacifists, refusing to support war. But this didn't stop John A. Zachary from being commissioned as Captain in the Surry County militia in 1816 and then promoted to Colonel in 1823. He and some members of his family were disciplined and ultimately disowned by the Quakers.

The family's move to the mountains of Western North Carolina was the result of a single bad decision that led to financial ruin. The Colonel put up his family's home and land in Surry County as collateral, and then co-signed a loan for a friend. The friend defaulted, and Zachary lost it all. Looking for a place to start over, he found that Cashiers Valley offered the perfect opportunity.

In January 1835, with the opportunity of securing free land grants, the Colonel and his wife, Sarah, moved their large family of eight boys and six girls from Surry County to settle in Cashiers Valley, nearly a 200-mile trip over tough roads from their former home. When they reached the mountains there often weren't any roads at all, so they needed to blaze their own trail.

Several land grants totaling 840 acres, located between the picturesque Chimneytop and Rocky mountains, each rising more than 4,800 feet on either side of a small valley, became the location for the family's farmstead.[576] There weren't Quaker meeting houses in their new community, but the Quaker sensibilities remained a deep-rooted way of life for the family.

Like most Western North Carolina homesteaders, they were subsistence farmers, growing what they needed right on the farm. In the first twenty-five years leading up to the Civil War, the family had the burning ambition of pioneers. Several of the Colonel's sons developed into excellent craftsmen known throughout the valley. Eldest brother Alfred was a haberdasher; Andy was a brick mason who, in addition to making his own bricks, ran a small general store and was the valley's postmaster; and brother Mordecai was a carpenter, stonemason, and skilled craftsman. The enterprising family also built Cashiers Valley's first sawmill.[577]

When the Civil War started in 1861, most of the large Zachary clan lived near the Colonel's homestead in Cashiers Valley, each having married and produced large families of their own. The Colonel was in his eighties and his wife, Sarah, was age seventy-six. Those sons and daughters that moved away didn't go that far, living relatively close by in a county east or south.

The Colonel himself was a staunch supporter of the Confederate cause as were most of his sons. But one of his sons, Andy Zachary, was a Unionist; like many families at the time, this caused a divide.

The Cashier Valley's third generation of young Zachary men of age volunteered for service in the Confederate army. The family saw two lose their lives in the first year of the war: one dying of disease in a hospital in Richmond and another killed in battle at Sharpsburg, Maryland.

Andy Zachary had four sons, three of conscription age when the war began, and two of his sons volunteered for Confederate army regiments.

Andy and Ibby's first-born son, twenty-six-year-old Christopher Columbus Zachary, enlisted in Company F of the 29th North Carolina infantry, CSA, and was soon promoted to Sergeant. But as the war progressed something changed, and he deserted the Rebel cause, switching sides to join Kirk's Raiders, part of the 3rd North Carolina Mounted Infantry (U.S.).

Twenty-five-year-old Alexander Washington "Wash" Zachary was an ardent Unionist. Though he never volunteered for a Union regiment, he risked his life acting as a guide for escaped Union soldiers and Rebel deserters and refugees wanting to get over the Union lines.

Nineteen-year-old James Madison Zachary enlisted in Company B of the 25th North Carolina Infantry, CSA, the same regiment as his cousins who were lost early in the war. He served the length of the conflict and survived.

The fourth and youngest son was just nine years old at the beginning of the war. Thompson Roberts "T.R." Zachary was named after his maternal grandmother, Catherine Thompson, and paternal grandmother, Sarah Roberts.[578] To T.R., becoming a soldier seemed like a great adventure. He stood in front of their small cabin with his parents and other siblings, watching his brothers Christopher and James march away down the country road that ran through the middle of their farmstead. T.R. noticed tears in his mother, Ibby's, eyes. His father's eyes had a sadness in them as well, but it was from the realization that the division in his family was more than just physical distance.

For the boy's father, Andy, the impact of the war on his family deepened his resolve for the Union cause, and when the time came, he would secretly do whatever he could to help.

ANDY ZACHARY'S FARMSTEAD WAS sheltered and protected in the narrow valley, which he had cleared with his own hands more than twenty-five years earlier. It was almost hidden away from the rest of the world, which offered some semblance of protection from bushwhackers and raiders. On the fertile valley soil the family raised all the crops they needed to survive, and over the years the trees in their orchard of apples, pears, persimmons, and plums had matured, producing bountiful crops with each season. Andy began selling his apple tree saplings to the surrounding community. The apples the three starving officers had so ravenously consumed had been harvested from their orchard that fall.

After a time standing in the road, Andy invited the Major, Page, and Hoffman into their cabin. When they got inside, they met five Zachary daughters ranging in age from nine to twenty-one. The girls had been curiously peeking out of a cabin window after their father had first gone outside. They helped their mother, Ibby, set about making dinner for their guests. The cabin's fireplace was a welcome luxury to the three officers, who sat huddled close by absorbing its warmth as Andy sat in a chair and talked with them about their journey.

"After sampling about all of his supper we sat by the fireplace and talked until 11 o'clock," said Hoffman. "He gave us directions and names of Union men for thirty miles ahead, although he advised to avoid Franklin. He said the rebel, Col. Thomas, was there with a company of rebel soldiers. In doing this it made our march about fifty miles longer."

The Colonel Thomas that Andy referred to was Colonel William H. Thomas of Thomas's Legion, a North Carolina infantry regiment and cavalry battalion made up of mountain men and indigenous Cherokee who had remained in the area after the Trail of Tears. There were several Zachary's in Thomas's Legion including Andy's forty-two-year-old brother Mordecai, who had built a stately Greek Revival style home in Cashiers Valley in the 1850s. Andy likely knew the whereabouts of his brother and, as a result, the rest of Thomas's Legion.

Late in the evening the officers knew they needed to move on; the cabin was full of the Zachary clan with no additional space other than the barn, but that was too close to the house, making it too dangerous a place for Andy to hide them. He told them to go about three miles west down the lone valley road where they would see another barn, the Zachary's corn crib. His sons, Wash and T.R., were working there.

"He said his two boys were husking corn and sleeping there. He told us to crawl in and sleep with the boys, and in the morning we would come to a house three miles further on where we could get breakfast," said Hoffman. "He said the man was in the rebel army, but the women would get our breakfast, and then we were free to continue our march in the day time instead of nights."

It was a relief to know they could safely travel by day when it was much warmer and they could see where they were going. The officers thanked Andy and Ibby for their hospitality and help and headed down the road in the darkness. Around midnight they found the barn that Andy had mentioned. They door's hinges creaked open, revealing a space filled with a mountain of shucked corn. When the door opened, it woke Wash and T.R., and the officers introduced themselves. Wash was a twenty-five-year-old man and experienced mountain guide. Fourteen-year-old T.R. rubbed sleep from his eyes and just stared.

The three officers told them they had just been at their family's cabin and that their father had sent them there to sleep for the night. Once finding that Wash was a guide, they asked whether he could get them into Tennessee. T.R. immediately got excited about the prospects of going on an adventure with his older brother, helping him guide these Yankees into Tennessee. But Wash explained he would have to talk with his father, which would delay things in the morning. So they all agreed that the Major, Page, and Hoffman could safely continue west without a guide and perhaps have an opportunity to pick one up once they got thirty miles ahead, around Fort Hembree, North Carolina.[579] Then the three officers each found a place within the mountain of corn and quickly fell asleep.

Throughout the night while the 5th Iowa Boys were sleeping, burrowed into a pile of shucked corn cobs, thirty miles to the east Flem Cison began guiding his group west from Dunns Rock toward them. They followed the West Fork of the French Broad River until its waters turned north, then parted from the river and continued on the western path, entering rugged mountains that averaged almost 3,000 feet in elevation. Flem's charges, which included Bassett, Young, Stewart, Dobbs, and several other refugees, followed a narrow valley road that eventually climbed and became a narrow trail along the spine of the mountain peaks. The entire way they contended with deep snow and endured temperatures below freezing. As the sun rose on Friday morning, they hid out in a hollow full of mountain laurel, where they would sleep during the daylight hours.

FRIDAY, DECEMBER 16, 1864

On Friday morning the Major, Page, and Hoffman said goodbye to Wash and T.R. at the Zachary corn crib and headed west. Once again it was brisk, but the morning sun warmed their backs as long as they weren't walking through shadowed forest. They were looking for the farmstead that Andy Zachary had told them about the night before, trying to get some breakfast. A few hundred yards from what appeared to be the right place, the officers noticed several people were standing on the porch watching their approach with keen interest.

"When within a hundred yards we saw a rebel major and two soldiers with guns standing on the porch," said Hoffman. "We were too close to them to run, so all we could do was face the music."

Since escaping Camp Sorghum nineteen days earlier, they had tramped some 150 miles and had several close calls along the way. Now there was no way out. The feeling of accomplishment they had had just the night before, having connected with Andy Zachary and what they hoped was the first in a series of Union sympathizers that could help them, came to a crashing end. Now they were POWs once again.

"The Rebels had arrived that morning and had just finished breakfast. We called for ours, which the lady proceeded to prepare, and after having eaten it all of us sat on the porch and talked matters over," said Hoffman. "We told them a straight, true story, who we were, and what a hard time we had in getting this far to liberty. They seemed to show and express a little sympathy for us."[580]

Page and Hoffman sat dejected while Marshall considered their options. He motioned to the Rebel major who got up and walked over to Marshall. They each whispered a few words not heard by the others, then Marshall got up, set down his breakfast plate on the porch floor, and walked away with the Rebel major, talking in hushed tones.

The two Rebel soldiers didn't move and seemingly had little to say. They sat on their end of the porch staring at Page and Hoffman on the opposite end, their rifles in their laps. Finally breaking the ice, the four men began making small talk about what they shared in common: their lives during the war, the battles they had fought in, and what was hardest for them all, leaving their families behind at home. The Rebels admitted that things didn't look too good for them. They were aware that Sherman was on the march in southeast Georgia. They also offered that it appeared that the Confederacy was on its last legs.

"The two Majors got off by themselves and talked quietly for over an hour," said Hoffman. "What they said, Page and I did not know, but when their conversation was finished we bid one another good-bye and parted, they going their way and we ares *(sic)*."

As the Rebels mounted their horses and began to ride away, the Rebel major paused for a moment and said to Major Marshall, "I hope you will make success of it." Then they left, and the Major, Page, and Hoffman watched until they disappeared over a rise in the road.

The hour that passed sitting with the two, armed Rebels sunning themselves on a porch in the North Carolina mountains had seemed like a year to Page and Hoffman.

The reason the three Rebels were in the mountains was to forage for their army. They were specifically looking for beef. Hoffman and Page knew that Marshall was a Mason and suspected that the Rebel Major was also one, which is why Major Marshall had been able to convince the other officer to let them go. Twenty-two years later when Hoffman visited the Major at his home, he asked him how he had been able to pull it off.

"There was nothing to it," said Marshall. "The reason they did not take us was that we were not worth the taking, and it would have been too much trouble for them to have taken care of us."[581]

There were no additional horses to carry three prisoners; the three Union officers were not beef, so the Rebels considered their options, left things be, and moved on. A short time later Marshall, Page, and Hoffman began moving west themselves, covering twelve miles before finding another Union stopping point that had been mentioned by Andy Zachary.

This farmstead was owned by a man named Keener. One of the members of the Keener family had married Andy Zachary's brother Mordecai, a member of Thomas's Legion, CSA. But this Keener was a Unionist—another example of families divided.

"He appeared to be glad to take care of us," said Hoffman. "We ate our suppers, chatted quite awhile, then climbed up a ladder to the loft and slept until morning."[582]

SATURDAY, DECEMBER 17, 1864

Throughout the night several miles to the east, the Bassett, Young, Stewart, and Dobbs group were being led by Flem Cison westward along the spine of the rugged mountains. By sunrise on Saturday they descended a mountain trail into Cashiers Valley and approached the Zachary farmstead.

Andy and Ibby welcomed this next group of Union escapees the same way as they had the Major, Page, and Hoffman two days earlier. The couple's two sons Wash and T.R. had come back to the main house after completing their work at the farmstead's corn crib. Truth be told, with five sisters in the small main house, they spent a lot of the time sleeping at the corn crib, even in the winter. They had arranged sleeping space at the barn and somehow managed to stay warm, with plenty of space to themselves.

Flem knew the Zachary's as part of the Unionist network. Andy was a "stationmaster" helping to connect parties with guides and others who would help them along the way. Flem asked Andy whether Wash could take over and guide the group west on the next leg of the journey to Fort Hembree, where there were other Unionists that could guide them on the final leg into Tennessee and Union lines. Wash, however, was sick and confined to bed. This left fourteen-year-old T.R., who was immediately excited by the opportunity and asked his father if he could help guide the men over the mountains. Andy thought about it and realized his youngest son had matured quite a bit, with the hardships the family had experienced during the war years. Andy agreed that if Flem would go, too, then T.R. could help him on the next leg of the journey over to Fort Hembree. Fifteen miles west of Flem's group, the 5th Iowa Boys had decided to spend a day at the Keener farmstead. It was a welcome break from the rigors of hiking through the mountains.

"We spent the day in an old log house of his, located up the side of the mountain on a small level piece of ground, and at night slept at his house on the left. Keener was a clever man, and had plenty to eat," said Hoffman. "We would go down to the house a little early and chat with him and watch Mrs. Keener get supper."

The Keener log cabin, like many cabins in the mountains, had no kitchen. On one end of the structure was a large stone fireplace where all the cooking was done. Several iron hooks could be swung into and away from the flames. For baking they used a Dutch oven, which was a deep heavy flat-bottomed pot with a solid lid that firmly sealed on top. Both parts were made of heavy-duty cast iron. The item to be baked was placed within the flat-bottomed pot, and then the lid was placed on it. Then the entire arrangement was placed directly onto hot coals in the fireplace, and more coals would be shoveled directly on the top of the pot.

"We saw Mrs. Keener bake the biscuits, then fry the meat in the oven for our supper, and then after supper the children, before retiring, would wash their feet out of it being nice and warm. In the morning it would again fry the meat and bake the biscuits," said Hoffman. "They did not, however, ask us to wash our feet. They knew where to draw the line."

Chapter Nineteen

Kit Ledford
December 1864

SUNDAY, DECEMBER 18, 1864

On the Sunday that the Major, Page, and Hoffman spent with the Keeners west of Cashiers Valley, a local man named Wood stopped by to visit. One of the first things he did upon meeting the three men was to comment about how much he liked Hoffman's Union-issued beat-up old boots. In short order Woods asked Hoffman if he would be willing to trade his boots and offered to barter with them for other possessions the officers were carrying. The Major sat chewing on his cigar and watching the man closely, his gut instinct telling him something was a little off with Mr. Wood.

"We traded him our old boots, which were worn out–except for the red tops, which he took a fancy to, for his shoes, which were more serviceable, and lasted us through our lines," said Hoffman. "We also cut the twelve brass buttons off our coat and sold them to him at $5 a piece Rebel money."

With the deal done, Mr. Wood offered to guide the officers through the next patch of particularly rugged mountains that would take them into the Hiwassee Valley. "These are a part of the Blue Ridge or Smoky Mountains, a broken, straggling lot of hills, running in spurs, peaks and chains, with an altitude of over 5,000 feet with valleys 3,000 feet below," said Hoffman. The Hiwassee Valley and the Unicoi Turnpike were their preferred route to the Union lines in Tennessee.

Around 8 p.m. the group left the Keeners, led by their new guide proudly wearing his newly swapped footwear.

"After going some ten miles we found that Wood did not know as much about the roads and country as we did. He did not know whether we were going north, south, east, or west. We did not either, for that matter, the night being quite dark," said Hoffman. "After tramping around for awhile without any success we spread our blankets and slept until morning."

MONDAY, DECEMBER 19, 1864

The Major's suspicions proved accurate. Mr. Wood was not the guide he made himself out to be; in fact, they really didn't know what to make of the man. When the sun rose, they let Wood know that they would continue on alone, thanking the man for his help.

Mr. Wood shrugged, and they all watched as the odd man wearing Hoffman's old boots disappeared eastward along the mountain trail in the direction they had all come overnight. Their parting quickly proved to be a smart decision.

"On examining our haversacks after Wood was gone we found he had stolen some little bone work I had whittled out while in Libby prison: a couple of napkin rings, two collar buttons, and a watch charm,"[583] said Hoffman who had spent countless hours whittling and filing the objects. They had little value, yet their loss stung; they were Hoffman's personal possessions that had memories of difficult times attached to them.

The three officers spent the day in the camp hidden away, determined to resume their march at night when they hoped to move stealthily without anyone's assistance. When night finally came the mountains were so rugged, and it was so dark and bitterly cold, that they could only manage a few miles. They stumbled across an old church where they sheltered for the night as the weather began to change.

TUESDAY, DECEMBER 20, 1864

The morning was gray with constant rain and drizzle and, as the day progressed it got colder with the rain turning to a heavy snow.[584] Bassett's group was west of Cashiers Valley, having left the Zachary's farmstead on Sunday. They continued to make progress, finding help along the way from some of the other Unionists' names mentioned by Andy Zachary.

T.R. Zachary was in heaven with his new job as a mountain guide, helping Flem find their way along the rugged trails as the group avoided the main roads near Franklin, North Carolina. Bassett, Stewart, and Young were impressed with the fourteen-year-old boy; he was a smart kid, and the three officers decided to offer him an added incentive. If he helped get them successfully over the Union lines, they'd all chip in some money to help him pay for a college education.[585]

Bassett, in particular, befriended the boy, whom he called Tommy. It no doubt made him think about his own son, six-year-old Nathaniel, back home in Illinois. It startled him that he couldn't remember how long it had been since he had last seen Nathaniel and, for that matter, his daughter, Sarah Jane, who wasn't even age two when he had left. He had never met his youngest son, Charles, who was born after he had left for the war. Most of the men he was now traveling with were single. Dobbs was a newlywed, so Bassett was the only one married with children. He internalized the pain that gnawed at his heart, missing a family he hardly knew. His family had fragmented and imploded when his wife, Lottie, who first thought he was dead, had given up on him. She probably thought he was never coming back. Bassett kept it all inside; none of his comrades had a clue.

The snow that began on Tuesday afternoon made the group decide to hold up for the evening and, in doing so, got some valuable intelligence from their hosts, who, as part of the Unionist network, were constantly on guard for all Rebel comings and goings around them. Word had been passed down the line of a small Rebel wagon train spotted on a path that would soon be moving through the valley. It was loaded with provisions that had been rounded up from the citizens in the mountains to help supply the Confederate army. The train was likely connected to the three Rebels in the foraging party looking for cattle that the Major, Page, and Hoffman had run into the day after they had left the Zachary's.

"Hearing through the 'natives' that a Confederate wagon train was coming through the valley loaded with provisions...we constituted ourselves a foraging party and made bold to attack the train which consisted of anywhere from three to six wagons with a span of mules, a driver and one guard to each," said Bassett.

The men who had been prisoners for so long, then desperate escapees, quickly returned to the job of being soldiers. The next morning the landscape was all white from the falling snow, which had begun to let up. The path of the road was covered in pristine white powder and unmarked, as if nothing had passed through. The only hint that there was a road there at all was a white, shallow depression. The men lay hidden behind snow-topped pines near where the road narrowed as it entered the forest. The heavy snow clung to the tops of the trees; occasionally, the weight would let loose with a muffled "wooossshh," showering the men in a blast of cold white from above like a snowball thrown by God. The snow muffled the sounds around them, but in the distance they could hear the wagons as they approached. The lead mule's hooves churned the snow on the road, and their breaths were visible as bursts of warm fog in the deep cold. When the wagons entered the narrowing in the road, Bassett's men quickly moved into their path, blocking their way, rifles pointed at the Rebels.

Bassett stood in the middle of the road with his rifle pointed at the approaching wagons. The wagons immediately halted, and the Rebels raised their hands up into the frigid air.

"We helped ourselves to hams, sides of bacon, jars of honey, chestnuts, home-made clothing from home-made cloth, quilts and blankets—a variety of substantial provisions which we carried to the secluded hut of some mountain dwellers for their and our refreshment. It is safe to say that the mules were not sorry for our raid, for it is wonderful what quantities of provisions we removed from these wagons," said Bassett.[586]

THE MAJOR, PAGE, AND HOFFMAN were miles ahead of Bassett's group during their successful raid. They were traveling high along a perilously narrow path that sat on the spine of the mountain with cold, wind-blown snow swirling all around them. They had come across another mountain man who was acting as their new guide, for which they were thankful because the weather made things particularly treacherous. Icicles hung from the sides of the rock and ice formed in places on the path itself. Mr. Watts was also a friend of both the Zacharys and Keeners and had both a better sense of direction and reputation than the now-infamous Mr. Wood. Watts had managed to guide them safely during the winter storm along the top of an eight-mile-long mountain ridge named Chunky Gal. The name was derived from a Cherokee legend about a chubby young woman who fell in love with a young warrior from another tribe, decided to follow her heart, and was thus abandoned by her family. Every culture seems to have a similar legend, though perhaps not a large mountain named for it.

"At last we came to the end of this mountain ridge...and could look perpendicularly almost 2,000 feet below. It was so steep a mule could not travel it," said Hoffman. "Here Watts pointed out a Mr. Al Moore's house down in the valley below, and said we should stop there, and that he was a Union man. After traveling thirteen miles for the day we came to Moore's. He had been having a considerable trouble with the rebels, they having killed two of his boys and having carried off all of his stock. He gave us our suppers, after which we slept in his barn, or fodder house, as all barns in the south are called."

THURSDAY, DECEMBER 22, 1864

In the morning the weather had cleared a little, revealing patches of blue sky, but it was windy and bitterly cold. The place that the escaped officers had entered after finding their way down the steep slopes of Chunky Gal Mountain was known as Shooting Creek. The further west the escapees went into North Carolina, the more isolated it became. There were no railroads, so everything needed to be brought in on wagons to the citizens who lived there.

This region where North Carolina, Tennessee, and Georgia all shake hands was at war with itself, and Mr. Moore's sons were caught in the crossfire.

Bands of men roamed the region, some loyal to the Confederacy and some to the Union. Each was viewed by the opposite side as criminal guerrillas or bushwhackers who were robbing, looting, and sometimes just killing for sport.

People were having a hard time trying to protect their loved ones and property, and neither side could do much to help. Things had spun out of control.

It was chaos in the mountains.

People had become paranoid, avoiding contact with any strangers and not knowing whose side they might be on. The day after their stay at the Moore farmstead, the Major, Page, and Hoffman stopped at another log cabin and could feel fear emanating from the man. "He was scared, and in return, scared us. He said the guerrillas were around the country. So we went up the side of the mountain, and lay there all day," said Hoffman.[587]

Christmas was just three days away. It would be the second Christmas the 5th Iowa Boys had been away from the comforts of civilization, either in prison or on the run. They moved westward from Shooting Creek, entering the Hiwassee Valley nearing Hayesville, North Carolina, and looking for a place where they could safely hide out and hopefully wait out the weather.

The Ledford's were a large family living in extreme Western North Carolina. In the 1860 census for Cherokee County there were twenty-nine individual Ledford households located in Murphy, Shooting Creek, and Fort Hembree, which was located in Hayesville, NC. In 1861 the area they lived in became Clay County, nestled against the Georgia border. One member of the Ledford's had married into the Moore family, which was how the officers came to find them.

Fort Hembree was the collection site for the removal of the indigenous Cherokee who lived in the upper Hiwassee Valley during the Trail of Tears in the 1830s. For the Ledfords', indigenous Cherokee blood flowed through their veins; as early settlers, several of the Ledford's had married local Cherokee neighbors.

When one family of the Ledford clan met the Major, Page, and Hoffman, they offered the men a place to shelter and wait out the weather. They also invited them to celebrate Christmas with their family. It was an unexpected blessing for the 5th Iowa Boys.

"Here we were at home and remained for five days, boarded at the house, and through the day we stayed up a ravine in his fodder house. It was now time for us to do a little washing. We needed it and the Ledfords knew it, too, besides, as we were to spend Christmas with them, a little fixing up was necessary, said Hoffman. "Mrs. Ledford furnished the soft soap and a big iron pot, so we went up to the fodder house and went at it. We had no change of clothing, so while washing we kept a sharp lookout down the valley so that no chance visitor should surprise us, or we them. The most important thing our clothes needed, so far as our peace and comfort was concerned, was to get the animated life out of them by a good scald."[588]

Since the early days of becoming prisoners of war, the men constantly fought a battle with the "animated graybacks" or body lice. Their clothing had become a mobile home for the pests, who endured and seemed to actually thrive in any kind of situation, no matter how hot or cold the temperatures were. As long as their home housed a warm-blooded human being beneath it, they were happy campers. The men's clothes were the same ones they had been taken prisoner in more than a year earlier and had deteriorated into rags. Some garments, made from anything they could find, were added to their wardrobe to try and provide warmth during the winter.

"The most durable garments we had were our over-shirts, and those were made out of rice bags by cutting a hole in the bottom to slip over our head, and holes cut out in the sides for our arms," said Hoffman.

Now their rice bag overshirts sparkled. They were probably the cleanest they had been in over a year.

SUNDAY, DECEMBER 25, 1864

The Major, Page, and Hoffman walked from the Ledford's fodder house down to the family's cabin for Christmas dinner as a cold wind blew. It seemed to snow a little every day, and they could tell more was on the way. Several other Ledford's arrived; a brother and a nephew joined the family and their guests. The three officers entered the cabin, filled by the warmth they felt in their hearts for their new friends. They may not have been celebrating Christmas at home with their families, but the Ledfords certainly made them feel welcomed, and the celebration of Christmas in the mountains during wartime became an unforgettable memory.

"Now we had a Christmas dinner all right. Among other things was venison, killed the day before, with an adjunct of apple brandy, called by them apple-jack," said Hoffman. "Distilleries were about as numerous in this country as the old cider mills used to be in Pennsylvania, and most every home like Ledfords had a quantity of apple-jack in store. It had one virtue. It was pure."[589]

Homemade apple-jack was a welcome treat, medicinally warming them in the cold. What the three officers were unaware of while they enjoyed their Christmas feast was the great hardships the Ledfords of Hayesville had experienced during the last year. Most all of them had been terrorized by neighbors they knew visiting their homes as Rebel guerrillas.

Many of the Ledford men of military age had followed the path of conscription into the Confederate army, then desertion, then enlistment in the Yankee army. With a family so large, it was nearly impossible for the war to have not caused division. It was also sometimes hard to keep track of who was on which side.

Three brothers—thirty-four-year-old Jason (known as "Big Jason"), thirty-two-year-old Center, and thirty-one-year-old David Ledford—and their cousins lived close by. Along with two other brothers—twenty-four-year-old William Cicero and nineteen-year-old Julius Ketron "Kit" Ledford—they they all enlisted together in a Union regiment on October 3, 1863, in Company D; 2nd North Carolina Mounted Infantry

(U.S.). By July 1864 only Kit's brother William Cicero Ledford, who went by Cicero, remained with the regiment, staying with it through the end of the war.[590] It was the same regiment, but Company F, that Flem Cison had joined and also deserted.

When word came from home of how bad things had become around Hayesville, Jason, Center, David, and their cousin Kit all deserted and rushed back to protect their farms and families. Fighting for either side was meaningless if, when you came back home, home wasn't there. Still trying to serve the Union cause while remaining on guard close to home, they began acting as guides for escaped officers such as the Major, Page, and Hoffman. Being a guide required being gone for less than a week; Hayesville was just seventy miles from the Union lines near Madisonville, Tennessee. To neighbors that supported the Confederacy, they became known as "Home Yankees."

Nearby the warm cabin where the Major, Page, and Marshall sat enjoying their Christmas dinner, there was a cluster of four more Ledford cousins' cabins sitting alongside each other, surrounded by their snow-covered farmstead. Jason Ledford and his Irish-born wife, Jane Ledford, both sixty-eight-year-olds, lived in one of the homes. The other three were the homes of their three sons, daughters-in-law, and a large, growing brood of grandchildren. Their sons were "Big Jason," Center, and David—the same three brothers that had deserted the Union regiment earlier in the year with their cousin Kit.

That Christmas instead of celebrating, the family was in mourning. Just a few weeks earlier David had been murdered by Rebel guerrillas while helping escaped POW officers get back to the Union lines.

On the evening of Friday, December 2, 1864, David Ledford met two Union officers who came knocking on his door seeking his help.

They were Captain John Collins Welch of Company F, 85th New York Infantry, and Lieutenant Adrian Symmes Appleget of Company C, 2nd New Jersey Cavalry, after escaping from Camp Sorghum on November 4, 1864, just six days before Bassett's group. The two officers had walked over 225 miles, taking a different route west into Georgia and then north up to Hayesville.

The men were in need of a scout to get them to the Union lines in Tennessee, and David agreed to help. They all left his home around 10 p.m. on Sunday night, December 4, 1864.

Soon afterwards Rebel guerrillas made a surprise visit to the family's home, looking for David. His wife, Dulcena, and nine-year-old son, Ranz, were hung by their thumbs from the rafters of their cabin and tortured while the men tried to pry information out of them. Much of their family's property and food stores were destroyed. Through it all, Dulcena and Ranz remained tight-lipped, revealing nothing.[591]

"It has been customary for the villains there, in making a descent on a Union man's house and not finding their prey, not only to rob him of his food, his bed clothing, wife's and children's clothing, knives, forks, dishes and everything transportable, but also to take out his wife and children and seek every expedient short of death to make them expose the whereabouts of the husband and father," wrote Captain Welch after the war.[592]

On Tuesday, December 6, the three men were being hidden in another Unionist's home located along the Unicoi Turnpike just twenty-one miles from the Union lines at Tellico Mountain in Tennessee. At around 10 p.m. a large group of armed men, some dressed in Union blue identifying themselves as Union militia, barged into the house.

Welch and Appleget identified themselves to the men as escaped Union officers. Ledford, thinking he was with like-minded men, identified himself as a member of a local organized group of Unionists (aka Yankee-leaning guerrilla group) that acted as a guide for escaped officers and also mentioned how the group had injured the prominent secessionists neighbors living in his area. Those words sealed David's fate.

The large group of armed men were lying. They were actually a Confederate army company, a group known as Abbott's Scouts, under the command of Captain William R. Abbott, sent to the area by Brigadier General John C. Vaughn.[593] Captain Abbott told the two men that he had no interest in escaped Union officers, letting Welch and Appleget go, but David was murdered, reported as hung and shot later that evening.[594]

His wife, Dulcena, and son, Ranz, rode their wagon along the Unicoi Turnpike into Tennessee and recovered David's body, carrying it back to Hayesville for burial a few days later.

Grief and mourning continued throughout the entire Ledford clan three weeks later. But it was kept private, hidden beneath the surface, with never a word mentioned to their three guests. But there was also a growing anger. This was not the first family member murdered during the war. In fact, a Rebel guerrilla group had visited the very home where the 5th Iowa Boys sat enjoying their Christmas dinner, raining down retribution on the family for being Unionists.

"The furniture and culinary departments at the Ledfords was very scant. We sat on benches, ate from broken dishes with broken forks and wooden spoons. Table clothes were also something they didn't have, but these inconveniences did not mar our pleasure any, and poor Mrs. Ledford who was so good and kind, knew that apologies were not necessary," said a grateful Hoffman. "There was but one needle in the house and this would go the rounds among the neighbors."[595]

Lieutenant Hoffman assumed it was just that their Ledford hosts were poor mountain folk suffering from the Confederacy's inability to provide, having been cut off from the Northern supply chain.

He never knew the truth.

MONDAY DECEMBER 26, 1864

The Ledford underground Unionist network needed to move the Major, Page, and Hoffman. Now that Christmas was over, the Rebel guerrillas would be back on the prowl, terrorizing the neighborhood. With the whole valley around Hayesville full of Ledford farmsteads, there were many options.

"We left this Ledford's and after going some little distance spent the rest of the day and night with the other Ledford," said Hoffman.[596]

The "other" Ledford farmstead that took in the 5th Iowa Boys was owned by fifty-eight-year-old Amos Ledford and his fifty-nine-year-old wife, Delilah. The three officers were excitedly greeted by their younger children, aged eight to fourteen. The eldest son, Cicero, had been promoted to sergeant and was away with his Union regiment; though unknown at the time to his family, he lay sick in a hospital bed at Cumberland Gap, Tennessee.[597] Then they were introduced to Amos and Delilah's second son, a twenty-one-year-old young man named Kit who had enlisted in the Union army but then quickly deserted, though he didn't mention that small fact to them because now he had a more important job.

Kit Ledford was the scout who would help them on the rest of their journey.

Chapter Twenty

After leaving the Amos Ledford farmstead on Tuesday, December 27, the Major, Page, and Hoffman marched just a few farmsteads away to have breakfast with the Curtis Ledford family. They hoped this would be the final leg to Union lines with Kit Ledford as their guide. They spent the rest of the day laid up in the mountains, sleeping the night in a preacher's house. On Wednesday, December 28, they marched eight miles over a mountain and down into the next valley. "We had heard of eleven more escaped prisoners over in another valley, so we went over to where they were, and found them very tired and footsore," said Hoffman.

The tired group of escaped prisoners the 5th Iowa Boys were paired up with included the group of Bassett, Stewart, and Young. After escaping on November 11, their trip had taken a couple of weeks longer than all the others. Also, there were Dobbs and Private Hall, who had escaped on November 21, and then were paired up with Bassett's group in Transylvania County by Flem Cison while they all waited for better weather to travel in. Tom Young, one of the three in Bassett's group, was in bad shape, still suffering the long-term side effects of typhoid fever from years ago. Traveling in the cold had really been difficult for him; he supported himself with a straight tree branch that served as a walking stick.

"We found young Zachary here also, one of the young men we had slept with in Cashiers valley some two weeks before," said Hoffman. "He wanted to come with us, but not having his father's consent we would not take him."

So after T.R. Zachary was turned down to go with the 5th Iowa Boys, two days later he got another opportunity when Flem Cison arrived with his batch of Union escapees. They all made their way into the Hiwassee Valley around Christmas and were waiting to make the dash toward the rail line at Sweetwater, Tennessee.

Also there were John McAdams, Henry Fowler, and four other escaped officers who had traveled sometimes together, sometimes on their own, knowing there were many other escapees around them.

Now they were all gathered together into a single group, ready to take on this last stretch of their escape route together. There was an excitement in coming together this way, having all shared the same miserable experiences as the Rebels' prisoners of war. They all had the knowledge that, one way or the other, the long, cold slog would soon be over. It gave them all a rush of adrenaline that temporarily helped them with the cold conditions.

Hoffman referred to the guides Flem, Kit, and T.R. as "refugees," like they were coming along with the officers to get away from a bad situation where they lived. He felt they didn't need them as guides; but, thus far, having a competent guide through the rough mountain terrain had indeed been valuable to his group. Also, once these three guides successfully got them to Knoxville, they were all coming back home to North Carolina.

"Including three refugees our party now numbered sixteen," said Hoffman. "We then moved along as fast as our sore feet would allow, making some thirteen miles, and towards the night going into a vacant house to sleep."

The winter weather was returning to add misery to each step they took. On Thursday, December 29, they managed just four miles. The temperatures in the early morning hours of Friday, December 30, were so numbingly cold that sleep in the vacant house where they had sheltered, without the benefits of a fire or blankets, had become impossible. So after an hour or two, they gave up on trying to get the sleep they sorely needed and kept moving. It was incredibly dark. There was no moon to provide light to help them see where they were going. In addition, though they were following the path of the main road toward Murphy, North Carolina, they tried to remain as hidden as possible, darting into the frozen woods along the way if they sensed anyone coming. Like blind men, they groped along and were only able to make it four miles before they gave up and hid themselves in the forest, sleeping all day when it was a little warmer.

As the sun began to set, the group was on the move again. They were close to the town of Murphy, which was full of Rebel home guards and militia groups. Murphy was just fourteen miles from Hayesville, and the men cautiously skirted their way around the town during the evening hours after Kit Ledford warned them of the danger.

In addition to the problems that the Ledfords had experienced down in Hayesville, in October 1863 Murphy was the site where John Ledford, another cousin, had been killed. John had been part of an "independent" Union company of more than 100 men known as the "1st Tennessee Scouts and Guides" commanded by Captain Goldman Bryson.[598] They were on a recruiting mission in Cherokee County by order of Major General Burnside.[599] Captain Bryson was killed in the mountains; his body was riddled with rifle shot by members of Company B, Walker's Battalion of Thomas's Legion CSA, which was made up entirely of Confederate indigenous Cherokee. After killing Bryson they captured Ledford and took him to Murphy, where they hung him from a tree on the courthouse square for all to see.[600]

They avoided Murphy as best they could, but a little after midnight on Friday, December 30, they still needed to enter the town's northern edge to gain access to the Unicoi Turnpike and Hunter's Ferry, which was located at the confluence of the Valley and Hiwassee Rivers. The route of the turnpike went right through the middle of Murphy and crossed with the ferry to the northwest. The Unicoi Turnpike was an indigenous trail dating back centuries, used for traveling from the mountains of North Georgia through Western North Carolina and into Eastern Tennessee. In the early nineteenth century it was expanded as a toll road and served as an important artery for commerce since there were no railroads. Once across the river, it entered more mountainous terrain, which would provide some cover for travel with a group so large. But as had been proved weeks earlier, roaming bands from both sides would attack one another with deadly effect.

"We awakened the ferryman, who took us across. We paid him a little rebel money," said Hoffman.

Once the ferryman had their money in his pocket and they reached the northern shore of the river, he told them to go up the road a ways looking for a man named Blythe. The Blythe family were Cherokees living northwest of Murphy. As the group tramped in the dark again along the turnpike in the early morning hours, the temperatures began to drop. They found the Blythe farmstead, and the hungry men were given all the meager food supplies the man had, yet nowhere near enough to feed sixteen hungry men. As it began to get light, they thanked him nonetheless, though the skies were gray and the weather had begun to change. They marched until the mid-afternoon, then sheltered in another vacant house as snow began to fall.

They were getting so close.

They stayed there until the next morning, Saturday, December 31. They had no fire for warmth, huddled together, spooning like their days at Libby Prison. After a miserable and restless night, the group awoke as it began to get light and looked outside to yet another snow-covered landscape. More than six inches of snow had fallen, and now a cold wind blew the white fine powder in small vortexes along the road's path.

As hard as it was to get moving, they had to. It was a choice of moving or freezing to death. The snowfall and cold actually provided them with cover. It was so damned cold as they traveled; they found no one else along the way so even though it was miserable, it was safe. They marched all day, covering miles, huddled together to try and keep warm. Tom Young found himself in the middle of the pack, the bodies of the others supporting him; had he been on his own, he would have collapsed and probably been unable to get up.

Kit Ledford knew they were very close to where his cousin David had been murdered a few weeks earlier at Tellico Mountain, but everything was a pristine white, so finding an actual landmark identifying the place was impossible. Kit was completely unaware when they walked right past the small cabin, now completely covered in snow, where David had been captured along with the two Union officers. The full story of what had happened to his cousin David wouldn't be known for a couple of years.

"We marched the rest of the day, and at night came to a little village. Here the citizens distributed us around to different houses, Page, Marshall, and myself in one house," said Hoffman. "They gave us a good supper. We apologized some for our ragged and dirty condition and told our hostess that if she would give us a couple of quilts we would sleep on the floor and not soil or pollute their beds. She remarked that sheets were easier washed than quilts, so we piled into bed–the best we had for years."

It was New Year's Day 1865. The exhaustion they felt was indescribable. The 5th Iowa Boys all woke that Sunday in a good bed for the first time in years and didn't want to move. Their bodies screamed as they got out of their bed. Outside the thermometer registered zero.

"I have never seen it so cold here before this," said one of the hosts as the three men inhaled their breakfast.

The ragged group all emerged from the homes they had been housed in and, once again, huddled together as they walked along the road, which had turned north into the wind.

So. Damned. Close.

"We were now in Union territory, and only nine miles to Sweetwater, a station on the Chattanooga & Knoxville railroad," said Hoffman. "In going there we found the road very circuitous around a low bottom land, so we took across the bottom, and while doing this we saw our first Union picket post a mile or so to the left of us, and to our surprise they let us pass without being questioned."

They had made it to safety.

The men on picket duty were as numb with cold as the sixteen men walked past them to one side. They stared at the sight of ragged men packed tightly together. One man on picket duty brought up his hand and gestured. Bassett stared at the man, unable to take his eyes off him, then turned his head back in the direction they were all walking as the wind blew hard and froze tears to his face.

It took what seemed like forever to walk nine miles. But those nine miles were under the protection of the Union army. They had made it over the Union lines. They felt tremendous relief. A huge burden of weight suddenly lifted from their shoulders, instantly gone.

"We arrived at the station at 2 o'clock p.m., Jan. 1, 1865, finding the place guarded by a company of Union soldiers," said Hoffman. "The captain in command asked us how we got around the picket post. We told him we flanked them, that we saw them, and they us."

The captain just shook his head and listened to the men's story for a few minutes, then ordered that the men at the picket line come back in, where he would deliver a verbal thrashing.

The next train north to Knoxville wouldn't be until 4 p.m. They walked toward the depot's entrance, all staring up at the American flag that was standing up almost at attention, stiffened in the strong blowing wind. A stove provided warmth inside the small depot. The men had to sit and wait. Some of the men sat on the floor, crowded right next to the stove trying to warm up. They stared at soldiers on guard outside, dressed in Union blue dotted with flecks of clean white snow. Some dozed off, no longer worried about their fate. After staring down the barrel of a gun pointed at them for so long, the fear and anxiety just melted away.

"After 16 months of imprisonment and 2 months of endeavoring to regain our liberty, evading all sorts of dangers from the elements as well as the enemy, we counted this the happiest New Year of our lives to be again among our troops, while above us waved 'Old Glory,'" said Bassett.[601]

Finally, the small passenger train arrived, and the men made a mad rush to get aboard. But there was a problem.

"Your pass and ticket," said the guard who stood on the platform, just doing his duty yet blocking the men's path to board the car. It seemed like a cruel joke.

"These we did not have. We had courage and perseverance, and enough of it to get us on the platform. Captain Page, who was generally known to have his own way, pushed the guard to one side and went in, the rest of us following," said Hoffman. "When the conductor came around we told him our old story that had now been repeated over a hundred times. This was equal to a pass to Knoxville."

The train pulled out of the station at Sweetwater, northbound for Knoxville, which was forty-five miles away. It would take a little over two hours. Trains were lucky to travel much faster than twenty miles per hour, and this particular route had had its tracks ripped up and bridges destroyed by both sides over the last few years, depending on which side controlled it. Now it was safely in Union hands.

The men stared out the windows at the snow-covered landscape and gray skies as the hypnotic sounds of the train's wheels click-clacked along the metal tracks. Many fell asleep to the sound. No one really had much to say.

Soon the afternoon light began to fade. The train rolled into the station at Knoxville right around dark. After exiting the train car and walking through the Knoxville depot, they found themselves on Gay Street, the town's main thoroughfare. A soldier directed them to the Asylum U. S. Army General Hospital or "Soldier's Hospital," which was a couple of blocks west. The men walked with temperatures hovering around zero, climbed up the impressive building's steep steps to the main entrance, and walked in. A staff was buzzing around the place, setting up for a big New Year's dinner extravaganza that was scheduled to be hosted at the hospital the next day.[602] This seemed so odd to men who had nothing to celebrate for so long.

"We reported to the post commander who gave us a supper, once again at the expense of the United States government," said Hoffman, "and at bed time they gave us each a nice little cot to sleep on. But we were so elated and lighthearted over our successful escape and the prospects of soon being at home that we could not sleep much."[603]

They had made it.

Chapter Twenty-One

1865

On Monday, January 2, after having their photograph taken, the men climbed down the stairs of the photographer's studio and reemerged onto Gay Street, then retraced their steps back to Asylum General Hospital where they had spent the previous evening. Even in the middle of the day it was still bitterly cold.

They were all still soldiers in the Union army and had reported to Provost Marshal General Samuel P. Carter's headquarters before having their photograph taken. A clerk recorded on official letterhead of the Provost Marshal each man's name, company and regiment, the date and place of their capture, the date and place of their escape, and the date of their reporting back: January 2, 1865.[604] Some were given a thirty-day leave, after which they could very well be issued orders to report to their regiments and possibly join the fight again. Most were emaciated and broken down from their POW experience and subsequent month-plus slog in winter conditions.

They were all anxious to get out of Knoxville and get home, but when they found out the train schedule, they discovered they were all going to have to spend one more night at the hospital sleeping on cots. Back at the hospital they got warm baths; some were given new uniforms, for which their military accounts were charged. Then they passed the time eating lunch, then dinner, and looking around the large building. The hospital staff was busy because of the New Year's dinner extravaganza hosted by the surgeons and stewards that was going to take place later that day.

Though they were not invited as guests to the big event, they were oddly placed on display after the New Year's dinner when the entire hospital was toured by those guests in attendance. Two days earlier the officers had a completely different appearance and smell, with unkempt hair and beards, dressed in dirty, ragged clothes. Now they were rubbing elbows with Knoxville's elite citizens, who were no doubt dressed to the max for the festive evening.

"There are 1,250 patients in the Hospital...the beds are clean and neat, the rooms well kept, and everything was as perfect as desired," reported the *Knoxville Whig,* which covered the affair.[605]

It was indeed perfect, but now that they were free, what they desired was to go home. That night at 9:20 p.m. a telegram went out from Knoxville to Washington, D.C.:

Office U.S. Military Telegraph, War Department
The following Telegram was received at Washington,
9:20 P. M. Jan 2nd, 186_ 20 from Knoxville.

General Thomas
 The following officers escaped from Columbia, S.C. have reported at the office since twenty ninth Dec.
 Maj Marshall fifth (5) Iowa Infantry
 Capt Mann fifth (5) Ill Cavy
 Page fifth (5) Iowa Infantry

1st Lt. Sutherland one hundred & twenty six (126) O.V.I and Potter, second Ky Infy & Strickland one hundred & fourteenth Ill Inf & Hoffman fifth Iowa Infy & McAdams tenth Wisconsin (sic) Vol Infy & 2d Lieuts Potts seventy fifth OVI & Turner second RI Cavy & Ziegler one hundred & fourteenth Ill Infy & Bassett fifty third Ill & Fowler fifteenth NJ Infy & Young fourth Ky Infy & Dobbs nineteenth USC and Stewart fourth Ky Infy

SP Carter
Br Gen Cmng[606]

Finally, the time had come to go home. The winter temperatures had warmed slightly, but it was still cold. "We received transportation, each for his destination and left at 7:30 a.m.," said Hoffman.

The route home for everyone meant that from Knoxville they had to head south before they could head north. To add to the anticipation of getting home after being gone for years, none of their families were aware that they had escaped prison, or that they would soon be home knocking on the front door.

The train rolled out of Knoxville headed toward Chattanooga. At around 10 a.m. they stopped at Sweetwater, Tennessee, where they had first gotten on the train headed north two days earlier. Their three guides got off there to take the Unicoi Turnpike back to North Carolina. Before Flem Cison, Kit Ledford, and T.R. Zachary disembarked the passenger car, they said their goodbyes, shaking hands and slapping each other on the back. Most of the officers would never see them again. The three guides all watched as the train slowly left Sweetwater depot headed south; then they turned and began their long walk home. Zachary was excited by the promise that was made by Bassett, Stewart, and Young to send funds to help in his education. The funds would never come.

Though Knoxville to Chattanooga was just over 100 miles, the train stopped at almost every depot along the way. The trip took all day, and they arrived in Chattanooga around 5:30 p.m.[607] For the Major, Page, and Hoffman, this was full circle. Chattanooga was the place where they were all captured a little more than thirteen months earlier.

They had no money and only owned the clothes on their back and the rags they had been wearing when they crossed Union lines. For some reason a few continued to wear some of the rags, perhaps not wanting to pay for new officer's uniforms that they might not need. As former prisoners of war, they all had back pay coming, but they needed to wait for the slow gears of the military bureaucracy to receive it, so they had limited options on where to stay and how to pay for things such as transportation, food, and additional warm clothing. Each man had Confederate money, but that wasn't worth anything in Union-controlled Chattanooga or, for that matter, in the remaining Confederacy as well. Many kept their Rebel currency as a nostalgic souvenir of the worst time of their life.

Most of the group went to the Soldier's Home in Chattanooga for a meal and lodging for the night. They would be sleeping on cots again.

Major Marshall, however, wasted no time. The moment he arrived in Chattanooga he headed straight to the Headquarters Department of the Cumberland and was issued "Field Order No. 3," granting him twenty days' leave signed by the Assistant Adjutant General Lieutenant Colonel Southard Hoffman.[608] He was also able to twist arms and have back pay issued through August 31, 1864, which must have been a decent sum, by the paymaster Major William N. McIntire.[609] The Major was set and headed to a nearby hotel for the evening. There would be no army cots for him.

Like other returning POWs, returning to the normal ways of life was like discovering gold, and they all reacted with newfound appreciation. "Went to a good hotel where we enjoyed the luxury of a bed, the first bed that I had slept in since June 1863," said one officer. "Went to a Barber shop and we had our beards trimmed and shampooed. Oh what a luxury!" said another.[610]

On Wednesday morning, January 4, after breakfast at the Soldier's Home, some of the men went to the Sanitary Commission in Chattanooga and were lent money so they could continue their journey home. The Sanitary Commission was a civilian-run organization, a forerunner to the Red Cross. It was recognized by the U.S. government and provided all kinds of assistance to military hospitals, distributing supplies where needed at no cost to the government. The organization existed on private donations. Once the officers' back pay was issued, they would reach out to the Sanitary Commission and return the loans they had been given. It was all done under the honor system.

The train departed Chattanooga headed north for Nashville at 1 p.m. on Wednesday afternoon. The distance between the two cities was only 148 miles; it was a very slow-moving train, and the men would not pull into the station at Nashville until 5:30 a.m. on Thursday, January 5.[611]

The next train to Louisville, Kentucky, would not leave until the next morning so the men had the day to spend in Nashville. Hoffman wrote in his diary that he went to the St. Cloud hotel, located in the heart of Nashville near 5th Avenue and Church Street, just a few blocks from the Cumberland River, for breakfast.

But while the Major, Page, and Hoffman were in Nashville, their old regiment, the 5th Iowa, was there, too. The three officers found where they were camped and visited them, catching up on the story of their capture and events that followed. Hoffman went looking for his older brother, Samuel, who had been in Company D with him but was told that Samuel had transferred to the 5th Iowa Cavalry in August 1864. Unbeknown to Michael at the time, his brother Samuel was in a Nashville hospital, having been wounded at Pulaski, Tennessee, on Christmas Day[612] at about the same time the 5th Iowa Boys were guests of the Ledfords for the memorable Christmas dinner in North Carolina.

Now that the experience of having been a POW was over, and because everywhere they went everyone wanted to know about it, the men began to craft the narrative of what had happened to them. For some, talking about it was cathartic and helped them move forward; for others, they didn't want to go into the details and held things in. They were all permanently scarred. At the time, the concept of post-traumatic stress disorder (PTSD) was completely unknown. Having been subjected to extreme stress for months on end, the former prisoners all suffered from it in some way. Most were emaciated and frail; they all had to regain their strength and health after being subjected to such horrible living conditions and diets. It would take some men the rest of their lives, and one wouldn't survive the rest of the year.[613]

The train left Nashville on Friday, January 6, at 7:30 a.m. headed for Louisville, Kentucky. This leg was 175 miles, and they would have to disembark at 6 p.m. Louisville was the main point where the men all split up and headed their separate ways. Many checked into Louisville House, once again telling the story of being POW Union soldiers awaiting their back pay. Most had to talk the clerk at the front desk into spotting them the cost of a few rooms, with the pledge that they would pay them as soon as their back pay arrived. Mike Hoffman recorded in his diary that he stayed in room 132.[614]

For Allie Stewart and Tom Young, they were almost home. Since they arrived after dark, they spent the night in Louisville, too. But the excitement of getting home was building, and both could hardly sleep. For Tom, the side effects from typhoid fever were debilitating, and his condition, though buoyed by the adrenaline rush of finally being free, had long worn away. He was exhausted. Danville, Kentucky, was just over eighty miles away, and with no railroad linking the two towns, they would take a wagon on Saturday and arrive home a few days later.

Thomas Young Jr. would never recover. His health continued to deteriorate. He received several thirty-day extensions to his original leave and was finally medically discharged from the 4th Kentucky on May 15, 1865, by order of the War Department.[615] His father, the Judge, and mother, Mary, could only watch in dismay. He survived the summer but died of heart disease on Friday, October 13, a lingering, long-term side effect of the typhoid fever he had contracted in December 1861. He was buried in Bellevue Cemetery in Danville, Kentucky. GAR Post #125 in Danville was named after him upon its founding in 1889.

ON SATURDAY, JANUARY 7, 1865, the rest of the men finally received some of their back pay and were able to buy additional clothing. That evening they paid a $3.50 fare to board a steamer bound for Cincinnati, Ohio. The voyage up the icy Ohio River would take all night and most of the next day, arriving in Cincinnati around 7 p.m. The 5th Iowa Boys all got rooms at the Spencer House hotel, which was located along Cincinnati's riverfront.[616]

Cincinnati was the hub from which the remaining officers went either east or west. Three of the men, John McAdams, Henry Fowler, and Lem Dobbs, would continue to the east up the Ohio River on a steamboat, watching the ship's bow push chunks of ice to either side as it gingerly moved upriver.

When John McAdams arrived at his home, his wife, Kate, opened the door to see a ragged-looking scarecrow-like man standing in their doorway. She barely recognized her husband, but after staring into his deep blue eyes, she embraced him in a hug and didn't want to let go. John looked down and saw three-year-old Charles standing behind his sobbing mother. That was all he could take; soon he was sobbing, too, an emotional release triggered by the indescribable feeling of being home and finally free.

"After he made his escape from the Rebel prison he was in very poor health," said his brother-in-law, Samuel Ryland, recalling John's return home. "He was generally broken down...he was crippled in his back with rheumatism, and his scurvy was so bad he lost all his teeth. He did not work for six months."[617]

Another lifelong friend went to John's home often to keep him company while he convalesced and said, "He was a mere skeleton when he came home."[618]

"Lieutenant John McAdams, of the 10th West Virginia Infantry, who was captured last winter while with Gen. Averill (sic) on the famous Salem raid, returned home yesterday, having escaped several weeks ago from a rebel prison in Columbia, SC," reported *The Wheeling Intelligencer*. "He escaped with several others and walked four hundred miles barefooted and almost naked."[619]

McAdams wouldn't be mustered out of service until May, having to make a trip to meet up with the rest of the regiment near Richmond, Virginia. Still in rough shape, he barely survived the trip. In the latter part of 1865 he successfully petitioned the Office of the Commissary General of Prisoners and received a claim of $185 for "Money Taken from Federal Prisoners of War Confined in Confederate Prisons." It was payback to the Turners at Libby who had picked his pockets.

Henry Fowler and Lem Dobbs continued on to Pittsburgh, then took the train east. Henry arrived in Washington, D.C., around January 16, and Lem continued on to Baltimore.

"Lieut. Fowler, of the 15th Regiment, N.J.V., who was reported killed in one of the battles of May last in the Wilderness, and whose mother has drawn a pension on that account for some months,[620]has reached home alive and well," reported the *Hunterdon Republican.* "Instead of being killed, he was taken prisoner, and has been detained in the horrible southern prisons, without being able to communicate with his friends. He escaped from the prison in Columbia, S.C., in November until three or four days ago in reaching Washington. His shoes and stockings gave out, and he entered Washington barefoot, with his pantaloons entirely worn away below the knees, and with a remnant of a coat made from an old sack. His health is better than would be supposed after so many hardships."[621]

From Washington, Henry returned home to New Jersey to be reunited with his mother on a thirty-day leave. About the same time Henry arrived home, his uncle, Colonel Samuel Fowler, who had raised the 15th New Jersey and was their first commanding officer, died.

During Henry's time at home, he was promoted to Captain of Company A of the 155th New Jersey. The war was not over for him, and he returned to his regiment in mid-February.

Lem Dobbs arrived at his wife, Kate's, late father's home in north Baltimore. They had been married for less than a year, and she had endured the devastating news that he had been killed in action at The Battle of the Crater on July 30, 1864, but then received the amazing news that he had survived and was a POW weeks later. She had ridden all the emotional waves caused by shock, and now Lem was home. But, like Henry Fowler, his war was not over. After a short leave he was back with the 19th USCI, though was fortunate enough to be given detached service with the special duty of recruiting in the Baltimore area until May. For the first time in their short marriage, the couple would be with each other.

In May Dobbs was sent back to the 19th USCI, which was serving in Brownsville, Texas. To Catherine, the loss of her husband again caused her to have a nervous breakdown. Immediately after arriving in Brownsville, Dobbs requested a leave to attend to his wife in Baltimore. Dobbs returned to his wife and brought her back to Brownsville to be with him. He would serve in Brownsville into the following year before being mustered out of service.[622]

On June 19, 1865, Dobbs' regiment was in Brownsville where he was acting quartermaster of the 3rd Brigade. Yet, 400 miles to the northeast in Galveston, Texas, a military general order written by General Gordon Granger was being read on the streets. "The people of Texas are informed that, in accordance with a Proclamation from the Executive of the United States, all slaves are free."[623]

The day became known as Juneteenth.

On Monday, January 9, 1865, Mark Bassett and the 5th Iowa Boys, Major Marshall,

Page, and Hoffman all caught a train headed for Chicago, arriving in the windy city late in the evening. At 11:30 p.m. they checked into the Fremont House. The next morning Mark Bassett caught a barge down the Illinois and Michigan Canal, then down to LaSalle, connecting with a steamer down the Illinois River on the final leg of his route home.

The 5th Iowa Boys spent all day Tuesday, January 10, running around Chicago before boarding a train, taking a sleeping car around 7:30 p.m. The Major got off early on Wednesday morning, January 11, at the Davenport, Iowa, depot. Wasting no time, Marshall was mustered out of service in the 5th Iowa the next day. Returning to civilian life, he began to pick up where he had left off, reaching out to his attorney friends in town.

Page and Hoffman arrived at the depot in Marshalltown, Iowa, around 1 p.m. on January 10.[624] A cold wind blew as they disembarked the train and walked down the platform alongside the tracks. When the locomotive steamed past headed westward, it was like drawing open a curtain, revealing a desolate, snow-covered landscape of the flat Iowa plain that seemed to go on forever, seamlessly merging with a cloudy sky at the horizon.

For Captain John E. Page, the arrival home that afternoon was bittersweet. His wife, Nan, embraced him tightly at the door with tears streaming down her face, deeply moved to have her husband finally home. His oldest son, Charles, stood wide-eyed at the sight of a tall man with a long beard, knowing this was his father but not at all recognizing the man looking back at him with a haggard, distant stare. Nan then told her husband the bad news. Their younger son, William, was deathly ill with diphtheria.[625] The boy wouldn't survive the month. Their emotions ran the gamut, and soon the Page family would be grieving over the loss of their youngest son while celebrating the return of their patriarch. Page was honorably discharged from the 5th Iowa on February 1, and in the spring the familiar sounds of his wagon-making business again emanated from the barn behind the house.

Michael Hoffman arrived at the home of his parents, John and Lydia Hoffman, at around the same time as John Page; the two men lived just a few blocks from each other. He heartily gave his mother a big hug and was soon mobbed by his four younger sisters, somehow finding a way to shake his father's hand at the same time. He mentally noted that his parents had aged in the three and a half years since he had left home, and they, too, noted how their son had also aged from more than a year's exposure to Rebel prisons. They also noticed he had a hard time hearing; they had to speak louder, and face to face, for them to communicate with him. Some of Hoffman's brothers were still fighting in the war. Now, for the first time, he was home and at peace. He couldn't remember the last time he had felt that way.

Also that Wednesday afternoon a steamship was heading southeast on the Illinois River. It was the final link en route to home for Mark Bassett. In the cold of winter, ice had formed along the riverbanks, and the fertile farmland was covered with snow. With a sense of foreboding, Bassett got off at Havana, Illinois, the same place he had gotten on to head north and enlist just over three years earlier. With thirty-day leave papers in his pocket, he would soon be home and confronting his wife, Charlotte. No one who knew him in the small, isolated farming community of Kerton Township had a clue he was coming.

After arriving in the early afternoon in Havana, Illinois, Bassett crossed over the river to Point Isabel and caught a ride on a wagon, taking him down the familiar country roads south to Kerton Township where he passed through the small town of Marbeltown. The whole trip was about ten miles, and he arrived at his home, a small farmhouse up the road from his father-in-law's place, around dark.

Mark Bassett never wrote down what was said when Lottie opened the door and saw her husband standing on the porch. Mark was a changed man. Three years of war and the effects of being a POW, combined with the stress of worry, ages a man. Lottie was a changed woman, and surely in a state of shock. He quickly realized that now that he was finally home, there was no way he could stay in his own house. Their first contact in three years was tense and painful for both. He briefly saw his children; but he knew his marriage had imploded and was over. They had lived in a tiny farming community where everyone knew what was going on. There were no secrets in Kerton Township.

Though Bassett was happy to no longer be a prisoner of the Rebels, there was no joy. Even though he was free, he had just a few weeks before his leave was up and he would have to return to the army. He needed to put on some weight and fill out his emaciated frame, desperately needing to rest and recover. What he was experiencing at home was far more stressful than what he had experienced in prison. He needed to think, clear his head, and figure out what to do next.

His sister, Mary Jane, and brother-in-law, Abram Markey, lived less than a mile from his house; for a while he stayed with them. Mary Jane and Abram had six children; one niece had been born after Bassett had gone off to war. Another niece was named after his estranged wife, Charlotte. Mary Jane had hinted in the letters he had received from her while at Libby Prison that there were problems at home. Now she was able to tell Mark in detail how devastated Lottie had been after she had first been told that he had been killed in action and then, months later, how she had reacted when she got the word that he was very much alive. Bassett knew he had but one option.

Samuel S. Tipton was a thirty-year-old attorney living in Lewistown, Illinois, where the Fulton County Circuit Court was located. Tipton was a war veteran, having served as the adjutant in the 103rd Illinois Infantry until June 1863 when he returned home to resume practicing law. After meeting with Mark at his law office in Lewistown, he took Bassett's divorce case.

Tipton filed the divorce papers on February 16, 1865. In the filings he argued that Charlotte Bassett was unfit to raise their three children.[626]

Two days later Bassett was given orders to report to General Lysander Cutler's headquarters at Camp Blair in Jackson, Michigan, on March 1, 1865. By the end of the war, Camp Blair was being used as a convalescence center for Union troops and as a draft rendezvous site. The camp's commander, General Cutler, had himself been seriously injured in 1864, struck in the face by a shell fragment and badly disfigured. The General was an invalid, still recovering from his wounds while serving as the camp's commander.[627]

Bassett arrived in Michigan as ordered on March 1. "I reported to Governor Oglesby and he commissioned me captain of the company and I noted as such until the close of the war," said Bassett. "But as I was not any time where there was a mustering officer I was mustered out as a First Lieutenant at Jackson, Mich, where I was in charge of draft rendezvous, where we were drafting men for the front."[628]

The next day Robert Johnson, the sheriff of Fulton County, knocked on the door of the Bassett farmstead in Kerton Township with a summons for Charlotte Bassett. She wasn't home.

"Not being able to find Charlotte Bassett, I gave W. H. Bassett, a member of her family, at her place of abode, a true copy within, explaining the contents," said the sheriff.

William H. Bassett, Mark's older brother, was the one who accepted and signed for Charlotte's summons. William, who was a farmer living in Indiana, made the 300-mile trip west with his family to Kerton Township to help support his brother during a very difficult time. It must have been awkward for him to sign the summons for his soon-to-be ex-sister-in-law. What became of Charlotte after Mark arrived back home is not known, though she probably returned to her father's farmstead.

For Bassett, his time in Michigan must have felt as a reprieve from the stress of the upcoming divorce proceedings had been scheduled to be held in Lewistown in mid-April. Though he was doing his job as a Union officer, things were fairly quiet in Michigan in the early spring of 1865. The camp covered eleven acres and was located a few miles west of the town of Jackson. It had a barracks and hospital that could each house up to 100 men, and there was also a bakery. The smell of fresh baked bread greeted the former POW each morning with a warm, luxurious aroma that Bassett found wonderful. At the camp he was able to convalesce, biding his time with assisting in the draft of new recruits into the Union army, of which there were not many. By the last days of March, it was apparent that the war had wound down to its last few weeks.

While he was stationed at Camp Blair, he met seventeen-year-old Annie Elizabeth Gould. She seemed like a breath of fresh air after the suffering he had been through. Though she had not had much education, Annie was intellectual and enjoyed writing poetry. Like Mark, her life had been very difficult, and she, too, had suffered greatly during the war.

Annie, the youngest of six, had lost her mother before her first birthday in 1848. Her father, David Gould, was a traveling cobbler, unable to take care of an infant, so he relied on the kindness of a cousin, Elizabeth, who had married John Haddock, a local wagon maker and lived nearby. David Gould moved his other children to Parma, Michigan, about five miles west. John and Elizabeth Haddock unofficially adopted Annie and raised her as their own, along with their two children. Annie's father, David, traveled around the region selling his shoes while continuing to stay in touch with his youngest daughter.

Throughout the 1850s Annie's siblings would fend for themselves while their father was away selling his wares. Then the war came, and shoes were one thing in great demand. The Union army had a draft rendezvous site right up the road, so David Gould didn't need to travel as much.

With the confusing family relationships and limited contact with her father and siblings, Annie managed to have a relatively happy childhood and grew up with a good set of values as an adopted member of her aunt and uncle Haddock's family.

Then tragedy struck in 1862. Sixty-year-old John Haddock died in February, and his thirty-one-year-old son, Silas Haddock, died in December. Having lost two other children before Annie came along, this left sixty-one-year-old Elizabeth Haddock a widow, living alone with fourteen-year-old Annie in the town of Sandstone, Michigan, and trying to survive in the middle of the Civil War. Less than five miles east from their home, Camp Blair offered a place they could both find work in order to survive.

In 1864 Annie lost two of her older Gould brothers in the war. On May 12 twenty-two-year-old Lieutenant James Gould of the 20th Michigan Infantry was wounded and captured at the battle of Spotsylvania Court House. It was the same battle in which Henry Fowler of the 15th New Jersey was wounded and captured. James was moved to Libby Prison and, in an odd coincidence, arrived just days after Bassett was moved from Libby, heading south to Macon. A month later on June 15, James Gould succumbed to his wounds and died at Libby. That same month his twenty-five-year-old brother, Frank Gould, was killed at Vicksburg.

Annie Gould made a lasting impression on Mark Bassett. The two had been through hell and back. They were kindred spirits. But first Mark needed to resolve things back in Illinois.

WHEN BASSETT ESCAPED FROM Camp Sorghum on November 10, 1864, he was part of a group of nine officers. Two weeks later after being pursued by Rebels on horseback, the group split into three different ones. It may have taken them fifty-one days but Bassett, along with Thomas P. Young and Allie Stewart, were the first to successfully make it to freedom.

The others didn't fare as well.

The second group was composed of four officers: Captains James A. Wilson and Alvah S. Skilton, both of the 57th Ohio, Captain Augustus Dusenberry of the 35th New Jersey, and Lt. William H. H. Welch of the 87th Pennsylvania. They had been hidden away until the beginning of January 1865 by members of Sheriff Robert Hamilton's Union sympathizers in Transylvania County, North Carolina. When they finally moved westward, they were in a large group of more than twenty that were all captured by home guards within ten miles of Ducktown, Tennessee, on January 18, 1865.

Dusenberry and Welch escaped their captors three days later and successfully found their way to the Union lines at Cleveland, Tennessee, on January 25. Wilson and Skilton were sent to a jail in Asheville, North Carolina, and eventually back to Libby Prison in Richmond.[629]

The third group was composed of Lieutenants Malcolm M. Moore of the 6th Michigan Cavalry and John G. Oates of the 3rd Ohio Cavalry. The two were also recaptured in North Carolina and ended up at Libby as well.

Captain Skilton was released on April 2 and headed by boat to Annapolis, Maryland, where he remained waiting to receive his discharge papers and having to deal with other responsibilities from his regiment.

At Appomattox Court House in Virginia on Sunday, April 9, General Robert E. Lee surrendered to General Ulysses S. Grant. It would take a few months for the word to get around and all hostilities to cease, but the war was over.

ON WEDNESDAY, APRIL 12, Mark Bassett was discharged from the 53rd Illinois in Jackson, Michigan. He had been captured in Jackson, Mississippi, and now his military service had come to an end in Jackson, Michigan. It had been quite an experience. After saying goodbye to Annie Gould, he started the grueling 380-mile trip back to Illinois by train, barge, steamboat, and wagon.

Two days later, on Friday evening, April 14, while Bassett was still traveling, President Lincoln was assassinated.

Stuck in Annapolis on Saturday, Bassett's fellow escapee, Skilton, would record in his diary: "This morning brings the sad news...of the assassination of the President of the

United States. He was killed in Fords Theatre shot by Wilkes Booth. All trains are stopped and no one is allowed to leave the city."

By Monday, April 17, Skilton had made it by train to Washington, D.C., and spent the day at army headquarters settling his regimental issues with the Quartermaster. Afterwards, he had planned on catching a train home to Pennsylvania, but the startling events of the last few days in Washington had compelled him to stay another day.

"I went to the White House this morning," Skilton recorded on Tuesday, April 18. "I saw the remains of the late President—he looked very natural."

Then he spent the remainder of the day doing what visitors normally do in Washington when the nation is not at war with itself. He went sightseeing, then finally caught a train home to Pennsylvania around 10 p.m.[630]

Back in Illinois, Mark Bassett had also made it home again, or what had once been his home in Kerton Township, in time for his appointed court date. On Tuesday, April 18, he traveled to Lewistown, Illinois, and spent the night. On Wednesday morning he met his attorney, Samuel S. Tipton, at the courthouse. Judge Chauncey L. Higbie was on the bench of the Fulton County Circuit Court.

The facts in the case against his wife, Charlotte "Lottie" Bassett, were open and shut. Tipton argued that Charlotte was not a fit or proper person to have the care and custody of the children. It was when Tipton interviewed the witnesses and their testimonies were written into the record that Charlotte's fate was sealed.

The most damning testimony was that of Mary A. Schreffler, the twenty-two-year-old friend of both the Bassetts, who had boarded in their home several times in the early 1860s. She was in the Bassett home between November 1863 and April 1864, helping Lottie with the children while Mark was away.

"The defendant (Lottie) told the witness (Mary) that she committed adultery with John H. Moore in August 1863, and that she was in a family way by him, that it was December 1863," testified Schreffler. "In January 1864 saw the defendant procure an abortion, that witness was in the house and in the same room when the abortion was procured, that there was a physician present at the time."[631]

The physician that performed the abortion was thirty-nine-year-old Dr. William Kirk who lived in nearby Marbles Mill, Illinois. Dr. Kirk was summoned to the court, but no record shows whether he actually appeared. Shortly after the proceedings, Dr. Kirk quickly left Illinois and moved with his wife and six children hundreds of miles west to Nebraska, seeking greener pastures to start things over with a new, untarnished reputation.

Mary Schreffler went on to testify, along with another neighbor, Elizabeth Kelley, that not only had Lottie had an affair with Moore, but also with Otis Richardson and four other men whom they each named—all lived in close proximity to the Bassett home. Kerton Township was one close-knit community, to say the least.

Remarkably, Moore, Richardson, and Dr. Kirk had all been privates in Company E of the 53rd Illinois and had been under Bassett's command. All three had been discharged with disabilities from battle in October 1862 and returned home. Bassett remained stoic when these particular names with their ironic military records came up in testimony. Their actions against the man they knew and answered to as their sergeant, which was Bassett's rank at the time of their departure from the 53rd Illinois, was devastating.

Judge Higbie issued his ruling, dissolving the marriage of Mark M. Bassett and Charlotte Severns Bassett. He further ordered that the care and custody of their three children, Nathaniel, Sarah Jane, and Charles, be given to Mark.

By late Wednesday, April 19, 1865, Mark Bassett was a newly minted divorcé with three young children. His children barely knew him, but the stress he had been under for what seemed like a lifetime was suddenly gone.

In post-Civil War America when a family with young children lost one of the two parents through death, it was common for the surviving parent to quickly remarry afterwards. The rare divorce was just like the death of a parent. Bassett needed a new wife. The person of definite interest was seventeen-year-old Annie Elizabeth Gould back in Sandstone, Michigan. Now that his divorce was final, Bassett would write Annie often. He would also rely on his brother and sister to help him with the children while he got his life back in order.

Thinking that the worst was finally behind him, suddenly, in the second half of 1865, Bassett's four-year-old son, Charles, unexpectedly died.[632] Childhood illness that led to death among young children was a common occurrence in the nineteenth century. So much had happened to Bassett in the last three years. The loss of Charlie, whom he was just getting to know since he had been born when Mark went off to war, was yet another devastating blow.

Bassett sought comfort in his letters to Annie, and by the fall of 1865 she had turned eighteen and agreed to marry him. He traveled back to Sandstone, Michigan, where the license was obtained and the simple ceremony conducted on Wednesday, November 22, 1865. The couple returned to Illinois and lived for a short time on Mark's farm with his two surviving children. But there were too many bad memories. He needed to get away from the small Kerton Township community where everyone knew everyone and everything that everyone did with everyone.

In addition, he was still convalescing from his time as a POW. Bassett found himself physically unable to do the things on his farm that he effortlessly had done before he went off to war.[633] It became apparent that he needed some other occupation to provide for his newly constituted family. He had been around lawyers so much, both in the military and through his divorce, that the study of the law began to intrigue him.

Back in 1861 Alonzo W. Bull, who was an attorney before the war, was the officer who signed Bassett's papers when he enlisted as a sergeant in the 53rd Illinois. Bull later became the captain of Company E, with Bassett as one of his lieutenants. After the war Bull had set up his law practice in Pekin, Illinois, which was just forty-five miles northeast of Kerton Township. At year's end Bassett and Annie and his two children, seven-year-old Nathaniel and five-year-old Sarah Jane, moved to Pekin, and Mark began to study the law under the tutelage of his old captain.

IT WOULD TAKE A WHILE FOR all the men to acclimate themselves to the concept of being free, to go about as one pleased, and not worry that they might be shot when doing so. Slowly to a certain degree with the passage of time, they recovered their health, though most were never got back to where they were before they became POWs.

They were all different men than before the war. Mental scars would continue to dog some for the rest of their lives. But they were survivors and, in the decades to come, would move on until the pain and suffering they had endured faded into the background and became distant memories.

Chapter Twenty-Two

After the War

Marsh Byers
Photographer unknown

The Poet – Samuel H. M. "Marsh" Byers (1838-1933)

While Marsh Byers did not make his escape at the same time as the others, his importance to their story, and the story of the Civil War, makes him worthy of mention here. After the large wave of escapees at Camp Sorghum in Columbia, South Carolina, in November 1864, the Rebels moved the remaining prisoners to Asylum Prison in the heart of Columbia on December 12.

Byers escaped for a third time from the Rebels by hiding out in the prison's attic as the other POWs were being moved by the Rebels when General Sherman approached the city. On February 17, 1865, Columbia, South Carolina, was taken by Sherman's troops. When Byers saw Union troops moving through town, he knew that after sixteen months of captivity he was finally free and was surprised to hear them actually singing the song he had written, "Sherman's March to the Sea," as they marched on by. Byers had no idea it had become so popular; he was a bona fide celebrity. Word got to General Sherman that Byers was in Columbia, and the general wanted to meet the man who had created a sensation with his words, telling the story about Sherman's famous March to the Sea.[634] "General Sherman sent for me, and, furnishing horse, saddle and tent, gave me a position, for a time, on his staff," said Byers. "I now had pleasant times, and I felt the contrast between starving in prison and living in the headquarters of a great army."

After the war Byers returned to Iowa and was brevetted a major. He married Margaret Gilmore in Knox, Illinois, in 1869 and was shortly after appointed as U. S. consul to Switzerland by President Ulysses S. Grant. The couple had two children, a boy and a girl, both born while the family was in Switzerland.

Byers spent almost twenty years in Europe before returning to the United States. He became a prolific writer and published several books on his Civil War experiences, some of which were based on the diary he kept while a POW, as well as books on other subjects.

Later in life Byers moved to Los Angeles, California, then died on May 24, 1933, at the age of ninety-four. His wife and two children pre-deceased him. At his passing he was the last surviving member of General Sherman's staff and the last surviving member of the 5th Iowa Infantry.

The Ex-Wife – Charlotte Severns Brown (1840-1914)

On December 30, 1865, Mark Bassett's ex-wife, Charlotte, married Charles D. Brown. Perhaps most interesting about the new couple was that Brown wasn't one of the many men's names recorded in court depositions during her divorce. Ironically, John H. Moore, one of the objects of Charlotte's attention while Bassett was a POW, continued to live with his parents just two doors down from the newly married Mr. and Mrs. Charles

D. Brown.[635] It might have been slightly uncomfortable, but it was oddly normal for Kerton Township.

Mr. and Mrs. Brown would continue living a few farmsteads from Charlotte's father, Daniel Severns, and produce eight children together. Charlotte's second husband was a farmer and had some small county government roles in Fulton County, Illinois.

It is not known if she ever had any further contact with the two children she had with Bassett, who both survived into adulthood. Charlotte died in March 1914 in Havana, Illinois, just across the Illinois River from Fulton County

The Antagonists – The Confederates in Charge of Union POWs

There were four men who made the lives of the POWs in this story miserable: General John H. Winder, who was in charge of all the Confederate prisons; Major Thomas Pratt Turner, the commandant of Libby Prison; Richard Randolph Turner, the warden of Libby Prison; and Erastus Willey Ross, the chief clerk at Libby Prison. All four were loathed by the Union officers they held as prisoners.

General John H. Winder (1800-1865)

General Winder was in charge of all Rebel prisons including Andersonville. Winder seemed to take pleasure in how Union prisoners were mistreated. He reportedly boasted that he was responsible for the "killing of more Yankees than twenty regiments in Lee's army."[636] It was Winder who had ordered for the mine to be placed under Libby Prison with additional orders to blow up the prison if Kilpatrick's Raiders got close. He is said to have given similar orders to open fire on the prisoners in 1864 if General Stoneman's Raiders got close to Andersonville.

General Winder died of a heart attack in Florence, South Carolina, on February 6, 1865.

General John H. Winder
Photographer unknown

"The rebel General Winder, the inhuman commander of all prisons in the south, died," said Marsh Byers. "On announcement of his death the prisoners greatly rejoiced, and some of them raised a mud monument in the center of camp, on which was inscribed the last words of the tyrannical general" 'Cut off their molasses, boys.'"[637]

Had Winder survived the war, he would very likely have been brought to trial like Andersonville's commander, Henry Wirz, who was found guilty of acts of personal cruelty and hung.

Major Thomas P. Turner & General Jubal Early
In Havana 1865
Photographer unknown

Major Thomas Pratt Turner (1840-1900)

When the outcome of the war became apparent, Commandant Turner burned the records held at Libby and fled, first south, ending up in Florida. Then he headed west, eventually making it to Galveston, Texas, where he boarded a ship headed for England, passing himself off as a Massachusetts Yankee. Turner landed in the Bahamas and caught another ship for Cuba, arriving in December 1865, where he took refuge at the Hotel Cabana in Havana where other Confederates expats were staying. He eventually ended up in Canada. After President Andrew Johnson had pardoned prominent Confederates in 1869, Turner returned to the United States.

"I do not know that the Yankees desired particularly to arrest me; for several months I saw no newspapers and am not posted," wrote Turner from his hotel digs in Havana to a friend, "but I knew enough of Yankee character, to be convinced, that no one connected with the Prisons, would be safe in their hands. If you see any of my Yankee friends, give to them my kindest regards, and say to them, that I would have allowed myself to have been taken, or arrested, but for several reasons, the principal one being, that I would have seen them d-d first."[638]

Turner became a dentist, with a home practice at the 200-300 block of Main Street in Memphis, Tennessee, beginning in 1872.[639] In an era of pedal-driven dental drills, the new job fit the sadistic former-commandant well. He never married, and Dr. Turner died on the day after Christmas in 1900 in Clarksville, Tennessee.

Richard Randolph Turner (1838-1901)

**Richard Randolph
Turner**
Later in Life
Photographer unknown

Libby's hot-tempered, belligerent warden was captured at the end of the war and, ironically, held as a prisoner for a time in Libby Prison, his old stomping grounds. He escaped Libby by sneaking out, then was recaptured and held in the Virginia State Penitentiary before finally being paroled in June 1866, when it was determined they couldn't find enough evidence to try him.[640]

After the war he became a lumber dealer and lived in Smithfield, Virginia, about seventy miles southeast of Richmond, until his death in December 1901.

His son published several articles about his father in 1929, attempting to improve upon his father's tarnished reputation. There is some question as to whether Turner was actually in the Confederate army; his son's account of his father's life claims that he was a captain under General Winder though no records for his military service can be found.

Erastus Willey Ross (1840-1870)

"Little Ross" was an enigma. He was universally despised by the Union prisoners at Libby but was later discovered to possibly have been a deeply placed spy in the Unionist spy network under Elizabeth Van Lew.

His uncle Franklin Stearns was a Richmond distiller and staunch Unionist, also known to be affiliated with Van Lew.

As Richmond fell on April 2, 1865, Lieutenant David B. Parker of the 72nd New York was tasked by General Grant with going to Van Lew's house on Gay Street to make sure she had protection. When he arrived at her home a few blocks from Libby Prison, she greeted him and welcomed him in. There were several people with her in the house, and one of them was Little Ross, right next to whom the lieutenant sat in conversation.

"You must think it a little strange to meet me here, but I don't dare be anywhere else. If I went on the streets of Richmond, perhaps some officer who had been a prisoner in Libby Prison might recognize me and put a stop to my career," said Ross.

"Would you be so unpopular as that with them?" asked the lieutenant.

"Oh, yes," said Ross, "I have cussed them up and down in the prison."

"Don't you believe all he says," interjected Ms. Van Lew. "I have had him in Libby Prison for years doing my bidding. These other gentlemen have been in affiliation with me, and you probably know that I have been in communication with General Grant all the time."[641]

For years after the war, former POWs would argue that there was no way Ross was a Unionist spy.

"Ross was insultingly, malignantly bitter towards prisoners at all times and under all circumstances, gnat-brained, pompous, and the ready tool of his brutal superiors. It will be within the limits of the truth to assert that three-fourths of all the officers who came into contact with Ross, while prisoners, utterly despised him," wrote one former prisoner in *The National Tribune*.[642]

The true answer will never be known, but lots of anecdotal evidence point to him acting to help POWs escape. The answer went to the grave with Little Ross, who died tragically trapped in his room on Christmas Day 1870 in a massive fire that destroyed the Spotswood Hotel in Richmond, where he was staying as a guest.[643]

Libby Prison Building (1845-1899)

Libby Prison itself had an interesting life after the end of the Civil War. After the Confederates used the building to house Union prisoners during the war, the Federal government for a short time used the building to house Confederate prisoners after the war.

In 1889 Charles Günther, a wealthy German-born candy manufacturer living in Chicago, bought Richmond's infamous Libby Prison.

During the war Günther had served as a purchasing agent and purser on a Confederate Navy on the steamer *Rose Douglas*. His ship was scuttled and burned on the Arkansas River in December 1862, and Günther became a POW himself. He was later exchanged and made his way to the north. After the war he became an obsessed collector of Civil War memorabilia, which included Libby Prison itself that in the 1880s still sat on the James River in Richmond. That didn't hold back Günther. He had the entire building disassembled brick by brick, all 600,000 of them, loaded onto rail cars, and shipped to Chicago. Aside from a train derailment along the way, which almost scattered Libby's bones across the Ohio countryside, the massive pile of bricks arrived in the Windy City and were reassembled in Chicago's Wabash Avenue between 14th and 16th Street.

Günther also built a rather odd medieval castle-like wall around Libby Prison and filled the building with his war memorabilia and a cache of kitschy unrelated nineteenth-century items that gave the entire museum a carnival-like vibe. Through this collection Günther became known as the "P.T. Barnum of Chicago." After the museum opened its doors on September 21, 1889, more than 250,000 visitors flocked to the place in the first year. Admission was 50 cents, with children half price.

Several former Libby POWs were involved in the operation of the museum, and one of them who knew Mark Bassett asked him to lend a copy of his prized photograph of the twelve ragged men to be displayed there.[644]

The museum enjoyed a ten-year run, and then interest waned. Libby was dismantled again for the last time in 1899, with a large portion of the bricks acquired by the Chicago Historical Society. Most of the structural timbers were sold to a Hamlet, Indiana, farmer who transported the wood eighty miles to his farm and built a large barn. The initials of

**Libby's third floor can be seen sticking out
to the right of the medieval turret gate**
Libby War Museum Postcard circa 1890s, Author's collection

Libby prisoners carved in the beams as well as stenciled words were visible in the completed structure. Over the years sightseers would visit the farm and carve out pieces of wood as keepsakes. The family finally had the barn taken down in 1963 and hidden away. In 2010 what timbers remained were sold in auction to a private individual, then purchased again by Pamplin Historical Park and The National Museum of the Civil War Soldier in Petersburg, Virginia. The last of Libby made the trek on a flatbed truck back to Virginia, where some are on display in the museum today.

The Men in "The Photograph"

Henry Mead Fowler (1846-1878) – After a short furlough, at the end of January 1865 Henry M. Fowler returned to the 15th New Jersey and was promoted to Captain. When the war ended and the 15th New Jersey was mustered out of service, Fowler enlisted in the United States Army and was stationed in Fort Leavenworth, Kansas[645]— the first of four of the officers in "The Photograph" that would find themselves living in the Kansas town.

He left the Army around 1874, then married Michigan native Sarah J. Payne. The couple relocated to New Orleans, Louisiana, where their son, Joshua, was born in September 1875.

That same year Henry took the job as superintendent of Chalmette National Cemetery, which was about six miles from the heart of New Orleans. The cemetery was located at the site of the Battle of New Orleans in the War of 1812, right on the Mississippi River. When Henry became superintendent, most of the interments at the cemetery were Civil War soldiers from both sides of the conflict.

Three years after the end of the Civil War, May 30 was established as "Decoration Day" by the Grand Army of the Republic (GAR), the veterans' group made up of Union soldiers. On that day the graves of their fallen comrades were decorated with flowers.

This day became the precursor to Memorial Day. In the south the southern veterans' groups had a similar day of remembrance, though each state had a different day to honor the fallen Confederate soldiers.

In the spring of 1877, a little more than 12 years after he had been a POW in a southern prison, Superintendent Fowler reached out to his Southern neighbors and suggested that at Chalmette National Cemetery they honor the fallen from both sides together on May 30, to which *The New Orleans Daily Democrat* heartily agreed with his thinking as "an invitation to join hands over the bloody chasm."[646] It was a gesture to promote healing proposed by a man who had himself been held as a POW by the people who were now his neighbors.

Each summer New Orleans suffered through its annual yellow fever season, which occurred between the months of July and October. At Chalmette the Fowler family lived in the superintendent's house, a one-story, three-room brick building located on the cemetery grounds. In 1874 the prior superintendent had complained the house "was damp and unfit for habitation."[647] A damp house with its view of the Mississippi River and nearby swamps was the perfect breeding ground for the mosquitoes that bore yellow fever. Its symptoms and the progression of the disease through the bodies of its victims were horrible.

Ultimately, the Fowlers both contracted the illness. On Friday, September 13, 1878, at age thirty-two, Henry succumbed to the disease. His wife, Sarah, would die just over three weeks later on October 8, 1878. The orphaned sole survivor, their three-year-old son, Joshua, whom Henry and Sarah had nicknamed Jack, was quickly sent by train, chaperoned by a family friend back to New Jersey, where he was raised by his grandmother, Sarah Fowler.

Both Fowlers were buried at Chalmette. The GAR erected a stone with the inscription: "A Gallant Soldier who fell at the Post of duty during the Epidemic of 1878 while Superintendent of Chalmette Cemetery."

John McAdams (1835-1913) – After returning to his family in January 1865, it would take McAdams most of the year to gain back his health. Shortly after returning home, he received a letter from General Sherman congratulating him on his successful escape.[648] The McAdams family lived in the house next to his father-in-law in a section of Wheeling with other Irish immigrants. His Irish cousins, who had immigrated to the United States in the 1850s and had established a successful painting business in Wheeling, lived nearby. His cousins included William, with whom John had enlisted in the 1st West Virginia Cavalry at the start of the war. Cousin Will had also safely returned to Wheeling, serving until the end of the war.

In November 1865 a daughter, Jessie Belle, was born. Soon opportunities in the east saw McAdams pulling up roots and moving from Wheeling to the outskirts of Philadelphia, where he found work as a traveling salesman. Another daughter, Nellie, was born there in 1870, and the family moved across the Delaware River to Camden, New Jersey, which they would call home for the next twenty years, with John oftentimes away traveling throughout the Northeast.

In the early 1890s his wife, Kate, died. With all three of his children grown and married, John moved west to Colorado where he remarried. He would work as a hotel keeper in Littleton, Colorado, just south of Denver. Then he and his wife, Rose, moved to a home on West Colfax Avenue in downtown Denver around 1909. McAdams was a GAR member there and would write in *The National Tribune* in 1910 that he would like to hear from some of his old comrades, listing his Denver address and hoping they would write.[649] But he never reconnected with any of the men he was photographed with in 1865 though, unbeknown to him, he often crossed their paths.

In July 1911 in declining health and mourning the death of his second wife, seventy-five-year-old McAdams was admitted to the hospital at the Western Branch of the National Home for Disabled Soldiers in Leavenworth, Kansas. The large 650-acre campus had been constructed primarily for Civil War veterans. John would spend six months there, recovering from a series of maladies, the most serious of which was a heart condition.

In January 1912 he was released from the hospital in Leavenworth, Kansas, and moved to Wichita where he went into the restaurant business. McAdams & Craig was the name of the lunchroom-style diner he ran with his partner, John R. Craig. Both men lived at Wichita's Baltimore Hotel, which was located on the same block as their restaurant. Though the restaurant was well received, the partners put it up for sale in June 1913.

On December 20, 1913, McAdams was found unconscious on the floor of his room in the Baltimore Hotel by an employee who awakened him every morning. He never regained consciousness and died that afternoon, the result of a stroke.[650]

Lemuel Davis Dobbs (1842-1918) – Captain Dobbs remained in service in Brownsville, Texas, until January 1867. He moved his wife, Catherine, from Baltimore to Texas, and they started a family that eventually totaled three boys and two girls. After he mustered out of the army, he farmed in Eagle Pass, Texas, a small community located on the Rio Grande River more than 300 miles northwest of Brownsville. It would have been an extremely isolated, tough life. For a man who was subject to bouts of heatstroke and an inability to tolerate heat, the choice of a homestead in southern Texas was surprising. In the early 1870s he moved his family to Kansas, taking part in the country's western expansion, where his father and several of his siblings had established homesteads.

Having been a teacher before the war, he took a job as the Kansas representative of the Philadelphia-based Thomas, Cowperthwait & Co, selling schoolbooks, desks, and other supplies to the small, one-room schoolhouses that were springing up in the prairie communities that grew out of the wave of new homesteaders. Dobbs traveled throughout the state over the next ten years, maintaining a farmstead in Gale, Kansas, for his family and elderly father. He was prosperous enough to afford a servant, and during the 1870s became very involved in the GAR veterans' group.

After the death of his father in October 1881, Dobbs changed. Having become familiar with all of Kansas in his travels, he also visited most of the GAR groups that had sprung up. The one-time teacher-farmer-salesman decided to become an actor; he also started writing and producing plays throughout the Midwest. It was no surprise that most all of Dobb's plays had Civil War–themed plots as they appealed greatly to the GAR audience. His plays became a sensation in a time when prairie communities were starving for entertainment.

The plays were performed in local GAR halls, with Dobbs himself acting in them. In addition, he was the plays' producer and would wrangle up locals to act in the other roles, then book the performances in the local venues centered around where the citizen-actors lived. One of his first plays was titled "The Spy of Atlanta," in which Dobbs himself played the villain. The entire state of Kansas seemed to rave about this play.

Advertisement for "The Tennessee Scout"
A play written by Lemuel D. Dobbs
March 11, 1886; The Weekly Argus; Clay Center, Kansas

"The Spy of Atlanta was played four nights in this city last week to full house... Capt. L.D. Dobbs is powerful in this play. He possesses the fire and force necessary for a great actor."
Cline's Press, Clyde, Kansas

"Capt. L.D. Dobbs, as Edward St. Clair, showed himself to be a cold-blooded, heartless villain–a thorough master of his difficult part."
Hiawatha Herald, Hiawatha, Kansas

"The popular and thrilling war drama The Spy of Atlanta *was played on Tuesday night in one of the largest audiences ever assembled in Turner Hall...The play has been under the management of Capt. L. D. Dobbs...his fine acting on the stage and his excellent management has won him a host of warm friends who will always welcome him back to Maryville."*
Marshall County News

"Thursday night closed The Spy of Atlanta. *It was a dramatic success, for it was well put on stage and the drilling of the amateurs by L. D. Dobbs, the manager, shows how thoroughly he was up in the business."*

Kansas City Times

In 1883 Dobbs premiered another play titled "The Tennessee Scout." Dobbs made Kit Ledford the lead character in the play and starred himself as a Rebel protagonist.

"We have carefully read the play and we can assure the readers it will be one of the greatest dramatic treats ever given to the people of Iola. Kit Ledford, the Scout, is a veritable East Tennessee Union man who on five different occasions piloted escaped prisoners and refugees into the Union lines, the last party being Captain L.D. Dobbs, the author of this play. who escaped from the rebel prison in Columbia, S.C., and who in gratitude has named this play in honor of his benefactor," raved the Iola Register.[651]
March 11, 1886
The Weekly Argus
Clay Center, Kansas

It was a case of art imitating reality except the real Kit Ledford was a veritable Union man from North Carolina. In making Kit a resident of Tennessee, Dobbs was clearly taking artistic license as "The Tennessee Scout" was shorter and would fit better in the advertisements.

Dobbs became a tireless self-promoter and acted as his own business agent. Over time his demeanor raised questions about his character and financial stability. "You know where to find him," commented one Kansas newspaper to the local police after one week's performance.

The bohemian lifestyle of an actor, writer, and producer suited Dobbs' personality. With it came the obvious accolades he cherished as he became well-known in the Midwest prairie towns. But it also contributed to personal difficulties, and traveling all the time took its toll on his marriage. In December 1885 Catherine filed for divorce on the grounds of abandonment in the district court of Marion County, Kansas, which was granted in March 1886.

On June 2, 1887, after another performance of "The Spy of Atlanta," Dobbs married a fellow actor, Rhoda F. Crouch, on stage in front of the theatre's remaining audience in Holton, Kansas. The event made for headline news across Kansas. The couple would have three children over the next ten years.

Finally, around 1895 after touring multiple plays throughout the Midwest for almost fifteen years, Lem and Rhoda settled in Garnett, Kansas, where he started a nursery business. Dobbs' nursery was located in a prominent spot in town with a flagpole flying a large American flag; Lem, now an expert in advertising himself, would advertise weekly in the newspaper to "Come to the Flagpole." The local newspaper would also publish his regular horticulture column. Dobbs' nursery was one of the first businesses in Garnett with a telephone; his phone number was 58.

The stability of Dobbs' mental condition was brought into question at the beginning of the twentieth century. His wife, Rhoda, brought him up on charges of insanity, a result of his old war wound in 1901, but the charges were dismissed. It was apparent from the testimony that Dobbs was a difficult man to live with and could be abusive and aggressive.

He was tried again on the same charge in May 1903, and this time was found to be "spasmodically unbalanced" and sent to the Osawatomie Kansas State Hospital for treatment. "He suffers from an injury to his head received in the civil war which, probably is the cause of his present problem," reported his hometown newspaper the *Kansas Agitator*.[652]

After treatment in the hospital for three months, Dobbs returned home in August 1903. But his behavior continued to be erratic, and Rhoda finally left him. In April 1905 she filed for divorce, charging Lem with extreme cruelty, adultery, and that he was wholly unfit to be charged with the care and custody of minor children. His own son, seventeen-year-old Logan L. Dobbs, testified that his father whipped him with a wire and riding whip whenever he got a temper.[653]

Before the final divorce proceedings were to take place, on June 11, 1905, Rhoda suddenly died at the home of a friend in Garnett. It was a shocking development, and a battle with Rhoda's family soon took place over the custody of Lem's ten-year-old daughter, Ura Maude Dobbs. Lem won, and Ura Maude returned home to live with her dad. During these years all the Dobbs' family struggles continued to play out in the local paper for all to see. It wasn't pretty.

In 1908 Dobbs moved himself permanently to the Western Branch of the National

Home for Disabled Soldiers in Leavenworth, Kansas. With the requirement that all occupants had to wear a military uniform, Dobbs must have felt right at home. He was surrounded by hundreds of fellow elderly veterans, which would have included John McAdams when he was in the hospital there for six months in 1911. He moved his then thirteen-year-old daughter to Leavenworth as well, where he got her a room in town as a boarder at the home of the family of the clerk-of-the-court.[654] Soon after Dobbs' arrival, he was elected as commandant of the Leavenworth GAR post. He also took on the role of patriotic instructor and was a member of the National Association of Union Ex-Prisoners of War. He created a leaflet that he would pass out flaunting his military record and providing the local newspaper with a Dobbs-generated press release, which included a regal picture of the former Captain wearing his GAR hat.

Lemuel D. Dobbs
GAR Photograph
Later in Life
*Photographer
unknown*

The local town newspaper in Garnett, Kansas, where he had made his home for thirteen years, had enough of the grandstanding Captain Dobbs, sarcastically commenting on his relocation to Leavenworth, "Several old soldiers in Garnett are in receipt of a copy of the Leavenworth Times,[655] from Capt. L. D. Dobbs...a half column extolling the virtues and character of the worthy gentleman (?) who hounded his wife with malicious stories of her character and actions...it makes us mad every time we read one of these self contributed articles of his that are wont to appear from time to time in papers at various points he makes his stopping places, who don't know the least part of his history except he wore blue. The fact that a man bore arms for his country covers a multitude of sins, but not his sins."[656]

On Saturday, May 19, 1918, even though he had been ill for a month, eighty-two-year-old Lem Dobbs made the 140-mile trip to Chanute, Kansas, arriving for the annual state GAR encampment. "I have never missed one of the state encampments since the first one was held," said Dobbs to a few of his fellow comrades on arriving, "and I want to go to the thirty-seventh because the sands of my life are running out."[657] The trip exhausted him, and the next afternoon Dobbs was stricken ill in his room at the Oriental Hotel and died of heart failure. The hourglass was empty. He was buried at Leavenworth National Cemetery with a military headstone.

The term post-traumatic stress disorder (PTSD) wasn't coined until the twentieth century. Like most wars, the majority of veterans went on to normal lives, though there is no doubt the experience of war changed all of them in some way. The statistics for divorce in the nineteenth century showed that Civil War veterans showed a fifty percent rise from pre-Civil war divorce. The US divorce rate in 1860 was 1.2 per 1,000; in 1866 it was 1.8 per 1,000.[658] For the small group of nine Union officers in "The Photograph," three would be divorced. After the war both John Page and Lemuel Dobbs suffered psychological stresses, emerging as different men and changing the course of their lives that followed.

The 5th Iowa Boys – Major Marshall, Captain Page, and Lieutenant Hoffman had escaped together, posed together in "The Photograph" on January 2, 1865, and then went their separate ways. Two prospered, and one suffered from the scars of the war for the rest of his life.

William Stanhope Marshall (1832-1891) – After he arrived in Davenport, Iowa, on January 11, 1865, Major Marshall was the first of all the officers to officially be discharged from the 5th Iowa. He quickly set his sights on a return to his law practice. He also reconnected with an old flame he had known before the war when he lived in Independence, Iowa, which was the county seat where the courthouse was located and which attorney Marshall knew well. Louise C. Bryant was the twenty-three-year-old daughter, and only surviving child, of Dr. Horatio and Lutheria Bryant. The family moved to Iowa in 1856 with roots going back many generations to Plymouth, Massachusetts. William and Louise began courting over the next couple of years while Marshall traveled throughout the Midwest on law business.

By 1867 Marshall had established Stanley, Wheeler & Marshall, a law practice located in the First National Bank building in Chattanooga, Tennessee[659]—an interesting choice in that the city was the location in which he had been captured in 1863. He soon

returned to Iowa and married Louise on July 8, 1868. The local newspaper reported the couple had left on a month-long "wedding tour" to St. Paul, Minnesota. On August 11, after the Midwestern honeymoon, they left for Chattanooga, where they had planned to make their home.[660] But things didn't go well for the new couple, and Louise became ill soon after arriving in Chattanooga. She returned to her father's home and died on October 27, 1868. Marshall was devastated; the couple had been married less than four months. He buried his wife in Oakwood Cemetery in Independence.

Grieving from loss, for eighteen months Marshall relocated to Lincoln, Nebraska, to practice law, primarily dealing with land sales. He returned to Chattanooga once and for all in August 1872 and reestablished his law practice with Xenophon Wheeler, one of his earlier Chattanooga partners. Wheeler, who went by "Xeno," had been a Captain in the 67th and 129th Ohio Infantry during the war.

William Stanhope Marshall
c1885
Chattanooga Times Collection,
1870-1991. Acc. 295.
Chattanooga Public Library
Photograph by Marceau Bellsmith Cincinnati, Ohio

As Marshall became more ingrained in the movers and shakers in Chattanooga, he was introduced to the Montagues, an Ohio family of lawyers and bankers who had also relocated to the southern town.

On November 6, 1873, Marshall married thirty-one-year-old Katherine Sophia Montague at the family home in Meigs, Ohio. The couple would build a stately mansion on Oak Street in the heart of Chattanooga, just four miles from where the Major had been captured at Tunnel Hill. Ironically, Marshall would eventually own some of the land on which he was captured. A son, Stanhope Stewart Marshall, was born in 1877.

As Marshall's law career flourished, he acquired real estate and was involved in business ventures that helped modernized the city, which included early electrification and bringing a streetcar system that connected Chattanooga to Lookout Mountain. "He has been prominently identified with growth and progress of Chattanooga for twenty years," noted the *Chattanooga Republican* in 1891.[661]

Marshall stayed in touch with other veterans of the 5th Iowa. On Friday, July 28, 1882, he visited Lieutenant Michael Hoffman at his home in Elk Point, South Dakota, where the two men spent the weekend reminiscing about the past. "After their escape from prison they were 35 days wandering through the mountains and woods before they reached Union lines for safety. They had not seen each other since the war, and the visit was a very pleasant and enjoyable one for both of them," reported the *Elk Point Courier*.[662]

The Major was active in the GAR, was the first post commander of "GAR Lookout Post No. 2," and would attend most of the major encampments held throughout the country. With the experiences of his escape as a POW and the help of the people loyal to the Union that lived in the mountains of Western North Carolina and Eastern Tennessee, Marshall championed their cause. Speaking at the 1884 GAR encampment in Minneapolis, he tried to persuade the national organization to allow membership of veterans who had been conscripted against their will in the Confederate army and later deserted to serve in the Union army.

"In Tennessee alone we have over 30,000 soldiers of the Union Army. Those soldiers left their families, their homes, their property, and everything that they had in the world," said Marshall, "and dodging rebel conscript officers, slipped through their picket lines on their way for hundreds of miles through the mountains to the Union Army, joined with it and staid [sic] with it, a great many of them to the end."[663]

He was also speaking personally for the benefit of the scouts from Western North Carolina who helped his own escape into Eastern Tennessee—namely, to Flem Cison, TR Zachary, Kit Ledford, and several others.

"They are mostly poor men. Loyalty was not a general product of the cotton belt. They are the men who drank the pure water and breathed the pure air of the mountain regions. They were poor then and they are poor yet and they always will be poor," said Marshall. "They cared nothing for riches, but they did take pride in their loyalty and they stood firm and true as the rocks around their mountain home; now after it is all over they have a very vivid recollection of those times."

The GAR turned down the proposal.

In September 1889 the Major and his wife held a reunion for the 5th Iowa at their home in Chattanooga. The *Chattanooga Daily Times* reported that in attendance were Marsh Byers, a valuable contributor to the *North American Review, Harper's Weekly*, and *Overland Monthly* as well as having a history in the 5th Iowa, along with Lieutenant M. Hoffman who had escaped during the war with the Major from the Columbia, South Carolina, prison and thirteen others who came from as far away as Pasadena, California, for the event.

Marshall was in discussions in the deposition room at the courthouse in Chattanooga on March 27, 1890, when one of his arms suddenly went limp, and he was unable to move it. Helped into a chair, a doctor was summoned. He had suffered a stroke. He would never fully recover. Less than a year later, on January 27, 1891, the fifty-eight-year-old major suffered a second stroke while at the home of his brother-in-law and died. He was buried in Chattanooga National Cemetery.

In all his work as a skilled, intellectual attorney, Marshall never took the time to put pen to paper and write about his experiences as a POW in the war.

"The experiences of our dear friend during his long prison life, were most interesting, and the history of his escapes forms one of the most thrilling episodes of the Great Rebellion. It was seldom, however, that he could be induced to talk about this period of his life, and few, save his intimate friends, knew anything about this remarkable chapter of his life-history," recorded the Chattanooga Bar as a tribute.

"The story of Maj. Marshall's escape and travels by night from Columbia to East Tennessee was a most thrilling one, but his innate modesty prevented him from often telling," commented a Chattanooga newspaper after his death.[664]

John Elijah Page (1832-1914) – Captain Page was officially mustered out of service in April 1865 though he had already been discharged from the 5th Iowa in February. He and his wife, Nancy, grieved through the spring over the death of their son, Peter, from diphtheria. Page attempted to return to the normal life he had before the war but was a damaged man. In 1866 he became the postmaster at Marshalltown, Iowa, and worked for a while as a clerk in the courthouse. In quick succession, he and Nancy had two more children, Euretta and Frank. By 1870 John had yet another job, working as a clerk in a retail store in town.

His wife, Nancy, was keenly aware of the difference in her husband. He had a brooding disposition, was frequently nervous, and often complained of vertigo and headaches in the left side of his forehead, where the gunshot wound had left its mark at Iuka, Mississippi, in 1862. He had a prominent diagonal red scar that ran several inches across his forehead toward his temple between his left eye and hairline. The scar would turn deeper red when he had his spells.[665]

In spring 1872 the Page family moved to Chicago in search of better work opportunities. He quickly returned to his original trade as a harness maker. Another daughter, Nellie, was born in 1874. On a steamy July 6, 1875, Page returned home after work, had his supper as usual, and settled in the family parlor as his wife, Nancy, attended to some sewing.

"He got up from the table and went in the sitting room, he spoke of the evening being very hot," said Nancy Page. "He took of his collar and tie and hung them up and then drew off his boots and put on his slippers...in a little while after that I saw him going out and thought he would be in soon."

John Page never came home.

His wife, Nancy, looked everywhere and thought he was dead, eventually filing for his soldier's pension benefits. At the time John disappeared, the couple's four children ranged in age from one to eighteen.

"I firmly believed him dead," said Nancy. "I believe he died from the effect of the wound in his head."

The pension benefits were denied because Page was not dead. He had abandoned Nancy and his four children, never providing an explanation for his actions.

On April 4, 1877, after no further contact with his first wife, he would officially be granted a divorce in an Indiana court 122 miles southeast of Chicago. Nancy was awarded $21.25 by the legal system.

On June 7, 1877, Page married Mary Ann Kelsey, a widow with two children, in Warsaw, Indiana, a small farming community where he had relocated. John and Mary Ann Page had three more children between 1879 and 1886, two of whom survived into adulthood. Page successfully plied his harness-making trade to the region's farmers for the next fifteen years.

Page's first wife, Nancy, continued to file for widow's pension benefits throughout the 1880s, claiming he was "suffering under the effects of insanity" and "of his unsound condition of the mind."[666] Each time she was turned down. It seemed she was never fully aware in the pension filings that John was still alive and had actually divorced her and remarried. John himself would successfully file for his own pension benefits in the late 1880s.

John and his second wife, Mary Ann, moved to Pueblo, Colorado, in the early 1890s. They would live in Colorado for the rest of their lives, with Page continuing to suffer the effects of his wartime injuries. He was able to find small jobs and at the end of his life was a railroad night watchman. He died on March 15, 1914, at age eighty-two. The cause of his death was recorded as senility.[667]

Michael Hoffman (1839-1918) – After Hoffman returned to Marshalltown, Iowa, he resumed the life he had prior to the conflict, living at his parents' home. Soon he joined his older brother Joseph's lumber business and moved to Rockton, Illinois, in 1868. The job required him to travel throughout the Midwest, and along the way he met twenty-year-old Mary Ellen Perry, whom he called Ella, in Tipton, Iowa. Tipton was halfway between Rockton and Marshalltown, and Ella's father was a retail merchant who owned a grocery, flour, and feed store, in addition to a mill. Mike surely took note that one of the big crops processed through the Perry family's mill, that they advertised and sold in their store, was the dreaded sorghum syrup. He managed to see Ella every time he passed through her town. In March 1869 the couple was married in Tipton, and Mike took his new bride back to Illinois.

Two years later they moved to Manistee, Michigan, a town halfway up the east side of Lake Michigan where his brother Joseph had built a new lumber mill as he continued to travel and sell lumber through the Midwest. [668] Over these years Hoffman met many retail merchants in his travels. Some were veterans like himself, making a good living running their own businesses in the small towns that were springing up. Every growing new town needed a place to buy the things required for day-to-day life on the growing American frontier.

Counting his time in the war, Mike had been traveling one way or the other for over ten years. He began to ruminate on the idea of owning his own store in a growing small town. He and Ella could settle down in one place, and he could stop leading the life of a traveling salesman.

In 1872 Mike found just the spot. The Hoffmans, taking advantage of opportunities presented by the migration of Americans westward, moved to Dakota Territory. They settled in the town of Elk Point, which was located twenty miles northwest of the confluence of the Missouri and the Sioux River at Sioux City. Soon after his arrival in Elk Point, he established Hoffman & Co., a dry goods store selling all kinds of merchandise from cast iron stoves, hardware, and agricultural implements to groceries and clothing. Over time his operations would eventually take up a whole block on Main Street in the rapidly growing town.

Michael Hoffman
Union County
Historical Society
Photographer unknown

Just over a year after their arrival at the start of 1874, tragedy struck when Ella suddenly died. Mike had her buried in the Elk Point cemetery. He grieved and focused on growing his business. Later that year he met an attractive schoolteacher.

Olivia, who was born in Cairo, New York, was the eldest child of Benjamin and

Phoebe Hayes. Her father, who was a surveyor, relocated the family to Wisconsin just before the Civil War where he also established a small farm. Thirty-year-old Olivia had come to Dakota Territory to teach school in 1874. In October 1875 Mike and Olivia were married; the couple would have four children together. Mike continued to suffer from maladies related to the poor conditions he endured as a POW. By the time he married Olivia, he was almost completely deaf and had developed severe arthritis in his knees.

Several other family members followed him to Elk Point, and Hoffman became a prominent citizen with a highly successful business and was involved in city government. Hoffman and his brother, Samuel, became active members of the Stephen A. Hurburt GAR Post in Elk Point, which had to be chartered by the Department of Iowa since South Dakota was not yet a state when it was first formed in May 1882.[669]

In 1883 people at *The Union Courier*, the local Elk Point newspaper, approached Hoffman to write about his Civil War experience. Mike wrote almost 5,000 words, detailing his time at Libby Prison, which the paper serialized into three separate articles. He closed his account by writing "In prisons of Macon, Ga., Charleston S.C. and Columbia S.C., we spend seven months more of prison life and it seems as though we would be there yet had we not with two others made our escape which also occupied thirty-five days or rather nights, travel. Of these we may say something some other stormy winter."[670]

It would take thirteen years for him to finish his account, writing about his escape from Camp Sorghum with Major Marshall and Captain Page, which was published in four separate articles in *The Union Courier* in 1896. To assure the readers that his account was accurate more than thirty years later, Hoffman wrote that "the reader may rest assured that it will be correct for we copy largely from a diary we carried all through the prison–and war, in fact." A copy of the diary in Hoffman's own handwriting is cherished by his descendants to this day. Hoffman copied the original into a larger-sized bound book later in his life. A typewritten transcript of the diary was given to the Union County Historical Society.

As the nineteenth century approached its last decade, he kept in touch with other members of the 5th Iowa including Major Marshall and Marsh Byers. In the 1890s, with his retail operations running smoothly with the help of family members, he and his wife took some time to travel, going back east for the reunion of the 5th Iowa at Major Marshall's Chattanooga home and heading to California to sightsee.

Hoffman retired in 1904, selling his retail business to his nephew. He and Olivia continued to live in their stately home on Main Street. Mike became more forgetful, and his life's memories began to fade and elude him. He kept a tattered scrapbook full of newspaper clippings he had carefully collected since the 1870s to try and help. He died of the results of senility on September 13, 1918, four days after his older brother Samuel, and was buried in Elk Point. His marker has the notation: Lieut. Co. D. 5th IA, 1861-1865; Prisoner 11 Mos - Escaped.

Alfred Shelby Stewart (1837-1920) – In January 1865 Allie Stewart returned on a thirty-day furlough to the place that had been his parents' old home, located on the road about a mile outside of Danville, Kentucky. His older brother, Robert, and his family now occupied the Stewart farmstead and welcomed him home. Like the other POWs, Stewart suffered from the effects of poor food, horrible hygiene, and exposure to winter elements. But unlike his neighbor and comrade Tom Young, his health rebounded rather quickly, and a little over a month later in March he caught a train south and rejoined his regiment.

The 4th Kentucky was a part of General James H. Wilson's cavalry corps, chasing Confederate General Hood's forces through Alabama and into Georgia as the war was winding down, with the entire regiment ending up in Macon on April 20, 1865. The corps were then pressed into the hunt for a fleeing Jefferson Davis in the center part of the state, with the 4th Michigan, another regiment in their corps, finally capturing Davis and his wife near Irwinville, Georgia, on May 10.

In this same cavalry corps as Stewart's 4th Kentucky was the 5th Iowa Cavalry, which included Michael Hoffman's brother, Samuel. In an odd coincidence Samuel Hoffman was detailed and in charge of twenty men that guarded the train car in which Davis and his family were held after their capture.[671] During his time back with the regiment, Allie received promotions to 1st Lieutenant and then to Captain. Finally, the 4th Kentucky returned to Macon and was discharged on August 20, 1865,[672] and Stewart's army career came to an end.

Allie got home for the second time in late August. He had money in his pocket and returned to work for his old boss William Lucas, a merchant in Danville. On November 25, 1865, his old boss became his new father-in-law when Allie married Lucas's daughter, Anna Jane Lucas, whom everyone called Nannie. The Lucas family had practically adopted Stewart after both his parents had died; Nannie and Allie had flirted with each other for as long as Nannie's other siblings could remember.

Allie spent the next few years studying to be a pharmacist. In 1866 his wife, Nannie's, sister married James Linney, another officer who had served along with Allie in the 4th Kentucky, and soon the couple headed west, settling in St. Clair County, Missouri, about 100 miles southeast of Kansas City.

In the summer of 1871 most all the other Lucas siblings, along with Allie and Nannie Stewart, had moved west to Missouri as well. Two of Nannie's brothers, William and John, were lawyers in Kansas City while the Linneys and two other brothers, Charles and James, settled in Oscoela, Missouri, along with Allie and Nannie Stewart. James Linney opened a grocery store while Charles Lucas ran the Osceola newspaper, and James Lucas owned the Johnson-Lucas Banking Company.

In July 1871, a month after arriving, Allie purchased a drug store in Osceola. He would run it until the early 1900s and sell a wide variety of items needed by the citizens of a bustling frontier town, including pure old Kentucky whiskey imported from back home—for medical use.

In the 1880s Stewart would run and be elected twice to the Office of the Collector in St. Clair County. In 1884 he and Nannie would visit Mark Bassett in Peoria, Illinois, on a trip back east, reconnecting with a fellow soldier who

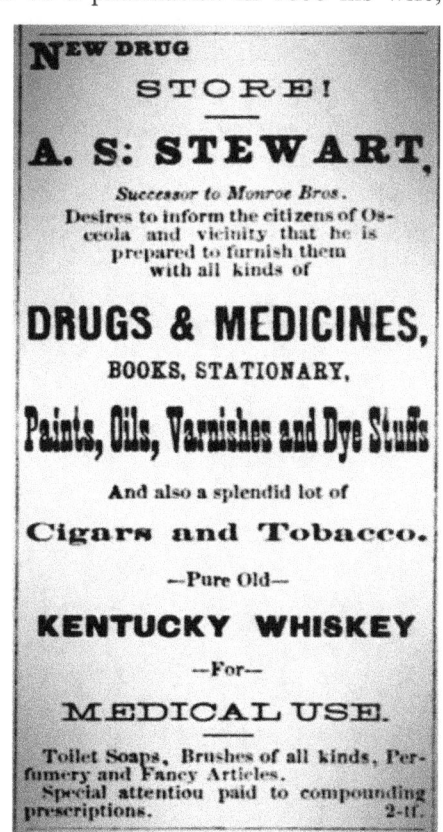

Allie S. Stewart
Drug Store Advertisement
7/20/1871 Osceola Herald

shared the same escape story from Camp Sorghum twenty years earlier as well as a photograph captured when they were finally free.

Throughout the years Allie and Nannie remained childless, though they were surrounded by plenty of nieces and nephews who took to calling them Uncle Al and Aunt Nannie. In 1909 Mark and Annie Bassett visited the Stewarts at their home in Osceola. Bassett would ask Allie if he would be willing to sign as a witness, and have notarized, an account that he had written of their Civil War adventures. Allie was happy to oblige and signed the account in 1910, having his brother-in-law and next-door neighbor James Lucas, who was also a notary, apply his stamp. In January 1910 Nannie suddenly died. Seventy-four-year-old Stewart continued living next door to James Lucas and his family on 2nd Street in Osceola for a time. Finally, old age caught up with him. As his health began to deteriorate, he developed senility and needed a higher level of care.

On October 27, 1916, Stewart became the fourth man in the 1865 photograph to find himself in Leavenworth, Kansas, entering the Western Branch of the National Home for Disabled Soldiers. The Soldier's home was a small town unto itself, featuring a large comfortable campus with many barracks-like buildings all filled with veterans. It also included a chapel, bandstand, hospital, mess hall, and employee housing.

When Allie arrived, Lemuel Dobbs was also a resident there. For the next eighteen months the two men lived near each other until Lem's death in May 1918. It's not known if the two old comrades ever met, or if they did, whether they passed the time discussing their exploits and adventures escaping through the Western North Carolina and Eastern Tennessee mountains in the company of Mark Bassett and Tom Young with the help of guides Flem Cison and T.R. Zachary. One could only hope they crossed paths, recognized each other, and reminisced.

In the last year of his life, his health deteriorated, and he became an invalid. At around noon on Saturday, June 5, 1920, Allie suffered a heart attack and died.[673] His body was returned to his Osceola, Missouri, home, where he was buried next to his wife, Nannie.

Western Branch of the National Home for Disabled Soldiers
c1900; Leavenworth, Kansas
Photographer unknown

The North Carolina Guides

After returning to North Carolina, both Kit Ledford and Flem Cison made their way back to their respective homes in the North Carolina mountains. Flem made sure that Tom Zachary made it back to Cashiers Valley before making the last hike over the mountain range east of the Zachary farmstead and returning to Transylvania County, North Carolina.

It would take several months for the war to end, but the tensions between neighbors who sided with the north and those who leaned toward the southern cause would take generations to heal. For those who had caused harm to their fellow neighbors throughout the war, they might face retribution; many would simply pack up and move west to start life anew.

Julius Ketron "Kit" Ledford (1842-1905) – Kit Ledford returned to the chaotic environment that permeated the mountains of Eastern Tennessee, western North Carolina, and North Georgia. Even after the war personal conflict continued to impact the Ledford family with a cousin ambushed and brutally murdered near a church known as Harris Chapel in March 1865, just west of Murphy, North Carolina.

In December 1866 Kit married eighteen-year-old Adaliza "Addie" Allen, whose family lived in Habersham County, Georgia, about forty miles south of where Kit's family lived near Hayesville, North Carolina. The couple had four children over the next decade, three of which survived into adulthood. Kit and Addie's relationship was unusual as Addie continued to live on her family's farmstead with their children, while Kit was never recorded in any of the official records as living with his family.[674] With so many cousins in the latter half of the nineteenth century, today there are many Ledford descendants in Eastern Tennessee, western North Carolina, and North Georgia.

Unlike most of the other men who had their picture taken on January 2, 1865, the man with indigenous Cherokee in his blood kept to himself in later years. He surely never knew he was the main character, "the veritable East Tennessee Union Man,"[675] who actually hailed from North Carolina, as featured in the Captain Lemuel Dobbs stage production playing all over Kansas in the 1880s. There is no record of his death and no known place of his burial. Family records record him as dying at about sixty-three years of age sometime around 1905. Somehow Mark Bassett and his wife were aware of his passing, as they became the keepers of the legacy of the twelve men in "The Photograph."[676] In the 1910 United States Census, sixty-six-year-old Addie is listed as a widow living alone with her brother on his farm in Habersham County, Georgia. Kit Ledford had simply faded away into mists of the Appalachian Mountains.

Joseph Fleming "Flem" Cison (1835-1916) – Flem Cison returned to East Fork in Transylvania County and went back to farming as the war came to a close. Things remained "hot" in his part of the mountains as neighbors carried grudges against fellow neighbors for years after the war was over.

"After a lapse of 30 years, in August 1895, I visited the vicinity of the memorable though tough time," said Mark Bassett writing in the *Peoria Herald Transcript* in 1910, just weeks before his death. "I went for pleasure, on comfortable trains to Asheville, N.C. Thense by a branch road to a little

Flem Cison - 1874
Courtesy of the
Cison Family
Photographer unknown

town further up the mountains. From that place I hired a man to drive me over to Flem Cison's." Bassett was reliving parts of his perilous traipse through the North Carolina mountains and firmly shook Flem's hand as Flem stared into the eyes of the excited man when recognition finally set in. "Flem was hale and hearty," said Bassett. "So was his wife, the woman who braved alone the dangers of winter and night and wild beasts of the mountains for him and us so long ago."

Sarah Ann Bagwell, the young fourteen-year-old woman who assisted Flem in hiding Bassett, Young, Stewart, and Dobbs, had become Flem's wife in 1867. Flem Cison's family also claims indigenous Cherokee in their lineage, where the Bagwells came from Europe. Flem and Sarah would have five children, four of whom would survive into adulthood. When Bassett visited the Cisons in 1895, their youngest son, Harrison, was just five years old, while their oldest daughter, Amy, was married and expecting her fourth child at any moment. It was a boy; Flem and Sarah's fourth grandchild was born on September 15. While visiting, Bassett advised Flem of the U.S. government's pension program for veterans of the Civil War, and right after his visit in September 1895, Flem filed for his pension, citing his service in Company F of the 2nd North Carolina Mounted Infantry. The U.S. government turned him down even though Flem claimed that in 1864 he was cut off by the Rebels in Transylvania County, preventing him from returning to his regiment. The government's view was that he had never been properly mustered into the 2nd North Carolina, so he was never officially a Union soldier.[677]

In May 1916 Flem died at age eighty-one of a heart attack. He is buried, along with Sarah, who survived him for more than eighteen years, at the Carson's Creek Baptist Church cemetery, within a couple miles of his small log cabin in East Fork that Mark Bassett visited in 1895.

Chapter Twenty-Three

Mark Bassett and T. R. Zachary

Thompson Roberts "T.R." Zachary (1850-1921) – Fourteen-year-old Tom Zachary was incredibly excited to get home. They had left Knoxville with the Union officers they had helped guide on January 3 and taken the same train back to Sweetwater, Tennessee. Kit Ledford, Flem Cison, and T.R. stepped off the train and said their goodbyes, then started their hike back east down the Unicoi Turnpike, heading home.

After leaving Kit at his family's farmstead outside of Hayesville, NC, Flem and T.R. continued hiking east climbing along the ridge of Chucky Gal Mountain and winding their way down into Cashiers Valley where the Zachary farmstead was located. The entire return trip of 180 miles had taken them a week. Flem shook hands with T.R.'s father, Andy, then continued east alone. It would be another thirty miles of hiking through mountainous terrain to get back to his home at Dunns Rock. T.R. walked into his parents' log cabin in Cashiers Valley bursting at the seams, ready to tell the tale of his great adventure to the whole family. The big news he saved for last. The officers he had become the closest to were Mark Bassett, Allie Stewart, and Tom Young. The three of them had promised T.R. that if they successfully made it to the Union lines, they would send him money so he could pursue an education.

T.R. was a smart young man who had experienced a lot during the war. His family had everything in life they wanted as subsistence farmers except money, which was scarce as gold. The months passed. and the war finally came to an end. T.R. waited, expecting a letter from either Illinois or Kentucky, but the letter never came, and life went on.

With the war's conclusion, his older brothers and uncles who had been away fighting returned to the valley. Each return home was a celebration for the family. But even though the fighting was over, the Zachary family remained deeply divided.

T.R.'s father, Andy, a staunch Unionist, had become estranged from his own father and most of his siblings, all of whom sided with the Confederacy. Andy Zachary's father, Colonel John Zachary, the family patriarch, was eighty-six years old in 1865 and knew he was in the twilight of life. The Colonel made sure his entire family was aware that he forbid any family members who supported the Union to be buried in the family cemetery. He was targeting his son Andy Zachary and his family. The Colonel would live another six years, to the ripe old age of ninety-two, passing in March 1872. He was buried in what then became known as the "Lower" Zachary cemetery, and his edict stood firm. No Yankee lovers at his final resting place. T.R.'s father cordoned off a plot on his own land located four-tenths of a mile up the road, appropriately to the north, and named it "Upper" Zachary cemetery, specifically for Unionist Zachary family members. Even in death, the Zacharys would remain divided for generations.

As the Civil War decade came to an end, the middle of the continent began opening up to homesteaders. Manifest destiny was a concept from before the Civil War; now the opportunity of free land in the west became popular. For many people who still were experiencing conflict with their neighbors and own family over the war, it offered an opportunity to start over and get away from the continuing unpleasantness. In 1868, when T.R. Zachary turned age eighteen, his oldest brother, thirty-three-year-old Christopher

Columbus Zachary who was known as "CC," was married with a small family living in Knoxville. CC had decided to become a homesteader in Kansas, and T.R. asked if he could come along.

Before T.R. left for Kansas, he met eighteen-year-old Julia Beazley, who lived in Greene County, Georgia, between Atlanta and Augusta. T.R. had met Julia when he spent the night at the Beazley farmstead while acting as a traveling salesman for his father, selling Zachary fruit trees throughout Georgia. The couple would correspond with each other, her letters providing most of the only contact he had with the outside world.

T.R. and CC's family headed west to Nashville, then St. Louis, and then through Kansas City, stopping just west of the city in Quindaro, Kansas. There they stayed for a couple of years while learning the lay of the land and waiting for the railroad to build its tracks west, set on establishing homesteads somewhere in the middle of Kansas once they could determine where the most promising land was.

In October 1874 both T.R. and CC had each secured 200-acre homesteads in Rush County, Kansas, about 275 miles west of Kansas City in an area known as Walnut Creek. It was about the same time that Lem Dobbs had settled 120 miles west of the Zachary brothers in Garnett, Kansas. They were all on the great prairie; initially, T.R. stayed with his brother's family, which by then had grown to six children. He helped to build a one-room sod house on the prairie where the nine of them lived. Then he built a sod home on his homestead and soon learned the pros and cons of solitude.

"I am so lonely hear *(sic)* all alone. Nothing to keep me company except the birds and my dog," he would write to Julia, and then describe what a sod house was. "(You) probably you don't know what I mean by sod? Well its prairie turf. The ground is first plowed to a depth of about 8 inches then the turf cut in peaces (sic?) about fifteen or twenty inches long and laid up on the wall like brick or stone."[678]

The Zachary brothers grew corn and wheat on their homesteads. For several years T.R. and Julia conducted a cross-country letter-writing courtship. He would describe the house he was building for her on the prairie and the quality of the land. She would respond, sending him her photograph for him to ponder from the solitude of his little

T.R. Zachary
Likely around the time of
his marriage in 1879
*Courtesy of the
Jane Gibson Nardy
Photographer unknown*

farmhouse as the Kansas winds blew across his rich wheat field. In February 1878, back in North Carolina, his mother died, and his father remarried a short time later.

T.R. and Julia's relationship as a couple was all in writing. They exchanged letters offering love and hope for a future together that finally culminated with his proposal of marriage, which she happily accepted. T.R. traveled 1,200 miles by train from his prairie home to Julia's father's home in Union Point, Georgia, for their wedding in October 1879. They were both twenty-nine years old. They traveled back by train to the little house he had built for his bride on the Kansas prairie just in time for winter. He was lonely no more, or so he thought.

They lived happily in Kansas for a couple of years, and their first child, Johnnie, was born in August 1881. For Julia, the going was tough, a lot tougher than on a farm in Georgia. She began to question if she could tolerate the lonely life of a prairie farmer's wife, suggesting to T.R. that maybe they should consider moving back east.

Back in Cashiers Valley, North Carolina, T.R.'s seventy-five-year-old father, Andy Zachary, had a similar idea and was lobbying for his son to come back to North Carolina, where he could use his help now that he was getting on in age. In the summer of 1881 he advised his son to sell his land after his next crop and come back to Cashiers Valley where he would find a place he would like better than the Kansas plains, or, "taking everything into consideration, your wife would."[679] Somehow, Andy Zachary had an inkling that his daughter-in-law, Julia, wasn't too thrilled living on the Kansas plains.

Homesteading in Kansas was difficult and successful farming a crap shoot, completely dependent on weather. After years of decent corn and wheat bounties, T.R. experienced crop failures in 1880 and 1881. He had to find work with a railroad construction company in New Mexico and Arizona in the winter of 1881 to try and keep his homestead afloat. Julia returned to her father's home in Georgia with their son; a woman alone on the prairie with an infant in the winter where the nearest neighbor was miles away was too much. Somehow she managed to get a letter to him in Arizona discussing their plight and again suggesting he come back east. Julia would write, "tell me that you will be here soon and then God helping, I hope we will never be so far or so long away from each other, again."[680]

T.R. got the message. In early 1883 he sold off his land in Kansas and finally returned to Cashiers Valley, much to the relief of his wife and father. He started a seed company called T.R. Zachary & Sons, and over the years would travel throughout western North Carolina and North Georgia selling apple trees. The family later called him the "Johnny Appleseed of Western North Carolina."

T.R.'s life in North Carolina was returning to what he had remembered when he was a boy; his father lived nearby, and his wife and growing family were content and happy. Then one day in late 1883 T.R. received a letter. It was from Mark Bassett.

Mark M. Bassett (1837-1910) – Captain Bassett had experienced the complete gamut of emotions in 1865. He had been a POW on the run, made it to freedom, gotten promoted to Captain,[681] divorced his first wife on account of adultery, gained custody of his three children, then experienced the death of his youngest child and remarried.

He and his new wife, Annie, relocated to Pekin, Illinois, with Bassett's two surviving children in 1866 where he took up the study of law with the help of another veteran, Alonzo W. Bull, who was a lawyer before the war. In September 1867 while Bassett was in the middle of his studies, his mentor Bull died. Bassett stomached through this new adversity and was admitted to the Illinois bar in 1868. He immediately began his practice through Bull's old law firm in Pekin.

Mark and Annie would have their first child together, a boy named Frank, in September 1869, but the child didn't survive his first birthday, passing in the summer of 1870.

In 1872 the family moved to nearby Peoria, and Bassett established his own law practice. In the years after the war ended, Bassett continued to suffer from various maladies that were a result from his years as a POW. They prevented him from returning to the more physical labor he had been used to before the war, but the law, where the muscles used were in his brain, suited him perfectly. He focused his law practice on civil cases but also was an advocate for Civil War veterans.

Mark M. Bassett
Abraham Lincoln
Presidential Library
& Museum
Photographer
and date unknown

When the pension system was established, he would help his fellow veterans file for their pensions. In addition, he, like most of his fellow veterans, became active in the Peoria GAR post.

Annie was the stepmother to Bassett's two other children, Nathaniel and Sarah Jane, who both grew up in Peoria. Sarah Jane was married in the Bassett's Peoria home in November 1882 and moved to New York City. Elizabeth Haddock, who took Annie in as an infant after her mother died and became the only mother Annie ever knew, lived in the Bassett's Peoria home until her death in December 1882.

When T.R. Zachary received the first letter from Mark Bassett, it took a few moments for him to understand who the letter was from. Then the memories of shaking hands with the then-Lieutenant Bassett as they said goodbye to him and the other soldiers at the train station at Sweetwater, Tennessee, came flooding back.

In January 1882 the Bassetts had received a visit from Allie Stewart when he was passing through Peoria. Allie visited them again, this time with his wife, Nannie, in June. The visits, seventeen years after their escape together, had stirred up memories in Captain Bassett, and he began to reach out to see how the others in his prized photograph were doing.

Circa 1900 – T.R. and Julia Zachary and their children
Courtesy of Jane Gibson Nardy
Photographer unknown

T.R. and Mark exchanged a couple of letters, telling each other the stories of their lives since they had last seen each other in 1865. Bassett was becoming busy in 1884, not only with his law practice, but with the Peoria Republican party, which wanted him to run for the Illinois state legislature later that year.

In a letter to Bassett in February 1884, T.R. provided details on the distance and exact route they had traveled, then inquired about the picture they had all taken together. He had never seen it. In the reply sent in April 1884, both Annie and Mark Bassett wrote to T.R.:

"I have been very much interested in your letters to Mr. Bassett-and for that matter in yourself also, ever since I became acquainted with the "boy-guide" in the group photograph that Mr. B. prizes so much," wrote Annie Bassett. *"I recall the years that have gone since that picture was taken and consider that I am not writing to a 'boy' at all."*

"It does not seem possible that we traveled 100 miles after getting with you but I suppose you are right," wrote Bassett, who was then struck with an idea, *"Well, now, in case we wanted to go back, as we do, over that route past your place, how would we go? I want to get two or three or all of the boys together if possible, and go back this summer if we can raise the funds, over the same grounds to Dun's (sic) Rock."*[682]

In addition, in his last letter to Bassett T.R. raised the subject of the promised money that was supposed to be sent nineteen years earlier to be used for his education, to which the Captain replied: *"Now I will not say we will be there this summer but will make an effort to do so, when we will try to make everything right with you. I have really forgotten what was said and done about the matter."* He also promised to send T.R. a copy of the photograph.

Thus began a correspondence between the Captain and his former guide that would continue off and on for the rest of their lives. Bassett was elected to the Illinois legislature for two terms in 1884 and 1886. Then in 1888 he was elected to the Illinois Senate from his district in Peoria. The district was a Democratic stronghold, and Bassett, a Republican, won the race primarily with the support of veteran soldiers.[683]

"I was a democrat too before the war but the dems shot all the democracy out of me—now I am a strong republican fully believing in the majority ruling—and guess your better not talk politics as we are good friends and I hope always will be," wrote Bassett to T.R. in October 1890. He had never made it back to North Carolina as he had contemplated in his letter six years earlier, but the thought of a trip taking him back to a time in the past still percolated in his mind. *"Hope to be with you if possible next summer some time. By the way—How far are you from a place called Highlands, what direction (how far) is it from where we staid (sic) at your fathers and did we go near it as we passed through?"*[684]

Tragically, in 1891 Bassett's oldest son, Nathaniel, who worked for the Rock Island Line Railroad, was seriously injured in a train accident outside of Chicago. The accident affected his mind, resulting in a permanent disability. At age thirty-two on June 7, Nathaniel took his own life.[685]

Bassett lost his bid for reelection to the Illinois State Senate in 1892, defeated by the Democratic candidate 7747 to 7486.[686] He would return to Peoria, where he would become a probate judge.

Finally, in August 1895 Bassett made the trip back to Western North Carolina for which he had been wishing. Traveling from Asheville, he spent time with Flem Cison and his family at Dunns Rock and then made his way into Cashiers Valley and was reunited with T.R. Zachary. The conversations were full of nostalgia and reminiscing about the dangerous journey they had all made together.

T.R. continued successfully farming while selling seeds and apple trees throughout Western North Carolina and North Georgia. He even became interested in photography when the new Kodak began to be marketed to the masses. He and Julia would have a total of six children together, with their last child born in 1906 when they were both fifty-six years old.

Then multiple tragedies struck when he lost one of his daughters in 1907, and then his wife, Julia, died in January 1911. T.R. would marry for a second time to forty-two-year-old Mary Rogers in June 1913, and they would have a son in August 1914 when T.R. was sixty-four years old. Then his oldest son, John, who had been born on the Kansas plains, died in 1919 from tuberculosis. It was all too much for T.R., causing his health to fail. He died in August 1921, the result of a nervous breakdown.[687]

At the beginning of the twentieth century Mark Bassett knew that his health was declining. He continued his work as a probate judge in Peoria, living in the home he and his wife had built around 1890.[688] At times he would take in boarders, not for the need of money but to provide help for others in need. Schoolteachers and wards of the state might have found a room at Mark and Annie's home. One of the boarders was a male nurse. He was specifically there for Mark Bassett, who had a stroke in 1906 and suffered some paralysis of the face and throat.[689]

In December 1908 Bassett's forty-seven-year-old daughter, Sarah Jane Frost, succumbed to cancer in New York City. He had survived all his children and was now entering the twilight of life.

With the memories rekindled from his correspondence and visits with other veterans including comrades from the 53rd Illinois, Bassett felt that he needed to put down his account of his wartime experiences in writing. Being the lawyer and judge that he was, he also wanted to have the account signed and notarized by two witnesses as proof of its authenticity and accuracy.

The Bassett Home at 1301 Glen Oak Avenue in Peoria, Illinois
Courtesy of the Peoria Public Library
Photographer and date unknown

He used a typewriter to draft his story, fourteen neatly typed pages dated December

14, 1909, which he signed and had notarized on the last page as M. M. Bassett. He then had J. D. Hatfield and Alfred S. Stewart sign and have their signatures notarized in early 1910. They were two comrades who had escaped with Bassett, though at different times, and had stayed in touch over all the years. Hatfield escaped with Bassett through the tunnel at Libby Prison, which was successful for Hatfield, though unsuccessful for Bassett. Stewart successfully tramped for fifty days with Bassett to make it to freedom.[690]

Then on May 31, 1910, he had his account published in the *Peoria Herald*.[691] It took up a full page and included the photograph of twelve men taken on January 2, 1865. He knew his time was short and, in fact, had just weeks to live.

Annie Bassett continued to trade letters with T.R. Zachary after her husband's death. The last one in September 1911 compared notes on the identities of the men in "The Photograph" and included a copy of the *Peoria Herald* newspaper clipping. She had other plans for his account, stating *"I expect to have the story of his capture and escape published for a wider field"*[692] By then her husband had been gone over a year. She was all alone.

It had happened on Thursday June 16, 1910, during the warm early days of a Peoria summer. Before the sun had set around 7:30 p.m., Mark had asked his private nurse, Robert Craig, to help him into the parlor so he could sit. He had become feeble and now needed help to walk, with a weakness on his left side dramatically affecting his arm and face. At 8:30 p.m.[693] he closed his eyes for the last time. Sitting in his chair with his head tilted slightly back, he had been looking up at the "rare relic" that sat resting on the mantle of the fireplace when he suffered the final stroke and he faded away.

"I have a photograph of twelve ragged men with determination strong in their faces…"

Captain Mark M. Bassett

Chapter Twenty-Four

The Archeology of a Photograph and Its Photographer

WHEN THIRTY-TWO-YEAR-OLD Prussian-born Theodore M. Schleier replaced the lens cap on his camera, finishing the exposure for the photograph he had just made of the men posing in his Knoxville studio, he never considered that the resulting photograph would somehow confuse future generations as to the identities of the group of twelve ragged men. Strangely, for some reason the photograph was misidentified right from the beginning. Each misidentification created a new narrative on who the men were and where the photograph was made. Each misidentification became the truth in the "photographic genealogy" that then followed that particular copy of the image. History is full of self-perpetuating mistakes.

Theodore M. Schleier
Date Unknown

In researching this book, one of my first objectives was to pin down the photographer who had made the fascinating image of the nine Union POW officers and their guides. It soon became apparent that this photograph has been the subject of confusion for more than 150 years. This is perplexing because the twelve subjects in "The Photograph" all knew where and when the image was made; they regularly spoke about it. Well into the twentieth century, several of them publicly spoke about having the image displayed on the mantle of their home; it was a prized possession. "I have a photograph of twelve ragged men with determination strong in their faces..." wrote Mark M. Bassett on December 14, 1909. This was part of the full, sworn, and notarized account of his experiences as a prisoner of war. The account appeared in the *Peoria Herald* on May 31, 1910, just seventeen days before his death. It was also written into the *Journal of the Senate of the State of Illinois*[694] after his death in 1911.

Two additional soldiers added their signatures to the end of the manuscript and had them notarized at Bassett's request. They were Captain Alfred S. Stewart of the 4th Kentucky, one of his fellow escapees who appears in "The Photograph." He signed it on April 14, 1910, and Captain John D. Hatfield of Bassett's own 53rd Illinois, who signed on April 7, 1910. Hatfield had escaped with Bassett through the tunnel at Libby Prison; though Bassett was recaptured, Hatfield made it to freedom.

Finding an explanation for the misidentification of the image has resulted in a scavenger hunt that continues to this day. Archeologists explore their subjects by looking at layers, which helps them to tell a story and assign a date when events took place. This photograph of twelve ragged men has many layers indeed.

Theodore M. Schleier: The Photographer
Piecing together a series of clues led me to the conclusion that Theodore M. Schleier had to have been the photographer who exposed the glass plate negative from which the

photograph of the twelve men was made. His identification is all based on circumstantial evidence, but the facts are sound and convincing.

The first clue was that the location of Schleier's studio on January 1, 1865, was in the building next to Provost Marshal General Samuel P. Carter's headquarters, on Gay Street in downtown Knoxville.[695]

Gay Street; Knoxville. Tennessee – circa 1866-69
T.M. Schleier's Picture Gallery relative to the location
of the Provost Marshal Samuel P. Carter's Headquarters.
The photograph has been attributed as taken in 1869, though the East Tennessee History Center
believes the photograph to be taken earlier, perhaps 1866-1867.
Photograph by T. M. Schleier

This would have been a busy place, with soldiers constantly passing through its doors. Schleier, who also had a studio in Nashville since the early 1860s, catered to soldiers who were far away from home and had a little bit of money in their pockets. A photograph was the perfect, affordable, keepsake for a soldier to send home to his mother or other loved one.

Schleier arrived in Knoxville around the beginning of 1864 to open a second studio. He advertised his new digs in *Brownlow's Knoxville Whig and Rebel Ventilator*. The editor was William G. "Parson" Brownlow, who was also a Methodist Episcopal minister. *Brownlow's Knoxville Whig* was a pro-Union newspaper; its publication was suspended by the Confederate government at the start of the war. Parson Brownlow was arrested, charged with high treason, and would eventually be allowed to go to Nashville, which was under the control of Union forces, in 1862.

On November 11, 1863, with a printing press provided by the Federal government, Brownlow's newspaper was relaunched with a bold, new name: *Brownlow's Knoxville Whig and Rebel Ventilator*. The newspaper's updated name took up the entire width of the masthead and was a journalistic dig at the Confederacy. Schleier's advertisement "Headquarters for Pictures" was published on page two of the January 9, 1864, edition and introduced Knoxville to his studio.

January 9, 1864 – Theodore M. Schleier Advertisement
Brownlow's Knoxville Whig and Rebel Ventilator

Being located right next to General Carter's headquarters was a boon for Schleier's business of photographing soldiers. Carter's headquarters was also the place where the motley crew of ragged Union officers checked in and had their names entered into the record as returning prisoners of war soon after they arrived by train in Knoxville on January 1, 1865.

Major William S. Marshall and Captain John E. Page
as recorded in the records of the Provost Marshal General's office in
Knoxville, TN on January 1, 1865.
The records show all nine officers from the photograph
and several others recorded at the same time.
National Archives – Courtesy of Lorien L. Foote

Lieutenant Michael Hoffman recorded in his January 2, 1865, diary entry: "got our likeness taken in group." In 1896 Hoffman also wrote about the details of his escape in his Elk Point, South Dakota, hometown newspaper, which included his recollection of having the photograph taken.

"The next morning he gave us an entire new suit of blue soldier clothes, but before discarding our old ones we put them on and went up town in search of a photographer. No caravan in passing through the streets would have excited any more curiosity than we did. There were twelve of us who had our picture taken in the group, four of our party for some reason or other not being with us. This picture can now be seen at the writer's home."

Michael Hoffman
The Union County Courier
May 7, 1896

The second and most important clue that points to Schleier as the photographer also took place in Knoxville and comes a little over a year after the photograph was made.

In April 1866 William G. "Parson" Brownlow, the newspaper editor of the *Knoxville Whig*, was elected the governor of Tennessee. The role of editor of the newspaper was passed on to his son, twenty-six-year-old Colonel John Bell Brownlow. Theodore M. Schleier was friends with the Brownlows. An astute businessman, he knew the value of political connections. As a leader in the Knoxville German population, he represented a block of voters of interest to the Brownlows, and they sometimes moved in the same circles. In 1867 Schleier served as a delegate to the Republican State Convention. He later served as an alderman in the city. In the early 1870s Colonel John B. Brownlow presented his friend with a gift. "It was probably the finest cane in Knoxville, and probably cost forty or fifty dollars. The name of Col. J. B. Brownlow is engraved on the head with the inscription, "Presented to T. M. Schleier." It certainly is the prettiest stick of the kind we have seen," reported the *Knoxville Daily Chronicle*.[696]

On Monday, May 21, 1866, a little over a month after Parson Brownlow became governor, Knoxville was visited by Benson J. Lossing, one of the most well-known historians of the nineteenth century. Lossing was touring the south by train, a year after Lee's surrender at Appomattox, and the journey through the war-torn region would take him months. Lossing was conducting research for what would become his seminal history book series of the Civil War. Leaving from Chattanooga by train on Monday morning, May 21, 1866,[697] Lossing traveled on the same railroad that the escaped Union officers had traveled seventeen months earlier, arriving at the same railway station in Knoxville.

"At Knoxville we were guests of Governor Brownlow, whose names and deeds are so conspicuous in the annals of the Civil War in Tennessee. While in Knoxville we visited the various localities of interest in and around the city, accompanied by John Bell Brownlow, then editing his father's newspaper, the Knoxville Whig," recorded Lossing in his book *Pictorial Field Book of the Civil War, Volume 3*, published in 1868.

Besides being a historian and writer, Lossing was a jack of all trades, having mastered the art of engraving and painstakingly producing them for the books he authored as well as for other publications.

Lossing created a sketch of the Governor's home, which he adapted into an engraving that was published in his book, while in Knoxville in May 1866,. In Knoxville for a little over two days, he visited and sketched everything from battle sites to homes in the area that were relative to the story he was documenting. He interviewed witnesses to the Battle of Knoxville and talked to people in the Brownlow's circle—like photographer Theodore M. Schleier.

In an era where photographs were not yet able to be reproduced in print, engravings ruled. During the Civil War publications such as *Harper's Weekly* regularly published engravings that were adapted from the photographs of Mathew Brady, Alexander Gardner, and many other photographers throughout the country. During Lossing's trip through the south, it would have been very common for him to reach out to the area photographers such as Schleier and ask to see what photographs of interest to his project they might have. He would then acquire a copy of these photographs to later make into an engraving.

UNION REFUGEES IN EAST TENNESSEE.[1]

Engraving by historian Benson J. Lossing of the photo in question
Pictorial Field Book of the Civil War, Volume 3, p130
Published in 1868

There is no specific record of Schleier meeting Lossing. Nor did Lossing credit Schleier or any other photographer for the image he used to create the engraving in *Pictorial Field Book of the Civil War. Volume 3.* When published in 1868 on page 130, Lossing would be the first to incorrectly identify the soldiers and their guides in "The Photograph" that he adapted into an engraving. He called them "Union Refugees in East Tennessee." We can assume that when Lossing was shown around Knoxville by Colonel Brownlow, he would introduce Lossing to his friend and photographer Theodore M. Schleier, who showed him something of interest: a photograph of twelve ragged men. Lossing would add in the footnote that he was presented the image in Knoxville as follows:

> *"This is a careful copy of a photograph presented to the author, at Knoxville, in which is delineated a group of returned refugees, at the time we are considering, They consisted, in large degree, of young men belonging to the best families in East Tennessee. Their sufferings had been dreadful. Their clothing, as the picture shows, was in tatters, and at times they had been nearly starved, Yet they held fast to hope, and resolved to save their country if possible."[698]*

It is also interesting that the context of Lossing's writing, in which the engraving was used, related to September 11, 1863, and the arrival of Union forces in the lead-up to the Battle of Knoxville. This is, of course, incorrect.

> *"The loyal inhabitants of that region received the National troops with open arms as their deliverers; and Union refugees, who had been hiding in the mountains, and Union prisoners from that region, who had escaped from the*

clutches of their captors, and had been sheltered in caves and rocks, all ragged and starved, now flocked to their homes, and joined in ovations offered to Burnside and his followers at Knoxville and elsewhere."[699]

Did Lossing get it wrong because Schleier himself didn't really know the story behind the men in the image? After the negative was made, it would likely have taken a few days for the prints to be made. By then, all the men in "The Photograph" had left Knoxville. Schleier would have had to mail photographic prints to the men who had ordered them. There are only two soldiers, Captain Mark M. Bassett and Lieutenant Michael Hoffman, who are known to have possessed original copies, likely obtained directly from Schleier shortly after the photograph was taken. Whether any of the other seven soldiers ordered copies from Schleier is unknown; the three guides never ordered original prints from the Knoxville photographer. Immediately after "The Photograph" was taken on January 2, 1865, everyone in it went their separate ways. Most received a twenty- or thirty-day leave and traveled to Chattanooga, then Nashville to connect to points north. Major William Stanhope Marshall, Captain John E. Page, and Lieutenant Michael Hoffman left Knoxville on January 3 at 7:30 a.m. and arrived in Chattanooga around 5:30 p.m. They then reported to the Headquarters of the Department of the Cumberland.[700] Hoffman recorded leaving Chattanooga on January 4 and arrived home in Marshalltown, Iowa, by way of Nashville, Cincinnati, and Chicago on January 10, 1865.[701]

Once Lossing's book was published, several of the officers in the picture became aware that the engraving incorrectly identified them. They would comment about it several times in the coming decades.

Lieutenant Michael Hoffman, in his hometown newspaper in Elk Point, North Dakota, wrote, "This picture can also be seen in Lossing's *History of the Rebellion.* He narrates on it as 'a group of refugees who fled from west North Carolina to escape persecution, and came into our lines for protection.' Mr. Lossing was off his base."[702]

Captain Mark M. Bassett also wrote in his hometown Peoria newspaper, "In Lossing's *History of the Civil War*, volume 3, page 130, is a copy of this picture, procured, no doubt from the photographer at Knoxville, Tenn."[703]

So was Theodore M. Schleier the man who took the photograph? There were only a couple of other professional photographers in Knoxville at the time, but the circumstantial evidence clearly points to Schleier. Absolute proof might be found in an original print of the photograph with an identifying photographer's back-mark affixed to it. In researching this book, I found only one original print that was owned by Michael Hoffman. Unfortunately, the Hoffman original print had no identification on its back. My research also identified two additional original prints; there may have been others as well; whether any of these survive today is a mystery.

It is also most likely that the original glass plate negative no longer exists. After Schleier left Knoxville, his original negatives were retained by the photographers that took over his business and maintained his negative archive.

"McCrary & Branson preserve and register all negatives. They have all negatives made in their gallery since 1865, including Schleier and Krutch," noted *The Knoxville Daily Chronicle* on Wednesday, March 31, 1880.

On Thursday, July 14, 1910, the *Knoxville Sentinel* ran an ad in the "Miscellaneous for Sale" classifieds.

> *"FOR SALE - All of the old negatives of McCrary & Branson Studio, up to 1900. These plates will be sold to green houses if not called for in 10 days. Cabinets, 8x10, 50c each."*

So the glass-plate negative made by T. M. Schleier of the nine Union officers and their three North Carolina guides likely had its emulsion scraped off and was installed in a Knoxville area greenhouse somewhere.

Versions of the Photograph

There are many different versions of the photograph found during the research of this book. Some are held privately by descendants of the men in the photograph, some are held in historical societies in the towns where the men lived before their deaths, and others are held by large institutions. All of the versions currently held by institutions are first-generation copy photographs made from the original photographs owned by two men—Mark M. Bassett and Michael Hoffman. The exception is the copy negative held by the National Archives.

Right as this book was going to press, an original albumen print made from the original negative was discovered. A digital capture of that original photograph was used on the cover of this book.

The following is a breakdown of all the known versions of the photograph today:

Original Michael Hoffman Albumen Print

The only known original albumen print is located in the Pacific Northwest and owned by the descendants of Charles S. Hoffman (1878-1941), Michael Hoffman's first-born son. When I first discovered it, the owner agreed to allow Lisa Duncan, a professional conservator based in Seattle, Washington, to visit their home to examine the image and make high resolution digital captures.

The photograph appears to be an albumen contact print from the original glass-plate negative. It measures approximately 7.5" x 5.375" and is mounted in a thin matte that overlaps the image by approximately 1/16" around all sides. The visible area of the print measures 7.375" x 5.25".

Michael Hoffman's handwriting appears on the bottom of the matte identifying the officers and their regiments. He got three of the men's regimental information wrong. L. D. Dobbs was listed as a member of the "9th U.S. Cav." He was actually a member of the 19th USCI when captured. T. P. Young was listed as a member of the "4 Kentuck. Cav." He was actually in the 4th Kentucky Mounted Infantry, an easy error to understand. J. McAdams was listed as a member of the "10th Virginia." He was actually a member of the 10th West Virginia when he was captured. Again, an easy to understand error. Prior to June 20, 1863 when West Virginia became a state, the regiment was known as the 10th Virginia. The three North Carolina guides are identified simply as "Refugee."

The original print displays beautiful sharpness, except for the men who move slightly when the exposure was made, as well as a beautiful tonal range and patina. It is the sharpest and most defined version of the photograph. Unfortunately, there is no photographer's mark on the back.

Also of interest was the double matte the photograph was housed in. Since the original matte was an odd size, and not easy to frame, Michael Hoffman at some point had a new 8x10" matte made that overlaid the first matte. He then wrote the identities of the men at the bottom, closely matching what he had done on the first matte. His descendant had the photograph and its two mattes archivally framed to display the bottom of both of the mattes with Michael Hoffman's handwritten identifications.

Original Michael Hoffman photograph with its double mattes
Photograph by Lisa Duncan - Courtesy of the Charles Hoffman family.

Version 1: National Archives Copy Negative – The National Archives in Washington, D.C., houses a misidentified copy of the photograph. It is not a photographic print but a copy negative of what is likely an original print contained within an oval matte. This negative was part of the purchase made by the War Department Records Office in July 1874 and April 1875 of almost 6,000 negatives from Mathew Brady studios. At this time Brady was in need of money, and it was decided by Congressional authorization to purchase his massive archive of negatives.

Many of the negatives are original Brady negatives, covering a wide range of subjects and famous people. But there are also copy negatives that were made by his studio of photographic prints by photographers who allowed his studio to make additional prints.

Version 1 – National Archives; Washington, D.C.
From the Mathew Brady purchase by
the War Department Records Office; made before 1874

This copy negative is poorly made. The left side of the image is slightly out of focus, whereas the right side of the image is not. It is also in bad condition, with many scratches made by the negative being poorly handled over the years. There is one scratch in the negative that was deliberately made. The words are seen when you reverse and turn the image sideways spelling out "Rebel Prisoners." The National Archives interprets this as Rebels who are prisoners, which is incorrect, rather than prisoners of the Rebels, which would be correct. Also on the surface is the imprint of some wooden planks that the photograph in its matte was affixed to when the copy negative was made.

It is interesting that this was part of the Mathew Brady cache as it places the date of its making prior to 1874. There is no other information related to whom the original photograph belonged, and no prints from the negative have been found. It is also curious that they did not remove the photograph from the matte to make the copy negative. Since the Brady studios made copy negatives frequently, it could have been from one of the soldiers in "The Photograph," including Mark Bassett.

It could also have been the copy of the photograph that Benson J. Lossing acquired in

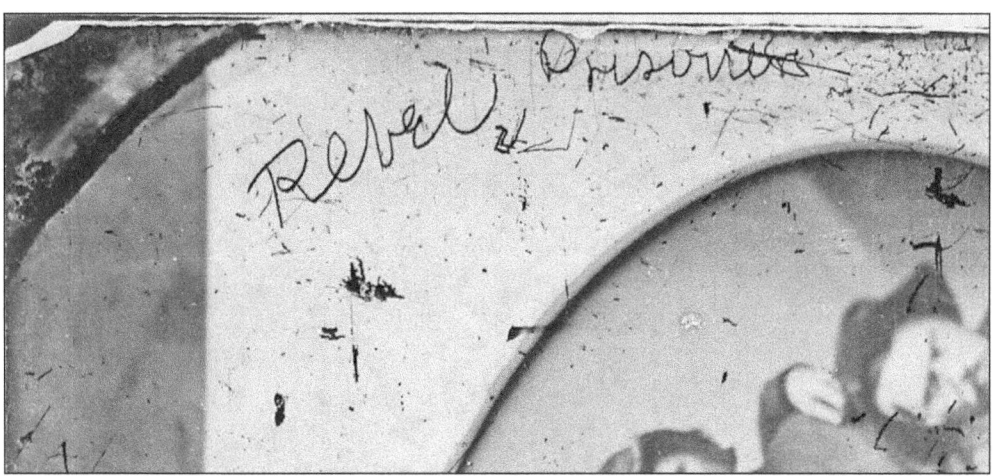

Version 1 – Image reversed, "Rebel Prisoners" scratched into the emulsion
National Archives, Washington, D.C.

1866 from the photographer when he traveled through Knoxville. Lossing had a relationship with Brady and lived in New York. The reason for Lossing to have wanted a copy made is unknown; perhaps it was part of his engraving process, or he did not have time while on his trip to make engravings of all the photographs he wished to use. Also of note, seen within this image is what appears as a vertical pipe in the studio, in the extreme right of frame. This is also visible in the Michael Hoffman original photograph and copy photograph, though not in the Mark Bassett copy photographs.

Version 2: Library of Congress Copy Photograph[704] – The Library of Congress in Washington, D.C., has a copy of the picture that was donated to the institution on August 17, 1944, by Mrs. Louise Sloan Ernst. Ernst and her family were living in Tacoma, Washington, at the time, having moved there in 1889 from Peoria, IL.

Ernst's father, Matthew Morrison Sloan, a grocer in Peoria, also moved to Washington state in 1889 and, upon his death, was returned for burial to Peoria. A relative of Mrs. Ernst, Dr. William T. Sloan, was Mark Bassett's doctor who is recorded in Bassett's Soldier's Pension Application as his physician and, at the time of Bassett's death, signed Bassett's Death Certificate. Dr. Sloan practiced medicine in Peoria from 1877 until his death in 1929. Matthew Morrison Sloan, Dr. William T. Sloan, and Mark Bassett are all buried in Springdale cemetery in Peoria, IL.

It is likely that Mark Bassett's physician, Dr. William T. Sloan, was given a copy made from Bassett's original photograph, and then, after the doctor's death, one of his relatives, Louise C. Sloan Ernst, acquired it. It is known that Bassett had copies made of his original photograph a couple of times.

Bassett also gave a copy of the picture to Thompson R. Zachary, the fourteen-year-old-boy in the photograph, sometime around 1884. Thompson, who went by "T.R.," had recently moved back to North Carolina after trying his hand at homesteading in Kansas from 1868 to 1883.

Version 2 – Library of Congress, Washington, D.C.
with missing emulsion in upper left and right
It is likely this is a copy that Captain Mark M. Bassett
had made from his original photograph.
Albumen photographic print 7.91 x 10 inches
Donated by Mrs. Louise C. Ernst on August 17, 1944.

Shortly after returning to North Carolina, he wrote to Captain Bassett (these letters no longer exist). On April 28, 1884, Bassett's wife, Annie, responded to a letter sent to them by T. R. Zachary. Annie Bassett's letter suggests that Mark Bassett's first attempt at copying the image was "enlarged" and the later attempt was not. This brings to question the original size of the photograph.

"Now about the picture that Mr. B. promised to send—he had the original one enlarged at one time and it is not distinct—looks blurred, and is therefore not as true as the first and I suggested that he try again to have several copies made without enlarging," said Annie.

In the same letter Mark Bassett added, *"As to the picture I am going to send you the one I had raised—it is a very good one and I think shows the parties as well as the original; they look a little coarser, that is all the difference I can see, I will have it tubed and send by mail."*[705]

> 440132

Groupe of Union Officers who escaped from Confed Prison at Columbia S.C. in the fall of '64 also Three guides procured in the mountains of Tennessee.

No 1. Capt M. W. Bassett Co E. 53rd Ills. Inf.

No 7. T. P. Young & A. S. Stewart 4th Ky. who with six others attempted to escape by running the guard at two oclock A.M. Nov. 10th 1864. The other 6. were recaptured & Killed.

No 2. Col. H.S. Marshall. No 3. Capt Dobbs. No 4. Fowler No 5. M. Hoffman No 6. Page. No 7. Jno McAdams.

Nos 10. 11. & 12. Guides =

Version 2 – Library of Congress; Washington, D.C.
Card that was attached with the photograph.
Donated by Mrs. Louise C. Ernst on August 17, 1944.

The Library of Congress image is identified by the institution as an albumen print. It exhibits a very good black and white tonal range with a sepia toning. It is mounted to a backing card that has a tear in the top center. The handwritten identification written in pencil appears to be in Annie Bassett's handwriting based on letters written to T. R. Zachary. The pencil crosses over from the backing matte and onto the actual photographic surface in a couple of places. The image also shows missing emulsion in the upper right corner, which is common with other first-generation copies of the photograph that point to being made from Mark Bassett's original.

Version 3: Union County Historical Society, Elk Point, South Dakota– Michael Hoffman was a successful retail businessman living in Elk Point, South Dakota, after his Civil War service. He was in the 5th Iowa Infantry, becoming a POW at the Battle of Chattanooga and then escaping Camp Sorghum in Columbia, South Carolina, and ultimately having his photograph taken on January 2, 1865. Hoffman lived until September 13, 1918. He is buried in the small South Dakota town.

Version 3 – Union County Historical Society; Elk Point, South Dakota
Hoffman is at the top of the photo, second from the right.
Donated to the Union County Historical Society in 2011

This is a first-generation copy photograph made of Hoffman's original albumen print contained in its "second 8x10 matte" that is currently owned by descendants of Hoffman's first-born son Charles S. Hoffman (1878-1941). It was donated to the Union County Historical Society in 2011 by descendants of Michael Hoffman's daughter Jess Hoffman McInerny (1880-1980) who lived in Sioux Falls, South Dakota.

When compared, the Hoffman original albumen print and this copy to the Library of Congress's copy photograph, this photograph shows more on the left and right side of the print revealing more of the photographer's studio. There is a vertical pipe on the right side of the image similar to the National Archives copy negative. The matte the photograph is contained within crops out part of the top and bottom of the image as compared to the Library of Congress version.

★ ★ ★

Version 4: Chicago History Museum – The museum of the Chicago Historical Society's version of the image is a first-generation copy photograph (albumen?) made from an original print. The copy photograph image size is approximately eight by ten inches, has sepia toning, and is mounted on backing card stock with a hole at the top that looks to have been made by a nail or pushpin. It is very similar to the Library of Congress image in that it is the same image size, crop, and is mounted to a backing

Version 4 – Chicago History Museum
Likely an albumen print – Date of acquisition is unknown

card stock. They may have been produced at the same time. The image also shows missing emulsion in the upper left and right corners, which is common among other first-generation copies of the photograph.

This first-generation copy was likely made from the original print owned by Captain Mark Bassett who lived in Peoria, Illinois, for most of his life after the war and served terms in the Illinois State House and Senate.[706] The reason for this conclusion is that there are several imperfections in the original photograph that show up on the first-generation copy that are also seen on other first-generation copies held by other institutions. When the photo was taken on January 2, 1865, then Lieutenant Bassett was seated in the far left, bottom row, with his arms crossed. He was promoted to captain on March 9, 1865, but not mustered.

Richmond, Virginia's Libby Prison was where Bassett was first housed as a POW. He was one of the 109 tunnel escapees who crawled sixty feet from out of the prison cellar on February 9, 1864, only to be recaptured four days later along the Virginia peninsula and returned to Libby. In December 1888 Libby Prison was purchased by a group of capitalists headed by Charles F. Günther, a wealthy candy manufacturer with the intent of turning it into a museum in Chicago.

Version 4 – Chicago History Museum - Reverse of print
Date of acquisition is unknown

The building in Richmond was taken apart, brick by brick, and transported to Chicago by train. The museum opened on September 21, 1889, and exhibited a wealth of Civil War memorabilia. One of the men who ran the Libby Prison Museum in Chicago was Major Robert C. Knaggs, who was also secretary of the Libby Prison Tunnel Association, even though he had not escaped through the tunnel himself.[707]

On April 7, 1897, Knaggs wrote to Bassett of Libby Prison Tunnel Association letterhead stating:

> *"Dear Comrade - Dont (sic) forget the Photograph you were going to send me last Saturday, it hasn't shown up". The letter is signed R. C. Knaggs, Sec. and continues with a notation handwritten at the bottom of the page: "They were all night getting through 1-0 left through this tunnel, 40 recaptured. Vol 3 -Page 130 Lossings History of the war M. M. Bassett, the lower left hand one as you look at the picture recaptured kept in dungeon 8 weeks sent to Columbia where he escaped Nov 10-64. First sent to Danville, Va to Macon G to Charleston SC the to Columbia & from here he made his final escape."*[708]

Annie Bassett also commented about the photograph displayed at the Libby Prison Museum in a letter she wrote to T.R. Zachary dated September 4, 1911:

> *"Mr. Bassett had sent with the group photo to be exhibited in Chicago in Libby*

Prison which had been removed to that city and was for years a center of attraction to patriotic people. When it ceased to be such - or when the property it occupied changed hands, the copy of the picture with the page of explanation was returned to him and he gave the copy to someone else."

When comparing the Library of Congress copy photograph to the Chicago History Museum's copy photograph, they have the exact same creases and dust spots, which points to them both being made from the same original photograph.

The Chicago History Museum (CHM) owns a second eight by ten copy of the photograph. It appears to be a second-generation copy made from their first-generation copy photograph. When copies of copies are made, they pick up contrast and lose subtleties in the tonal range of the image.

The second-generation copy photo shows some of the same crease marks in the photograph as the Library of Congress version except for the missing emulsion at the top right of the image, which is barely seen in the photo. This version is slightly cropped from the CHM's other copy.

The front of the photo has crop mark indicators in the white margin. There is a lot of writing on the back and several stamps. The stamp in the center of the back reads: "ORIGINAL IN CHICAGO HISTORICAL SOCIETY; CLARK ST. AT NORTH AVE.; CHICAGO 14 - PLEASE CREDIT." From this stamp you can derive an approximate date that the photograph was made. Two-digit postal codes such as "CHICAGO 14" were introduced in 1943 during World War II to handle the increased amount of mail. They were discontinued in 1963, replaced with the five-digit zip code.

The CHM's second version appears to have been used for public relations purposes, perhaps provided to newspapers, magazines, or books. Also written on the back of the photograph are some handwritten notations and captions:

"DETENTION FACILITIES; CONCENTRATION CAMPS –
CAMP DOUGLAS I"
"Confederate soldiers in clothing in which they where captured,
Camp Douglas 1862-1865."

A website titled "Civil War In Art," which is affiliated with the Chicago History Museum, displayed the CHM's copy (Version 4A) of the photograph as well as the following information:

These men were members of General John Hunt Morgan's Raiders, an infamous Confederate unit of the Civil War. They staged daring raids into the North, the most famous of which occurred in July 1863, when Morgan and 2,500 horsemen galloped through southern Indiana and Ohio, robbing banks, stealing horses, and skirmishing with Union troops. Eventually, Union forces captured Morgan and several hundred of his men, who were then imprisoned at Chicago's Camp Douglas. In late October 1863, twenty-six of them attempted to escape by digging a tunnel ten feet underground past the fence, right under the guards' noses. All of them were captured and returned, but their daring attempt made headline news, and they tried to get away again on more than one occasion. These men considered themselves an elite group, far superior to ordinary rebels, and this photograph clearly shows their sense of daring and comradeship, as well as the effects of army and prison life. You might wonder about how the photo was taken at all, and how it was that the prisoners had a rifle (center) in their possession! But the prison camp did boast a photography studio run by D. F. Brandon within its walls. Perhaps this is where Morgan's Raiders had their photo made, in which case one must assume that the rifle was unloaded and merely a prop! But it is also possible that the prisoners had the portrait taken when on the run in the city after one of their repeated, if ill-fated, escapes.

The rifle mentioned in possession of one of the men in the center of the photograph is actually a walking stick in the hands of twenty-year-old Second Lieutenant Thomas Payne Young Jr. of the 4th Kentucky Mounted Infantry. Young was seriously ill, the result of living in terrible prison conditions and the fifty-one days he spent traversing the mountains of Western North Carolina and Eastern Tennessee in the brutal cold of November and December 1864. Young returned home to Danville, Kentucky, on a medical furlough but never recovered.[709] He died at his family home, just over a month shy of his twenty-first birthday, of heart disease, perhaps a side effect from typhoid fever,[710] just over ten months after the photograph was made. He is buried at Bellevue cemetery in Danville. Grand Army of the Republic (GAR) post #125 was named after him in Danville.

The Chicago History Museum was also the source for the cover image of the book, *To Die in Chicago; Confederate Prisoners in Camp Douglas 1862-65* by George Levy, published in 1999. In addition to the cover photo, Levy used the image again on page 142 with the caption:

"Morgan's raiders at Camp Douglas. Probably by D. F. Brandon. Note their menacing look and ragged condition. A youngster is in the upper right." (Image courtesy of the Chicago Historical Society.)[711]

There is a bit of irony in the misidentification of the photograph as Morgan's Raiders at Camp Douglas. Mark Bassett, Illinois State Legislator, Senator, and Judge, first enlisted in February 1862, as a sergeant in the 53rd Illinois. One of the first duties of his regiment was guard duty at Camp Douglas, just as it was being turned into a prison for Confederate POWs.

As the research for this book progressed, I shared the findings and had multiple discussions with the Chicago History Museum. They have now updated their description attached to the photograph in their inventory to reflect the facts presented in this book:

Chicago History Museum ICHi-001805
Headline: Union officers and scouts who escaped from Camp Sorghum
Description: Portrait of nine Union officers who escaped Camp Sorghum in Columbia, South Carolina, along with three scouts, Sweetwater or Knoxville, Tennessee, circa 1865.

Version 5: Peoria Public Library – Local History and Genealogy Department, Peoria, Illinois. This version of the photograph is another copy likely made from the Bassett original. This copy also has the same identifying creases and emulsion loss in the

upper right corner like the Library of Congress and Chicago Historical Society copy photographs.

The library does not have any information regarding the acquisition of the photograph, although it is contained in a special custom folder from Venard Studio, which was active in Peoria from around 1914 to the 1970s. Mark Bassett had his portrait made late in life in Peoria by Bach Studios, which was run by Emil and Otto Bach. Bach Studios closed its doors in 1914. In 1915, for one year only, Otto Bach worked for Venard Studios. It is possible that Annie Bassett sought out Otto Bach to have a copy made of her original photograph. The medium that the photograph is printed on is unusual with its carbon-black contrast and tone. It is possibly a platinum print. Commercially made platinum photographic paper was available from Kodak through 1916.

Version 5 – Peoria Public Library – with missing emulsion in upper right
Date of acquisition is unknown; Possibly a Platinum print
Local History and Genealogy Collection,
Local History and Genealogy Collection, Peoria Public Library, Peoria, Illinois.

The name of the individual who provided the handwritten identification on this version of the photograph is unknown.

Version 5 – Peoria Public Library – in its custom Venard Studio folder
Local History and Genealogy Collection,
Local History and Genealogy Collection, Peoria Public Library, Peoria, Illinois.
Photo courtesy of Christopher Farris

After Mark Bassett died in 1910, his wife, Annie, wrote to T. R. Zachary in a letter dated September 14, 1911, giving him the names of all the men in "The Photograph." Zachary had inquired about getting another copy of it for a friend in North Carolina who was interested in Zachary's story of the events resulting in the picture being made. Not wanting to lend out her original photograph for fear of losing it, and knowing that Zachary was planning on having a copy made from the print Mark

Bassett had already given him, Annie indicated she wanted an additional copy herself as well, writing:

"For I want a copy—and do not want the original picture, which I still have; it is too rare a relic to run risk of getting lost."

The Peoria image is slightly cropped from the Library of Congress version. It displays the same creases and imperfections found in the Chicago History Museum and Library of Congress copy photographs. It also has increased contrast, a result of the copying process. The increased contrast helps enhance the print's sharpness, showing more detail of the creases and imperfections found on the original photograph.

Annie Gould Bassett died in Peoria on June 4, 1924. What became of the original Bassett albumen photograph she had kept on her mantle that was the source of so many copies is unknown. By 1924, the Bassett print had become quite weathered based on the looks of the last copy made from it. Upon her death, there were only a limited number of surviving family it might have been given to. I searched the Peoria Historical Society, which maintains an extensive amount of Peoria GAR items and turned up nothing.

Version 6: Thompson Roberts "T.R." Zachary copy – Acquired by Zachary from Mark Bassett most likely in the 1880s.

The original photograph that T.R. Zachary received from Mark Bassett is still owned by a member of the Zachary family, though the family's genealogist, Jane Gibson Nardy, is unsure which cousin has the original. Nardy has a copy made from the original that was made sometime in the last fifty years and is printed on Kodak color paper. This version has a very high contrast and an extreme crop from the original composition.

Are there are more copies of this photograph, and perhaps another original or two out there waiting to be found? Perhaps this book will raise awareness and the other known original prints will reveal themselves. One can only hope.

The remarkable image taken in a frigid Knoxville, Tennessee, on January 2, 1865, is a moment forever frozen in time. It is a rare photographic relic, and its emotional effect on those who see it, is evident in the fact that it has been copied so many times and has made its way into so many museums and books. Its effect on the men who posed for the photo can only be imagined, but we know that several of them kept the photograph and displayed it prominently in their homes throughout their lives. It caused the men to relive what they were thinking and feeling at that precise moment their likenesses were captured. It was an object they cherished for the rest of their lives because it captured freedom.

Acknowledgments

WHEN SAM HOUSTON SHARED his photograph of the twelve men with me in 2021, I had no plans to write another book with a Civil War theme. But the picture intrigued me so much that I had to dig into the background of his Ledford descendant. I immediately began calling the picture of the "twelve ragged men" as "The Photograph." Their faces were staring back at me from 157 years ago, each with a story to tell. Once down the rabbit hole, the scavenger hunt led in many directions. It has been a remarkable journey.

I first set out to find living descendants of the men in "The Photograph," and one of the first I found was a nine-year-old girl. Or rather a woman who was a nine-year-old girl in 1985. Anna Catherine Josephs won a contest writing about her three-times-great-grandfather, who happened to be the fourteen-year-old boy in "The Photograph." As the winner of the contest, they published her children's book titled *Mountain Boy*, which told the story of T. R. Zachary helping the Union officers through the North Carolina mountains. Thirty-seven years later, after much hunting, I located Anna Catherine Josephs Mirovic living in Australia. She put me in touch with her mother, Juliet Zachary DeMarko, who lived nearby in Florida. After a phone call with Juliet, she insisted the person to talk to was the Zachary family historian, Jane Gibson Nardy, who lived in Cashiers, North Carolina, right next to T. R.'s old family home.

Jane is a Cashiers Valley resident, genealogist, author, and octogenarian whose great-grandfather was Thompson Roberts Zachary. Jane and I spent countless phone calls discussing her ancestor and visualizing what his life must have been like—something she has thought about for a long time. She graciously sent me the original letters that her family still prized, some written more than a 130 years ago to T.R. Zachary by Mark and Annie Bassett, as well those correspondences between T.R. and his wife. T.R.'s life as a Kansas homesteader is a book unto itself. I have told Jane recently that this book would not exist without her help and enthusiasm.

Sam Houston's Ledford descendants led to many other Ledfords, many of whom live near me in North Georgia and Western North Carolina. These descendants include Michael Ledford and Gary Ross, who shared elements of their vast family tree, which, along with the diary and written accounts by some of the men in "The Photograph," helped to prove that the man identified as David Ledford was actually Kit Ledford.

At the time this book was going to press, I connected with Charles S. Hoffman IV and Linda Hoffman, descendants of Charles S. Hoffman (1878-1941), Michael Hoffman's oldest son. Incredibly, they had his original photograph (the only original photograph known to exist).

The image is an albumen contact print made from the original Theodore M. Schleier negative. They allowed Seattle-based art conservator Lisa Duncan to visit their home and do a full assessment of both the photograph and original Michael Hoffman handwritten diary copy. The result is the image on the cover of this book coming from the high resolution image captures made by Duncan.   I also thank other descendants for taking the time to talk, dig through their attics for family photographs and other memorabilia, and reach back to me. With some of them I have had ongoing correspondence and phone calls as they became as interested in the story as I was.

I give my thanks to Mark Bassett descendants Christine Mueller, Peggy McLaughlin, and Debra Clendenen. Flem Cison descendant Tena McKelvin provided me with a lot of insight regarding Flem; she, too, was researching him. I also acknowledge William Stanhope Marshall family members Dr. Norton T. Montague III and Lucy Ann McBain, Allie Stewart descendant Carolyn Crabtree, and Brad Bascom, descendant of Elias Bascom and Judy Gerrard, the descendant of Henry Fowler.

Thanks to Mark and Matt Tusken, the keepers of the George R. Lodge diary, which was originally acquired, transcribed, and deeply researched by their parents, Roger and Margaret Tusken, long ago.

I also thank Michael Hoffman family members Peter and Barbara Hoffman, Carolina Cooney, Jody Menk, and Barbara Wylde. Barbara was the Hoffman descendant who had ended up with a treasure trove of Hoffman material, including his diary and scrapbook. She donated these items to the Union County Historical Society in Elk Point, South Dakota, where Eric Rosenbaum is the point man. Eric shared a keen interest in the story. As a local historian, he had been giving walking tours of the local cemetery where Mike Hoffman is buried. Long before I reached out to him about this book and would carry a copy of "The Photograph," telling folks what he knew about the men. I would like to thank Eric for the numerous hours he spent copying Hoffman documents and sending them to me, as well as regularly trading emails with suggestions—always on the lookout for other Hoffman descendants.

Thanks to Steve Cunningham and Jimmy Casdorph for their help on Averell's Raiders. Jimmy is the descendant of one of the officers captured with John McAdams and an example of how oral tradition passed down can help triangulate the facts in a story.

Thanks to Bassett descendant David Parks, who questioned the evidence as to whether his five-times-great-grandfather William Hezekiah Lee was really related to Robert E. Lee. Then to Colin Woodward, PhD, the historian and editor of the Lee Family Digital Archive, who confirmed that David Parks' instincts were correct and that General Lee was, in fact, nowhere to be found in the Bassett family tree.

Thanks to John Kuhl and his amazing archive on the 15th New Jersey and insights on the Fowler family and to Robert Bartley for sharing his third Great Uncle Reuben Bartley's diary.

Thanks to Laura Gardner and Hale Durant of the North Carolina's Transylvania County Library and to Keith Parker, descendant of Sheriff Robert Hamilton.

Thanks to Linda Aylward and Joe Hutchinson of the Peoria Public Library's Local History and Genealogy Department.

Thanks to Dr. Lorien Foote, author of *Yankee Plague,* for sharing some of her original National Archives research from Provost Marshal Samuel P. Carter's headquarters in Knoxville. Her continuing research project through the National Council on Public History tracking the escape of Federal prisoners of war is remarkable.[712]

Thanks to my friend Kerik Kouklis, independent photographer, filmmaker, and instructor for the Ansel Adams Gallery at Yosemite National Park, for our discussions regarding the wet-plate collodion photographic process, albumen printing, and the camera and lenses of the 1860s used by T. M. Schleier.

In Knoxville, thanks to the Knox County Public Library including Vicky Bills at the library's McClung Historical Collection and Adam Alfrey at the library's East Tennessee History Center. Both helped pin down the location of the Provost Marshal's headquarters. Additionally, Adam's knowledge of the early photographers in Knoxville was instrumental in deducing that Theodore M. Schleier was the most likely man who, with a black cloth draped over his head and camera, peered onto the ground glass at an upside down image of the "twelve ragged men" on that cold January day in 1865.

Thanks to the Abraham Lincoln Presidential Library and Museum; Rutherford B. Hayes Presidential Library and Museum; Center for Archival Collections at Bowling Green State University; Carolyn Crabtree of the Boyle County Genealogical & Historical Society; The Centre College Archives; Chattanooga Public Library; The Cherokee Historical Society—Murphy, North Carolina; James H. Ogden, III, Historian at the Chickamauga and Chattanooga National Military Park; The East Tennessee Historical Society – Knoxville; Cathy Parsons of the Fulton County Historical & Genealogical Society; The Gilder Lehrman Institute; Kankakee Historical Society; Illinois University's Illinois History and Lincoln Collection; New York State Library Manuscripts and Special Collections; The North Carolina Civil War & Reconstruction History Center; Oakland University Libraries, Rochester, Michigan; Peoria Historical Society; Bryan Bush of the Perryville Battlefield State Historic Site; Library of Congress Manuscript Division; Platt County Historical Society; The Sautee-Nacoochee Cultural Center, Shiloh National Military Park; Streatorland Historical Society; David Reed and the Streatorland Historical Society University of Illinois at Urbana-Champaign; Virginia Museum of History & Culture; St. Clair County Library; Western Illinois University's Malpass Library. I found that people from most all the organizations out there were only happy to help me dig into this story and became as interested by "The Photograph" as I was.

My thanks to the many Civil War Facebook groups out there, in particular to Michael Huston the Iowa Civil War Images group. In addition, thanks to Ron Coddington, editor and publisher of *Military Images* magazine, and Ronn Palm of the Museum of Civil War Images at Gettysburg.

Thanks to Gary Benson and the late David L. Keller of the Camp Douglas Restoration Foundation who early on in my research skeptically listened to my argument that the "The Photograph" had been incorrectly identified by both the Chicago Historical Society and their foundation as "Members of Morgan's Raiders at Camp Douglas." Then they took the time to look into it for themselves and came to realize that something wasn't quite right with that identification. Keller went to the Chicago History Museum himself trying to find out when the photograph had been acquired.

Thanks to John Russick, Senior Vice President of the Chicago Historical Society, who listened as I presented the facts of the case regarding said "Morgan's Raiders" misidentification, then had the Chicago History Museum's records updated. Thankfully, now there is one less historical self-perpetuating error out there.

A special thanks to Clint Johnson who read the manuscript and became my "historical consultant" based on his extensive knowledge of all things Civil War. Clint and I were both members of Phi Gamma Delta at the University of Florida, and one of the few who I knew would appreciate that Major William Stanhope Marshall was also a Phi Gam from the Jefferson College in Canonsburg, PA. graduating just eight years after the fraternity was founded there in 1848. Perge!

To Tom Parson, park ranger at the Shiloh National Military Park, who read an advanced copy of the manuscript and provided me with valuable feedback and insight. His attention to detail was amazing, and I am incredibly grateful.

Thanks to my two independent researchers on the ground in Chicago and Washington, D.C., Ray Johnson and Sam Askew. Also, many thanks to my editor, Karen Hodges Miller, for reining me in and keeping me focused.

Finally, thanks to my wife, Lauren, and my daughter, Melissa, who were there to read another Civil War story without eyes glazing over.

Endnotes

About the Escape Route Map
[1] The information for the paths the men took comes from multiple diaries carried by the escapees and other escapees as well as accounts written by some of the men after the war.

Introduction
[2] James E. Murphy, "The New Journalism: A Critical Perspective," in *Journalism Monographs* no. 34, ed. Bruce H. Westley (Lexington, KY: The Association for Education in Journalism, May, 1974).

Every Picture Tells a Story
[3] The term "Prisoner-of-War" and "POW" were not used during the Civil War. They actually began being used in World War I. Since the term is so well known today, the author is using it in throughout this book written in the 21st Century because it helps the tell the story.
[4] George T. Ditto, *Statistical Roster of the 5th Iowa Infantry*; Smith's Iowa Times Print; Sigourney, Iowa, 1897, 23.
[5] "Break For Liberty," *Union County Courier*, 4.
[6] Lorien, Foote, *The Yankee Plague - Escaped Union Prisoners and the Collapse of the Confederacy* Chapel Hill, NC: The University of North Carolina Press, 2016 and Lorien Foote & Andrew Fialka, "Fugitive Federals: A Digital Humanities Investigation of Escaped Union Prisoners." National Council on Public History, April 29, 2021. https://ncph.org/project/fugitive-federals-a-digital-humanities-investigation-of-escaped-union-prisoners/.
[7] Foote, The Yankee Plague; Foote and Fialka, Fugitive Federals .
[8] "Break For Liberty," 4.
[9] "Break for Liberty," 4.
[10] "Break for Liberty," 4.
[11] "Break For Liberty," 4.
[12] Adam Alfrey, East Tennessee History Center. Personal Communication, Description of Schleier's studio space on Gay Street.

Chapter One: Mark M. Bassett – 53rd Illinois January 1862 to July 1863
[13] Frances H. Kennedy, *The Civil War Battlefield Guide, 2nd Edition* (Boston: Houghton Mifflin, 1998), 172-173.
[14] The measurement known as a rod equaled 16.5 feet in the United States, so 3 to 4 rods would be 49.5 to 66 feet. The term originates from the standardized length of a surveyor's tool.
[15] H.E. Ranstead, *A True Story and History of the Fifty-third Regiment Illinois Veteran Volunteer Infantry Its Campaigns and Marches*; Soldier's Diary, 1910.
[16] Ranstead, *A True Story*.
[17] Theo R. Marsters, "Talk of the Town," *Peoria Morning Star*, 1917.
[18] Bassett Family Genealogy.
[19] "Illinois River Road National Scenic Byway," Interpretive Plan, History & Culture, Sea Reach Ltd, 2015,24, https://www.illinoisriverroad.org/wp-content/uploads/2018/07/12.15.2015-Illinois-River-Road-Scenic-Byway.pdf
[20] Mark M. Bassett Compiled Service Records.
[21] Last Will and Testament of William Lee, 14, August, 1819. Will Records, Book A-C, 1818-1870, Madison, Illinois. The will specifically mentions Lee's children by name including "Mary Ann Carlock."
[22] Marion Pomery Carlock, History of the Carlock Family and Adventures of Pioneer Americans (Los Angeles: Wm. B. Straube Printing Company, Inc.,1929), 197.

[23] For the Society of Lees of Virginia, the gold-standard of who begat whom in the Lee family, the begats don't quite add up. They do not show the first cousin connection in their genealogical records. This conclusion is also supported by the Lee Family Digital Archive at Stratford Hall, home of the Lees of Virginia. Woodward, Dr. Colin, editor of Lee Family Digital Archive at Stratford Hall, home of the Lees of Virginia; in correspondence with the author: "I talked with Judy Hynson, who is the real authority on the Lees, and she confirmed my research: William Hezekiah Lee was not the brother of Light Horse Harry Lee."

[24] US Naturalization Records. Armand and his father Paulin Pallissard became US Citizens in November 1860.

[25] Armand Pallissard Compiled Military Records.

[26] Julia Bowe, The Generations, (1959). A history of the Lecour and Pallissard family published by a family member in a limited-edition of 500 copies. Letter written by Mark Bassett to Edward Lecour; May 27, 1896.

[27] Armand Pallissard. *Armand Pallissard to Paulin Pallissard, July 8, 1862*. Letter. Archives West, University of Montana, Mansfield Library, Archives and Special Collections, Armand Pallissard Letters.

[28] Armand Pallissard. *Armand Pallissard to Edward Pallissard, October 2, 1862*. Letter. Archives West, University of Montana, Mansfield Library, Archives and Special Collections, *Armand Pallissard Letters.*

[29] Ranstead, *A True Story.*

[30] Mark Bassett. *Mark Bassett to Edward Lecour, May 27, 1896*. Letter. Illinois History and Lincoln Collections; Manuscript Collections, *Bassett, Mark M., and John G. Reckord Papers, 1863-1865.*

[31] Bowe, *The Generations,* 97.

[32] Bowe, *The Generations,* 97.

[33] Bowe, *The Generations*, 97.

[34] Report of the Adjutant General of the State of Illinois, Vol. III (Springfield, Illinois, 1901)618-655.

[35] United States Department of War, The War of the Rebellion: A Compilation of Official Records of the Union and Confederate Armies Series1, Volume. XVII (Washington: Government Printing Office, 1890):-313.

[36] United States Department of War, Series 1, Volume XVII, 325.

[37] "Private Wilson Letter", The Ottawa Free Trader, January 31, 1863, 1.

[38] Report of the Adjutant General of the State of Illinois, Vol. III, 618-655.

[39] Edwin L. Hobard, *A Story of Vicksburg and Jackson* (Denver: Hicks-Fairall, 1909).

[40] Mark Bassett. *Mark Bassett 1863*. Letter. Illinois History and Lincoln Collections; Manuscript Collections, *Bassett, Mark M., and John G. Reckord Papers, 1863-1865.*

[41] Jim Woodrick, *The Civil War Siege of Jackson, Mississippi* (Charleston: The History Press, 2016), 69.

[42] Shreveport Journal, February 19, 1915, 1.

[43] Hobard, A Story of Vicksburg and Jackson. This was a detailed letter to Hobard by his fellow 28th Illinois Infantry comrade detailing the battle of July 12, 1863.

[44] *History of La Salle County,* vol. I (Chicago: Interstate Publishing Company, 1886), 313. Among the dead was Col. Seth C. Earl, the regimental commander.

[45] Report of the Adjutant General of the State of Illinois, Vol. III, 654.

[46] Ranstead, *A True Story and History of the Fifty-third Regiment.*

[47] Mark M. Bassett, *Mark M.Bassett and John G. Reckord Papers.*

[48] Memoir "Civil War Recollections" by Thomas Benton Ellis,1913, 1913-09-30, Florida Memory, State Archives of Florida, Tallahassee, Florida. .https://www.floridamemory.com/items/show/345924?id=1

[49] George R. Lodge, Letter. *George R. Lodge to Mrs. Lodge*, Aug. 2, 1863.

[50] Jesse Yancy, "Woodrick's 'The Civil War Siege of Jackson': A Review," *Mississippi Sideboard A Southern Gallimaufrey* (blog), *Jesse Yancy,* July 8, 2019. https://jesseyancy.com/woodricks-the-civil-war-siege-of-jackson-a-review/

[51] The Cooper family's Chickering "square" parlor piano played on July 12, 1863, survives to this day as well, preserved in a museum in New Orleans.

[52] United States Department of War, Series 1, Volume XVIV, chapter XXXVI, pt2, 574-576. Captain James Culbertson McCoy (1828-1875) was the aid-de-camp to Lt. Col John Henry Hammond (1833-1890) of the Fifth Division commanded by General William T. Sherman. McCoy was promoted to Major on July 4, 1863 following the victory at Vicksburg; Major General Ord was likely unaware of McCoy's promotion.

[53] Edward O.C. Ord, Headquarters Thirteenth Army Corps Near Jackson, Mississippi, "Special Order No. 19", July 12, 1863, RG 111 Records of the Office of the Chief Signal Officer, 1860 – 1985, National Archives, Washington.

[54] Isaac C. Pugh. *Isaac C. Pugh to Elvina Pugh, July 29, 1863.* Letter. Special Collections and University Archives. University of California, Riverside. *Isaac C. Pugh Papers* (MS 266), box 2, folders 11-14.

[55] Rinaldo Pugh. *Rinaldo Pugh to Elvina Pugh, July 13, 1863.* Letter. Special Collections and University Archives. University of California, Riverside. *Isaac C. Pugh Papers* (MS 266), box 2, folders 11-14.

[56] Jim Woodrick, *The Civil War Siege of Jackson, Mississippi* (Charleston: The History Press, 2016), 76.

Chapter Two: 53rd Illinois – Prisoners of War
July 1863 to November 1863

[57] Ranstead, *A True Story.*

[58] George R. Lodge, *Diary,* in Journal of the Illinois State Historical Society (1908-1984) 56, no. 2, Civil War Centennial, ed. Roger Tusken (Springfield: Illinois State Historical Society1963), 316-339.

[59] United States Sanitary Commission, Narrative of privations and sufferings of United States officers and soldiers while prisoners of war in the hands of the Rebel authorities, (Philadelphia: King & Baird Printers, 1864), 158.

[60] United States Census Bureau, U.S. Census, "Slave Schedule - Seventh Census of The United States," (Washington, DC: The National Archive, 1850); NARA Microform Publication: M432, Title: Seventh Census Of The United States, 1850, Record Group: Records of the Bureau of the Census, Record Group Number: 29.

[61] Thomas P. Turner Compiled Military Records.

[62] Turner Compiled Military Records.

[63] John Algernon Owens and Willard W. Glazier, *Sword and Pen: Or, Ventures and Adventures of Willard Glazier In War and Literature* (Philadelphia: P.W. Ziegler, & Company, 1889), 167.

[64] Owens and Glazier, *Sword and Pen,* 167. Glazier was an author of multiple Civil War books and was breveted a Captain for 'meritorious service' in 1867.

[65] United States Sanitary Commission, Narrative of privations and sufferings of United States officers and soldiers 151-152.

[66] "Ross was…": Miss Van Lew and Young Ross," National Tribune; September 27, 1883, 2.

[67] Frank Rauscher, Music on the March 1862-1865, with the Army of the Potomac (Philadelphia: 1892), 43.

[68] Thomas E. Rose and Samuel P. Bates, "A Celebrated Escape, A Thrilling Story of the Libby Prison Tunnel; Part II," *Worthington's Magazine* III, no. 2, (February,, 1894): 56.

[69] Earl Antrim, *Civil War Prisons and Their Covers,* (New York: Theodore vE. Steinway Memorial Fund/Collector's Club, 1961), 205.

[70] James M. Wells, *With Touch of Elbow; or Death Before Dishonor* (Philadelphia: John C. Winston Co. 1909), 133.

[71] Libby's actual dimensions were recorded as 103 feet by 42 feet.

[72] Mark M. Bassett.

[73] United States Sanitary Commission, Narrative of privations and sufferings of United States officers and soldiers.

[74] Mark M. Bassett, *Mark M. Bassett and John G. Reckord Papers*, First Lieutenant George D. Forsyth of Company B, 100th Ohio Infantry was killed by a guard at Libby Prison on April 13, 1864.

[75] *Daily Richmond Enquirer,* February 2, 1864, 3.

[76] George H. Starr, *Diary,* 1863, The Gilder Lehrman Institute of American History, *The Gilder Lerhman Collection.*

[77] George R. Lodge, *Diary,* 316-339.

[78] United States Department of War, Series II, Volume VI, 241-242.

[79] *New York Times,* November 28, 1863, 1.

[80] *The Ottawa Free Trader,* July 25, 1863, 2.

[81] *Chicago Tribune,* August 11, 1863, 2.

**Chapter Three: William Stanhope Marshall, John E. Page, and Michael M. Hoffman
5th Iowa – July 1861 to November 1863**

[82] Steven E. Woodworth and Charles D. Greer, *The Chattanooga Campaign* (Civil War Campaigns of the West) (Carbondale: Southern Illinois University Press), 2012, 58.

[83] Samuel H.M. Byers, *Iowa in War Times* (Des Moines: W.D. Condit & Co.,1888), 251.

[84] Samuel H.M. Byers, *With Fire and Sword* (New York: The Neal Publishing Company, 1911), 104.

[85] Frederick Way, Jr. *Way's Packet Directory, 1848-1983: Dictionary of Transports and Combatant Vessels Steam and Sail Employed by the Union Army 1861-1868,* 1st ed (Athens: Ohio University Press, 1983).

[86] Byers, *With Fire and Sword*, 13.

[87] Samuel Hawkins Marshall Byers Compiled Military Records. There is a discrepancy as to whether he mustered in as a corporal as his military records indicate, or as a private as was reported in his obituary in *The Courier*, Waterloo, Iowa on May 26, 1933.

[88] Colonel William H. Worthington Family Genealogy.

[89] Byers, *With Fire and Sword*, 14.

[90] *Chattanooga Daily Times*, January 28, 1891, 4.

[91] "Dissolution Notice," *The Buchanan County Guardian*, August 27, 1861.

[92] Department of Veterans' Affairs, "John Elijah Page Pension Application," January 1, 1983, Veterans' Service Records, National Archives, Washington.

[93] Michael Hoffman. Michael Hoffman Original Handwritten Diary, Courtesy of the Charles Hoffman family.

[94] Byers, *With Fire and Sword*.

[95] Hans Christian Adamson, Rebellion in Missouri, 1861 (Boston: Chilton Company, 1961), 17.

[96] *With Fire and Sword*,14.

[97] "The Cost of War: Killed, Wounded, Captured, or Missing, Civil War Casualties", American Battlefield Trust, November 16, 2012, https://www.battlefields.org/learn/articles/civil-war-casualties

[98] Michael Hoffman. *Michael Hoffman Transcribed Diary and Michael Hoffman Personal Scrapbook*, Union County Historical Society, Elk Point, SD.

[99] Byers, *With Fire and Sword*, 26.

[100] John Elijah Page Pension Application.

[101] W.H. Tunnard, *A Southern Record. The History of the Third Regiment Louisiana Infantry* (Baton Rouge, Louisiana: Salzwasser-Verlag, 1866), 183.

[102] *Report of the Adjutant General and Acting Quartermaster General of Iowa; Volume II* (Des Moines; P.W. Palmer State Printer, January 1, 1863): 807-808.

[103] John Elijah Page Pension Application.

[104] Hoffman, *Diary*.

[105] John Elijah Page Pension Application.

[106] Hoffman, *Diary*.

[107] Memoir. "My Civil War Memoirs and Other Reminiscences" by William Eddington, Madison County Historical Society, Edwardsville, Illinois, 11-12.

[108] Byers, *With Fire and Sword*, 74.

[109] Byers, *With Fire and Sword*, 74.

[110] Byers, *With Fire and Sword*, 74.

[111] Hoffman, *Diary*.

[112] Byers, *With Fire and Sword* 96. Also "Robert Bain Obituary", *LA Times*, February 27, 1923, Section II, 12.

[113] "10 Facts: Battles for Chattanooga -November 23-25, 1863". American Battlefield Trust. Accessed November 22, 2021. https://www.battlefields.org/learn/articles/10-facts-battles-chattanooga.

Chapter Four: 5th Iowa – Prisoners of War November 1863

[114] United States Department of War, Series I, Volume XXXI, Part 2, Serial No. 55, "Report to Headquarters by Colonel Jabez Banbury, Fifth Iowa; Larkinsville, Alabama" December 29, 1863.

[115] Byers, *With Fire and Sword*, 107.

[116] Byers, *With Fire and Sword*, 108.

[117] United States Department of War, Series I, Volume XXXI, Part 2, 633-34.

[118] William S. Peck, *William S. Peck to William Codling*, January 4, 1864. Letter.

[119] Byers, *With Fire and Sword*, 109.

[120] John Whitten. *Diary in pencil*, 110 pages, August 4, 1863-May 17, 1864. Diary. Library of Congress, Civil War Manuscripts Division. John Whitten Papers 1857-2010.Diary kept by Whitten during his Civil War service with the 5th Iowa Infantry Regiment, U.S. Army.

[121] Samuel H.M. Byers, *Marsh Byers to John Byers, December 8, 1863*. Letter written at Libbey Prison.

[122] Hoffman, Diary.

[123] Samuel H.M Byers, *What I Saw in Dixie -or- Sixteen Months in Rebel Prisons* (Dansville: Robbins & Poors, Printers, Express Printing House, 1868), 9.

[124] Michael Hoffman, *The Union County Courier*, January 31, 1883; February 7, 1883; February 14, 1883..

[125] Private John H. Moore Compiled MilitaryRecords.

[126] Mary A. Schreffler, *Deposition*, "In the Matter of Mark Bassett vs. Charlotte Bassett," Mark Bassett Divorce Records, Fulton County Illinois: Circuit Court of Fulton County, Illinois, February 1865.

[127] Byers, What I Saw in Dixie,12.

[128] Michael Hoffman, "In Libby", *The Union County Courier*; January 31, 1883, 3.

[129] Michael Hoffman, *The Union County Courier;* January 31, 1883; February 7, 1883; February 14, 1883.

[130] Byers, *What I Saw in Dixie*, 13.

Chapter Five: John McAdams – 10th West Virginia December 1863

[131] Francis Smith Reader, "History of the Fifth West Virginia Cavalry, Formerly the Second Virginia and Battery G First West Virginia Light Artillery," *Daily News,* 1890, 226..

[132] William Woods Averell's military rank timeline from his compiled military records: Brig-General 9/26/1862 of volunteers; Major 3/17/1863 by Brevet (For Kelly's Ford, VA); Lt Colonel 11/6/1863 by Brevet (For Droop Mountain, VA); Colonel 12/15/1863 by Brevet (For Salem, VA); Major-Gen 8/7/1864 by Brevet (For Moorefield, VA); Brig-General 3/13/1865 by Brevet ; Major-Gen 3/13/1865 by Brevet (For Moorfield, VA). The spelling of his name also appears in the records and publications of the time as Averill.

[133] Edward K. Eckart. and Nicholas J. Amato, *Ten Years in the Saddle: The memoir of William Woods Averell 1851-1862* (San Rafael, California: Presido Press, 1978), 80, 203-8, 211.

[134] United States Department of War, Series I, Volume XXIX, Chapter XLI, Part 1, 952.

[135] J. Gray McAllister, Sketch of Captain Thompson McAllister, Citizen, Soldier, Christian (Petersburg: Penn & Owen Printers and Binders)., 1896.

[136] Darrell L. Collins, *General William Averell's Salem Raid;* (Shippensburg, PA: Burd Street Press,1998), 87.

[137] United States Department of War, Series I, Volume XXIX, Chapter XLI, Part 1, 924,929.

[138] McAdams Family Genealogy.

[139] Since all cities and towns located in West Virginia prior to the Civil War were a part of Virginia, from this point forward, locations will be labeled with their post-Civil War West Virginia identification.

[140] United States Department of War, Series I, Volume XXIX, Chapter XLI, Part 1, 954.

[141] John and William McAdams, Compiled Military Records

[142] Francis Smith Reader, *History of the Fifth West Virginia Cavalry.*

[143] The Medical and Surgical History of the War of the Rebellion; Part III, Volume II, Surgical History(Washington: Government Printing Office, 1883), 948-950.

[144] Christina Fisanick, "The Wheeling Ambulance: A Civil War Hero." Weelunk. April 16, 2018. https://weelunk.com/the-wheeling-ambulance-a-civil-war-hero/

[145] Francis Smith Reader, History of the Fifth West Virginia Cavalry, 224.

[146] Jacob M. Rife, Article, National Tribune, September 8, 1887, 1. Rife enlisted April 20, 1861, and served as a Sergeant in Company F, 18th Ohio Volunteer Infantry, through August 28, 1861. He then re-enlisted in Company C, 8th West Virginia Mounted Infantry which became the Company A, 7th West Virginia Cavalry in early 1864.

[147] Rife, *National Tribune*, p1.

[148] Francis Smith Reader, *History of the Fifth West Virginia Cavalry,* 223-224.

[149] United States Department of War, Series I, Volume XXV, Chapter XXXVII, Part 1, 928.

[150] United States Department of War, Series I, Volume XXV, Chapter XXXVII, Part 1, 929.

[151] Daniel H. Polsley had resigned the position as Lieutenant-Governor on June 8, 1863, just prior to West Virginia officially becoming a state on June 20, 1863 to become a judge in the 7th judicial circuit of West Virginia

[152] *Richmond Sentinel,* December 22, 1863, story by correspondent named "Rambler".

[153] Reader, *History of the Fifth West Virginia Cavalry* 227.

[154] Reader, *History of the Fifth West Virginia Cavalry*, 122.

[155] William Davis Slease, *The Fourteenth Pennsylvania Cavalry in the Civil War* (Pittsburgh: Art and Engraving Printing Company, 1915), 121.

[156] Reader, *History of the Fifth West Virginia Cavalry,* 224. It is interesting that in the summer of 1884, Seaman returned to Sweet Springs and after making several inquiries and searching through the area, found Polly. He did not reveal his true identity, but had a short conversation with her and learned that she had never remarried after losing George.

[157] Darell L. Collins, General William Averell's Salem Raid, 93.

[158] *The National Tribune*, September 27, 1883, 7.

[159]United States Department of War, Series I, Volume XXV, Chapter XXXVII, Part 1, 932. Private Starcher's account was written nearly 20 years after the event, so his POW numbers are likely slightly off. In Averell's official report, by Will Rumsey, Assistant Adjutant-General, the casualty list of the First Separate Brigade had the following totals for those captured near Covington, Virginia on December 19, 1863: 3 officers and 116 enlisted men. The report reflected numbers from the 2nd, 3rd, and 8th West Virginia Mounted Infantry, 14th Pennsylvania Cavalry, Gibson's battalion and Ewings' West Virginia Battery G. The United States Department of War record does not reflect the individual compiled military records of each of the 5 officers that were captured. Additionally, Lt. McAdams was detached from the 10th West Virginia, so perhaps not subject to Averell's report.

[160] Reader, *History of the Fifth West Virginia Cavalry*, 236. In 1890 Francis Smith Reader reported the number captured as 5 officers and 119 men.

[161] The 8th West Virginia mounted Infantry became the 7th West Virginia Cavalry on January 26, 1864.

[162] "Markbreit Interview", *The Sunday Oregonian*, June 28, 19081.

[163]Jacob G. Matlick, *Army and Prison Reminiscences During the Civil War 1861 to 1865*. West Virginia University, West Virginia Collection. Written in November and December 1903.

[164] Francis Smith Reader, History of the Fifth West Virginia Cavalry.

Chapter Six: Libby Prison December 1863 to February 1864

[165] Lieutenant Federico Fernández Cavada, *Libby Life: Experiences of a Prisoner of War in Richmond, Va, 1863-64* (Philadelphia: King & Bair, 1864), 100.

[166] George Duncan Forsyth. Letter. Toledo Blade December 31, 1863. 2.

[167] *New York Times*, February 15, 1891, 10.

[168] John E. Fisher, *They Rode with Forrest and Wheeler: A Chronicle of Five Tennessee Brothers* (Jefferson, NC: McFarland, 1995), 44.

[169] *New York Times*, February 15, 1891, 10.

[170] Frank E. Moran, "Colonel Roses Tunnel at Libby Prison", Century Illustrated Monthly Magazine Vol XXXV, No 5, March, 1888,770-790.

[171] Lodge, *Diary*,316-339.

[172] Michael Hoffman, *The Union County Courier*, February 7, 1883. Article series.

[173] Byers, *What I Saw in Dixie*, 16.

[174] Lodge, *Diary*; 316-339.

[175] *Peoria Herald*, May 31, 1910,21.

[176] Cavada, *Libby Life*, 102.

[177] Historynet Staff. "William Averell's Cavalry Raid on the Virginia & Tennessee Railroad. June 12, 2006. https://www.historynet.com/william-averells-cavalry-raid-on-%20%20%20%20%20%20the-virginia-%20%20%20%20tennessee-railroad/

[178] Markbreit was a 1st Lieutenant & Adjutant at the time of his capture. He was promoted to captain on 4/24/1864 but never mustered.

John J. Polsley. *John J. Polsley to Major Hedgeman Slack, January 21, 1864*. Letter. Library of Congress, Civil War Manuscripts Division *John J. Polsley Collection*, Gift of William F. Wagner, 1959.

[180] *Richmond Enquirer*, April 1, 1864, 3.

[181] Lodge. *Diary*,316-339.

[182] Alva C.Roach, *The Prisoner of War and How Treated* (Indianapolis: Railroad City Publishing House, A. D. Streight, Proprietor, 1865), 88.

[183] Thomas P. Turner, *Thomas P. Turner to Mrs. Van Lew*. Letter. National Archives, Washington: RG109, CH 9, Vol. 199½. *Letters & Orders Issued, Confederate Military Prison, January, 1862 – December, 1863*", 68..

[184] I.N. Johnston, *Four Months in Libby and the Campaign Against Atlanta* (Cincinnati: R.P. Thompson, Printer, Printed at the Methodist Book Concern for the Author, 1864), 52.

[185] Douglas Miller, *The Greatest Escape, A True American Civil War Adventure* (Guilford, CT: Lyons Press, 2021), 38.

[186] Robert P. Watson, *Escape! The Story of the Confederacy Infamous Libby Prison and the Civil War's Largest Jail Break* (Blue Ridge Summit, PA: Rowman & Littlfield, 2021),102-105.

[243] *The National Tribune*; May 14, 1885, 3, Colonel Thomas E. Rose's account of the Libby Tunnel.

[188] Andrew G. Hamilton, *Story of the Famous Tunnel Escape from Libby Prison* (Chicago: SS Boggs, 1893), This 14-page pamphlet was created for the Libby Prison Museum in Chicago.

[189] *The National Tribune*, May 14, 1885, 3.

[190] Miller, *The Greatest Escape*, 87.

[191] Byers, *What I Saw in Dixie*, 20.

[192] *The National Tribune*, May 14, 1885l, p3.

[193] *The National Tribune*, May 14, 1885,3.

[194] Thomas E. Rose. and Samuel P. Bates "A Celebrated Escape, A Thrilling Story of the Libby Prison Tunnel; Part I," *Worthington's Magazine* III, no. 1 (January, 1894): 55-64.

[195] Hamilton, *Story of the Famous Tunnel Escape from Libby Prison.*

[196] David B. Parker, *A Chautauqua Boy in '61 and Afterward: Reminiscences by David B. Parker* (2nd Lieut., 72nd NY)(Boston: Small, Maynard & Company, 1912), 54-64. Author's note: Many books on Libby Prison have identified the escapee as Captain William H. Lownsbury of the 74th New York. Captain William H. Lownsbury was seriously wounded in May 1863 at Chancellorsville and was never a prisoner at Libby. In Parker's account, he never mentions Lownsbury's first name or regiment, but he does mention that at the time he met him after the war, "Lowensbury" was a grocer living in Jamestown, New York. He also misspelled his name. After the war, Captain Benjamin F. Lownsbery of the 10th New York Cavalry along with his brother Jared D. Lownsbery owned a grocery store named Lownsbery & Grant in Jamestown. Captain Lownsbery was captured on July 2, 1863 at Gettysburg and was imprisoned and escaped from Libby Prison.

[197] Owens and Glazier, *Sword and Pen*,70-171.

[198] Miller, *The Greatest Escape*, 99.

[199] Johnston, *Four Months in Libby* 69.

[200] Carlock, *History of the Carlock Family*,147.

[201] Rose, and Bates, *A Celebrated Escape*, Part II, 161-172.

[202] Joseph Wheelan, *Libby Prison Breakout - The Daring Escape from the Notorious Civil War Prison*, (New York: Public Affairs, 2010), 161.

[203] Rose and Bates; *A Celebrated Escape, Part II,* 161-172.

[204] *The National Tribune*, March 17, 1892, 2.

[205] John H. Moore Compiled Military Records.

[206] *The Ottawa Free Trader*, July 25, 1863.

[207] Schreffler, *Deposition*

[208] Carlock; *History of the Carlock Family* 147-148.

[209] Bernhard Domschcke, *Twenty Months in Captivity: Memoirs of a Union Officer in Confederate Prisons*. Trans. Frederic Trautman (Madison, NJ: Farleigh Dickinson University Press, 1987), first published 1865,63.

[210] Moran, "Colonel Ross Tunnel at Libby Prison," 770-790.

[211] Mark Bassett, *Journal of the Senate of the 47th General Assembly of the State of Illinois, Senate Resolution No. 75* (Springfield, Illinois: Illinois State Journal Co, State Printers, 1911),; 1301.

Chapter Seven: Freedom and Return to Libby Prison February 1864

[212] Carlock, *History of the Carlock Family*,147.

[213] Byers, *With Fire and Sword* 115.

[214] Hamilton, *Story of the Famous Tunnel Escape from Libby Prison.*

[215] Bassett *Journal of the Senate of the 47th General Assembly of the State of Ilinois,*1301.

[216] Wheelan, *Libby Prison Breakout,* 184.

[217] The two drowned men were never identified, which is odd because most all of the men held as POWs at Libby were known, so it wouldn't be difficult to determine from Little Ross's count, the names of the men missing. Captain George R. Lodge of the 53rd Illinois, who had been captured with Mark Bassett in July 1863, though he did not escape through the tunnel, would record his fellow POWs being recaptured right after the escape, and of two dead men in his diary dated Wednesday, February 10, 1864 "They have already brought back five of them and we have seen two dead reb. soldiers brought in; but whether they were killed by our force on the peninsula or by fugitives we don't know". These two may account for some of the confusion in the total number of escapees - 107 vs 109. Could it be that the two dead Confederate men may have been thought by others to be two dead tunnel escapees that were reported as drowned? (Diary owned by the Tusken family).

[218] Watson, *Escape!,* 185.

[219] *New York Times*, March 15, 1891, 10.

[220] Hoffman. *Diary.*

[221] *The Daily Inter Ocean*, November 27, 1891, 12.

[222] *The Daily Inter Ocean*, November 27, 1891, 12

[223] United States Department of War, Series I, Volume XXXIII, 565.

[224] Roach, *The Prisoner of War and How Treated*, 118.

[225] *Richmond Dispatch*, March 11, 1882.

[226] Rose and Bates, *A Celebrated Escape*, Part II, 161-172.

[227] Moran, "Colonel Roses Tunnel,"770-790.

[228] Moran, "Colonel Roses Tunnel", 770-790

[229] Carlock*, History of the Carlock Family*, p149.

[230] Lodge, *Diary.*

[231] Watson, *Escape!,* 49.

[232] *Philadelphia Weekly Times*, October 28, 1882, 1.

[233] *Peoria Herald,* May 31, 1910, 21.

[234] Asa B. Isham, Henry M. Davidson, and Henry B. Furness, *Prisoners of War and Military Prisons* (Cincinnati: Lyman and Cushing, 1890), 34.

[235] Cavada, *Libby Life*, 189.

Chapter Eight: The Grand Raid February 1864 to March 1864

[236] Hamilton Gay Howard, *Civil-War-Echos: Character Sketches and State Secrets by a United States Senator's Son and Secretary* (Washington: Howard Publishing, 1907), 214.

[237] General Hugh Judson Kilpatrick Genealogy.

[238] Naval History & Heritage Command, "Civil War Prosthetics; Ulric Dahlgren's Leg," You Tube Video, 00:03:48. March 19, 2022. https://www.youtube.com/watch?v=kvuNBlM018U

[239] Ulric Dahlgren. *Urich Dahlgren to Admiral John Dahlgren, 1859-1864* Letters. Library of Congress, Civil War Manuscripts Division..

[240] Gene Paleno, "Chapter 85: Rat Hell," "Chapter 86: The Tunnel," "Chapter 87: Helped by a Slave," "Chapter 88: Free at Last," "Chapter 89: Home Is the Hero" in Lake County History *The Bloom*, May 21, 2020-June 18, 2020, https://www.lakecountybloom.com/category/history-literature/lakecountyhistory-history-literature/page/2/. Account of his escape from Libby Prison related to his daughter Mary Scudamore Akers (1898-1987) by Captain Scudamore. Scudamore was promoted to Captain on July 10, 1864..

[241] Bruce M. Venter, *Kill Jeff Davis - The Union Raid on Richmond, 1864* (Norman: University of Oklahoma Press, 2016). There are several accounts giving Martin's last name as Roberson or Robinson. No definitive proof exists of the exact last name of this man. Written accounts from the time and in the years afterward clearly referred to the guide simply by his first name, Martin, without recording his last name.

[242] United Department of War, Volume XXXIII, 221. Though the Richmond newspapers would later report him as an enslaved man owned by Mr. David Meems, this did not seem to be accurate. Martin was able to freely travel wherever he wanted, something that would have been very difficult for him to do if he were enslaved.

[243] Gene Paleno, *Lake County History*, Chapters 85-89.

[244] Gene Paleno, *Lake County History,* Chapters 85-89.

[245] United States Department of War, Series I; Volume XXXIII, 221.

[246] Richmond Dispatch, March 11, 1882, 2.

[247] Robert P. Watson, *Escape,!* 174.

[248] *New York Times*, March 4, 1864. 8.

[249] John Elijah Page Pension Application.

[250] Jack Coggins, *Arms and Equipment of the Civil War* (New York: Doubleday & Company, 1962), 51.

[251] McLean, George. Encyclopedia Virginia, s.v. "Virginia Railroads during the Civil War." (2021, May 13). https://encyclopediavirginia.org/entries/virginia-railroads-during-the-civil-war/.

[252] Laura Maria Knaggs and Katherine Anderson Knaggs, Major Robert Clark Knaggs, His Life and Times (1836-1927) (New York: Carlton Press, 1992), 107.

[253] Byers, *What I Saw in Dixie*, 27.

[254] Roach, *The Prisoner of War and How Treated* 123.

[255] Lieutenant Robert C. Knaggs was a member of the 7th Michigan Infantry and Aide-de-Camp on the staff of General Henry Baxter. He had been captured at Gettysburg in July 1863.

[256] Lodge, *Diary*. 316-339.

[257] Cavada, *Libby Life* 195-196.

[258] Cavada, *Libby Life,* 195-196

[259] Hoffman, *Diary*.

[260] Byers, *What I Saw in Dixie* p26.

[261] R. Bartley, "The Dahlgren Raid", *Detroit Free Press*, March 4, 1882, 8.

[262] Richmond Sentinel, March 3, 1864, "One of the prisoners, on being searched at the Libby prison yesterday, was found to be possessed of two forks and a spoon, of pure silver, and a beautiful China dish, which he said was doubtless stolen by some of the party, but not by himself. On one of the forks were the initials "J. M. M.," supposed to be the property of J. M. Morson, of Goochland county."

[263] *The National Tribune*, March 29-April 5, 1894, 3.

[264] *The National Tribune*, March 29-April 5, 1894, 3.

[265] *New York Times,* April 5, 1891, 10.

[266] Byers, *What I Saw in* 26.

[267] United States Department of War, Series I, Volume XXXIII, 618.

[268] United States Department of War, Series I, Volume XXXIII, 185.

[269] New York Times, April 5, 1891, 10.

[270] Cavada *Libby Life*: 196.

[327] *The National Tribune,* March 29 – April 5, 1894, 3.

[272] United States Department of War, Series I, Volume XXXIII, 205.

[273] Merriwhether Stuart, "Colonel Ulric Dahlgren and Richmond's Underground: April 1864," The Virginia Magazine of History and Biography; Volume 72, No. 2, April 1964, 152-204.

[274] R. Bartley, "The Dahlgren Raid," Detroit Free Press March 4, 1882, 8

[275] Reverend Alfred Bagby, *King and Queen County*, Virginia (New York: Neal Publishing Company, 1908), 184.

[276] United States Department of War, Series I, Volume XXXIII, 205.

[277] Bagby, King and Queen County, Virginia; 136.

[278] William J. Jones, "Sworn Statement by Edward W. Halbach," *Southern Historical Society Papers* XIII (January-December 1885): 546-551.

[279] United States Department of War, Series I; Volume XXXIII, 208.

[280] Lieutenant James Pollard Compiled Service Records.

[281] Venter, Kill Jeff Davis..

[282] *New York Times*,April 5, 1891, 10.

[283]John J. Polsley. *John J. Polsley to Ellen Polsley,, 1864*. Letter. Library of Congress, Civil War Manuscripts Division: *John J. Polsley Collection*, Gift of William F. Wagner, 1959..

[284] Venter Kill Jeff Davis.

[285] United States Department of War, Series I, Vol XXXIII, 170.

[286] United States Department of War, Series I, Vol XXXIII, 218.

[287] Michael Hoffman. "In Libby," The Union County Courier,,January 31, 1883, February 7, 1883, February 14, 1883.,

[288] Reuben Bartley, *Reuben Bartley Diary*, Diary. Bob Bartley Private Collection..

[289] United States of War, Series I, Vol XXXIII, 222.

[290] John Wilder Atkinson,"Col. Ulric Dahlgren, the Defeated Raider," *Southern Historical Society Papers* XXXVI (1909): 351-353.

[291] Corporal Richard P. Armstead's Widow's Pension Application. Armstead and his fellow USCI soldiers were captured by the Confederates when several companies were sent up to Virginia peninsula in search of Kilpatrick's forces. After a few weeks at Libby, he was transferred to a prison at Salisbury, NC, where he died on February 12, 1865 from starvation and exposure.

[292] Department of Veterans' Affairs, Corporal Richard P. Armstead's Widow's Pension Application, Veterans' Service Records, National Arvhives, Washington.

[293] John Y. Foster, New Jersey in the Rebellion (Newark: Martin & Dennis Co, 1868), 744.

[294] Several POWs recorded the incident, and how incensed it had made everyone, in their diaries.

Chapter Nine: Libby Life March 1864 to May 1864

[295] Roger Pickenpaugh, "Confederate Prisons," Essential Civil War Curriculum, Virginia Board for Civil War Studies at Virginia Tech, 2010-2023,
https://www.essentialcivilwarcurriculum.com/confederate-prisons.html&lang=en

[296] David E. Herrold and Benn Pittman, The Assassination of President Lincoln and the Trial of the Conspirators: 1865 (New York: Moore, Wilstach & Baldwin), Testimony of Captain Frederick Memmert,58-59.

[297] Hoffman, *Diary*.

[298] United States Department of War, Series I, Vol XXXIII, 176.

[299] Marsena Rudolph Patrick; *Inside Lincoln's Army: The Diary of Marsena Rudolph Patrick, Provost Marshal General, Army of the Potomac*,ed. David S. Sparks (New York: Thomas Yoseloff,, 1964).

[300]Lodge, *Diary*, 316-339.

[301] Bartley, *Reuben Bartlett Diary*.

[302] Private Enoch F. Lewis Compiled Military Service Records.

[303] Private James W. Corne Compiled Military Service Records.

[304] United Stated Department of War,Series I; Vol XXXIII, 178.

[305] George Meade, The Life and Letters of George Gordon Meade, Major-General United States Army (New York. C. Scribner's Sons, 1913),190-191.

[306] United States Sanitary Commission p44.

[307] Stuart, "Colonel Ulric Dahlgren", 152-204.

[308] *New York Times,* April 13, 1891; April 19, 1891..

[309] *New York Times,* April 12, 1891; April 19, 1891..

[310] *The Union County Courier*, February 14, 1883, 2.

[311] Emeric Szabad, The Libby Prison Diary of Colonel Emeric Szabad, ed. Stephen Beszedits, (Toronto: B & L Information Services, 1999), 37.

[312] United States Department of War,, Series II Volume VII, 457. Markbreit's friends and family lobbied for his release for the remainder of 1863. President Lincoln's endorsement to negotiate Markbreit's release is on a letter from Frederick Hassaurek, September 17, 1864, enclosing a letter from his half-brother, Lieutenant Leopold Markbreit. This same letter from Markbreit is printed elsewhere in the Official Records with the following endorsement by Charles A. Dana, October 10, 1864: "Respectfully referred to the Commissary-General of Prisoners, with directions to subject the officer held as hostage for the within-named prisoner to the same treatment." (United States Department of War,, Series II Volume VII, 457). Not until January 5 was an exchange effected, on which date General Grant telegraphed Stanton, ``Will you please say to the President that Lieutenant Markbreit has been released from prison and is now on his way North." (United States Department of War, Series II Volume VIII, 811).

[313] Byers, What I Saw in Dixie, - 31-32.

[314] Herrold and Pittman, The Assassination of President Lincoln, 86.

[315] Hoffman, *Diary.*

Chapter Ten: Henry M. Fowler – 15th New Jersey August 1862 to May 1864

[316] Joseph G. Bilby, Three Rousing Cheers - A History of the Fifteenth New Jersey from Flemington to Appomattox, (Hightstown, NJ: Longstreet House, 2001), 32.

[317] Bilby, *Three Rousing Cheers,* 32.

[318] Alanson A. Haines, History of the Fifteenth Regiment New Jersey Volunteers (New York: Jenkins & Thomas , 1883), 31-34.

[319] Ellis S. Hamiltion, Letter, Rutgers University: Special Collections and University Archives, *Captain Ellis S. Hamilton Letters.* Hamilton was just sixteen-years-old when he enlisted as a 2nd Lieutenant on August 25, 1862. He was promoted to captain on November 4, 1863 at age eighteen.

[320] Sergeant-Major John P. Fowler's remains were sent to Washington, D.C., where they were embalmed and then sent home to Hamburg, New Jersey for burial. His tombstone was erected by his cousin, Colonel Samuel Fowler and reads: In memory John P. Flower Sergeant Major 15th Regt NJ Vol born Nov 13, 1813 and killed at the Battle of Fredericksburg Va Dec 13, 1862. He fell gallantly fighting for the Constitution, the Union and the enforcement of the laws.

[321] Henry R. Pyne,; The History of the First New Jersey Cavalry; (Trenton: J.A. Beecher, 1871), 2-24.

[322] *Trenton Time*s, June 8, 1883, 5.

[323] Charles Robson, ed., Biographical Encyclopaedia of New Jersey of the 19th Century (Philadelphia: Galaxy Publishing Company, 1877), 405.

[324] Robson, *Biographical Encyclopaedia,* 405.

[325] Pyne,; The History of the First New Jersey Cavalry 11.

[326] Haines,; History of the Fifteenth Regiment New Jersey Volunteers, 19.

[327] Pyne, The History of the First New Jersey Cavalry, 44.

[328] Hunterdon Republican, February 13, 1863..

[329] Haines, History of the Fifteenth Regiment New Jersey Volunteers38-40.

[330] Haines, History of the Fifteenth Regiment New Jersey Volunteers45.

[331] Bilby, Three Rousing Cheers, 117.

[332] Haines, History of the Fifteenth Regiment New Jersey Volunteers, 56.

[333]Robson, Biographical Encyclopaedia, 406.

[334] United States Department of War,, Series I, Volume XXV; Chapter XXXVII, Part 1, 571-573.

[335] United States Department of War,, Series I, Volume XXV; Chapter XXXVII, Part 1, 189.

[336] Bilby, Three Rousing Cheers, p73.

[337] Haines, *History of the Fifteenth Regiment New Jersey Volunteers*, 70-71.

[338] Haines, *History of the Fifteenth Regiment New Jersey Volunteers*, 86-87.

[339] Pickett's Charge is also known as the Pettigrew-Pickett-Trimble Assault or Charge, named after the three commanding generals on the field. Major General George Pickett was only in command of Virginians; less than half the total troops involved. General James Johnston Pettigrew's division marched to the left of Pickett. General Isaac Ridgeway Trimble's division also advanced from the left of Pickett behind Pettigrew. Trimble was wounded during the battle which resulted in his left leg being amputated. Pettigrew was wounded in the arm and would die a couple of weeks after Gettysburg during the Confederate retreat when he was shot in the abdomen while his division was still north of the Potomac River.

[340] Haines, *History of the Fifteenth Regiment New Jersey Volunteers,* 95.

[341] Haines, *History of the Fifteenth Regiment New Jersey Volunteers,* 379-380.

[342] From 1855 until around 1869, the game was spelled as two separate words: "base ball". It wasn't until 1870 that the *NY Times* began using the term "base-ball" with a hyphen. In 1884, the NY Times eliminated the hyphen and the game became known as one word: "baseball."

[343] Hamilton was evacuated by ambulance to Fredericksburg on May 8. Wounds began to hemorrhage on Sunday morning, May 15. In an attempt to save him, they amputated his right leg, but he had lost too much blood, and he died the next day. He was eighteen years old.

[344] Shelby Foote, The Civil War: A Narrative. vol. 3, Red River to Appomattox (New York: Random House, 1974), 203.

[345] Curtis D. Crocket, "The Union's Bloody Miscue at Spotsylvania Muleshoe American Battlefield Trust, n.d. n.d.https://www.battlefields.org/learn/articles/unions-bloody-miscue-spotsylvanias-muleshoe.

[346] Haines, History of the Fifteenth Regiment New Jersey Volunteers,180.

[347] Haines, History of the Fifteenth Regiment New Jersey Volunteers, 172.

[348] United States Department of War, Series I, Volume XXXVI, 144.

[349] Crocket, *The Union's Bloody Miscue.*

[350] Haines, *History of the Fifteenth Regiment New Jersey Volunteers,* 176.

Chapter Eleven: POWs in the Heart of the South May 1864 to July 1864

[351] James I Robertson Jr., "Houses of Horror: Danville's Civil War Prisons," *The Virginia Magazine of History and Biography* 69, no. 3 (July 1961). 329-345.

[352] Department of Veterans' Affairs, Mark M. Bassett Pension Application, Veterans' Service Records, National Archives, Washington.

[353] Hoffman, *Diary,*

[354] Haines, *History of the Fifteenth Regiment New Jersey Volunteers,* 176.

[355] Hoffman, *Diary*. The entire timeline and route of the POW train from Richmond to Macon was recorded in Hoffman's diary.

[356] *Macon Daily Telegraph*, May 17, 1864, 2.

[357] United States Department of War, Series, Volume VII, 607.

[358] *Macon Daily Telegraph*, May 18, 1864, 2.

[359] Asa B. Isham, Henry M. Davidson, and Henry B. Furness, Prisoners of War and Military Prisons (Cincinnati: Lyman and Cushing, 1890), 44.

[360] Byers, *What I Saw in Dixie,* 34.

[361] Isham, Davidson, and Furness, *Prisoners of War and Military Prisons,* 41.

[362] "A Fighting U.S. Navy Paymaster," *Army & Navy Journal,* December 13, 1919, 443.

[363] Memoir. "Memoir of Luther Guiteau Billings" by Luther Guiteau Billings, 1880, Library of Congress, Civil War Manuscripts Division, ,58.

[364] Domschcke, *Twenty Months in Captivity,* 81-83.

[365] Willard W. Glazier, *The Capture, the Prison Pen and the Escape: Giving a Complete History of Prison Life in the South* (Hartford: H. E. Goodwin. 1869), , 110.

[366]National Park Service, "Omnipresent and Omniscient: The Military Prison Career of Captain Henry Wirz." National Park Service. September 21, 2022.
https://www.nps.gov/ande/learn/historyculture/captain_henry_wirz.htm#:~:text=He%20was%2C%20as%20one%20prisoner%20wrote%20in%201862%2C,as%20a%20part%20of%20his%20prison%20management%20team.

[367] Byers, *What I Saw in Dixie,* 34.

[368] Billings, *Memoir,* 78.

[369] Byers, *What I Saw in Dixie,* 35.

[370] Stephen Hoy, and William Smith,; *Camp Oglethorpe, Macon's Unknown Civil War Prisoner of War Camp, 1862-1864* (Macon: Mercer University Press,2019), 70.

[371] United States Department of War, Series I, Volume XXIX, Pt 2, 625.

[372] *Annual Report of the Adjutant General of the State of New York: Forty-Fifth Infantry*, 1900 (Albany: James B. Lyon State Printer, 1901): 298.

[373] Byers, *What I Saw in Dixie,* p35.

[374] Michael Hoffman, *Diary.*; Priest's body was disinterred in 1866 along with other Camp Oglethorpe dead and reburied at Andersonville Prison in grave number 12975.

[375] Byers, *What I Saw in* 38-47. This includes Byers' full account of his ten-day escape.

[376]United States Department of War, Series II, Volume VII, 472.

Chapter Twelve: Alfred S. "Allie" Stewart and Thomas P. Young Jr. July 1864

[377] David Evans, Sherman's Horsemen: Union Cavalry Operations in the Atlanta Campaign (Bloomington: Indiana University Press, 1996), 217.

[378] United States Department of War, Series I, Volume XXXVIII, Part 5, 260-261.

[379] United States Department of War, Series I, Volume XXXVII, Part 5, 265.

[380] Evans; *Sherman's Horsemen* 229.

[381] United States Department of War, Series I, Volume XXXVIII, Part 2, 762.

[382] Stoneman, a Democrat, was elected to one-term as the Governor of California from January 10, 1883 through January 6, 1887.

[383] United States Department of War, Series I, Volume XXXVIII, Part 2, p775-777.

[384] Lowell H. Harrison, *The Civil War in Kentucky* (Lexington: University of Kentucky Press, 2010), 27.

[385] Daniel Butterfield, *Camp and Outpost Duty for Infantry,*1896, Reprint, (Mechanicsburg, VA: Stackpole Books, 2003), 47-48.

[386] *The National Tribune*, June 22, 1893, 3.

[387] Zollicoffer Bond, Octavia, The Family Chronicle and Kinship Book of Maclin, Clack, Cocke, Carter, Taylor, Cross, Gordon, and Other Related American Lineages (Nashville: McDaniel Printing Company, 1928), 387.
 Zollicoffer Bond, 387.

[389] Anna McKinney, ""F. K. Zollicoffer - First and Last Battle," Confederate Veteran XVIII, no.o.4 (April 1910): 163. Account of Dr. D. B. Cliffe, a surgeon who examined Zollicoffer's body.

[390]United States Department of War, Series I, Volume XVI, Pt2, 514.

[391]United States Department of War, Series I, Volume XVI, Part 2, 471.

[392] Thomas J. Wright, *History of the Eighth Kentucky Volunteer Regiment* (St. Joseph, Missouri: Steam Printing Company, 1880), 97.

[393] Robert S. Cameron, Robert S., *Staff Ride Handbook for the Battle of Perryville*, 8 October 1862 (Fort Leavenworth, KS: Combat Studies Institute Press, 2005),; 114.

[394] United States Department of War, Series I, Volume XVI, Part 1, 20.

[395] Stuart Sanders, "Literally Covered with the Dead and the Dying: Leonidas Polk and the Battle of Perryville," American Battlefield Trust, n.d. https://www.battlefields.org/learn/articles/literally-covered-dead-and-dying.

[396] Wright; History of the Eighth Kentucky Volunteer Regiment, 103.

[397] Thomas P. Young Compiled Service Record.

[398] Thomas P. Young Compiled Service Record.

[399]. Thomas P. Young Compiled Service Record.

[400] Steve Procko, *Rebel Correspondent* (Chambersburg, PA: Blue Ridge,2021).

[401]United States Department of War, Series I, Volume XXXI, Part 2, p27.

[402] Henry Yates Thompson, *An Englishman in the American Civil War: the Diaries of Henry Yates Thompson 1863*, ed. Christopher Chancellor (New York: New York University Press, 1971), 155.

[403] Peter Andrews, "The Rock of Chickamauga," *American Heritage Magazine* 41 issue 2 (March 1990): 41. Quote attributed to Major General Gordon Granger in an exchange with General Ulysses S. Grant and General George H. Thomas.

[404] Company A's Lieutenant James H. Linney had resigned on March 9, 1864, so a lieutenancy had become available.

[405] Thomas P. Young Compiled Service Record.

[406] Evans, *Sherman's Horsemen*, 230.

[407] *The National Tribune*, January 16, 1890, 3.

[408] United States Department of War, Series I, Volume XXXVIII, Part 2, 770-771.

[409] United States Department of War, Series I, Volume XXXVII, Part 2, 770-771.

[410] John B. Vaughter, *Prison Life in Dixie: Giving a Short History of the Inhuman and Barbarous Treatment of Our Soldiers by Rebel Authorities* (Chicago: Central Book Concern, 1880), 23.

[411] United States Department of War, Series I, Volume XXXVIII, Part 2, 771.

[412] United States Department of War, Series I, Volume XXXVIII, Part 2, 773.

[413] "Battle of Brown's Mill," Coweta County Parks and Recreation, n.d. https://www.coweta.ga.us/departments-services/departments-f-q/parks-recreation/facilities/brown-s-mill/battle-of-brown-s-mill

[414] Vaughter, *Prison Life in Dixie,* 25-27.

[415] Evans, *Sherman's Horsemen*, 249.

[416] United States Department of War, Series I, Volume XXXVIII, Part 2, 780.

[417] *The National Tribune*, January 16, 1890, 3. The anxious Yankee officer was identified as Adjutant Charles Schable, who managed to get away.

[418] United States Department of War, Series I, Volume XXXVIII, Part 2, 771.

[419] United States Department of War, Series I, Volume XXXVIII, Part 2, 779-780.

[420]United States Department of War, Series I, Volume XXXVIII, Part 2, 775.

Chapter Thirteen: Lemuel D. Dobbs – 19th USCI July 30, 1864

[421] Byron M. Cutcheon. *The Story of the Twentieth Michigan Infantry, July 15th, 1862, to May 30th, 1865* (Lansing.: Robert Smith Printing Co., 1904), 139.

[422] Stephen M. Weld, "The Petersburg Mine," *Papers of the Military Historical Society of Massachusetts* 5(1918): 207.

[423] L. Allison Wilmer, J. H. Jarrett, and Geo. W. F. Vernon, *History and Roster of Maryland Volunteers, War of 1861-5, Volume 2.* (Baltimore. Guggenheimer, Weil, & Co., 1899). L20937-2.; 213-215.

[424] Henry Goddard Thomas, *Battles and Leaders of the Civil War – Volume 4* (New York: The Century Co., 1887-1888), 563–67.

[425] Howard C. Westwood, *Black Troops, White Commanders, and Freedmen During the Civil War.* (Carbondale: Southern Illinois University Press, 1992), 426-427.

[426] Kate M. Scott, *History of Jefferson County Pennsylvania* (Syracuse: D. Mason & Co., 1888), 230.

[427] Scott, *History of Jefferson County*, 117.

[428] Scott, *History of Jefferson County*, 117.

[429] United States Department of War, Series I, Volume XI, Part 1, 32.

[430] Scott, *History of Jefferson County,* 123.

[431] Scott, *History of Jefferson County*, 119.

[432] Department of Veterans' Affairs, Lemuel D. Dobbs Pension Application, Veterans' Service Records, National Archives, Washington.

[433] Lemuel D. Dobbs Pension Application.

[434] Lemuel D. Dobbs Pension Application.

[435] Lemuel D. Dobbs Pension Application.

[436] Scott, *History of Jefferson County,* 121.

[437] United States Department of War, "General Orders Number 143," May 22, 1863, RG 143 War Department Adjutant General's Office; National Archives, Washington. https://www.archives.gov/milestone-documents/war-department-general-order-143

[438] United States Department of War, Series III, Volume III, 100-101.

[439] "19th Regiment, U.S. Colored Troops." 19th USCI/USCT Research Site. http://ranger95.com/civil_war_us/us_color_troops/infantry/19usct/19th_regt_inf.html

[440] William A. Dobak, *Freedom by the Sword: The U.S. Colored Troops; 1862-1867*) Washington: Center of Military History, United States Army, 2011), 338.

[441] James H. Rickard, *Services with Colored Troops in Burnside's Corps: Soldiers and Sailors Historical Society of Rhode Island, Fifth Series,* no. 1 (Providence, Snow & Farnham, 1894): 29. also *The National Tribune,* February 10, 1910, 10.

[442] Joint Committee on the Conduct of the War, *Report of the Joint Committee on the Conduct of the War: The Attack on Petersburg on the 30th Day of July 1864* (Washington, DC: Government Printing Office, 1865), 2, 11.

[443] Augustus Woodbury, *Major General Ambrose E. Burnside and the Ninth Army Corps: A Narrative of Campaigns in North Carolina, Maryland, Virginia, Ohio, Kentucky, Mississippi and Tennessee, During the War for the Preservation of the Republic* (Providence: S.S. Rider & Brother, 1867), 430.

[444] United States Department of War, Series I - Volume XL - Part 1, 60.

[445] John F. Schmutz, *The Battle of the Crater: A Complete History* (Jefferson, NC: McFarland & Company, 2009), 99.

[446] United States Department of War, Series I - Volume XL - Part 1, 137.

[447] Rickard, *Personal Narratives*, 26-27.

[448] Schmutz, *The Battle of the Crater* 54, 128.

[449] United States Department of War, Series I - Volume XL - Part 3, 659.

[450] United States Department of War, Series I - Volume XL - Part 1, 118-119.

[451] Rickard, *Services with Colored Troops in Burnside's Corps.*

[452] "W.J. Andrews, Company K., 23rd South Carolina Volunteers In the Civil War from 1862-1865, oral history interview recorded at Sumter Courthouse May 18, 1909 transcribed by D. Whitesell," *South Carolina Genealogy Trails* from the University Libraries Digital Collections, http://www.genealogytrails.com/scar/coK23sc_vol.htm

[453] John Cheves Haskell, *The Haskell Memoirs* (New York: Putnam's Sons 1960), 77.

[454] Richard Slotkin, *No Quarter: The Battle of the Crater* (New York: Random House, 2009), 292.

[455] Sumner Upham Shearman, "Battle of the Crater and Experiences of Prison Life," *Personal Narratives of Events in the War of the Rebellion, Being Papers Read Before the Rhode Island Soldiers and Sailors Historical Society. Fifth Series.* no. 8 (Providence: The Society, 1898).

[456] Slotkin, *No Quarter,* 292.

[457] Rickard, *Services with Colored Troops in Burnside's Corps*; 29. also *The National Tribune*, February 10, 1910, 3.

[458] Shearman, "Battle of the Crater."

[459] *The Leavenworth Times*, May 12, 1908, 3.

[460] Shearman, "Battle of the Crater."

[461] Shearman, "Battle of the Crater."

Chapter Fourteen: Charleston, South Carolina August 1864 to October 1864

[462] *Charleston Mercury,* June 14, 1864.

[463] United States Department of War, Series II, Volume VII, 895.

[464] Alvah Stone Skilton, *Diary* Rutherford B. Hays Presidential Library and Museums, Fremont, OH.

[465] Joseph Perkins, *Report to Headquarters 19th USCT*, September 13, 1864, RG 111 Records of the Office of the Chief Signal Officer, 1860 – 1985, National Archives, Washington.

[466] John Azor Kellogg, *Capture and Escape - A Narrative of Army and Prison Life* (Wisconsin History Commission, 1908), 55-57.

[467] Byers, *With Fire and Sword,* 140-142. It is interesting that Marsh Byers' account of the Pocotaligo escape attempt is slightly different than Colonel Kellogg's account. Both men were members of the "Secret Band," but more than forty years later when they both wrote about it, their memories of the circumstances were not the same.

[468] Byers, *With Fire and Sword,* 140-142.

[466] Byers, *With Fire and Sword,* 140-142.

[470] Kellogg, *Capture and Escape,* 55-57.

[471] Byers, *With Fire and Sword,* 143.

[472] Byers, *With Fire and Sword,* 142.

[473] United States Department of War Series II, Volume VII, 817.

[474] United States Department of War Series II, Volume VII, 687.

[475] United States Department of War Series II, Volume VII, 616-618.

[476] Skilton, *Diary*.

[477] Hoffman, *Diary*.

[478] United States Department of War, Series II, Volume VII, 881.

[479] United States Department of War, Series II, Volume VII, 914.

[480] Byers, *What I Saw in Dixie,* 61.

[481] United States Department of War, Series II, Volume VII, 881.

[482] United States Department of War, Series II, Volume VII, 909.

[483] John G.B. Adams, *Reminiscences of the Nineteenth Massachusetts Regiment* (Boston: Wright, Potter Printing Company, 1899), 131.

[484] Kellogg, *Capture and Escape,* 98.

[485] Luther Samuel Dickey, *History of the 103d regiment, Pennsylvania Veteran Volunteer Infantry, 1861-1865* (Chicago: L.S. Dickey, 1910), 107-108.

[486] Elias B. Bascom, *Diary of Captain Elias B. Bascom*, Diary. Private Collection.

Chapter Fifteen: Camp Sorghum – Columbia, South Carolina
October 1864 to November 1864

[487] Skilton, *Diary.*

[488] Adams, *Reminiscences of the Nineteenth Massachusetts Regiment,* 131.

[489] Chester DePratter, "Camp Asylum Update," *Legacy,* South Carolina Institute of Archeology and Anthropology newsletter, November, 2013.,.

[490] Byers, *What I Saw in Dixie,* 67.

[491] Adams, *Reminiscences of the Nineteenth Massachusetts Regiment,* 132.

[492] Adams, *Reminiscences of the Nineteenth Massachusetts Regiment*132.

[493] Hoffman, *Diary.*

[494] United States Department of War, Series II, Volume VII, u986-987.

[495] Glazier, The Capture, The *Prison Pen, and the Escape,* 197.

[496] Glazier, *The Capture, The Prison Pen, and the Escape,* 197.

[497] Adams, *Reminiscences of the Nineteenth Massachusetts Regiment* 133.

[498] Hoffman, *Diary.*

[499] Adams, *Reminiscences of the Nineteenth Massachusetts Regiment,* 133.

[500] Adams, *Reminiscences of the Nineteenth Massachusetts Regiment,* 135.

[501] Hoffman, *Diary.*

[502] Hoffman, *Diary.*

[503] Adams, *Reminiscences of the Nineteenth Massachusetts Regiment*135. and Lieutenant Alvin George Youngs, Compiled Military Records.

[504] United States Department of War, Series II, Volume VII, 1046.

[505] *Peoria Herald,* May 31, 1910, 21.

[506] United States Department of War, Series II, Volume VII, 1030.

[507] United States Department of War, Series II, Volume VII, 930, 975, 1062.

[508] United States Department of War, Series II, Volume VII, 1047.

[509] *Edgefield Advertiser, November 30, 1864,* 1.

[510] Byers, *What I Saw in Dixie,* 65-69.

[511] Byers, *What I Saw in Dixie, 65-69.*

Chapter Sixteen: Escape November 1864

[512] Hoffman, *Diary.*

[513] Michael Hoffman, "Story of Prisoner's Escape," *Union County Courier,* April 16, 1896, 4.

[514] Adams, *Reminiscences of the Nineteenth Massachusetts Regiment,* 136.

[515] John A. Reed, *History of the 101st Regiment Pennsylvania Veteran Volunteer Infantry 1861-1865* (Chicago: L. S. Dickey, 1910), 48-49.

[516] *The Leavenworth Weekly Times,* August 26, 1909, 3.

[517] Ditto, *Statistical Roster of the 5th Iowa Infantry,* 159-173.

[518] Daniel Avery Langworthy, *Reminiscences of a Prisoner of War and His Escape* (Minneapolis: Byron Printing Company, 1915), 26-27.

[519] Glazier, The Capture, The Prison Pen, and the Escape, 197.

[520] Michael Hoffman, "Story of Prisoner's Escape,", *Union County Courier,* April 16, 1896, 4.

[521] *Reading Eagle, August 30, 1907,* 8. and Bassett, *Journal of the Senate of the 47th General Assembly of the State of Illinois,* 1298-1305.

[522] *Reading Eagle, August 30, 1907,* 8.

[523] *Journal of the Senate of the 47th General Assembly of the State of Illinois,* 1298-1305.

[524] *The Daily Inter Ocean,* November 28, 1891, 12.

[525] Bassett, *Journal of the Senate of the 47th General Assembly of the State of Illinois,* -1305.

[526] Bassett, *Journal of the Senate of the 47th General Assembly of the State of Illinois,* 1305. Bassett recalls feasting on "yams", but yams were, and still are imported from Africa. The correct vegetable he feasted on would be "sweet potatoes".

[527]Johnson, "Fugitive Federals.".

[528] Stanley Waterloo, *The Story of a Strange Career* (New York: D. Appleton and Company, 1902), 293.

[529] United States Department of War, Series II, Volume VII, 611.

[530] Skilton, *Diary*.

[531] Harold B. Birch, *The 101st Pennsylvania in the Civil War: It's Capture and POW Experience* (Bloomington: Authorhouse, 2007), 145.

[532] Three different Conscription Acts were passed during the war by the Confederate government. The first on April 16, 1862set the age as 18 to 35 for three years of service. The second on September 27, 1862 expanded it to age 45. The third on February 17, 1864set the age as 17 to 50 for an unlimited period of service.

[533] *The Daily Inter Ocean*, November 28, 1891, 12.

[534] United States Department of War, Series II, Volume VII, 1145.

[535] United States Department of War, Series II, Volume VII, 1151.

[536] United States Department of War, Series II, Volume VII, 611-612.

[537] United States Department of War, Series II, Volume VII, 611-612.

[538] Bassett, *Journal of the Senate of the 47th General Assembly of the State of Illinois,* 1305.

[539] Johnson, "Fugitive Federals."

[540] *The Daily Inter Ocean*, November 28, 1891, 12.

[541] Lithograph part of a larger poster titled "The Southern Prisons of U.S. Officers," (Cincinnati: R. J. Fisher, 1865).

[542]Department of Veterans' Affairs, Michael Hoffman Pension Application," January 1, 1983, Veterans' Service Records, National Archives, Washington.

[543] Ditto, *Statistical Roster of the 5th Iowa Infantry;* 159-173.

[544] United States Department of War, Series II, Volume VII, 1196.

[545] Ditto, *Statistical Roster of the 5th Iowa Infantry,* 159-173.

[546] Michael Hoffman Pension Application.

[547] Michael Hoffman, "Story of Prisoner's Escape", *Union County Courier*, April 23, 1896, 4.

[548] Hoffman, "Story of Prisoner's Escape."

[549] Hoffman, "Story of Prisoner's Escape."

[550] Henry Clay Work, *Kingdom Coming*, Song) Chicago: Root & Cady, 1862).

Chapter Seventeen: Flem Cison December 1864

[551] William R. Trotter, Bushwhackers! The Civil War in the North Carolina Mountains (Winston-Salem: John F. Blair Publisher, 1988), 29.

[552] George D. Harmon. and Edith Blackburn Hazlehurst, "Captain Isaiah Conley's Escape From a Southern Prison, 1864," *The Western Pennsylvania Historical Magazine*, (April and May 1964): 236. Hazlehurst was a relative of Conley and published Conley's manuscript she thought he had probably written in 1865 while waiting to be discharged from the Army.

[553]Harmon and Hazelhurst, "Captain Isaiah Conley's Escape," 236.

[554] Harmon and Hazelhurst, "Captain Isaiah Conley's Escape," 236.

[555] Harmon and Hazelhurst, "Captain Isaiah Conley's Escape," 236.

[556] John Collins Welch, An Escape From Prison During The Civil War - 1864 (Fairfield, WA: Ye Galleon Press;1995), 49-50.

[557] William W. Hamblen Compiled Service Records.

[558] Harmon and Hazelhurst, "Captain Isaiah Conley's Escape" 238.

[559] Carlock, *History of the Carlock Family,* 143-144.

[560] Hoffman, , "Story of Prisoner's Escape," 4.

[561] Hoffman, "Story of Prisoner's Escape," 4.

[562] Hoffman, "Story of Prisoner's Escape," 4.

[563] Hoffman, *Diary*.

[564] Hoffman, "Story of Prisoner's Escape" 4.

[565] Skilton, *Diary*.

[566] Bassett, Journal of the Senate of the 47th General Assembly of the State of Illinois1298-1305.

[567]*Greenville Chapter Journal* 2, no. 1,; South Carolina Genealogical Society (Spring 1991).

[568] Johnson, "Fugitive Federals."

[569] Hoffman, "Story of Prisoner's Escape," 4.

Chapter Eighteen: T. R. Zachary: December 1864

[570] Bassett, *Journal of the Senate of the 47th General Assembly of the State of Illinois,* 1298-1305.

[571] Hoffman, "Story of Prisoner's Escape," 4.

[572] Hoffman, "Story of Prisoner's Escape," 4.

[573] Michael Hoffman Pension Application.

[574] Hoffman, "Story of Prisoner's Escape," 4.

[575] Hoffman, "Story of Prisoner's Escape,' 4.

[576] "Settling the County's Southern End," The Sylva Herald and Ruralite, July 24, 2019 and Jane Gibson Nardy, great-granddaughter of T.R. Zachary, "Zachary Family History," oral history, interviewed by Steve Procko.

[577] Mark Arthur and John Preston Western North Carolina: A History from 1730-1913 (Raleigh: Edwards & Broughton Printing Company, 1914), 497-498.

[578] Nardy, oral history interview by Steve Procko.

[579] Hoffman, "Story of Prisoner's Escape," 4.

[580]Hoffman, "Story of Prisoner's Escape, 4.

[581] Hoffman, "Story of Prisoner's Escape," 4.

[582] Hoffman, "Story of Prisoner's Escape," 4.

Chapter Nineteen: Kit Ledford December 1864

[583] Hoffman, "Story of Prisoner's Escape," Union County Courier, 4.

[584] Skilton, *Diary*. Skilton was in Transylvania County being sheltered by a group that was probably associated with Sheriff Hamilton about 30 miles to the east of Bassett's group. He recorded the weather conditions frequently in his diary.

[585] Nardy, oral history interview by Steve Procko.

[586] Carlock, History of the Carlock Family, 143-144.

[587] Hoffman, "Story of Prisoner's Escape," Union County Courier, 4.

[588] Hoffman, "Story of Prisoner's Escape," 4.

[589] Hoffman, "Story of Prisoner's Escape," 4.

[590] David, Center, Jason, William Cicero, and Julius Ketron Ledford Compiled Service Records Company D; 2nd North Carolina Mounted Infantry (U.S.).

[591] Ledford family oral history, interviews with two descendants by Steve Procko and Department of Veterans' Affairs, Widow's Pension Application filed by Nancy Dulcena Ledford, January 19, 1867, Veterans' Service Records, National Archives, Washington.

[592] Welch, "An Escape from Prison," This is the transcribed version of Welch's account, which according to an unnamed descendant was written by "Grandfather Welch" in 1868. In his written account, Welch spells Appleget's name as Applegate. Welch's account parallels the Ledford family's oral tradition regarding the incident. Also, David Ledford's widow's claim for pension documents filed January 7, 1867 in Towns County, Georgia.

[593] Larry Gordon, The Last Confederate General: John C. Vaughn and his East Tennessee Cavalr. (Minneapolis: Zenith Press, 2009), 21.

[594] Ledford family oral history, interviews by Steve Procko.

[595]Hoffman, "Story of Prisoner's Escape," Union County Courier, 4.

[596] Hoffman, "Story of Prisoner's Escape," 4.

[597] William Cicero Ledford Compiled Service Records.

Chapter Twenty: Freedom January 1, 1865

[598] The company was also known as "Bryson's Boys" and the "1st Tennessee National Guard", somewhat of an outlier, independent Union guerrilla group in Eastern Tennessee and Western North Carolina that was never officially mustered into the service of the United States government. After the war was over, they were recognized by an Act of Congress on March 1, 1869 for pay, bounty and pension.

[599] United States Department of War, Series I, Volume XLIII, ar Pt 1, 235.

[600] Cherokee Scout, April 8, 1865, 5.

[601] Bassett, *Journal of the Senate of the 47th General Assembly of the State of Illinois,* 1304.

[602] *The Knoxville Whig*, January 11, 1865, 2.

[603] Hoffman, "Story of Prisoner's Escape," Union County Courier, 4. and Ditto, Statistical Roster of the 5th Iowa Infantry159-173. Sources for all of Michael Hoffman's dialogue in this chapter.

Chapter Twenty-One: 1865

[604] RG 393; Records of United States Army Continental Commands, 1821-1920, National Archives, Washington. Copies supplied by Lorien Foote. There are two versions in existence today of this registration. The first is on formal "Office Provost Marshal General of East Tenn." letterhead addressed to Brigadier General C. W. Wessel, Commanding General of Prisons, Washington, D.C., and signed by Brigadier General S. P. Carter. The second is on "Office U.S. Military Telegraph, War Department" letterhead.

[605] "Knoxville Whig, January 11, 1865, 2.

[606] S.P. Carter, Telegram, January 2, 1865. RG 393; Records of United States Army Continental Commands, 1821-1920, Telegrams Sent by the Provost Marshal, District of East Tennessee, National Archives, Washington. Copies supplied by Lorien Foote.

[607] Hoffman, *Diary.*

[608] No relation to Lieutenant Michael Hoffman.

[609] W. S. Marshall Original 20-day Leave Orders, January 3, 1865, Steve Procko collection owned by the author.

[610] Starr, *Diary.*

[611] Hoffman, *Diary.*

[612] Samuel Hoffman Compiled Service Records.

[613] The later pension applications of Mark M. Bassett, John E. Page, John McAdams, Alfred S. Stewart, Michael Hoffman and Lemuel D. Dobbs offer an insight as to their physical and mental conditions immediately after they arrived over Union lines.

[614] Hoffman.

[615] Thomas P. Young Jr. Compiled Service Records.

[616] Hoffman, *Diary.*

[617] Samuel Ryland, *Affidavit of Samuel Ryland*, "John McAdams Pension Application", January 23, 1864.

[618] Ryland, "Affidavit."

[619] *The Wheeling Intelligencer,* January 13, 1865.

[620] Sarah C. Fowler, Claim for Widow's Pension, May 13, 1864. *The Hunterdon Republic* was probably incorrect in that Henry's mother was collecting a pension for his reported death. Sarah C. Fowler had applied for a Widow's pension in May 1864 after her husband's death at Fredericksburg in December 1862 and was awarded a retroactive $8 per month pension. There are no records showing that she applied for a pension for her son, Henry.

[621] *The Hunterdon Republic,* January 20, 1865.

[622] Lemuel D. Dobbs Compiled Service Records.

[623] Gordon Granger, District of Texas, General Order No. 3, June 19, 1865, RG 393, Records of United States Army Continental Commands, 1821-1920, Part II, Entry 5543, District of Texas, General Orders Issued, National Archives, Washington

[624] Hoffman, *Diary*.

[625] John Elijah Page Pension Application.

[626] "In the Matter of Mark M. Bassett vs. Charlotte Bassett," Mark Bassett Divorce Records Fulton County, Illinois: Fulton County Circuit Court, February, 1865). The records are 21 pages of detailed depositions, summons and decrees."

[627] John H. Eicher and David J. Eicher, *Civil War High Commands* (Stanford: Stanford University Press, 2011), 196-197.

[628] Mark Bassett, Pension Application. Richard J. Oglesby was the Governor of Illinois in his first term of office (January 16, 1865to January 11, 1869).

[629] "Account of W.H.H. Welch," *Reading Eagle*, July 30, 1907.

[630] Skilton, *Diary*.

[631] Mark Bassett Divorce Records

[632] Charles Bassett's exact date of death was not recorded, but it can be deduced that it happened sometime between May and October 1865. He was buried in Morning Star Cemetery in Enion, Illinois, the same cemetery where Mark Bassett's older brother, Nathaniel (1833-1854), was buried. Enion is located 3 miles north of Kerton Township.

[633] Mark M. Bassett Pension Application

Chapter Twenty-Two: After the War

[634] Byers, What I Saw in Dixie 88.

[635] United States Census Bureau, U.S. Census, "Year: 1870," Census Place: Kerton, Fulton, Illinois; Roll: M593_223; Page: 110A.

[636] John McElroy, *This was Andersonville* (New York: McDowell, Obolensky Inc.), 296.

[637] Byers, *What I Saw in Dixie*, 77-78.

[638] *New York Times*, July 7, 1895, 28.

[639] 1872-1900 Memphis City Directories.

[640] Frank L. Byrne, *The Journal of Southern* History 24, no. 4. (November 1948): 430-444.

[641] Parker, A Chautauqua Boy in '61 and Afterward, 54-64.

[642] *The National Tribune*, September 27, 1883, 2.

[643] *The Abingdon Virginian,* December 30, 1870, 1.

[644] Annie Bassett, *Annie Bassett to TR Zachary September 4, 1911,* Letter. Jane Gibson Nardy Collection and Robert C. Knaggs, *Robert C. Knaggs to Mark Bassett, April 7, 1897,* Letter Peoria Historical Society.

[645] United States Census Bureau, US Census, "Year: 1870".

[646] *The New Orleans Daily Democrat*, May 20, 1877, 8.

[647] "Chalmette National Cemetery, Jean Lafitte National Historical Park and Preserve" *Superintendent's Lodge, Historic Structure Report* (Atlanta: National Park Service, Southeast Regional Office, Historical Architecture, Cultural Resources Division, June 2006) , 11.

[648] *The Democrat*, December 27, 1913, 1.

[649] *The National Tribune*, February 17, 1910, 8.

[650] *The Wichita Daily Eagle,* December 21, 1913, 5.

[651] *Iola Register*, November 19, 1883, 2.

[652] *Kansas Agitator,* May 8, 1903, 2.

[653] Logan L. Dobbs, *Deposition.* "Rhoda Dobbs vs. L.D. Dobbs," Rhoda Dobbs Divorce Records, Anderson County, Kansas: Anderson County District Court, January 7, 1905.

[654] U.S. Census, "Year: 1910," Census Place: Delaware, Leavenworth, Kansas; Roll: T624_444; Page: 20A; Enumeration District: 0085; FHL microfilm: 1374457.

[655] *The Leavenworth Weekly Times*, February 27, 1908, 8.

[656] *Garnett Journal Plaindealer*, May 6, 1908, 2.

[657] The Chanute Daily Tribune, May 21, 1918, 1.

[658] Paul H. Jacobson, *American Marriage and Divorce* (New York: Rinehart & Company, 1959).

[659] *The Daily Republican*, April 28, 1869, 4.

[660] *Buchanan County Bulletin and Guardian*, August 14, 1868, 2.

[661] Chattanooga Republican, February 1, 1891, 1.

[662] Elk Point Courier, August 2, 1882, 2.

[663] "Eighteenth Annual Encampment," *Journal of the National Encampment of the Grand Army of the Republic* (1884): 164-166.

[664] *Chattanooga Republican*, February 1, 1891, 1.

[665] John Elijah Page Pension Application.

[666] John Elijah Page Pension Application

[667] John E. Page, State of Colorado Death Certificate, Pueblo County, Colorado, March, 1914.

[668] Michael Hoffman Pension Application.

[669] Gevik, Brian. "The Grand Army of the Republic in South Dakota,: National GAR Records Program, South Dakota Public Broadcasting (SDPB), April 9, 2021, https://www.sdpb.org/blogs/images-of-the-past/the-grand-army-of-the-republic-in-south-dakota/.

[670] *The Union County Courier*, February 14, 1883, 2.

[671] Samuel W. Hoffman account in a newspaper clipping from the Michael Hoffman scrapbook held by the Union County Historical Society, Elk Point, South Dakota.

[672] Report of the Adjutant General of the State of Kentucky (Frankfort, KY: 1866), 683.

[673] Registers of Members 1885-1934, Alfred S. Stewart Record NAID 2124725 Record Group 15: Records of the Department of Veterans' Affairs: Veterans Administration. National Homes Service. Western Branch (Leavenworth, Kansas). National Archives: Washington.

[674] The US Censuses of 1870, 1880 and 1900 show Addie as living with either her father and mother or widowed mother and brothers along with all of her and Kit's children. But Kit is not recorded as living with them.

[675] The Iola Register, November 19, 1883, 2.

[676] Annie Bassett letter from Annie Bassett to TR Zachary, August 5, 1911 The letter mentions all who were in the 1865 photograph who were dead. She records them as Capt. Bassett, Major Marshall, Lieut. Young, and Kit Ledford. She didn't mention Captain Henry Fowler, who had died in 1884, which seems to indicate Fowler never corresponded with any of the men in the photograph after the war.

[677] Department of Veterans' Affairs, Joseph Fleming Cisson Pension Application. January 1, 1983, Veterans' Service Records, National Archives, Washington. The actual application spells his name Cisson as opposed to Cison.

Chapter Twenty-Three: Mark Bassett and T. R. Zachary
[678] T.R. Zachary, *T.R. Zachary to Julia Beazley May 26, 1877,* Letter. Jane Gibson Nardy Collection.

[679] Andy Zachary, *Andy Zachary to T.R. Zachary, July 18, 1883,* Letter. Jane Gibson Nardy Collection.

[680] Julia Zachary. *Julia Zachary to T.R. Zachary, January 1, 1882,* Letter. Jane Gibson Nardy Collection.

[681] Though he received a promotion from the Governor, he was never mustered in. Later in life he was referred to as Captain Bassett.

[682] Annie Bassett, *Annie Bassett to T.R. Zachary, April 28, 1884,* Letters. Jane Gibson Nardy Collection.

[683] The Daily Inter Ocean, October 22, 1891, 2.

[684] Mark Bassett. *Mark Bassett to T.R. Zachary, October 2, 1890,* Letter on State of Illinois. 36th General Assembly letterhead. Jane Gibson Nardy Collection.

[685] *Omaha World-Herald,* June 10, 1891, 4.

[686] Chicago Tribune, November 11, 1892, 3.

[687] T.R. Zachary Death Certificate, State of North Carolina, Raleigh, August 1921...

[688] Illinois Urban Architectural Survey, 1301 Glen Oak, Special Collections, Peoria Public Library, Peoria, Illinois, May 14, 1990.

[689] Mark Bassett Pension Application.

[690] The original document is held by the Illinois History and Lincoln Collections of the University of Illinois at Urbana-Champaign.

[691] The same account was published in the *Journal of the Senate of the 47th General Assembly of the State of Illinois* Senate Resolution no. 75;,1298-1305.

[692] Annie Bassett, *Annie Bassett to T.R. Zachary, August 5, 1911,* Letter. Jane Gibson Nardy Collection.

[693] Mark Bassett Death Certificate, State of Illinois, Peoria, June 1910 and Mark Bassett Obituary, Special Collections, Peoria Public Library, Peoria, Illinois.

Chapter Twenty-Four: The Archeology of a Photograph and Its Photographer

[694] Bassett, Journal of the Senate of the 47th General Assembly of the State of Illinois, 1298. Sworn account by Mark Bassett witnessed by Alfred S. Stewart and J.D. Hatfield.

[695] 1982 Application for the National Register of Historic Places, Mechanics Bank and Trust Company Building NAID: 135818873, Record Group 79: Records of the National Park Service, Series: National Register of Historic Places and National Historic Landmarks Program Records, File Unit: National Register of Historic Places and National Historic Landmarks Program Records: Tennessee, National Archives, Washington. https://catalog.archives.gov/id/135818873 and Personal Communication, Adam Alfrey of the East Tennessee History Center, discussion related to location of Theodore M. Schleier photography studio.

[696] Knoxville Daily Chronicle, November 85, 1872.

[697] Brownlow's Knoxville Whig, May 23, 1866.

[698] Benson J. Lossing, Pictorial Field Book of the Civil War, Volume 3, (Hartord: Thomas Belknap, Publisher, 1986), Footnote, 130.

[699] Lossing, 129.

[700] William Stanhope Marshall, Leave of Absence Papers, Steve Procko collection.

[701] Hoffman, Diary.

[702] The Union County Courier, May 7, 1896, 2.

[703] Peoria Herald, May 31, 1910, 21.

[704] Library of Congress Group of Union officers who escaped from Confed. prison at Columbia, S.C., in the fall of '64 also three guides procured in the mountains of Tennessee No. 1. Capt. M.M. Bassett, Co. E 53rd Ills. Inf. No. 7. Capt. T.P. Young & A.S. Stewart, 4th Ky. who with six others attempted to escape by running the guard at two o'clock a.m. Nov. 10th . The other 6 were recaptured & killed. No. 2. Col. W.S. Marshall. No. 3. Capt. Dobbs. No. 4. Fowler. No. 5. M. Hoffman. No. 6. Page. No. 9 Jn. McAdams. Nos. 10, 11, & 12 guides. South Carolina United States Tennessee Columbia Knoxville, 1865. Photograph. https://www.loc.gov/item/2013649089/.

[705] Bassett, Mark. Mark Bassett to T.R. Zachary April 28, 1884. Letter. Jane Gibson

[706] Bassett was elected in 1884 to the Illinois (34th-1885) House of Representatives and elected to the Illinois State Senate (36th-1889 & 37th-1891). He later served as a judge in Peoria.

[707] Hamilton, Story of the Famous Tunnel Escape from Libby Prison. Hamilton was the author of "Eighteen Months a Prisoner under the Rebel Flag," (Chicago: Libby Prison Museum, 1893). Knaggs does not show up in the list written by Major Hamilton of all the prison escapees and does not show up in other recognized lists of the escapees, as well as through the author's research.

[708] Annie Bassett, Letter and Knaggs, Letter.

[709] Thomas P. Young Compiled Service Records and Original Bellevue Cemetery Records, Danville, Kentucky, Mary Hamlin Collection.

[710] Mayo Clinic, "Typhoid Fever," https://www.mayoclinic.org/diseases-conditions/typhoid-fever/symptoms-causes/syc-20378661.

[711] George Levy, To Die in Chicago; Confederate Prisoners in Camp Douglas 1862-65 (Gretna, LA: Pelican Publishing, 1999).

[712] Johnson, "Fugitive Federals."

Bibliography
Primary Sources Noted With *

Articles (Encyclopedia, Journal, Magazine, Newspaper, Web)
"19th Regiment, U.S. Colored Troops." 19th USCT/USCI Research Site.
    http://ranger95.com/civil_war_us/us_color_troops/infantry/19usct/19th_regt_inf.html
"A Fighting U.S. Navy Paymaster." *Army & Navy Journal* 57, Part 1. (December 13,
    1919).
American Battlefield Trust. "10 Facts: Battles for Chattanooga." American Battlefield
    Trust. November 23-25, 1863. Accessed November 22, 2021.
    https://www.battlefields.org/learn/articles/10-facts-battles-chattanooga
American Battlefield Trust. "The Cost of War: Killed, Wounded, Captured, and
    Missing." Civil War Casualties. American Battlefield Trust. November 16, 2012.
https://www.battlefields.org/learn/articles/civil-war-casualties
Andrews, Peter; "The Rock of Chickamauga"; American Heritage Magazine 41, Issue 2
    (March 1990): 41.
Atkinson, Lieutenant Colonel John Wilder. "Col. Ulric Dahlgren, the Defeated Raider."
    Southern Historical Society Papers XXXVI. (1909): 351-353 Battle of Brown's Mill".
    Coweta County Parks and Recreation.
    https://www.coweta.ga.us/departments-services/departments-f-q/parks-
    recreation/facilities/brown-s-mill/battle-of-brown-s-mill
    Battle of Brown's Mill | Coweta County, GA Website
Byrne, Frank L. "Libby Prison: A Study in Emotions"; *The Journal of Southern History*
    XXIV, no 4. (November 1958).

Crocket, Curtis D. "The Union's Bloody Miscue at Spotsylvania Muleshoe". American
    Battlefield Trust.
    https://www.battlefields.org/learn/articles/unions-bloody-miscue-spotsylvanias-
    muleshoe
DePratter, Chester; "Camp Asylum Update." *Legacy*, South Carolina Institute of
    Archeology and Anthropology newsletter. November 2013.
Fisanick, Christina. "The Wheeling Ambulance: A Civil War Hero." Weelunk. April 16,
    2018. https://weelunk.com/the-wheeling-ambulance-a-civil-war-hero/
Gevik, Brian. "The Grand Army of the Republic in South Dakota,: National GAR
    Records Program, South Dakota Public Broadcasting (SDPB), April 9, 2021,
    https://www.sdpb.org/blogs/images-of-the-past/the-grand-army-of-the-republic-in-
south-dakota/
Harmon, George D. and Hazlehurst, Edith Blackburn, "Captain Isaiah Conley's Escape
    From A Southern Prison, 1864." *The Western Pennsylvania Historical
    Magazine*, (April and May 1964).
Historynet Staff. *William Averell's Cavalry Raid on the Virginia & Tennessee Railroad*
    June 12, 2006.
    https://www.historynet.com/william-averells-cavalry-raid-on-the-virginia-tennessee-
railroad/
*Johnson, Kate. "Fugitive Federals: A Digital Humanities Investigation of Escaped
    Union Prisoners." National Council on Public History, April 29, 2021.
    https://ncph.org/project/fugitive-federals-a-digital-humanities-investigation-of-
    escaped-union-prisoners/
Jones, J. William. "Sworn Statement by Edward W. Halbach." *Southern Historical
    Society Papers* XIII, (January-December 1885): 546-551.
    Mayo Clinic, "Typhoid Fever," Mayo Clinic. n.d.
    https://www.mayoclinic.org/diseases-conditions/typhoid-fever/symptoms-causes/syc-
    20378661
McKinney, Anna; "F. K. Zollicoffer - First and Last Battle". *Confederate Veteran* XVIII,
    no.4 (April 1910): 163.

McLean, George. Encyclopedia Virginia, s.v. Internet. "Virginia Railroads during the
    Civil War". (May 13, 2021).
    https://encyclopediavirginia.org/entries/virginia-railroads-during-the-civil-war/

Moran, Frank E.; "Colonel Rose's Tunnel at Libby Prison"; *Century Illustrated Monthly
    Magazine*; Vol XXXV, No 5; March 1888.

Murphy, James E. "The New Journalism: A Critical Perspective." In *Journalism
    Monographs* no. 34 edited by Bruce H. Westley, Lexington, KY: The
    Association for Education in Journalism, May, 1974
    https://www.battlefields.org/learn/articles/civil-war-casualties

National Park Service. "Omnipresent and Omniscient: The Military Prison Career of
    Captain Wirz. National Park Service. September 21, 2022.
    https://www.nps.gov/ande/learn/historyculture/captain_henry_wirz.htm#:~

History & Heritage Command. "Civil War Prosthetics; Ulric Dahlgren's Leg."
    You Tube Video. 00:03:48. March 19, 2022.
    https://www.youtube.com/watch?v=kvuNBlM018U&ab_channel=NavalHistoryandHe
ritage

Paleno, Gene. in *Lake County History. The Bloom*, May 21, 2020-June 18, 2020,
    "Chapter 85: Rat Hell,"
    https://www.lakecountybloom.com/lake-county-history-chapter-85-rat-hell/
    "Chapter 86: The Tunnel,"
    https://www.lakecountybloom.com/lake-county-history-chapter-86-the-tunnel/
    "Chapter 87: Helped by a Slave,"
    https://www.lakecountybloom.com/lake-county-history-chapter-87-helped-by-a-slave/
    "Chapter 88: Free at Last,"
    https://www.lakecountybloom.com/lake-county-history-chapter-88-free-at-last/
    "Chapter 89: Home Is the Hero."
    https://www.lakecountybloom.com/lake-county-history-chapter-89-home-is-the-hero/

Pickenpaugh, Roger. "Confederate Prisons." Essential Civil War Curriculum. Virginia
    Center for Civil War Studies at Virginia Tech, 2010-2023.
https://www.essentialcivilwarcurriculum.com/confederate-prisons.html&lang=

*Reader, Francis Smith. "History of the Fifth West Virginia Cavalry, Formerly the
    Second Virginia and Battery G. First West Virginia Light Artillery." *Daily
    News.* New Brighton, Pennsylvania: 1890.

Robertson Jr., James I. "Houses of Horror: Danville's Civil War Prisons." *The Virginia
    Magazine of History and Biography* 69, no. 3 (July 1961): 329-345.

Robson, Charles, editor. *Biographical Encyclopaedia of New Jersey of the 19th Century.*
    Philadelphia: Galaxy Publishing Company, 1877.

*Rose, Thomas E. and Bates, Samuel P.; "A Celebrated Escape, A Thrilling Story of the
    Libby Prison Tunnel; Part I"; *Worthington's Magazine* III, no. 1,
    (January 1894):55-64.

*Rose, Thomas E. and Bates, Samuel P.; "A Celebrated Escape, A Thrilling Story of the
    Libby Prison Tunnel; Part II"; *Worthington's Magazine* III, no. 2
    (February 1894): 56, 161-172.

Sanders, Stuart. Stuart "Literally Covered with the Dead and the Dying: Leonidas Polk
    and the Battle of Perryville," American Battlefield Trust,
    https://www.battlefields.org/learn/articles/literally-covered-dead-and-dying

Shearman, Sumner Upham. "Battle of the Crater and Experiences of Prison Life;
    Personal Narratives of Events in the War of the Rebellion, Being Papers Read
    Before the Rhode Island Soldiers and Sailors Historical Society, Fifth Series. no.
    8.* Providence: Snow & Farnham, 1898.

Stuart, Meriwether. "Colonel Ulric Dahlgren and Richmond's Union Underground: April

1864"; *The Virginia Magazine of History and Biography* 72, no. 2, (April 1964): 152-204.

*Thompson, Henry Yates. *An Englishman in the American Civil War: the Diaries of Henry Yates Thompson 1863*. London: William Clowes & Sons, 1971.

Tusken, Roger; "In the Bastile of the Rebels"; Journal of the Illinois State Historical Society (1908-1984) 56, no. 2, Civil War Centennial; Summer 1963.

Weld, Stephen M. "The Petersburg Mine". *Papers of the Military Historical Society of Massachusetts* 5 (1918).

Yancy, Jesse. "Woodrick's 'The Civil War Siege of Jackson of Jackson': A Review." *Mississippi Sideboard A Southern Gallimaufrey* (blog), *Jesse Yancy*. July 8, 2019. https://jesseyancy.com/woodricks-the-civil-war-siege-of-jackson-a-review

Books

*Adams, John G. B. *Reminiscences of the Nineteenth Massachusetts Regiment*. Boston: Wright, Potter Printing Company, 1899.

Adamson, Hans Christian. *Rebellion in Missouri: 1861 Nathaniel Lion and His Army of the West*. Boston: Chilton Company, 1961.

Antrim, Earl. *Civil War Prisons and Their Covers*. New York: Theodore E. Steinway Memorial Publication Fund/Collector's Club. 1961.

Arthur, Mark and Preston, John. *Western North Carolina: A History from 1730-1913*. Raleigh: Edwards & Broughton Printing Company. 1914.

Bagby, Alfred Rev. *King and Queen County, Virginia*. New York: Neal Publishing Company, 1908.

Belcher, Dennis W. *The Cavalry of the Army of the Cumberland*. Jefferson, North Carolina: McFarland & Company, 2016.

Bilby, Joseph G. *Three Rousing Cheers - A History of the Fifteenth New Jersey from Flemington to Appomattox*. Hightstown, New Jersey: Longstreet House, 2001.

Birch, Harold B. *The 101st Pennsylvania in the Civil War: It's Capture and POW Experience*. Bloomington: Authorhouse, 2007.

Bowe, Julia. *The Generations*. 1959.

*Byers, Samuel H. M. *Iowa in War Times*. Des Moines: W.D. Condit & Co. 1888.

* Byers, Samuel H. M. *What I Saw in Dixie -or- Sixteen Months in Rebel Prisons*. Dansville, New York: Robbins & Poors, Printers, Express Printing House, 1868.

*Byers, Samuel H. M. *With Fire and Sword*. New York: The Neal Publishing Company. 1911.

Butterfield, Daniel. *Camp and Outpost Duty for Infantry*. 1896. Reprint. Mechanicsburg, VA: Stackpole Books. 2003.

*Cameron, Robert S. *Staff Ride Handbook for the Battle of Perryville, 8 October 1862*. Fort Leavenworth, Kansas: Combat Studies Institute Press, 2005.

Carlock, Marion Pomery. *History of the Carlock Family and Adventures of Pioneer Americans*. Los Angeles: Wm. B. Straube Printing Company, Inc. 1929.

*Cavada, Lieutenant Federico Fernández. *Libby Life: Experiences of a Prisoner of War in Richmond, Va, 1863-64*. Philadelphia: King & Baird, 1864

Coggins, Jack. *Arms and Equipment of the Civil War*. New York: Doubleday & Company, 1962.

Collins, Darrell L. *General William Averell's Salem Raid*. Shippensburg, PA.: Burd Street Press, 1998.

Cozzens. Peter. *The Darkest Days of the War - The Battles of Iuka & Corinth*. Chapel Hill & London: University of North Carolina Press, 1997.

Cutcheon, Byron M. *The Story of the Twentieth Michigan Infantry, July 15th, 1862, to May 30th, 1865*. Lansing, Mich.: Robert Smith Printing Co., 1904.

Dickey, Luther Samuel. *History of the 103d regiment, Pennsylvania Veteran Volunteer Infantry, 1861-1865*. Chicago: L.S. Dickey, 1910.

Ditto, George T. *Statistical Roster of the 5th Iowa Infantry*. Sigourney, Iowa: Smith's Iowa Times Print, 1897.

Dobak, William A. *Freedom by the Sword: The U.S. Colored Troops; 1862-1867*. Washington, D.C.: Center of Military History, United States Army, 2011.

Eckart, Edward K. & Amato, Nicholas J. *Ten Years in the Saddle: The memoir of William Woods Averell 1851-1862*. San Rafael California: Presido Press, 1978.

Eicher, John H. and Eicher, David J. *Civil War High Commands*. Stanford: Stanford University Press, 2011.

Evans, David. *Sherman's Horsemen: Union Cavalry Operations in the Atlanta Campaign*. First Edition, Bloomington: Indiana University Press, 1996.

Fate, W. H. H. *Historical Glimpse of the Early Settlement of Union County, South Dakota*. Sioux City: Perkins Brothers, 1924.

Fisher, John. *They Rode With Forrest and Wheeler: A Chronicle of Five Tennessee Brothers' Service in the Confederate Western Cavalry*. Jefferson, NC: McFarland Publishing, 1995.

Foote, Lorien. *The Yankee Plague - Escaped Union Prisoners and the Collapse of the Confederacy*. Chapel Hill, NC: The University of North Carolina Press, 2016.

Foote, Shelby. *The Civil War: A Narrative. vol. 3, Red River to Appomattox*. New York: Random House, 1974.

Foster, John Y. *New Jersey in the Rebellion*. Newark: Martin & Dennis Co, 1868.

Gibbs, Joseph. *Three Years in the "Bloody Eleventh*. University Park, Pennsylvania: The Pennsylvania State University Press, 2002.

Glazier, Willard W. *The Capture, the Prison Pen and the Escape: Giving a Complete History of Prison Life in the South*. Hartford: H. E. Goodwin. 1869,

Haines, Alanson A. *History of the Fifteenth Regiment New Jersey Volunteers*. New York: Jenkins & Thomas, 1883.

Hamilton, Andrew G. *Story of the Famous Tunnel Escape from Libby Prison*. Chicago: SS Boggs, 1893.

Harrison, Lowell H. *The Civil War in Kentucky*. Lexington: University of Kentucky Press. 2010.

Haskell, John Cheves. *The Haskell Memoirs* (New York: Putnam's Sons1960), 77.

Herrold, David E. and Pittman, Benn, *The Assassination of President Lincoln and the Trial of the Conspirators: 1865*. New York: Moore, Wilstach & Baldwin, 58-59.

History of La Salle County, vol. I. Chicago. Interstate Publishing Company. 1886.

Hobard, Edwin L. *A Story of Vicksburg and Jackson*. Denver: Hicks-Fairall, 1909.

Howard, Hamilton Gay. *Civil-War-Echos: Character Sketches and State Secrets by a United States Senator's Son and Secretary*. Washington, D.C.: Howard Publishing, 1907.

Hoy, Stephen and Smith, William. *Camp Oglethorpe, Macon's Unknown Civil War Prisoner of War Camp, 1862-1864*. Macon: Mercer University Press, 2019.

Isham, Asa B., Davidson, Henry M., and Furness, Henry B. *Prisoners of War and Military Prisons - Personal Narratives of Experience in the Prisons at Richmond, Danville, Macon, Andersonville, Savanah, Millen, Charleston and Columbia*. Cincinnati: Lyman & Cushing, 1890.

Jacobson, Paul H. *American Marriage and Divorce*. New York: Rinehart & Company, 1959.

Johnston, I. N. *Four Months in Libby and the Campaign Against Atlanta*. Cincinnati: .P. Thompson, Printer, Printed at the Methodist Book Concern for the Author, 1864.

Jones, Robert C. *McCook's Raid and the Battle of Brown's Mill*. RCJ Books.com, 2013.

Jones, Virgil Carrington. *Eight Hours Before Richmond*. New York: Henry Holt and Company, 1957.

Josephs, Anna Catherine. *Mountain Bo*y. Milwaukee: Raintree Publishers, 1985.

Kellogg, John Azor. *Capture and Escape - A Narrative of Army and Prison Life*. Wisconsin History Commission, 1908.

Kennedy, Frances H. *The Civil War Battlefield Guide, 2nd Edition*. Boston: Houghton Mifflin, 1998.

Knaggs, Lara Maria and Anderson, Katherine Knaggs, *Major Robert Clark Knaggs - His Life and Times (1836-1927)*. New York: Carlton Press, 1992.

Langworthy, Daniel Avery. *Reminiscences of a Prisoner of War and His Escape*. Minneapolis: Byron Printing Company, 1915,

Lanier, Robert Sampson. "The Decisive Battles," *The Photographic History of The Civil War in Ten Volumes*, Volume Three. New York: The Review of Reviews Co. 1911.

Levin, Kevin M. *Remembering the Battle of the Crater - War as Murder*. Lexington: University of Kentucky Press, 2012.

Levy, George. *To Die in Chicago; Confederate Prisoners in Camp Douglas 1862-65*. Gretna, LA: Pelican Publishing, 1999.

Lloyd's Steamboat Directory. Cincinnati: James T. Lloyd Co., 1856.

Lossing, Benson J. *Pictorial Field Book of the Civil War, Volume 3*. Hartford: Thomas Belknap, Publisher, 1868.

Mazzagetti, Dominick. *True Jersey Blues*. Madison, Teaneck: Fairleigh Dickenson University Press, 2011.

McAllister, J. Gray. *Sketch of Captain Thompson McAllister, Citizen, Soldier, Christian*. Petersburg: Penn & Owen Printers and Binders, 1896.

McElroy, John. *This Was Andersonville*. New York: McDowell, Obolensky Inc., 1957.

Medical and Surgical History of the War of the Rebellion; Part III, Volume II. Washington D.C.: Government Printing Office, 1883.

McKenzie, Robert Tracy. *Lincolnites and Rebels - A Divided Town in the American Civil War*. Oxford: Oxford University Press, 2006.

*Meade, George. *The Life and Letters of George Gordon Meade, Major-General United States Army*. New York: C. Scribner's Sons. 1913.

Miller, Douglas. *The Greatest Escape - A True American Civil War Adventure*. Guilford, CT: Lyons Press, 2021.

Noe, Kenneth W. and Wilson, Shannon H. editors. *The Civil War in Appalachia*. Knoxville: The University of Tennessee Press, 1997.

*Owens, John Algernon and Glazier, Willard W. *Sword and Pen: Or, Ventures and Adventures of Willard Glazier In War And Literature*. Philadelphia: P.W. Ziegler, & Company, 1889.

*Parker, David B. *A Chautauqua Boy in '61 and Afterward: Reminiscences by David B. Parker (2nd Lieut., 72nd NY)*. Boston: Small, Maynard & Company, 1912.

Parker, G. Keith and Borhaug, Leslie Parker. *To Stand on Solid Ground*. My Easy Read Books, 2020.

Parker, Sandra V. *Richmond's Civil War Prisons*. Lynchburg, Virginia: H. E. Howard, 1990.

Portrait and Biographical Album Peoria County, Illinois. Chicago, IL, USA: Biographical Publishing, 1890.

Procko, Steve. *Rebel Correspondent*. Chambersburg, PA: Blue Ridge, 2021.

*Pyne, Henry R. *The History of the First New Jersey Cavalry*. Trenton: J.A. Beecher, 1871.

Rauscher, Frank. *Music on the March 1862-1865, with the Army of the Potomac*. Philadelphia: Press of W. F. Fell &Co. 1892.

Reed, John A. *History of the 101st Regiment Pennsylvania Veteran Volunteer Infantry 1861-1865*. Chicago: L. S. Dickey, 1910.

*Rickard, James H. *"Services with Colored Troops in Burnsides Corps"; Soldiers and Sailors Historical Society of Rhode Island, Personal Narratives of Events in the

War of the Rebellion; Fifth Series. No. 1. Providence: Snow & Farnham, 1894.

Roach, Alva C. *The Prisoner of War and How Treated*. Indianapolis, Indiana: Railroad City Publishing House, A. D. Streight, Proprietor, 1865.

Sarris, Jonathan Dean. *A Separate Civil War - Communities in Conflict in the Mountain South*. Charlottesville and London: University of Virginia Press, 2006.

Schmutz, John F. *The Battle of the Crater A Complete History*. Jefferson, North Carolina: McFarland & Company, 2009.

Scott, Kate M. *History of Jefferson County Pennsylvania*. Syracuse, New York: D. Mason & Co. 1888.

Slotkin, Richard. *No Quarter: The Battle of the Crater*. New York: Random House, 2009.

*Slease, Rev. William Davis. *The Fourteenth Pennsylvania Cavalry in the Civil War*. Pittsburgh: Art and Engraving Printing Company, 1915.

Speer, Lonnie R. *Portals to Hell, Military Prisons of the Civil War*. Pennsylvania: Stackpole Books, 1997. "StackPath," n.d. https://www.essentialcivilwarcurriculum.com/confederate-prisons.html.

Summers, Robert. *Maryland's Black Civil War Soldiers, 19th Regiment U.S. Colored Troops*. Seattle: Amazon Digital Services, LLC, 2020.

Thomas, Henry Goddard. *Battles and Leaders of the Civil War – Vol 4*. New York: The Century Co., 1887-1888.

Trotter, William R. *Bushwhackers! The Civil War in the North Carolina Mountains*. Winston-Salem: John F. Blair Publisher, 1988.

Tunnard, W.H. *A Southern Record. The History of the Third Regiment Louisiana Infantry*. Baton Rouge: Salzwasser-Verlag, 1866.

Varon, Elzabeth R. *Southern Lady, Yankee Spy - The true story of Elizabeth Van Lew, The Union Agent in the Heart of the Confederacy*. Oxford University Press, 2003.

Vaughter, John B. *Prison Life in Dixie: Giving a Short History of the Inhuman and Barbarous Treatment of Our Soldiers by Rebel Authorities*. Chicago: Central Book Concern, 1880.

Venter, Bruce M. *Kill Jeff Davis - The Union Raid on Richmond, 1864*. Norman: University of Oklahoma Press, 2016.

Waterloo, Stanley. *The Story of a Strange Career*. New York: D. Appleton and Company, 1902.

Way, Frederick, Jr. *Way's Packet Directory, 1848-1983: Passenger Steamboats of the Mississippi River System Since the Advent of Photography in Mid-Continent America*. 1st ed. Athens: Ohio University Press, 1983.

*Welch, John Collins. *An Escape From Prison During The Civil War – 1864*. Fairfield, WA: Ye Galleon Press. 1995.

*Wells, James M. *With Touch of Elbow; or Death Before Dishonor*. Philadelphia: John C. Winston Co. 1909.

West, Granville C. *Military Order of the Loyal Legion of the United States, Commandery of the District of Columbia, War Paper 29 - McCook's Raid in the Rear of Atlanta and Hood's Army, August, 1864*. 1898.

Westwood, Howard C. *Black Troops, White Commanders, and Freedmen During the Civil War*. Carbondale: Southern Illinois University Press, 1992.

Wheelan, Joseph. *Libby Prison Breakout - The Daring Escape from the Notorious Civil War Prison*. New York, New York: Public Affairs, 2010.

Wilkinson, Warren. *Mother, May you never see the sights I have seen - The 57th Massachusetts Veteran Volunteers in the Last Year of the Civil War*. New York, New York: Harper & Row, 1990.

Wilmer, L. Allison, Jarrett, J.H., and Vernon, Geo. W. F. *History and Roster of Maryland Volunteers, War of 1861-5, Volume 2*. Baltimore: Guggenheimer, Weil, & Co., 1899.

Woodbury, Augustus. M*ajor General Ambrose E. Burnside and the Ninth Army Corps: A Narrative of Campaigns in North Carolina, Maryland, Virginia, Ohio, Kentucky, Mississippi and Tennessee, During the War for the Preservation of the Republic.* Providence: S.S. Rider & Brother, 1867.

Woodrick, Jim. *The Civil War Siege of Jackson, Mississippi.* Charleston: The History Press, 2016.

Woodworth, Steven E. and Greer, Charles D. *The Chattanooga Campaign (Civil War Campaigns of the West).* Carbondale: Southern Illinois University Press. 2012.

Wright, Thomas J. *History of the Eighth Kentucky Volunteer Regiment.* St. Joseph, Missouri: St. Joseph Steam Printing Company, 1880.

Zollicoffer Bond, Octavia. *The Family Chronicle and Kinship Book of Maclin, Clack, Cocke, Carter, Taylor, Cross, Gordon, and Other Related American Lineages.* Nashville, Tennessee: McDaniel Printing Company. 1928.

Government Documents

*1982 Application for the National Register of Historic Places, Mechanics Bank and Trust Company Building. Record Group 79: Records of the National Park Service. National Archives, Washington. https://catalog.archives.gov/id/135818873

Annual Report of the Adjutant General of the State of New York: Forty-Fifth Infantry, 1900. Albany: James B. Lyon State Printer, 1901.

*Bassett, Mark. Death Certificate, State of Illinois, Peoria, Illinois, June 1910.

*Bassett, Mark. *Journal of the Senate of the 47th General Assembly of the State of Illinois.* Springfield, Illinois: Illinois State Journal Co., State Printers, 1911.

*Bassett, Mark. Obituary Notice. Special Collections, Peoria Public Library, Peoria, Illinois.

"Chalmette National Cemetery, Jean Lafitte National Historical Park and Preserve" *Superintendent's Lodge, Historic Structure Report* (Atlanta: National Park Service, Southeast Regional Office, Historical Architecture, Cultural Resources Division, June 2006) , 11.

*Department of Veterans' Affairs, Civil War Veterans Pension Records: Mark M. Bassett, John McAdams, Alfred S. Stewart, John E. Page, Lemuel D. Dobbs, Joseph F. Cison, Michael Hoffman. Veterans' Service Records. National Archives, Washington, DC.

*Granger, Gordon. District of Texas, "General Order No. 3", June 19, 1865, RG 393, Records of United States Army Continental Commands, 1821-1920, Part II, Entry 5543, District of Texas, General Orders Issued, National Archives, Washington.

Illinois Urban Architectural Survey, 1301 Glen Oak, Peoria, Illinois, May 14, 1990 Special Collections, Peoria Public Library, Peoria, Illinois.

*"In the Matter of Mark M. Bassett vs. Charlotte Bassett." Mark Bassett Divorce Records. Fulton County, Illinois: Fulton County Circuit Court, February, 1865.

*Joint Committee on the Conduct of the War. *Report of the Joint Committee on the Conduct of the War: The Attack on Petersburg on the 30th Day of July, 1864.* Washington, D.C.: Government Printing Office, 1865.

Journal of the Senate of the 47th General Assembly of the State of Illinois. Springfield, Illinois: Illinois State Journal Co., State Printers, 1911.

*Ord, Edward O.C. Headquarters Thirteenth Army Corps Near Jackson, Mississippi, "Special Order No. 19", July 12, 1863, RG 111 Records of the Office of the Chief Signal Officer, 1860 – 1985, National Archives, Washington, DC.

*Page, John E, State of Colorado Death Certificate, Pueblo County, Colorado, March, 1914.

*Perkins, Joseph. "Report to Headquarters 19th USCT, September 13, 1864, RG 111

Records of the Office of the Chief Signal Officer, 1860 – 1985, National Archives, Washington.

Sea Reach Ltd. "Illinois River Road National Scenic Byway." Interpretive Plan History & Culture. 2015. https://www.illinoisriverroad.org/wpcontent/uploads/2018/07/12.15.2015-Illinois-River-Road-Scenic-Byway.pdf

*Registers of Members, 1885-1934. Alfred S. Stewart. Record Group 15: Records of the Department of Veterans' Affairs: Veterans Administration. National Homes Service. Western Branch (Leavenworth, Kansas). National Archives: Washington.

Report of the Adjutant General and Acting Quartermaster General of Iowa; Volume II. Des Moine: P.W. Palmer State Printer, January 1, 1863.

Report of the Adjutant General of the State of Kentucky. Frankfort, KY: 1866.

Report of the Adjutant General of the State of Illinois, Vol. III. Springfield, Illinois, 1901.

* "Rhoda Dobbs vs. L.D. Dobbs," Rhoda Dobbs Divorce Records. Anderson County, Kansas: Anderson County District Court, January 7, 1905.

*United States Census Bureau. *United States Census Records,* 1840, 1850, 1860, 1870, 1880, 1900, 1910, 1920

*United States Census Bureau, U.S. Census, "Slave Schedule - Seventh Census of The United States," National Archives: Washington,

*United States Department of War. Collection of Confederate Records. RG 109 Letters & Orders Issued, Confederate Military Prison, Letter to Mrs. Van Lew by Thomas P. Turner, Capt. Commanding

*United States Department of War. Records of the Adjutant General's Office. "Military Records." RG 94 Book Records of Volunteer Union Organizations:, 4th Kentucky Infantry, 4th Kentucky Mounted Infantry, 19th USCI Infantry. National Archives: Washington.

*United States Department of War. Records of the Office of the Chief Signal Officer, 1860 – 1985. RG 111. National Archives: Washington.

*United States Department of War. RG 393 Records of United States Army Continental Commands 1821-1920. Letters Sent, April 1864-March 1866, District of East Tennessee. National Archives: Washington.

*United States Department of War. RG 393 Records of United States Army Continental Commands 1821-1920. Register of Letters Sent by the Provost Marshal, District of East Tennessee, July 1864-August 1865. National Archives: Washington.

*United States Department of War. RG 393 Records of United States Army Continental Commands. Telegrams Sent by the Provost Marshal, District of East Tennessee. National Archives: Washington.

*United States Department of War. The War of the Rebellion: A Compilation of the Official Records of the Union and Confederate Armies. Washington.: Government Printing Office, 1880–1901.

*United States Department of War. War Department General Order 143. RG 143. National Archives. Washington, DC. https://www.archives.gov/milestone- documents/war-department-general-order-143

United States Sanitary Commission. *Narrative of privations and sufferings of United States officers and soldiers while prisoners of war in the hands of the Rebel authorities.* Philadelphia: King & Baird Printers, 1864.

*Zachary, T.R. State of North Carolina Death Certificate, Raleigh, North Carolina, August, 1921.

Images

*Chattanooga Public Library. Chattanooga Times Collection, Chattanooga, Tennessee.
*Chicago Historical Society, Chicago History Museum, Chicago, IL. Libby Prison
    Museum Association Records, Events - Wars - Civil War (1861-65) - Prisons –
    Photos, ICHi-001805.
*Library of Congress. Civil War Manuscripts Division, Washington Selected Civil War
    Photographs, 1861-1865.
Peoria Historical Society. Local History and Genealogical Department, Peoria, IL.
    Copy of refugee photograph

Miscellaneous (Diaries, Genealogies, Letters, Memoirs, Oral Histories, Wills)

*Bartlett, Reuben. *Reuben Bartlett Diary* Bob Bartley Private Collection.
*Bascom, Elias B. *Diary of Captain Elias Bascom.* Private Collection.
*Bassett, Annie. *Annie Bassett to T.R. Zachary, April 28, 1884; August 5, 1911;
    September 4, 1911,* Letter. Jane Gibson Nardy Collection.
*Bassett, Mark. *Mark Bassett to Edward Lecour, May 27, 1896.* Letter.
    Illinois History and Lincoln Collections; Manuscript Collections. *Bassett, Mark M.,
    and John G. Reckord Papers, 1863-1865*
*Bassett, Mark. *Mark Bassett to T.R. Zachary October 2, 1890.* Letter. Jane Gibson
    Nardy Collection.
*Benton, Thomas Ellis. Memoir "Civil War Recollections". 1913. Florida Memory.
    State Archives of Florida, Tallahassee, Florida.
    https://www.floridamemory.com/items/show/345924?id=1
*Billings, Luther Guiteau. Memoir. "Memoir of Luther Guiteau Billings." 1880. Civil
    War Manuscripts Division. Library of Congress, Washington, DC.
*Eddington, William. Memoir. "My Civil War Memoirs and Other Reminiscences."
    Madison County Historical Society. Ewardsville, Illinois.
Greenville Chapter Journal 2, no. 1. South Carolina Genealogical Society (Spring 1991).
Hamiltion, Ellis S. Captain Ellis S. Hamilton Letters, Letter. Rutgers University: Special
    Collections and University Archives.
*Hoffman, Michael. *Michael Hoffman Transcribed Diary and Michael Hoffman
    Personal Scrapbook.* Union County Historical Society. Elk Point, SD.
*Lee, William Henry. *Last Will and Testament of William Lee, 14, August, 1819.* Will
    Records, Book A-C, 1818-1870, Madison, Illinois.
* Lodge, George R. *Diary.* Roger and Margaret Tusken Private Collection
*Marshall, William Stanhope. Leave of Absence Papers, Steve Procko collection.
 *Matlick, Jacob G. Memoir. "Army and Prison Reminiscences During the Civi War
    1861 to 1865." Matlick Family Papers. West Virgina Collection. West Virginia
    University. Morganton, West Virginia.
Nardy, Jane Gibson. "Zachary Family History." oral history interview by Steve Procko.
*Original Bellevue Cemetery Records. Danville, Kentucky, Mary Hamlin Collection.
*Pallissard, Armand. *Armand Pallissard to Edward Pallissard and Paulin Pallisard, July
    8 and October 2, 1862.* Letters. Archives West, University of Montana,
    Mansfield Library, Archives and Special Collections. *Armand Pallissard Letters,
    1862.*
Patrick, Marsena Rudolph. *Inside Lincoln's Army: The Diary of Marsena Rudolph
    Patrick, Provost Marshal General, Army of the Potomac.* Ed. David S. Sparks.
    New York: Thomas Yoseloff, 1964.
*Peck, William S. *William S. Peck to William Codling January 4, 1864.* Letter. Private
    Collection.
*Polsley, John J. *John J. Polsley Papers.* Letters. Civil War Manuscripts Division.
    Library of Congress, Washington, DC.
Pritzker Military Museum and Library. *Diary.* Chauncey S. Aldrich Collection. Chicago.
Procko, Steve. Oral history interviews with Ledford Family descendants.
*Pugh, Isaac C. *Isaac C. Pugh Papers* (MS 266). Special Collections and University

Archives, University of California, Riverside.

*Ranstead, H.E. *A True Story and History of the Fifty-third Regiment Illinois Veteran Volunteer Infantry Its Campaigns and Marches*. 1910. Soldier's Diary. https://history.illinoisgenweb.org/civilwar/scrapbk/ransteaddiary.html

*Stilton, Alvah Stone. *Diary*. Rutheford B. Hayes Presidential Library and Museums, Fremont, OH.

*Starr, George H. *Diary*. The Gilder Lehrman Institute of American History. *The Gilder Lehrman Collection*.

Szabad, Emeric. *The Libby Prison Diary of Colonel Emeric Szabad*. Ed. Stephen Beszedits, Stephen. Toronto: B & L Information Services, 1999.

*"W.J. Andrews, Company K., 23rd South Carolina Volunteers In the Civil War from 1862-1865, oral history interview recorded at Sumter Courthouse May 18, 1909 transcribed by D. Whitesell," *South Carolina Genealogy Trails* from the University Libraries Digital Collections, http://www.genealogytrails.com/scar/coK23sc_vol.htm

*Whitten, John. *John Whitten Papers*. Diary. Civil War Manuscripts Division, Library of Congress, Washington, DC.

Zachary Andy. *Andy Zachary to T.R. Zachary July 18, 1883*. Letter. Jane Gibson Nardy Collection.

Zachary Julia. *Julia Zachary to T.R. Zachary January 1, 1882*. Letter. Jane Gibson Nardy Collection.

Zachary, T.R. *T.R. Zachary to Julia Beazle,y May 26, 1877,* Letter. Jane Gibson Nardy Collection.

Newspapers

Brownlow's Knoxville Whig, May 23, 1866, Knoxville, TN

Brownlow's Knoxville Whig and Rebel Ventilator, January 1, 1864; January 9, 1864, . Knoxville, TN

Buchanan County Bulletin and Guardian, August 27, 1861; August 14, 1868, Independence, IA

Charleston Mercury, June 14, 1864, Charleston, SC

Chattanooga Daily Times, January 28, 1891, Chattanooga, TN

Chattanooga Republican, February 1, 1891, Chattanooga, TN

Cherokee Scout; Cherokee County, April 8, 1865, Cherokee, NC

Daily Richmond Enquirer, February 2, 1864, Richmond, VA

Detroit Free Press, March 4, 1882, Detroit, MI

Edgefield Advertiser, November 30, 1864, Edgefield, SC

Garnett Journal Plaindealer, May 6, 1908, Garnett, KS

Hunterdon Republican, February 13, 1863, Hunterdon County, NJ

Iola Register, November 9, 1883, Iola,KS

Kansas Agitator, May 8, 1903, Garnett, KS

Knoxville Daily Chronicle, November 8, 1872, Knoxville, TN

Knoxville Whig, January 11, 1865, Knoxville, TN

Los Angeles Times, February 27, 1923, Los Angeles, CA

Macon Daily Telegraph, May 17, 1864; May 18, 1864, Macon, GA

New York Times, November 28, 1863; March 4, 1864; February 15, 1891; March 15, 1891; April 5, 1891; April 12, 1891; April 19, 1891; July 7, 1895 New York, NY

Omaha World-Herald, June 10, 1891, Omaha, NE

Peoria Herald, May 31, 1910, Peoria, IL

Peoria Morning Star, January 1, 1917, Peoria, IL

Philadelphia Weekly Times, October 28, 1882, Philadelphia, PA

Reading Eagle, July 30, 1907, Reading, PA

Richmond Dispatch, March 11, 1888, Richmond, VA

Richmond Enquiror, January 1, 1864, Richmond, VA

Richmond Sentinel, December 28, 1863; March 3, 1864, Richmond, VA

Shreveport Journal, February 19, 1915, Shreveport, LA

The Abingdon Virginian, December 30, 1870, Abingdon, VA

The Buchanan County Guardian, August 27, 1861, Independence, IA

The Chanute Daily Tribune, May 21, 1918, Chamute, KS

The Chicago Tribune, August 11, 1863; November 11, 1892, Chicago, IL

The Daily Inter Ocean, January 27, 1891; November 28, 1891, Chicago, IL

The Daily Republican, April 28, 1869, Marion, IL

The Democrat, December 27, 1913, Wichita, KS

The Hunterdon Republic, January 20, 1865, Hunterdon County, NJ

The Knoxville Whig, January 11, 1865, Knoxville, TN

The Leavenworth Times, May 12, 1908, Leavenworth, KS

The Leavenworth Weekly Times, February 27, 1908; August 26, 1909, Leavenworth, KS

The National Tribune, September 5,1885; September 8, 1887; January 16, 1890; December 29, 1891; June 22, 1893; March 29, 1894; April 5, 1894; February 10, 1910; February 17, 1910, Washington, DC

The New Orleans Daily Democrat, May 20, 1877, New Orleans, LA

The Ottawa Free Trader; May 30, 1861; January 31, 1863; July 25, 1863, Ottowa, IL

The Sunday Oregonian, June 28, 1908, Portland, OR

The Sylva Herald and Ruralite, July 24, 2019, Sylva, NC

The Wheeling Intelligencer, January 13, 1865, Wheeling, WV*The Wichita Daily Eagle*, December 21, 1913, Wichita, KS

Toledo Blade, December 31, 1863, Toledo, OH

Trenton Times, June 28, 1883, Trenton, NJ

*Union County Courie*r, January 31, 1883; February 7, 1883; February 14, 1883; April 16, 1896; April 23, 1896; April 30, 1896; May 7, 1896, Elk Point, SD

Index

About the Author

Steve Procko is a filmmaker and photographer with a love for history.

He particularly loves learning about the small, everyday events in the lives of little-known people and the small towns they lived in. *Captured Freedom* offered Steve a chance to go on a great scavenger hunt, pinning down the facts about a more than 150-year-old photograph, whose story had been lost to the ethers.

His first book, *Rebel Correspondent* told the true story of the everyday life of a lowly cavalry private struggling to survive one of the greatest events in American history.

A native of Florida, Steve, along with his wife, Lauren, and their dog, Rigby, splits his time between a home in Ocala, Florida and a mountain log cabin nestled next to Stanley Creek near the town of Blue Ridge, Georgia, just a few miles down the road from the neighbor who first shared "The Photograph" with him.

Websites

For more on *Captured Freedom*, follow the book's Facebook page or visit the website, where additional stories about the subjects in the book and their remarkable lives can be found.

Captured Freedom's Facebook Page

https://www.facebook.com/capturedfree

Captured Freedom's Website

https://CapturedFreedom.com